TRINITY UNIVERSITY

A TALE OF THREE CITIES

TRINITY

A TALE

UNIVERSITY

OF THREE CITIES

R. DOUGLAS BRACKENRIDGE

Foreword by JOHN BRAZIL, *President of Trinity University*

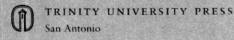

TRINITY UNIVERSITY PRESS
San Antonio

Published by Trinity University Press
San Antonio, Texas 78212

Unless otherwise noted, all photographs are from the Trinity University Archives or the Trinity University Office of Public Relations. Book and jacket design by Barbara Jellow

The paper used in this publication meets the minimum requirements of the American National
Standard for Information Sciences—Permanence of Paper for Printed Library Materials, ANSI
Z39.48-1992.

ISBN 978-1-59534-789-3 (paperback)
ISBN 978-1-59534-790-9 (ebook)

Library of Congress Cataloging-in-Publication Data

Brackenridge, R. Douglas.
   Trinity University : a tale of three cities / R. Douglas Brackenridge.
      p. cm.
Includes bibliographical references and index.
ISBN 0-911536-00-0 (hardcover : alk. paper)
1. Trinity University (San Antonio, Tex.)—History. I. Title.
LD5361.T62B73 2004
378.764'351—dc22   2004017998

Printed in the United States of America
20   19   18   17   16   5   4   3   2   1

CONTENTS

FOREWORD

by President John Brazil

ORIGINALLY COMMISSIONED IN 1998 by then President Ron Calgaard and the board of trustees, this history of Trinity University has been more than five years in the making. During these years, Douglas Brackenridge conducted exhaustive documentary and archival research, took a stunning number of oral histories, and assembled data on every era and facet of Trinity's winding past. Like all gifted writers, he wrote, rewrote, revised his revisions, and revised again.

The result is nothing short of masterful. The pages that follow are a compelling blend of historical narrative, sketch, portraiture, anecdote, analysis, evaluation, and contextual setting. Beyond its satisfying detail, Professor Brackenridge's history of Trinity, in the broad, sweeping contours of its 135-year story, tells a quintessentially American tale—of faith and idealism confronting hard reality, of ambition and aspiration pulsing with the ebb and flow of fortune, and of generosity and commitment animating visions of educational excellence that may have varied in their particulars but that, at their core, were identical in the value placed on the highest personal and intellectual standards. This is not hagiography: it is at times critical—controversies, mistakes, and imperfections are fully covered. Despite this, or perhaps partially because of it, the book is inspiring, particularly to those who have known Trinity both from the outside and from within.

Clearly, this was the proverbial labor of love for Professor Brackenridge. He loves history; he loves the scholarly process; he loves Trinity.

That many, many people have loved Trinity and have made it their personal labor of love is a recurring theme in this history.

After Nature, wrote Emerson, "the next great influence into the spirit of the scholar is the mind of the Past. . . . Books are the best type of the influence of the past. . . . Books are the best of things, well used; abused, among the worst. What is the right use? . . . They are for nothing but to inspire." Professor Brackenridge writes inspiringly of an inspiring history, rendering the influential minds of Trinity and, through them, the university's past. This is sound scholarship, a story—or more precisely, stories—well told, and a book that, well used, will be among the best of things.

It is altogether fitting that the recently revived Trinity University Press is publishing *Trinity University: A Tale of Three Cities* among its first, highly anticipated, and what promise to be critically well received books. This foreword is followed by a preface that, in turn, is followed by Trinity's past. As past is prologue, the story of Trinity to date is preface to the Trinity of tomorrow. The collective labors of those of us privileged to work at Trinity or to be part of the university's family of alumni and friends will, it is fervently hoped, add in commensurate measure to Trinity's continuing ascension while reflecting the history and traditions embodied in the pages that follow.

PREFACE

FOUNDED IN 1869, TRINITY UNIVERSITY is a paradigm of the century from which the institution emerged. Nineteenth-century Americans had an organic, pragmatic space—the space of action and freedom. Those who encountered problems could simply pick up, move on, and start anew. Likewise, Trinity has exhibited a mobility unmatched by few, if any institutions of higher learning in the United States today, occupying three different Texas settings: Tehuacana, Limestone County (1869–1902); Waxahachie, Ellis County (1902–1942); and San Antonio, Bexar County (1942–present). In San Antonio, Trinity merged with the University of San Antonio, a Methodist institution, and for ten years held classes on its Woodlawn campus. In 1952, the university moved to the city's north side, where it built a distinctive modern campus.[1]

Fiscal issues that threatened to close the institution precipitated each move. In Tehuacana, a small village of only a few hundred inhabitants, Trinity taught elementary, grammar, and high school students, as well as the collegiate group, and relied on the precollegiate tuition to balance the institution's operating budget. By the end of the century, with a public school system in place, that income was no longer available. Unable to attract endowment funds and lacking adequate transportation, Trinity relocated to Waxahachie, a relatively thriving town of approximately 7,500 inhabitants that was connected by rail to the nearby metropolitan areas of Dallas and Fort Worth. There the university experienced a period of some prosperity following World War I, during which it increased enrollment, accumulated a modest endowment, and erected a compact campus.

The Depression of the 1930s, however, brought economic chaos to Waxahachie, a town heavily dependent on the cotton industry. Plunging enrollments forced Trinity trustees to eliminate faculty and staff positions, reduce salaries, abandon building projects, and use endowment funds to meet operating expenses. As a result, in 1936 the Southern Association of Colleges and Universities withdrew Trinity's accreditation and placed it on probationary status.

By 1940 university officials concluded once again that Trinity would have to move or close its doors. For a time, it appeared that Trinity might merge with Austin College, a Presbyterian institution in Sherman, Texas, but those negotiations failed. On 8 December 1941, the day after the bombing of Pearl Harbor brought the United States into World War II, the San Antonio Chamber of Commerce issued a communication asking Trinity to relocate to its city. Responding affirmatively, the university moved to San Antonio in 1942 and began a new phase of its history in an expanding metropolitan environment.

Geographical relocation has clearly had a heavy effect on the formation of Trinity's institutional identity; however, in the final analysis, it has been people—trustees, administrators, faculty, staff, students, alumni, benefactors, and friends—who have shaped the university's destiny. In particular, during the last half of the twentieth century in its current location, Trinity made strides toward becoming one of the nation's premier undergraduate institutions.

Under President James W. Laurie (1951–1970), Trinity erected forty-two buildings, increased its endowment from less than $1 million to $42 million, expanded enrollment, and improved the quality of faculty and students. Growth continued during the tenures of Duncan Wimpress (1970–1976) and acting president Bruce Thomas (1976–1979) as Trinity secured a Phi Beta Kappa chapter, built a spacious, well-equipped library, and enhanced its reputation as a quality regional university.

During the twenty-year presidency of Ronald K. Calgaard (1979–1999), the institution adopted as its mission the goal of providing an excellent undergraduate program in the liberal arts and sciences, enhanced with selected professional and pre-professional programs. Trinity elevated admission standards, recruited a diverse and outstanding faculty and staff, established a residential policy, upgraded and increased campus facilities, and accumulated an endowment of approximately $540 million dollars.

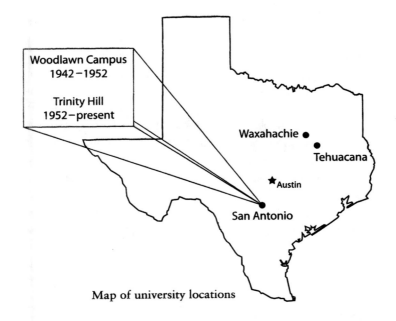

Map of university locations

Trinity moved into the new century under the leadership of John R. Brazil, former president of Bradley University in Peoria, Illinois. An experienced scholar, educator, and administrator, Brazil has undertaken the task of raising Trinity to a new level of achievement. Despite unfavorable economic conditions prior to and following the events of September 11, 2001, he has implemented programs designed to improve the academic, fiscal, and community dimensions of university life.

During the first one hundred years of its existence, the university maintained legal ties with various Presbyterian denominations. Founded in 1869 by Cumberland Presbyterians, Trinity became affiliated with the Presbyterian Church in the United States of America (PCUSA) in 1906 when the Cumberland Presbyterian Church reunited with its parent organization. A subsequent denominational merger in 1958 created the United Presbyterian Church in the United States of America (UPCUSA).

At the initiative of the UPCUSA, Trinity entered into a covenant relationship with the Synod of Texas in 1969 that involved no legal relationship, but affirmed a common heritage and pledged mutual cooperation. In 1983 the UPCUSA united with the Presbyterian Church in the United States (PCUS), to create the Presbyterian Church (U.S.A.). The university is currently related by covenant to the Synod of the Sun, Presbyterian Church (U.S.A.). In modern times, Trinity honors its historical roots through an ecumenical campus ministry based in the Margarite B. Parker Chapel and a commitment to the intellectual, moral, physical, and spiritual growth of its students.[2]

In the narrative that follows, I have attempted to place Trinity's institutional development within its regional setting and within the broader context of private, church-related institutions of higher learning. Similar to its counterparts, Trinity was influenced by national trends that affected pedagogy, social dynamics, and economic conditions. The endnotes and selected bibliography provide some relevant secondary sources for readers who are interested in examining these relationships in more depth.

Support for this history project has been provided by university funds authorized by the board of trustees in 1998 at the initiative of President Calgaard. During the 1999–2000 and 2000–2001 academic years, the university granted me academic leaves that enabled my full-time research and writing. President Brazil has provided additional funding for equipment, travel, and editorial assistance. I have been given unfettered access to all official documents and other materials in the university archives and have been free to determine the scope and content of the narrative. Although underwritten by university funds, the history is solely the work of the author and does not represent official positions of the board of trustees or the administration.

In the process of writing this history, many individuals, too numerous to mention here, have provided cooperation and support. I am especially grateful to the late Professor Emeritus Donald E. Everett for his wise counsel. His monograph, *Trinity University: A Record of One Hundred Years,* published by Trinity University Press in 1968, has been foundational to my research. My friend and colleague, Lois A. Boyd, has worked closely with me in preparing the manuscript for presentation to the editorial board of Trinity University Press. Thanks is also due to Barbara Ras, director of Trinity University Press, and Sarah Nawrocki, assistant to the director, for their editorial expertise.

Throughout the process of producing this history, Trinity's Public Relations Office, led by Sharon Jones Schweitzer, has been exceptionally cooperative and helpful. Associate Director Mary Denny, Sports Editor Justin Parker, Web Editor Scott Sowards, and Public Information Officer Russell Guerrero have assisted me in locating photographs and providing new ones as requested. In addition to public relations staff, Helen Terry, the visual resource curator of the Department of Art and Art History, performed image restoration and Margaret Miksch, Department of Religion secretary, provided typing and printing services.

Daily I have relied on the diligence and expertise of University Archives Coordinator Janice Sabec. Her willingness to interrupt projects in progress to assist me with searches for documents and photographs has greatly facilitated my work, and her genuine interest in all aspects of university history has been a joy to observe. Similarly, I have frequently called on Media Technician Pat Ullmann for advice regarding scanning and repairing photographs and for creating map illustrations and other images for use in speaking engagements and in the book. On numerous occasions, she has come to the rescue when computers and scanners have refused to obey my commands.

I am indebted to the staffs of the Presbyterian Historical Society and the Historical Foundation of the Cumberland Presbyterian Church for their hospitality and advice and to the trustees, administrators, faculty, staff, students, and alumni/ae who participated in oral history interviews during the course of my research. I also appreciate the willingness of George Boyd, Coleen Grissom, Jack Stotts, and Bill Walker to read parts of the manuscript and offer suggestions for improvement.

Finally, I want to thank my wife and colleague, Diane Saphire, associate vice president of Information Resources, for her sustained support and encouragement. She provided valuable statistical information and helped me to interpret it contextually. Despite demanding administrative and teaching responsibilities, she made time to accompany me on visits to Tehuacana, Waxahachie, and other locations, where she participated in interviews, took photographs, and interacted with residents and alumni/ae. On numerous occasions she assisted me in preparing and presenting visual aids for talks on Trinity history. Her ability to ask critical questions and to give constructive criticism has helped me to improve the manuscript throughout its many revisions. Above all, her optimism, enthusiasm, perseverance, and unqualified affirmation are gratefully acknowledged and deeply appreciated.

In writing this institutional history, I have come to know and admire countless individuals who have contributed to the advancement of Trinity University. They include trustees and administrators whose wise leadership guided the university during difficult times, faculty who challenged students to think critically and live responsibly, staff who kept the institution functioning smoothly, students whose accomplishments have brought honor to their alma mater, and benefactors and friends whose financial support enabled the university to survive and flourish. Unfortunately, all their names and stories cannot be included within the limited pages of this historical overview. To these individuals, who loved and served Trinity University during the Tehuacana, Waxahachie, and San Antonio eras, I dedicate this book. Without them, there would be no history to write.

R. Douglas Brackenridge, *Professor Emeritus*
Department of Religion, Trinity University
August 2004

PART ONE

TEHUACANA

It is thought that no more desirable location could have been
selected than Tehuacana. It is proverbial for its healthfulness,
supplied with an abundance of living water, surrounded
with a beautifully romantic scenery and fertile country,
capable of sustaining a dense population, central, and easy
of access, being on the line of the Central Railroad and now
with a short day's ride of the Terminus, and free from the
temptations to vice abounding in the various towns of the
country.

Trinity University Catalogue, 1869–1870

A UNIVERSITY OF THE HIGHEST ORDER

Unanimously resolved that it is proper and expedient that steps be taken at once to locate and establish in the State of Texas, a University of the highest order, to be controlled by the Synods in said state.

SYNOD LOCATION COMMITTEE, 6 DECEMBER 1867

THE CREATION OF THE REPUBLIC OF TEXAS in 1836 marked the beginning of an era of colonization that dramatically changed the area's social fabric. The expression "Gone to Texas" (or simply G.T.T.) chalked on the doors of houses in the southern states announced the departure of families to the frontier area. Despite lack of resources and conflict with Native Americans, immigrants responded to a generous land policy, and the population burgeoned. By the time Texas attained statehood a decade later, the Anglo population had grown from an estimated 34,470 to 102,961 and the slave population from 5,000 to 38,753. Growth accelerated further, and on the eve of the Civil War, Texas had a population of more than 600,000 residents.[1]

Among the new arrivals were significant numbers of Cumberland Presbyterians who immigrated from Tennessee, Kentucky, Virginia, Alabama, and other southern states. The Cumberland Presbyterian Church had its origin in the milieu of the early nineteenth-century frontier revivalism referred to by historians as the Second Great Awakening. While some members of the mainstream Presbyterian Church in the U.S.A (PCUSA) embraced revivalism as a valid means of church renewal, others criticized its emotional excesses and lack of decorum.

In dire need of clergy because of the rapid growth of church membership, the Cumberland Presbytery in Kentucky ordained ministerial candidates who lacked college degrees and formal theological training but who had been privately tutored by educated and experienced ministers. As a result, however, the Synod of Kentucky suspended the revivalist supporters for acting "contrary to the rules and discipline of the Presbyterian Church." After efforts at reconciliation failed, the revivalist Presbyterians separated from the PCUSA and created an independent presbytery in 1810, marking the beginning of a new denomination.[2]

Characterized by spontaneity and mobility, Cumberland Presbyterians nevertheless valued both experiential religion and higher education. Although they espoused a religion of the heart that emphasized radical conversion and a personal relationship to Christ, they also respected education as a means of producing informed clergy and responsible citizens. To prepare individuals for life and for eternity, Cumberland Presbyterian educational institutions considered the Bible to be foundational to all learning and employed only faculty whose moral values and theological beliefs coincided with denominational perspectives.[3]

Call for Ministers

If your heart is drawn out by the love of souls, and if you want a field where your labors will tell to the next generation how, and for what purpose you have lived, then go to Texas. But note this fact—the Texans are, and will be, a race of high-minded, ardent, enterprising freemen of the genuine southern stamp—very different from the rude simple-hearted backwoodsman of the west; and therefore it is desirable that he who would minister to such a race in holy things should possess not only ardent piety and a meek Christ-like spirit, but such intellectual advantages as will enable him to grapple with minds of the first order.

The Cumberland Presbyterian, 25 March 1837

Despite a late entry into the field of higher education, the Cumberland Presbyterians founded and/or controlled about thirty-nine institutions identified as colleges or universities during the nineteenth century. Scattered from Pennsylvania to California, including ten in Texas, all but two of the twenty-two institutions established before the Civil War had failed by the end of the war. Between the end of the Civil War and the beginning of the new century, the Cumberland Presbyterians opened the doors of fifteen new schools. Among those that endured were Bethel College

Sumner Bacon,
"The Apostle of Texas"

(Tennessee), Waynesburg College (Pennsylvania), Lincoln University (Illinois), Trinity University (Texas), and Missouri Valley College (Missouri).[4]

Although lacking physical comforts, financial resources, and pastoral leadership, Cumberland Presbyterians adapted well to frontier conditions in Texas. Their evangelical piety and ecumenical spirit enabled the denomination to take root and outpace the growth of other Presbyterian bodies. As early as 1829, colorful Cumberland lay evangelist Sumner Bacon crossed the Sabine River into Texas and embarked on a missionary career that earned him the sobriquet "the Apostle of Texas." Defying a Mexican law that permitted only Roman Catholicism, Bacon surreptitiously distributed Bibles and conducted revival meetings in fields. Forced to flee from Mexican troops on numerous occasions, Bacon found conditions more favorable when colonists banded together and drove the Mexican garrisons from Texas soil. After serving as a chaplain and courier for General Sam Houston during the war against Mexico and having secured ordination, Bacon organized one of the first Cumberland Presbyterian churches in Texas during the summer of 1836.[5]

Following Bacon's example, pioneer Cumberland clergymen such as Samuel Corley, Andrew Jackson McGown, and Richard O. Watkins commenced evangelistic ministries in the Republic of Texas. Together they recruited members and organized small, rural congregations in east and central Texas. In 1837, Bacon and two other ordained ministers established the Texas Presbytery in a meeting held near San Augustine, Texas. Five years later, two additional presbyteries, Red River and Colorado, were created, and representatives of the three governing bodies met to form Texas Synod in 1843. Because of continuing immigration, Cumberland Presbyterianism experienced remarkable growth in Texas during the antebellum era. In 1840, only a single presbytery existed, with 10 churches, 200 communicants, and 6 ordained ministers. Ten years later, the denomination reported 2 synods (Texas and Brazos), 6 presbyteries, 83 congregations, 2,850 communicants, and 64 clergymen. Just prior to the Civil War, statistics reveal 3 synods (Texas, Brazos, and Colorado), 12 presbyteries, 155 congregations, 6,200 communicants, and 126 ministers.[6]

Despite their increasing numbers, most Cumberland Presbyterians lived in isolated rural settings that precluded the establishment of large congregations. Cumberland churches usually had communicant rolls of fewer than thirty members and often lacked adequate buildings or permanent pastors. Itinerant ministers depended almost solely on the generosity of people who were able to eke out only a meager existence in dryland farming. Milton Estill reported an annual salary of $145.25 in 1851, and William Travelstead of Red River Presbytery collected only $45.00 in 1854.[7] Traveling more than a thousand miles in Stephens County, O. W. Carter held 200 religious services and revival meetings for which he received $75 in remuneration and a promise of $250 for the following year. Fortunately, few ministers reported, as did W. M. Speegle of Elgin, Texas, in 1883, that they "preached fourteen times at twelve different places and received one dollar and that too from a half-drunk man."[8]

Nevertheless, Texas Cumberland Presbyterians initiated a number of educational endeavors prior to the Civil War that bore the name of academy, institute, or college. Most were little more than grammar or secondary schools with only a few collegiate-level students in attendance. At the first meeting of Texas Presbytery in 1837, Bacon and his compatriots resolved to establish at an early date "a seminary of learning" primarily for ministerial candidates. Reminiscent of other pioneer Presbyterian educational institutions, the proposed school was to combine "manual labor and literary pursuits."[9] Although the school never materialized, others provided formal education for future Cumberland leaders. In 1846, Red River Presbytery reported to Texas Synod that an academy at Clarksville was operating under its supervision. At the same time, the Texas and Colorado presbyteries were taking steps to enter the educational field in the near future. Other presbyteries instigated similar ventures, although, in

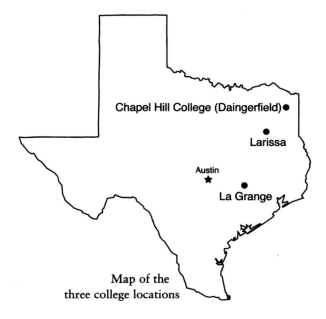

Chapel Hill College (Daingerfield)●

● Larissa

Austin ★

● La Grange

Map of the
three college locations

many cases, the precise relationship between the school and the governing body is obscure.[10]

Three schools that attained collegiate rank under the care of the Cumberland Presbyterian Church in Texas—Larissa College, La Grange Collegiate Institute (later Ewing College), and Chapel Hill College—are considered to be the forerunners of Trinity University. Although some sources refer to the "merger" of these three institutions to form Trinity University, in fact, there is no legal connection between Trinity and the three schools.[11]

All three institutions shared similar characteristics and met identical fates. Each was located in a rural village, free from what were deemed the negative influences of city life and in close proximity to a cluster of Cumberland Presbyterian settlers. Each school sought the formal endorsement of a governing body (synod or presbytery) and secured a charter that granted legal ownership and "general supervision" to its respective ecclesiastical body. "General supervision" consisted primarily of receiving an annual institutional report and approving charter amendments and trustee appointments. Otherwise, the schools retained considerable autonomy regarding internal operations such as faculty appointments, curricular decisions, and fiscal policies.[12]

Commencing operations with little or no endowment, the three colleges relied almost exclusively on tuition income to cover operating expenses.

Consequently, any drop in enrollment imperiled institutional stability. Over time, gifts of land and cash from Cumberland supporters generated income for buildings and equipment but were insufficient to provide the endowment needed to acquire a strong faculty and to maintain and upgrade facilities. Like most other peer institutions in Texas, the three schools would never recover from the economic impact of the Civil War and Reconstruction and, after hostilities ceased, were unable to resume collegiate operations.

The origins of Larissa College date back to 1846 when a group of Cumberland Presbyterians from Tennessee led by Thomas N. McKee emigrated to Cherokee County, Texas. Eight miles northwest of what is now the town of Jacksonville, they established the village of Larissa. Utilizing a small log hut on the outskirts of the village, McKee's sister, Sarah Rebecca Erwin, opened a school in 1848 under the auspices of Trinity Presbytery. The following year, Brazos Synod reported that the school was in a "permanent and flourishing condition" and urged congregations and individuals to give financial support to the new educational venture.[13] In 1850, completion of a two-story frame building enabled the school, initially known as Larissa Academy, to attract students from surrounding towns and villages.[14]

The institution entered a new phase of educational activity in 1855 when it obtained a charter and incorporated as Larissa College under the ecclesiastical supervision of Brazos Synod. Although the synod granted administrative autonomy regarding faculty and curriculum, it retained the right to veto what it deemed "improper appointments" to the school's board of trustees.[15] Immediately following incorporation, Larissa College enjoyed a brief period of prosperity and growth under the leadership of Franklin L. Yoakum, president and professor of languages and physical science.[16] During the 1856–57 academic year, the college reported 144 students in attendance, including three ministerial candidates, and assets of more than $13,000. With the endorsement of Brazos Synod, college trustees contemplated endowing a theological department with contributions from local congregations.[17]

When W. G. Parsons visited Cherokee County in 1860, he described Larissa as a "beautiful, thriving, quiet, religious village" that offered an excellent environment for academic and collegiate studies. Although the library contained fewer than one hundred volumes, Parsons extolled the college's faculty and student body and praised its fine scientific equipment, especially a large telescope purchased in New York at an approximate cost of fifteen hundred dollars.[18] In 1860, Larissa College awarded diplomas to

Larissa College, c. 1850

its first and only graduating class of four members. With the outbreak of civil strife in 1861, Yoakum suspended classes at Larissa "until such time as it can resume its career of usefulness."[19] Efforts to reopen the college in 1865 were unsuccessful, and Brazos Synod voted in 1867 to dissolve any connections existing between the two bodies because Larissa had "in effect gone into private hands."[20]

During the same year (1848) that Larissa College commenced operations, La Grange Collegiate Institute opened in La Grange, Fayette County, under the auspices of Colorado Presbytery. The local Cumberland Presbyterian pastor, A. H. Walker, and several elders raised the initial capital and formed the nucleus of a board of trustees that was empowered to procure the services of a suitable professor. They selected Marcus A. Montrose, a native Scotsman and reputed graduate of the University of Edinburgh who had acquired a regional reputation as a scholar and educator. A colorful and frequently controversial figure, Montrose had held brief presidencies at San Augustine University and Nacogdoches University in east Texas, where he promoted his "Electic [sic] System of Universal Education."[21] As the sole faculty member for a period of time at San Augustine University, Montrose taught classes in mathematics, Latin, Greek, history, navigation, astronomy, rhetoric, logic, political economy, natural philosophy, chemistry, botany, and geology. Concurrent with his teaching duties, Montrose participated in public debates on various theological and pedagogical topics.[22]

During Montrose's brief tenure as president and professor, La Grange Collegiate Institute catered mainly to primary and preparatory students. Later, as enrollment improved, the staff consisted of four professors and an assistant. After a decade of operations, the Institute advised Colorado Presbytery that all debts had been liquidated and that "seventy-six students [were] drinking from its scientific faucets."[23] In 1859, the Institute came under the jurisdiction and control of Colorado Synod and changed its name to Ewing College in honor of Finis Ewing, one of the founders of the Cumberland denomination. When the Civil War began, however, all hopes of financial stability for the college ended. In 1862, Colorado Synod noted that the school had been suspended and that President R. P. Dechard had been granted permission to use the facilities to operate a private school.[24] The college subsequently functioned briefly under Methodist auspices, although Cumberland Presbyterians retained legal ownership and control of institutional assets. In 1868, Colorado Synod sold the greatly deteriorated property for $500 and later turned the proceeds of the sale over to Trinity University.[25]

Chapel Hill College, located in Daingerfield, Titus County, secured a charter under the auspices of Marshall Presbytery in 1850 and four years later came under the control of Texas Synod.[26] Classes for preparatory students began in an unfinished frame building under the instruction of S. R. Chaddick, a Cumberland Presbyterian minister. By invitation of the board of trustees, William E. Beeson arrived from Logan County, Kentucky, in March 1852 to serve as professor and president of the fledgling institution. The board reported in 1854 that the college had matriculated ninety-six students and was "free from financial embarrassment" with a surplus of a thousand dollars in the treasury. Four years later, work began on a new brick building, standing two stories high, costing approximately three thousand dollars, and containing six recitation rooms and a chapel. Texas Synod set an endowment goal of twenty thousand dollars, well over half of which had been pledged before the Civil War brought operations to a halt.[27]

"This institution is located at Dangerfield [sic], Titus County, Texas, a pleasant, healthy and romantic village, far from any large water course. And on account of its remoteness from anything calculated to vitiate the morals, or draw off the mind from study, and its elevation and abundance of pure spring water, it is a delightful location for a Literary Institution.

The *Texas Presbyterian*, 10 July 1852

At Chapel Hill College, the academic year was divided into two sessions of five months each, the first beginning in September and the second in February. Students in the preparatory department paid tuition ranging from eight to sixteen dollars per session, while those in the college paid twenty dollars. Board, including light, fuel, and washing, amounted to approximately eight dollars per month. In the preparatory department, pupils studied orthography, reading, writing, arithmetic, geography, and English, Latin, and Greek grammar. The college division concentrated on a classical education, featuring languages, mathematics, and sciences. Courses on the Bible and a senior capstone course entitled "Evidences of Christianity" reportedly prepared students to defend Christian truth against all opposition. Upon completion of the four-year course, students received a Bachelor of Arts degree. The college granted only five degrees in more than two decades of operation.[28]

When rumors circulated in 1861 that Texas was about to be invaded by Union forces, President Beeson dismissed all classes except the preparatory department and offered his services to the Confederate States of America. Taking with him a number of Chapel Hill students as recruits, Beeson assisted in the organization of the Daingerfield Grays. Rising from the rank of captain to lieutenant colonel, he fought in a number of battles, including the bloody conflict at Shiloh. After Appomattox, Beeson returned to Daingerfield to resume his presidency and attempted to revitalize Chapel Hill College. Unable to collect on the financial pledges made before the Civil War or to secure new funding, Beeson maintained a small preparatory department for a time on income generated solely from tuition. In 1869, Brazos Synod returned ecclesiastical oversight of the school to Marshall Presbytery, which retained secondary and preparatory classes until the 1890s, when public schools made its work redundant.[29]

At the close of the Civil War, Cumberland Presbyterians began to reassess their strategy for higher education in Texas. Among others, A. J. McGown, editor of *The Texas Presbyterian,* considered it shortsighted to establish multiple educational institutions, none of which was able to attain statewide support. As a trustee of La Grange Collegiate Institute, McGown had experienced the futility of sustaining an institution that lacked broad denominational support. Citing the advice of a noted Cumberland educator, "Have but one first-class school—locate it in the midst of its friends," McGown urged his peers to establish an institution of higher learning that would serve the entire state of Texas. If agents had solicited land for such a project twenty-five years ago, he observed, Cumberland Presbyterians would now have an endowment of more than half a million dollars to underwrite the college.[30]

Other advocates of a central institution urged caution, arguing that the economic and political instability of the times was not propitious for establishing a college. The years that followed the Civil War proved difficult for plantation owners as well as small landowners and farmers. Land values fell to 20 percent of 1860 prices, and cotton, the basic money crop, declined in value from thirty-one cents per pound in 1866 to seventeen cents in 1870.[31]

Richard Beard, a theology professor at Cumberland University in Tennessee and a highly regarded authority on educational matters, deplored the proliferation of weak denominational colleges and advised against opening new schools before adequate finances could be procured. Referring specifically to the Texas Cumberland church, Beard thought that a first-class university, while a possibility in twenty years, was not feasible under Reconstruction conditions. "At this distance," Beard commented, "an observer would judge that [the] true policy at present would be to multiply their missions, strengthen their congregations, lay a broad and deep foundation, socially, ecclesiastically, and religiously, and then build up a great Texan University."[32]

Texas Cumberland clergymen's optimism, however, transcended reality, and they mobilized to promote an educational venture that would fill the vacuum left by the demise of Larissa, Chapel Hill, and Ewing Colleges. Clergymen Andrew Jackson Haynes and Henry F. Bone played pivotal roles in marshalling support for a new university. The two men "agitated the idea" among Cumberland leaders throughout the state in correspondence and in speeches at presbytery and synod meetings. Bone and Haynes had recently taken up residence in Dallas, a site they deemed auspicious for a denominational university. Nevertheless, they acknowledged that questions of location and organization should be decided only after all three synods had agreed to participate in the joint venture.[33]

At a meeting held in October 1866 at Tehuacana in Limestone County, Brazos Synod endorsed the cooperative project. Commissioners approved a report from the synod's Committee on Education that called for the establishment of a university "at some point as nearly central to the church in the State as soon as practicable" for the education of young men and women and "especially for our candidates for the ministry." The synod also recommended that a standing committee be appointed to correspond with similar standing committees from Texas and Colorado Synods regarding the creation of a new university. By emphasizing the need for a central location, however, the report heightened the likelihood that the proposed institution would be located in Brazos Synod. Bounded by Colorado Synod on the west and Texas Synod on the east, Brazos Synod was situated between the Brazos and Colorado Rivers, an area that encompassed the heartland of Texas Cumberland Presbyterianism. Not surprisingly, three of the four finalists for the university site were in Brazos Synod and the fourth was on its periphery.[34]

With little debate, both Texas and Colorado Synods enthusiastically endorsed the Brazos Synod initiative. As a result, representatives from the three synods agreed to meet in Dallas on 6 December 1867 to formulate procedures for implementing the joint venture. A week prior to the Dallas meeting, Bone and Haynes convened a public meeting to stimulate interest in locating the proposed university in Dallas. Emphasizing the economic and cultural advantages of hosting an institution of higher learning, John W. Swindells, editor of the *Dallas Herald,* endorsed the project. "It is now time for action, prompt, vigorous action, to manifest an interest commensurate with the importance of the enterprise."[35]

The Cumberland representatives arrived in Dallas the following week to begin deliberations. Willis Burgess, M. P. Modrall, and W. G. L. Quaite represented Brazos Synod; J. H. Wofford, Alpha Young, William M. Dillard, and Alfred Smith, Colorado Synod; and R. O. Watkins and R. R. Dunlap, Texas Synod. Anxious to move forward, the participants appointed a committee of three—Quaite, Young, and Watkins—to solicit propositions from towns desiring to underwrite the initial expense of locating a university in their community. To merit consideration, a town had to make a minimum offer of $25,000 to cover expenses for property, buildings, and equipment.[36] The representatives also agreed that an additional $30,000 should be raised to endow two chairs in the male department and one in the female department and that further donations of land should be solicited to provide long-term endowment resources. Once proposals had been secured, each of the synods was to appoint members to still another committee composed of twelve men (four from each synod) who were deemed "free from local prejudices and sectarian influences" to finalize the location, apply for a charter, and arrange to commence classes.[37]

Eager to secure the denominational university, Dallas citizens closely monitored the actions of the Cumberland delegates. At one point during the deliberations, a group of local businessmen met with the committee to present arguments for Dallas. Situated on the Trinity River in the midst of a rich agricultural region, the city had became the county seat in 1850, heightening its political influence in the surrounding area. Growing rapidly, Dallas had a population of about 3,000 by 1870, and as the contemplated point of junction for several major railroads, it would soon become an important commercial center. Moreover, Cumberland Presbyterians were among the first Protestants to establish churches in Dallas. Under Haynes's leadership, they had organized a congregation in 1867 and opened an academy with Henry F. Bone as the lone faculty member.[38]

Although Dallas supporters had their campaign well underway even before the Cumberland commissioners adjourned their conference, other Texas communities subsequently expressed interest in providing a home for the new university. Among those, however, only three locations—Waxahachie, Tehuacana, and Round Rock—met the $25,000 qualification. Committee members H. F. Bone, William E. Beeson, and S. R. Chaddick from Texas Synod, Alpha Young, William M. Dillard, and W. A. Davis from Colorado Synod, and W. G. L. Quaite and D. M. Prendergast from Brazos Synod met in Tehuacana on November 4, 1868, to begin the selection process. Following their examination of local facilities, the committee members planned to conduct on-site inspections of the other three towns before reaching a final decision.[39]

Named after the Tawakoni Indian tribe that once occupied the territory, Tehuacana was first settled by Major John Boyd, a veteran of the army of the Republic of Texas and a representative of the Sabine district in the first and second congresses of the new republic. In 1845, he staked out his veteran's claim in what became Limestone County, choosing a picturesque setting with panoramic views of the surrounding prairies, a healthy climate, abundant water supply, and fertile prairie lands. Following a dramatic conversion during a revival led by Cumberland Presbyterian evangelist Andrew J. McGown, Boyd joined the church and became one of its staunchest supporters. An advocate of education, he encouraged the establishment of Tehuacana Academy, a preparatory school that featured Daniel Malloy, Franklin L. Yoakum, and Samuel King as faculty members. Commencing classes in 1852, the school closed during the Civil War and never reopened. Nevertheless, the academy had attracted a number of Cumberland Presbyterian families who settled in the area to be close to educational facilities.[40]

From the outset, Tehuacana was the favored location. According to Cumberland folklore, Tehuacana was destined to become a university town. Reuben E. Sanders, one of the first Cumberland Presbyterian missionaries to be ordained by Colorado Presbytery, traversed the area around Tehuacana in 1848. Impressed by the beauty and tranquility of the location, Sanders reportedly climbed one of the prominent limestone formations and wrote in bold letters on a large rock, "Build a

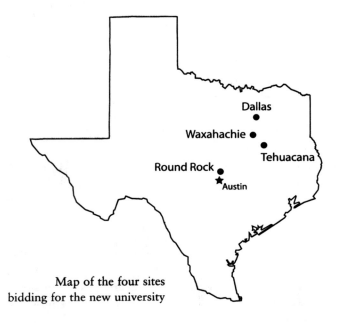

Map of the four sites
bidding for the new university

Cumberland university on these hills." The writing eventually faded, but the words remained vividly etched in the minds of pioneers who settled in the vicinity.[41]

Beyond sentimentalism, Tehuacana's pastoral setting offered a healthy and sheltered environment for young scholars, a primary consideration to a generation of adults who viewed urban life with fear and disdain. In Tehuacana, students would be shielded from the temptations of rowdy frontier towns and would be surrounded by a solitude conducive to study and reflection. Because of its high elevation, Tehuacana also provided protection from malaria and other diseases that often plagued low-lying areas. With abundant fruit trees, vegetable gardens, and grain fields, students could be well fed without relying on other communities. In addition, Tehuacana residents were proud that "the sale of ardent spirits, in or near the place, is prohibited by law."[42]

In 1849, Major Boyd had campaigned vigorously to make Tehuacana the capital of Texas. Traveling on horseback throughout the countryside and distributing tracts, he extolled the advantages of his home territory. Although unsuccessful, Boyd enabled Tehuacana to finish third in the process and to acquire a positive image among Texas residents. Moreover, despite its rural setting, Tehuacana was only an hour's buggy ride from Mexia, the nearest station on the Texas Central Railroad. In keeping with evangelical terminology, the new university could be "in the world but not of the world."[43]

Tehuacana also offered an attractive financial package. The donation of Boyd's home, a prominent site of 130 acres in town, and 1,500 acres of prairie land, as well as other individual gifts of land and money, were valued conservatively at $30,000. Certain to increase in value with the establishment of a university and the influx of population, the property around Tehuacana seemed likely to generate income that would produce a substantial endowment. The Boyd home, a spacious two-story building with eight rooms and columned verandas, could be converted into classrooms ready for immediate occupancy, thus avoiding a costly building program.[44]

Despite what they considered obvious advantages, Tehuacana residents knew that the search committee would give careful consideration to the other sites. Nearby Waxahachie had some ardent supporters, including one of the committee members, W. G. L. Quaite, pastor of a thriving Cumberland congregation in the town center. One contemporary described Waxahachie as a "thrifty, neat little place, beyond all doubt one of the healthiest places we have ever seen" and inhabited by an "order loving and order encouraging people."[45] Located thirty miles south of Dallas in Ellis County, Waxahachie was a cotton-producing center that grew rapidly after becoming the county seat in 1850. By the time of the search committee's visit in 1869, the town had an academy, a newspaper, a bank, several Masonic lodges, and churches of various denominations, including Methodist, Baptist, and Cumberland Presbyterian. On the negative side, Waxahachie Methodists planned to open Marvin College in the fall of 1870. Whether two church colleges could prosper in such close proximity was a question that no one could answer with certainty.[46]

A return visit to Dallas found its citizens eager to impress committee members with the advantages of their location. Largely through the efforts of Bone and Haynes, gifts and pledges amounting to approximately $25,000 had been received from Dallas citizens.[47] In addition, Dallas supporters offered a 13-acre site north of the city center and additional prairie lands in the immediate vicinity. However, many Cumberland Presbyterians still viewed the proximity of a university to a growing urban center to be a liability.[48]

A spell of bad weather in February 1869 made it impossible for the full committee to reach Round Rock, but those who managed to traverse the muddy roads and ford the swollen creeks reported that they were satisfied with its "liberal and eligible" proposals.[49] Sixteen miles north of Austin in

Major John Boyd

Williamson County, Round Rock (originally called Brushy Creek) had been settled in 1848 and soon became a prosperous village. Among the early settlers, Cumberland Presbyterian families established several congregations in the area. In 1853, Brazos Synod created Little River Presbytery to care for the growing number of communicants who were moving north from Austin to occupy the territory between the Brazos and Colorado Rivers. Greenwood Masonic College, an institution that later became known as Round Rock College, had opened in 1867, and again the presence of a functioning college raised questions about the viability of establishing a rival institution.[50]

After inspecting all four sites, committee members agreed to meet in Waco on April 20, 1869, to make a final decision. For a variety of reasons, including health and travel restrictions, some of the members did not make it to Waco for the decisive meeting. Bone was the sole representative from Texas Synod, with Quaite, Renfro, and Prendergast from Brazos Synod, and Dillard, Wofford, and Davis from Colorado Synod. During several meetings held over a four-day period, the representatives discussed the relative merits of each location. "After earnestly, calmly, and . . . prayerfully considering the claims of the different points, the interests of the church, and the future prospects of the proposed school," the committee unanimously voted for Tehuacana as the university site.[51]

Following the selection of Tehuacana, the committee adopted the name Trinity University, elected a nine-member board of trustees, who were required to be communicants of the Cumberland Presbyterian Church, and appointed agents to raise money for faculty salaries. The committee set ambitious, if unrealistic, contribution goals of $15,000 over a five-year period for Colorado Synod and $20,000 each for Brazos and Texas Synods. They also empowered agents to sell perpetual scholarships at $500, payable in two years with interest of 10 percent, and five-year scholarships at $150 with the same rate of interest.[52]

Before adjourning on April 23, 1869, the committee elected a president and faculty members, designated their salaries, and appointed a committee to draft a charter and secure its approval from the state legislature. Their presidential choice, Thomas B. Wilson, had served as a Cumberland pastor and for two decades had been president of the Masonic Female Institute in Marshall, Texas. A former moderator of the Cumberland General Assembly, Wilson was well known throughout the denomination as an educator and theologian.[53] For his services, Wilson was to receive $2,000 in coin annually. Each of the three professors selected, William E. Beeson, S. Doak Lowry, and William P. Gillespie, was assigned a yearly salary of $1,500.[54]

The name *Trinity University* was an unusual choice for nineteenth-century Presbyterians. Traditionally, they chose names for institutions of higher education that were either regional (Princeton, Wooster, Missouri Valley), individual (Calvin, Lafayette, Macalester, Washington and Jefferson), or historical (Geneva, Westminster). Sources from the early twentieth century attribute the appellation "Trinity" to Henry F. Bone, a Texas Synod representative, who reportedly deemed the name appropriate for an institution founded by three synods in the name of the Holy Trinity (Father, Son, and Holy Spirit) and designed to train students in body, mind, and spirit.[55] An article written less than a year after the event by J. H. Wofford, who was present at the Waco meeting, states that they chose the name because of "the joint work of the three Synods, in the name of the Holy Trinity." His account makes no mention of the relationship to body, mind, and spirit.[56]

Employment of the term *university* in the charter belies the configuration of the new institution. According to accepted use of the term, *university* implied a central degree-granting board of trustees with a number of individual schools or colleges, such as law, medicine, or engineering. While Trinity's founders had no immediate plans to implement such an educational program, the term expressed their aspirations. Later in the century, the university had a short-lived law school and, for a brief period, offered master's and Ph.D. degrees, but these programs were tangential to the primary focus on undergraduate studies.

Having completed its work, the committee directed the trustees to convene at the earliest date possible and to make preparations for the beginning of classes on the first Monday in September, a scant four months away. At their initial session on 1 May 1869, after "invoking the blessing of the Deity," the trustees took steps to designate a town center on a part of Boyd's land donation, reserving certain choice lots for future university buildings. While temporarily utilizing the Boyd home for classes, the trustees indicated that after other buildings were erected, the residence would be transformed into "one of the most tasteful, beautiful, and attractive female schools in our country." This statement would be later cited by opponents of coeducation as proof that Trinity's founders envisioned separate male and female departments rather than "promiscuous" mixing of men and women in the same classrooms.[57]

"We will not live to see Trinity arrive at maturity, but our children may, and the seed we have planted here with trembling hand, yet with an humble trust in God, may be made to spring up and fill a place in the South similar to that which Princeton and Yale fill in the east."

Brazos Synod Minutes (CP), 1870

Other actions soon followed. Receiving word that Thomas B. Wilson had declined the position of president, the trustees selected William Beeson, former president of Chapel Hill College, to lead Trinity University. As part of his duties, Beeson was requested to deliver "a public lecture to the students every Sabbath and to require the students to attend the same." The trustees also ordered that candidates for the ministry in "all orthodox denominations" who applied for admission were to be received into the school tuition free. Finally, they adopted as their official seal a circle on which the words *"Nil Cruce Nil Corona"* (No Cross No Crown) and "Trinity University" were emblazoned. After three years of resolutions, proposals, and deliberations, the long anticipated denominational university was about to become a reality.[58]

CHAPTER TWO

FOUNDATION WORK

He [William E. Beeson] was the Stonewall of Manassas to Trinity
University. He held the ground at a time when other men would have
wavered and lost the day. His work was foundation work. It will endure,
for he laid the foundation deep and broad.

S. M. TEMPLETON

WITH LITTLE FANFARE AND MUCH ANTICIPATION, Trinity University commenced classes in Tehuacana on 23 September 1869, later
than the scheduled opening on the first Monday in September because car-
penters still were renovating the former Boyd residence to use for classrooms. Even so, seven students presented themselves to the five-member
Trinity faculty at the opening session. By the end of the first term, nearly a hundred had enrolled, including part-time and precollegiate-level
students.[1]

Almost half of the initial matriculates listed Tehuacana as their home
address, with others arriving by horse-drawn hack from nearby Mexia.
Only five were non-Texans: one each from Louisiana, Kentucky, and
Arkansas, and two from Alabama. Twenty-four women enrolled in the
music department, and four men registered as ministerial students, of
whom two had preaching assignments in nearby congregations as they
continued their education in preparation for ordination.[2]

Since only the converted Boyd residence was available in 1869, men
and women enrolled and recited in the same classes, a blending of the male
and female departments that would precipitate a prolonged debate among
Texas Cumberland Presbyterians regarding the operation of Trinity as a
coeducational institution. With no residential facilities on campus, students sought boarding accommodations in the homes of faculty members
and other families in the immediate vicinity at monthly rates ranging from
$10.00 to $12.50.[3] Although private lodgings were limited, Tehuacana cit-

izens announced their determination "to do all in their power to provide facilities for boarding all that may come."[4]

President William E. Beeson and a faculty of four constituted the initial instructional staff of the male and female departments. Beeson served as professor of mental and moral science, William P. Gillespie as professor of ancient languages and literature, and S. Doak Lowry as professor of mathematics and natural philosophy. As was customary, a male (Lowry) served as principal of the female department, assisted by faculty spouses M. Kate Gillespie and Margaret F. Beeson, teachers of instrumental music. Joining the staff the following year were David A. Quaite, professor of rhetoric and *belles lettres*, and William Hudson, professor of penmanship, bookkeeping, and commercial law.[5]

Beeson was the dominant personality on the Trinity campus. With both admiration and consternation, trustees, faculty, students, and townspeople revered yet feared him. An experienced educator at the age of forty-seven, the Virginia native had taught for several years in Bowling Green, Kentucky, and for seventeen years at Chapel Hill College in Texas, where he also served as president. His status as a decorated Civil War veteran drew receptive audiences when he traveled on behalf of the new educational enterprise.[6]

Students spoke fondly of him even though he demanded adherence to university rules and regulations. Because of his ability to "ferret out the clandestine sports of the boys" whose penchant for recreation encroached on study hours, male students called him "Jack" for jackrabbit. At revival meetings, where spiritual fervor sometimes distracted the devout, Beeson maintained a vigil for potential misconduct among students. At one campus revival meeting in 1879, a student noted that although participating actively in the service, Beeson "can't help cutting one eye around to see if the students are behaving themselves."[7] Others described how Beeson and his spouse routinely gave significant portions of their meager salaries to help young ministers receive an education and quietly befriended the poor and needy in and nearby Tehuacana.[8]

At the same time, Beeson was an unconventional figure in an age that prized propriety and decorum. Described by a former student as "a short, stout man, with stubby whiskers covering his face, a gleaming eye, a firm, quick step" and "somewhat careless in his dress," Beeson lacked the social graces typically identified with presidential status.[9] Impulsive and single minded, he never allowed formalities to hinder the task at hand. If Beeson needed a sack of flour, he would push his wheelbarrow down to the local general store and trundle the load back to his residence rather than wait for delivery. Such behavior caused some villagers to criticize him as peculiar and lacking in dignity, but most Cumberland Presbyterians respected him as a kind-hearted, fearless, and independent administrator and teacher.[10]

Beeson presided over an institution that, although chartered, possessed few features in common with modern universities. Trinity did not provide advanced degrees nor did it have graduate school programs. The school maintained a preparatory department for students requiring additional course work before beginning their college careers. Depending on their previous educational experience, such students would spend from one to three years in high-school-level classes in order to remove academic deficiencies. Since Texas lacked an adequate public school system, Trinity also maintained a primary department to accommodate village children. Trinity charged collegiate students $20 for each five-month term during the freshman and sophomore years and $25 during the junior and senior years. Preparatory students paid an annual fee of $30, and primary students were billed $12.50 for each five-month term.[11]

Candidates for the ministry were admitted tuition free and paid only a contingent fee of one dollar. Later, trustees granted women preparing for careers as missionaries and the sons and daughters of clergymen the same consideration. During the Tehuacana years, from twenty-five to forty students annually received free tuition. At the end of the nineteenth century, Trinity still charged only $25 in tuition for undergraduate collegiate students.[12]

Trinity's curriculum mirrored the pattern of classical education of most peer institutions. Courses of study were definitive and prescriptive with no electives permitted. The primary department used various levels of the *McGuffey's Readers,* while the preparatory department employed them to the sixth level during the first two years, emphasizing writing, history, geography, arithmetic, and Latin. The third year, referred to as sub-freshman, featured algebra, Latin, English grammar, natural philosophy (physics), and courses in Old and New Testament history.[13]

In the collegiate department, men enrolled in a course of study that emphasized Greek and Latin classics, mathematics, physical and life sciences, philosophy, and theology. Although Trinity faculty encouraged females to take the same academic courses as males, they recognized that most Texas families preferred a less rigorous and more domestic course of study for their daughters. Accordingly, women omitted Greek, Latin, and advanced mathematical studies but were permitted to attend other classes with men. Their curriculum featured English language, composition and literature, history, philosophy, and rhetoric. In addition to courses leading to a diploma (rather than a degree), women received instruction in "the various ornamental branches of learning," such as music, art, and needlework.[14]

Trinity gradually deviated from the classical curriculum at the collegiate level to include more professionally oriented courses. In doing so, it followed the pattern of peer institutions that became "multipurpose colleges" in competition with other types of schools, including high schools, normal schools, institutes of technology, and commercial colleges.[15] The commercial department, offering courses in penmanship, bookkeeping, and commercial law, opened in 1871 with Professor William Hudson as the sole instructor. Tuition was ten dollars for "fair and elegant penmanship" and three dollars for "practical penmanship" per term. According to Hudson, students under his tutelage learned not only to draw correctly, but to "gradually become more patient, more persevering, more intelligently observing, more exact and orderly in everything, and altogether more refined in taste."[16] Under Hudson's leadership, the commercial department became one of the university's most popular programs. He asserted that his classes were the only ones at Trinity in which the students exclaimed daily, "Oh Professor, let us not leave yet!"[17]

In 1874 Trinity established a law department under the direction of Judge H. C. Ewing and Judge D. M. Prendergast, the latter a Trinity trustee and prominent Mexia lawyer. Tuition was fifty dollars per session, two dollars as a contingent fee, and five dollars for a diploma. Ewing and Prendergast assigned students readings in standard legal texts and conducted daily oral examinations in the presence of their peers. In addition, the two judges presided over moot courts in which students were drilled and instructed in the forms of pleading and practice.[18]

Minimal entrance requirements permitted ambitious law students to complete their studies in only five months, a course that the university's catalogue stated was "as extensive as most young gentlemen can be induced to take before commencing practice." Hampered by poor economic conditions, the law department closed in 1878 after only four years of operation. During that time, twenty-two men completed the course and set up law practices in Texas.[19]

In 1872 the trustees approved the establishment of a medical department to be located in Galveston and known as the Galveston Medical College. The faculty was to be entirely dependent on tuition income for salaries and operating expenses. When financial support for the project failed to materialize, however, the trustees abandoned the project.[20] Four years later, Trinity's trustees held discussions with representatives of two

D. M. Prendergast, Trinity trustee and law department professor

sister schools, Cumberland University in Lebanon, Tennessee, and Lincoln University in Lincoln, Illinois, regarding the formation of a cooperative medical college in St. Louis, but they ended negotiations due to lack of financial resources.[21]

In their initial report to Brazos Synod, Trinity's trustees boasted, "No institution of our church has ever started under as favorable auspices as this one does." In 1869, the university listed assets of $52,305, which consisted primarily of 5,743 acres of land and the Boyd homestead. Other items listed were a revolving telescope and a cabinet of fossils and minerals worth $1,200; laboratory equipment, including an electrical machine, air pump and fixtures, compound blow pipes, retorts tubes, two galvanic batteries, pyrometers, and other apparatus deemed sufficient "to illustrate nearly all the principles of chemistry," valued at $300; and 250 books and a collection of fossils donated by President Beeson. Sales of lots in Tehuacana amounted to $1,795, but only a fourth of that amount was in cash.[22]

Despite their initial optimism, Trinity's trustees quickly experienced cash-flow problems that threatened the future of their educational enterprise. Other than the modest tuition, which the trustees were reluctant to increase, the university's greatest asset was land, which had potential value but could not be readily converted into cash. A decade after the opening session, financial agent E. B. Crisman reported that the university had an endowment of approximately $21,000, of which only $2,550 was legal tender. Land valued at $10,000 and "non productive endowment not in hand partly doubtful" estimated at $6,500 constituted the remaining assets. Trinity University maintained a balanced budget by prorating faculty salaries and deferring purchase of needed supplies and equipment.[23]

Financial agents representing the university explored a variety of fund-raising methods. In 1875 J. H. Wofford placed a series of advertisements in denominational publications requesting donations of grain and livestock. He noted, "There are a great many who could give from one to five hundred head of cattle to this enterprise and hardly know that virtue had gone from them."[24] Crisman related stories of sacrificial giving and encouraged others to do the same. He told of four young women from Corsicana who pledged small amounts to the university's endowment fund and resolved to raise the money by picking cotton. Lauding their efforts, Crisman commented, "Imagine, will you, the hand of beauty pulling the locks of cotton from the bole, and every now and then that hand is pricked by the burr of the bole. But with an indomitable will they persevered to the end, and paid the sum promised."[25]

Although the need for endowment funds remained, the issue of faculty salaries was even more pressing. With the second year's session underway, faculty members had received less than half of their contractual income. During the first year, only $2,180.50 was available for faculty salaries, leaving a deficit of $2,819.50. University trustees received little assistance from the three Cumberland synods. In 1870 Texas Synod raised only $80, Brazos Synod $512, and Colorado Synod $40.[26] The synods passed the responsibility for faculty salaries back to the university trustees, stating that they understood that the goals set by the location committee in 1869 were to be attained by the university's financial agents.[27]

During Trinity's first thirty-three years, faculty salaries rarely were paid on time and in full. Burdened by a costly building program and lacking predictable income, trustees dispersed faculty salaries only after janitorial expenses and bills for coal, wood, and repairs had been paid. Shortages in faculty salaries were not carried forward as a continuing debt. To compensate, the treasurer doled out delinquent promissory notes and pledges to faculty who attempted to collect from individuals. Most often the faculty were unsuccessful in attaining cash and received farm produce, clothing, or other items in its place. One professor accepted a baby carriage because it was exceptionally large and in excellent condition.[28]

The trustees tried a variety of ways to improve the cash flow. They had initially accepted land in payment for scholarships, setting $600 as the minimum estimated value of land required for a perpetual scholarship. Be-

TRINITY UNIVERSITY

TEHUACANA, LIMESTONE COUNTY, TEXAS.

Certificate for Perpetual Scholarship.

This is to Certify that _Mr. John Boyd_ *his heirs or assigns, in consideration of the sum of* _Five Hundred Dollars_, *to be paid within* _ten_ *years from this date, to the Treasurer of the Board of Trustees of Trinity University, at Tehuacana, Limestone County, Texas, with interest at the rate of ten per cent. per annum from date, payable semi-annually in advance, (for which he has this day executed his obligation,) is entitled to a Perpetual Scholarship in the Literary Department of said University, free of tuition fees. The payment of said principal sum, or the interest thereon, will be necessary to the enjoyment of this privilege.*

Given under my hand this _21st_ **day of** _____ **A. D. 187_**

J. B. Meyer

Agent Board of Trustees.

Perpetual Scholarship Certificate

ginning in 1873, they no longer accepted payments in land, eliminated perpetual scholarships, and offered five-year scholarships for $150 and twenty-five-year scholarships for $300, both payable in gold. Purchasers could pay cash or use an installment plan that required a down payment of one-third and the remainder in two annual installments with interest at 10 percent per year. Failure to pay either of the installments within six months of maturity resulted in forfeiture of the amount previously paid and loss of scholarship privilege.[29]

Concurrent with revising scholarship policies, the trustees issued a twenty-five-year scholarship to anyone taking out a $1,000 life insurance policy with Trinity University as the beneficiary. Subsequently they gave exclusive right for the sale of such policies to the Nashville Life Insurance

Company.[30] Although the agent sold $25,000 worth of insurance during his first month in Texas, the program produced more students than income because the university benefited only at the demise of the insured. Several years later, the trustees dropped the insurance offer and substituted a plan of scholarship sales that required a specific sum of money before students could be admitted.[31]

In order to borrow money from individuals, the trustees utilized land as collateral. In 1871 they borrowed $1,000 in gold at 15 percent annual interest, secured by mortgaging 400 acres of land in Limestone County, 320 acres in Navarro County, and 160 acres in Freestone County. A few months later, they borrowed $1,000 at 10 percent interest, mortgaging the college building and eleven acres of land surrounding it. The trustees continued to authorize similar transactions in their desperation to secure operating capital.[32]

Although efforts to accumulate endowment funds fell short of expectations, several individual contributions added to the university's assets. In 1870 Colorado Synod sold the Ewing College property for $500, turning over the proceeds to Trinity's endowment fund. Two endowment gifts totaling $14,000 from Cumberland laymen James Aston of Farmersville, Texas, and the Johnson brothers of Corsicana and Hubbard, Texas, enabled the school to establish the Aston chair of theology and homiletics and the Johnson chair of mathematics. Three additional contributions provided support for ministerial students. William Saunders gave $500, the interest from which was awarded annually to the most deserving freshman divinity student. R. O. Watkins and other family members contributed a residence for divinity students known as Watkins Hall and a small sum of money for its maintenance. T. F. Fowler donated $8,000 with the stipulation that the annual interest be employed to defray the living expenses of Watkins Hall residents.[33]

The need for building funds in addition to permanent endowments and operating expenses placed a heavy burden on university trustees. Even with alterations, the Boyd residence could not provide adequate classroom space for the growing student population. Early in 1870, the trustees authorized the public sale of 2,050 acres in five tracts of land to secure funds for a new building, provided that satisfactory prices could be obtained. However, they soon abandoned the public auction, hoping to obtain better returns through private sales.[34]

When appeals to the Cumberland synods for building funds produced no results, the trustees resolved to go forward with what little money they had in hand. As the site for the new building, they selected a rocky elevation about one-fourth of a mile from the Boyd home in block 12 of the Tehuacana survey that local residents called College Hill. The board invited "all good Masons, Christians, and friends of Learning" to cornerstone-laying ceremonies on 19 May 1871, under the direction of C. M. Winkler, Grand Master Mason of the State of Texas. Utilizing readily available limestone from the hills surrounding Tehuacana, construction crews under the direction of William Rees, a skilled craftsman, laid the foundation in the shape of a capital T, symbolizing both Trinity and Tehuacana. Because funds were tight, Rees did the stonecutting himself, a task usually left to laborers. The first phase of the building project called for the erection of the two-story stem of the T with the wings to be added at some future date.[35] Twenty years would pass before the project was completed.

As work proceeded, mounting expenditures forced the board to authorize the sale of additional university-owned lands near Tehuacana to replenish the building fund. The trustees also asked faculty members to solicit contributions for the building during the summer recess. Despite these measures, the trustees had to draw from the school's endowment in order to continue construction. At the same time, they agreed to set aside some acreage as security in order to replenish the endowment fund.[36]

The first phase of the building project dragged on for more than two years. Finally, in the fall of 1873, classes began in the new building even though much interior work was incomplete. Construction costs to that date amounted to $26,700, of which all but $3,800 had been paid.[37] Despite repeated appeals for funds to finish the project, the "large and commodious" building, containing twelve recitation rooms and an ample chapel, lacked interior appointments for more than a decade.[38]

From the onset, the building program had been adversely affected by an unresolved dispute over the propriety of coeducation at Trinity. Prior to the Civil War, Texas had no coeducational colleges or universities, but after 1865, teaching both sexes in the same classroom gradually became more common. Most coeducational institutions established separate male and female departments that were housed in different buildings but supervised by one set of trustees. Many Texans, however, opposed even such a limited form of coeducation. As a result, a number of female institutions, such as Baylor Female College, Marshall Masonic Female Institute, and Chappell Hill Female Institute, catered exclusively to women.[39]

Despite shifting public sentiment in favor of coeducation, Cumberland Presbyterians debated the propriety of "mixing the sexes" up to the closing decade of the nineteenth century. Opponents of coeducation argued that it violated natural order established by God and would inevitably pre-

New building under construction, 1872

cipitate a decline in moral behavior. They feared that competition with males would adversely affect fragile feminine psyches. Proponents of coeducation countered that the interaction of males and females in the same learning environment fostered the formation of intelligent relationships between the sexes, thus preparing them for later life. Moreover, they asserted that coeducation guaranteed all persons, regardless of sex, their democratic right to be taught all branches of knowledge.[40]

Although Trinity's founders designated the university as coeducational, they apparently envisioned separate facilities for men and women as soon as a proper building could be erected.[41] During the first two years, men and women attended classes under the same roof with no difficulties except for space limitations. Shortly after the cornerstone-laying ceremony, however, the trustees reported that "public mind and individual interest in and around Trinity has demanded an expression relative to the division of the school and the continued use of the present house now occupied." At that time, the trustees affirmed their intention to use both the Boyd house and the new building "for the instruction of both sexes as the exigencies of the case may demand."[42] That decision was called into question in 1872 when a delegation of ministers and elders from Texas Synod visited Tehuacana to attend the public examinations and commencement exercises. Concerned about the overcrowded conditions in the Boyd residence, the synod dignitaries recommended that men and women be separated as soon as the new building was ready for occupancy.[43]

Motivated more by economic than pedagogical or cultural considerations, the trustees agreed by a 5–2 vote to use the Boyd home for the primary and preparatory departments and to conduct coeducational collegiate classes in the new building. The two dissident trustees, A. Barry and J. H. Bell, along with a number of Tehuacana residents, petitioned Brazos, Colorado, and Texas Synods to "remove the evil [of coeducation] and give us the school you promised us when you created Trinity University. We cannot educate our daughters in a coeducation school. It violates all our ideas of propriety."[44]

In a counter petition, the Trinity faculty unanimously endorsed coeducation on the grounds of its precedence, expediency, and economy. They pointed out that some of the best universities in the country, including other Cumberland Presbyterian institutions, had adopted the coeducational system and were prospering. Moreover, economic factors left no other choice. Trinity had no means to sustain two separate faculties. A division of the school would require an increase in staff without a corresponding increase in tuition.[45]

At their fall meetings in 1873, members of the three synods considered the merits of both petitions. After extended discussion, each synod adopted resolutions endorsing the action of the Board of Trustees in regard to coeducation and expressing confidence in its loyalty, devotion, and service. Synod commissioners found nothing in the university charter to prevent the board from utilizing its discretionary powers to sustain coeducation and recognized the financial necessity that mandated such a decision.[46]

Opponents of coeducation were unwilling to compromise their principles to accommodate pragmatic considerations and continued to agitate for separation of the sexes at Trinity University. In 1877 several board members again challenged the appropriateness of coeducation on the Trinity campus. Although the board reaffirmed its commitment to coeducation, it acknowledged that "a difference of opinion in regard to the education of the sexes in the same school" existed among Cumberland Presbyterians in Texas. Noting that financial considerations were paramount in maintaining coeducation, the board also observed that the system had worked well overall on the Tehuacana campus. Promising to enforce existing rules regulating the social interaction of male and female students, the trustees affirmed their openness to reconsidering "the entire separation of the sexes . . . should the circumstances at any time seem to demand it."[47]

With the passing of time, opposition to coeducation diminished and challenges to university policy on this issue ceased. Trinity repeatedly af-

Advertisement in *The Cumberland Presbyterian*, August 1889

firmed its unqualified commitment to coeducation in notices in denominational newspapers. One such advertisement in *The Cumberland Presbyterian* proclaimed in bold letters, "Trinity University For Both Sexes," and boasted that it employed "the best and most approved methods of instruction."[48] Trinity catalogues in the 1890s lauded the university's longstanding commitment to coeducation and boasted that such an arrangement over the years had produced "more womanly women, more manly men."[49]

Concurrent with the coeducation dispute, Trinity trustees and faculty became embroiled in another controversy that brought the university to the brink of closure. Unfortunately, official records offer few clues about the precise nature of the disagreement, and denominational and regional newspapers provide no supplemental information. Trustee minutes refer enigmatically to "the want of harmony among the members of the Faculty of the Literary Department," but do not specify what triggered the discord. According to trustee minutes, "partisan feelings waxed warm in many sections, until the revolution seemed to threaten the very foundations of the Institution." In an effort to resolve the conflict, trustees dismissed the faculty of the literary department, removed Beeson from the presidency, and altered the charter to permit wider representation on the university board.[50]

Signs of unrest among the literary faculty emerged as early as September 1876, when the Board of Trustees approved new rules for institutional governance. Apparently dissatisfied with Beeson's ad hoc administrative style, faculty members wanted to formalize certain academic procedures. The new bylaws specified faculty prerogatives, including the authority to set class schedules, select textbooks, and grant excused absences. They also specified that "no professor shall be interrupted, without his consent, while engaged in hearing recitations, in order to examine a student or to attend a called meeting of the faculty" and that "nothing affecting the interest of the school shall be decided upon unless at a regular meeting of the faculty."[51]

In conjunction with the new bylaws, the trustees informed faculty members that they were henceforth solely dependent on tuition for salary support. The board declared itself under no obligation to supplement faculty salaries out of institutional funds except from interest accruing on the endowment and stated that "all former resolutions seeming to contradict this idea be and are hereby modified to this extent."[52]

Despite the institution's chronic financial exigency, the trustees were considering the creation of a theological department for divinity students, a project favored by Beeson but questioned by others on economic grounds. Underpaid and overworked, faculty members responded to these developments by inviting the trustees to join them in a weekly prayer meeting "for the purpose of asking God to bless our efforts in building up this great interest, and especially to put it in the hearts of the people to give of their means for its endowment."[53]

New regulations and prayer meetings notwithstanding, the relationship between Beeson and members of the literary department continued to deteriorate. Seeking outside assistance, the trustees corresponded with leaders in the three synods, asking their advice and counsel "in reference to the troubles in our faculty."[54] In January 1877, after synod leaders failed to produce a solution, the trustees requested and received the resignations of Beeson and the three other literary department faculty members, R. P. Decherd, W. P. Gillespie, and T. M. Goodknight. At the same time, they elected E. B. Crisman of St. Louis as president and arranged for him to visit the campus. The trustees also approved the creation of a theological department and authorized Beeson to travel throughout the state to solicit endowment funds for the new program.[55]

By now, Trinity's troubles had become public knowledge in the denomination and were generating discussions among Cumberland Presbyterians. Hoping to establish closer links with Cumberland Presbyterian governing bodies and to obtain a more objective assessment of Trinity's problems, the trustees amended the university charter to increase and broaden its constituency to include board members from the three synods who lived a greater distance than the previously prescribed twelve miles from Tehuacana.[56]

At the initial meeting of the enlarged board, the trustees received word that Crisman had declined their invitation to become president. Feeling pressure from students and townspeople and needing a president, the trustees invited Beeson to return to his old position, but he rejected the offer.[57] A subsequent effort to recruit B. W. McDonnold, former president of Cumberland University, also was unsuccessful. Leaving the presidential vacancy unfilled, the trustees appointed Col. Robert W. Pitman as vice president with authority to act as president for the 1877–78 academic year.[58]

When students returned in the fall of 1877, new faculty members, an acting president, and a divided campus community greeted them. Support for Beeson and the departed faculty members remained strong, especially among Tehuacana residents and members of Brazos Synod. Because the new literary department faculty accepted their appointments "under embarrassing circumstances," the board pledged to pay them the full amount of the salaries for the academic year.[59]

Included in their number was the first and only woman to occupy a Trinity University collegiate professorial chair in the nineteenth century. Initially hired as an assistant teacher for precollegiate students, Miss S. J. McCord was appointed by the board of trustees as professor of mathematics in November 1877, a position she had already been filling on a temporary basis "with credit to herself, and satisfaction to the faculty and students." While noting that "circumstances are such as forbid raising her salary for the present session," the trustees promised to increase her remuneration when financial conditions improved. McCord's tenure was brief. When mathematics professor S. T. Anderson arrived early in 1878, she was assigned to the chair of natural sciences at a salary of $800, approximately half of what male professors were paid for similar positions. The trustees subsequently rescinded her appointment, however, "for want of means to pay her salary."[60]

After a shaky start, enrollment stabilized, unrest lessened, and new faculty members performed effectively. A member of Texas Synod who attended the commencement week final examinations in 1878 reported that student-faculty morale remained high despite the difficult circumstances under which the university had been operating.[61] Nevertheless, students and university patrons clamored for the reinstatement of Beeson as president. During the 1877–78 academic year, he had maintained a high profile by traveling throughout the state attempting to raise money for a chair in theology. Responding to public sentiment, the trustees voted unanimously in June 1878 to reappoint Beeson to his former office, an invitation that he accepted. Despite their apparent unanimity, the trustees were ambivalent about yielding to public pressure, concluding, "Whether such a demand is a wise one, the future alone can reveal."[62]

While the trustees and faculty wrestled with fiscal, personnel, and curricular problems, Trinity students also worried about meeting expenses. Most were dependent on their parents' income from farming to meet tuition and living expenses. Only a handful of students from each entering class actually graduated with a baccalaureate degree. For example, thirty-four first-year collegiate students entered Trinity in the fall of 1880, but only three graduated four years later. Figures for the period from 1895 to 1900 are comparable, indicating that attrition was a long-standing problem. Between 1870 and 1900, 199 men and women received degrees from Trinity, an average of slightly under seven graduates a year.[63]

Correspondence between Winstead Bone and his parents (1879–1883) illustrates how one Trinity student coped with financial problems. Bone, who graduated from Trinity and later became president of Cumberland University in Lebanon, Tennessee, frequently expressed fears that he might have to drop out of school. On one occasion he wrote, "I know that I cannot go to school here without means. I can say that I shall be grateful for what I get and if you find that it will be taxing you too much for me to go the spring session, I would not be so unkind as to desire to go under the circumstances."[64] Bone sought out the least expensive boarding house, purchased second-hand textbooks, and avoided courses that required extra fees or supplies.[65] His parents frequently covered boarding expenses by dispatching goods from their farm near Larissa, Texas. In November 1879, they sent 42 pounds of sugar, 20 pounds of coffee, 37 pounds of lard, and 38 pounds of bacon as a substitute for cash.[66]

The Trinity faculty conducted classes in an academic culture that featured rote learning, prescribed curricula, and strict discipline. Like parents writ large, the faculty regulated virtually every aspect of student life. When a parent complained that his two children were kept so busy at Trinity that they did not have time to write home, Professor S. M. Templeton responded with a lecture on parental detachment. Although students have a duty to keep parents informed, Templeton explained, they also have a duty to acquire "mental culture" at Trinity. If the two duties collide, mental culture must come first. Templeton urged the parents to "exile them [the children] from you, turn them over to other people for all their association, counsel, and encouragement."[67]

On campuses such as Trinity where males and females frequently intermingled, administrative oversight was especially scrupulous. The initial *Trinity University Catalogue* provided the following terse summary of the behavior expected of Trinity students.[68]

Trinity University Catalogue, 1869–70

According to one Trinity student, President Beeson had a single rule regarding deportment on campus: "Every boy or girl is expected to be a gentleman or a lady."[69] During the Beeson years, however, the list of regulations expanded until it reached nineteen in number. Except for meals,
study embraced virtually all of students' waking hours, from rising in the
morning until retiring in the evening. Students were charged not to be absent from their rooms during study hours except to attend classes and not
to leave town when school was in session without permission from the
faculty. Prohibitions against intoxicating liquors and gambling were extended to include tobacco and the possession of deadly weapons. Students
were also forbidden "to loiter about the post office or stores during study
hours" or "to engage in any diversion, or amusement, or correspondence
which will be detrimental to their rapid acquisition of knowledge."[70]

Believing that indolence was a "most pernicious habit," Trinity faculty
endeavored to keep their charges employed at all times "except such hours
as are necessary for refreshment and recreation."[71] Holidays were kept to
a minimum. Christmas recess, for example, lasted only one day and students were expected to remain on campus. Parents and guardians were
"earnestly requested not to permit their sons, daughters, or wards to visit
them and spend an entire week, as is customary, in idleness. Teach them
the value of time, and let not a week, in the midst of the Fall Session, be
squandered."[72]

From time to time the faculty imposed a variety of campus dress codes,
all of which were directed solely at women. In 1871 a detailed description
of uniforms for members of the female department included leather shoes
from the first of November until the last of April, everyday dresses of
worsted goods (solid maroon) for winter and pink calico and pink delaine

for fall and spring, and hats of plain straw with green ribbon for winter and blue ribbon for summer. Flowers were not to be worn on hats or dresses. Emphasizing that the uniform policy would be "rigidly enforced," faculty members advised that women "will be required to appear on all occasions in the uniform adopted for the school."[73] Gradually, however, the dress code became less prescriptive. By the end of Beeson's tenure as president, the *Trinity University Catalogue* recommended only that parents and guardians "not allow extravagance in dress or otherwise."[74]

Religion featured prominently in the lives of Trinity students. Although the university avoided sectarianism, it promised to expose students to a "highly religious culture" that would prepare them for a life of useful service in vocation and community. Required daily chapel services centered on Bible studies and homilies delivered by various faculty members, punctuated with hymn singing and prayers. Mandatory Sunday school and morning services also held in the college chapel brought students in contact with a wide range of speakers, including visiting dignitaries from the Cumberland denomination. On one occasion, students heard a minister and his spouse speak on their belief in total sanctification. According to a student who attended the service, the woman "said she could not sin, nor do anything wrong." Her remarks were refuted by Trinity trustee J. H. Wofford, "who quoted scripture just the opposite to what had been quoted by the previous speaker." Such theological discussions introduced students to the complexity of Biblical interpretation.[75]

Beyond these experiences, students frequently attended revival meetings and other special services conducted by visiting Cumberland Presbyterian clergymen. Referred to as "protracted meetings," the services were held daily for a week, usually in the evenings when everyone in the community could attend. At one revival meeting, a correspondent to *The Cumberland Presbyterian* reported that there had been eighteen professions of faith and "considerable interest, religiously, among the students on the Tehuacana campus."[76] Trinity officials kept count of student conversions and included the total in their annual reports to synods and the General Assembly.

Within the classroom, Trinity students experienced a tutorial method of instruction that featured group memorization and recitation. Lecturing, when it occurred, usually consisted of reading from a book rather than giving an individually prepared presentation. Faculty commonly used the more advanced students as tutors, thereby making it possible to have relatively large classes composed of students working at different academic levels. Professors periodically suspended individual study and memorization to allow class members to engage in a round of declamations and recitations that demonstrated what they had learned. The tutorial method seemed suited to the classical nature of Trinity courses that emphasized knowledge of English, Greek, and Latin grammar and mathematical skills.[77]

But not all Trinity faculty members conformed to traditional pedagogical methodologies. One notable exception was Professor William Hudson, who was deemed eccentric by his peers because of his interactive teaching style. Broadly educated, Hudson cited his ability to "lecture on almost any subject," including natural history, moral philosophy, logic, rhetoric, evidences of Christianity, physics or natural theology, geology, mineralogy, political economy, international law, zoology, chemistry, and botany.[78] Evidence of Hudson's penmanship survives today in the art lettering on early Trinity diplomas, some of which are on display in the Trinity University library.[79]

As headmaster of the Commercial Department, Hudson set high standards for the new enrollees. His departmental motto, "What is acquired too rapidly sometimes fails to be permanent," encapsulated his philosophy of education. "No one, *except a brilliant genius* will be allowed to graduate in this department in less than two years."[80] Hudson emphasized the importance of discipline in mastering techniques of writing and drawing. In a course featuring pencil and crayon drawing and watercolor painting, Hudson reported that it constituted "a powerful means of so disciplining the mind as to promote patience, refined taste, control of the temper, a love of order, and exactness of observation."[81]

Hudson emphasized the importance of adaptability and innovation in the classroom. A Trinity faculty member, he said, had to "cultivate a contented spirit, be readily inventive and adept in imparting knowledge, and ever ready to make the best of everything." He also stressed that classroom recitations must be much more than simply repeating information derived from a textbook. Hudson encouraged students to develop a habit of daily self-examination of ideas and practices and to express rules, facts, and principles in their own words. He concluded, "The faculty of Trinity University do their best to incite their scholars to understand rules and principles, and to clearly express them in chaste language."[82]

Despite the formality of the times, Trinity students enjoyed close relationships with teachers both within and outside class. Faculty members routinely gave personal attention to students who were working on special projects such as laboratory experiments, orations, and student publications. Winstead Bone related how Professor R. W. Pitman helped him make preparations for an oration during the spring term of 1880: "After I prepared my piece, he would go to the chapel with me every few nights (2 or 3 times a week) and give instructions as to the delivery. Such kindness I am not used to." On another occasion, at Pitman's residence when Bone had a sore throat, Pitman read aloud for him, illustrating proper inflections and gestures. Bone told his parents, "I thanked him for his kindness and attention and regretted that I had no way of repaying." Pitman responded, "Make a *man* of yourself, and I will be *more* than repaid."[83]

Most female students omitted Latin and Greek and settled for the truncated curriculum that led to a diploma rather than a degree, although a few ambitious women accepted the challenge of the full curriculum. When Jessie Bone arrived on campus in the fall of 1882, Dr. S. T. Anderson persuaded her to take the same course of study as the male students. She kept her parents updated as the semester progressed: "I am the only girl in Latin and Greek, and I am determined to keep up with those boys." Bone found the classroom work to be rigorous but rewarding. Anderson was a demanding taskmaster who pushed students to work at full capacity. "The Dr. can plague you to death sometimes," Jessie recounted to her parents. "When I worked all the examples but one, he wanted to know what my object was in not working it two [sic]. He kept on till I felt like creeping out of the room or that I had done some awful crime. I only wish I knew as much as he does."[84]

Apparently not all students were as attentive as Jessie Bone. One professor lamented the large number of mediocre and dull Trinity students who often said, "I would rather plough than study so hard."[85] Professor Anderson reported an incident involving a female student who was "laughing and talking in my room so as to disturb the recitation." When asked to recite, the student frequently said that she was not prepared. As a result, Anderson assigned her a low grade in the course. The student came to his office and demanded to know why she had not received a higher mark. Informed that it was because of her behavior, the student responded that she had "laughed and talked as much as she pleased in other recitation rooms and that the other teachers had given her high marks." This situation, Anderson said, "was the mildest case. The others were worse, more insulting."[86]

Beyond the classroom and religious exercises, student literary societies enjoyed undisputed pre-eminence at Trinity. Because of the emphasis on recitation and lecturing, students had few opportunities in the classroom to express themselves freely. Functioning primarily as debating organizations, the literary societies provided an outlet in which student discussion

Ratio-Genic and Maeonian Literary Societies, 1889

could develop without curricular restraint.[87] Moreover, because public speaking played a prominent role in the various professional pursuits for which students were preparing, such as sermonizing, pleading a case in court, and teaching, they needed all the oratorical practice they could manage. Literary societies commanded the passionate student loyalty that was later accorded to fraternities and athletic teams.[88]

Both male and female literary societies on the Tehuacana campus vied for social and academic recognition. During Trinity's first session, men organized the Philosophronian Literary Society, the oldest society connected with the university. Two female societies, the Sappho and the Adelphian, were established in 1873 and merged a decade later to form the Sappho-Adelphian Society, a sister society to the Philosophronian. Although "joined in a firm league of fraternal and sisterly feeling," each group maintained its own autonomy. Organized in 1870, the Maeonian Literary Society for women emphasized acquiring "self-control and originality in public addresses and essays," and the Ratio-Genic Society for men, formed in 1874, claimed that "the practical lessons given by the society exercises and business proceedings" prepared its members to participate more effectively in their chosen vocations. All of these groups maintained libraries that provided students with reading and research materials during a time when the university itself had limited library facilities.[89]

The literary societies held weekly meetings, usually on a Friday or Saturday evening, to conduct debates, declamations, and other public speaking events. Debates between the Ratio-Genic and Philosophronian societies held semiannually at the end of the fall term and during commencement week were major events on the college calendar. Students from both groups diligently prepared in order to impress a panel of visiting dignitaries (ministers or lawyers) from various Texas locations who served as judges. On these special occasions, the Maeonian and Sappho-Adelphian societies performed in conjunction with the other organizations. Commencement programs also included various society offerings of music, declamation, and essays, with students making presentations to appreciative audiences of families and townspeople.[90]

Excerpts from the "Critic's Book" of the Ratio-Genic Society suggest that few Trinity students came from family environments where polite speech and proper diction had been stressed. Critics rated the speakers as tolerable, good, and very good and chastised student orators for grammatical shortcomings such as "cat-asstrophe," "fur" (far, for), "he taken her," "sich" (such) "cheer" (chair), "ruther," and "coleeg." Some students were criticized for laughing at their own mistakes and "using the name of our Saviour in vain." General criticism of meetings included "too much frivolity and laughing" and "writing all kinds of foolishness on ballots" such as a motion to buy the American Book Exchange, which was deemed "a very foolish motion." The last entry in the "Critic's Book" reminded members of their obligation to seek self-improvement. "Fellow Ratios, while we remember and realize that for a season the criticisms of this book is [sic] closed, and that for a season we shall not hear its contents of rebuke and corrections, let us remember the great critics book of the world is ever being read out against us and that we strive ever to live pure."[91]

Students at the Ratio-Genic meetings debated a wide range of topics. Contemporary issues such as the enfranchisement of women, Sunday blue laws, and prohibition of the sale of alcohol generated considerable interest among society members.[92] On other occasions, the topics were of a different nature. Students debated, "Does the mental capacity of man exceed that of woman's [sic]?" and "Is an old bachelor's life more dreary than an old maid's?"[93]

In 1877, members of the literary societies published the *Trinity Collegian*, self-designated as "the oldest College paper in the State" and devoted to "the General Diffusion of Practical Knowledge." An editorial staff consisting of a member of each literary society published a monthly paper that contained discussions of literary topics, biographical and historical sketches, and "reminiscences of College Life." Although short lived, the paper provided an outlet for student creativity and imagination. One article entitled "Chronicles," set in medieval times, portrayed life under "King Jack of Trinity," who punished those who rebelled against his laws. This thinly veiled lampoon of President Beeson apparently was accepted in good humor by the Trinity faculty. Other articles featured reflections on contemporary issues, original poetry and prose, and a potpourri of campus gossip.[94]

In addition to the male and female literary societies, other student organizations flourished on the Tehuacana campus. Chartered in 1877 by W. B. Preston, the Trinity chapter of Young Men's Christian Association (YMCA) held the distinction of being the first such group to be formed at any Texas college.[95] Professing the motto, "Every student in this College for Christ this year," the YMCA met monthly for programmatic and recruitment purposes. Other meetings included daily Bible study and prayer sessions and a Sunday morning devotional service that sought "to culture the spirituality of its members and to win others to the way of life." In addition to its evangelistic efforts, the YMCA also supplied Trinity's reading room with newspapers, religious journals, and magazines such as *The Century, Harper's, Review of Review,* and *Forum.* A Young Women's Christian Association (YWCA) also functioned on campus. Being in a "disorganized condition," it was reorganized in January 1897 and reported to be "heartily at work developing the piety and Christian activity of its members."[96]

During the early years of Trinity's existence, university officials permitted the Greek-letter fraternities Phi Delta Theta and Beta Theta Pi to function on campus. Denominational authorities opposed such groups on the grounds that they fostered atheism, immorality, and subversion causing Trinity trustees to reconsider their toleration of secret societies. In 1882 a faculty committee reported to the board that the groups were "a cause of more trouble than they had done good, their effect being to divide members of each society in cliques or clans by which the harmony of the school is destroyed."[97] The following year, the faculty advised that they had squashed the secret societies and had inserted a clause in the *Trinity University Catalogue* forbidding the existence of such organizations.[98]

As Trinity entered the decade of the 1880s, it faced an uncertain future, but there were reasons for optimism. Trinity had survived disputes over its policy of coeducation and dissent among faculty members that threatened its credibility among denominational supporters. Approximately eighty students had received university degrees since classes commenced in 1869, and many more had attained the equivalent of a high school education. Most important, institutional loyalty among students, faculty, alumni, and

William Beeson's grave marker in Tehuacana Cemetery. The Biblical inscription reads: "I have fought a good fight, I have finished my course, I have kept the faith." II Timothy 4:7. Photo, *Mexia Daily News*.

townspeople held remarkably firm in the face of discouraging financial problems and disagreements regarding university policies.

The death of President Beeson on 5 September 1882, marked the end of Trinity's first phase of development. While attending a presbytery meeting in Hillsboro, Beeson suffered a stroke and passed away two weeks later in the home of a local physician. As he lay dying, Beeson's last words were about Trinity University. "It is a child of God—ultimate success." [99]

When news of Beeson's death reached Tehuacana, members of the university community went into an extended period of mourning. One student wrote home, "Everyone is taking the death *very* hard. You don't know how much we miss our beloved departed Dr. Beeson." [100] In a display of affection, Trinity students established a fund to erect a suitable monument for Beeson in the local cemetery. It remains today as a memorial to a remarkable man who helped to lay the foundation of a great university. [101]

CHAPTER THREE

PROGRESS WITHOUT PROSPERITY

> In fulfilling its mission, the University has had, as most young institutions
> do have, a fluctuating history, sometimes enjoying a large degree of pros-
> perity, at other times a less; yet its general movement may be truly denomi-
> nated one of progress.
>
> *TRINITY UNIVERSITY CATALOGUE (1896–97)*

FOR TWO DECADES FOLLOWING THE DEATH OF BEESON, Trinity
University clung to a marginal existence on the Tehuacana campus. A prolonged drought in Texas and an extended national economic recession un-
dermined efforts by trustees and administrators to marshal adequate financial resources for the struggling institution. Additionally, school
officials detected a growing sentiment among Cumberland Presbyterians
that Trinity's founders had erred in selecting a remote setting such as
Tehuacana. Advocates of relocation proposed an accessible urban environment with the amenities of city life that would attract a more diverse
student body. Such rumors within the Cumberland denomination regarding Trinity's possible move discouraged potential donors.[1]

On his deathbed, Beeson had requested that Professor Samuel T.
Anderson serve as acting president until the trustees could conduct a
search for a successor. Complying with his wishes, the board of trustees
moved cautiously to select a new leader, cognizant that their choice might
well determine the institution's failure or success, given the university's
precarious fiscal situation.[2]

In July 1883, after a protracted search, Trinity trustees selected Benjamin G. McLeskey, pastor of the Cumberland Presbyterian Church in
Sherman, Texas, to assume the presidency. After a brief law career,
McLeskey had graduated from Bethel College in McKenzie, Tennessee,
and entered the ministry. Following service in the Civil War as an army
chaplain, he held a number of pastorates in Tennessee before coming to

Texas in 1881. Standing six feet three inches tall and possessing "a manly form, pleasant face, expressive eyes, and a loud, clear, musical voice," the fifty-year-old McLeskey's credentials indicated his prowess as an evangelist rather than his abilities as an educator. While president, McLeskey also served as pastor of the Tehuacana Cumberland Presbyterian Church, lectured weekly to theological students, and functioned as their faculty mentor.[3]

McLeskey's immediate task was to restore denominational confidence in the school, boost faculty morale, and reactivate an unfinished building project.[4] One of his first acts was to establish the *Trinity Herald*, a monthly newspaper designed to promote the university and "to urge its claims upon the church and the public." It included articles by faculty and staff as well as stories and essays by students, whom the literary societies appointed as associate editors.[5] In an effort to increase tuition revenue, McLeskey persuaded the trustees to expand the music and commercial departments and to create a fine arts department.[6] Inheriting a number of faculty vacancies, McLeskey recruited several young professors, including Luther Apelles Johnson, who would play a pivotal role in the university's future.[7] Largely through McLeskey's efforts, the university acquired sufficient funds to plan additional wings on the main building, and, in the fall of 1885, the trustees appointed a committee to employ an architect and receive bids from contractors.[8]

Despite these encouraging signs, rumor and innuendo regarding McLeskey's leadership abilities marred his presidency. Early in his tenure, McLeskey came under attack by trustee J. H. Wofford, editor of the *Texas Observer* and the university's former financial agent.[9] Wofford had abstained from voting for McLeskey, who did not meet his criteria of being a promising scholar and a native Texan.[10]

In a series of scathing editorials and in private correspondence, Wofford charged the Trinity president with administrative incompetence, scholarly deficiencies, and a questionable work ethic. Wofford accused McLeskey of committing "literary blunders" that subjected the institution to scorn and ridicule. As an example, Wofford claimed that McLeskey made an address in the chapel in which he referred several times to an "autobiography" of the late President Beeson written by W. G. L. Quaite. Wofford also asserted that Trinity students frequently posted notices of the president's spelling and grammatical errors in the college halls.[11]

Dismayed at the unfavorable publicity and fearful that he had lost the confidence of the university community, McLeskey tendered his resignation early in September 1885. The trustees, deeming Wofford's charges

President McLeskey and ministerial students

"frivolous" and "misrepresentations and perversions of facts," endorsed
McLeskey's administration and "expressed confidence in the future of the
School under his Charge." Noting that McLeskey enjoyed the esteem and
confidence of the Tehuacana community, the Board of Trustees voiced its
"decided disapproval" of Wofford's efforts to undermine the reputation of
the Trinity president.[12]

Six weeks after receiving the vote of confidence, McLeskey died unexpectedly of a heart attack in his Tehuacana residence. Eulogies praised him
for his commitment to the church and to Trinity University and affirmed
that his brief presidency had brought vitality and hope to an institution in
need of leadership. Faced with the difficult task of seeking a replacement
at the beginning of an academic year, Trinity's trustees appointed Luther
Apelles Johnson, principal of the preparatory department, to serve as president pro tem while they conducted a search.[13]

Johnson's appointment signaled a generational shift in faculty leadership. During the Beeson years, the Trinity faculty had been drawn primarily from the ranks of Civil War veterans who used the prescribed classical
curriculum of their own educational experience. Resisting change, they
were not amenable to new forms of pedagogy emerging during the last
three decades of the nineteenth century. In contrast, Johnson and his peers
stressed learning rather than memorization, choice rather than prescription, and innovation rather than the status quo.[14]

A parallel change occurred in the student body. During Trinity's early years, students were almost exclusively from Tehuacana and surrounding rural counties. Between 1885 and the end of the century, however, increasing numbers of students came from small towns and developing urban centers throughout Texas. These students did not readily accept traditional customs and resisted the institutional regulations more persistently and vocally, occasionally organizing demonstrations. Student activism also led to a rising interest in organized athletics, clubs, and musical organizations in addition to the traditional campus literary societies.

More than any other individual, Johnson shaped the educational environment of Trinity University during the closing decades of the nineteenth century. Born in Mississippi in 1858, Johnson spent his formative years in Tennessee, where he resided with family friends after the death of his mother. There he came under the influence of Cumberland Presbyterian evangelists and was converted at a revival in Giles County, Tennessee, at the age of thirteen. Johnson attended Cumberland University in Tennessee and Southern Illinois Normal University and served as principal of Lawrenceburg High School in Tennessee and Veal's Station High School in Texas prior to coming to Trinity. Like his predecessors at Trinity, Johnson was an ordained Cumberland Presbyterian minister who viewed college teaching as an ecclesiastical and a professional calling.[15]

Johnson's experience at Southern Illinois Normal University was influential in his career. The Illinois normal school system, one of the most progressive in the country, was established in 1857 under the leadership of Professor Richard Edwards. Influenced by European educational trends that repudiated rote drilling and abstract textbook memorization, Edwards impressed on prospective teachers the philosophy that students must educate themselves through their own activities rather than being passive receptors of information. He also encouraged graduates to take leadership roles in curricular reform at all levels of public and private education.[16] Subsequent changes at Trinity, including the abandonment of outdated textbooks, the introduction of electives, and the establishment of a faculty leave system, reflect Johnson's pedagogical training.[17]

Two months after his arrival in Tehuacana, at the age of twenty-seven, Johnson was thrust into a position of leadership that he neither desired nor sought. As principal of the preparatory department, Johnson had anticipated that he would be able to do graduate work in English literature at Trinity, and at the time of his appointment as president pro tem, he was already working on a master's degree, a goal that he achieved the following year. Convinced that good classroom teaching depended on constant upgrading of one's knowledge of subject matter, Johnson subsequently earned a Ph.D. degree from Bethel College in Tennessee in 1891 and an A.M. degree from the University of Chicago in 1894.[18]

In one of his first curricular decisions, Johnson separated the preparatory department from collegiate-level work. Prior to his arrival, preparatory students were permitted to enroll simultaneously in college classes even at the junior and senior levels. While realizing that ending this practice might result in the loss of some students, Johnson contended that in the long term the university would benefit: "[Trinity] will have no poor spellers and grammarians in its senior class as so many schools do."[19] Furthermore, beginning with the 1885–86 academic year, Trinity no longer carried a description of the primary and grammar departments in its catalogues, instead dispensing information regarding these programs in a separate circular.[20]

Johnson also added a section into the annual catalogue on teaching methodology and expected performance levels of students. Mathematics courses stressed "culture of the power of deductive reasoning, and practical skill in the application of mathematical principles." In order to pass geometry and calculus, students had to demonstrate the truths, derive the formulas, and present the discussions "independently of the book." English and philosophy courses emphasized original expression of ideas "obtained by investigation and systematic analysis" and criticized and discussed by other students and the professor. In the natural sciences, students were trained "to acquire the habit of methodically cultivating [their] powers of observation" and "become so thoroughly enlightened as to be *exact and faithful* in describing everything which comes under the cognizance of their natural senses." Although professors gave brief lectures on all subjects, they emphasized "enlightening experiments."[21]

Johnson's interest in pedagogy led to the establishment of a normal school to prepare teachers for the expanding Texas public school system. Entrance requirements for the two-year program that resulted in a Licentiate of Instruction diploma were limited to "familiarity with the common school branches, one year in Latin, and a thorough mastery of the elements of Algebra." In addition to methods courses, students of the normal school studied a wide range of subjects such as mathematics, chemistry, physics, biology, literature, history, and philosophy. Johnson believed that a solid grounding in traditional academic disciplines provided potential teachers with the necessary tools to develop their full intellectual capacities.[22]

Trinity's business college commercial department, which had previously limited its offerings to courses in penmanship, drawing, and bookkeeping, expanded its curriculum under Johnson's supervision to become a business college. Advertising itself as "The Model School of the South-west," the business college designed a curriculum that combined both practical and theoretical aspects of commercial life. The program integrated courses in business theory with courses in penmanship, correspondence, and commercial law and included field trips to various business establishments. Students were also required to set up a model business operation, a task that they had to perform with "neatness, dispatch and accuracy" before receiving a diploma. Noting that demands for female accountants were rapidly increasing, Johnson opined that Trinity's program was "peculiarly adapted to ladies" and encouraged them to participate alongside their male counterparts.[23]

After two years as president pro tem, Johnson had impressed trustees with his pedagogical expertise and administrative skills. A search committee charged with the responsibility of canvassing the denomination for suitable presidential candidates declined to make a nomination. Accordingly, in June 1887, the trustees unanimously elected Johnson as the third president of Trinity University. Requesting a day in which to decide whether he would accept the nomination, Johnson answered affirmatively after "prayerful consideration."[24]

Over the next several years, Johnson completed a major reorganization of the collegiate program that, with a few modifications, Trinity maintained during the closing decade of the century. Under the new configuration, the president's teaching responsibilities were reduced to three hours per day so that he could "study the school and give that personal supervision to the various departments their needs and importance may require." The professorships of English language, chemistry, and natural science were combined and designated as the professorship of English and natural science. He implemented a maximum teaching load of five hours a day that allowed instructors time to do research and oversee laboratory work in the sciences.[25]

The curriculum was centered around four departments. The collegiate department embraced the traditional classical and scientific track, featuring courses in philosophy, mathematics, English, ancient languages, physical science, and natural science. The professional department included Biblical instruction, civil engineering, and teacher certification. The Biblical program functioned as a supplement for preministerial students preparing for seminary and pastoral careers. The civil engineering course entitled students to a degree of Civil Engineer (C.E.) and included courses in geometry, railroad engineering, road alignment, mechanics of engineering, and map and topographic drawing. In the department of fine arts, stu-

Advertisement in *The Cumberland Presbyterian*, 1887.
Note reference to type-writing.

dents received training in oratory, music, painting, ornamental needlework, and penmanship. The university department offered postgraduate
work at the masters (arts, sciences, and philosophy) and doctoral (Sc.D.
and Ph.D.) levels. Requirements for admission to this department consisted of either graduation from "a reputable college," a degree in one of the
learned professions, or "three years of study devoted to literary pursuits."
In addition to specified course work, candidates had to present an acceptable dissertation on a subject assigned by the faculty. The fee for each of
the graduate degrees, including diploma, was thirty dollars.[26]

Although Johnson resigned as president in 1889, citing a desire to concentrate on teaching and research, he continued to play a prominent role
in academic policy making during the last decade of the century as chairman of the faculty and professor of English and science.[27] One of the most
contested national educational battles in the nineteenth century centered
on granting students the right to select some of their courses. Breaking
with the tradition of a curriculum that had total course requirements,
Johnson introduced the option of electives at the junior and senior levels.
Entire class cohorts, rather than individuals, determined most electives.
The only restriction was that classes could not elect more than one-half of

their work in any one department. Convinced that the elective system permitted individuals to enjoy the freest range of choice "consistent with breadth of culture," Johnson stated that under Trinity's elective system, "a young lady may become an intelligent, refined and cultured member of society [and] a young man may give himself the best training preparatory to entering business or one of the learned professions."[28]

In 1893 Johnson persuaded the trustees to adopt a policy for paid faculty leaves. According to his plan, one faculty member per year was to be granted a year's leave of absence to do graduate work in his particular field of expertise at a major university. Colleagues carried heavier teaching loads so that the leaves required no additional institutional funds. As recipient of the first academic leave, Johnson attended the newly opened University of Chicago, which was led by the innovative educator William Rainey Harper. Recruiting a topflight faculty from premier educational institutions throughout the country, Harper created a novel American university that quickly became an educational icon.[29] The intellectual ferment on the University of Chicago campus made lasting impressions on Johnson and his Trinity colleagues who attended in subsequent years on their leaves: Samuel L. Hornbeak, Jesse Anderson, George Newton, Rhea Miller, and B. Eugene Looney. These faculty members brought back to the Tehuacana institution updated information and new ideas regarding teaching methods, curricular reform, and the campus social environment.[30]

The faculty members, with their commitment to their continuing education, served as role models for undergraduate students who previously had viewed professors as authorities who possessed all knowledge and tolerated no questions. Editorials in the student newspaper spoke of them as "living scholars–teachers who are not satisfied with past achievements, but who read new books and think modern thoughts and expect to expand in soul as long as they live." Noting that Trinity faculty had done graduate work in some of the country's best universities, a student editor observed, "They are still students—and ambitious ones at that."[31]

Several important curricular changes at Trinity can be traced to the influence of President Harper's educational philosophy. Harper made a sharp distinction between collegiate and graduate work, insisting that the latter should be confined to large state or private institutions where opportunities for research and scholarship attracted outstanding students and faculty. In support of this position, Johnson published a monograph in which he advocated that small denominational "universities" like Trinity "drop the title and become colleges in name as well as in fact, and make college life full, rich, and interesting." Instead of aspiring to graduate

Professor L. A. Johnson (standing, far right) and English literature class, 1893

work, Johnson advocated that small colleges should work closely with high school educators to develop a curriculum that would prepare students for a meaningful college experience.[32]

For a time, Trinity faculty and trustees contemplated changing the institution's name to Trinity College to reflect its actual status. In 1892 the Committee on Education of the Cumberland General Assembly suggested that the trustees of Trinity and Lincoln Universities "consider the propriety and feasibility" of correcting the misnomer.[33] With strong support from the faculty, the trustees concurred with the General Assembly and requested that the Synod of Texas approve a change in the charter to include the new nomenclature. When the synod's Committee on Education opposed the change and urged the university not to abandon its graduate aspirations, Trinity's trustees did not pursue the matter further.[34]

Nevertheless, Johnson and his faculty colleagues altered the curriculum to emphasize Trinity's commitment to undergraduate education. In 1898, at the request of the faculty, the trustees removed all graduate courses from the catalogue.[35] At the same time, Trinity dropped all courses of study below the second year of high school, continuing the later years only because so few Texas localities offered this level of education. Although the decision resulted in a sharp decline in revenue, Johnson reaffirmed his conviction that Trinity should concentrate its efforts on becoming a premier four-year liberal arts institution.[36]

Following Johnson's resignation as president in 1889, the trustees turned again to the Cumberland Presbyterian homeland of Tennessee for a new president. They selected John L. Dickens, a native Tennessean who served as president of Bethel College in McKenzie, Tennessee, prior to his call to Texas. His arrival on the Tehuacana campus coincided with concerted efforts by the Trinity faculty to address what it perceived to be declining student morality.[37]

Although Trinity had maintained a policy of "strict but parental" discipline throughout its existence, changing community social values made it increasingly difficult for university officials to monitor off-campus student activities. Faculty were concerned about reports of parties held in Tehuacana homes in which male and female students interacted without proper supervision. Moreover, weekend trips to nearby Mexia exposed students to the "temptations of city life," such as the saloon, train station, and theatre. To address the situation, the faculty requested and received permission from the board of trustees to impose a new set of regulations that included a dress code for men and women and increased restrictions on the interaction between male and female students.[38]

When students learned about the proposed disciplinary regulations, they took to the streets in protest during the closing weeks of the semester in May 1890. President Dickens bore the brunt of student anger. Minutes of a trustees' meeting indicate "quite a number of students assembled together and paraded the street and fired pistols near the residence of some of the citizens and of the president and then marched to the college where they were guilty of other indignities at the room of the president." Shaken by the raucous student behavior, Dickens peremptorily resigned and accepted a position at the newly opened Texas Female Seminary in Weatherford, where campus conditions promised to be less confrontational.[39]

In a public display of authority, the board of trustees assembled the student body in the chapel to express its displeasure over the events that led to the president's departure. Speaking for the trustees, R. M. Castleman decried what he termed "lawless conduct" and called upon local citizens to assist in suppressing "such disgraceful methods of resistance to authorities placed in the management of the institution." Promising that the trustees would "watch with a keen eye" for any irregularities in behavior, Castleman threatened to expel any students who participated in "future acts of violence toward the faculty." Although the board ordered no suspensions or expulsions, it sent an unequivocal message: new regulations would be put in place, and they would be rigorously enforced.[40]

The responsibility of implementing the new rules fell to Dickens's successor, Benjamin D. Cockrill, who accepted the presidency in August 1890. A pastor of a Cumberland Presbyterian Church in Louisville, Kentucky, and a native of Kentucky, Cockrill spent much of his early life in Tennessee, where he received his education first at Cumberland University and later at the University of Nashville. From 1876 to 1878 he studied at Union Theological Seminary in New York, after which he held pastorates in Mississippi and Kentucky. Like several of his predecessors, Cockrill also was appointed the Aston Lecturer on Theology and Homiletics and served as pastor of the Tehuacana Church. During his six-year stay at Trinity, he was much in demand for popular and inspirational addresses at churches and civic organizations throughout the state.[41]

Subtle but striking changes in university regulations first appeared in the 1890–91 *Catalogue*. Previously there had been no reference to boarding arrangements, but now students were permitted to reside only at faculty-approved residences. Householders were required to abide by college rules and to report all violations to college authorities. Moreover, men and women were not allowed to board in the same house unless parents or guardians accepted responsibility for such arrangements. Students were now "required," rather than "expected," to attend weekday chapel and worship on Sunday. Whereas students were previously not permitted "to leave town" without permission, they now could not "leave the immediate premises" without approval. A new demerit system penalized unexcused absences, failures to prepare lessons, and "other misdemeanors." Any student who accumulated twenty demerits faced suspension or expulsion at the pleasure of the faculty. In addition to these changes, students were expected to observe "implicit obedience to all the rules, whether published in the *Catalogue* or announced orally by the president," and to maintain "regular, faithful, and thorough work, punctual attendance upon every recitation, and thorough preparation of every lesson."[42]

Part of the disciplinary reformation was the implementation of uniforms for dress occasions. A committee of female teachers chose styles for the young women at the start of each season that were "neat and stylish" but less expensive than non-uniform clothing of the same quality. In 1893 the fall and winter attire consisted of "confederate-gray flannel dresses trimmed with the same and hats of a suitable style to match." Spring called for gray chambray dresses with gray embroidery and "inexpensive hats suited to the season." For commencement season, cream mull

Male and female students in uniforms, c. 1896

dresses with cream lace ("trimming must not be elaborate") and cream hats were deemed appropriate. The uniform for young men consisted of dark blue coats and "blue-gray pantaloons of good material and made in seasonable college styles with caps to match the coat." The full suit was not to cost more than fifteen dollars.[43]

"Rule Nine," the most unpopular and least enforceable regulation, evoked the most negative response from Trinity students in the 1890s. "Students of the opposite sex are strictly forbidden all communication with each other of every kind; and they are considered under this rule from time of their arrival at the University until they leave."[44] On special holidays such as Thanksgiving, Christmas, and Washington's Birthday, for religious events such as prayer and revival meetings, and during commencement week activities, presidents usually suspended the rule. Even at these times, however, adults watched for behavior deemed unbecoming a member of the Trinity community. To students, Rule Nine represented the ultimate challenge of their undergraduate career, and their efforts to circumvent the regulation became cherished contributions to Trinity's student folklore.

Recalling their experiences on the Tehuacana campus during the last decade of the nineteenth century, Trinity alumni described various strategies designed to overcome the prohibition of social communication between the two sexes. Notwithstanding meticulous adult chaperoning, male and female students maintained an elaborate system of communication. Mandatory chapel services during the week and on Sunday evenings provided regular opportunities for social interaction. Boys used the left flight of stairs leading to the second-floor chapel and girls entered from the right flight of stairs, closely followed by the boarding hall matron who guarded her flock until they reached their seats in the auditorium. Segregated seating arrangements made contact difficult but not impossible. A wall from the tops of the pews to the floor divided the middle tier of seats so that when a young man sat on one side of the middle tier and a young woman on the other side, a blank wall separated them. But chapel provided opportunities for exchanges of smiles and glances and notes passed from one side of the partition to the other. Students sitting next to the wall accepted this potentially dangerous task as part of their common responsibilities.[45]

Although segregated seating prevailed in the classroom, students managed to communicate even under the watchful eyes of the instructors. Undergraduates left notes tucked in the folds of wooden chairs to be removed during the next recitation period by the addressee or passed on by a third party. One venturesome senior, who was teaching a class for an indisposed professor, borrowed a book from a female student and returned it several days later with a love note tucked inside.[46] Other opportunities for clandestine meetings occurred on Sundays after morning services when students entertained themselves by taking long walks, often ending at the local cemetery, which offered a panoramic view of the countryside. Young men and women left their boarding houses separately but managed to end up "accidentally" at the cemetery away from the prying eyes of adults. The rocky campus provided students with a variety of repositories for strategically placed love notes, including the rocks at nearby Love's Spring and Barry's Spring, favorite gathering spots for Trinity students.[47]

When faculty or staff intercepted notes, the students endured public humiliation and demerits or expulsion. At one chapel service, the president read a confiscated love letter, spicing it with his own derisive comments. Both culprits endured their chastisement in the presence of their

The TRINITONIAN

VOL. II. TEHUACANA, TEXAS, APRIL, 1902. NO. 7.

Etiquette for Students

FOR MEN.

Have neatness in your personal habits—the first mark of good breeding.

Never leave your room for school or public place without dressing the hair, cleaning the skin, the teeth, the nails; having spotless linen and a tasteful tie, well brushed clothing and tidy boots.

Don't appear on the streets in shirt sleeves, or with no collar or tie, and never approach a lady in such an ill bred toilet.

Before escorting a lady, or before coming into their presence, be sure that you have taken a thorough bath; that your breath is not offensive, or any part of your person. (How disgusting for the man or woman to be in company with one whose body smells foul, and whose breath is painfully offensive.) Air your clothing frequently, especially before coming into the presence of others.

Avoid excessive use of strong perfumes; a very little of some mild odor may be permissible.

Don't sit sideways, or cross-legged, or slip halfway down in the chair.

Scratching the head or ears and picking the teeth are operations to be attended to in one's room.

Blowing the nose in the presence of company or at the table is unpardonable. Be courteous at all times to the ladies.

Do not be "fresh" unless you are, and then your face will show it without any effort on your part.

Tip your hat when meeting, speaking to, or leaving a lady, and at any time when speaking to any one, where a woman is one of either party.

Bathe and change your clothing oftener, for one is dirty enough at best. Daily baths are not too frequent for this weather.

Keep your hair cut close, head clean and face shaven.

Be a man, mannerly and polite at all times.

---

peers and then were sent home in disgrace.[48] Sometimes demerits were dispensed to groups. An astronomy class studying the stars at a professor's home one Friday evening "coupled off according to choice" before they reached their respective boardinghouses. Observed by an alert faculty member, the students received ten demerits each the following Monday in chapel.[49]

Although consumption of alcohol apparently did not constitute a major problem on campus, anecdotal evidence indicates that at least some Trinity students were not total abstainers. A boarding student confided to his parents that some of his friends drank whiskey when they visited one

FOR THE WOMEN.

Let us caution you that a neat toilet is first and fundamentally essential. Before leaving your room see that your hair is neatly dressed, the skin fresh and clean, the teeth well kept, the nails trimmed and polished, the dress clean and free from wrinkles. See that your dress is properly fastened, the belt in its place, that the dress skirt hangs even; that the skirt bands and the fastenings do not show above or below the belt, or show at all; that the placket hole is properly fixed (anything but a girl's placket hole gaping"; that the petticoats and underskirts do not extend below the outside dress skirt; that your feet are as well dressed as your head, and that your clothing is clean. Keep pins, hairpins and toothpicks out of your mouths. Such is disgusting.

Be sure that neither your person nor your breath are offensive.

Do not wear the same shirtwaist a week at a time. Have an ample supply and laundered frequently.

Do not keep a young man waiting for you to dress.

Avoid familiarity and boisterousness. Do not be loud on the street; don't be loud at any time.

Take the gentleman's arm; do not permit his taking yours.

Say "Thank you" for any and every courtesy shown you by the men, no matter how small.

Do not be so susceptible to flattery, and rebuke the man who "taffys" you.

Remember that you are not a man, so avoid anything mannish; be a woman, a lady, at all times.

Opposite and above: "Etiquette for Students," the *Trinitonian*, April 1902

of the nearby towns. Among them was his roommate, who frequently returned to campus drunk and "raised a ruckus" with other Trinity students.[50] On one occasion Trinity officials turned an incident of student drinking into a windfall for the university. Word reached campus that a saloonkeeper in Mexia had sold intoxicating drinks to some Trinity students in violation of Texas law. Sensing potential income, the trustees hired a lawyer who took the case on contingency and filed a $1,000 suit against the saloonkeeper. Rather than face a public hearing, the offender settled out of court. As one faculty member later expressed it, "That year, a saloon keeper paid off at least most of the deficit in the budget of a Christian institution."[51]

Aside from violations of specific university rules, Trinity students of the 1890s reveled in practical jokes, frequently directed at faculty and staff. An unidentified student placed a sheet of tin over the chimney of Professor Gillespie's boardinghouse on a cold, snowy night, causing the fire the next morning to drive all the occupants out into the yard. When Professor B. E. Looney arrived in Tehuacana with his bride, students had removed the slats from his bed and fastened cowbells to the springs. On one Halloween night, school officials had to summon the Mexia Fire Department to remove a donkey that appeared on top of the university building. On another occasion, pranksters tied the end of a long rope to the bell at the top of the building, extended the rope across a fence, and attached it to a heifer. Whenever the heifer moved, the bell rang in time with its steps.[52]

By the end of the decade, however, members of the Trinity faculty were having second thoughts about micromanaging students' social life. Influenced in part by some of their colleagues' experiences at the University of Chicago, where President Harper granted students considerable autonomy, they realized that many of the rules, especially Rule Nine, were unenforceable.[53] Monitoring misconduct was time consuming; moreover, the trend was that students should take more responsibility for their own behavior. Accordingly, in 1898 the faculty recommended to the trustees that "there be no rules or regulations respecting the conduct of the pupils after this year." Instead, incoming students would be required to sign the following pledge: "I hereby solemnly promise upon my honor as a gentleman (or lady) to allow nothing to interfere with a diligent prosecution of my studies, and also to deport myself at all times in a way becoming to a young gentleman (or young lady)."[54]

Although the trustees conceded the difficulties of student discipline, they were not prepared to take the radical step advocated by the faculty. Instead, they modified the existing regulations to make them more realistic. They listed attendance at chapel and Sunday worship as "desired" rather than required, removed a statement prohibiting students to incur debt, and amended the wording of Rule Nine to read, "Students of opposite sexes are strictly forbidden all communication with each other of any kind *except the common courtesies of life*" (italics added). The trustees empowered the faculty to make additional revisions and to eliminate any rules that they considered impracticable, but they requested that the faculty "strictly enforce" the remaining rules.[55]

Beginning with the 1899–1900 *Catalogue*, the section entitled "Suggestions and Regulations" contained a much abbreviated and unnumbered list of regulations dealing primarily with boarding arrangements and admission policies. Rule Nine, even in modified form, no longer appeared in print. Returning to earlier nomenclature, the faculty expected the students to "conduct themselves as ladies and gentlemen" and to obey all regulations whether published in the *Trinity University Catalogue* or announced by university officials. Although students continued to lead extremely regimented lives, they enjoyed a social freedom unknown to previous student generations. In 1901 the *Trinitonian* applauded "the more natural forms of government such as the social relations between sexes, permission to leave town, and personal independence of students" that characterized official policies at the beginning of the new century.[56]

Trinity students found outlets for social interaction and personal development in extracurricular activities. During the 1890s the literary societies continued to be strong, with the Philosophronian, Maeonian, Sappho-Adelphian, and Ratio-Genic Societies attracting wide followings. Their field of activities expanded in 1894 when representatives of Austin College, Baylor University, Southwestern University, Add-Ran University (predecessor of Texas Christian University), and Trinity University met in Fort Worth to found the Texas State Oratorical Association. This intercollegiate group stimulated competitive rivalries among the various institutions in debate and declamation.[57]

Leaders in the literary societies initiated a new student newspaper in 1888, the *Trinity Exponent*, published monthly "in the interests of education in general and literary culture in particular." The *Exponent*, which evolved into the *Trinitonian* in 1900, showcased outstanding student essays and orations and kept students informed regarding campus events. The initial publication contained articles on the techniques of oratory, a history of literary societies, the meaning of wisdom, and the lives of great men and women in American history. On the lighter side, a column entitled "Dots" offered accounts of events in the lives of students and faculty. Unlike previous school papers that lacked adequate financial support, the *Exponent* contained a full page of paid advertisements from Tehuacana and Mexia merchants.[58]

New organizations provided additional choices for students. The Timothean Society, which initially functioned as a theology class for preministerial students, reorganized in 1891 under a new constitution and conducted weekly meetings similar to those of the other literary societies. Members were fined 25 cents for tardiness, speaking, whispering, moving a chair without permission, clapping their hands, spitting on the floor, or similar transgressions. Debates typically focused on religious subjects, such as "Resolved, that it is possible for one to attain to a state of sinless perfection in this life" (affirmative); "Resolved, that women are called and should be ordained to preach the gospel" (affirmative); and "Resolved, that the evolution theory of man's origin from some lower animal is highly probable"(affirmative). Other issues had broader social and political implications: "Resolved, that every American citizen should know how to read and write before voting" (affirmative); "Resolved, that education will solve the race problem" (negative); "Resolved, that the liquor traffic is the greatest evil of our country" (negative); and "Resolved, that marriages should be prohibited where there is a possibility of the parties engaged suffering from poverty" (affirmative).[59]

Students of natural history organized the Exploration Society, a group that combined weekly campus meetings with periodic field trips to wilderness areas in Limestone and surrounding counties. During the summer of 1885, faculty sponsor William Hudson and a group of students searched for rock and mineral specimens and fauna and flora to be added to the university's collection. Traveling on horseback and sleeping in tents, the party traversed the area between Tehuacana and Waco, resting only on Sundays, when they spent the day in prayer and Bible study. According to Hudson, "Our minds and hearts are deeply impressed with the solid fact that if we spend Sunday well, we shall prosper better for it the week after."[60] Along the way, they hunted the bears, panthers, jaguars, ocelots, lynxes, antelopes, and black-tailed deer that roamed the area along Devil's River in Crockett County. Arriving in the small town of McGregor, Hudson decried the presence of the Sunny South Billiard Hall, which featured the sign "Beer on Tap." How much better, Hudson moralized, "if the sign said the Public Library of McGregor and Good Bread and Ham on Hand."[61]

Students also displayed interest in musical groups during the last decade of the century. Under the leadership of Professors Eugene E. Davis, a graduate of the Imperial Conservatory of Music in Vienna, Austria, and William W. Campbell, a graduate of the Westminster Conservatory of Music in Pennsylvania, Trinity organized several musical organizations. A Mandolin Club, composed of men who gathered weekly to play popular music, had an enthusiastic following. Students who displayed proficiency in their respective instruments (violin, mandolin, guitar, cello, and piano) joined the university orchestra that performed at numerous campus events. A male glee club, directed by Campbell, represented Trinity at various church and civic gatherings throughout the state, "winning the highest praise" from receptive audiences.[62]

Intercollegiate athletics gradually became an important part of campus activities. Although Trinity's founders viewed organized athletics as an intrusion into the academic routine, the younger faculty encouraged exercise and athletic competition as a means of developing individual discipline and promoting school spirit.[63] Members of the campus YMCA raised

Glee Club, the *Trinitonian*, April 1906

money for exercise equipment for the student body and in 1900 furnished two rooms with parallel and horizontal bars, a punching bag, hand weights, Indian clubs, and tumbling mats. S. L. Wear taught a class in calisthenics to prepare students for athletic competition.[64]

Team sports on the Trinity campus during the 1890s consisted primarily of recreational baseball games, foot races, and occasional football contests with local residents. In September 1898, a pick-up Trinity team played a game of football with the "Tehuacana Town Boys." According to a participant, "the game was very good at first, but the University boys 'played out' before the game was ended, and, therefore, lost the game." Music Director Campbell entered the fray and won the admiration of his students for a stellar performance.[65]

The origins of Trinity University's first intercollegiate football team can be traced back to the turn of the century at the University of Chicago, where legendary coach Amos Alonzo Stagg produced a series of outstanding teams. While pursuing graduate work in 1898–99, Trinity faculty member B. Eugene Looney observed the prominent role given to athletics at the University of Chicago and became especially interested in football. Coach Stagg encouraged Looney to promote the sport when he returned to Texas and gave him some tips about gridiron strategy. Following his return to the Tehuacana campus, Looney organized and served as faculty manager of the first university football team in 1900.[66]

Looney found it difficult to form a team because football was not a popular sport in Texas, and few students knew much about its rules. On the first Trinity team, one man had played football but never with a regular team, several men had watched a few games, and the rest simply had to use their imaginations. Before practice could begin, Looney and a group of students carved a playing field out of the rocky Tehuacana campus. Using borrowed crowbars, hammers, and shovels, they dug up stones and filled holes with dirt. Rocks too big to move were simply crushed to ground level, while those that could be moved became reserved seats on the sidelines for faculty and female students. Other spectators sat on the ground.[67]

On 17 November 1900, the Trinity Warriors participated in their first intercollegiate match, traveling to Waco to scrimmage the Baylor University eleven.[68] The Trinity uniforms consisted of white pants, white jerseys with maroon stripes, and "old shoes with strips of leather nailed on the soles for cleats." The most important part of the uniform, however, was the nose guard, a hard rubber contraption narrow enough at the top to fit between the eyes and wide enough below to encompass the nose, with a piece of rubber extending into the mouth to protect the teeth. Team Captain George Stoker, class of 1901, recalled that the inexperienced Trinity players suffered from stage fright and were unable to remember their field positions. After being directed into place by Stoker, one of the players said, "Now what do you want me to do?" Stoker yelled back, "Catch the ball and run like hell!" Despite individual efforts by Warrior players during the bruising encounter, Baylor shut out the visiting Trinity team 17–0.[69]

Other sports such as tennis, basketball, and baseball also attracted students. Considered a "gentleman's game," tennis meshed well with Trinity standards of decorum. Under Looney's supervision, a thirteen-member male tennis team was organized in 1898. One team member, Frank Wear, later became president of Trinity University at Waxahachie. Baseball, which enjoyed a wide following among Trinity students, became a popular spring sport. In 1901 the *Trinitonian* reported that Trinity had "one of the best baseball teams to be found anywhere. Manager McCain is arranging for inter-college games and our boys expect to do honor for themselves and school."[70] Trinity is also reputed to have been the site of one of the first indoor basketball games in Texas. During recent renovations in the old Tehuacana classroom building, workers uncovered a basketball backboard mounted on the attic wall. Structural beams had been moved in order to accommodate the new sport.[71]

Despite an active student environment, Trinity faculty and trustees had serious concerns about the university's future in Tehuacana, and fear of relocation hovered over the campus. In September 1888, Cumberland Presbyterians dissolved the Brazos, Colorado, Texas, and Trinity Synods and

Trinity's first football team, 1900

University tennis team, 1898

established a single governing body called the Synod of Texas. At the opening session of the new synod in Dallas, several presbyteries recommended that Trinity be moved to an urban setting. Anticipating this, a large contingent of Tehuacana townspeople arrived to oppose relocation. Their presence and the support of Trinity trustees and faculty had a measurable impact on the commissioners in attendance. The synod's Committee on Education reported that agitation for removal was "hurtful to the institution" and urged all ministers and laypersons "to do all in their power to increase the efficiency of the institution at its present location."[72] To confirm their support for Trinity, commissioners designated the first Sunday in December as Trinity University Day, requesting that congregations take up special offerings for the Tehuacana campus.[73]

Having temporarily sidetracked the relocation movement, trustees and townspeople continued to refute charges that Tehuacana did not warrant a denominational university. Although the town consisted only of three churches, two gristmills and cotton gins, and 500 residents, it was incorporated by 1890 with a mayor-council form of city government and was linked to the outside world by telegraph and telephone. City officials engaged in conversations with Mexia residents concerning the establishment of rail connections between the two localities. Negotiations for an electric streetcar line looked promising but were contingent on the ability of Tehuacana residents to raise sufficient cash ($14,000) to underwrite a portion of the expenses. When the funds failed to materialize, residents reluctantly abandoned the project.[74]

Trinity trustees moved forward with a campus master plan that included completing and furnishing the existing building and erecting dormitories for men and women, a gymnasium, a music hall, a museum, a science building, and a divinity hall for preministerial students. Following the erection of the north wing of the "T" in 1887, the main building was completed in 1892 with the addition of the south wing, a high mansard roof, and a cupola. Referred to as the "Pride of Limestone County," the building in its final form measured 63 feet in height, excluding the cupola, and 116 feet in length. In addition to the chapel, which seated 600, the building contained 26 large rooms designed for classrooms, laboratories, society halls, and a library.[75]

Largely through the efforts of Luther Apelles Johnson, Trinity acquired facilities to house female students. In 1895, at a cost of $6,000, the school purchased, remodeled, and enlarged an adjacent residence to accommodate thirty women. Johnson and his spouse lived in the house as supervisors. House rules required residents to "provide their own sheets and towels, make their beds, and sweep rooms and keep them tidy." Servants handled other duties such as "making morning fires, bringing water and fuel, carrying out slops, sweeping out halls, etc." The building was off limits to males unless their sisters lived in the dormitory. Brothers could visit on Friday afternoons between 4 and 6 o'clock.[76]

In addition to campus improvements, Trinity officials launched a public relations campaign, targeted at denominational periodicals, to make constituents aware of Trinity's new facilities and outstanding faculty. The articles emphasized the uniqueness of Tehuacana as a university town and, without mentioning the issue of relocation, urged Cumberland Presbyterians to give generously to new building projects. In 1896, a profusely illustrated article in the *St. Louis Observer*, a widely read Cumberland newspaper, featured biographies of the seven full-time faculty members and detailed descriptions of various programs of instruction.[77] As a follow-up, the editor of the *Observer*, D. M. Harris, extolled the virtues of Trinity and urged readers to support campus expansion at Tehuacana. He wrote, "Trinity University takes first rank among the colleges of Texas, and the Cumberland Presbyterian Church in the State should enlarge the facilities of the institution without delay."[78]

University and civic officials came up short, however, in their drive for campus expansion. The Panic of 1893 triggered an extended period of national economic depression that negatively impacted railroad development and agricultural operation, especially in the western states. Other factors, such as an impending denominational reunion of the Cumberland Presbyterian Church with the Presbyterian Church in the U.S.A. and competition from the newly opened Cumberland Texas Female Seminary in Weatherford, caused many Cumberland church members to adopt a wait-and-see attitude regarding Trinity's future. As a result, collections from Trinity University Day netted only about $150 annually during the 1890s, and hopes of securing large sums from Texas benefactors evaporated. A movement by the Cumberland Presbyterian General Assembly in 1899 to secure one million dollars for higher education raised hopes on the Trinity campus, but the movement never generated denomination-wide support.[79]

Declining faculty morale, decreasing student enrollment, and chronic financial shortfalls marked the university's final years on the Tehuacana campus. From 1896 to 1901, the trustees were unable to recruit a qualified candidate to accept the position of president. During that period, the chairman of the faculty, Johnson, and his successor, Samuel M. Hornbeak, functioned as the chief executive officers. Between 1899 and 1902, combined enrollment in the preparatory and collegiate departments averaged only 162, and graduating classes were consistently in single digits. Heavily dependent on tuition income and reluctant to raise tuition and fees, Trinity faced mounting budget deficits that were addressed by reducing faculty salaries and deferring all but essential maintenance work.[80]

In the midst of all this, Johnson succumbed to typhoid fever in July 1900. Widely respected in church, civic, and educational circles, Johnson's death removed the university's most eloquent and effective spokesperson from the relocation debate. Hornbeak, Johnson's colleague and close friend, summarized his contributions: "From the time he was first connected with the school till he was stricken low with the fatal illness, he was the leading spirit of Trinity University. He was a clear, accurate and powerful thinker, reinvestigated thoroughly and studied exhaustively. . . . Broad in scholarship, ripe in experience, clear in conception of educational values, well rounded in character, seemingly psychologically complete, he was universally sought when wise counsel was needed. He magnified the office of teaching."[81]

Following Johnson's death, Cumberland Presbyterians intensified efforts to remove Trinity from Tehuacana. Meeting in Sherman in November 1900, synod commissioners received overtures from Bonham, Dallas, Guthrie, Red Oak, and San Saba Presbyteries recommending that Trinity secure a more suitable home. Opponents of removal deemed the move unfair to people who had invested so much time and money in the Tehuacana campus, while supporters countered that neither students nor financial support could be attracted to such an isolated hamlet. After lengthy debate, the synod passed a resolution, by a 53–44 vote, affirming that the educational progress of Trinity would best be conserved "by the removal of said institution from its present location, to some good city within our bounds." Two Trinity trustees, D. M. Prendergast and R. M. Castleman, resigned their posts, providing the synod with an opportunity to replace them with members favorable to relocation.[82]

Following the precedent established in 1869, the synod appointed a committee to receive sealed bids from all cities in the state who might wish to have Trinity University relocate to their community. Due by 1 June 1901, bids were to cover any losses that might be entailed in the process of vacating the Tehuacana campus.[83] Even before the committee published its call, Waxahachie citizens organized to secure the institution that it had failed to attract in 1869. Led by local businessman W. H. Getzendaner, a committee of community leaders selected a ten-acre site less than a mile from town and began to raise subscriptions for the funding. The nearby communities of Itasca and Corsicana also joined in the bidding, making it a three-town race for the new Trinity University.[84]

After visiting each of the towns that had submitted sealed bids, the synod's locating committee voted unanimously to accept Waxahachie's proposition, which amounted to $80,000. Of that sum, two local banks guaranteed $50,000 in cash and a group of fifty-two Waxahachie citizens pledged a total of $15,000 in deferred payments. Also included were ten acres of land valued at $7,500 and equity in notes amounting to $7,500.[85] Although the Cumberland Synod of Texas had yet to act on the committee's decision, Waxahachie citizens held a "jollification meeting" in the district courtroom accompanied by music from the Firemen's Band and "spellbinding" addresses by local orators. The *Waxahachie Enterprise* proclaimed in a banner headline, "Trinity Comes to Waxahachie."[86]

When the Cumberland Synod of Texas convened at Hillsboro on 12 September 1901, S. M. Templeton, chair of the relocation committee, presented the report that recommended the acceptance of the Waxahachie proposal for Trinity. For the last time, opponents and proponents of removal argued the issue in a debate that carried over into the next day's session. Following impassioned oratory on both sides, the moderator called for a vote. Eighty-four commissioners responded affirmatively and twenty-eight negatively; thus, after a third of a century in Tehuacana, Trinity would open the 1902–1903 academic year in Waxahachie.[87]

However, the controversy did not end with the final vote. Opponents of the move threatened a court injunction. Heading off a costly and time-consuming court case, synod commissioners proposed the donation of the Tehuacana campus and building to the local community "for the peaceful and harmonious accomplishment" of the removal of the campus to Waxahachie. Tehuacana residents accepted the offer, and Trinity trustees immediately took steps to complete the legal papers.[88] Under the auspices of the Methodist Protestant Church in 1902, Tehuacana became the site of Westminster College, a four-year liberal arts institution formerly located in Collins County, Texas.[89]

Trinity's last year on the Tehuacana campus evoked mixed emotions among faculty and students. Students were excited about the move to Waxahachie. An editorial in the *Trinitonian* affirmed that Trinity would "soon be the leading denominational educational institution in the state . . . Arouse ye, Cumberland Presbyterians! Let's boom this thing right now!"[90] Faculty morale, however, reached a low ebb, a fact not unnoticed by students. In a letter to his sister, Robert Bone wrote: "We counted 106 old students that are not here. Tehuacana is a dead town. Even the teachers seem like they are half asleep all the time."[91] Faculty who opposed relocation presented their resignations to the trustees, including Jesse Anderson, who had accepted the presidency in June 1901 after the death of Johnson. A native Texan, Anderson graduated from Trinity in 1889 and became the professor of Latin and Greek in 1891. Awarded a Ph.D. from Cumberland University in 1894, Anderson also did graduate work at the University of Chicago. In stepping down as president, Anderson expressed his support for the university, but stated that he believed his opposition to relocation would prejudice his ability to perform satisfactorily as chief executive officer. He agreed, however, to perform presidential duties during Trinity's last semester in Tehuacana.[92]

The search for Anderson's replacement proved difficult. After negative responses from several prominent Cumberland Presbyterian clergymen, including Ira Landrith, editor of *The Cumberland Presbyterian*, trustees turned in January 1902 to a local minister, thirty-five-year-old Leonidas C. Kirkes, pastor of the Third Presbyterian Church of Corsicana. A graduate of Cumberland University in Lebanon, Tennessee, and Union Theological Seminary in New York, Kirkes took graduate courses at Columbia University and subsequently received a master's degree from Trinity University. "After a free discussion of the matter," trustees set a salary for Kirkes at $1,800 and allowed for traveling expenses payable out of funds raised while soliciting on behalf of the university.[93]

During the spring of 1902, Waxahachie citizens made preparations for the arrival of the university. Hubble and Green, Dallas architects, submitted plans for a four-story structure with a capacity of 500 students. By the time of the cornerstone-laying ceremony on 21 March 1902, the Waxahachie street-railway company had extended its track, the telephone company was stringing telephone lines to the campus, workers were drilling a well, and newly planted shade trees graced the avenues approaching the university grounds. A group of Trinity faculty and students arrived on a special train from Mexia and "promenaded the streets, taking in the town" before the afternoon ceremonies. Schools and businesses closed, and Waxahachie citizens turned out in large numbers to witness the event, which resembled a Fourth of July celebration.[94]

Trustees and faculty participated in exercises that culminated with the insertion of a sealed copper box in the cavity of the cornerstone. Among the items contained in the box were copies of the Bible; the Presbyterian Confession of Faith; a Trinity catalogue; a roll of graduates, faculty, and students; and various church newspapers. Waxahachie citizens hoped that the event would lead to a long and productive relationship with Trinity University.[95]

Back in Tehuacana, commencement week in the spring of 1902 brought closure to the prolonged and painful relocation process. At the final chapel service on 30 May, graduating seniors and faculty members spoke "tender and enthusiastic parting words" as they severed cordial relations with the Tehuacana community. Retiring President Anderson appealed to the students to "rekindle the fires of your youthful oratory and renew your enthusiastic vows of devotion to musical culture, art, classics, literature, science, philosophy, and mathematics" on the Waxahachie campus. Following the chapel service, the YMCA gave a "mirth-provoking entertainment," and later the campus community gathered for a music recital.[96]

The last Sunday on the Tehuacana campus featured two worship services and a memorial tribute to Luther Apelles Johnson. In the morning President-elect Kirkes preached a sermon on the theme of "The Spirit and Method of Christian Thinkers," and in the evening the Reverend J. T. Molloy of Waco spoke to the students on "Life: Its Purposes and Responsibilities." On Sunday afternoon, the faculty led a solemn procession of students and townspeople to the village cemetery, where they dedicated a monument honoring Johnson.[97]

"When the history of Trinity University is written, high upon the lists of its greatest scholars and leaders will stand the name of *Luther Apelles Johnson.*"

Trinity University Trustees Minutes, 19 July 1900

Commencement week concluded with other traditional events. The literary societies held their annual exercises on Monday evening, and the Alumni Association met on the following day. On Wednesday, June 4, Trinity graduated a class of nine, five of whom were preministerial students. Describing the events in *The Cumberland Presbyterian,* the writer concluded his nostalgic account on a positive note: "With these exercises closed the thirty-third annual commencement of Trinity University. The next session opens in September in Waxahachie, Texas, under most promising environments."[98]

PART TWO

WAXAHACHIE

Waxahachie, the county seat of Ellis County and a major
railway center, is located in the richest black land belt of
Texas and stands as one of the most flourishing cities of the
State. With so strong a commercial basis, unexcelled religious
and educational advantages, and with a constituency of
intellectual, industrious and thrifty agricultural people,
Waxahachie has a guarantee of stability and prosperity.

Trinity University Catalogue, 1902–1903

CHAPTER FOUR

BRIGHTER DAYS AHEAD

We expect to work with all our might for the abundant success of
Trinity University in the midst of those big-hearted and liberal people at
Waxahachie. And we feel that there are brighter days and more glorious
possibilities ahead of us in the educational work of our beloved church
in this great state.

JESSE ANDERSON, PRESIDENT OF TRINITY UNIVERSITY, 1901

GEOGRAPHICALLY, THE MOVE from Tehuacana to Waxahachie
covered only seventy-five miles, not a great distance even at the turn of the
century. Physically, it required only one horse-drawn wagon to transport
a few desks, some geological and botanical specimens, several hundred library books, and limited laboratory equipment. Sociologically, however, it
represented a quantum leap from rural isolation into urban surroundings.
As one Tehuacana alumnus expressed it, "Trinity University is now moving out of the woods into a town where her possibilities will be grander
and her influence will be extended to a wider scope."[1]

Although Waxahachie was too small to be called a metropolis, it was a
county seat and a commercial center of 7,500 inhabitants in which Trinity students would be exposed to a wider variety of cultural experiences.
Described by the local chamber of commerce as the "Queen City of the
Cotton Belt," Waxahachie sat thirty miles south of Dallas and forty miles
southeast of Fort Worth at the junction of two railways, the Houston &
Texas Central and the Missouri, Kansas, & Texas. In 1902 the town reported bank deposits of $1,750,000, thriving flour and cotton mills, elec-
tric lights, a street railway, and a public sanitary system.[2] Noted for its religious ethos and abundance of churches, Waxahachie was a "dry town,"
with "no dives to lure students" because of a recent local option election
that closed all the saloons in Ellis County.[3]

Like other Texas towns at the turn of the century, Waxahachie was a
segregated community, with "colored" schools and demarcated residential

Downtown Waxahachie, 1905
Photo, the Ellis County Museum, Waxahachie

areas for nonwhite populations. Accounts of beating, lynching, and burning of African Americans in surrounding communities periodically appeared in the *Waxahachie Enterprise*.[4] Neither local citizens nor school officials contemplated the presence of African American students in the new university setting except as groundskeepers, janitors, and cooks. During the last two decades in Waxahachie, however, a few Hispanic students added some diversity to the otherwise all white enrollment.[5]

Six months before Trinity University opened its doors in Waxahachie, President-elect Leonidas Kirkes embarked on a money-raising tour in the Synod of Texas. Commissioned by university trustees to secure funds for the construction of a women's dormitory, Kirkes contacted Cumberland Presbyterian clergy, hoping that they would lead him to potential donors. Many ministers, however, were resistant to his overtures for assistance. Some were not college graduates or had attended small colleges that relied almost exclusively on tuition fees for income, so requests for endowment and building funds ranked low on their list of stewardship priorities. Others resented the fact that Trinity had left Tehuacana or thought that it should have moved to a larger center like Dallas or Fort Worth.[6]

Kirkes launched his campaign in the summer of 1902 in the midst of a prolonged drought that threatened the north Texas economy. Consequent-

Interurban trolley advertisement, the *Trinitonian,* February 1914

ly, he found it awkward to ask for donations from farmers and ranchers
whose fields had turned into swirling dust bowls. Kirkes appealed for
funds from one cattleman who took him on an extended tour of his
ranch, which was littered with the carcasses of dead livestock. Kirkes left
with neither a pledge nor a donation. Although Kirkes persisted in soliciting funds for Trinity, he raised only about $5,000 toward the construction
of the women's dormitory, primarily from personal friends in and around
Corsicana.[7]

Fearful that the campus would not be functional for the scheduled
opening date of September 6, Kirkes recommended that the move to Waxahachie be postponed for one year. Trinity trustees, anxious to exit the
Tehuacana environment, added $12,000 from the endowment fund to the
money that Kirkes had raised so that construction could begin. Realizing
that time was short, however, they set back the opening of classes by two
weeks so that work could be completed.[8]

At opening ceremonies on 9 October 1902, Trinity had enrolled 225
students and more were expected to arrive within the week. Kirkes, J. C.
Smith, a local Cumberland Presbyterian minister, and Judge M. B. Templeton, a trustee and member of the building committee, spoke to an assembly of students and local citizens. A reporter who was present expressed hope that those who opposed relocation would now "find cause
to change their opinions and see light where they suspected darkness."[9]

Mule-drawn streetcar, 1906

At one of the first board meetings on the Waxahachie campus, Trinity trustees clarified the relationship between the president and the faculty, an issue that had surfaced from time to time in Tehuacana but had never been resolved. The trustees gave the president "full authority in the government, management, and control of the university, including the selection and dismissal of all teachers and instructors," subject to the final approval of the trustees. They further specified that "in matters of *importance*" the faculty should be considered as advisors to the president, similar to the relationship of cabinet members to the President of the United States.[10] The trustees also authorized the president to hire a person "at a salary he deems appropriate" to serve as university registrar. The job description included service as secretary to the president, secretary to the Board of Trustees, registrar, and accountant and the responsibility "to take care of and preserve all university property."[11]

Despite initial optimism, the university did not function smoothly in its new location. With the construction of an artesian well and the campus sewer system still in progress, Trinity staff had to haul water from town. When the well was completed, the wind was insufficient to activate the pump, so it was not until workmen installed an electric pump during the summer that the campus had an adequate water supply. Heating systems, put in belatedly at the end of the first semester, failed to operate properly. Professors complained that the "knocking and popping and cannonading and squirting of water from the radiator valves" made it difficult to conduct classes. For temporary relief, Kirkes purchased a number of kerosene stoves for rooms and halls.[12]

The drought finally ended in November and was replaced by persistent rains that continued until the following spring and thus slowed construction. Unpaved streets and walks turned into quagmires, so faculty and students left a trail of mud throughout the building. Women struggled to keep their long dresses clean and prevent the mud from sucking off their overshoes. A mule-car line furnished transportation from the university to the town center but experienced numerous derailments. Its passengers frequently had to disembark to pull, push, or lift a car back onto its tracks.[13]

The trustees had originally planned to board male students in the homes of nearby families until they could raise funds to build accommodations, but there were more men than families willing to take them in. The university purchased an old building adjacent to the campus formerly used as a private school and converted the classrooms and study halls into sleeping quarters. Although it provided shelter and an opportunity for the men to participate more fully in university social life, primitive living conditions in the hastily renovated structure elicited frequent complaints about meals and sleeping arrangements.[14]

Despite efforts by faculty and staff to improve the quality of campus life, the student body and the Waxahachie community appeared discouraged and disillusioned. The second-year's enrollment fell from 322 in 1902–03 to 231 in 1903–04. While affirming their support for Trinity, leaders in the Synod of Texas expressed dissatisfaction that the school was not expanding as rapidly as anticipated. Local citizens who had purchased property near the college in hopes of turning a quick profit complained because the anticipated influx of new residents failed to materialize.[15]

President Kirkes became increasingly pessimistic about his ability to reverse the university's fortunes. In addition to fund-raising ventures, Kirkes taught classes when emergencies arose, and he and his spouse were resident supervisors of the women's building. Although a synod visitation committee reported that the university was "in good and competent hands," it parenthetically commented, "and brethren should withhold any unkind statements or advice until they are asked for it."[16] In May 1904, Kirkes submitted his resignation to the Board of Trustees. En route to the meeting, he remarked to one of his colleagues that if he had to choose between earning a living as president of Trinity University or by digging mesquite stumps, "it would be awfully hard on the mesquite stumps."[17]

Unlike previous presidential searches, in which viable candidates

Trinity University advertisement, the *Trinitonian*, April 1907

emerged only after extended inquiries, the quest for Kirkes's successor quickly centered on Archelaus E. Turner, who had impressive academic credentials from Cumberland institutions and would shortly be in Dallas to attend a meeting of the Cumberland General Assembly. Turner had a B.A. degree with honors from Lincoln College in Lincoln, Illinois, and a Ph.D. from Milliken University in Decatur, Illinois. After further experience in Illinois as the principal of Ashmore Seminary and superintendent of the Oakland public schools, Turner returned as president at age twenty-seven to his undergraduate alma mater, where he served with distinction for twelve years. In 1900 Turner accepted the presidency of Waynesburg College in Pennsylvania, another Cumberland institution. During his brief tenure, the college increased its enrollment, enlarged its endowment, and raised its academic standards. An active layman in the Cumberland denomination, Turner served on numerous General Assembly committees, appearing frequently as a spokesman for various causes, including reunion with the Presbyterian Church in the United States of America and ecumenical relationships with Presbyterian denominations overseas.[18]

Trinity trustees interviewed Turner in Dallas and were impressed with his communication skills and intellectual acumen. They immediately offered him the Trinity presidency, but he rejected a salary of $1,600 as unacceptable.[19] Later in the week, however, a group of Waxahachie citizens offered to supplement his annual salary by $900 if he would agree to a five-year contract. Turner accepted and notified Waynesburg College officials of his decision.[20]

Turner's presidency was unprecedented in several respects. For the first time, Trinity University's chief administrative officer was not an ordained Cumberland Presbyterian minister. Although raised in a Cumberland manse and a devout churchman, Turner's academic perspectives were not shaped by a seminary education. Moreover, because of his previous executive experience and participation in educational associations, Turner brought national visibility to his position.[21] Expectations among Trinity constituents regarding his presidency were high even before he took office. Trustees thought they had a man "who would lead the college out of the wilderness into green pastures." One senior faculty member said, "A strong, scholarly, cultured, polished, magnetic personality, he is an inspiration to all who are associated with him."[22]

Before taking up residence in Waxahachie, Turner and his spouse spent the summer touring historical sites in Greece and Italy. Turner collected stereopticon slides to use in popular lectures that he believed would enhance his scholarly reputation and interest potential donors. His inauguration, conducted in conjunction with the dedication ceremonies of the new Sims Library, attracted a large audience and received adulatory coverage in local, regional, and denominational publications. The daylong event featured six major addresses in which each speaker extolled Turner's leadership abilities. President S. P. Brooks of Baylor University said, "Who hereafter studies the history of Trinity University will take into account this day, the day of President Turner. . . . The greatest single catch Waxahachie has ever made is Trinity University. The greatest catch Trinity has ever made is President Turner."[23]

Once the initial euphoria subsided, Turner encountered the same obstacles that hindered his predecessors. Verbal affirmation for Trinity abounded throughout the state, but financial support remained elusive. Turner's oratorical eloquence and academic proficiency impressed audiences, but his ability to attract wealthy benefactors proved negligible. In 1905, the only gifts he reported were an electric clock valued at $200, a table, twelve office chairs, a settee, a cork carpet for the auditorium platform, and a bequest estimated to be worth approximately $2,000.[24] By the time he resigned in 1907, the endowment had only increased from $38,681 to $41,107.[25]

Although Turner received a guaranteed salary, other faculty members labored on a pro rata basis as they had in Tehuacana. In 1905 the university dean received $1,000, and other faculty salaries ranged from $600 to

$900. Despite such low figures, the trustees reserved 18 percent of tuition revenues as a contingency fund for operating expenses. They were especially unhappy about soaring electricity bills, caused "by turning lights on earlier than necessary, leaving them on longer than useful, and using more lights at times than needed."[26] At the end of the next fiscal year, faculty members learned that while the contingency fund had covered operating expenses, it also had decreased by 18 percent the money available for faculty salaries.[27]

In addition to increasing the endowment, Turner intended to raise $20,000 toward building a dormitory for male students. At the end of the 1905–06 academic year, however, after visiting presbyteries and congregations throughout the synod, he had secured only $4,000, and Trinity trustees once again tapped the endowment, contributing $11,500 so that construction could begin. On September 19, 1906, Turner presided over the dedication of Beeson Hall, a three-story brick-veneer structure named in honor of Trinity's first president. Described as "one of the best-equipped dormitories in Texas," the building featured steam heat, gas lighting, and "all the appliances for the comfort and conveniences of the students." Each room was furnished with a carpet, two iron beds, and an oak dresser. It included a dining hall, a kitchen, and a study hall where residents could prepare their lessons under the supervision of a faculty member.[28]

Turner did not necessarily use poor strategy, nor did he lack effort in his fund-raising plans, but he was adversely affected by denominational rivalries and schisms in Texas. Since the last decade of the nineteenth century, members of the Cumberland Presbyterian Church and the Presbyterian Church in the U.S.A. (PCUSA) had discussed reunion. Although the two denominations shared a common theological tradition, they had substantial doctrinal and cultural differences. Doctrinally, Cumberland Presbyterians believed that the PCUSA denomination espoused teachings on predestination and election that precluded human choice. Even though the PCUSA revised its Confession of Faith in 1903 in an effort to eliminate such an interpretation, many Cumberland members remained unconvinced.[29] Segregation was also a contentious issue. The PCUSA denomination officially endorsed integration, while members of the Cumberland Presbyterian Church, most of whom resided in the south, advocated separation of the races. As a result, when the Cumberland Presbyterian and PCUSA General Assemblies achieved the reunion in May 1906, many Cumberland Presbyterians walked out in defiance and formed a continuing Cumberland denomination.[30]

Beeson Hall for male students

In the long run, Trinity's new relationship with the PCUSA brought the university considerable financial and educational benefits. The PCUSA had a million adherents in churches spanning the continent. It also had a Board of College Aid, with offices in Chicago and New York, that supplied colleges with grants and loans, assisted with fund-raising projects, recruited teachers, arbitrated territorial disputes, and set academic standards for all aid-receiving institutions. Between 1906 and 1922, Trinity received almost half a million dollars in funds channeled through the Board of College Aid and the General Board of Education.[31] In addition, the Presbyterian College Union, an annual meeting of Presbyterian college presidents, provided a national forum for discussion of issues in higher education, such as curriculum, tenure, investment policies, fund-raising, and student activities.[32]

In the short term, however, reunion resulted in serious problems for Presbyterian higher education in Texas. For more than two years, dissident Cumberland Presbyterians appealed to civil authorities, citing voting irregularities and violations of the Cumberland *Book of Government*, and called into question property rights of churches and educational institutions throughout the denomination. Whether Trinity belonged to the continuing Cumberland Presbyterian Church or to the PCUSA cast uncertainty on the university's future. Many Texas Presbyterians refrained from committing financial resources to an institution mired in litigation and wavering between denominational affiliations.[33]

In the meantime, self-styled "true-blue" Cumberland Presbyterians made Turner and other prominent reunionists targets of ridicule and disdain. The *Texas Cumberland Presbyterian* relentlessly denigrated Cumberland Presbyterians who entered the reunited church, referring to them as "traitors," "heretics," and "turncoats." They also influenced their young people to withdraw from Trinity and enroll in other Texas schools. In response to Turner's plea for funds to raise faculty salaries, the *Texas Cumberland Presbyterian* queried: "Why does Dr. Turner not call on his rich Northern Church for funds instead of calling on Cumberland Presbyterians who have been robbed of their property which the Doctor now has in charge? The learned Doctor who hails from Pennsylvania is wasting postage in sending out appeals to Cumberland Presbyterians for funds to help pay fat salaries to men who are trying to destroy the church."[34]

Efforts by Presbyterian clergyman W. G. Claggett to establish a university in Dallas posed another serious threat to Turner and Trinity University. Claggett advocated the creation of Texas Presbyterian University, a cooperative venture to be sponsored by the PCUSA (northern) and the Presbyterian Church in the United States (PCUS) (southern). Having secured a charter, located property, and raised a modest endowment, Claggett marshaled support for the project even though Trinity University, now under the aegis of the PCUSA, was situated only thirty miles away in Waxahachie.[35]

During Turner's presidency, Claggett corresponded regularly with executives of the PCUSA Board of College Aid in an effort to secure their approval of his proposed university. Claggett argued that the Texas Presbyterian University would not compete with Trinity University. Trinity would remain a small, liberal arts, undergraduate institution while Texas Presbyterian University would emphasize graduate studies and offer specialized programs.[36] Board of College Aid executives contended that competition would exacerbate Trinity's financial problems and fragment institutional loyalties. Following a series of heated exchanges, Secretary J. S. Dickson of the Board of College Aid informed Claggett, "We have now belonging to the Presbyterian Church an institution at Waxahachie, and *nothing* must be done in any way to interfere with the growth of that institution."[37]

Not dissuaded, Claggett traveled throughout Texas and surrounding states to promote his cause at presbytery meetings, conferences, and civic gatherings. After Dallas businessmen lost interest in the project, he tried unsuccessfully to locate the university in several other Texas towns. Eventually Claggett relinquished his quest, but not without cost to Trinity's efforts to secure the financial support of Texas Presbyterians.[38]

Unable to increase enrollment or to generate endowment funds, Turner's popularity waned. Waxahachie citizens who had pledged to supplement the president's salary in anticipation of dramatic growth threatened to withdraw their support. Turner knew that if Trinity could not demonstrate evidence of financial backing within its own state, eastern benefactors would not invest in the university. Moreover, in his estimation, the financial burden of providing free tuition for pre-ministerial students and children of ordained clergy precluded a balanced budget. In April 1907, with two years of a five-year contract remaining, Turner tendered his resignation to the Board of Trustees.[39]

Turner's sudden departure left Trinity trustees in a quandary. If someone of his stature and experience had failed, it would likely be difficult to attract another prominently known candidate. Deciding against a national search, Trinity trustees made a "cautious, considerate and discriminating" survey of local talent to find a candidate who could rekindle confidence in a troubled institution. They selected Samuel Lee Hornbeak, an alumnus whose extensive association with the university had prepared him to take the reins of leadership. In contrast to Turner's sophistication, culture, and national visibility, Hornbeak's mannerisms, speech, and dress reflected his Texas roots. He routinely sprinkled his addresses with colloquial expressions and colorful stories and had a self-deprecating humor that conveyed values derived from rural life and evangelical piety. His appointment resonated favorably with all segments of the university community.[40]

Samuel Lee Hornbeak was born on January 13, 1865, in Bosqueville, Texas. His parents, of Dutch and French Huguenot extraction, moved to Tehuacana, where their children could have an opportunity for a college education. Samuel's relationship with Trinity began in 1873, when he was eight years old. Entering Trinity's primary department, Hornbeak continued his education through the collegiate level. After securing a B.A. degree in 1885 and an M.A. the following year, Hornbeak went to Northern Indiana Normal School in Valparaiso, where he became familiar with modern curricular trends and explored new teaching methods in chemistry and physics.[41]

Returning to Texas, Hornbeak taught at Wooten Wells in Robertson County and later served as superintendent of public schools in Franklin. In 1891 he accepted an appointment at Trinity as professor of science, a position he held for sixteen years. Working closely with his mentor and close friend, L. A. Johnson, Hornbeak helped to modernize Trinity's curriculum. Following Johnson's death in 1900, he served as chairman of the faculty and dean during the last years on the Tehuacana campus.[42]

When Trinity moved to Waxahachie, Hornbeak played an important role as dean of the university in reconfiguring Trinity to serve its new constituency. In 1907 he resigned to become superintendent of the Texas State School for the Blind in Austin, an appointment made by Governor Thomas Campbell, a Trinity alumnus and close friend. During his year in Austin, Hornbeak was a member of Trinity's Board of Trustees, thus keeping intact his record of continuous service to the university.[43]

Before accepting the presidency, Hornbeak insisted that trustees end the practice of prorating faculty salaries and agree to guarantee payment on the first day of each month. Even though salaries were meager, Hornbeak knew that faculty morale would suffer in the face of uncertainty over remuneration. Assurance of a guaranteed salary would reduce the threat of losing capable teachers to higher-paying state institutions and make it easier to recruit new faculty members.[44]

As a progressive educator, Hornbeak believed in adjusting the curriculum to reflect educational trends and to meet the growing needs of Trinity students. Hornbeak selected Trinity alumnus James M. Gordon, a professor in the Department of Classical Languages, to serve as Dean of the University during his presidency. Gordon had recently returned from a year's leave of absence at the University of Chicago, where he received a master's degree. During his thirteen-year tenure as dean, Gordon strengthened the faculty, broadened the curriculum, and solidified Trinity's standing with a number of accrediting agencies, including the National Council on Education, the Presbyterian General Board of Education, and the Association of Texas Colleges.[45]

Under the combined leadership of Hornbeak and Gordon, Trinity made advances in its curricular development and in admission policies. The university codified basic entrance requirements for all degree-seeking students on the basis of high school units, with a unit being equal to one year of successful work at a recognized high school. Trinity required three units of English, three units of mathematics (two algebra and one geometry), two units of history (one general and one Greek and Roman), and two units of science (one-half unit physiology, one-half physiography, and either one physics or one chemistry). Although students were accepted with deficiencies, after 1910 they had to fulfill all entrance requirements before being permitted to take junior-level courses.[46]

As a solely undergraduate institution, Trinity offered bachelor of arts, bachelor of science, and bachelor of letters degrees. Although the curriculum for first- and second-year students continued to be prescribed, juniors could choose electives by class vote, and, for seniors, all classes except philosophy and Bible were elective, with a limit of six hours in any one department.[47] The faculty required degree candidates to submit a thesis based on work done during their junior and senior years. Monitored by the department head and approved by the general faculty, the thesis had to display "indications of individual and broad thinking and the ability to express these thoughts in elegant literary style." Thesis subjects included "The Development of Nominalism in the Middle Ages and Its Influence on Philosophy," "The Influence of Horace in the Establishment of the Regime of Augustus," "Browning's Philosophy of Life," and "The Application of Differential Calculus in the Solution of Maxima and Minima Problems."[48]

Trinity's increasing number of electives reflected a trend in American higher education that had profound implications for curricular development. The previously prescribed course of study promoted generalization among teachers and students in a variety of subjects rather than specialization in specific fields. Electives permitted both professors and students to pursue specific interests, encouraging the accumulation of concentrated knowledge into the world of learning. By 1905 Trinity listed ten departments: mathematics and astronomy, English, Greek, Latin, chemistry and physics, biology and geology, history, modern languages, Bible study, and philosophy.[49]

Responding to community needs and economic pressures, Trinity offered a four-year high school curriculum to prepare students for college work, to train potential public school teachers, and to "give those who have not a college education in view, a general education."[50] As Waxahachie public schools improved, Trinity dropped the first two years of its high school program in 1915, noting that this gave the institution "a more distinctively college atmosphere."[51] Five years later, the third year was discontinued, and in 1923, Trinity eliminated all preparatory work, accepting only students who had completed an accredited high school program.[52]

Several new departments emerged during the first two decades of the twentieth century. In 1908 the separate departments of philosophy and Bible study were combined to form the single Department of English Bible and Philosophy. A bequest of $20,000 from the estate of Martha L. Dunn, a Waxahachie resident, provided the department with an endowed chair. New courses included a survey of Biblical prophecies and a contextual study of the life of Christ. As a rationale for the merging of the departments, the *Trinity University Catalogue* stated that the two fields had certain common elements: "The Bible contains the true philosophy of life and all existence. Philosophy seeks the fundamental principles of life and the world. They are both concerned with the ultimate realities and final meaning of things."[53]

In the same year, Trinity created a Department of Education with courses in school management and organization, teaching methods, educational psychology, and child development. The department anticipated a law passed by the Texas legislature in 1909 that recognized such work completed in "Colleges of the First Class." Trinity graduates who had taken four courses in education and pedagogy were eligible to apply for a permanent teaching certificate in Texas public schools.[54] In conjunction with a new summer school, first offered in 1910, Trinity initiated a program that gave prospective teachers an opportunity to be certified without taking a four-year college course. Utilizing members of the Trinity faculty and experienced public school teachers, the program emphasized teaching methods, permanent certificate subjects, and courses in the sciences. Enrollees for the eight-week session paid $8.50 for tuition and $1.00 for an examination fee.[55]

Other new offerings reflected a growing interest in the social sciences. Classes in economics explored the development of modern business and laws of economic forces and featured a course on "Foundations of National Prosperity" that dealt with conservation of natural and human resources. Psychology courses, taught in the education and philosophy departments, covered such topics as the structure and function of the brain, stages of a child's life, and development of personality.[56] In sociology, a survey of general principles of social evolution and progress and of current social problems brought students in contact with contemporary societal issues.[57] Trinity also offered classes in home economics "to assist in developing full capable young woman-hood." Instruction in cookery, household administration, dietetics, first aid, home nursing, and sewing were designed "to make more efficient home makers."[58]

During the first decade on the Waxahachie campus, the university provided a gymnastic room in the basement of the administration building where students could exercise on an informal basis. Physical education became an official component of the Trinity curriculum in 1911 when the Board of Trustees approved a recommendation that all students below the junior class be required to take some kind of physical exercise. The proposal included hiring a full-time director of physical education and mandated annual physical examinations of all incoming students.[59] To foster better relationships with the Synod of Texas, Trinity created several continuing education courses for clergy and laypersons, such as "Religious Education in the Local Church," "Social Principles of Education," and "Old and New Testament History." The university also sponsored a Preachers' Summer Institute and Conference, featuring lectures by qual-

Student Army Training Corps, 1917

ified instructors on subjects such as "Presbyterian History and Traditions," "Prayer Habits of Jesus," "Religious Education," and "The English Bible."[60]

In compliance with U.S. War Department regulations, Trinity initiated a Department of Military Science during World War I. Any accredited college with an enrollment of one hundred physically fit men received government assistance, which included issue of uniforms, rifles, and ammunition, provision of instructors, and reimbursement for related expenses incurred by the school. Although Trinity could not immediately supply one hundred men, Hornbeak decided in 1917 to start and develop such a department until it could qualify as a Senior Reserve Officers' Training School. About forty men initially volunteered to purchase their own uniforms and textbooks and devote six hours a week to intensive drill and study.[61]

Although the trainees maintained order when under the direct supervision of military personnel, their behavior elsewhere on campus created problems for faculty and staff. Free from military restraints, they disrupted classes, badgered students, and annoyed townspeople. When the corps disbanded in December 1918 and military discipline ended, the trainees "went wild," according to Hornbeak. Describing the situation to members of the Board of Christian Education, Hornbeak said, "We have had more vexational problems than ever before in one term. If you hear of any body that has a S.A.T.C. [Student Army Training Corps] to let, do not send them to me. I have had a sufficient amount of it."[62]

Indirectly, the troublesome trainees prompted Trinity officials to hire the university's first full-time librarian. At that time, the library consisted of one large room in the east wing of the administration building staffed by senior students who served as monitors. The 3,000-volume collection had no catalog and no systematic arrangement of books. Hired initially on a temporary basis to keep order, Theresa R. Simms subsequently became a trained librarian and served Trinity for thirty-five years in that capacity.[63]

Despite its low salary scale and southwestern setting, Trinity managed to attract instructors with excellent credentials to its expanding faculty. Most held advanced degrees from highly respected universities and colleges, including the University of Chicago, Ohio State University, Princeton University, the University of Michigan, Columbia University, Oberlin College, the College of Wooster, and Bryn Mawr College. In 1914, for example, Hornbeak announced the appointment of Howard W. Wolfe, a graduate of Hanover College and the University of Wisconsin, to the Department of Modern Languages; Florence Beckwith, an Oberlin graduate, as head of the Department of Piano; and John W. Barton, with a graduate degree from Columbia University, to the Department of History. Many appointees devoted most or all of their academic careers to the Waxahachie institution.[64]

Trinity's ability to recruit outstanding classroom teachers depended to a great extent on contacts with the Board of College Aid, which served as a placement office for Presbyterian colleges throughout the United States. With offices in Chicago and New York, the board's executives had access to applicants who were graduates of eastern and midwestern institutions. Hornbeak once asked a board official to meet with a candidate from Brooklyn, New York, "size him up as to his personality and character," and assess what impression he would make on Trinity students.[65] When hiring a professor for the Department of Philosophy and Bible, Hornbeak specified, "I want a man who is reasonably conservative in so far as what he teaches is concerned. I want him to believe all he teaches, but he need not teach all he believes if any of it would be inclined to stir up questions."[66]

As a condition for receiving assistance, the Board of College Aid required that Presbyterian institutions meet certain educational and financial standards, such as quantity of library holdings, number of full-time faculty with graduate degrees, and an adequate endowment. In addition, institutions were required to affirm on their application forms that they employed only faculty members who would "exert a positive Christian influence" on the campus. Although college officials enjoyed considerable latitude in interpreting the latter standard, they sometimes had to justify questionable appointments. Hornbeak explained his retention of a teacher in the Department of Music, "a young lady of excellent teaching ability," who was a Christian Scientist, an organization deemed a "cult" at that time by most Protestant denominations. Hornbeak assured the Board of

College Aid executives that she would not "give expression to the views of her organization" to students and expressed confidence that "her influence will stand for Christianity."[67]

Although Trinity sought faculty whose primary interest was classroom teaching, the university also encouraged professional development. During the summer months, faculty not engaged in teaching summer school pursued graduate work, took enrichment courses, or attended workshops and professional meetings. In 1905, for example, mathematics professor Luther Wear spent the summer with the Harvard Engineer Corps in New Hampshire, music director William Campbell and pianist Nona Yantis studied with tutors in New York City, and biology instructor Edwin Powers studied botany at the University of Chicago. Although Trinity maintained no formal system of academic leaves, the trustees periodically approved unpaid leaves of absence to enable professors to complete graduate degrees.[68]

Trinity faculty had teaching loads, student advising, and committee assignments that required them to be on campus six days a week. The academy staff at the high school level taught between twenty and twenty-five hours per week, and college professors' teaching loads ranged from fifteen to twenty hours, depending on departmental needs and other assignments. In regard to academic freedom, Hornbeak reported that Trinity faculty, with few exceptions, had no restrictions on course content. Biology and geology professors were expected to teach those subjects "in accordance with the Christian faith," however, and sociology instructors were not permitted to teach "socialism, bolshevism, or anarchism except for condemnation." Bible professors were cautioned to "be sane in interpretation, not destructive or ultra-conservative." Trinity had no system for granting tenure, and all full-time faculty received one-year contracts. When asked if cause must be given for dismissal, Hornbeak responded, "not compulsory but is a matter of courtesy." Trinity's policy, he said, "was to retain all teachers who do satisfactory work."[69]

After 1910, in addition to Hornbeak, only one faculty member from the Tehuacana era remained on the Waxahachie campus. David S. Bodenhamer, a Civil War veteran, had joined the Trinity faculty in 1883 as an assistant instructor and two years later became the Johnson Professor of Mathematics, a position he held until the move to Waxahachie. On the new campus, he served as professor of Greek, Bible, and astronomy and later as the Aston Lecturer on Theology and Homiletics. Described by one graduate as "the most saintly spirit that I have ever met," he was beloved for his gentle demeanor and his personal concern for students.[70] When he retired in 1914 after thirty-one years on the faculty, Trinity trustees designated him professor emeritus, the first such honor bestowed on any Trinity faculty member, and awarded him an annual pension of $200, "with sincere regrets that finances of the school would not enable us to do more."[71]

Although Hornbeak preferred to give priority to academic and curricular issues, he spent most of his time on financial matters such as meeting the payroll and increasing the endowment. Realizing that administrative responsibilities precluded giving adequate attention to his classroom duties, Hornbeak relinquished his teaching position in 1911 to Professor Jesse B. Ford.[72]

Through careful management of revenues from increased enrollment, Hornbeak reduced a debt of $4,000 to less than $1,000 and gradually increased faculty salaries. The university's income from tuition and fees covered about 63 percent of the annual expenses, endowment income paid 12 percent, and the remaining 25 percent had to come from other sources. Because the school was so heavily dependent on tuition revenue, however, a decrease in enrollment, unexpected expenditures, or a poor economic environment could jeopardize the institution's ability to maintain its programs.[73]

However, increased enrollment, with the added tuition revenues, had its downside. The unexpectedly large number of female students could not be accommodated in Prendergast Hall. Early in 1911, with assistance from Waxahachie citizens, Trinity trustees planned a new women's dormitory. Waxahachie agreed to raise $25,000 for the project if the university matched with at least $50,000. Within six weeks, Waxahachie reached its goal, but as the semester drew to a close, Trinity was $8,000 short of its share. At a meeting of the PCUSA General Assembly in May, Hornbeak secured a promise from the secretary of the Board of College Aid, Robert McKenzie, that if Trinity raised $4,000 before commencement day, June 7, the board would match that sum.[74]

Largely through Hornbeak's last-minute efforts, Trinity met the challenge. Adding a touch of drama to the occasion, Hornbeak arranged to have Western Union deliver a telegram during the commencement ceremonies announcing the board's contribution and the successful conclusion of the financial campaign. Hornbeak told the audience how difficult it had been to raise money for the dormitory. At the end of the first day of solicitation, he reported to trustee chairman Frank Drane that he had raised $230 in cash and pledges. Drane, not impressed, promised to eat a bale of hay when the total amount was in hand. Hornbeak created "considerable merriment" by producing a small bundle of hay tied in university colors that he presented to Drane.[75]

Workers completed a scaled-down version of the new dormitory in less than one calendar year. Trinity officials originally envisioned a modern, fire-resistant building with a capacity of 150, but construction costs were much higher than anticipated. Consequently, they built the main section and a north wing, leaving a south wing to be added at a later date. Named in honor of Drane, a major contributor, the two-story dormitory provided forty-eight rooms for female students. Each room featured hot and cold water, electric lighting, and steam heat. Basement facilities included a kitchen, a refectory, and a large room for club and recreational activities. The *Waxahachie Evening Herald* termed the building "a great asset for the university and a monument to the energy and the enterprising spirit of the men who have made this splendid institution of learning a possibility."[76]

In 1912 B. F. Yoakum, president of the Frisco Railroad System, agreed to purchase ten acres north of the campus for use as an athletic field. Named in memory of the donor's father, F. L. Yoakum, who was a former president of Larissa College, Yoakum Athletic Field became a hub of activity during the school year. In 1913 Waxahachie citizens contributed sufficient funds to grade the grounds, prepare a running track, and erect a board fence.[77]

Despite these improvements, Hornbeak knew that Trinity faced continuing financial problems. Drane Hall remained uncompleted, Beeson Hall needed extensive renovation or replacement, and the school lacked a gymnasium, science hall, and library. Moreover, the construction costs of Beeson and Drane Halls had so eroded endowment funds that the trustees had to borrow money from the Board of College Aid and several local banks to pay outstanding bills. Unless financial resources could be dramatically increased, Trinity's future looked bleak.[78]

With the approval of the Board of Trustees and the Synod of Texas, Hornbeak launched a campaign in October 1912 to secure $325,000 for permanent endowment funds. Of that sum, $150,000 was to be raised in the Synod of Texas and $175,000 from out-of-state sources. As campaign manager, Hornbeak assumed responsibility for all the publicity. For more than a year, he published a biweekly university bulletin sent to a mailing list of approximately 5,000 people. He also kept the state newspapers informed of the progress of the campaign and organized a team of speakers to visit each presbytery in the Synod of Texas. By January 1, 1915, when the campaign was scheduled to close, Hornbeak hoped that Trinity would celebrate its first successful endowment solicitation.[79]

Although the campaign began with much fanfare and high expectations, it soon encountered unexpected obstacles. World War I erupted in Europe, and a period of economic depression impacted the entire country. In Texas, prices for cotton and other agricultural goods fell sharply. As he traveled throughout the state and visited potential donors in the eastern United States, Hornbeak expressed confidence that the campaign's goals would be met or exceeded. Privately, however, he acknowledged that out-of-state donations were virtually nonexistent. In a letter written to a denominational official during a visit to New York City, Hornbeak confided, "I have not received any money on this trip, but I am not disappointed, for I did not expect to receive any."[80]

Most discouraging, however, was Hornbeak's inability to attract major benefactors within the Synod of Texas. Pledges averaged only about $100 and were due in equal payments over a five-year period. At one point, he had two Texas businessmen lined up to give $25,000 to endow a faculty chair, but they withdrew their promises when cotton prices plummeted. "We are going to fight until the last minute to succeed," he told Robert McKenzie of the Board of College Aid, "but if there is anything lying loose around in the East that the College Board could turn our way if we are in distress, I hope you will keep us in mind."[81]

As the deadline of 1 January 1915 approached, it appeared that Trinity would fall short of its $150,000 target in Texas. During the last two weeks of December, however, Hornbeak and committee members managed to reach the goal. At a victory celebration in the university auditorium, speakers addressed the student body on topics such as "How May the Alumni Help Trinity," "What Trinity Has Done for Waxahachie," and "How Students May Help Trinity University." Students concluded the program with fifteen "rahs" for Waxahachie and by singing "Trinity Will Shine Tonight." University and civic dignitaries then moved to the Hotel Rogers in downtown Waxahachie for a banquet honoring Hornbeak.[82]

While public releases heralded the successful completion of the in-state portion of Trinity University's financial drive, Hornbeak privately acknowledged that "qualified success" was a more appropriate term. Most of the cash received had gone to pay off debts to local banks and to repay loans from the Board of College Aid.[83] Despite some substantial individual gifts, the university continued to accumulate operational deficits, and board members complained that because they were legally responsible for the university debt, it burdened their own business dealings and interfered with their credit.[84] Faculty members continued to receive flat salaries, and Hornbeak worried that they would seek employment elsewhere.[85]

Million-dollar campaign advertisement, 1919

It soon became evident that not all pledges to the endowment campaign would be fulfilled. At the end of 1915, only $23,175 had been received, and two years later only two presbyteries had paid as much as one-half of the amount promised. Of the total amount pledged, Trinity had received slightly less than $67,000.[86] At the end of 1919, 30 percent ($46,000) remained unpaid, and requests for payments went unanswered.[87] As late as 1928, university officials were still trying to collect "a considerable number of outstanding pledges," but they subsequently agreed that further attempts would be unproductive.[88]

Trinity could not begin another capital campaign because the Synod of Texas had decided to channel its financial resources into an effort to save Texas Fairemont Seminary (formerly known as Texas Female Seminary) in Weatherford. In January 1919, however, the seminary closed its doors and used its assets to pay existing debts. From the remaining balance, Trinity received $1,500, and the seminary's graduates were received as alumnae of Trinity University.[89]

Hornbeak thought that Trinity's best hope for endowment funds rested with wealthy friends of the university and national philanthropic organizations such as the Carnegie and Rockefeller foundations. He utilized the semicentennial anniversary of Trinity University in 1919 for the beginning of a drive to raise the endowment to the million-dollar level. With hundreds of graduates and former students in attendance, the two-day cele-

Student caricature of Hornbeak,
the *Mirage*, 1942

bration included a memorial service for students who had died in the recent war, meetings of the Alumni and Former Students' Association, and
a pageant depicting "Fifty Years of College Life."[90]

Before the anniversary celebrations drew to a close, the board of trustees had plans in place to launch the new campaign. They enlisted the clergy in attendance to organize a committee that would ask all pastors in the
Synod of Texas to support the endowment-fund drive. The trustees also
budgeted funds to publish a semimonthly newsletter for a mailing list of
6,000 names.

The trustees appointed Hornbeak to head up the campaign. He hoped
to accomplish his goal within a year and "retire to the quietude of a professor's chair, if the Board will let me."[91] Hornbeak was convinced that he
could capitalize on the oil boom that was creating overnight millionaires
in Texas. Several members of the Chapman family, especially James A. and
Oscar H. Chapman, who had long associations with Trinity, were high on
his list of potential donors. Hornbeak had been quietly cultivating them
for several years, and he felt that the time was right to seek a major gift.
Following his presentation of Trinity's needs, they promised to participate

in the campaign, but were reluctant to specify an amount because of fluctuating market prices for oil.[92] Other Presbyterian oilmen were less responsive to Hornbeak's appeals. Frustrated with their recalcitrance, he confided to a friend, "We have a few Presbyterians in Texas who have made large money from oil, but they have not yet learned to give money readily."[93]

Beyond Texas, Hornbeak applied for major grants from the Presbyterian General Board of Education, successor to the Board of College Aid, and the Rockefeller Fund. After World War I, the PCUSA launched the New Era Movement to raise funds for a variety of causes, including two million dollars for higher education.[94] If their campaign succeeded, the General Board of Education promised to give Trinity $200,000 provided that Trinity acquire $800,000 in cash, property, and pledges from other sources. John D. Rockefeller established the Rockefeller Fund with a gift of fifty million dollars to supplement the salaries of college professors throughout the United States. With Trinity's high academic standing in Texas, Hornbeak was optimistic that the Rockefeller Fund would look favorably on his request, and a visit to Waxahachie by a representative of the fund heightened his hopes that Trinity would receive $200,000 to underwrite faculty salaries. Unfortunately, the New Era Movement never attained its goal, and the Rockefeller Fund did not include Trinity among its grant recipients.[95]

Discouraged that the anticipated "big money" never materialized and exhausted by travel and administrative responsibilities, Hornbeak decided to turn the presidency over to a younger person. "I feel like the frazzled end of a calf rope," he told an acquaintance. "I presume you have been on a farm and know what that looks like."[96] He missed classroom teaching and wanted to do graduate work in the field of sociology, his new academic interest. Moreover, he was aware that some leading figures in the synod were advocating new leadership for Trinity, preferably an experienced clergyman with expertise in soliciting wealthy donors.[97] After initially rejecting Hornbeak's resignation, the board of trustees acceded to his request, effective at the close of the school year in June 1920. Hornbeak agreed, however, to continue as campaign director until the new president assumed that responsibility.[98]

In commencement week ceremonies, Trinity honored Hornbeak for his service to the university. Designating him Trinity's first president emeritus and awarding him an honorary doctor of laws degree, the board of trustees acknowledged Hornbeak's outstanding contributions to the university. During his presidency, Hornbeak broadened the curriculum, expanded campus facilities, and enhanced accreditation. Despite unfavorable economic conditions, he had substantially increased the university's endowment and managed to meet operating expenses.[99]

The following year, during the Golden Jubilee commemorating Hornbeak's association with the university, Trinity students bestowed on him the title of "The Grand Old Man of Trinity," a gesture that he cherished more than any honor he had received.[100] Hornbeak continued to serve Trinity for two decades as a classroom teacher and student advisor and, when the occasion arose, as interim president. He is best remembered, however, as the person whose administrative skills, academic expertise, and fund-raising abilities enabled Trinity to survive the transition from Tehuacana to Waxahachie.[101]

CHAPTER FIVE

BALLYHOO AND BONDING

Every year there is the usual blah about "spirit" until some have come to feel that it exists only by ballyhoo. But as every real Trinity student knows, there does exist here at Trinity an unexplainable thing, an intangible something which binds every Trinitonian to his fellow students.

TRINITONIAN EDITORIAL, SEPTEMBER 1932

Dᴜʀɪɴɢ ᴛʜᴇ ꜰɪʀsᴛ ꜰᴏᴜʀ ᴅᴇᴄᴀᴅᴇs of the twentieth century, student life at Waxahachie reflected patterns of social change common among colleges and universities throughout the United States. Early in the century, as Victorian moral codes diminished, university officials gradually relaxed institutional prohibitions against "mixing of the sexes" and permitted more opportunities for male and female interaction. Students also assumed more responsibility for shaping their academic careers and, through the creation of student councils, began to have a voice in campus governance. The formation of honor codes, student courts, and national honorary societies indicated growing student maturity. By the beginning of World War I, most college campuses had dropped dress codes, mandatory church attendance, and card-playing prohibitions and had entered enthusiastically into the world of intercollegiate athletics.[1]

During the "Roaring Twenties," an era characterized by automobiles, motion pictures, illegal alcohol, and liberalized sexual mores, university officials had to accommodate to changing times. The pace of campus life across the United States accelerated as a generation of fun-loving, free-spirited students began their undergraduate careers. Colleges elected beauty queens and designated men and women as most popular, most likely to succeed, most intelligent, and most athletic and devised elaborate ceremonies to reward them for their accomplishments.[2]

The prewar and depressed economy of the 1930s muted the optimism of the previous decade but did not diminish the students' quest for fun and freedom. Limited by financial resources and thoughtful about life after

Trinity students in automobile, 1914

graduation, they seemed more serious about academic achievement than many of their predecessors. While dances, parties, and sporting events remained popular with a wide range of students, interest in activities such as hazing and interclass rivalries lessened. The demise of the old literary societies and the rise of new professional, academic, and social clubs and societies signaled the end of an era of university life that had roots in the previous century.[3]

Throughout the Waxahachie era, intercollegiate athletics played a primary role in fostering school spirit. Although baseball, basketball, track, and tennis attracted student interest, football was the premier sport, as it was on many college campuses. While only a recreational sport in Tehuacana, football assumed increasing significance in Waxahachie, a town filled with sports-minded enthusiasts who wanted winning teams.[4]

Wary of unregulated collegiate athletic programs, Trinity joined the Southern Intercollegiate Athletic Association in 1902 and fielded teams in football, basketball, and track.[5] At the same time, university trustees established an Athletic Board, composed of three faculty members appointed by the president and managers of the various athletic teams selected by the students, that established eligibility criteria for participation in intercollegiate sports. Student-athletes had to carry a full academic load of fifteen hours and receive passing grades in all their classes. Those who were under discipline for missing classes or who had received financial remuneration from any previous collegiate or professional team were barred

Trinity University football team, 1903

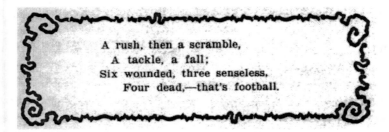

A rush, then a scramble,
A tackle, a fall;
Six wounded, three senseless,
Four dead,—that's football.

The *Trinitonian*, October 1902

from competition. Students under twenty-one had to secure written permission from a parent or guardian in order to play football.[6]

During the early years in Waxahachie, Trinity football teams faced opposing teams from Baylor University, Texas Agricultural and Mechanical College (Texas A&M), the University of Texas, and Texas Christian University. In 1902 Trinity battled to a scoreless tie with Texas A&M in a game that featured a dramatic goal line stand in the closing minutes of the contest. According to the *Trinitonian*, team captain Fred Fuller rallied his teammates by shouting, "For Trinity's sake men, hold hard, it's now or never!" After the final whistle, Trinity supporters rushed on the field "whooping and shouting and cheering the eleven happy but battered men who were worn to a frazzle with the fierceness of the contest." In contrast, the A&M fans "filed down in silence and wended their way sadly off the field."[7] Aggie coach Charlie Moran paid tribute to Trinity with these words: "We of Texas A&M schedule annual games with your Trinity football teams because, regardless of the heavy odds which may be against them, the little devils never give up and never quit fighting."[8]

Football at the beginning of the century was a dangerous game. Rules permitted tactics such as the flying wedge, hurdling, and flying tackles, and, often without helmets and padding, players were susceptible to crippling and life-threatening injuries.[9] In 1903 the Trinity faculty cancelled the last two games of the season due to the excessive number of players' injuries. Students complained that the faculty's unilateral action embarrassed the Trinity players, who were branded "cowards" and "cry-babies" for not honoring schedule commitments. In protest, Trinity students conducted a mock funeral for the football team, proceeding with a casket from the administration building to the football field chanting, "Ashes to ashes and dust to dust, if the Faculty won't have him, the Devil must."[10]

Play resumed in 1904, a season that marked the beginning of an extended home and away series with Austin College, a peer Presbyterian institution in Sherman, Texas. Scheduled on Thanksgiving Day as a season-ending game for both teams, the series evolved into an intense rivalry that continued throughout most of the century. Two hundred Trinity students traveled to Sherman for the first encounter, which resulted in a 23–0 victory for Trinity. "One pleasing feature of the game," reported the *Trinitonian*, "was the gentlemanly behavior and perfect good will exhibited between the two teams. Trinity and Austin College have always sustained toward each other the friendliest of relations, and will undoubtedly prove of mutual benefit to each other."[11]

The annual Trinity University and Austin College encounter generated new traditions in both schools, including parades, pep rallies, bonfires, signs such as "Kick the Kangaroos" and "Sink Austin College," and the tradition that a victory freed the first-year class from wearing "slime caps" for the remainder of the semester. A season's success or failure hinged on the outcome of the Austin College contest, regardless of the win-loss record. When the teams played in Sherman, special interurban streetcars conveyed a large contingent of Trinity students and Waxahachie townspeople to the game.[12]

Although football became increasingly popular on the Trinity campus and elsewhere, it had its detractors. During the 1905 season, eighteen Americans died playing the sport, and hundreds more suffered concussions and broken limbs. President Theodore Roosevelt warned college administrators that if they did not quickly remedy the situation, he would abolish football by executive order. In response to the presidential admonition, college officials eliminated many controversial practices and mandated supervised training and coaching as well as the use of protective padding.[13]

Despite reforms, many institutions suspended football indefinitely or cancelled the 1906 season. Along with Baylor University and Northwestern University, Trinity faculty unanimously opted for indefinite suspension "in view of the general dissatisfaction which has arisen in regard to football" and because revision of the rules "does not seem to us to eliminate all the evils of the game."[14] However, pressure from students and townspeople influenced the faculty to lift the ban in 1907, and, consequently, Trinity annually fielded teams except in a period of travel restrictions and lack of personnel during World War I. Trustees authorized the hiring of physical education instructors and coaches to ensure that Trinity student-athletes would receive proper training and instruction in all sports.[15]

During the suspension of football in 1906, Trinity students turned their attention to intramural and recreational outdoor sports, especially tennis and basketball. The faculty encouraged male and female students to participate because they were "extremely suited to develop the physical natures, but in a mild and unharmful way."[16] The *Trinitonian* reported that tennis and basketball were fast becoming the most popular extracurricular activities on campus.[17] Nevertheless, when intercollegiate football resumed, it quickly became the dominant sport on campus, a position it maintained throughout the Waxahachie years.

Football fever at Trinity reached its apex in the 1920s after a decision by the board of trustees to increase the athletic budget and hire "a first-class coach" for the major sports.[18] In the spring of 1925, Barry Holton, a protégé of Knute Rockne of Notre Dame, arrived on campus as the new football coach. At Notre Dame, Holton played center as an undergraduate and coached the famous "Four Horsemen" backfield during their freshman year. Inheriting a nucleus of talented players at Trinity, Holton introduced them to the innovative Notre Dame backfield shift designed to confuse traditional defenses. Effectively utilizing the new technique during the 1925 season, Trinity won nine games and lost only one, a grueling 20–10 defeat by a powerful Texas A&M team coached by Dana X. Bible. With wins over defending Southwestern Conference champion Baylor (10–3) and third-place finisher Rice (13–0), Trinity gained national recognition for its gridiron accomplishments.[19]

During the ensuing seasons, Trinity's football fortunes dwindled as opposing teams adjusted to the Trinity offense and scored decisive victories. Despite Holton's efforts to recruit top players and revamp his strategies, Trinity never repeated its outstanding 1925 season. The trustees, concerned about "the growing tendency on the part of athletics in the violation of the rules and regulations of the conference, the subsidizing of players, and the incurring of increased expenses," concurred with a decision by the faculty in 1930 not to retain Holton.[20]

Acknowledging that "athletics constitute a real problem in college life," Trinity trustees appointed a committee composed of faculty and ex-students to select an athletic director who would also coach the football team. Their unanimous choice, Leland J. Wilkins, was a former outstanding Trinity athlete who came highly recommended as an administrator and hands-on instructor.[21] Hired with a mandate to have an "absolutely clean" athletic program, Wilkins promised to field competitive teams that played by the rules. "Winning games is not the chief objective of our athletic activities," he told the student body, "but rather inculcation of basic moral principles."[22]

Despite these high ideals, football was a costly sport in terms of scholarships, staff salaries, and travel and equipment expenses. During the Depression, the football coach received more in remuneration than the dean of the university. On several occasions, trustees contemplated dropping football, but in each instance they were dissuaded by groups of former students and alumni who promised additional financial support. Before Trinity left the Waxahachie campus in 1942, the football program was running a deficit of more than $10,000 annually during a period when the institution could ill afford such an expense.[23]

Basketball remained primarily an intramural sport because Trinity had no gymnasium in which to host games. Trinity played all its intercollegiate matches on the road and conducted practices outdoors on a concrete pad that doubled as an exercise area for physical education classes. Because Trinity's teams had limited familiarity with hardwood floors, their opponents had an overwhelming home court advantage. When Trinity built Watkins Gymnasium in 1928, the team had indoor facilities for the first time. Ironically, players attributed their poor record the first year in the new gymnasium to the difficulty of making the transition from concrete to wood.[24]

Baseball's popularity on campus was second only to football. Trinity teams fared well against larger schools by emphasizing skill and speed rather than size and power. During the 1920s, they were a perennial power in the Texas Conference, winning back-to-back league championships in 1924 and 1925. Baseball in the early days of the century was not a power-hitting sport, so Coach Roy Aiken took advantage of the dead ball and drilled his Trinity team on the art of bunting. In a contest with A&M in 1905, facing the Aggie's star hurler, Aiken inserted his six best bunters to start the fifth inning. All six bunted successfully and enabled Trinity to score three runs and shut out A&M even though no hit went through the infield.[25]

Indirectly, baseball accounted for the acquisition of a new nickname for Trinity athletic teams. During the early years in Waxahachie, school papers and the local press referred to the teams as "the Trinitonians" or sometimes "the Presbyterians." Their mascot, a bulldog, paced the sidelines on leash dressed in Trinity maroon and white. In 1916 a major league team, the Detroit Tigers, led by manager Hugh Jennings, came to Waxahachie for spring training. The *Waxahachie Daily News* carried numerous stories about the Tigers, including detailed accounts of exhibition games and interviews with team members. As a hospitable gesture, Waxahachie officials named the local municipal ballpark "Tiger Field" to commemorate the town's connection with the team.[26]

During their month-long stay in Waxahachie, Tiger personnel watched Trinity baseball games, offered tips to the players, and signed Chuck Watson, a Trinity hurler, to play for a Detroit farm team.[27] Appreciative of the attention given to their baseball team, Trinity students adopted the nickname "Tigers" in honor of the Detroit ball club. The local press first referred to Trinity as the Tigers on 27 September 1916, when the *Waxahachie Daily Light* reported, "the Trinity Tigers will meet Tarleton on local gridiron in their first battle."[28] Although newspapers continued to use Presbyterians and Trinitonians, Tigers eventually prevailed. Student publications such as the *Trinitonian* and the *Mirage* featured Tiger logos and used the term to refer to all athletic teams.[29]

In the opening decades of the new century, Trinity women displayed a growing interest in sports and physical education. On the new campus, they took up tennis, fencing, and basketball as intramural sports. Initially barred from using the exercise room in the basement of the administration building, they aired their displeasure in the *Trinitonian*. "The boys seem to be the only persons in the University who have an opportunity for athletics. We girls are getting tired of such partiality. We would enjoy a few swings on horizontal bars ourselves."[30] Following the construction of Drane Hall in 1912, women acquired facilities for gymnastics and other indoor exercise activities.

Because female students were not permitted to leave campus, their games were limited to contests between students living in town and those in the dormitory. Basketball, which required agility rather than physical contact, was especially popular among Trinity coeds. In an era of long skirts and concealed limbs, female basketball players' outfits were expansive bloomers with long "middle blouses" designed to ensure that no flesh except the hands and face could be seen. During a game with the Dodgers (the town girls), Grace Haynes, a Prendergast Hall resident, fell and ripped her bloomers from seam to seam. Time was called and she "gathered up the yardage with a safety pin borrowed from a spectator, pinned it to her belt, pulled the middie down over the hump, and reentered the game."[31]

Male and female pep leaders organized rallies to support Trinity teams and maintain school spirit. In the early years of the century, brief pep rallies were held outdoors after morning chapel. In 1916, students instituted evening rallies conducted in the college auditorium. Local newspapers reported that "Yells and songs will be practiced, pep speeches made, and everything conducive to stirring up enthusiasm will be done."[32] At a subsequent pep rally, 300 "lusty voices" sang "Trinity Will Shine Tonight" followed by yells that "seemed for a time would literally lift the roof off the building." Students then boarded special streetcars that took them to the railroad station, where songs and cheers honored the football team as it left for an away game.[33]

During the 1930s, pep squads diminished in size and importance as school officials de-emphasized intercollegiate athletics. Once composed of a large group of upperclassmen, the pep squad reorganized in 1937, including only fifteen first- and second-year students, and the following year changed its name to the Lancerettes.[34] At the same time, a new group, The Bengal Lancers, composed of first-year male students, organized "to keep Tiger Spirit an omnipresent and active reality" on the campus. Dressed in military uniforms, the Lancers became a fixture at Trinity sporting events for many years.[35]

College songs, including an official alma mater, evolved into Trinity traditions for generations of students. The university alma mater, with words and music composed by John Bert Graham, director of music, was first performed by the Young Men's Glee Club at chapel services on September 19, 1914. The *Trinitonian* hailed the song as being "noble and inspiring" with "an easy air and swing to it that adds much to its attractiveness."[36]

Intramural competition among the four student classes became an increasingly important aspect of athletics during the 1920s and 1930s. In 1922, students formed an intramural council composed of a male and female member of each class. The Waxahachie Rotary Club donated a cup that was awarded to the class with the best athletic record during the school year. Later, Coach Wilkins expanded the intramural program to include organized interclass competitions in tennis, golf, swimming, basketball, and track.[37]

Official Foot-Ball Song

Trinity will shine tonight,
Trinity will shine,
Trinity will shine tonight,
Trinity will shine.
When the sun goes down, and the moon comes up,
Trinity will shine.
    (Followed by fifteen Rahs for Trinity)

OFFICIAL YELL

Hoo Ray Rah Roo,
Wahoo, Wahoo,
Hullabaloo, Hullabaloo,
Trinity! Trinity! Trinity!

FIGHT YELL

Yeh——————Trinity.
Yeh——————Trinity.
Yeh——————Trinity.
   Fight! Fight! Fight!

WHISTLE YELL

Whistle (Thrusting arms above the head)
Boom! (Bringing arms down smartly)
Hullabaloo, Hoo Ray, Hoo Ray,
Hullabaloo, Hoo Ray, Hoo Ray,
   Hoo Ray, Hoo Ray,
    Varsity! Varsity!
    T————U!

LOCOMOTIVE YELL

U Rah Trin-i-ty,
U Rah Trin-i-ty,
U Rah Trin-i-ty,
Buom Rah Trin-i-ty.
   (yell)

PREACHER'S DELIGHT SONG

(Girls sing and the Boys whistle)
Hail, Hail, the gang alls here.
So————(whistle)
So————(whistle)
Hail, Hail, the gang alls here.
So————(whistle)

Yells and Cheers, 1914

Grace Haynes, Cheerleader, 1911

In addition to athletics, the move to Waxahachie stimulated other new traditions as faculty and students adjusted to different surroundings. In early fall, the faculty held a reception for students in the administration building to mark the beginning of the social calendar. Following a formal reception line of "beaming and bowing professors," male and female students were "matched up" at random. Once they located their partners and the music began, they marched through the library, down the corridors, up and down the stairs, and through the president's office. The faculty transferred these ceremonies to Drane Hall, the residence hall for women, when it opened in 1912.[38]

Another annual fall event, the Trinity YMCA Stag Roundup, attracted large numbers of new and returning male students. Gathering on the athletic field to play games, they heard student leaders and civic officials encourage membership in the YMCA and participation in other extracurricular activities. In closing ceremonies, students circled a large bonfire and each received a freshly baked pie, a tradition that newspaper accounts indicate was "the most popular feature of the evening."[39]

Trinity women developed traditions that would be maintained for many generations. "Swing-In," sponsored by the YWCA, began in 1924 to welcome first-year women to campus and partner them with "big sisters" who became their unofficial mentors. The event commenced with a picnic supper on the Drane Hall lawn, followed by a lantern-lighted procession to the gymnasium consisting of big and little sisters and female faculty. There the little sisters were "swung in" to the club after a brief ritual conducted by the YWCA officers and faculty sponsors.[40] At the close of each year, Trinity women held Swing-Out, described as "one of the most beloved traditions of the Trinity Family," which consisted of a dinner and candle-lighting ceremony to honor graduating seniors.[41]

Each February Trinity senior women observed the birthday of the nation's first president by decorating the parlors of Drane Hall with flags of various sizes and red, white, and blue bunting. The program consisted of a "merry game of Blind Man's Buff," followed by a question and answer session about George Washington ("Why did Washington resemble a piano? Because he was grand"; "Why did he sleep standing up? Because he could not lie;" etc.) The seniors distributed napkins, some of which were printed with subjects relating to an aspect of Washington's life and character, and recipients made impromptu speeches on their assigned topic. "After dainty refreshments," they "played more jolly games."[42]

Students, faculty, and townspeople observed Founders' Day on the Saturday closest to April 20, the date in 1869 when church officials selected Tehuacana to be the university site. Faculty dismissed classes at 9:30 in the morning so that students could attend a program of music and skits led by various campus organizations. The afternoon featured intramural sports events between classes competing for honors. In the evening, the university community gathered in Getzendaner Park for a picnic supper honoring ex-students and alumni.[43] In 1938 the Trinity faculty introduced a new format for Founders' Day in which a motorcade of students, faculty, and alumni drove to Tehuacana for a program of singing and reminiscing in Texas Hall, followed by a picnic on the grounds.[44]

Commencement week activities combined old Tehuacana traditions, such as literary society debates and music recitals, with new events. On Ivy Day, members of the senior class planted a sprig of ivy near the college walkway. The seniors remembered "the memories of happy days, pledging themselves to be true to truth and duty and do good to all men."[45] In "faculty-take off," seniors impersonated faculty members' voices and mannerisms in their various activities. Attending the event in 1915, a local reporter said, "It was clever acting, and kept the audience in constant laughter."[46]

Despite assurances in the annual *Trinity University Catalogue* that women enjoyed the same social advantages as men, university regulations nevertheless reflected a double standard. Women were sequestered in residence halls at the end of the school day and not permitted to leave the campus without a chaperone. They were not allowed to meet guests at the train station even if accompanied by an adult. Men, however, moved freely about the campus and town, except for freshmen, who had specified evening study hours under adult supervision. Women residing in Prendergast Hall were also required to attend Sunday school and church, while no similar regulation existed for men.[47]

Although the university dropped dress codes for males, it continued to impose them on females. Women wore a "simple inexpensive uniform" consisting of dress and cap for daily use and a "simple white dress" for school entertainments. Regulations specified that "low neck and short sleeve dresses will not be permitted." This dress code remained in effect until World War I, when cultural practices among women began to change.[48]

Continuing a trend from the last years on the Tehuacana campus, students had more social freedom but with close adult supervision. Men and women interacted in classrooms, chapel services, and public events such as lectures and music recitals. The university allowed "suspension nights" in Prendergast Hall on the second and fourth Monday night of each month when women could receive calls from males. Men's boarding residences also had periodic open houses to which town and resident women came. On special occasions, such as the "Spook Reception" at Halloween, university women in ghostly masks and flowing white robes invited male students to a party featuring games and refreshments.[49]

During the period before and after World War I, clubs ranging from serious to frivolous flourished on the Trinity campus, and many students became engrossed in extracurricular activities to the detriment of academic pursuits. A contributor to the *Trinitonian* admitted, "We find that dramatics, athletics, and clubs are demanding so much time that we have to cram in our courses wherever we can and gloss them over with the promise to ourselves that someday we will review the whole business and find out what it is all about."[50] To regulate participation in these activities, the Trinity faculty introduced in 1915 a point system with values assigned to each major campus organization. No student was allowed to perform duties or hold offices that totaled more than five points. Positions valued at three points included YMCA or YWCA president, editor or business manager of the *Mirage*, editor of the *Trinitonian*, president of one of the literary societies, and manager of the football or baseball teams. Debaters, students with major roles in dramatic performances, and class presidents accumulated two points. Participation in athletics and holding offices in other student organization had a one-point value.[51]

Membership in local chapters of national honor societies became an important prestige symbol for Trinity students in the 1920s. Highly visible on campus, the groups honored students for displaying qualities of scholarship, character, leadership, and service. During the academic year, the organizations sponsored lectures, discussions, and a variety of social events. Active groups on the Trinity campus included Blue Key (senior men), Pi Kappa Delta (forensics), Alpha Chi (senior men and women), Pi Gamma Mu (social sciences), Alpha Psi Omega (drama), and Delta Kappa Phi (senior women). The Scholarship Society, organized in 1923, was affiliated with the Scholarship Societies of Texas and dedicated to "the promotion of scholarship among undergraduate students in the academic division in Texas Colleges."[52]

During the same time period, students formed clubs on the basis of geographical origins. The Town Club, organized in 1921 and one of the largest and most active student groups on campus, automatically enrolled any woman attending Trinity but not living in Drane Hall. The group held dinners, teas, and theater parties.[53] The West Texas Club, made up of students from Grayson and Collin Counties, and the Interurban Club, composed of commuters who traveled by streetcar, met periodically for dinners and picnics. The Out-of-State Club, formed in 1927 to promote interest in Trinity University among non-Texas residents, began with twelve charter members from eight states.[54]

Reflecting the growing importance of individual departments and special academic programs, Trinity students also took part in associations that fostered discipline-related skills and activities. The French, German, and Spanish Clubs met regularly with faculty advisors to discuss books, plays, and poems and to prepare musical or dramatic performances for student and town audiences. The Philosophical Club held meetings in which they considered subjects such as "The Origin of Religion" and "Through Science to Faith" and debated perennial philosophical issues such as "Determinism and Free Will" and "The Meaning of Evil."[55] The Script Crafters, the university journalism club, discussed the works of various authors and often presented original stories and poems.[56] Organized in 1925, the Citizenship Club discussed contemporary social problems related to course work in the social sciences.[57]

Other clubs proclaimed no particular purpose or elected to keep their objectives secret. Among the latter were The ? Club, The Chumps, The Bohemian Club, The Wandering Jews, and The KFK Club, a group of first-year females living in Drane Hall that had "no particular purpose and bends all of its efforts toward the accomplishment of this end." The Chronothanatoletron Club, its name derived from the Greek words for "ladies of leisure," limited its membership to women who had been nominated as campus favorites and stated in the *Mirage* that otherwise it had no reason for existing. The Whites, a small group of Trinity males, kept membership criteria secret, but claimed as their emblem "the honored and ancient corkscrew" and promulgated the motto, "To hell with Mr. Volstead, God save the King!"[58]

Early in the century, the four literary societies retained the prominence they had acquired on the Tehuacana campus, but in 1904 they combined into coeducational groups called the Ratio-Maeonian and Philo-Sappho Societies. Their meetings featured debates, orations, essays, original stories, declamations, and extemporaneous speaking.[59] Every year two intersociety contests highlighting the "intellectual giants" from each group had the trappings of athletic events with "yells" and blue and white banners for the Philo-Sapphos and gold and white for the Ratio-Maeonians.[60]

Interest in the literary societies waned in the 1920s because of competing activities and organizations. Despite various attempts by students and alumni to revitalize the organizations, membership declined to a point where officers often outnumbered the adherents. In 1923 the *Trinity University Catalogue* noted that the literary societies ceased to function because "the needs are met by other organizations," and their names were dropped from the list of campus organizations.[61]

Superceding the literary societies were groups such as the male-only Trinity Debating Club and the Bryan Dialectican Society, which began holding regular meetings in 1909 to sharpen debating skills. Triangular debates among Texas Christian University, Southwestern University, and Trinity that commenced in 1912 received considerable publicity and wide student support. In 1924 the debate topics were "Resolved, That France was Justified in the Occupation of the Ruhr" and "Resolved, That the United States Should Enter the League of Nations as it is now Constitut-

Trinity Tramps, the *Mirage*, 1925

ed." During the same year, the Trinity debate squad conducted a 150-mile tour through Oklahoma, Kansas, and Missouri, competing with the University of Tulsa, the College of Emporia, and Park College.[62] In acknowledgment of their importance on campus, debaters and orators in intercollegiate contests were granted the privilege of wearing a "T" (university letter) in 1923.[63]

Physical education and athletics groups attracted students who were involved in intercollegiate and intramural activities. Membership in the Order of the Tiger, formed in 1920 to honor Trinity athletes who had excelled in intercollegiate sports, was coveted. The "T-men" pledged to support Trinity athletics both financially and as recruiters of student-athletes and to publish a quarterly newsletter, "The Tiger," to keep members in-

The *Mirage,* 1920

formed of the order's activities.[64] Women's organizations, such as the Trinity Tramps, specialized in hiking and outdoors activities. The faculty approved the group's constitution with the proviso that they conduct no overnight hikes and carry no firearms. The Women's Athletic Association formed in 1927 to promote female athletic activities and outdoor sports, especially volleyball, baseball, and tennis.[65]

After the move from Tehuacana to Waxahachie, Trinity alumni organized the Association of Former Students at a meeting held in Dallas in 1904. The association's objectives included holding reunions each year during commencement week and serving as ambassadors for Trinity University in their workplaces and communities.[66] By the university's fiftieth anniversary in 1919, 6,500 students had matriculated and 500 bachelor's degrees had been granted. The graduates included 175 teachers, 115 ministers, 45 lawyers, 12 physicians, and 9 foreign missionaries. Of those who did not graduate, it was estimated that at least 100 entered the ministry.[67]

Religious organizations offered a variety of programs for Trinity students. The YMCA and the YWCA, two of the oldest campus groups, sponsored weekly devotional meetings and frequently invited prominent ministers and laypeople as speakers. YWCA members held mission study classes that informed members about national and international missionary activities and encouraged them to consider a vocation in these fields.[68]

Other religious groups focused on social issues and evangelistic outreach. The Prohibition League, organized in 1914, emphasized "the study of the economic, social and moral effects of the liquor traffic throughout the nation." Affiliated with The Intercollegiate State Prohibition Association, the group annually offered a $25 prize for the best oration on some phase of the liquor traffic.[69] The Christian Service Club, which included 25 or 30 students, visited congregations in neighboring communities on weekends, teaching Sunday school classes and assisting in worship services.[70]

Students who planned to become ministers and/or missionaries formed the Life Work Recruits. Although their numbers had diminished since the Tehuacana era, they maintained a membership of 15 to 20 students during the last decade on the Waxahachie campus. Their announced goal was "to keep members in the best spiritual condition, and to foster the spirit of Christ throughout the student body."[71] Through the efforts of student president John Shell, the group procured in 1935 an official meeting place, known as "The Upper Room," in the main building for meditation and prayer. The tradition of the Upper Room carried over to the Woodlawn and Trinity Hill campuses as a focal point for private meditation and personal devotions.[72]

The Religious Life Council, composed of faculty and students, supervised campus religious activities.[73] What had been termed a week of revival services became known as Spiritual Emphasis Week by the 1930s. No longer highly charged emotional services led by evangelists, the meetings usually featured sermons by visiting Presbyterian clergymen.[74] Sometimes professionals with expertise in areas other than religion were invited to participate. In 1938 Howard McClusky, associate professor of psychology at the University of Michigan, led Spiritual Emphasis Week by "presenting religion in a new form, joyously and skillfully presenting this vital matter in terms of psychology and other sciences."[75]

During the 1920s and 1930s, observers noted a decline in student religiosity as secularism infiltrated college campuses. Trinity President John Harmon Burma, who succeeded Hornbeak in 1920, acknowledged that the spiritual life of many Trinity students was "at low ebb" and that "a spirit of worldliness and irreligion was sweeping the young people of the land."[76] In 1930, a synod visitation team chaired by Trinity alumnus Illion T. Jones reported that it found little evidence of religious activity on campus. The committee proposed that Trinity employ a college chaplain or release the president "from the task of begging for money" so that he could attend to the spiritual needs of the student body.[77]

Student publications played increasingly important roles in providing

Student editors of the 1927 *Mirage* surreptitiously inserted their rules of conduct into the advertisement section of the yearbook.

Freedom Of The Press.

Our modern scholars sometimes condescend
Humor with logic in their works to blend,
Our lawyers pungently each other "chaff"
Till judge and jury over-tickled laugh;
Our politicians who for office strive
Like clowns, with jokes the canvass keep alive;
Our statesmen deal in stories quaint and queer
That tell, well told upon the public ear,
And e'en the merchant, leaning o'er his desk,
Hums some light ditty from the latest burlesque,
While we poor, misguided, Trinity sheep
Must not give vent to a single bleat,
About the Faculty actions, in our sheet.

Student protest of faculty "censorship" of the *Trinitonian,* 1914

outlets for literary and artistic creativity. The *Trinitonian,* which first appeared in 1900 as a monthly magazine, featured student essays, works of fiction, and poetry, providing only minimal coverage of campus and world events. Following journalistic trends on other campuses, student editors shifted in 1915 to a newspaper format and issued the *Trinitonian* every

Tuesday morning. With the exception of a brief period during World War I and occasional lapses during the Depression, the *Trinitonian* kept the Trinity community informed regarding campus, local, and world news.[78]

When photography became readily available during the first decade of the century, Trinity students followed the example of peer institutions in producing a student yearbook. Students planned to issue the inaugural edition, called the *Corral*, in 1911, but were unable to secure sufficient financial backing to complete the project. When it appeared a year later as the *Mirage* (perhaps a pun on the previous failure), the yearbook included class histories, fictional essays, and a section on campus humor, along with extensive photographs.[79]

During the first two decades of the twentieth century, university administrators throughout the nation shifted some of the disciplinary and regulatory burden from the faculty to the students. Consequently, student councils, intrafraternity councils, and other varieties of student government became widespread. This movement was in part a move to treat students as adults as well a response to the disinclination of professors to be involved with matters of discipline and extracurricular activities.[80]

Although encouraged by the faculty to establish a student government structure, Trinity students voted down such opportunities twice prior to World War I. In 1923, however, students approved a constitution that afforded them a major role in matters of self-governance regarding social and academic behavior. The 1923 constitution affirmed the students' desire "to maintain a higher standard of honor . . . and to assume a greater responsibility in the government of the University." In addition to officers elected by the student body at large, members of the Student Association included representatives from the *Mirage,* the *Trinitonian,* and the Pep Squad. The women in Drane Hall had a separate council that established house rules and handled internal disciplinary matters.[81]

The new structure featured an honor system that embraced academic performance and social behavior. Students promised to abide by standards of behavior that included academic integrity in their own work and an obligation to report any observed violations of the honor code. Affixed to every examination and/or written assignment was a statement, "I pledge my word of honor as a gentleman (or a lady) that I have neither given nor received aid in this written work." Monitoring of examinations was left to the discretion of individual faculty members, and decisions of the Student Court involving suspension or expulsion could be appealed to the university faculty.[82]

Although students modified the constitution periodically, the honor

Left to right: William E. Beeson (1869–1882);
Benjamin G. McLeskey (1883–1885);
Luther A. Johnson (1885–1889), chairman of the faculty (1896–1900)

Left to right: John L. Dickens (1889–1890); Benjamin D. Cockrill (1890–1896);
Jesse Anderson (1901–1902)

TEHUACANA PRESIDENTS

Hack en route from Mexia to Tehuacana

Tehuacana town center in the early 1870s

The Boyd House, c. 1870

First unit of new building, c. 1873

"The Pride of Limestone County," completed in 1892 by the addition of a south wing, a high mansard roof, and a cupola.

Boarding students and family of Professor and Mrs. William Gillespie at their Tehuacana home in 1902

Trinity University faculty, 1889–1890.
President L. A. Johnson is seated front center.

Science laboratory on the Tehuacana campus

Chemistry students, early 1890s

Surveying class in 1901. Eula McCain is the lone female student.

Primary students and teacher. For a time, Trinity offered classes ranging from kindergarten to high school in addition to college-level work.

Female students and chaperone at Love's Spring in 1898

Trinity's graduating class of 1899

Left to right; Leonidas C. Kirkes (1902–1904);
Archelaus E. Turner (1904–1906);
Samuel L. Hornbeak (1907–1921)

Left to right: John H. Burma (1921–1933);
Raymond H. Leach (1934–1937);
Frank L. Wear (1937–1942)

WAXAHACHIE PRESIDENTS

Waxahachie main administration and classroom building, c. 1910

Campus scene, c. 1930

Drane Hall women's dormitory, 1920

Drane Hall women, 1923

Trinity men spoof forbidden vices in 1914

May Fest celebration, c. 1928

Trinity men ready for an outing

Trinity pep squad, 1924

Tehuacana alumni/ae meeting on the Waxahachie campus, early 1900s

Paul Schwab, Professor, Department of Religion (1928–1961)
and Dean of the University (1935–1947),
Maude B. Davis, Dean of Women (1923–1948)

Texas Intercollegiate Athletic Association championship baseball team, 1925

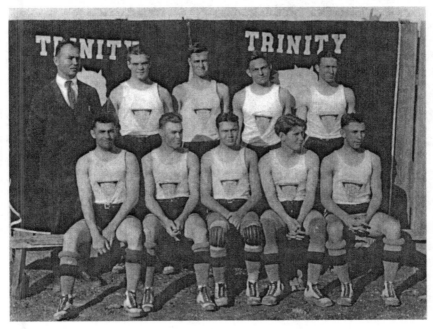

Trinity basketball team, 1922. Note the "hook 'em horns" gesture at top right of fence, which was cropped out of the *Mirage* photograph.

Trinity University choir leaving for annual tour, 1935

Trinity band 1937–1938

system appears to have functioned well, especially during its early years of operation. References in the faculty minutes indicate that the Student Court routinely handled cases of honor code violations and assigned punishments. In 1923 the court suspended a student for procuring liquor with a medical prescription and bringing it into Beeson Hall.[83] A few years later the Trinity faculty endorsed a court decision to put a student on probation and disbar him from all extracurricular activities for an unspecified violation of the honor code.[84] Even minor violations of the code warranted consideration. One first-year student received censure because he gave his football ticket to a friend who was not matriculated at Trinity. Noting that the individual was "probably not aware of the seriousness of the act," the Student Court warned, "if any such act shall be committed again, the council shall take action against the party involved."[85]

The women's Fellowship Council of Drane Hall, under the supervision of Dean Maude Davis, met regularly to consider cases of infractions of dormitory regulations. The most frequent offenses were smoking, dancing, riding in automobiles with members of the opposite sex, and dating irregularities. One woman who did not return to Drane Hall from a car ride with a male until just before midnight was denied social privileges for a month.[86] Two women observed dancing at a local establishment were "strictly campused for three weeks."[87] Some residents caught smoking in Drane Hall claimed that the cigarette "had been lit without touching their lips." Deeming their excuse unacceptable, the Fellowship Council placed the women on probation and removed all social privileges for the remainder of the semester. Other women present at the time of the alleged incident were disciplined for not rebuking the offenders.[88]

On rare occasions misconduct resulted in suspension or expulsion. One such instance occurred in 1926 when two Trinity coeds spent a Saturday night at the Adolphus Hotel in Dallas "under assumed names and without permission." Placing the offenders under strict probation, the Fellowship Council recommended that the Faculty Discipline Committee expel the two students. After considering the case, the faculty adopted a lesser penalty of suspension for the remainder of the semester.[89]

The Fellowship Council expended considerable time and effort defining and regulating the frequency of dating. The questions included: Did a serendipitous encounter with a young man downtown constitute a date? What if a couple attended a church meeting and walked home together? Did a stroll to the library punctuated with conversation on a campus bench count as a date? In 1925 the council agreed on definitions that covered most situations. For example, "To go to the show in the afternoon

THE purpose of the Students' Honor Association of Trinity University is fittingly expressed in the preamble of the constitution and by-laws: "Desiring to maintain a higher standard of honor at our Alma Mater and to assume greater responsibility in the government of the University, etc." The Honor Association is the most important self-governing body in the institution, the Drane Fellowship and Beeson Hall Club being subordinate divisions of the Association. All bona fide students of Trinity University are considered members of this Honor Association, and the honor system is the prevailing and fundamental doctrine of the Association as expressed through its constitution and by-laws.

Student Honor Code Statement, the *Mirage,* 1927

with a boy is not considered a date and it is not necessary to sign it up in the date book. Freshmen and Sophomores must not meet young men in town at night. Juniors and Seniors may meet them and come out to the hall with them. However, if the date is not signed up, the Junior date must leave as soon as they reach the hall and the Senior date must report to the hostess if he stays."[90]

During the early 1930s a sequence of events tested the ability of students to maintain the honor system. The first involved the behavior of a group of Trinity students who traveled on a special train to Brownwood to watch a football match between Trinity and Howard Payne College. Apparently a number of them became intoxicated and behaved badly during and after the contest. Based on a report furnished by the Student Council, the faculty suspended ten men for the remainder of the semester and placed fifteen others on probation. Several other students, including the president's son, were permitted to make a public apology for their unruly behavior because they had not been found guilty of drinking alcohol. Sending a stern message to the student body, the faculty ordered the campus closed to "loitering" after seven in the evening and threatened more severe punishment to any future violators of campus regulations.[91]

After this incident, the student government conducted its own investigation of hazing and drinking activities among Trinity students. In April 1930 the Student Council recommended to the faculty that twenty-two men be suspended for hazing, three for drinking, and one for "contempt of council and conduct unbecoming a gentleman." In concurring with the council recommendations, the faculty voted to report their action to the student body at morning chapel.[92]

Resentment surfaced regarding the role of "student informers" in caus-

"Cutest Girl," the *Mirage,* 1922

ing the discipline of popular students and the imposition of a campus curfew. A number of students signed a petition requesting a campus referendum on whether to retain the honor code. A contributor to the *Trinitonian* commenting on the controversy claimed, "When two or more Trinity
students get together nowadays, the topic of discussion is nothing except
the honor system." He questioned whether the honor code could continue because "the prevalent attitude of the student body is in favor of ostra-
cizing the conscientious student who would report any violation of the
honor system."[93]

Although the honor code survived, it faced a second crisis three years later, this time involving hazing. Practiced both on and off campus, hazing was difficult to control because many students considered it an integral aspect of college life.[94] Parents frequently complained about hazing activities and asked college administrators to take action against offending upperclassmen. In response, Trinity officials admitted that hazing was a common practice but they were unable to suppress it because students refused to inform on their peers.[95]

An intense rivalry existed between the freshman and sophomore classes, with first-year students being subject to a variety of rules and regulations tolerated by university officials. Traditions such as making first-year students wear "slime caps," denying them the right to sit on the steps of the front entrance of the administration building, requiring them to give up their seats to upperclassmen, and limiting their dating to members of their own class were common practices on college campuses. As such, they appeared to adults as juvenile but harmless routines. Other aspects of the rivalry, however, such as painting class numerals on the water tower, disrupting class meetings, engaging in class fights, paddling, and abandoning victims on country roads, raised concerns among university officials that students were unnecessarily distracted from their studies and subjected to bodily harm.[96]

Matters came to a head in the fall of 1933 when a group of sophomores beat three freshmen with brooms, transported them to a neighboring town, and abandoned them, bruised and bleeding, to walk home in their underwear. The three families withdrew their sons from Trinity and demanded a thorough investigation by local and campus authorities. A dozen students, all well-known members of the campus community, were identified as the perpetrators. The faculty suspended some for the remainder of the year and placed others on probation, depending on the extent of their involvement.[97]

When students learned of the faculty's action, they protested by walking out *en masse* at a morning chapel service. Class and student government leaders later apologized to the faculty for the incident, however, and promised a cessation of hazing during the remainder of the school year. They also petitioned the faculty to reinstate the suspended students, whose punishment they deemed to be excessive for the nature of the wrongdoing. After considerable discussion, the faculty denied the request for clemency and "in a courteous communication to the student petitioners, gave full explanation of the reasons for such refusal."[98]

As a result of these events, campus enthusiasm for the honor code rapidly faded. Discussions between faculty and the Student Council committees led to a decision in 1935 to revise the student constitution to eliminate the honor code. According to the 1935–36 *Trinity University Catalogue*, "the discipline of the institution is [now] in the hands of the President and the faculty." The details of administering discipline were assigned to a Student Affairs Committee, appointed by the president and consisting of the president (ex officio), the dean of the university, two faculty members, and "two outstanding members of the student body." While students were expected to "conduct themselves like ladies and gentlemen," they no longer would have the rights and responsibilities that accompanied a campus honor system.[99]

During the closing years on the Waxahachie campus, hazing gradually diminished due to strict enforcement of rules and a student body more concerned about the Depression and growing war clouds in Europe than in class traditions. A *Trinitonian* editorial in 1934 lamented the "changing customs and more rigidly enforced regulations" that caused incoming freshmen not to take "Slime" activities seriously.[100] By 1940 only remnants of "Slime Week," now referred to as Freshman Week, remained. Friendly rivalry between the freshmen and upperclassmen continued but lacked the intensity of previous years. "There is no doubt about it," a *Trinitonian* editorial noted. "The rock 'em sock 'em days have just about disappeared."[101]

Trinitonian surveys of student attitudes and life styles during the 1930s shed light on other aspects of college life. In 1934 first-year students revealed that the *Dallas Morning News* was their favorite newspaper and *Colliers* was their choice of magazine reading. Most respondents indicated that they studied about an hour a day outside of class during the semester and read fewer than five books not assigned by professors. Time spent in "courting members of the opposite sex" ranged from zero to five hours per day. Most freshmen reported that they attended Sunday school and church regularly and that they regarded the most esteemed campus office to be the president of the student body, followed by class officers and the captain of the football team.[102]

Another survey conducted in 1939 asked Trinity students "Who is the Most Outstanding Man Alive?" The overwhelming favorites were Franklin D. Roosevelt and Albert Einstein, the former because of what he had done for the country's economic situation and the latter because he was "the greatest scientist alive at this time." Other choices of many students included Arturo Toscanini, the world famous symphony orchestra director; Henry Ford, the automobile manufacturer; and British Prime Minister Neville Chamberlain, "because of his efforts to retain world peace."[103]

In a related survey, students endorsed a third term for President Roosevelt, fearing that a change in administration would be harmful in such critical times. In the Willkie-Roosevelt presidential contest, they favored the incumbent FDR by a four-to-one margin.[104]

When queried regarding the war in Europe, students expressed an isolationist preference. Several editorials in the *Trinitonian* stressed the importance of neutrality when it came to another nation's battles. Citing the experience of World War I, a student editor concluded, "our participation will not help that continent solve its problems. It is their problem and only they can work out an ultimate settlement."[105] Despite such sentiments, students overwhelmingly approved supplying Britain with equipment and finances in its struggle against Nazi oppression. When the Japanese attacked Pearl Harbor, student support for the war effort dramatically increased. Trinity men enlisted and were drafted into military service or left school to take jobs in defense-related industries.[106]

Despite occasional clashes with authority and resistance to rules and regulations, most Trinity students reported favorable experiences during their college years on the Waxahachie campus. Testimonies from Waxahachie alumni confirm their appreciation of a dedicated faculty and a sense of community that characterized their college experience. A graduate who later received a Ph.D. in chemistry from Texas A&M said, "One of the most valuable factors in the training that I received at Trinity University was the personal contact and association with a faculty composed of the highest type of Christian men and women. Such a faculty as Trinity's is not found in institutions in which scholarship is considered the sole element in education."[107] Another student expressed a sentiment that many Trinitonians felt toward their alma mater. Reminiscing about his years on the Waxahachie campus, he recalled the names of faculty and staff whom he termed "caring men and women." Without their support, he concluded, "I don't think I could have made it through the university."[108]

CHAPTER SIX

RUMORS AND FEARS

It is my firm conviction that sometime in the not distant future some noble minded visionary persons in Waxahachie will increase substantially the endowment of Trinity University . . . and will thereby forever silence rumors of removal and fears of dissolution.

PRESIDENT FRANK L. WEAR, MAY 1939

TRINITY UNIVERSITY'S LAST TWO DECADES on the Waxahachie campus began with high expectations and significant achievements only to end in discouragement and uncertainty. In the 1920s, trustees, faculty, and students were optimistic about the university's future. The elusive quest for economic stability appeared attainable as the United States entered a period of growth and prosperity following a brief recession at the end of World War I. Under new leadership and with increased enrollment, the administrators anticipated benefactors who could ensure the institution's financial future.

For a time it appeared that goal might be realized. In 1923 Trinity dropped all preparatory classes and became a *bona fide* collegiate institution for the first time in its history. Although the million-dollar endowment campaign fell short of its goal, by 1929 Trinity's endowment reportedly reached almost $700,000 and generated approximately $35,000 annually. With enrollment approaching 600, an all-time high, and accreditation enhanced by membership in the Southern Association of Colleges and Secondary Schools in 1925, Trinity's status among the elite private denominational colleges in Texas seemed secure.[1]

Confidence vanished in the economic environment of the 1930s. National unemployment rose to 25 percent during the winter of 1932–33. Banks failed, businesses closed, retail sales plunged, and bread lines became commonplace throughout the country. Survival rather than expansion became the campus watchword, and only the sacrifices of faculty and staff enabled Trinity to maintain operations.

To lead Trinity as Hornbeak's successor, the board of trustees in 1920 selected John Harmon Burma, a large, gregarious, and energetic man whose imposing countenance and booming voice earned him the nickname "Bull" from Trinity students. A deeply religious man with considerable administrative abilities, Burma established a network of beneficial contacts in the Synod of Texas and throughout the denomination. He optimistically told the Trinity faculty in 1922, "We are going to build big for the future. We are going to be a big school as well as a good school."[2]

The son of German immigrants who settled on a farm in northern Iowa, Burma attended Dubuque University where he received a B.A. degree in 1896 and a B.D. degree in 1899. Securing ordination as a minister in the Presbyterian Church in the United States of America (PCUSA), Burma served pastorates in Illinois and Iowa before coming to the Second Presbyterian Church in Dallas in 1908. Burma was a dynamic speaker and conducted evangelistic revival services in small rural mission congregations and large city churches with equal success. For twenty-five years he represented the PCUSA at the Bloys Cowboy Camp Meeting near Fort Davis, Texas, an annual gathering that attracted people from throughout the southwest.[3]

Following a six-year pastorate in Dallas, Burma returned to his alma mater and became vice-president of Dubuque University. At Dubuque, Burma devoted much of his time to fund-raising and led the university's successful endowment campaign. He also did volunteer work to assist the settlement of German immigrants who were moving into the midwest during that time period. In acknowledgment of his accomplishments, Trinity awarded Burma an honorary Doctor of Divinity degree at commencement services in 1917.[4]

During his thirteen-year tenure at Trinity, Burma fulfilled a wide range of duties. A respected member of the Synod of Texas, Burma functioned as a minister-at-large with the state as his parish even as he immersed himself in the day-to-day responsibilities of being the university's president. His extensive correspondence reveals that he traveled widely, preached almost every Sunday to a different congregation, and advised and counseled ministers, businessmen, alumni, and church members.[5]

Burma repeatedly conveyed his convictions about Trinity's institutional purpose to faculty and staff. "Your personal conduct should be in line with the principles and the teachings of Evangelical Christianity. Your teaching and your character should in every way conform to those ideals and teachings." No matter what the subject matter, Burma proclaimed, teachers should do nothing to "unsettle young people in their religious training," but rather "lead them gradually into what may be a more mature conception of things." Cognizant that the country was caught up in a modernist-fundamentalist struggle that involved both scientific theory and religious faith, Burma cautioned faculty to be careful in discussing sensitive issues: "Let us try to talk to our young people in such a way that they will not go home and say we are a bunch of heretics and the like."[6]

Burma held faculty members accountable when they failed to heed his admonitions. A religion professor once selected a textbook that included what Burma deemed "teachings which are not in accord with what we wish to inculcate in the students of Trinity University." Burma confiscated the textbook, replaced it with one he considered more theologically acceptable, and, at the end of the semester, did not renew the professor's contract.[7]

Although Burma deemed teaching, scholarship, and research important, he most valued service to the university community. When determining faculty salaries, he gave priority to activities such as advising and counseling students, supporting university programs, and fulfilling committee assignments. "If you men and women do not take a personal interest in the student, you make me out a liar, and if a school goes before the community with a president as a liar, that is fatal," he told a faculty assembly. "Trinity University is a business place and every student is a customer. Every student is a customer because each student pays a fixed amount of money for a certain commodity, intellectual, moral, spiritual, and athletic, that Trinity University offers."[8]

When hiring new faculty, Burma inquired about religious and moral standards alongside academic credentials, welcoming only candidates who belonged to mainline Protestant denominations.[9] One of Burma's acquaintances recommended a young Roman Catholic Ph.D. as a potentially excellent undergraduate science teacher. While affirming his own broad-mindedness, Burma nevertheless claimed, "many in the rank and file of our ministry take a very different attitude. This is more especially true with the Ku Klux situation to which a great many of our ministers belong and one of their strong features is anti-Catholicism." Burma feared that "our Church would rise up if they should know that we have a Roman Catholic on our faculty."[10]

An Iowa native, Burma ironically preferred southerners who were familiar with regional customs and traditions. Most northerners and easterners, Burma observed, "simply cannot hit it off" on southern campuses. All things being equal, Burma said, "We prefer southern professors, notwithstanding the fact that our dean, our registrar and I are all northern men. . . . When people of the east go south or west they go with a sort of missionary spirit and with a measure of superiority. They act as though they had to set things right in the south and in the west. This is always resented and ought to be."[11]

In the early years of his presidency Burma rejuvenated the one million dollar endowment fund drive that had lapsed in 1920. Hampered by poor economic conditions, the campaign languished until 1924 when Trinity received the largest single gift in its history, a contribution of $100,000 from the estate of Philip A. Chapman, prominent rancher and oil producer whose family had long ties with the university.[12] Chapman's gift stirred fresh interest in supplementing the endowment, especially among Waxahachie residents who mounted an effort to match the donation. Although other contributions followed, the campaign never gained sufficient momentum to justify continuation. With goals only partially fulfilled, Trinity trustees closed the endowment fund drive in March 1924.[13]

Trinity received another unexpected gift in 1925 from the Presbyterian Board of Christian Education in Philadelphia (formerly General Board of Education). The board promised $50,000 to establish endowed chairs in a department of religious education if Trinity raised a matching amount by March 1926. With help from pastors and laymen in the Synod of Texas, Burma secured the needed money, and Trinity opened the new department in 1927. The religious education program prepared students to do graduate work in the field and enabled laypeople to become more effective teachers in local church situations.[14]

At the suggestion of members of the Board of Christian Education, Burma hired a woman to teach in the religious education department "since women play so large a part in religion and since so many students in the department would be women." The new professor had a master's degree in religious education from Boston University and seemed to be "most capable and beloved, deeply religious, and in every way a fine character." Despite her credentials, work ethic, and teaching expertise, many students chose not to enroll in her classes apparently because they rejected the idea of a woman teaching religion. When enrollment patterns failed to change after two years, Burma reluctantly dismissed her and hired a male instructor.[15]

Because of the quality of Trinity's educational programs in the first part of the twentieth century, various accrediting agencies, such as the National Council on Education, the Presbyterian Board of General Education, and the Association of Texas Colleges, included Trinity on their lists of accredited colleges and universities. By 1920, however, the Southern Associ-

Trinity faculty, 1930

ation of Colleges and Secondary Schools had attained prominence as the major regional accrediting agency. Although Burma insisted privately "Trinity has no zeal for membership in this association," he admitted that its omission from the list of accredited institutions affected recruitment and retention. He frequently received letters from parents who were concerned about accreditation and from Trinity graduates who had been rejected by top graduate schools because their degree was from an institution not affiliated with the Southern Association. Accordingly, in 1923 he instructed Dean Edward P. Childs to make inquiries regarding the procedures and criteria required for admission to the regional accrediting agency.[16]

Southern Association representatives encouraged Trinity to make a formal application for membership. In 1924 the university met the Southern Association's stringent criteria, which included financial stability, quality of its library and other physical plant facilities, qualifications and remuneration of its faculty, and size and content of its classes. Before final approval, however, the accrediting agency required Trinity to remove an $18,000 operating deficit, which it accomplished with assistance from the Presbyterian Board of Christian Education and from Waxahachie citizens. To maintain its standing, however, Trinity knew that the Southern Association expected it to increase faculty salaries, enlarge its library holdings, and build a gymnasium.[17]

When word of the successful accreditation application became public, enrollment soared, even though Trinity turned away a number of students

The Watkins Gymnasium

who did not meet minimal Southern Association entrance standards. A prominent Trinity alumnus wrote, "This is far more important for the actual welfare of the purpose of the school than its fine standing in football, as much as we rejoice in that record."[18]

Under Burma's leadership, the university demonstrated quantifiable progress in meeting Southern Association expectations. When Burma became president in 1921, Trinity had an enrollment of 335 students, an operating income of $52,000, and an endowment of $340,000. By the end of the decade, enrollment had doubled and retention had significantly increased, the operating income had reached more than $130,000, and the endowment totaled approximately $700,000. The size of the faculty grew from twenty in 1920 to thirty-five in 1929, and salaries doubled from two to four thousand dollars. During the same time period, library holdings increased from approximately 7,000 to 12,500 volumes.[19]

Accreditation pressures also spurred efforts to upgrade campus facilities. In 1928 the university completed construction of a new gymnasium for physical education classes, indoor sports, and conditioning and training facilities. Erected at a cost of approximately $40,000, the gymnasium seated 1,000 and provided locker rooms for men and women. The donation of a 240-acre farm by the R. S. Watkins family and contributions from Waxahachie citizens and former students financed its construction. Trustees named the building in honor of Richard O. Watkins, a pioneer Cumberland Presbyterian clergyman and longtime Trinity supporter.[20]

The institution took a sharp decline, however, when the stock market crash of 1929 ushered in the Depression of the 1930s. As Trinity trustees

Student searching for personal belongings after the Beeson Hall fire

grappled with declining income and decreased enrollment, they faced an additional crisis. On the morning of 28 October 1929, a fire razed Beeson Hall. Breaking out at breakfast time, the fast-spreading blaze left little opportunity for residents to carry out their belongings. Waxahachie citizens made generous contributions to replace personal possessions, and many nearby residents opened their homes to dispossessed students.[21]

Burma attempted to view the conflagration positively. "In place of this old fire trap," he told a friend, "there must rise a fire-proof building that will be adequate to the needs of Trinity, a credit to the Presbyterian Church, and an honor to our Lord."[22] Because the insurance paid only $16,000, a little more than the amount originally borrowed from the endowment fund to complete construction of the building, Burma initiated a campaign to finance construction of a new dormitory for one hundred students. Hampered by the poor economic conditions, the project languished for nine years despite efforts to secure donations. In 1938, Trinity trustees conceded defeat and returned collected funds to the donors.[23]

As the Depression deepened, a decline in tuition revenues and income from the endowment produced mounting deficits. Making sharp cuts in the budget, Trinity trustees placed a moratorium on repairs and improvements and did not fill faculty and staff vacancies caused by resignations or leaves of absence. In 1931 faculty members accepted a request by Trinity trustees to "donate" 10 percent of their salaries to alleviate the institution's financial pressures. Trustees asked for a second 10 percent reduction in 1932, with which the faculty again complied. Describing Trinity's financial condition two years later, the president told a church official, "Our faculty generally has accepted the situation, and excellent morale has been maintained. Only two members of the entire staff sent communications to the Board regarding their salary situation—the two Deans!"[24]

Attempts to collect unpaid tuition and fees produced limited results. Correspondence in the business manager's files reflected the plight of students and parents unable to meet their financial obligations. One student dropout reported that he was working on the family farm, and, if it showed any profit during the year, he assured officials that "his debt to the university will come first." One of many parents, embarrassed by his outstanding debts, wrote, "I have tried very hard to pay you this money, and will some day pay you, but I have three families with children to keep up this year and it has taken about everything I could rake and scrape to keep them in necessities of life." Another parent wrote, "In these stringent times we have all got to do our best, keep up our courage, and be helpful to one another. Please write me by return mail your reaction, as it is financially impossible to pay you now." In each instance, the business manager granted the parties an extension without interest.[25]

During the Depression, some Trinity students qualified for financial aid from the university and from the U.S. government through the Federal Emergency Relief Association (FERA), later known as the National Youth Administration, which permitted 10 percent of the student body to be employed at the rate of $10 to $20 per month. Of the 154 students receiving work grants in 1934, FERA supported 34. Although these aid programs did not meet the needs of all students, they enabled many men and women to continue their education rather than drop out of school. Trinity publications stressed, however, that all students had to work for what they received. "We consider giving 'something for nothing' injurious to the individual student, and most of our scholarships are, therefore, opportunities to work."[26]

Between 1929 and 1932, Trinity's enrollment decreased by 209, resulting in a reduction of $29,970 in revenue from student tuition and fees and $7,352 from Drane Hall residents. At the same time, endowment income declined by $13,282. All told, these factors resulted in an accumulated deficit of $40,269.25 for the three-year period. Trinity trustees covered the indebtedness by withdrawing money from the endowment fund, a practice they employed throughout the remainder of the Waxahachie period.[27]

At the close of the 1932–33 academic year, after thirteen years and the longest tenure of any previous Trinity president, Burma submitted his res-

Student worker picking up litter on campus during the Depression

ignation to the board of trustees. Citing weariness of his role as "ecclesiastical beggar" and "living out of a suitcase," Burma accepted a call to be pastor of the Central Presbyterian Church in Sherman, Texas, a position that he held until his death in 1938.[28]

Securing a successor to Burma in the midst of the Depression proved to be challenging. Some trustees preferred an ordained minister with extensive denominational connections and others called for an experienced educator with administrative and business skills. In Raymond Hotchkiss Leach, the search committee found an individual who appeared to fulfill both desires.

An ordained Presbyterian minister, Leach graduated from Oberlin College in 1904, attended Princeton Theological Seminary, and later did graduate work at Stanford University. After teaching at the Mid-Pacific Institute, a mission school for Asian boys, he served as president of the Hawaiian Pineapple Company until 1918 when he resigned to become a volunteer YMCA chaplain to U.S. troops in France. Returning to the United States, Leach served as academic dean at the University of Nevada from 1922 to 1929 and then accepted an appointment as an executive of the Council of Church Boards, an interdenominational educational agency that advised denominational colleges and universities on curricular and administrative issues. From this position, Leach became Trinity University's eleventh president in the fall of 1934.[29]

In an unusual introduction to the Trinity community, Leach arrived on campus incognito several months before his assumption of the presidency. Strolling around campus, he inspected the facilities and conversed informally with students. Thinking Leach to be a textbook representative, an applicant for a faculty post, or an inspector from an accrediting agency, they freely offered their opinions about student and faculty affairs. When he was introduced as the president-elect three days later, students learned the true identity of the inquisitive campus visitor.[30]

Inheriting a deteriorating fiscal situation, Leach tried to no avail to secure funds from the Synod of Texas and various philanthropic organizations. He clashed with trustees, who, despite their purported desire for an economic savior, bristled at his aggressive administrative style. In particular, he differed with Oscar H. Chapman, a Waxahachie businessman who had served as trustee and treasurer for two decades. According to Leach, the college had been "practically the personal possession of one man [Chapman] for the past twenty years." No one but Chapman, Leach alleged, had any real knowledge of the university's investment strategies or annual endowment income. Leach asserted that the board relied on Chapman to determine the total amount of money that was available for operating expenses without a detailed accounting of income and expenses. Although he did not question Chapman's integrity, Leach thought that the plenary board and the president should be more involved in determining the annual budget. Only by an independent audit, Leach contended, "will we know the real condition of affairs—something nobody has known for twenty years except the treasurer himself."[31]

At Leach's urging, the Presbyterian Board of Christian Education conducted an investigation of Trinity's financial records and investment policies. While finding no fiscal impropriety, the committee recommended that Trinity centralize all financial records in the business manager's office and that Trinity's Investment Committee minutes record complete information as to actions taken concerning investments and endowment. Despite Trinity's changes in fiscal procedure, Chapman maintained his considerable influence with board members regarding financial matters and continued to serve as treasurer, and the breach between him and the new president widened.[32]

Leach also encountered opposition from some board members over a decision to reverse longstanding university regulations that banned social dancing on campus. During the 1920s, dance halls and speakeasies afforded students opportunities for dancing away from the oversight of university authorities. For those not inclined to frequent such establishments, the increasing availability of phonographs allowed dancing in private homes. Aware that such events were widespread, the Trinity faculty had passed a regulation in 1925 "strictly prohibiting dancing or attendance at dances by non-resident students." Appealing to local citizens not to permit dancing in their residences when Trinity students were present, the faculty based its request on pragmatic rather than moral grounds, stating that "it has simply been demonstrated that students cannot go to dances at night and accomplish the work that must be done at the University."[33]

Regulations notwithstanding, Trinity students danced in homes and halls and periodically agitated for the right to hold such functions on campus. In 1929 a student committee presented to the faculty a petition signed by 75 percent of the student body asking for permission to hold dances in the gymnasium "under proper supervision and rules." After a heated discussion and a divided vote, the faculty rejected the petition but recommended that a committee be appointed to study social relations in the college.[34]

Subsequent attempts by students to end dancing restrictions ended in failure even though in 1932 the faculty approved dancing as "an acceptable diversion in the school's social calendar" and received permission from the Board of Trustees to permit dancing "under faculty authority."[35] However, because of pressure from then President Burma, who feared opposition from church members and ministers in the Synod of Texas, the board rescinded its action. Deeming the time "not propitious for any modification of our attitude as a faculty toward the problem of dancing," the faculty voted to reinsert a statement prohibiting dancing into the university's catalogue.[36]

In Raymond Leach, however, Trinity students found an advocate willing to challenge social convention. At his urging, a majority of the faculty voted to grant Trinity students permission to hold dances on campus "under regulations adapted to each circumstance."[37] In November 1934 the Student Affairs Committee sponsored a dance in the gymnasium. Approximately seventy-five couples danced to the music of a popular local orchestra, dined on finger sandwiches, and sipped nonalcoholic punch served by observant chaperones.[38] A *Trinitonian* editorial noted, "We see a complete change in attitude, spirit, social life, in fact everything that goes to make up a successful university. The student body of Trinity is completely behind its new president."[39]

Several members of the board of trustees, including Samuel L. Templeton, a prominent Presbyterian clergyman, Trinity alumnus, and former faculty member, opposed the decision. In response to Templeton, Leach pointed out that the vast majority of Trinity students favored the proposal and that several other church-related schools, including Southern Methodist and Texas Christian Universities, had recently removed the ban on dancing. In a scathing reply, Templeton rejected the principle of deciding social issues by student vote and argued that policies of sister institutions had no relevance unless Trinity was competing with them for dancing patronage. "These debutantes into the dancing world cut a sorry figure in the light of Christian ethics." Templeton concluded that conceding this issue "would make it a Christian duty to have a dance in every home, and would convert our churches into dance halls—dancing everywhere like the frogs of Egypt."[40]

At a trustee meeting in February 1935, Templeton moved to rescind the faculty's action regarding dancing. After considerable discussion, a substitute motion to uphold the president and the faculty prevailed by a roll-call vote of eight to five. Although dances continued to be held on campus, students were aware of the pressures on Leach and the faculty. An editorial in the *Trinitonian* observed that "a great deal of prejudice against this form of recreation" had emerged since the policy change became effective. Noting that the dances were well supervised and free from problems, the writer commended the administration for "meeting in a beneficial manner a long-discussed problem." It is impossible for university officials to prevent dancing off campus, the editorial concluded, "but it is not impossible for Trinity to provide for regulated dances."[41]

During the spring and summer of 1935, numerous church sessions and presbyteries sent petitions to the Synod of Texas in advance of its annual October meeting expressing displeasure with Trinity's revised dancing policy. Bowing to the overwhelming sentiment against dancing expressed by synod commissioners, the board of trustees held a called meeting and rescinded its previous action. To inform the churchgoing public, the trustees published their decision in several denominational papers and in the *Dallas Tribune*.[42] Trinity students continued to sponsor dances at off-campus locations, and Trinity authorities did not challenge them. They insisted, however, that such events not be advertised in the *Trinitonian*.[43]

The dancing controversy paled in significance to accreditation deficiencies that threatened Trinity's membership in the Southern Association. When Trinity's financial resources plummeted during the Depression, loss of accreditation appeared inevitable.[44] Leach told a colleague, "It will be necessary for us to crack a bank vault or else lose our Class A standing, since they [Southern Association] are going to begin to put the screws on next year about advancing staff salaries."[45] In 1936 the Southern Association placed the university on probation, citing a variety of problems, most of them fiscal. The association reported that Trinity's salaries were "next to the lowest paid by any member of the Association." It also pointed out that many faculty members lacked required advanced degrees and found it difficult to pursue graduate studies because of heavy teaching loads. The association said, "In expenditures per student, in stable income, in all library statistics, and in other vital matters, the university is very nearly at the bottom of the list in our membership."[46]

Efforts to remove the probationary status between 1936 and 1942 proved unsuccessful. Although library holdings increased and the percentage of faculty with advanced degrees reached a satisfactory level, Trinity's financial crisis precluded reducing institutional debt and raising faculty salaries.[47] At one point, treasurer Chapman proposed dropping football in order to economize, but protests from members of the Tiger Club and student and alumni organizations caused the trustees to maintain the status quo.[48] Despite the Southern Association's "sympathy and familiarity with our problems," Dean Paul Schwab reported that Trinity would remain on probation until financial conditions improved. In the meantime, the university could only hope for an economic miracle to occur.[49]

Leach did not anticipate the occurrence of such a miracle. He told a staff member in Philadelphia that "the Board of Christian Education may just as well cross Trinity off her list of colleges. It is just that bad."[50] Moreover, Leach's relationship with synod officials and trustees had seriously deteriorated. At a trustee meeting early in June 1936, he presented his resignation effective at the end of the month. During his brief administration, Leach improved budgeting and investment procedures and supported students in seeking a liberalization of social restrictions.[51]

In the wake of Leach's controversial presidency, Trinity trustees turned to one of their own members for leadership. The valedictorian of Trinity's class of 1899, Frank Lucian Wear obtained a B.D. degree from Cumberland University in 1902 and was ordained as a Cumberland Presbyterian minister the same year. Following graduate work at Columbia University and Union Theological Seminary in New York, Wear held pastorates in Alabama and Texas, the last one at Central Presbyterian Church in Paris, Texas, from 1921 to 1937. He served as field secretary for Trinity's million-dollar endowment campaign from 1919 to 1921 and was a member of the Board of Trustees for sixteen years (1921 to 1937). Well regarded in the Synod of Texas as a pastor, administrator, and scholar, Wear's appointment resonated favorably among Trinity supporters.[52]

In spite of economic problems, accreditation concerns, and student unrest, Trinity faculty members remained focused on their responsibilities as teachers and scholars. During the last two decades on the Waxahachie campus, Trinity's academic program underwent revisions influenced by two strong academic deans committed to progressive educational standards, Edward P. Childs (1920–34) and Paul J. Schwab (1935–47). Childs, a graduate of Denison University in Ohio, held a master's degree from the University of Michigan and did graduate work at Harvard and Columbia. Before coming to Trinity, he served three years as president of Cumberland University in Lebanon, Tennessee. Implementation of his academic principles in Trinity's undergraduate program diversified the curriculum, created a student government and honor code, and paved the way for membership in the Southern Association of Colleges and Secondary Schools.[53]

By the 1920s Trinity's curriculum bore little resemblance to the simple literary and classical format of the early days in Tehuacana. Under Childs's leadership, students had more options for majors, minors, and electives. At the end of the sophomore year, students selected a major group: Language and Literature (English), Foreign Language (French or Spanish), Social Science (economics or history), or Scientific (biology, chemistry, mathematics). Students also were required to choose a minor field of study from a group of designated departments. For example, an English major could minor in Bible, business administration, education, German, history, home economics, journalism, music, or public speaking.[54]

By 1934 Trinity had adopted the two-semester structure used on most college campuses throughout the country. The university offered three degrees (B.A., B.S., and B. Music) and majors in art, biology, chemistry, physics, business administration, English, education, home economics, history and political science, journalism, mathematics, music, voice, violin, band, physical education, psychology, religion, sociology, and speech. Graduation requirements included a major (thirty hours), one long minor (eighteen hours) or two short minors (twelve hours each), and sufficient electives to total 125 semester hours.[55]

Trinity's curricular program diversified and expanded under the leadership of Schwab, Childs's successor. A Nebraska native, Schwab received much of his early education in Illinois, graduating from North Central College and the Evangelical Theological Seminary. After graduate work at the University of Chicago and Northwestern University, Schwab received a Ph.D. in church history from Yale University in 1928. Awarded a Sterling Fellowship for study abroad in Germany, Switzerland, and France on completion of his degree requirements, he came to Trinity in 1928 as professor of religious education. Students and peers recognized Schwab as an outstanding classroom teacher who encouraged critical thinking and as a dean who handled student problems with authority and understanding.[56]

Despite his reputation for academic rigor, Schwab taught one of the most popular courses in the curriculum, The Bible as Literature, which attracted outstanding students from a variety of academic majors. Graduates remembered Schwab as "a good scholar and excellent teacher" who introduced students to a critical study of the Bible in interactive class sessions that incorporated discussions, lectures, and research projects. One student who later earned a Ph.D. in English from Cornell University ranked Schwab as one of her most stimulating professors, noting that his approach to learning helped broaden her intellectual and religious perspectives. At the end of her own career, she still remembered the text of one of Schwab's chapel talks, "If you have two loaves of bread, sell one and buy white hyacinths to feed your soul."[57]

Shortly after becoming dean, Schwab initiated semimonthly faculty meetings devoted to the discussion of important educational topics. Paired off in teams of two, faculty members assigned readings and led discussions on current issues in their particular teaching fields, such as "New Developments in College Curricula," "Improving the Reading and Study Habits of Students," "Learning from Lectures and Readings," "Professional Ethics," and "Orientation Versus Freshman Week." In addition, Schwab required instructors to make weekly reports on students who were doing unsatisfactory work "or otherwise in need of admonition" and to submit self-evaluations of their classroom teaching and research activities at the end of each semester.[58]

The Trinity faculty formed a cohesive group of scholars and teachers committed to the university and to one another during a period of economic adversity and social stress. The thirty faculty members shared common goals and simple pleasures. During the academic year faculty gathered socially at a series of dinners, picnics, and concerts. One year they held "an old-fashioned social" in the music hall that featured a one-act play by selected faculty performers, a George Washington's Day banquet with musical entertainment, and a picnic in Getzendaner Park with recreational activities such as baseball and tennis. Faculty minutes note that expenses for these events were to be borne "by special assessment upon each member for each event."[59]

Throughout the Waxahachie era, Trinity faculty developed programs that involved student participation and interaction with the local community. Samuel Hornbeak's sociology class gathered data in African-American neighborhoods about living conditions, economic levels, and religious practices. As a result of these surveys, the sociology club, with Hornbeak's approval, invited an African-American clergyman to speak at one of the YMCA-sponsored student chapel programs. School officials became concerned that some townspeople or students might be offended by the appearance of a "colored man" at a Trinity chapel service, but the speaker was well received with no complaints from Waxahachie residents or the student body.[60]

In 1923 the biology department conducted a survey of homes in Waxahachie regarding mosquito infestation. In teams of two, students instructed homeowners on removing possible breeding places and received a letter of commendation from the State Board of Health for participating in the program.[61] In 1938, the home economics department sponsored a three-hour "play school" under the supervision of college students and faculty members to help preschool children develop social skills."[62]

When war began in Europe in 1939, Trinity established a flying school under the supervision of the Civil Aeronautics Authority that operated out of a nearby airport. Initially ten students qualified for enrollment, including Dorothy McDonald, who received special attention in the local press for entering and completing the demanding ground and flying courses. The class celebrated when she completed her solo flight, the last of the group to do so. By 1941 Trinity had two certified ground school instructors and twenty-five graduates engaged in some type of flying career.[63]

The faculty designed programs to assess the quality of new students and prepare them for life after graduation. In 1935 Trinity introduced an orientation week for incoming students that emphasized academic preparation rather than social events and hazing. For the first time, entering students were given standard I.Q. tests and aptitude examinations in English grammar, reading, and vocabulary, and a special laboratory section, taught by a member of the English department, provided assistance for students who scored low.[64] One of Trinity's more interesting matriculates during this era was Sue Allyn Stripling, who graduated from high school in 1937 at age eleven and entered Trinity in the fall of that year. Believed to be the youngest high school graduate in the United States at the time, she was at the top of her first-year Trinity class in aptitude and psychological tests and in academic performance. A gifted dramatic artist and poet, Stripling attended Trinity for two years and later graduated from Texas Christian University.[65]

Trinity Flying School, 1940.
Dorothy McDonald was the first woman to complete training.

Trinity faculty instituted a program in 1940 to improve the language skills of upper-division students. A representative faculty committee on English standards prepared a list of the most frequently misspelled words and directed department chairs to include an additional 100 words. The chairs distributed the lists among their majors to learn the spelling and meaning of each word. During January all upper-division students took a spelling test and wrote a 30-word impromptu essay that was graded by an English standards committee. Department chairs tutored majors who performed poorly and gave them an opportunity to retake the test.[66]

The faculty also provided vocational guidance for Trinity students preparing to enter graduate school or the work force. According to a study conducted in 1934, approximately 25 percent of Trinity graduates sought advanced degrees.[67] In 1939 the university instituted a "Vocational Counseling and Personnel Advisory Program" that brought guest speakers from a variety of professions to campus for public lectures and individual counseling sessions.[68]

Along with these new programs, Trinity faculty periodically reevaluated the university's mandatory chapel requirement. Students with unexcused absences lost academic quality points, and, in extreme cases, were suspended or expelled. Many students fulfilled the requirement with resignation and resentment, often displaying disinterest and boredom during the services. As one student expressed it, chapel speakers are "usually an unpleasant necessity to the college students. They usually have nothing to say and take up twenty or thirty minutes of allotted time telling of it in their most stilted and bore some [sic] manner."[69]

By the 1930s, faculty had reduced required chapel services to three days a week. On Fridays, unattended by faculty, student organizations were in charge of services that usually had little or no religious content. Even this arrangement, however, failed to satisfy the majority of students, who deemed the concept of required chapel to be anachronistic and detrimental to the cultivation of personal piety.[70]

The faculty always conducted discussions about chapel with an eye to the university's relationship to the Synod of Texas. Although revised denominational guidelines for colleges and universities did not refer to required chapel, most Texas Presbyterians viewed the practice as an important symbol of Trinity's religious heritage. After considerable debate, the faculty voted in 1937 to drop required chapel and hold one voluntary weekly religious service presided over by a faculty member. In taking the action, however, faculty members warned students that a general attendance count would be taken and that the program would be periodically reevaluated for its effectiveness.[71]

Although students applauded the decision as an indication of institutional maturity, they were not inclined to attend chapel even on a voluntary basis. Apparently the same was true for some faculty members, whom Schwab periodically reminded to set an example by being regular in their own chapel attendance. In 1939 Schwab informed students of the reinstatement of compulsory chapel, citing lack of attendance, confusion in the halls during chapel period, and "taking excess advantage of the voluntary privilege given [you] this year."[72]

As university president, Wear had little time to devote to curricular issues or student concerns regarding chapel and social activities. He traveled extensively to solicit endowment funds and operating income, visiting presbyteries, churches, and individuals throughout the southwest. The pace affected his health, and physicians advised Wear to reduce his travel and speaking engagements. Pushing aside these concerns, Wear achieved some success but could not surmount the economic malaise that gripped the university. Trinity managed to keep its doors open only by taking repeated appropriations from its shrinking endowment corpus. Enrollment, after rising briefly during the 1938–39 academic year to 444, steadily declined, and by the spring of 1942, only 167 students were taking classes on the Waxahachie campus.[73]

Even to the most sanguine observers, Trinity's future in Waxahachie looked bleak. In 1939, the Synod of Texas appointed a commission "for the purpose of making an extensive survey of the service, needs, and possibilities of Trinity University." The commission's assignment also was to discover "the measures and means of advancing and maintaining our beloved university," a task that members knew would require considerable ingenuity and good fortune.[74]

In their search for a solution to Trinity's economic problems, commission members turned to Austin College, a peer institution in Sherman, Texas. Founded in 1849 at Huntsville, Texas, Austin College relocated to Sherman in 1876, a move prompted largely by economic necessity.[75] Trinity University and Austin College both had Presbyterian roots but were affiliated with different denominations, Trinity with the Synod of Texas of the PCUSA ("northern"), and Austin College with the Synod of Texas of the PCUS ("southern"). Both denominations shared common historical roots but were separated by lingering theological and regional differences dating back to the Civil War. These attitudes, unarticulated in official documents but commonly discussed in private, formed an undercurrent of mutual mistrust that complicated the complex merger negotiations.[76]

In the midst of a financial crisis of similar proportions to Trinity's, Austin College officials expressed a willingness to explore a united institution either in Waxahachie or Sherman or at another site in the state. In 1940 the PCUS and PCUSA synods authorized the commencement of discussions regarding a possible merger of the two institutions. Administrators from both Trinity University and Austin College, however, advised constituents that each school would continue to function should the talks fail.[77]

When word of these discussions reached campus, Wear reiterated that the talks were informal and had no binding effect on university or synod officials. Speaking to an attentive chapel audience in October 1940, Wear emphasized that the merger proposal was "in principle only" and "was nothing to get excited about." Even if it did take place, the president said, it would not affect the academic careers of any current students, but would enlarge the resources and financial conditions of the institution in a dramatic fashion.[78]

During 1940 and 1941, representatives of each institution's boards of trustees explored merger conditions that would be mutually acceptable. At a meeting in Dallas on 30 September 1941, the joint committee issued a statement favoring a union of Trinity University and Austin College "at the very earliest possible date." The committee proposed to form a college of 600 to 1,000 students, "capable of developing safely, sanely, and soundly as needs may arise and means may be supplied." Because they were not legally empowered to make commitments to communities interested in hosting the merged institution, committee members recommended the appointment of a joint committee of ten persons, five from each synod, who would function as trustees to implement the merger and select a location.[79]

At their meetings in October 1941, both synods approved the formation of a joint committee to complete negotiations and select a site for the new institution. Before doing so, however, the PCUS synod commissioners debated the merger, emphasizing what they termed "the spiritual, moral, social, class-room and campus effects involved." Some suggested that Austin College's spiritual atmosphere would be lowered if it left the community of Sherman and merged with Trinity University. Others resisted breaking ties with their alma mater that reached back before the Civil War.[80] Meeting in San Antonio, the PCUSA synod was more receptive to merger than its southern counterpart. Almost unanimously, the commissioners approved a resolution to combine Austin College and Trinity University "unless insurmountable obstacles prevent."[81]

At various times during merger discussions, representatives from Waxahachie, Sherman, Tyler, Corpus Christi, San Antonio, and Houston expressed interest in hosting a consolidated institution. Presidents Frank Wear and Everett Tucker favored San Antonio as the most advantageous location for the new entity, but sensed a lack of enthusiasm for the project among the city's civic leaders. Working through a San Antonio clergyman, Arthur V. Boand, Tucker and Wear attempted to discern the community's interest. Boand's contacts with the San Antonio Chamber of Commerce responded positively, assuring him that adequate support could be enlisted for a new institution of higher learning in the Alamo City.[82]

In the meantime, Boand, Tucker, and Wear contacted Will W. Jackson, president of the University of San Antonio, a Methodist college facing financial problems similar to those of Trinity and Austin College. Founded as Westmoreland College, a two-year women's school in 1918, the institution became coeducational in 1932. Four years later, it changed its name to the University of San Antonio and began issuing baccalaureate degrees as a four-year institution. Jackson suggested that they consolidate all three institutions and indicated that the Southwest Conference of the Methodist Church might give the campus, buildings, library, endowment, and goodwill of the University of San Antonio to the merged institution. Ecumenical in outlook, Methodist leaders surmised that Presbyterians, with substantial state and national connections, might muster sufficient financial resources to succeed.[83]

At the request of David Powell, president of the San Antonio Chamber of Commerce, Boand addressed the chamber's board of directors on 28 January 1941, regarding the proposed relocation of Trinity and Austin College. Noting that San Antonio had three Catholic colleges (St. Mary's University, Incarnate Word College, and Our Lady of the Lake University) and that Methodist leaders were willing to turn over the assets of The University of San Antonio to the new school, Boand predicted that this would be San Antonio's chance to obtain a strong Protestant university supported by three major denominations. Responding to Boand's speech, Powell appointed a committee, chaired by Cecil W. Miller, a local Sears and Roebuck executive, and including Boand and James H. Calvert, president of the local Joske Brothers department store, to investigate the proposition and report back to the board of directors.[84]

Between February and October, Miller and his committee received favorable responses from prospective donors to support the new institution in San Antonio.[85] After the two synods met in October 1941 to approve in principle the merger of Austin College and Trinity University, the San Antonio Chamber of Commerce reaffirmed its interest in locating the school in San Antonio.[86] Receiving word on 25 November 1941, that San Antonio was the official choice of the joint synod committee, the new president of the San Antonio Chamber of Commerce, Calvert, called a special meeting of the board of directors for Monday, 8 December 1941, at noon. As the directors gathered at the Gunter Hotel, President Roosevelt was addressing Congress, calling for a declaration of war against the Empire of Japan because of its surprise attack on Pearl Harbor the previous day.[87]

Faced with this new set of political, social, and economic conditions, members of the chamber debated the wisdom of entering negotiations to bring the new university to San Antonio, but a majority favored moving ahead without reservations. Miller reported that the Presbyterian synods wanted the chamber to deliver one million dollars under the following conditions: The University of San Antonio, with all its assets, valued at $400,000; a five-year annuity of $25,000 per year, underwritten and guaranteed by the chamber; a campaign to secure funds to purchase or lease the so-called Wesleyan property adjacent to the University of San Antonio, valued at $475,000 and consisting of approximately twenty acres and two buildings; and options on other property contiguous to the University of

Advertisement, the *Mirage*, 1942

San Antonio campus to secure a total of at least 150 acres. The chamber approved the report and its recommendations, paving the way for the move to San Antonio.[88]

Meeting the next day, a majority of the joint synod committee, including all of the PCUSA representatives, voted six to four to proceed and accepted the San Antonio proposal, "with qualifications making it immediately effective except as to campaigns in San Antonio and in the synods for enlarged funds." The minority, all members of the PCUS, refused to accept the majority decision, insisting on an extended delay due to uncertain wartime conditions.[89] Fearing that the merger could not be effected without unanimous support from both synods, the committee subsequently supported a motion declaring the existence of an "insurmountable obstacle" that made implementation of the merger impossible at the present time.[90]

Although the two synods continued to discuss the possibility of a three-way-merger, the San Antonio Chamber of Commerce pursued conversations with representatives of Trinity University and the University of San Antonio. The chamber offered a package of land and cash that amounted to $575,000 with the understanding that Trinity or the Synod of Texas would raise an additional $20,000 a year to supplement Trinity's current annual income of approximately $30,000. Assured that the Methodist Church would turn over the University of San Antonio campus and adjoining Wesleyan Institute property to the Presbyterians when the merger of the University of San Antonio and Trinity was finalized, the PCUSA Synod of Texas accepted the offer at a called meeting on 25 February 1942, in Temple, Texas. The synod also directed the board of trustees to dispose of the Waxahachie property and transfer records, monies, and movable assets to San Antonio at the conclusion of the academic year.[91]

Deeming the completion of the university project "a major accomplishment," San Antonio Chamber of Commerce President Calvert welcomed the school "as a splendid addition to the community's institutions and cultural life."[92] Citing the Chamber's tireless efforts "against formidable competition" to bring Trinity to the Alamo City, an editorial in the *San Antonio Express* claimed that the new university was the city's most important acquisition since Randolph Field. In anticipation of the material, civic, social, and cultural benefits that would result from Trinity's presence, the editorial concluded, "Certainly it will become a force for building a greater San Antonio."[93]

Shortly after its last commencement exercises for thirty-eight graduates in Waxahachie on 1 June 1942, members of the Trinity faculty and staff prepared for the transfer to San Antonio. A half-million pounds of classroom and office furniture, laboratory and recreational equipment, library books, current and archival records, and anything else of value were transported on more than thirty train cars to the Woodlawn campus. After a third of a century in Tehuacana and forty years in Waxahachie, Trinity University moved to San Antonio, a city where it planned to establish permanent foundations.[94]

PART THREE

SAN ANTONIO

For two centuries San Antonio has been a center of historical
interest. The missions, which served in part as schools for
Indians, were begun in the seventeenth century by Franciscan
monks and were sponsored by the King of Spain. The Cathedral
of San Fernando lies in the heart of the city. Here, also, is the
far-famed and revered Alamo, Cradle of Texas Liberty. San
Antonio is the hub of an enormous agricultural, industrial, and
fruit and vegetable raising territory consisting of approximately
fifty Texas counties. Railroad lines reaching directly two-fifths
of the population of the United States serve the city.

Trinity University Catalogue, 1943–1944

CHAPTER SEVEN

HOUR OF REBIRTH

An increment of power has come with the realization of this, Trinity's great hour of rebirth. . . . We have a greatly improved outlook, but we have just begun to work. We are now committed to a great enterprise which will require that we be all at it, altogether at it, for the glory of God and the service of youth.

TRUSTEE JASPER MANTON, OCTOBER 1942

A COSMOPOLITAN CITY OF 300,000 IN 1942, San Antonio bore little resemblance to the agricultural-based county seat of Waxahachie. With diversified commercial interests, excellent transportation facilities, and a dominant military presence, San Antonio would almost double in size before the end of the decade. Founded by Franciscan monks in 1718, the city represented a blend of Hispanic, German, and southern Anglo-American cultures that made it distinctive among southwestern municipalities. At Mission San Antonio de Valero, commonly known as the Alamo, defenders fought to gain autonomy from Mexican hegemony, an encounter that resulted in the establishment of the Republic of Texas and later statehood. In San Antonio, Trinity University moved away from its roots of rural and small-town Presbyterianism and from many of the families who had supported the institution for seventy-five years.[1]

The sixty-acre Woodlawn campus consisted of a four-story administration and classroom building, a women's dormitory (Mary Catherine Hall), and two buildings on long-term lease from the adjoining Wesleyan Institute property, Onderdonk Science Hall and McFarlin Hall, a men's dormitory. As enrollment increased, portable buildings obtained from nearby military bases provided temporary facilities. Two of these situated near the science building held chemistry laboratories, three close to the main building served as offices for student publications and the veterans' guidance center, and a large Quonset hut housed the library. There also was a large frame gymnasium and five apartment buildings for returning veterans.[2]

Aerial view of Woodlawn campus, c. 1945.
None of these buildings is standing today.

Trinity's newly constituted board of trustees had little time to savor the move to San Antonio. Their agenda included securing a new president, combining the Trinity and University of San Antonio faculties and staffs, deciding on the location of a permanent campus, and regaining accreditation with the Southern Association. Beyond these issues, the board needed to nurture its relationship with the Synod of Texas, which had become strained over the decision to leave Waxahachie, if church ties were to be maintained.

The trustees first had to appoint a new president. During the negotiations between Austin College and Trinity, both Tucker of Austin College and Wear of Trinity said that they would not be candidates for the presidency of the merged San Antonio institution. When talks collapsed, Wear told Trinity trustees that he would not continue as chief executive, citing health factors and a desire that Trinity begin with new leadership in the new location.[3] Desiring someone with extensive academic and fund-raising experience as well as denominational recognition, the trustees turned for counsel to the Board of Christian Education in Philadelphia. Board executives recommended Monroe G. Everett, a PCUSA minister who was then a campus minister at Drexel Institute and the University of Pennsylvania in Philadelphia, for the Westminster Foundation.

Everett's background, educational experience, and professional credentials indicated a match with the trustees' desires. A Tennessee native with a Cumberland Presbyterian background, Everett attended Bethel College, receiving a B.S. degree in 1908. Following additional degrees from Whitworth College in Washington State and McCormick Theological Seminary in Chicago, Everett was ordained to the ministry in 1915. After serving pastorates in Washington and Oregon from 1917 to 1922, Everett focused on campus Presbyterian student ministries and university fund-raising activities as director of Westminster Foundation for Oregon (1922–1931) and for Philadelphia (1931–1942). During the decade in Philadelphia, he became a familiar figure to Board of Christian Education officials and broadened his knowledge of colleges and universities affiliated with the PCUSA.[4]

At the invitation of the trustees' search committee, Everett came to San Antonio in June 1942 to preach in Madison Square Presbyterian Church and to meet privately with committee members. After interviewing him on leadership style and goals for the university, the committee offered fifty-seven-year-old Everett the presidential position at a salary of $6,000 and with contributions to his Presbyterian Ministers' Pension Fund. In accepting the presidency, Everett indicated that he intended to retire at age sixty-five unless conditions warranted an extension beyond that date.[5]

Even as Trinity was settling into the new campus, some leading members of the PCUS Synod of Texas, including President Tucker of Austin College, sought to renew merger negotiations. On the initiative of the PCUS Synod of Texas, discussions between representatives of Trinity University and Austin College resumed in December 1942. Although Trinity officials were less enthusiastic than they had been previously, they agreed to the merger on the condition that the university remain in San Antonio and be jointly owned and controlled by the two synods. Austin College's endowment and equipment would become part of the merged institution, and the Sherman faculty and administration would be incorporated into the staff so far as possible. If approved by both synods, the merger could become effective as early as September 1943.[6]

A week after negotiations concluded in January 1943, PCUS synod commissioners met to consider the proposed merger. After extended discussion, a vote resulted in a sixty-seven to sixty-seven tie. The synod parliamentarian ruled the vote invalid, however, because the moderator, who was not supposed to vote except in the case of a tie, apparently had participated in the ballot. Results of a second ballot, with additional commissioners present, was sixty-nine to sixty-seven against the merger. By that narrow margin, Austin College loyalists preserved the school's continued existence in Sherman and brought to a close the possibility of a united Presbyterian college in Texas.[7]

During Trinity's first academic year in San Antonio, Everett met with campus personnel and prioritized what seemed to be the pressing issues. Working closely with former University of San Antonio president Will W. Jackson, who served as vice president and director of public relations, the new president began to blend the two institutions. He and others recognized that both Methodists and Presbyterians among the faculty and students regretted relinquishing certain traditions and found it difficult to create new ones. In particular, the former students of the University of San Antonio, returning to their old campus, encountered new administrators, faculty, and students and felt sometimes that Trinity students from Waxahachie, though small in numbers, constituted a favored group.[8]

During the early months of the first semester, the combined faculty established new rules and regulations for academic and social life. One of the first items addressed was dancing, an issue that had been widely contested on the Waxahachie campus. The faculty approved the installation of a juke box in the coffee shop and dancing from eleven in the morning to two in the afternoon. To attend off-campus dances, however, female students were required to file written parental permission with the dean of the university. Smoking was restricted to dormitory rooms and the coffee shop, but an effective mechanism for enforcement eluded the administration. A majority of the faculty voted to retain mandatory chapel attendance, at least for the immediate future. They also specified that no campus events other than religious-oriented meetings or services could be held on Sunday.[9]

Under the direction of the dean, Paul Schwab, the faculty worked out a basic curriculum and other academic regulations. Requirements for all degrees included twelve hours of English, eight hours of laboratory science, six hours each of social science, Bible, and physical education, and three hours of psychology or philosophy. Candidates for the bachelor of arts and bachelor of science degrees also took twelve hours of a foreign language as well as other major and minor departmental requirements. A

Students at juke box in campus lounge

strict attendance policy specified one semester hour of negative credit for the first seven unexcused absences and one semester hour of negative credit for each additional two absences. Overarching academic considerations, Schwab reminded faculty that they were expected "to give wholehearted support to the Christian way of life" as reflected in "regular chapel attendance, general classroom attitude, and all relations to students."[10]

Despite initial difficulties, students and faculty attempted to create a campus community. Shortly after the first semester in San Antonio began, university officials declared a partial holiday designated "Clean Up Day" when faculty, staff, and students donned work clothes to wash windows, mop and sweep floors, and do landscaping. Later, male students volunteered to paint rooms and furniture in the men's dormitory, and town students offered to furnish their own lounge furniture if university officials provided the space. Other such renovation and repair projects improved campus facilities and encouraged better relations among students and faculty.[11]

In a year-end report to trustees in May 1943, Everett indicated that although the process of integrating the two institutions was filled with "acute and, at times, trying problems," students and faculty had cooperated remarkably well. Civic response to Trinity had been extremely positive, especially from the chamber of commerce and church groups, including the "kindly reception of our Catholic friends." Enrollment reached 456 for the 1942–43 academic year, including summer school, a 60 percent increase over the first term of the previous year and the largest increase reported by any college in the state.[12]

On the negative side, Trinity ended the year with a budget deficit, principally because of maintenance, and with much more yet to be done. Equipment and laboratory space were scarce and could not support disciplines such as geology, petroleum engineering, and home economics. The library collection, decentralized in several buildings, continued to utilize both catalogs of the merged institutions. The approximately 75 percent of the student body who were nonresidential needed a place where they could congregate and study, and as for recreational facilities, Everett summarized, "We have no gymnasium, no useable tennis courts, no swimming pool, and no athletic field."[13]

Everett neglected to report that the main administrative and classroom building had seriously deteriorated due to an extended period of deferred maintenance and needed major structural repairs. According to Bruce Thomas, the building quivered and shook when classes changed and students moved in large numbers through the halls. Music professor Albert Herff-Beze recalled that a grand piano once crashed from the fourth floor to the third. "What was that?" a professor exclaimed. "B-flat, I think," came a student's reply."[14]

Campus activities between 1942 and 1945 reflected wartime conditions in the United States. Male intercollegiate sports were limited, so students relied on intramural activities for recreation. Because San Antonio was a major military center, students and faculty hosted social events for local servicemen and rendered service to the Red Cross and U.S.O. In October 1943 the Spurs, a women's social organization, sponsored a dance for officers at Randolph Field and later presented a two-act musical show to soldiers in Brooke General Hospital.[15] Many students and faculty maintained contact with former classmates in the armed forces by means of a weekly column in the *Trinitonian* entitled "Uncle Sammy's Trinitonians." Readers were encouraged to donate blood, write letters, and serve as volunteers in local U.S.O canteens.[16]

During the course of World War II, more than thirty Trinitonians died

Captain Henry T. Waskow

serving their country. One casualty, Captain Henry T. Waskow, a native of Belton, Texas, and graduate of the class of 1939, received national recognition for his heroism. Waskow was a company commander in the 36th Division that fought in North Africa and participated in the invasion of Italy. Articles by noted war correspondent Ernie Pyle describing Waskow's character and courage appeared in *Reader's Digest* and *Time Magazine* and led to the production of the highly acclaimed movie *The Story of G. I. Joe,* directed by William Wellman in 1945. Robert Mitchum played the part of Waskow (who is called Bill Walker in the movie), a role that earned him an Oscar nomination for Best Supporting Actor and paved the way for future stardom.[17]

"In this war I have known a lot of officers who were loved and respected by the soldiers under them. But never have I crossed the trail of any man as beloved as Captain Henry T. Waskow of Belton, Texas. Captain Waskow was a company commander in the 36th Division. He was young, in his middle 20's, but he carried in him a sincerity and gentleness that made people want to be guided by him."

Ernie Pyle, "Captain Waskow's Men Say Good-Bye,"
Reader's Digest (March 1944)

Lacking facilities and hampered by wartime restrictions, Trinity students had limited social activities. One of the first all-campus social events was the "Jig-Jamboree," an evening of dancing, games, and refreshments sponsored by the Heels, a new campus organization dedicated "to sublimate the spirit on the Trinity campus."[18] Another typical program, the "Harvest Festival, Hayseed Carnival, and All College Game Party," brought students and faculty together for bridge, bingo, dominoes, checkers, and athletic games. Musical performances and a white elephant sale raised money for the publication of the *Mirage*, the student yearbook.[19]

Despite such efforts, campus leaders reported difficulties in attracting students to community events. A campus survey revealed that less than half of the student body was involved with any campus organization.[20] The nonresidential students were not inclined to participate in campus social life. Referring to the town students, an editorial in the *Trinitonian* commented, "It is they who evidently look upon the school merely as a cafeteria for education—one may pass by, choose his menus, and depart to assimilate his solitary meal."[21]

Commencement in 1945 marked the last class of students who began their college careers either at the University of San Antonio or on Trinity's Waxahachie campus. The class of 1946, having entered as first-year students on the new campus, had four full years to establish its own traditions. Their commencement experience became unique in the annals of both Trinity University and the University of San Antonio when an outbreak of polio in San Antonio prompted the City Health Department to shut down all educational facilities for two weeks just as final examinations were scheduled to begin. As a result, the faculty exempted all fifty-four seniors from final examinations and granted their degrees in absentia. Underclass students, however, received study guides for the completion of courses and reviews for final examinations by mail and returned after the quarantine to finish the semester.[22]

As the war ended, Trinity officials anticipated an influx of both returning veterans and civilians entering college. The Veterans Administration selected Trinity as a counseling center for discharged veterans, and members of the education and psychology departments assisted the government employees in setting up campus operations. Professor Dale N. Morrison became the coordinator of veterans' work at Trinity as servicemen began to return to campus. By September 1945, enrollment climbed to 814, and by the end of the school year, it had reached a total of 1,525. After the initial years of transition, Trinity now faced a period of unprecedented growth and expansion.[23]

Trinity library housed in army Quonset hut

Trinity had lost its probationary accreditation status in 1942 when it merged with the University of San Antonio, which was not a member of the Southern Association. Attaining full accreditation was crucial to securing Trinity's future in San Antonio. Without the certification, Trinity could not compete with peer institutions for quality students or attract the financial support necessary to complete the relocation process. The university realized, however, that despite the combined resources, Trinity showed deficiencies in endowment, library facilities, and faculty salaries just as it had in the past.[24]

Schwab bore the responsibility of keeping the lines of communication open with Southern Association officials. Even though Trinity was not a member, Schwab attended annual association meetings, maintained a steady correspondence with committee members, and kept them informed of Trinity's progress toward readmission. By 1946 a freestanding library of 30,000 books was in place in an army Quonset hut, which was sufficient for association standards. Faculty salaries, ranging from $1,800 to $2,400 for instructors and $3,500 to $4,000 for professors, while low in comparison with peer institutions, now met minimal association standards. The endowment remained under a million dollars, but Trinity's annual income from endowment interest, tuition, and gifts of approximately $800,000, with a major financial campaign underway, indicated progress toward fiscal stability.[25]

In February 1947, Trinity regained full membership in the Southern Association of Colleges and Secondary Schools. In granting reaccreditation, association officials advised the university that it must continue improving academically and financially in order to avoid future probationary status. The trustees would be expected to address continuing issues, such as faculty tenure and retirement programs, which Trinity had not done previously.[26]

Within a few hours of receiving assurance that Trinity would be readmitted to membership in the Southern Association, Schwab resigned as dean of the university. He had previously given notice to Everett of his desire to concentrate on teaching and research either at Trinity or a denominational seminary. Everett reluctantly accepted the resignation with thanks for Schwab's academic leadership during a difficult thirteen-year period that included the Depression years, the move to San Antonio, and the merging of two institutions' traditions.[27]

In quest of a dean, Everett contacted members of the Presbyterian Board of Christian Education and officials of the Southern Association for possible candidates. He indicated, "There would be some preference given to men of equal ability to the one who is a member of the Presbyterian Church, although that would not be a deciding point."[28] Sifting through a number of candidates, Everett settled on Marion Bruce Thomas, dean of Brenau College in Gainesville, Georgia, a candidate who came highly recommended by M. C. Huntley, executive secretary of the Southern Association. An Alabama native, thirty-six-year-old Thomas held a baccalaureate and master's degree in English from the University of North Carolina in Chapel Hill and a Ph.D. from Vanderbilt University. From 1939 Thomas taught in the English department at Brenau, leaving in 1942 to serve as field director for the Red Cross in the South Pacific during World War II. Returning to Brenau, he served as academic dean for two years before coming to Trinity in 1947. With the exception of one year (1957–58) when he was a staff member of the Texas Commission of Higher Education, Thomas spent the rest of his academic career at Trinity.[29]

During the same year, Everett created a new position, public relations officer, and appointed Leon M. "Tex" Taylor, who was employed by a large firm in Des Moines, Iowa. Taylor, from Tennessee, had extensive experience in the field of public relations and came highly recommended as "a publicity genius" by Trinity football coach Bob Coe, who had known Taylor when he served as public relations officer at Hondo Air Field during World War II. Taylor's career at Trinity spanned more than four decades, a period in which he influenced the institutional image, fund-raising strategies, and intercollegiate athletic programs.[30]

During the transitional years in San Antonio, the university engaged in recruiting and retaining competent faculty members. Only a few professors made the move from Waxahachie to San Antonio, but faculty from the University of San Antonio brought strength and diversity to the newly combined faculty. Some served for decades with distinction, including Albert Herff-Beze, music history and music appreciation, William and Ina Beth McGavock, chemistry and English, Frances Kellam Hendricks, history, and Felix Ullrich, education. In 1942 each of the thirty-one faculty members held a master's degree, but only a few held doctorates. Four years later, eleven of sixty-seven faculty members held a Ph.D.[31]

To meet curricular demands, Everett and Schwab engaged instructors who would not have been employed on the Waxahachie campus. This was especially true in the case of part-time faculty, some of whom were Roman Catholics or members of the Jewish faith. Job seekers who appeared on campus were often hired on the spot. Marion Stiles, chair of the English Department during the 1940s, related how an ex-serviceman with a master's degree in English approached her after class one day seeking employment. She took him immediately to Schwab, who found the applicant's academic credentials satisfactory but was concerned that he acknowledged being a social drinker. Schwab offered him a position if he promised not to drink alcoholic beverages while a member of the Trinity faculty, which he accepted. When he told Stiles about his bargain with Schwab, she offered a solution that enabled him to keep his promise and still drink socially on the weekends. She "fired" him every Friday and "rehired" him every Monday. The arrangement worked during his brief stay on the Trinity faculty.[32]

As enrollment swelled and campus facilities filled to capacity, Trinity opened a downtown division in September 1947 for part-time students who wanted late afternoon and evening classes. Housed in the old *San Antonio Express* building that had been offered rent-free by publisher Frank Huntress, the evening program rapidly expanded. Within two years, more than nine hundred students were enrolled in approximately eighty classes. Eighty percent of the students were twenty to thirty-nine years old, with most of the remainder being forty to sixty-nine years old. Because of space limitations, Trinity professors also taught extension courses at Lackland Air Force Base, Fort Sam Houston, Madison Square Presbyterian Church, and a local high school. While these arrangements lasted only a few years, the downtown program continued until 1955, when the evening courses were moved to the main campus.[33]

In 1949 Trinity took steps to begin a limited graduate program by offering master's degrees in English, history, biology, sociology, and education. Surveys indicated a need for graduate studies in the San Antonio area, and Thomas assured trustees that Trinity had grown sufficiently in library holdings and faculty strength to warrant entry into new academic areas. Although graduate work would require even more library growth and expansion, Thomas estimated that by June 1950 Trinity could have a graduate program in place.[34]

Under the direction of Jacob Uhrich, professor of biology, Trinity offered its first graduate classes in San Antonio during the summer session of 1950. In addition to degree programs in five areas at the master's level, students could take courses in the departments of art, economics, mathematics, religion, and speech and drama. Within a year, more than five hundred students had commenced graduate studies at Trinity, and by May 1951, eight degrees had been awarded. Uhrich, who directed the program for the next decade, acknowledged that library and laboratory needs limited the number of graduate offerings.[35]

With curricular expansion, Trinity's intercollegiate athletics program, which had been dormant during the war years, received considerable attention on campus and in the local media. Some university officers felt that a successful football team and excellence in other sports, such as basketball, baseball, and tennis, could be a powerful recruiting tool for new students and a bonding agent for alumni and former students. Many ex-students and denominational officials viewed the resumption of athletics as essential to the preservation of the "Trinity spirit."

J. Hoytt Boles, president of the Trinity Alumni Association and a field representative for the Synod of Texas, wrote President Everett on several occasions during 1946, urging him to resume intercollegiate athletics as soon as possible. Such action, Boles said, "is essential to salvaging any sense of unity, loyalty, and happiness in the present student body." He concluded with a plea for action: "Let's start on a small, safe scale and work toward the Southwest Conference, but LET'S START."[36] Impetus for an enlarged intercollegiate athletic program came from a number of other sources as well. Members of the San Antonio Chamber of Commerce viewed the entrance of Trinity into the athletic scene as a stepping-stone into the NCAA Division I Southwest Conference and a status symbol for the San Antonio business community.

Everett was hesitant to undertake an ambitious athletic program in the light of Trinity's limited financial resources and while embarking on a major building program. In a letter to board of trustees Chairman Rasmus Thomsen, he reported pressure from students to commence intercollegiate football activities. "When I ask students where are we going to get the money for 25 or 30 scholarships, they reply, 'Why not take some of the money from the new campus buildings?'" From Everett's perspective, the most difficult students were those from Waxahachie, "who keep harkening back to the good old days when Trinity was a college with spirit."[37]

Although deciding against intercollegiate athletics, in 1946 the trustees hired Bob Coe, an experienced coach, to field a team of volunteer players to compete with local military service gridiron teams. In its opening game in Alamo Stadium, Trinity beat the San Marcos Army Air Field Mustangs 92–0. With a squad of forty men, Trinity won six games and lost two during its first football season since 1941.[38] Taking the case further, the board's Athletics Committee chairman, T. Frank Murchison, an oil magnate and prominent university benefactor, launched the modern era of Trinity football by announcing plans to secure funding for forty-five athletic scholarships for students possessing superior athletic skills. Murchison provided the first contribution for the athletic program and assured trustees that a winning team would attract sufficient local interest to make the venture profitable.[39]

Trinity's football program generated problems relating to finances, recruitment, and scheduling that plagued the university for more than a decade. Before Trinity even fielded an intercollegiate team in 1947, Coe faced accusations of recruitment irregularities that caused its first scheduled opponent, Texas Agricultural and Industrial University (Texas A&I) in Kingsville, to cancel the game. This triggered an investigation by the Lone Star Conference, of which Trinity was a member, and evoked negative comments from Rice University coach Jess Neely, who claimed that Trinity representatives had contacted Rice athletes to attract them to the San Antonio team.[40]

Trinity nevertheless returned to intercollegiate football competition on 20 September 1947, when they were defeated 39–0 by the Hardin-Simmons University Cowboys in Alamo Stadium before a crowd of 15,000. Following a second loss, assistant coach Jack Sanders replaced Coe. After a losing season, the Lone Star Conference put Trinity on probation, citing recruiting irregularities and a lack of faculty oversight of the athletic program. A year later, Trinity withdrew from the Lone Star Conference and, with North Texas State Teachers College, Hardin College (later Midwestern State University), and the University of Houston, established the Gulf Coast Conference. Sanders resigned, and in 1948 Bill James, former line coach at Texas A&M, came to Trinity as both football coach and athletic director.[41] Echoing widely held sentiments among Trinity supporters, James affirmed his intention to upgrade Trinity's performance to merit a place in the Southwest Conference with such institutions as the University of Texas, Texas A&M University, Baylor University, Texas Christian University, and Rice University.[42]

Despite positive coverage from the San Antonio press, football failed to attract community support and received mixed reviews on the campus. Everett's public declaration that Trinity hoped to attain membership in the Southwest Conference evoked a rare student demonstration. Women climbed out of dormitory windows and joined other students marching through the neighborhood, carrying placards, and chanting, "We want good faculty, not a big football team."[43] On the other hand, editorials in the *Trinitonian* consistently endorsed an expanded athletic program and urged students to attend games and boost school spirit.

Football placed a heavy burden on Trinity's financial resources. Only substantial contributions from trustee Murchison enabled the institution to maintain the program on a year-to-year basis. Even with his support, however, Trinity failed to meet athletic expenses that exceeded $100,000 by the end of the decade. In 1950 the deficit for all sports during the fiscal year was $31,200, causing concern among some trustees and church officials about the "possible excessive emphasis being placed on athletic scholarships." When Murchison and Tex Taylor assured trustees that adequate financial support would be forthcoming, trustees decided to continue the quest for national recognition as an athletic power.[44]

Besides athletics, students formed organizations and adapted traditions to fit the new surroundings during the postwar years. With many older students on campus, for example, the hazing of freshmen underwent change. In 1945 school officials made hazing voluntary and forbade any rituals involving physical harassment or public intimidation.[45] As the veteran population dwindled toward the end of the decade, however, students called for the reinstatement of hazing, arguing that it boosted "school spirit." The administration submitted to the request, and, once again, there were flag-raising contests, bonfires, fights, country rides, and all-night escapades between first-year and upper-division students.[46]

Both older and younger students were involved in restructuring the student government. In April 1946, a new constitution gave students the right to review all cases of discipline and dismissal formerly handled solely by administrative groups. The new structure had three branches (a stu-

First-year students endure hazing by upper-class students

dent council of nine members, a legislative assembly, and a student court) and provided students with more of a voice in decisions that affected their campus life.[47] In 1949 the Trinity Student Council played a leading role in the formation of the Texas Inter-Collegiate Student Association and became an active participant in the organization's programs over the next several decades.[48]

Other organizations reflected the growing diversity of the Trinity campus. The International Relations Club met monthly to discuss current problems, such as France's postwar pattern, Latin America, and the Dumbarton Oaks Conference.[49] The Trinity University Latin American Club (TULAC), a service and social group for Hispanic students, first met in 1946. During its initial year of operation, the group held a reception for visiting officials from Mexico and sponsored a Pan American Ball honoring professors from the National University of Mexico.[50] Older male students formed the High Twelve Masonic Club, which consisted of master masons united for fellowship and the promotion of values associated with their organization.[51]

The postwar era also saw a resumption and expansion of speech, drama, and other programs that had been popular on both former campuses. The Trinity University Players, under the direction of professor Clayton McCarty, presented seasons of more than 150 public performances, including seven major productions. Twice a year the group performed a three-act play on a thousand-mile tour of southwestern cities.[52] In 1945 McCarty and professor Ralph Ewing of the music department launched a weekly variety program on radio station KABC, and the following year they introduced dramatic and musical programs on KYFM, the first FM station in San Antonio.[53] Under the direction of speech instructor Frances Richter (Swinny), the Trinity University Invitational Speech Festival for area high school students became an annual event at Trinity for many years.[54]

As in previous years, debate was a highly regarded campus organization. Given extensive coverage in student and local newspapers, the Trinity team, a member of the southwestern division of the national Pi Kappa Delta, participated in regional and national debates with consistent success. One of the outstanding debaters of the forties, John Silber (Class of '47) later attained national recognition as a philosophy professor, dean at the University of Texas in Austin, and president of Boston University.[55]

By the end of the decade, the new medium of television began to make an impact on the Trinity campus. In 1949, students and faculty participated in a series of half-hour variety programs on the local station, WOAI-TV. Featured on the first program were Professor Brownie McNeil, folklorist and guitarist; Professor Robert Winn and his marionettes; and the Trinity Trio, composed of Pat Evans and Nancy Findly of Fort Worth and Bonnie Schmick of San Antonio.[56] Two years later the Student Council installed a sixteen-inch black-and-white television set, equipped with a meter to play one hour for twenty-five cents, in the campus lounge on a trial basis. Students were asked not to adjust the set except to change channels. If problems occurred, users were directed to contact a member of the Student Council.[57]

Trinity students also expressed opinions regarding social and political problems. Although the civil rights movement did not gain momentum in Texas until the late 1950s, some students voiced opposition to racial segregation much earlier. They particularly criticized segregation on local public transportation. Because many students rode the bus to and from campus, they objected to the rear seats being marked and set aside for "colored people."[58] Responding to President Harry S. Truman's civil rights program, junior Bruce Faulkner wrote in the school newspaper in 1948 that "voicing opinion is very much avoided around these parts. Most of us are afraid everyone will start looking down his nose and calling us 'nig-

Dr. Mary Bethune visits Trinity campus. Left to right: President Monroe Everett, Bethune, Miss Artemesia Bowden, and sociology professor Dr. Charles Burrows

ger lovers' if we give voice to our ethical opinion." Referring to efforts to provide separate but equal higher education for African Americans as "BUNK," the writer urged students to write their congressmen in support of integration. "Let us be the ones to step up the progress towards the equality of man, no matter what his color, race, or creed."[59]

Other students supported Faulkner's stand but advocated a long-range program of change based on education rather than short-term tactics employing public demonstrations or force. While they deplored segregation as unfair and unproductive, they believed that coercion would heighten rather than diminish racial tensions in Texas. "The solution will not be found by agitation, war or devastation," one student averred, "but rather by a serene motivation, sincere thought, and education."[60]

The Trinity faculty provided forums in which the subject could be openly discussed on campus. In 1948 sociology instructor Mildred Rosenthal's class on race relations hosted fifteen African-American delegates from the local St. Phillip's Junior College to discuss interracial issues, civil rights, and the higher education of African Americans in Texas. Rosenthall called this experience one that reinforced "the bonds of human relationships."[61] On another occasion, Mary Bethune, a noted African-American educator, spoke to an overflow crowd in the university auditorium and urged people to "find the real meaning of the Constitution as it applies to every citizen." According to the *Trinitonian*, Bethune stated that she was depending on the audience "as whites to give equal opportunity to blacks."[62]

Other issues evoking editorial comment in the *Trinitonian* included support for the Marshall Plan, opposition to isolationism, concerns about the Soviet "Iron Curtain," and fears that opposition to communism might impinge on academic freedom.[63] One editorial protested the investigation of Clarence E. Ayres, professor of economics at the University of Texas at Austin, who was charged with advocating socialism and being an enemy of "free enterprise."[64] When the *Trinitonian* published the results of a student poll in 1951 indicating strong approval of President Truman's decision to remove General Douglas MacArthur from his command, reader response was divided and prolonged.[65]

Student religious life during the war years of the 1940s followed patterns from the Waxahachie campus. Compulsory chapel services held once a week in the university auditorium identified Trinity's religious affiliation with the Presbyterian Church. Spiritual Emphasis Week, featuring yearly special services and informal discussions conducted by prominent Presbyterian clergymen, continued. Established groups such as the YMCA, YWCA, and the Life Work Recruits promoted religious activities on campus and in the wider community. Although church attendance was not mandatory, resident students were expected to attend the church of their choice for both Sunday school and morning worship.[66]

During the postwar era, campus religious practices changed significantly. Compulsory chapel attendance ended in 1946, more for practical than philosophical considerations, because, with an enrollment approaching one thousand, Trinity had no meeting facility large enough. In any event, only about 150 to 200 students attended chapel, prompting frequent pleas in the *Trinitonian* from faculty and student leaders for support of the program.[67] To encourage attendance, the Student Religious Association in 1947 introduced a two-tiered chapel program that featured a traditional liturgy in the auditorium and an informal music-oriented service in the student lounge.[68] As a further inducement to participate in religious services, during the chapel hour all administrative and business offices closed, including the post office, coffee shop, practice rooms, and bookstore. Despite these measures, less than a third of Trinity students engaged in the weekly worship services.[69]

Responding to complaints from some students and faculty about diminishing religious interests among students, Trinity trustees, at the behest of Everett, in 1948 created the office of university chaplain. Such a position had not been considered in Tehuacana or Waxahachie, because the president, faculty who were ordained clergy, and other interested faculty and staff supervised campus religious life. In addition to administrative and counseling activities, the new chaplain would be expected to teach several undergraduate religion classes.[70]

On 29 September 1948, Carlton Allen, a Trinity alumnus and Princeton Seminary graduate who had served overseas as a military chaplain during World War II and as a missionary to India, became the first officially designated chaplain in the university's eighty-year history.[71] Possessing an engaging personality, interpersonal skills, and familiarity with university traditions, Allen utilized a variety of formats to increase student involvement and significantly improved attendance at the weekly gatherings. Beginning in 1949, Trinity chapel programs became available to a wider audience through weekly broadcasts on local radio station KYFM.[72] The Life Work Recruits of the Waxahachie days became the Christian Service Fellowship and grew from only a few members in 1948 to almost one hundred in 1949. The YMCA and YWCA were combined into the Student Christian Association for students who wanted to be involved in campus religious work but were not contemplating full-time church vocations. In 1950 Allen organized the Committee on Religious Life and Work, composed of faculty, staff, and students, to coordinate and support all campus religious activities. Even though many Trinity students remained aloof from organized religious activities, the general consensus was that Allen's ministry had made a significant impact on campus life.[73]

Although Trinity retained its ties with the Synod of Texas after the move to San Antonio, relationships between the two bodies became increasingly ambivalent, especially after World War II when the university grew rapidly in size and diversity. Some synod leaders thought that Trinity was losing the religious ethos that had characterized campus life in Tehuacana and Waxahachie. Board of trustees Chairman Thomsen confided to Everett that there was a "whispering campaign" circulating around the synod that Trinity had lost its sense of direction and was more interested in raising tuition than in cultivating piety. Allegations surfaced that Presbyterians were underrepresented on the faculty and staff and that newcomers were not well grounded in Presbyterian history and theology.[74]

Some synod leaders also expressed concern that the leadership of the board of trustees had fallen primarily to local businessmen, many of whom were not Presbyterian. They felt that their opinions, once deemed important, no longer had influence when it came to critical issues facing the institution. Trinity, they said, was being marketed like a chamber of commerce production rather than a church institution. Feeling their control slipping away, a few synod officials complained to Board of Christian Education officials in Philadelphia about the rapid growth and apparent secularization of Trinity during the postwar era.[75]

Everett, Thomsen, and several other trustees feared that complaints about administrative policy and leadership coming from synod sources would alienate San Antonio businessmen, such as Cecil W. Miller, James Calvert, and Robert Witt, whose membership on the board they deemed crucial to the university. Through correspondence and personal contact, they reassured denominational officials that Trinity continued to affirm its church relationship and that the new San Antonio trustees supported efforts to preserve historic institutional ties to the Presbyterian Church. If the San Antonio trustees were to sense a lack of confidence on the part of church leaders, one board member wrote, they "will cease to be available. Should this occur the Trinity University that is now envisioned and almost assured could not possibly be materialized."[76] Trustee Frank Murchison bluntly said, "We do not want some small conniving group of our synod to come in and completely wreck this university."[77]

From Everett's perspective, synod officials wanted to replicate the Waxahachie campus in San Antonio. Everett told a trustee, "It is easy for me to understand their feelings about Trinity being different here from what it was in Waxahachie. We want to preserve the best of the old, but a great deal of new life has to be injected into the organism of this institution." If Trinity was to succeed, Everett maintained, it would have to adapt to changing higher education standards and environments. Everett cited new guidelines for Presbyterian colleges and universities issued by the PCUSA General Assembly in 1945 that emphasized academic excellence, freedom of intellectual inquiry, and theological inclusiveness.[78]

Trinity's changing institutional identity is reflected in a revised statement of institutional aims and purposes that first appeared in the 1951–52 *Trinity University Catalogue*. The previous version, written in 1936, expressed the purpose in terms of a religious environment that featured a dedicated Christian faculty and emphasized Biblical studies, worship experiences, and personal attention to spiritual growth. In contrast, the new statement, while continuing to use such words as *Christian, church-*

related, spiritual, and *religious* to describe the university's connection and dedication, did not use them to describe the primary educational goals. Instead, it emphasized the university's function to be an academically oriented, Christian, liberal arts institution serving in the contemporary culture.[79]

Everett and Synod Executive Boles periodically clashed over the management of the school. Tensions between the two men surfaced at synod meetings, where they differed on issues of university funding strategies and the development of church relationships. Their correspondence indicates unresolved disagreements despite efforts by both parties to reconcile viewpoints. In May 1947, Everett told Thomsen that "it is very clear that he [Boles] is on the warpath and I am not going to fight back." Everett handed an undated resignation to Thomsen and told him to submit it to the board anytime he wanted to do so. "Life is too short," Everett said, "and there are too many other jobs to be done for me to hold this one through tension and conflict."[80] Although Thomsen refused to accept the resignation, Everett's relationship with Boles and other synod leaders remained tense during his final years at Trinity University.[81]

While focusing on academics, intercollegiate athletics, campus social life, and church relationships, Trinity administrators recognized the importance of a campaign to secure funds for the construction of a modern physical plant. The Trinity trustees initially envisioned expanding and modernizing the Woodlawn campus, but studies indicated a high cost for remodeling existing structures and purchasing residential property in the area. They concluded that the "Greater Trinity" envisioned when the university moved to San Antonio in 1942 would be located somewhere other than the Woodlawn campus.[82]

When the Synod of Texas met in January 1944, Trinity trustees reported that they had not yet decided on a permanent location, although several in the northern part of the city appeared promising. After further studies, a trustee committee chaired by C. W. Miller reported in May 1944 that three sites merited consideration. The first consisted of 210 acres approximately four miles north of the city center between San Pedro Avenue and Blanco Road. The second was a tract of 240 acres on the Austin Highway about five miles northeast of downtown San Antonio. A smaller parcel of land of about 75 acres near Alamo Stadium on the near north side of town had also recently come to their attention. The committee recommended that all three sites be scrutinized for suitability and cost.[83]

The Alamo Stadium site offered interesting possibilities for architectural development. San Antonio architect Bartlett Cocke reported that the irregular shape of the property and the seventy-foot difference in slope between low and high points did not lend themselves to a traditional campus building design. Nevertheless, Cocke envisaged a campus with rock steps, informal terracing, retaining walls, pools, and winding walkways. He recommended an informal arrangement of buildings, irregular in shape and designed to fit the terrain. Utilizing local materials as far as possible, Trinity could become one of the most distinctive campuses in the country—"informal, definitely Texas, picturesque, charming, yet functional, living, useful."[84]

With information in hand, the site committee met to decide on a location in September 1944. The Austin Highway site was abandoned because a local title company could not guarantee a clear title to the property. Ruling out the Woodlawn campus, the committee considered only the San Pedro Avenue and Alamo Stadium sites. The former, readily accessible and on even ground, provided the best opportunity to build a campus along formal gothic lines. The latter, more varied topographically, offered possibilities for architectural innovation. After lengthy discussion, the committee voted six to four in favor of the Alamo Stadium site. Despite their differences, the committee members pledged their full cooperation and support when the report was presented to the full board in October.[85]

At the October board meeting, the trustees approved the report and directed the committee to expeditiously obtain ownership of the property. Trustee Miller advised that the university hoped to acquire by trade about seventy acres owned by the City of San Antonio, twenty-five acres of adjoining property valued at $120,000 to $135,000, and five additional acres valued at $20,000 to $45,000. The San Antonio City Council agreed to trade part of its city property near Alamo Stadium for fifty-five lots owned by Trinity and needed by the city for the expansion of Bandera Highway. Although the stadium acreage was valued higher than the Trinity lots, Mayor Gus B. Mauermann assured San Antonians that "it would be a good exchange for San Antonio as the city could get a first class educational institution to boot."[86]

By the spring of 1946, the site committee successfully completed negotiations for the additional pieces of land to give the university a 107-acre campus bounded by Shook Avenue on the west, Hildebrand on the north, Stadium Drive on the east, and a line north of Mulberry Avenue on the south. By means of a gift of $27,000 from the Pioneer Flour Mills in memory of Erhard R. Guenther, the university acquired approximately six acres adjoining the northeast corner of the new campus. City officials wanted a right of way across this tract to straighten Hildebrand Avenue and paid Trinity $10,000 for the required portion of land. Through a combination of trade and purchase, Trinity had acquired an exceptional tract of land, which previously had been a working quarry. Running from east to west and dividing the campus, a rugged tree-covered limestone bluff offered a spectacular view of downtown San Antonio. The upper level would accommodate the majority of administrative and classroom facilities, the library, student union, and chapel. Below the bluff, an abandoned gravel pit provided sufficient space for athletic facilities and residence halls.[87]

With property negotiations in progress, the trustees began selecting architects to draw up a master plan for the new campus. After an extended search, they chose local architects Harvey P. Smith and Bartlett Cocke. They also selected as consultants the Boston firm of Perry, Shaw, and Hepburn, noted for its work on the library and rare book annex of Harvard University and for its supervision of the Rockefeller reconstruction project at Williamsburg, Virginia.[88]

During the spring of 1945, President Everett accompanied Smith and Cocke on a tour of college campuses, including Cornell University, Grove City College, the University of Virginia, and the University of Pennsylvania. At a meeting of the board of trustees in May 1945, the architects outlined their plans for construction materials, type of architecture, and campus layout. Cocke and Smith projected "a general colonial type of architecture modified to incorporate local atmosphere and design, with construction of stone although other construction material is not ruled out." Their traditional design would necessitate leveling much of the irregular site to accommodate the new structures.[89]

With the site and architectural plan in place, the university launched a $1,500,000 campaign to construct the buildings, employing the New York firm of Marts and Lundy to direct financial operations. Concentrating on the state of Texas, Trinity trustees proposed to raise enough funds to erect six buildings: a liberal arts building and auditorium ($550,000), a chapel ($125,000), a library ($225,000), residence halls ($250,000), and a science building ($200,000). At the request of Trinity alumni, the trustees added a student union building for social and recreational events. Utilizing professionally designed promotional materials that contained photographs of the Alamo Stadium site and illustrations of the proposed colonial-style buildings, Trinity officials urged donors to contribute generously to the ambitious building program.[90]

Riding the crest of local and synodical enthusiasm, the campaign gained momentum, and by Christmas 1946 San Antonio residents and

Presbyterian churches throughout the state had pledged almost one million dollars. During the following months, the campaign waned despite conscientious efforts by trustees, alumni, and Trinity supporters. By the close of Trinity's fiscal year in August 1947, the new campus fund totaled $1,112,000, but unpaid pledges and campaign expenses reduced that figure to approximately $700,000 in available cash.[91] Efforts to collect pledges and seek new donors eventually added $33,000 to the building fund, but as months passed it became evident that the campaign had run its course. Chairman Thomsen said that the common question addressed to him was, "When are you going to put up new buildings?"[92]

Aware of the deteriorating institutional image, trustees felt in early 1948 that an immediate start on the new campus might produce a "desired psychological effect on securing payment of pledges and additional contributions." However, cost projections based on the proposed architectural plans during an inflationary postwar economy prohibited major construction. Realistically, Trinity had sufficient funds to erect only one or possibly two major buildings, hardly enough to warrant moving operations to the new campus. In frustration, Presbyterian clergyman Harry Sarles warned his fellow trustees that unless the board took action quickly, Trinity's credibility in the community and throughout the synod would be greatly compromised. "Let's get going," he implored, "let's do something now!"[93]

At this point, trustee Tom Slick proposed a radical change in architectural design and construction methods that reduced initial costs, sped up the building program, and established Trinity as a pacesetter in imaginative campus planning. Conceived by Philip N. Youtz, a New York architect, and Slick, a San Antonio businessman, and developed by the Southwest Research Institute, an innovative lift-slab construction technique enabled workers to build concrete slabs at ground level and lift them into place. The actual lifting was accomplished with tension screws fastened to the top of the building's upright beams and powered by hydraulic pressure. Trinity's administration and classroom building (later Northrup Hall) was the first major building in the country to be erected by this method.[94]

Because this building process necessitated abandoning previous architectural proposals, the trustees retained as a consulting architect William Wurster, dean of architecture and planning at Massachusetts Institute of Technology. When Wurster first visited the site and its unique view of the surrounding landscape, he insisted, "Don't negate this site—that would be a tragedy. Let its hills design your buildings."[95] Wurster also recommended that local architect O'Neil Ford, whom he called "the best functional architect in the Southwest," be appointed as his chief designer. Ford, whose name would become synonymous with the campus, worked with Wurster and Cocke to devise a master plan that would harmonize with the site, "preserving its beauty, utilizing its unique topography—not altering it except where absolutely necessary."[96]

Trustees differed on the sequence of the initial building projects. Leaders in the Synod of Texas favored the erection of a chapel as symbolic of the institution's commitment to Christian higher education. More practical minds, however, called for classrooms, administrative offices, residence halls, and a library to precede the chapel. The immediate need for a chapel diminished when Austin Presbytery decided to purchase property adjacent to the campus and establish a congregation, which became University Presbyterian Church. A gift to build a library from Louise J. Lips and her son Charles enabled Trinity to move forward with plans for that project. By November 1949, Building Committee chairman Slick presented detailed plans for the administration and classroom building and Murchison Dormitory. At the same time, he described general proposals for the student union, library, and science building.[97]

Throughout the process of raising money and developing plans for the new campus, Trinity public relations officer Tex Taylor prepared press releases and planned events to keep the San Antonio community informed about progress on relocation. At Trinity's homecoming game with Sam Houston State College in October 1947, Taylor publicized the first official use of the campus with a barbecue supper, band concert, bonfire, and pep rally prior to the contest on the lower campus below the bluff where the present university center stands. He also secured press coverage of faculty and students clearing brush and removing rubbish on the new site.[98]

At a kickoff meeting for the new Trinity Booster's Club in the downtown Gunter Hotel in September 1948, Taylor unveiled the architects' scale model of the proposed campus. Accompanied by photographs and including an aerial shot of the stadium property, the exhibit was displayed for two weeks in the Gunter Hotel and then for a week each in local department stores.[99] At Founders' Day celebrations on 21 April 1949, a group of about five hundred Trinity supporters assembled to dedicate the ground on which the campus would be built. On Bushnell Avenue near where residence halls now stand, Everett led a brief worship service that featured music by a student brass sextet. In his remarks, Everett said, "We are dedicating ground and not buildings. We want the teachings of Trinity to be as endurable as the rock upon which we are standing."[100]

"When I was hired as the basketball coach in 1949, President Everett took me to the new campus site. We went up on the bluff and were looking down on San Antonio. He said to me, 'That's a beautiful sight and right down there in front of it is going to be one of the most attractive campuses in the United States.' Of course, all I could see was a lot of debris, rubbish, bottles, bricks, paper, and garbage. To tell you the truth, I couldn't quite get the picture."

Houston Wheeler, Trinity coach and physical education instructor (1949–88)

Delayed by a shortage of building materials, actual construction did not begin until January 1950. An article in the *Trinitonian* informed readers, "If Trinitonians are like Missourians and have to be shown, then they can either take a ride down Stadium Drive or believe us—work was begun this week on the first unit of the new campus."[101]

By April crews were ready to raise the initial concrete slabs into place, and crowds of spectators came to see the Youtz-Slick construction technique employed for the first time on a full-sized structure. Over a period of time, slabs weighing 165 tons each were hoisted into place with hydraulic jacks to form the roof and floor of the two-story building.[102] When the slabs were about ten feet off the ground, O'Neil Ford, Everett, and a number of trustees and civic leaders were on hand. At Ford's urging, Everett joined him in an inspection stroll under one of the rising slabs. "What if it should fall?" Everett queried. Never one to lack a response, Ford retorted, "If it does, this is the best place for us to be."[103]

Although Trinity would not occupy the new campus until May 1952, construction of the first four structures (a dormitory, administrative and classroom building, student union, and library) quieted the critics and energized the students and faculty. Even before workmen had completed their tasks, Trinity students scheduled events on the new campus. In May 1951 the Student Council sponsored a dance in the unfinished administration/classroom building for the traditional Tigerland Coronation of campus royalty including a King of Prosperity and a Queen of Peace along with other members of the court. The semiformal event featured the appearance of Tommy Dorsey's seventeen-piece orchestra at a cost of $1,500. A financial and social success, the dance was long remembered by Trinity students and school officials as a housewarming for the new campus.[104]

Northrup Hall under construction, viewed from the west with Alamo Stadium
in the background. The road on the right is a continuation of
Bushnell Avenue, now a cul-de-sac.

The administration and classroom building also provided a temporary
sanctuary for the newly organized University Presbyterian Church. In August 1950, the board of trustees granted the congregation permission to
worship on the premises while they were building a church on a three-acre
site at the corner of Bushnell and Shook Avenues. When purchasing the
property from Trinity, the congregation agreed to make its building available as a university chapel until the new campus had its own edifice. The
cross presently on the chancel wall in the University Presbyterian Church
sanctuary was crafted out of discarded lumber from the campus construction site and used initially in their temporary quarters.[105]

As the arduous relocation process neared completion, Everett showed
signs of physical and mental strain and reiterated his wish to retire when
he reached sixty-five in May 1950. Anticipating this event, the trustees informally gathered a committee in the spring of 1949 to commence a pres-

idential search. Because Everett was cultivating donors to fund the new campus and expected some large gifts in the near future, the trustees hoped to keep his pending retirement secret until the last possible moment. Everett became ill during the summer and fall of 1949, however, and word of his poor health and retirement plans reached both Dallas newspapers and commissioners at a Synod of Texas meeting in October. While Everett recuperated in a private hospital in Temple, Texas, the trustees retained him as the titular president but gave Bruce Thomas authority to manage the university's affairs.[106] When Everett returned to campus early in 1950, the trustees directed him to devote himself full time to fund-raising and leave administrative and academic management of the university in the hands of Thomas. This arrangement proved difficult for both Everett and Thomas, who had adjoining offices. Staff members were never quite sure on what desk to deposit mail marked "University President." In August the trustees eased tensions by renting office space for Everett in downtown San Antonio and designating Thomas acting president.[107]

During his eight-year presidency, Monroe Everett guided Trinity through a crucial period of transition and the reconfiguration of its institutional identity. Major decisions regarding relocation, curriculum, athletics, and student life set the stage for Trinity's future identity as a fully accredited undergraduate and graduate institution. An effective fund-raiser, Everett played a key role in cultivating donors, including some who continued to support the university long after his departure. Under his leadership, from 1942 to 1950, the annual operating budget grew from $132,000 to $1,000,000, the student body increased from 400 to 1,500, and the faculty expanded from 26 to 80.[108]

As the university searched for a new president, Thomas displayed considerable skill in keeping students, faculty, staff, and trustees positive regarding the university's future. He also delivered an exceptional bit of good news to the community in January 1951 when he announced that Trinity had become the beneficiary of the annual income from an endowment fund valued at $500,000, the largest single gift in the university's history. Insisting that "absolutely no publicity" be given to the gift, the benefactors, James A. and Leta M. Chapman of Oklahoma, whose family had long associations with the university, indicated that future additions to the fund would be forthcoming.[109]

Although Trinity's future appeared brighter than at any time in its previous history, serious problems loomed. After the surge of returning veterans in 1945, enrollment gradually declined, exacerbated by low birth rates during the Depression. Hampered by an inadequate endowment and limited operating income, Trinity struggled to maintain a balanced budget and secure funds to complete the construction of the new campus. Noncompetitive faculty salaries made it difficult to attract and keep quality instructors. Other unresolved issues involved relationships with the Synod of Texas, the role of intercollegiate athletics, and the future of graduate education.

The most immediate challenge was finding a suitable candidate for president of the university. Guided by trustees Frank Murchison and Jasper Manton, the Personnel Committee commenced a two-year search for Everett's replacement. In the meantime, Bruce Thomas and acting dean Paul Schwab led Trinity faculty and staff in maintaining operations on the Woodlawn campus, awaiting a move to the new campus and the arrival of a new president.

CHAPTER EIGHT

A COMPANY OF NEW PIONEERS

Each student who enters Trinity this fall will do so as one of a company of new pioneers. With the fall of 1952 Trinity enters a thrilling new adventure in the field of Christian Higher Education.

JAMES W. LAURIE, JUNE 1952

H AVING SURVIVED TWO RELOCATIONS, a merger, and almost ten years in temporary quarters, Trinity University entered the 1950s in yet another period of transition and uncertainty. Building projects, held up by a shortage of construction materials, made occupancy of the new campus unlikely before the summer or fall of 1952, and financial problems caused skeptics to predict that the institution might face bankruptcy or absorption into a municipal university system.

While supporters were not so pessimistic, they recognized that Trinity's future hinged on its securing professional and visionary leadership during the next decade. With the country involved in the Korean conflict and confronted with inflation, Trinity's new president would begin in an environment of challenging political circumstances as well as internal concerns. Trinity's checkered history, however, indicated that such conditions were neither unusual nor unexpected. As trustee C. W. Miller told an audience in 1953, Trinity "was born in a crisis and frankly, ladies and gentlemen, it has been in a crisis ever since."[1]

Despite the need for continuity in leadership following Monroe Everett's resignation, Trinity's presidential search committee made little progress. Plagued by crippling arthritis and poor health, Chairman Murchison relinquished his position to trustee Jasper Manton, a prominent Dallas clergyman and Trinity alumnus. For different reasons, neither expedited the search process. Murchison wanted to wait until Trinity occupied the new campus before settling on a permanent replacement, believing that with buildings in place and academic routines established, outstanding candidates would more likely be attracted to the position.[2] Manton, on the other hand, moved slowly because he favored a ministerial president of national stature and thought that the candidate pool was weak. Moreover, he sensed strong support among faculty, students, and trustees for acting president Bruce Thomas, who was neither ordained nor widely known in denominational circles. Although he had high regard for Thomas as an academician and administrator, Manton hesitated to bring his candidacy to a vote, fearing that the popular dean would be elected president. As a result, he employed what he termed "stalling tactics" to allow time for someone else to emerge.[3]

As the months passed with no apparent progress in the presidential search, synod officials and university trustees pressed Manton to accelerate the process. Turning to denominational leadership, Manton invited Paul C. Payne, general secretary of the Presbyterian Board of Christian Education, to meet with the search committee. Visiting San Antonio in March 1951, Payne urged the committee to seek a ministerial candidate who had broad denominational recognition. Committee members asked Payne to study Trinity's situation and compile a list of three names, ranked in order, for their consideration. He agreed to do so after the General Assembly of the national church ended its annual session in May, although he immediately suggested one name: Eugene Carson Blake, pastor of the Pasadena Presbyterian Church in California and a former Princeton football star with strong interpersonal skills and administrative ability. He became unavailable, however, due to his election that year as Stated Clerk of the Presbyterian General Assembly. Blake served as the denomination's chief officer until 1966 when he was elected General Secretary of the World Council of Churches.[4]

After this suggestion, instead of sending three names, Payne presented as the sole nominee James Woodin Laurie, pastor of the Central Presbyterian Church in Buffalo, New York. (Laurie had been Blake's chief competitor for the stated clerk's position.) "I don't believe there's a more competent business executive among the men of our Church than Jim Laurie," Payne informed Manton. Extolling Laurie's organizational skills and money raising abilities, Payne concluded that "he is respected by business men, he is loved by all who know him, he has been one of the key men in the councils of the church and is recommended as one of the most brilliant figures in the Church at present."[5]

Laurie belonged to a family noted for a long and distinguished record of service to Presbyterian enterprises. Laurie's father and grandfather conducted pioneering ministries in Minnesota, Washington State, and Iowa, and other family members had served as missionaries and educators at home and abroad. A native of Bellingham, Washington, Laurie received his B.A. degree from Coe College in Cedar Rapids, Iowa, in 1924, a B.D. degree from Princeton Theological Seminary in 1927, and an M.A. degree from Princeton University, also in 1927. Laurie served pastorates in Elizabeth and Rahway, New Jersey, and Wilkinsburg, Pennsylvania, before joining Central Presbyterian Church in Buffalo, New York, in 1942. He was active in presbytery and synod committees and also held national denominational positions, serving for a number of years on the General Council of the General Assembly and the Council on Theological Education.[6]

At the invitation of Murchison, the Laurie family drove from Buffalo to San Antonio in August 1951 to meet with the search committee and other university officials. The "new campus" consisted of a few buildings under construction and an abandoned stone quarry covered with brush and cactus. "Standing in the middle of nothing," Dorothy Laurie recalled, "Jim gathered the family together and asked what they thought about Trinity and living in San Antonio. Most were favorable to moving, but it was daughter Jean who sensed the challenge involved in the new position. 'If you want to go on doing something you do well and are sure of, you'll stay in Buffalo. But if you're young enough to take a dare, you'll come here.'"[7] After reflection, Laurie "took the dare" and agreed to become the fourteenth president of Trinity University, beginning October 1951.

The first Trinity president to be born in the twentieth century, Laurie was forty-eight years old when he arrived in San Antonio. He brought to his new assignment personal qualities that made his presidency one of the most productive in Trinity's history. Driven by a work ethic rooted in a theological sense of vocation, Laurie viewed the presidency as a "calling" rather than an administrative position. He once wrote, "I am convinced that there is a divine pattern and that success in life ultimately is measured by the accuracy with which we find and follow it."[8]

Laurie frequently invoked the image of the pioneer in describing the position of university president. In particular, he perceived the move from the Woodlawn campus to Trinity Hill as comparable to a wagon train of settlers leaving familiar surroundings in order to break new paths and develop new territories. Speaking to a national radio audience shortly after he assumed the Trinity presidency, Laurie gave a sermon entitled "The Beckoning Frontier," based on the biblical text (Hebrews 12: 1–2) that referred to Jesus as "the pioneer and perfecter of our faith." Affirming that frontiers are not concerned only with geography and adventure, Laurie spoke

Laurie family in the early 1950s

of "frontiers of the spirit," especially in the field of higher education, that had the potential to change society and stimulate the endless search for truth. Enlarging on the pioneer motif, Laurie envisioned a university informed by Christian values and characterized by academic excellence.[9]

Articulated with eloquence and conviction, Laurie's mission captured the imagination of potential benefactors, denominational leaders, trustees, faculty, and staff. Possessing remarkable stamina, an outgoing personality, and distinguished good looks and combining the qualities of salesman, pastor, administrator, and educator, his energies were directed to one all-consuming goal—the advancement of Trinity University.

Laurie's commitment surfaced in comments written in small notebooks that he carried in his coat pocket. During his daily routine, Laurie would jot down reflections regarding personal qualities that he deemed appropriate for upcoming tasks. Not meant for public eyes, the scribbled musings reveal a piety that shaped his private and public life. As he commenced his work in San Antonio, for example, Laurie wrote, "Accepted the Presidency of Trinity University. God will be my co-pilot. Have no fear. This can be the center of gravity for a wide area. Be sincerely Christian. You are entering a new field. God will guide you in it all. Move as fast as you can. No need for lagging. God is at the controls." Later he commented, "Never expect full appreciation for anything you do—God knows—serve him," and "Go forward so fast that my errors don't catch up."[10]

With the vigor that characterized his nineteen-year presidency, Laurie prepared to lead the university. Before leaving Buffalo, he studied photographs in college yearbooks and other university publications so that he could associate names and faces. Consequently, at a formal reception for trustees, faculty, and staff, Laurie was able to identify everyone by name and position, which made a lasting impression and smoothed his acceptance in the San Antonio community and the Synod of Texas. For many years at the annual president's dinner that marked the beginning of the school year, Laurie introduced faculty and staff, including spouses, by sight.[11]

During the first months of his presidency, Laurie presided over Trinity's closing days on the Woodlawn campus. In a time of confusion and insecurity, Laurie encountered a stream of people anxious to register complaints and offer solutions. Attempting to create a positive atmosphere, Laurie called a faculty and staff meeting in the university chapel. He told his audience, "At the moment I don't presume to know a great deal, but I am learning fast. What happened before I came is ancient history. Do your own job and don't worry about anyone else." His words helped alleviate tensions and rejuvenate community morale.[12]

Laurie initially attempted to restore good relationships with the Synod of Texas, which had deteriorated during the early years in San Antonio. He and Dorothy Laurie spent many weekends traveling across Texas in an automobile without air conditioning to meet Presbyterian clergy and congregations. They visited small churches in communities such as Hochheim, Cheapside, Cisco, and Red Oak, as well as the large urban congregations. Once, when Laurie was in El Paso to speak at a prominent church, he learned that a nearby Hispanic congregation was scheduled to have a pastoral installation service. He postponed his return to San Antonio so that he could attend the event. Because the presbytery representative never arrived, Laurie, with the help of an interpreter, gave an impromptu sermon on "The Nature of the Church." Church members appreciated his participation and left the service with a favorable impression of Trinity University.[13]

At his first briefing with key staff members, Laurie received mixed news regarding short-term university finances. The transfer of the Woodlawn property to the Catholic Archdiocese of San Antonio, effective 4 June 1952, would net Trinity approximately $250,000. The agreement, however, required the university to vacate the premises before that date.[14] Cash flow from the Chapman Trust would be less than anticipated because the donor had specified that a portion of the accumulated income be withheld in order to ensure corpus growth. Declining enrollment mandated that thirteen full-time faculty members be released, and salaries remained at the low end of Southern Association minimum standards. While considering a substantial tuition increase, Laurie mulled the wisdom of promoting an expensive athletic program at a time when the university was unable to attain a balanced budget.[15]

Trinity's most immediate concern was to secure funding for the building program on the new campus. The financial campaign begun during the Everett administration had lost momentum, and hopes of revival were improbable. As moving day approached, the new campus, referred to as Trinity Hill or the Skyline campus, consisted of a men's dormitory, a classroom building that lacked a heating system, an empty library building, an uncompleted student union, and a women's dormitory under construction.[16]

To facilitate relocation, Laurie urged trustees to participate in the federal government's program of low-interest loans for college housing, even though the board had rejected such an idea on two previous occasions. In 1948 board members had voiced "generally a negative feeling" about accepting federal aid, and two years later, when Everett recommended that the university file a loan application, they again demurred.[17] Speaking individually to key trustees and then to the full board, Laurie defended federal loans, referring to judicious use of government funding as good stewardship and sensible economics. Emphasizing the ramifications if campus construction did not proceed expeditiously, the trustees, with one dissenting vote, granted him authority to negotiate federal loans for student housing not to exceed one million dollars.[18]

Laurie also recognized an unresolved issue involving the establishment of a Reserve Officers Training Corps (ROTC) on the new campus. In 1948 the board of trustees hesitantly proposed to introduce a voluntary ROTC unit, but feared possible opposition from churches in the Synod of Texas. Before implementing the program, the trustees polled the presbyteries in the Synod of Texas regarding their views. When Bruce Thomas reported early in 1951 that a majority favored the establishment of some type of military training on campus, the trustees made applications for an Army, Marine, or Air Force ROTC unit. By the time Laurie arrived, negotiations for a military unit were progressing, but no contract had been signed.[19]

The Army agreed to tender an offer to establish a unit if the university required all males who enrolled at Trinity to participate in ROTC during their first two years on campus. With the Korean conflict at its height,

ROTC unit at drill on the lower campus

the ROTC unit also would give males an automatic draft deferment. Although campuses with large male enrollments could adopt voluntary programs, Laurie knew that Trinity's small male population warranted mandatory participation. After considerable discussion, a motion authorizing the administration to enter into a contract with the Army carried unanimously. The ROTC program began in the fall of 1952 and was estimated to cost the university approximately $1,000 annually in addition to providing office and classroom facilities. The compulsory aspect of the program engendered sustained opposition over the years, but in the long run it stabilized male enrollment and provided scholarships for men who opted for the four-year course and subsequent enlistment as commissioned officers.[20]

As the spring semester drew to a close, the campus community prepared for moving day on 13 May 1952, two days before final examinations. Five hundred students, faculty, and staff assisted workers from the San Antonio Association of Motor Carriers to transfer more than one-half million pounds of supplies and equipment in the fifty-one vans, trailers, and trucks furnished by the association. In less than five hours, Trinity moved from the Woodlawn campus to Trinity Hill, conducted entirely

Students taking a break during moving day

with volunteer labor and donated equipment. The move saved the university an estimated $19,000, provided an occasion for extensive media coverage, and promoted community spirit.[21]

Laurie signaled the beginning of moving day with a farewell ceremony on the Woodlawn campus. By 10:00 A.M., the loaded vans were ready to depart. The 307th MP battalion of Fort Sam Houston provided four jeeps with two-way radio equipment for communications during the move. Students and faculty wore hats fashioned from the Trinity moving signs. As the procession of vans and cars moved down Hildebrand Avenue and approached the new campus, a San Antonio Police Department vehicle led the parade with its siren wailing.[22]

When the vans arrived, a ribbon-cutting ceremony took place that included the national anthem, prayers, and speeches by C. W. Miller, chairman of the chamber of commerce, and Mayor Samuel Bell Steves. The event went as planned except for one minor obstacle. Trinity band members could not remember in which van they had packed their instruments. After a fruitless search, they hurried over to Edison High School to borrow some instruments in order to provide appropriate music for the occasion.[23]

Following the brief ceremonies, the volunteers ate a picnic lunch. Participants in the move recalled that Trinity's finances were so meager that no dessert was served. At the reception honoring Laurie's retirement eighteen years later, Professor Paul Walthall, who had assisted with the move, reminded Laurie of this omission and presented him with a large cake, which he termed "a delinquent dessert" for the picnic lunch almost two decades previously.[24]

By 4:00 P.M., most of the unloading was completed and the vans had departed. Caught up in the excitement of the event, the faculty and students dispersed only after Thomas announced, "There is nothing else to be done. Won't you please go home and get some rest?"[25]

Once the euphoria of moving subsided, members of the Trinity community faced the realities of life on a campus in progress. In an understatement, Laurie informed faculty members at their first meeting in the new location that they would experience some "discomforts" with unfinished buildings and facilities. For more than a decade, two or three faculty members shared the same office and a single telephone that accessed the outside world through a campus switchboard operator. Restricted to one or two bookcases, faculty members had shelf space for only their most frequently used resources. With some exceptions, offices and classrooms lacked air conditioning, a situation that prompted students and faculty alike to schedule early morning classes, especially during summer sessions.[26]

Academic support services were minimal. Full-time departmental secretaries were the exception rather than the rule, and most departments functioned with part-time student workers whose availability was limited by class and laboratory schedules. Although a few departments had ditto machines, faculty relied primarily on a small post office staff to duplicate syllabi and other class materials on an electric mimeograph machine.[27]

"I used to tell Jim Laurie, after this I could operate a college
in a jungle."

Dean Bruce Thomas

For a number of years, the Laurie home at 139 Oakmont Court served as a meeting place for various organizations and social gatherings. The board of trustees met at the president's residence. After their deliberations, they had a lunch graciously prepared and served by Dorothy Laurie. On Sunday mornings, the Lauries provided breakfast and the use of their living room for college students from University Presbyterian Church for Bible study and prayer sessions.[28]

Although presidential spouses, usually silent and invisible partners in the educational enterprise, contributed much to community life throughout Trinity's history, their activities were rarely recorded in official records or university publications. With Dorothy Augustine Laurie, however, sufficient written and oral sources exist to document her activities. Having functioned during three pastorates as the minister's spouse, "an unpaid professional," she adapted these skills to the campus arena. Dorothy Laurie performed a variety of pioneering tasks at Trinity, such as cultivating donors and trustees, nurturing students and staff, and assuming leadership roles in community and denominational activities. When new faculty arrived in town, she assisted them in locating a home, recommended dentists and physicians, and even arranged to secure credit cards with local businesses. Always current with campus events, she had appropriate words of encouragement, praise, or consolation for members of the Trinity family.[29]

In the midst of becoming acclimated to the new campus, the Trinity community celebrated the inauguration of James W. Laurie as the university's fourteenth president on 8 October 1952. At a civic dinner the previous evening attended by some five hundred guests in the student union building, Henry R. Luce, editor-in-chief of *Time*, *Life*, and *Fortune* magazines, was the featured speaker. Luce also spoke at the inaugural ceremony in the Travis Park Methodist Church, attended by the Trinity University Board of Trustees, faculty, students, representatives from 125 academic institutions, leaders of learned societies, civic officials, and other university supporters.[30]

To provide adequate facilities for students, faculty, and staff, Laurie initiated a series of financial campaigns during the first decade on Trinity Hill. Unlike some presidents of struggling church-related colleges, he never emphasized institutional poverty as an incentive for contributions. Rather, he stressed the opportunity to participate in a venture destined to succeed. Describing the future role of Trinity University in Christian higher education in private conversations and public addresses, Laurie proclaimed his vision of an institution that would bring recognition to benefactors and provide quality education for countless student generations. Laurie told a group of church people, for instance, "Someone down in Texas is going to have the thrill of a lifetime in building a Science Building for Trinity, for twelve hundred students a year for the next hundred years will go to confront God's universe in a Christian setting. It will be a thrilling investment, and a good thing to do if properly motivated by a desire to serve the Lord as a steward of his bounty."[31]

Two years after moving to the new campus, Laurie announced a long-range ten million dollar development program, half of which would be devoted to buildings and half to endowment. Concurrently, he proposed to raise $250,000 annually to cover operating expenses not met by tuition and fees. Because of escalating costs and expanding needs, the board of trustees enlarged the long-range development program in 1957 to fifteen million dollars, including $3,485,000 for plant facilities and operating funds. Under the leadership of trustee C. W. Miller, the development campaign was successfully completed in May 1962, less than five years after it had begun. Seizing the momentum, Laurie announced that Trinity would immediately embark on a fifty million dollar academic and campus development campaign to be completed in time for the centennial celebration in 1969.[32]

Guided by architect Ford and consultant Wurster, Trinity devised a master campus plan that featured integrated architecture and use of the land only for academic, student housing, and recreational purposes. Plans called for the continuing use of "Bridgeport pink" bricks, which would became the hallmark of Trinity buildings, walls, and curbs, and the creation of small, informal, circuitous roads that discouraged public use. Resisting mass parking areas, the architects devised small cluster areas where automobiles could be discretely accommodated. As a result of such planning, the Trinity expansion process was completed expeditiously, with consideration for environmental and aesthetic principles.[33]

Even as the building program gained momentum during the 1950s, the campus still lacked the necessary facilities for an expanding residential university community. Trinity housed only 190 students during the 1953–54 academic year, but the construction of a new men's dormitory and the completion of unfinished portions of the women's dormitory and lounge provided space for an additional hundred students in the fall of 1954. The following year, a gift from Mr. and Mrs. Vernon F. Taylor underwrote the construction of a music building and concert hall. The completion of an Olympic-sized swimming pool in 1959 was made possible by a contribution from Dallas student D. Harold Byrd, Jr. in memory of his parents. During the same year, contractors put the finishing touches on the Marrs McLean Science center. In addition, the university obtained several residential properties on Oakmont Court, adjacent to the campus, which later served as homes for Trinity administrators.[34]

Although the building program generated interest, it placed a heavy burden on Trinity's financial resources. During eight of the thirteen years between 1952 and 1965, operating expenses exceeded current fund revenues, and the financial status of the current fund varied from a surplus of

$77.11 in 1952 to a cumulative deficit of $400,000 in 1964. By 1966 the plant fund debt had reached $8.5 million, not including unpaid amounts for contracts already signed on buildings under construction. When cash-flow problems occurred, Laurie utilized a revolving line of extended credit from three local banks to cover immediate operating expenses.[35]

If Laurie had doubts about deficit spending, he never indicated them. He broke ground for new buildings with modest sums in hand, confident that he could secure the balance in time to complete the project. Work on the science building, for example, was conducted on a month-to-month basis, depending on the availability of funds. Laurie told one trustee, "We have two commitments which will keep the Science Building going for a month or so. Now I must have $50,000 to furnish the girl's dormitory or we will be in a bad way this fall. So it goes—from one need to another, but there seems to come help in the nick of time."[36]

On another occasion, he informed Tex Taylor that he needed $40,000 before the end of the week in order to meet the payroll and other outstanding debts. Laurie fortuitously met an individual willing to loan Trinity that amount at bank rates if the university promised to repay the loan in four months. Laurie accepted the offer even though he was not certain how he would raise the $40,000 in such a short time, but he successfully repaid the loan.[37]

When the Cowles Life Science Building was in its planning stages, Laurie learned that a local contractor and his crew were idle because of construction problems on a nearby job. Laurie asked the contractor to move his heavy machinery to the Trinity campus and do rough excavation work until the other job resumed. Although the contractor resisted the proposal, he finally relented and asked Laurie to send the necessary engineering plans. Laurie informed him that they didn't have any plans, but there was a lot of rock that needed to be moved before construction could begin. "But we don't do things that way," the contractor replied. Not to be dissuaded, Laurie convinced the contractor "to move some rock" in order to speed up work on the anticipated life science building.[38]

Behind the scenes, business manager Carl Parker and his successor Derwood Hawthorne struggled to keep pace with Laurie's financial brinksmanship. Hawthorne later confirmed that on numerous occasions he held back paychecks until the banks closed for the weekend so that Trinity had extra time to cover the checks. He also let requisitions for supplies and equipment approved by Laurie languish in his office. A department chair related how he had gone to Hawthorne to inquire about a requisition for laboratory equipment that Laurie had authorized months earlier.

Hawthorne opened a desk drawer and pointed to a stack of signed requisition forms saying, "I have a drawer full of ones just like yours, but they aren't going anywhere."[39]

"Laurie had a real concept of dealing with finances. He was one who had all the confidence that if money wasn't here today it would be tomorrow. But that made it difficult to spend."

Derwood Hawthorne, the *Trinitonian*, 16 April 1979

Although Laurie devoted considerable time to fund-raising and campus construction projects, he and Thomas made efforts to address other aspects of university life as well. As the civil rights movement gained momentum in the early 1950s, they devised a strategy to integrate African Americans into the university community. Although Trinity had begun admitting African Americans to its downtown evening school in 1949, no such policy existed on the Woodlawn or Trinity Hill campuses.[40]

Before raising the issue with the trustees, Laurie and Thomas consulted the Trinity faculty in January 1953. During what the minutes termed "a most interesting discussion," faculty members supported the admission of African-American students to university classes but established no timetable for such an event. Aware that the Supreme Court had directed the University of Texas in 1950 to admit African Americans to graduate and professional schools, they also agreed that Trinity should start with graduate rather than undergraduate students. Thomas cautioned that it would be judicious to prepare the board of trustees for such a change rather than confronting them with an ultimatum, believing that "a negative vote would be a complete defeat."[41]

Developments on a national scale assisted Trinity's integration process. The Supreme Court case *Brown v. the Board of Education* in 1954 ended the "separate but equal" educational practices and provided civil rights activists with leverage for change. Moreover, the Presbyterian Church, which had for more than a decade advocated an unsegregated church and an unsegregated society, urged its denominational colleges and universities to revise their admission policies to reflect this standard.

Supported by these actions, Laurie proposed at a trustees meeting in October 1954 that Trinity begin admitting African Americans. Noting that nothing in the charter precluded their admission, Laurie referred to a "long established precedent" of denying them access to classes on the main campus. He urged trustees to initiate the integration process rather than waiting for outside pressures to develop. On a motion by ministerial board member Thomas Wilbanks, the trustees appointed a special committee to consider "some modification of university admission policies."[42]

When the committee reported six months later, it stated an inability to "resolve all of the details involved in possible complete integration." It did recommend, however, that "qualified mature non-residential" African-American graduate students and members of the Armed Services who had previously enrolled at Trinity's evening division be admitted to the main campus. The committee also suggested that the admission of African Americans as residential undergraduate and graduate students be studied carefully before making additional policy decisions. By a voice vote, the trustees accepted the recommendations.[43]

Moving cautiously, Laurie and Thomas reported periodically on the implementation of the new admissions policy. In October 1955 Thomas informed trustees that seven African-American undergraduates had attended Trinity during the summer and that seven more were taking evening graduate courses during the fall semester. Satisfied that integration was proceeding smoothly, Thomas and Laurie decided to take an additional step. Not waiting to form another investigative committee, the two men agreed that at the board meeting in May 1956, the president would recommend that trustees delegate full authority for admitting undergraduate and graduate minority students to university administrators.[44]

Because of major surgery, Laurie was unable to attend the board meeting, so Thomas presented the integration proposal. As a southerner, Thomas felt that he could speak candidly to board members. After re-reading the original charter and subsequent modifications, Thomas put the subject in historical context. In his remarks to the board, Thomas stated that, after examining all the relevant documents, he could find no exclusionary statements regarding admission of African Americans or other minorities. If the board wished to exclude African Americans, he concluded, it would have to amend the charter.[45]

Noting that he did not anticipate any large influx of African-American students, Thomas "recommended" that the trustees delegate authority with power to act to the administration (president and dean) regarding the admission of African-American students to Trinity University. When queried by a board member about whether administrators intended to admit only qualified African Americans, Thomas replied, "Those are the only kinds of students we admit, either white or black." Thomas informed the trustees, however, that neither he nor Laurie envisaged "in the near future" having African-American students living in dormitories or participating in intercollegiate athletics. With that caveat, the trustees approved the dean's request.[46]

At the board of trustee level, other important changes took place during the first decade on the new campus. Since 1869, every chair of the board of trustees had been either a Presbyterian layman or a minister with close ties to the Synod of Texas. When Chairman Clint Small stepped down in 1957, Laurie encouraged the trustees' nominating committee to submit the name of Cecil W. Miller, a Methodist layman, as Small's successor. Elected in May 1957, Miller became the first non-Presbyterian and first San Antonio resident to serve in this capacity.[47]

Together with James H. Calvert and Robert R. Witt, Miller had played a leading role in promoting the university among civic leaders. Although the three vice chairmen of the board were Presbyterians, many in the Synod of Texas interpreted Miller's election as another sign that Trinity's future would be determined by San Antonio businessmen rather than by synod leaders. As a result of Miller's election, several longstanding clergymen board members chose not to continue when they came up for reappointment.[48]

At the same meeting, the trustees established another precedent by selecting a woman to serve as an officer of the board. Ruth Chapman Cowles, a Waxahachie alumna and a member of the Madison Square Presbyterian Church in San Antonio, was elected third vice chair. She and her husband Andrew were Trinity benefactors. Elected as a trustee in 1950, Cowles was responsible for much of Trinity's landscaping and for furnishings in the student union building and the Chapman Graduate Center. One of her major projects was to redesign, remodel, and refurnish the Cowles House at 130 Oakmont Court as a residence for the dean of Trinity's graduate school. Cowles remained active as a member of the board until her death in 1964.[49]

Recognizing that adequate compensation and a stable working environment encouraged faculty morale and stimulated productivity, Laurie and Thomas advocated higher salaries, retirement benefits, and clearly defined tenure procedures. By incorporating annual goals for increased compensation into the budget process, the university doubled nine-month salaries in all ranks between 1954 and 1964. Although average salaries were competitive with Texas state institutions for that time period, they still fell below national calculations produced by the American Association of University Professors, especially at the ranks of associate and full professor.[50]

Faculty fringe benefits improved considerably during the same time period. In 1957, Trinity trustees gave faculty members the opportunity to participate in one or both of the programs offered by the Teacher Insurance and Annuity Association (TIAA) and College Retirement Equities Fund (CREF). Initially, the university contributed 5 percent of a faculty member's salary, but by 1963 the amount had increased to 10 percent. Group hospitalization and medical service benefits and a group life insurance program were in place by the early 1960s. Beyond these programs, Trinity operated on an informal understanding that faculty salaries would not be withheld due to extended illness. Colleagues were expected to cover classes for an absent professor "when such substitution is reasonable."[51]

Throughout its history, Trinity had no formal policies governing promotion and tenure, and trustees displayed no inclination to take action on the subject. Although the Southern Association periodically urged the university to formulate a tenure policy, board members deferred action on several occasions. At a meeting in 1944, for example, after considering a tenure proposal submitted by the faculty, some trustees opposed it because they considered tenure to be an imposition from the Southern Association, an organization in which they had no representation. After considerable debate, the trustees incorporated the proposal into the minutes "for the information of its members" but took no formal action.[52]

Discussions regarding tenure resumed in 1952 when Laurie and Thomas proposed the creation of a faculty senate composed of faculty members who held the rank of professor and had served the university for at least two years. As an advisory body with no legislative powers, the senate would serve as an executive committee of the faculty to consult with the administration (president and dean) on issues such as tenure and promotion. After extended study and debate, the faculty approved the formation of the Faculty Senate in 1953 and drew up bylaws that established tenure and promotion criteria and procedures.[53]

The Faculty Senate was to have only limited consultative influence regarding tenure decisions. The power to make tenure decisions on probationary faculty would remain vested in the administration, i.e., the academic dean and the president. Faculty members with the rank of assistant, associate, or professor would receive tenure automatically upon appointment for their fifth year of service. Tenure criteria included "demonstrated compatibility with the Christian aims of the university"; good moral character; evidence of teaching ability, training, and experience; and acceptability to the department. The criteria also specified that a candidate for tenure should possess "a personality which suits him to the demands of the classroom and association with his colleagues."[54]

Initially, the Faculty Senate was directly involved in promotion decisions. Criteria for promotion emphasized classroom teaching and campus, community, and professional service rather than scholarly research. "Effective teaching" as determined by student evaluations, observations of the department chair, and "the collection of information concerning the records and achievements of Trinity graduates," were to be the primary considerations. Mechanics for gathering and evaluating these criteria, however, were not specified in the bylaws.[55] Acknowledging that working conditions at Trinity made research and publishing extremely difficult, the bylaws stated "scholarly production, though looked upon favorably, is not a requisite for promotion."[56]

After receiving the tenure and promotion document as "information," the board of trustees affirmed its approval of "the generally recognized principle of tenure for faculty members after a probationary period."[57] Following the document's approval by the general faculty, the Faculty Senate met periodically to consider promotions, exceptions to policy, and recommendations from the administration regarding new faculty appointments above the rank of instructor.[58] In 1957 the Faculty Senate modified its bylaws to assign the responsibility for promotion decisions to the dean and the president in consultation with department chairs. As a result, such actions were often handled informally with varying interpretations of standards by individual chairs and administrators.[59]

Shortly after settling in on the new campus, Trinity faculty began to reconfigure the basic curriculum that had been adopted when the university moved to San Antonio in 1942. The new curriculum, implemented in September 1958, was designed to expose students to a variety of academic disciplines and encourage them to integrate acquired knowledge and skills. The curriculum consisted of nine groups of studies from which students selected a variety of courses amounting to approximately one half of the hours required for graduation. Although most faculty and students responded favorably, some thought that it required too many hours and limited opportunities for integration of accumulated knowledge.[60]

While continuing a commitment to the liberal arts undergraduate curriculum, Trinity introduced several new professional programs and expanded its graduate program during the first decade on the new campus. Encouraged by trustee Tom Slick, Trinity offered the country's first comprehensive program in home building in 1952. Supervised by the department of business administration and offering a Bachelor of Science degree, the home-building program featured lectures by visiting craftsmen and a junior summer apprentice experience with professional supervision. "In

The home-building department

inaugurating this course to help the home builders of the future become more skilled and expert in their chosen field," said Laurie, "we believe Trinity is making a major contribution to the future well-being of our society as a whole."[61]

The university introduced an engineering science program in the fall of 1961 under the direction of Robert V. Andrews, the former dean of engineering at Lamar Technological College in Beaumont, Texas. The four-year degree program combined engineering and science courses with work in the humanities and social sciences, similar to programs previously adopted by Northwestern University and the University of Texas at Austin. Entrance requirements demanded that students have a minimum of three years of mathematics and either chemistry or physics as one of two laboratory sciences in addition to the other usual requirements. Because the program consumed 139 semester hours, engineering students were not required to meet all of the basic curriculum requirements and were instead allotted twelve hours of electives in the humanities and the social sciences.[62]

Trinity enhanced its curricular offerings through affiliations with several research and professional organizations. The Southwest Foundation for Research and Education (later, Southwest Foundation for Biomedical Research) and Trinity agreed to exchange personnel, libraries, and laboratory facilities to conduct graduate education programs. Founded in San Antonio by Trinity trustee Tom Slick as a nonprofit scientific institution, the Southwest Foundation received grants over the years from the National Institute of Health and private donors to expand its program. Many members of the foundation's staff served on the Trinity graduate faculty, and Trinity science faculty members participated in research projects of the Southwest Foundation.[63]

The Seagle Colony of Music in Schroon Lake, New York, directed by John D. Seagle, a Trinity faculty member, offered music students an opportunity to train with professional musicians during the summer months. Trinity also affiliated with the Instituto Tecnológico of Monterrey, N. L., Mexico, where students could take summer courses in a variety of subjects, including language, history, literature, folklore, and philosophy.[64] After several years of an informal relationship, Trinity assumed full operational responsibility and control of a nonprofit agency for the hearing impaired, Sunshine Cottage, situated adjacent to Trinity. Sunshine Cottage teachers held adjunct status on the Trinity faculty through Trinity's Department of Education.[65]

Despite campus growth and program expansion, Trinity in the late 1950s retained many of the traditional hallmarks of a denominational university. Faculty members, nine of whom were ordained clergymen, were predominantly Protestant (Presbyterian and Methodist), and 75 percent were church officers, Sunday school teachers, or leaders of various church organizations. Only 4.3 percent of undergraduate students reported no church affiliation, and about half of the student body was either Presbyterian (30 percent) or Methodist (20 percent).[66] Approximately fifty students were preparing for church vocations as ministers or directors of Christian education. Twenty-seven of Trinity's thirty-six trustees were Presbyterians who were either active church members or ordained clergy.[67]

The curriculum and campus religious life reflected a commitment to Presbyterian higher education. All students were required to take six hours of religion (Old and New Testament history). The university also offered a degree in Christian education for students preparing to serve as directors of religious education in local congregations. Scholarships were available for preministerial students, many of whom attended Presbyterian seminaries and returned to serve at churches within the Synod of Texas. Under the guidance of Chaplain Carlton Allen, the daily early morning Upper Room devotional service, the weekly chapel service, and the annual Spiritual Emphasis Week remained fixtures on the religious calendar. The Student Christian Association and the Church Vocations Fellowship offered interested students programs of spiritual training and service.[68]

President Monroe G. Everett (1942–1950)

Leon "Tex" Taylor, Director
of Public Relations and Vice
President for University
Relations (1947–1972)

Marion Bruce Thomas, Dean of
the University and Vice President for
Academic Affairs (1947–1975)

Administration and classroom building on the Woodlawn campus

President's home on the Woodlawn campus

Trinity faculty at commencement in 1945.
President Everett is seated at left on first row.

Music Professor Albert Herff-Beze with students on the Woodlawn campus

Undeveloped campus site viewed from Stadium Drive looking north

Informal groundbreaking ceremonies on new campus site. With students are (left to right) President Everett and Vice President Will W. Jackson.

The Youtz-Slick lift slab building process was used on Trinity Campus.

Aerial view of campus in early 1950s looking south. Stadium Drive, lower left.
Clockwise from center: Northrup Hall, Student Union Building, Murchison
Dormitory, Storch Library, McFarlin Dormitories, and first unit of the
Marrs McLean Science building

James Woodin Laurie, President (1951–1970)

13 May 1952—Moving day from the Woodlawn campus to Trinity Hill
Top: Vans are loaded in preparation for move.
Middle: Trinity band performs on new campus with borrowed instruments.
Bottom: Students carry books into the Storch Library.

Laurie and architect O'Neil Ford combined skills to develop a distinctive, modern campus on Trinity Hill.

Storch Library

South side of the Student Union Building.
Note the lack of landscaping below the bluff.

East front of Northrup Hall prior to a later addition

T. Frank Murchison,
Trinity trustee and
benefactor

Murchison Dormitory, donated by T. Frank Murchison and
named in honor of his father, John W. Murchison.
Designed as a residence for men, it was initially used by female students
pending completion of their facilities.

Chapman Memorial Graduate Center, completed in 1964

Members of the Chapman family at the dedication of the Chapman Graduate
Center in 1964. Seated (left to right): James A. Chapman, Ruth Chapman Cowles,
Fred Chapman; standing (left to right): Leta Chapman, Elise Chapman,
and Andrew G. Cowles

Malcolm McCown, professor of mathematics, and students examine an early
model computer in the early 1960s.

During the 1950s and 1960s, Trinity held its summer commencement exercises
outdoors in Brackenridge Park at the Sunken Gardens.

Trinity Skyline Swing Band in the 1950s

Director Claude Zetty and the Trinity Choir in 1963. The annual spring choir tour
and concert were important events on the university calendar.

Left to right: Trustees Robert R. Witt, Cecil W. Miller, and James H. Calvert, referred to as "the three wise men" for their leadership during Trinity's formative years in San Antonio.

Derwood Hawthorne, Trinity's chief financial officer (1958–1979), played a key role in the university's growth and development during two crucial decades.

Left: Laurie and Chuck McKinley, the nation's number one ranked singles player, 1962. Right: Laurie and Trinity Little All-American Larry Jeffries, 1968.

Coach Clarence Mabry with tennis team members, left to right:
Cliff Bucholz, Al Hill, Butch Newman, and Andy Lloyd

The Lauries leaving Parker Chapel at the conclusion of their
retirement ceremony in 1970

Aerial view of Trinity University at the time of Laurie's retirement.
Note Laurie Auditorium under construction in the lower left of photograph.

Laurie believed that the president should be the titular head and the faculty the collective promoters of campus religious life. Working in conjunction with the faculty Committee on Religious Life and Work, Laurie played a leading role in shaping Trinity's church relationships and defining the scope and nature of campus religious activities. He supported the annual visits to Trinity by the Synod of Texas and the Synod Youth Workshop, events that brought nearly a thousand people to campus, including many potential students. On the other hand, because he believed that student denominational groups on campus (including Presbyterian) fostered sectarianism and discouraged ecumenical cooperation, he prohibited the establishment of such campus organizations and encouraged students to make denominational contacts through local churches.[69]

On the fifth anniversary of the move to Trinity Hill, Laurie summarized the university's progress between 1952 and 1957. In part because of the successful building program, the university had almost doubled its net worth (from $2.5 million to $4.9 million) and had received more than $4 million in gifts and contributions. Despite downturns in enrollment during the Korean conflict, Trinity had maintained an average student population of approximately 1,000 on the main campus. Although faculty size remained substantially the same (seventy full-time faculty members), the number who held an earned doctorate rose from 25 percent in 1952 to approximately 40 percent in 1957. With the graduate program fully accredited by the Southern Association and a major curriculum revision underway, Trinity was making strides in solidifying its academic reputation. "In all honesty," Laurie said, "we might say that God has never seen fit to bless any institution more richly than Trinity."[70]

Absent from Laurie's optimistic report were any references to professional and personal problems that characterized the early years of his presidency. With self-esteem and confidence that were sometimes seen as arrogance, Laurie aggressively pursued his goals, sometimes disregarding academic protocol. When he did seek formal approval of his decisions, it was often after the fact. Laurie patterned his academic administrative style on that of pastorates in which ministers functioned as staff professionals and lay people served under their oversight. Although this model usually worked well in congregations, it generated unrest in Trinity's academic environment. Some viewed Laurie as a micromanager whose decision making ranged from major policy issues such as church relationships and budget priorities to minor items such as purchasing a typewriter and making office assignments.[71]

Laurie once asked faculty members to serve as fund-raisers and assigned them to solicit various local businesses. The faculty responded with a mixture of incredulity and anger. An irate professor confronted Laurie and accused him of turning faculty members into development officers. When Laurie responded that it was not unusual for Presbyterian elders to assume key roles in congregational financial campaigns, the professor retorted, "You may know something about elders, but I know something about professors!" Encountering sustained opposition from faculty members, Laurie quietly abandoned the project.[72]

Laurie heightened tensions in 1953 when he abolished the position of university chaplain held by Carlton Allen. A popular faculty member and recent moderator of the Synod of Texas, Allen had differed with Laurie on a number of issues, including religious activities, compulsory ROTC, and budgetary priorities, but they had maintained a cordial relationship. The campus community and synod officials were shocked, therefore, when they learned that Laurie had informed Allen that Trinity would no longer need his services as university chaplain. Although Laurie invited him to remain as a member of the department of religion, Allen decided to seek a position elsewhere.[73]

Unhappy with Laurie's treatment of Allen, a group of students and recent graduates organized to secure his removal. Trinity alumni attending McCormick Seminary in Chicago addressed a letter to the stated clerk of the Synod of Texas listing their complaints and calling for the appointment of an investigative committee. In San Antonio, some residential students held clandestine meetings at late hours with various trustees and synod officials in the foyer of the downtown St. Anthony Hotel. Together they discussed strategies to remove Laurie from office.[74]

Adding to Laurie's problems, Bruce Thomas and Carl Parker resigned in 1957 to accept positions with the Texas Commission on Higher Education, citing "a tremendous opportunity for enlarged service."[75] Despite repeated efforts by trustees to dissuade Parker and Thomas from leaving, the two men said their decision was irrevocable. "With reluctance and real regret," board of trustee Chairman Miller accepted their resignations and noted that Trinity "was suffering a real loss in the resignation of two men who had contributed so much to Trinity."[76]

As Parker's replacement, Laurie selected Derwood L. Hawthorne, who held degrees from the College of Emporia in Kansas and New York University and had served for more than a decade as bursar of the Newark branch of Rutgers University. Recruited during one of the president's trips to Princeton Theological Seminary, Hawthorne quickly became a key figure in Trinity's administrative structure. His fiscal expertise and manage-

Trinity billboard heralding the new campus

ment of university resources served Trinity well during a career of more than two decades.[77]

Laurie left the dean's position unfilled and appointed a dean's council consisting of eight faculty and staff members to direct academic affairs on an interim basis. In the meantime, Thomas's family remained in San Antonio while he commuted to Austin and conducted research for the Texas Commission on Higher Education.[78]

After seven months in Austin, Thomas determined that the position was too politicized and, in his estimation, held no long-term professional possibilities. Having promised Laurie that he would consider the option of returning to Trinity if the Austin position proved unsatisfactory, Thomas met with the president to discuss his future plans. Talking into the small hours of the morning and both acknowledging the issues between them, they reached a mutual understanding that worked remarkably well in subsequent years and forged a bond of lasting friendship.[79]

In the midst of his professional difficulties, Laurie had encountered serious health problems. During a routine physical examination in the spring of 1956, physicians detected colon cancer and advised a colostomy, which was successful, but the slow recovery process stretched over several months. Afterward Laurie rarely mentioned his condition except when he counseled people facing a similar operation.[80]

Following the cancer surgery, Laurie suffered a detached retina, which led physicians to immobilize him in a hospital bed and sandbag his head so that he could make no sudden moves. Even in this situation, Laurie promoted Trinity. He asked Tex Taylor to have sketches of proposed buildings brought down to his hospital room for display. Although unable to see clearly, Laurie memorized the location of each picture and pointed them out to his frequent visitors. He mentioned only incidentally that the sketches would not become buildings unless they received financial support. Laurie quipped to his visitors, "They're there for you to enjoy until I can see them, too."[81]

Laurie's health problems had a significant impact on his interpersonal relationships within the Trinity community. Although he lost none of his sense of urgency to move the university to new levels of accomplishment, Laurie acknowledged that his recovery from cancer was both a gift and a message from God. After the operation, he wrote in his notebook, "Let this be a symbol of a new day and a new beginning of partnership with God and His power. Be much more positive, appreciative, stick to that for a while, not the failures, the negatives. God will give all the health and strength He feels I need. Let love be your watchword and token."[82]

Laurie also vowed to be more sensitive to criticism in his role as university president: "There is nothing magical about this, just keep working. There is support to be had and it will come. It is your job to help men make their own right decisions. Neither domination nor abdication." Responding to campus tensions, he wrote, "Do not be annoyed. Our program is sound—it will require a little more time to put it into operation. It is always right to maintain a Christian attitude of love—no bitterness, no flipness, gracious good will is the answer. Keep your attitudes right and all else will fall into place. Do not fear."[83]

Aware of tensions in the university community, Laurie took steps to address issues of campus morale. He invited a select group of students, faculty, and staff to his home to express their opinions. Promising to listen and respond without recrimination, Laurie listened for more than an hour to a variety of complaints. Most centered on the view that he made arbitrary decisions without having consulted administrative units or student organizations. Acknowledging that his desire to achieve immediate results often caused him to bypass established procedures, Laurie agreed to rectify such matters. He then led the group in a positive discussion regarding what could be done to improve campus morale. Although tensions did not end immediately, the meeting proved pivotal in improving Laurie's relationship with the campus community.[84]

After returning to his duties, Laurie had to use both tact and ingenuity to deal with intercollegiate athletics. Despite mounting deficits, Trinity trustees continued to support efforts by Frank Murchison and Tex Taylor to promote the institution as a football powerhouse. A major step in that direction occurred in 1952 when William B. McElreath, formerly an assistant at Tulane University, was hired as head football coach. McElreath gathered an experienced staff, recruited transfer and high school athletes, and quickly assembled highly competitive teams.[85]

During the 1953 season, Trinity lost only one game, and that by a single point to East Texas State University, a team that brought a record of twenty-one consecutive victories to the contest. The same season marked the introduction of a new Trinity mascot, Lee Roy, a Royal Bengal tiger purchased by local builder and developer L. R. (Lee Roy) Pletz. Housed in the San Antonio Zoo, Lee Roy appeared at pep rallies and football games in a portable display cage escorted by the Bengal Lancers social club. Transported around the track after every Trinity touchdown, Lee Roy became a familiar figure to San Antonio sports enthusiasts for nearly a decade.[86]

In 1954 Trinity enjoyed its most successful football season in more than fifty years of intercollegiate competition, ending the season with a 9-0 record and outscoring its opponents by 227 to 41 points. The Associated Press selected star quarterback Alvin Beal as a first-team Little All-American, and the Texas Sports Writers Association named McElreath as state coach of the year. In receiving the honor, McElreath beat out notables such as Paul "Bear" Bryant of Texas A&M University, Chalmer Woodard of Southern Methodist University, and George Sauer of Baylor University.[87]

Trinity's gridiron success proved to be short-lived, however. When the Gulf Coast Conference folded in 1956, Trinity played as an independent against schools such as Texas A&M University, Mississippi Southern University, and the Air Force Academy. Although Trinity's teams performed well, their disappointing season records failed to attract fans, and box office receipts dramatically declined. With the death of Frank Murchison in 1955, Trinity's athletic program also lost one of its most enthusiastic advocates and financial supporters.[88] Trustees began to question the wisdom of continuing the quest for national recognition as a football powerhouse.

Above: Trinity's mascot, Lee Roy
Below: Lee Roy's cubs

During a discussion in 1956, trustee Robert Witt observed, "It looks like Trinity can't afford a football team," and trustee Margarite Parker commented, "It appears that San Antonio doesn't want it."[89] Other observers cited disciplinary problems and special treatment as negative aspects of the athletic program.[90]

Despite their reservations and the fact that in 1957 Laurie reported an accumulated five-year institutional deficit of $255,000, of which intercollegiate athletics accounted for $180,000, Trinity trustees hesitated to downsize a sport that was popular among many students, alumni, and members of the San Antonio business community.[91] Trinity continued to play major opponents and acquired National Collegiate Athletic Association (NCAA) recognition as a major football team. As criticism of athletic budget deficits mounted, however, the Athletic Council acknowledged in 1958 the improbability of breaking into big-time football and recommended that Trinity concentrate on maintaining existing sports at "a moderate level" while broadening the program to include other sports.[92]

Laurie (right) receiving the Golden Deeds Award, 1960

Even though de-emphasizing football evoked some negative comments in the local press, Trinity in general enjoyed favorable relationships with the San Antonio community, in large part because of Laurie's status as a university administrator and civic leader. From 1953 to 1956, he served as a member of the Board of Directors of the San Antonio Chamber of Commerce and in 1959 was elected president, the first minister and educator ever to hold that position in San Antonio. Laurie also served as director and president of the San Antonio Rotary Club, trustee and president of the San Antonio Public Library, a trustee of the Southwest Foundation for Research and Education, a member of the Council for Educational Television, a director of the San Antonio Fiesta Commission, and a member of the Greater San Antonio Development Committee. His other positions included the Texas Foundation of Voluntarily Supported Colleges and Universities, the Commission on Christian Higher Education of the Association of American Colleges, and the Conference of Church-Related Colleges of the South.[93]

Laurie's work in San Antonio did not go unrecognized. In 1960 the retiring mayor of San Antonio indicated publicly that he could think of no better person than Jim Laurie to succeed him in that office. Although Laurie dismissed the possibility of a political career, he enjoyed the publicity generated by the mayor's remarks. Official recognition of his civic labors came in 1960 when the Exchange Club named him the recipient of the Golden Deeds Award. Given annually to a member of the community who had rendered service "over and beyond the call of routine civic duty," the award demonstrated how much San Antonians appreciated Laurie's work as a university administrator and responsible citizen, especially in the area of civil rights.[94]

After a decade under the leadership of James W. Laurie, Trinity University had made remarkable strides. Trinity's endowment rose from less than one million to more than six million dollars and the operating budget increased from some six hundred thousand dollars to more than three million dollars. Most obvious were the dramatic physical changes that took place on the 107-acre campus. By 1961, Trinity had twenty-two buildings in place and three more under construction. Four new dormitories and the Charlotte Mayfield Home Economics Cottage rounded out the major projects on the new campus.[95]

Among the campus additions was a new wing of the main administration building, named Northrup Hall in 1960 in honor of Preston Gaines Northrup, a deceased San Antonio rancher and independent oil operator. Northrup bequeathed a substantial portion of his estate to the university, providing major financial support at a crucial point in its history.[96] His widow, Gretchen Gaines Northrup, served for many years as a university trustee and established a foundation to provide for the maintenance and upkeep of Northrup Hall and to support faculty salaries. In 1988 she received a Distinguished Service Award in recognition of her outstanding service to the university.[97]

Under the combined leadership of Laurie and Thomas, progress touched all aspects of academic life: classrooms, faculty, and curriculum. Teachers with earned doctorates reached 60 percent of the faculty in 1960, compared with 19 percent in 1951. Moreover, expenditures for faculty salaries, library needs, and supplies for classrooms and laboratories were twice those of the previous ten years. New departments, a major curriculum revision, and increased library holdings enhanced Trinity's reputation as a quality educational institution. The addition of a guidance program and a job placement service as well as a professionally staffed office of student life provided students with more personal attention.[98]

Laurie's optimism permeated all levels of university activity. He talked so persistently and eloquently about excellence and creativity that it seemed to become a self-fulfilling prophecy. At the "Decade of Achievement" dinner held in December 1961 to honor Laurie, Bruce Thomas summarized the uniqueness of Laurie's leadership and its impact on the Trinity community. "The qualities that characterize a great university president are present in Dr. Laurie to a degree that I have seen in no other man. Coming from the ministry to the presidency of Trinity, he accomplished a major career transition with skill and efficiency, tempering a natural tendency to move rapidly and decisively with a warm, friendly, and understanding nature. He caught on to the problems of the educational world more rapidly than anyone I have known not brought up in it. I can speak for the faculty when I say that everyone at Trinity gratefully realizes that we have an educator as a president.[99]

CHAPTER NINE

THE MIRACLE OF TRINITY HILL

The reason we believe we can do the impossible
is because we have already done it.

JAMES W. LAURIE, JUNE 1953

THROUGHOUT ITS HISTORY, FROM TEHUACANA to Waxahachie to San Antonio, Trinity's leaders invoked words such as "dream," "hope," and "promise," but they invariably saw their aspirations falter. Despite relocations, financial campaigns, and leadership changes, Trinity continued to be inadequately housed, marginally staffed, and insufficiently funded. Under James W. Laurie's leadership, however, it was nearing a point where rhetoric might become reality. Although national acclaim remained elusive, Trinity had shed its image of a peripatetic institution on the cusp of closure and attained recognition as a quality regional university. In the press, on television, and from the podium, the encomium "the miracle of Trinity Hill" described the university's dramatic transformation.[1]

While Laurie worked toward a "new Trinity," administrators hoped that his policies would catch up with his procedures. Trustees wondered who was going to pay the bills. Benefactors wondered if there would be an end to blueprints for new buildings earmarked for their generosity. And students and faculty wondered what academic life would be like without a succession of groundbreakings, dedications, and construction projects. According to one account (possibly apocryphal), a power failure caused all the construction machinery suddenly to become quiet. The silence was overwhelming. Accustomed to the steady background noise, students, faculty, and staff were unable to concentrate. Only when the drills, hammers, and bulldozers started up again did Trinity return to normal.[2]

Implementing the master building plan represented only one aspect of the changes that reconfigured Trinity's identity during the 1960s. After years of vacillation, Trinity adopted a selective admissions policy and raised entrance requirements. Concurrently, a new generation of Trinity students challenged the entrenched *in loco parentis* approach to student life and called for more rights and responsibilities. The changing faculty, more committed to academic disciplines than denominational affiliations, took an increasingly active role in the process of setting institutional policies and goals. Like their students, they questioned administrative paternalism and formalized procedures relating to equity in hiring and due process in employment practices. Beyond these developments, Trinity and the Presbyterian church entered into a bilateral agreement that ended legal ties, establishing a covenant relationship based on shared histories and common goals.

To outside observers, the most obvious indication of progress on Trinity Hill was the rapid transformation of the former quarry site into a distinctive and modern campus. Between 1964 and 1968, a major part of Trinity's master plan reached completion. At one point during that time span, seven buildings were in various stages of construction. In 1964 the T. Frank Murchison Memorial Tower with the Carolyn Calvert Bells became a campus landmark. During the same year, the Chapman Graduate Center and the Earl C. Sams Memorial Athletic Center were finished. The Refectory (now Mabee Hall) opened in 1965, and three other buildings became available for use in 1966: the Margarite B. Parker Chapel, the Ruth Taylor Theater, and the William L. Moody Jr. Engineering Building. Construction of the E. M. Stevens Field in 1967 and the erection of the Ruth and Andrew G. Cowles Life Science Building, the Ewing Halsell Administrative Studies Center, and the Robert R. Witt Reception Center followed in 1968. In addition, the Eugenia Miller Fountain and the Cowles Fountain graced two of the principal entrances to Trinity's upper campus.[3]

During this extended building program, Laurie and O'Neil Ford developed a close working relationship. Ford, liberal and outspoken, and Laurie had different styles and perspectives, but they respected one another's qualities of leadership, energy, and vision. Laurie especially appreciated Ford's artistic sensitivity, and Ford recognized in Laurie a man who combined deep religious convictions with the ability to make wise tactical and business decisions.[4]

The team of Laurie and Ford also succeeded in attracting donors and securing commitments to fund new buildings. When Laurie recruited dramatist Paul Baker to join the Trinity faculty in 1963, he promised him a new theater with three stages, a set shop, dressing rooms, and produc-

Construction accelerated during the 1960s. Above: Murchison Tower.

Air hammers
were required to
dig in limestone
bedrock.

tion offices. To accomplish this, Laurie attracted the interest of Vernon and Ruth Taylor, mining millionaires who had recently funded a music building and fine arts center at Trinity. Reportedly, they had planned to give $600,000 to the project, but were considering withdrawing their offer. Ford, in his usual casual manner, showed up thirty minutes late for his first meeting with the couple and launched into an animated presentation. In describing the charms of the theater, he claimed it would be one of the most prestigious buildings on the campus. By the time Ford finished, he had convinced the Taylors to pledge $1.5 million to the project.[5]

By 1968 forty-two buildings had been erected and only an auditorium remained to round out the university's master plan. With a projected seating capacity of 3,000, the auditorium would function as the site for university and civic cultural programs as well as annual commencement ceremonies. Laurie hoped to have the building available in time to celebrate Trinity's centennial in 1969 and to host the General Assembly of the United Presbyterian Church in the U.S.A., scheduled to meet that year in San Antonio. That aspiration died when the university failed to raise sufficient funds to activate a federal loan. Undaunted, Laurie told the board of trustees in 1968, "I am sure the auditorium will come, but if it comes too far down the road I shall remember Moses as he stood looking over into the promised land, but not having set foot thereon."[6] Although Laurie announced a year later that a Texas foundation had contributed enough money to warrant breaking ground for the new auditorium, he did not live to see the finished product.[7]

In contrast to the first phase of the building program, which resulted in annual operating deficits, Laurie completed the final elements of the master plan with a balanced budget. Laurie told trustees in 1967, "Some have thought we have always lived a bit dangerously in our building program, and if this has been true, then I would say we are living a little less dangerously than we have in the past."[8] For the fiscal years 1965–66 through 1969–70, Trinity avoided operating deficits, due primarily to a substantial increase in the endowment. Although long-term indebtedness grew, primarily for buildings, the trustees included provisions for repayment in the general operating budget.[9]

Other campus improvements made life more comfortable, efficient, and safe. All buildings were air-conditioned, offices were furnished with modern furniture and equipment, and poles and wires were replaced by underground utility lines. A new telephone system enabled faculty, staff, and students to make campus calls without going through a Trinity operator.[10] As buildings became available, most faculty gained private offices, file cabinets, and adequate shelving space for books. Although only executive secretaries and department chairs were issued electric typewriters, other staff had, for the first time, modern manual equipment that did not resemble imports from the Woodlawn campus.[11]

A growing campus necessitated increased security measures. With incidents of theft and physical assault reported on campuses throughout the country, Trinity examined liability issues that might arise from failure to provide adequate protection for students and their personal property. In the early 1950s, Trinity employed one night watchman who patrolled the area around the women's dormitories. By the end of the decade, the services of six part-time off-duty police officers supervised by Lt. William "Smoky" Stover of the San Antonio Police Department supplied campus protection. Their attention centered on writing traffic tickets and attempting to reduce the number of break-ins and car thefts in campus parking lots.[12]

Trinity employed the services of the Smith Detective Agency in 1965 for twenty-four-hour campus coverage. It also installed new campus lighting to make it safer to walk at night and added an emergency telephone number to put students in immediate contact with security officers. New rules closed all buildings except the library at 10:00 P.M. on weekdays and Sat-

SAN ANTONIO *Evening* **NEWS** **FINAL** LATE MARKETS

48th Year — No. 183   Wednesday, May 18, 1966   San Antonio, Texas   Tel. CA 5-7411 — Classified CA 5-1611   80 Pages

Police Cool Off Midnight Raiders
Trinity Boys Howl for Panties

A panty raid made headlines in 1966.

urday and all day on Sunday. During these times, no entrance was allowed without obtaining special access from university authorities. Some users lamented the loss of freedom, but others expressed appreciation for the new campus safety measures. Security officers reported that their most exacting assignments were to monitor several panty raids during which a large number of male students gathered at the women's dormitories. After women tossed some garments from the balconies, the crowd quickly dispersed.[13]

Trinity entered the computer age in 1960 when the mathematics department acquired a rebuilt Royal Precision Digital LGP-30 model at a discount price of $18,000. The size of an office desk, the computer had the ability to add two ten-digit numbers in approximately two-thousandths of a second. Used primarily by faculty and graduate students for research projects, the computer also enabled Trinity to offer courses in elementary and advanced computer programming, the first such courses available at any San Antonio college or university.[14] In 1966 Trinity received a $75,000 grant from the National Science Foundation to rent a high-speed IBM 1800 computer that was installed in the new Engineering Science Building. This instrument enabled the university to automate a number of campus operations, such as payroll distribution, account records, and data processing for laboratory experiments.[15]

With the completion of the Ewing Halsell Administrative Studies Center in 1968, Trinity expanded its use of computer technology. The purchase of an IBM model 360-44, the first series to employ integrated circuits rather than transistors, widened the range of possibilities for educational use. Trinity conducted its first partially automated registration process in May 1968 utilizing computer punch cards.[16] Laurie reported that the new technology "had its problems" but on the whole promised to be a more efficient method of operation. The initial registration closed on

Wednesday evening at eight o'clock, and faculty members received a print-out of their class rolls early the next morning.[17]

In concert with the accelerated building program, Trinity was taking steps to improve the quality of the student body. Historically, the university had operated under a *de facto* open admissions policy. Virtually all high school graduates and transfer students who applied were accepted either provisionally or without reservation.[18] Although the university required College Entrance Examination Board (CEEB) scores for the first time in 1959, the admissions committee still exercised considerable discretion in evaluating their importance in the decision-making process. Standards for admission included graduation in the upper half of the class from a secondary school, a verbal score above 475 on the CEEB Scholastic Aptitude Test, and a total of 900 on the combined quantitative and verbal tests. Applicants were also required to submit writing samples as part of the admissions process.[19]

Trinity modified its admissions criteria in 1966 to require two units of a single foreign language and three achievement tests, including English composition, for all students. The university also employed a freshman grade prediction formula using weighted values for high school grades and test scores. Consequently, the number of students accepted for admission declined, and the number of first-year students placed on probation dropped sharply. At the same time, CEEB scores rose significantly for both men and women.[20] Reporting to the board of trustees in 1966, Thomas hailed the progress of Trinity's admission program as "the beginning of a new era" for the university. During the previous seven years, average CEEB scores had increased approximately 100 points, along with a corresponding improvement in average high school grades. With mean scores of 1068 for males and 1051 for females, the quality of the incoming freshman class exceeded that of any previous year on record. As a result, as Thomas concluded, "more demanding and more exciting educational programs are both possible and mandatory."[21]

Director of Admissions Walter P. West noted three significant changes in Trinity's enrollment trends. First, the number of part-time students was decreasing and full-time students increasing. Second, there had been a sharp rise in resident students with the erection of several new dormitories. Third, the former predominance of students from San Antonio and Bexar County was changing to a larger representation from other Texas areas and surrounding states.[22]

In faculty recruitment, Trinity's quest for academic excellence received impetus from an unprecedented availability of scholars with Ph.D. degrees from some of the country's most highly regarded universities. By the end of the 1960s, 70 percent of Trinity's 168 full-time faculty members had earned doctoral degrees. Bruce Thomas described the new recruits as "the backbone of the present faculty" and said, "The maturing of a young faculty should produce a quality of academic work in the next few years for which we have been earnestly striving for a long time."[23]

The new faculty members differed from their predecessors in terms of religious commitment and denominational loyalty. Although most were aware of Trinity's church affiliation, they viewed themselves as *educators* at a Christian university rather than as *Christian* educators at a denominational institution. Faculty hired during this era recalled that neither department chairs nor the academic dean raised the issue of religious preference during the hiring process. Faculty members were attracted to Trinity by the possibilities of building departments, developing curricula, and experimenting with pedagogy and by promises of increasing commitments of university resources to faculty development and research.[24]

Early in his presidency, Laurie had envisioned a faculty consisting solely of evangelical Christians. He later modified this vision to include qualified scholars who had little or no religious commitment or who were members of other religious traditions as long as they were tolerant of Trinity's historic church relationship. When one candidate informed Laurie that he was an atheist, Laurie asked him if he had read the institution's statement of purpose and could work comfortably within that framework. An affirmative response from the candidate ended the conversation about religion. Another candidate mentioned that he was a Unitarian, to which Laurie jokingly responded, "That's not a religion." Nevertheless, he approved the appointment and welcomed the professor to the Trinity community.[25]

Scholarly activities assumed more importance as faculty members wrote, edited, and translated books and published scholarly articles in their disciplines.[26] In 1964 Thomas reported that Trinity faculty had published six books in recent months with several others soon to be published. Two outstanding works came from English professor Thomas F. Gossett and drama instructor Robert L. Flynn. Gossett's book, *Race: The History of an Idea in America*, was published by Southern Methodist University Press in 1963, won the Phi Beta Kappa Ralph Waldo Emerson Award, and was favorably reviewed nationally. The *New York Times* recognized Flynn's satire on the vanishing West, *North to Yesterday*, released by Alfred Knopf in 1967, as one of the twenty outstanding novels of the year.[27] A survey of faculty publications indicated that between 1960 and

1969 approximately 102, or half, of Trinity professors had published scholarly articles and/or books in their particular fields of specialization.[28]

New faculty members encountered an informal tenure and promotion system. Much of the process required minimal documentation and no input from the faculty at large. Faculty at the rank of assistant professor or above were awarded tenure with their fifth-year contract, while those with two or more years of service elsewhere acquired tenure with their fourth-year contract. With no specified time frame for promotion, much depended on the initiative of the chair, dean, or president. Because of limited funds for faculty salaries, the administration often offered promotions, rather than significant raises, for outstanding achievements.[29]

To be promoted, faculty members often had to raise the issue themselves. One professor related how she secured her promotion to associate professor. She first talked with her department chair, who told her that he had recommended a promotion to the administration but had received no response and advised her to talk to the dean. Bruce Thomas said that he did not recall any communication from the chair, but based on her outstanding teaching record, he thought she merited promotion. However, if she was willing to wait a year, he promised both a promotion and a $1,000 raise. He asked her to think it over and let him know. As the interview ended, Thomas said, "If you decide to take the promotion now, just tell Barbara [the executive secretary]. She will take care of it."[30]

The same professor's elevation to department chair occurred with a similar casualness. Thomas met her in a corridor of Northrup Hall and said, "We need a new chair in your department, and you will make a good one. Let me know if you are interested in the position." She later accepted the offer after he promised a full-time secretary and an electric typewriter. Because the incumbent was not aware of this decision, her first task as chair was to inform him of his change in status.[31]

The dismissal of a popular nontenured faculty member made headlines in the *Trinitonian* and highlighted the need for more formal tenure and promotion procedures. In December 1967, Thomas notified philosophy professor Sherman Stanage that he would not receive tenure. No official reasons were given for the decision, but rumors were that Stanage's political activism and his reputation for "generating sparks" on campus were underlying factors. "It seems obvious to me," Stanage told student reporters, "that due process for students and faculty does not exist on this campus. In my case, if there were due process for faculty, I would have had the opportunity to answer any possible charges that might have been lodged against me."[32] In support of Stanage, the student government adopted a "statement of concern about administrative-student-faculty relationships" and held open forums to discuss issues of academic freedom.[33]

Responding to the public clamor over Stanage's dismissal, Thomas assigned the investigation of the matter to the Faculty Senate. A committee chaired by religion professor Guy Ranson followed the guidelines established by the American Association of University Professors (AAUP) and heard testimony from both Thomas and Stanage. In its report to the senate, the committee concluded that Stanage had not demonstrated "probable cause" or "reasonable grounds" to believe that not receiving tenure constituted a violation of his academic freedom. The senate approved the report and forwarded it to the dean and the president. Stanage did not appeal the decision and left Trinity at the end of the semester.[34]

For several years prior to the Stanage controversy, the Faculty Senate had been intermittently engaged in revising its constitution and bylaws to deal with issues of representation and due process. During the summer of 1968, it completed this task. The new constitution provided for a senate of eighteen members (six professors, six associate professors, and six assistant professors or instructors) elected by their peers. The constitution also redefined the academic faculty as consisting exclusively of full-time faculty members whose primary responsibility was teaching, research, or librarianship. The bylaws contained an expanded policy statement on academic freedom, responsibility, employment, tenure, and due process that gave faculty members a greater degree of involvement in decisions affecting their professional careers.[35]

In presenting the new constitution to the board of trustees, Laurie acknowledged that Trinity lacked adequate procedures to handle "unhappy situations between the academic administration and faculty staff members." Previously, he said, it had always been possible to proceed "in a climate of trust and understanding," but changing times required more formal channels of representation.[36] Laurie called the faculty a "very responsible group" and commended it for making its organization more meaningful to the university and the total academic community. The trustees approved the plan with the caveat, "Nothing in this statement is intended to protect an incompetent or negligent faculty member."[37]

In other areas, the conditions for faculty greatly improved during the decade of the 1960s. The trustees approved modest funds for faculty research and development, including opportunities for advanced study, completion of dissertations, and attendance at professional meetings. Some money was also available to enable a few professors to conduct university-supported research or to secure reduced teaching loads while working on particular projects.[38] In 1955 teaching loads ranged from fifteen to eighteen hours a week. A decade later, the standard teaching load was twelve hours for the general faculty and nine hours for department chairs. The establishment of a faculty club in the new addition of Northrup Hall, tuition waivers for faculty spouses and children, and a summer sports program for younger faculty children, proved to be positive factors in attracting new faculty.[39]

Recognizing the pivotal role of the library in academic life, Trinity administrators devoted increased financial resources to improve the collection and to secure professional staff. In 1955, Trinity had a book collection of only 61,000 volumes, and its annual book budget of $10,000 fell below the Southern Association's minimum guidelines of 5 percent of the educational budget. Directed by James G. Govan (1961–65), the library staff was expanded with the employment of a cataloger, a circulation librarian, and several assistant librarians. Book resources increased 18 percent, and the library budget grew from $21,000 to approximately $170,000.[40]

Under Govan's successor, Robert A. Houze, who had been the library director at Texas A&M University for sixteen years, the library underwent a series of changes that permitted a higher volume of material to be processed without proportional staff increases. During the spring and summer of 1967, the library converted from the Dewey decimal system to the Library of Congress classification system, and staff keypunched the library holdings for future computer use. The installation of an NCR posting machine increased the efficiency of the library's bookkeeping system. In the fall of 1967, Houze established the Committee on Automation, which coordinated the library's use of data-processing equipment. Library staff began to distribute a monthly list of acquisitions and provided selective subject bibliographies at the request of faculty members.[41]

The library continued its growth in the late 1960s aided by donations of private collections and more than a quarter of million dollars in cash gifts and grants. Between 1964 and 1968, the library's share of the university's educational budget increased from 5.3 percent to 10 percent, and the number of shelved volumes grew from 126,000 to more than 260,000. By the end of the decade, the collection totaled 365,000 volumes and the library had fourteen professional librarians and a staff of twenty-six nonprofessional employees.[42]

Nevertheless, the growth of the library remained a central and continuing project, especially as Trinity contemplated expanding graduate programs. Reporting to Trinity trustees in 1964, Thomas stated that conversations with department chairs invariably focused on the library's inability to support both student and faculty research. Trinity's future as an educational institution, Thomas concluded, would depend greatly on its ability to develop adequate library facilities.[43]

Undergraduate curricular innovation characterized academic developments during Trinity's centennial decade. Instituted in the fall of 1963, the Independent Study Program attracted gifted first-year students to the Trinity campus. To be eligible for consideration, students had to achieve a secondary school average of 2.65 on a 3.0 scale and a total of 1250 on CEEB tests. From the list of candidates, approximately twenty-five students were accepted and assigned to an instructor in the department of their choice. The program featured a three-hour colloquium for all participants and a conference and reading course with individual professors. The colloquium emphasized study and discussion in some broad area of human knowledge, such as "The Effect of the Scientific Revolution on Twentieth Century Civilization," "Social Anthropology," and "American Civilization by Its Interpreters." In addition to the Independent Study Program, a system of honors courses for qualified juniors and seniors permitted students to proceed at an individual pace under the guidance of a faculty tutor.[44]

Following an intensive institutional self-study in 1965, Trinity faculty moved to craft a new basic curriculum that was appropriate for the rising quality of entering students.[45] Implemented in 1968, "The Trinity Plan," unlike the previously structured curriculum, emphasized academic goals rather than required courses and stressed competence in a subject matter rather than a specified number of hours. Within the framework of satisfying a number of goals such as language facility, mathematical and logical reasoning, historical perspective, natural sciences, and the nature of religion, students could choose courses of study to meet these goals. Some courses satisfied more than one goal, so students were able to reduce the number of hours committed to the general curriculum studies. Because the Trinity Plan enabled students to broaden their range of electives, they could graduate with double or even triple majors. With periodic modifications, this curriculum proved to be popular with both faculty and students for more than a decade.[46]

The Trinity Plan heightened the role of faculty advisors in course selection and degree planning. The flexibility of the Trinity Plan gave more leeway to faculty advisors' judgment and students' responsibility in fulfilling goals and selecting majors. In 1965 the office of the academic dean, rather than admissions, assumed responsibility for the assignment of faculty advisors for first-year students. Assuming that any faculty member could advise first-year and sophomore students under the Trinity Plan, students were assigned randomly rather than by anticipated majors or fields of interest. The only exceptions to this policy were students with a declared interest in Engineering, Speech and Drama, or Music.[47]

"There were all kinds of prophets of gloom. You may not think this flexible degree program sounds very radical, but to our faculty in 1968 it was sort of like the Communist Manifesto. Imagine the English department that had existed for a hundred years on a twelve-hour requirement in English being suddenly told that we were not going to require this any longer!"

Dean Bruce Thomas describing the Trinity Plan
at the Southern University Conference in 1973

Trinity's undergraduate offerings included a growing number of innovative courses that attracted large numbers of students. The newly established Department of Geology, for example, combined lectures, laboratories, and extended field trips. Excursions to Enchanted Rock and surrounding areas enabled faculty to integrate information gleaned from the classroom and laboratory with first-hand observation and exploration. Led by chair Don McGannon, the department quickly acquired a reputation for demanding scholarship and interactive learning. Both McGannon and his colleague Edward Roy received "outstanding teacher" awards from student organizations in recognition of their accomplishments.[48]

Trinity's speech and drama department underwent a sudden transformation in 1963 when nationally acclaimed dramatist and Trinity alumnus Paul Baker became the department chair. As head of Baylor University's drama department since 1939, Baker had acquired a national reputation for his artistic creativity, having designed the famous Baylor Theater, the first in the United States to incorporate conventional staging and theater-in-the-round in flexible staging.[49] Baker and his twelve-member drama staff resigned en masse from Baylor University in the spring of 1963 after an extended controversy over the use of profanity in Eugene O'Neill's autobiographical *Long Day's Journey into Night*. Baylor's president forced the production to close in mid-run by banning plays that contained "vulgar, profane or blasphemous language" or "ridiculed the Christian religion." Baker brought with him to Trinity five staff members (Eugene McKinney, Dugald MacArthur, Jearnine Wagner, Robert Flynn, and Mary

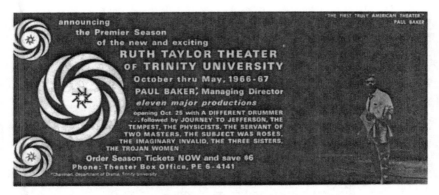

Trinity's theater program generated wide interest with the
arrival of Paul Baker and his staff.

Sue Fridge) whose professional talents generated an interest in performing
arts that was unprecedented in Trinity's history.[50]

Baker's course entitled "Integration of Abilities" introduced students to
exercises in space, rhythm and time, direction, line movement, and sound
and silence that enhanced their creativity and self-understanding. "We
have a vision that is individually ours, that comes from our very unique
background," Baker said. "My job is to help rediscover that individual
country and landscape, help establish an inner dialogue for the student involved, and let the environment remain friendly long enough for that person to test and communicate his ever-growing vision, be it as an actor,
writer, designer, musician, scientist, whatever."[51]

Along similar lines, journalism professor David Burkett's course in
mass communication attracted large numbers of students from a variety
of majors and disciplines. Burkett designed the course to help students increase their awareness and creativity. Along with lectures and discussions,
the course featured "growthful games" based on human awareness and
several extended off-campus retreats. Students kept journals of their experiences and completed assignments in creative writing. The class generated several student-organized "reunions," in which former participants
gathered to share experiences and renew friendships.[52]

Students accustomed to traditional physical education courses encountered something quite different at Trinity. Department chair Jesse
MacLeay, who held a Ph.D. from the University of Illinois, developed a
curriculum of theory and activity courses for Trinity students. MacLeay
designed the basic required course, P.E. 100, to educate students in the latest scientific findings pertaining to sports, exercise, and dance.[53] Featuring

lectures on subjects such as "Hereditary and environmental factors in human performance," "Analysis of motor function and its relationship to mental and social accomplishments," and "Procedures for developing motor, cardiovascular, and aesthetic fitness" and combining them with individualized exercise and recreational programs, MacLeay encouraged students to integrate physical fitness into lifetime activities. A relentless taskmaster, MacLeay evoked ambivalent responses from Trinity students, but even his critics admitted that P.E. 100 was a memorable learning experience, one that challenged them to take seriously the interdependence of physical, mental, and emotional health.[54]

Perhaps the best known and most sought after course on campus was music appreciation, the only departmental offering in the *Trinity University Catalogue* with an asterisk indicating "no previous knowledge of music required." Taught by Albert Herff-Beze, one of the most popular members of the Trinity faculty, Music Appreciation 316 was always filled to capacity with a diverse group of students. "Beezie," as students referred to him, had been a member of the San Antonio University faculty before it merged with Trinity in 1942. Active as the sponsor of the Triniteers, Blue Key, and the T Association, Herff-Beze captivated, engaged, and inspired Trinity students for more than three decades. As a tribute to his extended impact on the Trinity community, one of Trinity's residence halls bears his name. Typical of many comments, one student said, "Beezie's classes are a joy to attend. A place where freedom of the spirit abounds, shoes have been known to be discarded, and smoking is allowed. . . . If the composition is an opera, Beezie becomes actor, singer, interpreter and narrator. He may be up on a chair portraying a giant or dancing along performing Carmen's flirting scene." Another student signed Beezie's *Mirage*, "Thanks, Beezie, for giving long-hair music a crewcut."[55]

"The reward of Albert's courses was obviously not the grade, but the experience, the exciting hours in his company. He placed emphasis not on grades or threats, but only experiences, on treats of the spirit. He had something better to do than discipline students: he had to transform barbarians into civilized persons. Spartan discipline, for all its power, was still barbaric. Albert sought to instill in us the free Athenian love of beauty, truth, and goodness."

John Silber, the *Mirage* (Spring 1974): 38–39

Albert Herff-Beze, Professor, Department of Music, University of San Antonio
(1937–42) and Trinity University (1942–76)

Trinity engaged in its first experiment of teaching by television as part
of a ten-college system organized by the University of Texas and the Ford
Foundation. The initial program presented in 1961 was a lecture on "The
Great Plains" by University of Texas historian Walter Prescott Webb. During the following months, a series on language was offered. Although the
project aroused considerable interest initially, the overall student and faculty response to the project was disappointing. After a trial period, the
project was discontinued.[56]

Beyond undergraduate programs, the most controversial component in
Laurie's vision of a "greater Trinity" was a growing emphasis on graduate education. When Bruce Thomas first raised the subject of graduate
school expansion with the faculty in 1958, he envisioned a "slow, orderly
process" that would involve strengthening undergraduate departments,
increasing the quantity and quality of master's programs, and "in the distant future" the undertaking of selected doctoral programs. Although
Thomas set no specific timetable for implementing doctoral work, Laurie
expressed hope that this might be achieved before the end of the decade,
in time for the centennial celebrations. Received with mixed emotions by

a wary faculty, the increased stress on graduate studies generated considerable discussion over the next decade.[57]

Armed with a positive feasibility study by consultant Roger P. McCutcheon, dean of Tulane University's graduate school, Laurie initiated the expanded graduate program. In 1959, he presented a proposal to the trustees that called for the creation of a graduate school administered by a graduate dean and assisted by a director of research who would work concurrently as director of the Southwest Foundation for Research and Education. The proposal also included plans for securing funds to construct a graduate center and to increase library holdings.[58] Citing increasing demand for trained scholars and researchers, Laurie advocated a "gradual approach" that would include doctoral work in English, history, biology, chemistry, psychology, and possibly education. He estimated that an initial cost of $250,000 would be necessary to operate the program and that additional funds would be required to provide scholarships and improve library holdings. The trustees enthusiastically adopted Laurie's proposal and approved the necessary faculty additions.[59]

To oversee the graduate school, Laurie selected Leonard A. Duce, who had a Ph.D. from Yale University and was a professor of philosophy and the dean of Baylor University's graduate school. At Trinity, Duce administered a graduate program that lacked adequate facilities, finances, and faculty and that served mostly part-time students. Working within a tight time frame, Duce concentrated on adding new majors at the master's degree level and revising admission standards, degree requirements, and thesis regulations. He also set the target dates of 1962 through 1966 to construct graduate facilities and begin doctoral work in the biomedical field and several other areas.[60]

During the 1960s, the university added three new graduate degree programs. Originally a part of Baylor University's graduate school, the Dallas Theater Center affiliated with Trinity in 1963 when Paul Baker came to Trinity. Composed of a company of resident artists, the theater center presented an annual season of plays that included classics, modern drama, musicals, and a variety of experimental productions. Under the direction of Baker, who commuted between San Antonio and Dallas, the two-year master's of arts degree offered a program that integrated historical, theoretical, and social aspects of theater with the technical aspects of dramatic creation and production.[61]

A program leading to a master's degree in hospital administration commenced in the fall of 1965, and the first degrees were awarded in August 1967. Beginning with twenty-five students, the program had 101 candidates for degrees five years later. Requirements included twelve months of full-time course work on campus and twelve months of residency in an approved hospital. The program received full accreditation in 1969, and Trinity was admitted as a member of the Association of University Programs in Hospital Administration. In 1970 the Graduate Council changed the name of the program to Health Care Administration.[62] Over the years it acquired a reputation of being one of the strongest programs in the country, producing graduates who readily found administrative positions throughout the United States.

In 1968 Trinity announced the appointment of Earl Lewis to direct a two-year graduate program in urban studies, partially endowed by the George W. Brackenridge Foundation. The first African-American member of the Trinity faculty, Lewis held a doctorate from the University of Chicago. He came to Trinity from Prairie View A&M, where he served as chair of the political science department. Highly regarded as an educator and participant in public service, Lewis initiated a program in the fall of 1969 with a diverse student population that included significant numbers of African Americans and Hispanics. In addition to specific urban studies courses, students took courses taught by instructors in the departments of sociology, economics, psychology, political science, health care administration, and journalism. Students were also required to serve a nine- to twelve-month apprenticeship in a private or public community agency. By 1971, when the first degrees were conferred, the program had an enrollment of sixty-six students.[63]

The expanding graduate program received much-needed impetus in 1962 when Laurie announced that Oklahoma philanthropist and longtime Trinity benefactor James A. Chapman had agreed to build a $1.5 million graduate center to be named in honor of his parents, Philip and Roxana Chapman. Designed by architects O'Neil Ford and H. G. Barnard Jr. of Tulsa, the Chapman Graduate Center was envisioned to be the central building in an evolving graduate studies complex. Although not a Trinity graduate, Chapman was a member of a family that had associations with the university dating back three generations to the Tehuacana era. Eighty-nine members of the extended Chapman family attended the graduate center's dedication ceremonies on 29 May 1964, during which Rice University Chancellor Carey H. Croneis served as principal speaker.[64]

Despite his gift of the Graduate Center, Chapman had misgivings about Laurie's ambitious building program, which he thought placed an excessive debt burden on the university. Fiscally conservative, Chapman considered removing Trinity from his testamentary trust, but eventually decided otherwise.[65] At his death in 1966, Chapman left the university 25 percent of a fortune worth more than one hundred million dollars. Laurie estimated that the Chapman Trust would bring Trinity $1.5 million in income per year, stabilize undergraduate work, and enable the university to launch doctoral work in the near future. The gift marked a turning point in Trinity's fiscal history. By 1970, the year of Laurie's retirement, the endowment had reached an estimated $42 million, making Trinity one of the most substantially endowed private universities in the country.[66]

"The Chapman family ordered furniture for the Great Hall in the Chapman Center from a cabinet maker in London. Because of tight scheduling, the furniture arrived in the Port of Houston on a Thursday with the dedication of the building scheduled for Saturday. Jud Abernathy, director of the Physical Plant, called the federal official who controlled the Port of Houston and requested immediate delivery of the furniture. The response was that it was impossible to unload the shipment, clear customs, and deliver the items to San Antonio by Saturday. Abernathy concluded the conversation by saying, 'If you can't do it, there's nothing more to say except that the president will be very unhappy.' Saturday morning, a few hours before the dedication program was scheduled to begin, a truck loaded with wooden crates arrived from Houston. On one of the crates, lettered in red paint, was this message: Unless these boxes are delivered to Trinity University by 10 O'Clock Saturday, President Johnson is going to be very unhappy."

(Anecdote related by Jud Abernathy)

Questions persisted, however, regarding the wisdom of prematurely implementing a doctoral program. The Southern Association's visitation team in 1965 expressed concern over the paucity of existing library resources and recommended greatly increased expenditures on books and periodicals before undertaking additional graduate work: "In the proposed projection of graduate studies to the Ph.D., the pace has been speeded up to a point where there is grave danger of the library being overrun and trampled." The team also noted that enormous financial capital would be needed to assemble a viable graduate faculty and to provide scholarships to attract a quality student body. "Under no circumstances should work begin at the doctoral level until the library, faculty, and buildings have been built to the required level, and Trinity has enjoyed successful operation for a few years of several highly respected master's programs."[67]

Undeterred by this cautionary note, Laurie remained optimistic about the future of graduate education at Trinity. If Trinity moved quickly, he believed it could have a viable doctoral program in place before competitors emerged on the local scene. "It will take a few 'extra miracles' to be able to announce the doctoral program in the Centennial Year," he told trustees in 1967, but he expressed confidence that Trinity would begin to award Ph.D.s before the end of the decade.[68]

Despite Laurie's optimism and Duce's expertise, the doctoral program never went beyond the planning stage. Laurie could not obtain the requisite financial resources within his self-imposed time frame. Distributions from the Chapman Trust were slow to materialize, and when they did come, they were used to pay debts and support existing programs. Duce expressed hope that a few selected doctoral programs such as hospital administration, education, biology, and chemistry could be initiated sometime during the 1970s. To do so, however, he estimated that Trinity would need an additional $1 million for its instructional budget and $1.5 million for library resources.[69]

In concert with its emphasis on graduate education, the university in 1961 acquired Principia Press of Illinois, a small private press with titles primarily in mathematics, economics, and philosophy.[70] To give more visibility to the university, the name was changed in 1967 to Trinity University Press. Among the early titles published under the new name were *Baronial Forts of the Big Bend* by Leavitt Corning Jr., *Zosimus: Historia Nova* by James J. Buchanan and Harold T. Davis, and *Creating Theater* by Ruth Byers.[71]

Operating with a small staff and a limited budget, the press published about a half-dozen books a year, primarily in the fields of religion, history, art and architectural history, bibliography, and regional subjects. In spite of its small-scale operation, the press brought regional and national recognition to the university through its scholarly books and monographs. Under the leadership of Joe W. Nicholson and Lois A. Boyd, the press published manuscripts by scholars from institutions such as the University of Notre Dame, the State University of New York, Rice University, the University of Texas, Harvard University, Yale University, and the University of North Carolina as well as by members of the Trinity University faculty. By 1975, the press had produced almost a hundred titles, including two major series: *The Trinity University Monograph Series in Religion* and *Checklists in the Humanities and Education.*[72]

As Trinity pondered its future in graduate education, it also was reconsidering its identity as a Presbyterian church-related university. Always a staunch advocate of close denominational relationships, Laurie ironically presided over the dissolution of legal ties between the university and the Presbyterian church.[73] Impetus for the change, however, came from the denomination rather than from the university. A study document entitled "The Church and Higher Education," approved by the General Assembly in 1961, resulted in the development of new guidelines for Presbyterian church-related colleges and universities.[74] Faculty, rather than being active members of some evangelical Christian church as previously required, were asked only to be "dedicated to the [university's] declared institutional purpose." Instead of mandating a course on the Bible, the guidelines recommended "a mature classroom encounter with the Judaic-Christian heritage." Finally, schools were expected to secure accreditation by a regional association as a sign of academic quality."[75]

The document reflected national trends in higher education among church-related colleges that by mid-century had adopted many of the values of secular universities, such as academic specialization and research. It also indicated the dominance of more liberal theological views in mainline Protestant churches and a growing acceptance of cultural pluralism. Subsequent General Assembly reports informed the colleges that a decline in benevolent giving precluded new funds from the Board of Christian Education for the escalating needs of higher education. Increasingly, denominational colleges had to rely on individual gifts and government and private foundation funding for support. It followed that if the denomination could not produce financial support, then it should not insist on any form of legal control either through election of trustees or ownership of property.[76]

In place of legal ties, the General Assembly recommended that Presbyterian colleges establish voluntary covenants with their respective synods. Under this arrangement, each partner acknowledged the autonomy of church and college and agreed to cooperate and support one another to the best of their ability. The Assembly left details of how best to work out these arrangements to the parties involved.[77]

Laurie raised the question of church relationship with the trustees early in 1968 by reviewing various General Assembly pronouncements on higher education and showing that institutions such as Austin College, Lewis and Clark University, and Nebraska Wesleyan University had already entered into covenant relationships with their respective denominations. Aware that many trustees cherished the longstanding church relationship, Laurie assured them that he envisaged no precipitous action on the subject. "Trinity must face this change with wisdom and without any sense of pressure or panic," he said. "It seems inevitable that there may be a new kind of relationship established, but this should be carefully thought through and clarified."[78]

After extended conversations between a joint committee of Trinity University and Synod of Texas officials, both parties agreed in 1969 to end legal ties and enter into a voluntary covenant relationship. In effect, Trinity became an independent institution under the control of a self-perpetuating board of trustees. Although the synod no longer had the power to confirm the election of trustees, it was given representation on the trustee nominating committee. Trinity would continue to submit an annual report to the synod, and university trustees would welcome an annual visitation by an appropriate synod committee for conference and counsel. Laurie urged approval of the proposed covenant, expressing hope that Trinity's relationship with the Presbyterian Church would remain firm and that the university and the synod would continue to work together to promote Christian higher education.[79]

Significantly, the change in church relationship occurred during Trinity's centennial year as the university reflected on its origins and staged a series of celebratory events to mark the occasion. Beginning with a Founders' Day centennial flag-raising ceremony and an all-school picnic, the campus community honored the pioneers who established Trinity in the village of Tehuacana in 1869. Other events included a symposium on "The Impact of Technology on Higher Education"; the publication by Trinity University Press of a trilogy of university histories—*Trinity University: A Record of One Hundred Years* by Donald E. Everett, *Voice in the Wilderness: A History of the Cumberland Presbyterian Church in Texas* by R. Douglas Brackenridge, and *One Hundred Years of Challenge and Change: A History of the Synod of Texas of the United Presbyterian Church in the U.S.A.* by George H. Paschal Jr. and Judith A. Benner; and a ceremony marking the return of the Waxahachie main building's cornerstone to the Trinity campus.[80] *Follow the Sun,* a musical dramatization of Trinity's first one hundred years presented in conjunction with the Dallas Theater Center, was performed for Trinity audiences and members of the United Presbyterian General Assembly meeting in San Antonio.[81]

In the midst of centennial celebrations, Laurie announced his intention to step down as president and requested that the board commence a "vigorous and intelligent transition of administrative authority." The trustees designated the board's long-range planning committee to serve as a search committee for a new president, a process they estimated would take at least one year. At the same time, the board created a new position, Vice Chairman of the Board in Charge of Special Development, and announced that Laurie would hold that office for a three-year term after his presidential successor had been appointed.[82]

Impetus for doctoral work rapidly diminished after Laurie announced his impending retirement. He had been the chief proponent of the doctoral program, and without his continued leadership, prospects that momentum could be maintained appeared slim. Moreover, word that the University of Texas system planned to open a campus in San Antonio within the next three to five years indicated that competition with a state-funded graduate program held little promise of success. As a result, the board of trustees decided it was prudent to wait for the selection of a new president before making any decisions about the future of Trinity's graduate program.[83]

During his last years in office, Laurie maintained a frenetic pace as administrator, fund-raiser, churchman, and community leader. Following the recommendations of the Southern Association's visitation team, Laurie requested that the trustees elevate Bruce Thomas (Academic Affairs), Derwood Hawthorne (Fiscal Affairs), and Leon Taylor (Administrative) to vice-presidential status and approve the establishment of the Schools of Engineering and Business Administration with Robert V. Andrews and Jarrett E. Woods, respectively, as deans. The trustees also announced tentative plans to create a college of arts and sciences with appropriate divisions and deans.[84] Trinity faculty and staff learned about these changes in the local papers, prompting members of the Faculty Senate to question the administration's commitment to involve them in the university's decision-making process.[85]

At the same time, Laurie acceded to the growing dissatisfaction among students and faculty regarding compulsory ROTC in the university curriculum. Acknowledging that a voluntary program was both feasible and appropriate, Laurie endorsed the report of a faculty committee that recommended the abolishment of mandatory participation in the military program. He made a public announcement of the curricular change at a Parents' Weekend gathering in April 1969, stating that the voluntary program would begin in the fall of 1970.[86]

From the outset, the presidential search committee maintained a low

Laurie giving the centennial medallion to Duncan Wimpress, 1 August 1970

profile on the progress of its deliberations. Even the trustees complained that they were not being adequately informed. The search committee, chaired by Wichita Falls lawyer Joseph Sherrill, took such complaints "under advisement" but continued to be sparing with information regarding the names and number of potential candidates.[87]

As a member of the presidential search committee, Laurie played a major role in the selection of his successor. During the first six months, Laurie cultivated James I. McCord, president of Princeton Theological Seminary. An acclaimed denominational educator and theologian who was noted for his administrative skills and fund-raising abilities, McCord had Texas roots and a deep commitment to maintaining close relationships with the Presbyterian church. In Laurie's estimation, McCord would provide the leadership necessary to make Trinity foremost among Presbyterian institutions of higher learning in the United States.[88] Early in 1970, however, McCord informed the committee that it should look elsewhere for a president because he felt compelled to remain at Princeton.

Laurie then turned to another candidate, Duncan Wimpress, president of Monmouth College in Illinois, a small, liberal arts, Presbyterian church-related institution. Wimpress had caught Laurie's attention as a progressive administrator at meetings of the Presbyterian College Union, a gathering of Presbyterian college presidents. Wimpress later acknowledged that he had been "handpicked" by Laurie for the position.[89]

At baccalaureate services for the class of 1970, Laurie gave his last public address as president of Trinity University. Entitled "The Beginning of Wisdom," he used as a text Proverbs 1:7, "The fear of the Lord is the beginning of knowledge, but fools scorn wisdom and discipline." Speaking during a time when the nation was torn by racial strife and the war in Vietnam, Laurie urged the graduating class to avoid both apathy and violence in seeking social and political change. He also reflected on the meaning of their Trinity experience in terms of the institution's religious heritage. Noting that the founders of Trinity believed that students deserved the best skills and knowledge available, Laurie affirmed that the university offered something of greater significance: "I trust, in the spirit of this institution, there will be this Trinity tradition or spirit, this reverence for God which is the foundation of wisdom, which makes us respect and honor each other as children of God."[90]

The Trinity community gathered to bid the Lauries farewell on 13 May 1970, with more than a thousand people honoring them at a garden party on the Skyline campus. Activities began with a brief service in the Parker Chapel in which longtime professors Paul T. Walthall and Frances Swinny paid tribute to James and Dorothy Laurie. Walthall praised Laurie for his dynamic leadership that had turned dreams into realities and singled out qualities such as persistence, determination, sensitivity, and creativity as major factors in his success. Walthall quipped, "President Laurie has always insisted that Trinity live within its means, even if it has to borrow the money to do it."[91]

Swinny recognized Dorothy Laurie for her tireless service to the entire Trinity community that had touched the lives of so many people in such different ways. "Your warmth of sincerity flows freely, the door to your home and to your heart is never closed. You are a respecter of life and love and these you give in abundance."[92]

At the conclusion of the service, Trinity trustee and benefactor Andrew G. Cowles announced that the new auditorium then under construction would be called the Dorothy A. and James W. Laurie Auditorium, the first building on campus to be named after a Trinity president.[93]

On July 31, Laurie left his office as president of Trinity University. Following a European vacation, Laurie planned to assist with university development operations, working out of an office in downtown San Antonio. He wrote in his personal notebook: "Do not try to do too much this summer. Get away. Let it be clear that you are leaving the Presidency but not leaving Trinity." He reminded himself, however, that he should "answer questions and withhold advice! Change will be good for all concerned." His final note was underlined to emphasize its importance. "Remember, you are only a trustee after August 1st."

While visiting Scandinavia, Laurie suffered a recurrence of viral hepatitis, canceled the remainder of the vacation, and returned to San Antonio. He underwent surgery at Nix Hospital on September 2, which confirmed that the hepatitis had irrevocably damaged his liver. Laurie died in his sleep on 9 September 1970, on the eve of his sixty-seventh birthday. Raymond Judd, minister in charge of the Margarite B. Parker Chapel, and T. Stewart Coffman, pastor of the University Presbyterian Church, conducted his funeral service two days later in the Parker Chapel.[94]

Profuse tributes to Laurie came from academic, civic, and religious sources emphasizing his tremendous impact on Trinity and the San Antonio community, and time has not diminished their observations. With an exceptional physical plant, a substantial endowment, and a growing reputation for academic excellence, Laurie gave Trinity a solid foundation on which others would build. He also left a cadre of benefactors who continued through the years to support major university projects with gifts and bequests.

Beyond these accomplishments, however, James and Dorothy Laurie left something far more significant and enduring—a sense of community spirit and a feeling of confidence in the university's future. *Trinitonian* editor Cheri Crapster aptly described the Lauries with these words: "The future of Trinity may stretch far beyond the lifetimes of these two fine Christian citizens, but their influence and guidance will mold university tradition for years to come."[95]

CHAPTER TEN

UNIVERSITY IN THE SUN

The University's PR tag, "University in the Sun," is the epitome of
blandness. the sense of it is not the hot, searing heat of the sun; it is,
rather, a feeling of warmth evenly spread over the whole body—no rains,
no storms, no troubled weather, and no troubled mind. A sense of
sweetness, fellowship, fun.

PROFESSOR PHILIP F. DETWEILER

DURING THE LAURIE ERA, TRINITY BECAME widely known as
"The University in the Sun," a description conceived by Director of Public Relations Leon "Tex" Taylor to capture the institution's new vitality.
For several decades, university publications combined this encomium with
a circle surrounded by emanating rays of light, intended to convey energy
and excitement linked with academic rigor and intellectual inquiry. To the
chagrin of some faculty, however, the wording and logo also conveyed to
prospective students an impression of leisure and relaxation associated
with the southwestern Sun Belt. In retrospect, students of the Laurie-
Thomas era reflected both aspects of the ubiquitous designation. While
many concentrated on academics, some came to have fun in the sun while
obtaining a degree. Still others, a small but growing minority, identified
with movements for empowerment that were emerging on campuses
throughout the country.[1]

Social historians place students of the 1950s and students of the 1960s
in two distinct groupings. Following World War II, the returning veterans
who flooded college campuses were intent on pursuing their studies and
obtaining employment, and they spent little time in cultural and societal
involvement. Although some students expressed criticism of racial segregation and voiced concerns about atmospheric testing and the escalating
arms race, the majority remained relatively uninvolved in larger social
concerns. This passivity caused contemporary observers of the higher education scene to describe students of the 1950s as "the silent generation."[2]

Students of the 1960s were the first of a group born after World War II, the "baby-boomers," who entered colleges and universities as the decade began. Fueled by issues such as civil rights, feminism, and opposition to the war in Vietnam, student discontent erupted into protest and rebellion on campuses throughout the country. Activists, who tended to be children of middle-class parents, often had been student leaders in high school and sought to continue that role in college. While only a small minority belonged to radical organizations, many more questioned the established order.[3]

Insulated geographically and culturally from the centers of social activism, Trinity students seemed not to identify with the radicalism that characterized many of the larger universities. The legacy of the World War II and Korean War veteran-students' hard work continued to influence student behavior. Looking back on his experience at Trinity during the 1960s, student government president Jim Jones described Trinity as a "hotbed of political rest," and history professor Donald Everett commented, "Mainly at Trinity the protest has been that there has been no protest."[4]

The chief administrators, Laurie and Thomas, however, played a key role in influencing student decorum during a period of national campus unrest. Their accessibility and openness to students defused potentially disruptive situations and facilitated incremental rather than explosive social change. As academic dean, Thomas established a reputation for fairness and firmness among both faculty and students. Never one to equivocate, he responded decisively when students raised questions about academic policies. Assistant Dean Paul Busch, who was referred to by a student as "the ultimate surrogate grandfather for hassled students," resolved day-to-day problems in a low-key manner.[5]

After a shaky start with student relationships, Laurie utilized his pastoral skills to cultivate an avuncular image that satisfied parents and appealed to a broad spectrum of Trinity students. A Rice University trustee who visited Trinity in 1966 expressed amazement at the tranquility on campus in light of student unrest throughout the country. "What a happy experience it is to walk across your campus and see all of the kids with a smile on their face and a gleam in their eye, speaking to the President just like he was one of them. It is even more thrilling to see the President and Deans exchanging felicitations with the students and in most instances calling the students by their first names."[6]

Laurie's open-door policy facilitated dialogue with student leaders, who found the president willing to listen to their concerns. Student association president Art Sundstrom related how he would regularly go to

Laurie's office with an agenda of items on which he wanted action. He admitted, however, "I always left the sessions feeling upbeat and satisfied, only to realize later that I never got anything that I wanted."[7]

Invitations to dine at the Laurie home on Oakmont Court enabled students to meet the president and his spouse in relaxed surroundings where opportunities for formal discussions emerged out of casual conversations. After attending one such dinner, a Trinity student praised the president's "honesty and straightforwardness" and Dorothy Laurie's "genuine friendliness and concern" and described them collectively as a "team marked by diplomacy, grace and intelligence."[8]

During the initial academic year on the new campus, students were taken by bus to their science courses at Onderdonk Hall on the Woodlawn campus. On Trinity hill, classes met in buildings that had no air conditioning and were surrounded by noisy construction projects, unpaved roads and sidewalks, and a bleak landscape devoid of trees and greenery. During dry spells, the campus swirled with dust. When it rained, the caliche soil turned into a quagmire of mud that clung to shoes and left footprints in halls and classrooms.[9]

Women occupied the only available residence hall, and athletes were housed in a large home on Mulberry Street that had been purchased by the university. Other male students lived in the nearby Grande Courts, a no-frills tourist accommodation. Because the student union building remained unfinished, resident students were shuttled three times a day to Damon's Restaurant on Austin Highway, where they ate in shifts in a private dining room.[10] As the months passed, resentment mounted, and Laurie feared that a "food riot" would ensue unless meals could be served on campus. With the concurrence of Blanche King, director of food services, Laurie informed students that dining facilities on campus would be available before the end of the fall semester. With no glass in the windows, no refrigeration, and no gas cooking ranges available until five hours before the first meal, King commenced operations. Despite the workers pounding and drilling on every side, students preferred the surroundings over the time-consuming bus rides.[11]

The university's residential population in the 1950s was a small and close-knit community in which inhabitants knew their peers by name and shared common cultural and religious backgrounds. "The townies," the largest group of students, commuted from their homes in San Antonio and surrounding Bexar County. For the most part, they studied at home or worked at part-time jobs, with some attending the large number of evening classes that Trinity offered to accommodate part-time undergrad-

Students were bused to meals three times a day.

uate and graduate students. Although the office of student life and student government organizations made efforts to bridge the social gulf existing between those students who lived on campus and those who lived off campus, none proved successful.[12]

Social life at Trinity during the 1950s functioned under a set of administrative rules and regulations. All events had to be scheduled on a master calendar at least one month in advance at times that did not conflict with other campus activities and required the presence of two faculty chaperones. Functions held on Monday through Thursday evenings ended at ten in the evening and those on weekends at midnight. Sunday social events were prohibited unless students secured special permission from the dean of student life.[13]

After World War II, homecoming resumed as a major event on the university's social calendar. Helene Scrivener, Trinity's first homecoming queen in San Antonio, presided over festivities in 1948, including a bonfire and a postgame "Tiger Dance" in the university gymnasium on the Woodlawn campus. In 1950 the homecoming celebration expanded with a Friday evening downtown snake dance and a pep rally on Alamo Plaza. On Saturday morning students set up club booths and art exhibits to greet returning students and visitors. A parade featuring nearly fifty floats and bands began in mid-afternoon in front of the Gunter Hotel. Afterward

Homecoming and fiesta parades were important events during the 1950s.

there was lunch on campus before the football game at Alamo Stadium. At halftime, the president introduced the homecoming queen and her court to the crowd.[14]

Other established all-school activities also were on the social calendar. Each year Trinity participated in San Antonio's annual Fiesta Week parades with floats, bands, drill teams, and a campus queen.[15] Founders' Day in April hearkened back to celebrations held in Waxahachie. Beginning with an all-school assembly in the morning that featured speeches by candidates for various student offices, the day continued with an ROTC parade and inspection and a Founders' Day Carnival on the Slab that included a dunking tank, pie-throwing booths, croquet, and dart-throwing. One of the most popular attractions, a car-demolishing booth, gave students an opportunity to swing sledgehammers at an old automobile. The day concluded with a barbecue supper and a western swing dance.[16]

Dances and parties sponsored by the student council or one of the social clubs during the school year attracted large numbers of students. The Tigerland Coronation Dance, sponsored by the Town Club, featured royalty, including a duke and duchess and a prince and princess from each class and from the faculty. Presiding over the court were a campus king and queen elected by the student body.[17] The junior-senior prom held at

Trinity students in the 1950s

the San Antonio Country Club brought closure to the social year. With "formal dress the prescribed attire," attendees enjoyed a festive banquet, humorous farewell speeches, and an evening of ballroom dancing.[18]

Traditional activities associated with freshman orientation began to encounter resistance from entering students who deemed them juvenile, demeaning, and time-consuming.[19] Responding to repeated criticism, student senate representatives modified the interclass program in 1953. Incoming students were permitted to substitute participation in orientation rituals with campus improvement projects such as landscaping, painting, and decorating.[20] Even this measure, however, failed to quell opposition to the program. In 1954 a majority of women in McFarlin Hall elected not to participate in orientation activities. Their action prompted the Student Senate to halt all interclass activities for the year and to reappraise the entire new student orientation program.[21]

Beginning in the fall of 1955, first-year students voluntarily participated in a six-week orientation program that emphasized the academic, social, and spiritual dimensions of student life and retained only a few traditional activities such as wearing beanies and learning the alma mater.[22] Selected upper-class students conducted mentoring sessions on academic activities, including degree requirements, class scheduling, and study habits. Other meetings introduced students to the functions of student government and various social activities. Picnics, dances, and variety shows provided opportunities for students to mix informally, and intramural sports competitions generated friendly rivalry among the classes. Although some students expressed dissatisfaction with such a "tame program," they admitted that it seemed to produce a harmonious group of new students without the negative aspects of previous routines.[23]

As interclass rivalries diminished in popularity, local fraternities and sororities emerged to fill the social gap. By the early 1960s, Trinity had five men's clubs (the Triniteers, Theta Tau Upsilon, the Bengal Lancers, Sigma Kappa Epsilon, and Chi Delta Tau) and five women's organizations (Chi Beta Epsilon, Gamma Chi Delta, Kappa Psi Omega, Sigma Theta Tau, and the Spurs). The organizations formed the Inter-Club Council and the Board of Women's Social Clubs to coordinate the growing number of group activities and projects. Reports of hazing incidents among the clubs caused Thomas to extend previous interclass regulations to include all campus social fraternities and sororities. He warned that policy violations could lead to suspension or dissolution of offending organizations. Despite repeated admonitions against hazing, however, university officials acknowledged their inability to curtail such activities without the support of fraternity and sorority leadership.[24]

One of Trinity's most enduring social traditions began in 1958 when the Chi Beta Epsilon sorority sponsored the first school "Sing Song" in the Ruth Taylor Concert Hall. Other participants included Delta Kappa Phi, Sigma Theta Tau, the Spurs, the Bengal Lancers, and the Triniteers. Each club presented three songs within a fifteen-minute time period, and the Spurs won the first-place trophy with a Christmas theme. Subsequently, the event became associated with Parents (now Family) Weekend, instituted in 1960, which for many years was presided over by Coleen Grissom, dean of student life and later vice president for student affairs. Sometimes controversial because student presentations stretched the bounds of propriety, Sing Song was reconfigured in 1986 as the "Best of Trinity Spotlight," cosponsored by the Trinity Activities Council and the Office of Student Affairs and open to all students wishing to audition.[25]

Resident students in the 1950s lived under the scrutiny of adult supervisors who monitored their activities and enforced university policies regarding behavior and dress. Although men had no curfews, their rooms were subject to unannounced inspections, and they were required to notify the dormitory supervisor before leaving campus overnight or for an extended period. Failure to do so could result in suspension. Male students had considerable freedom in their campus attire, although T-shirts, cut-off pants or shirts, and shower shoes or thongs were not deemed appropriate dining room attire.[26]

Trinity women were denied the range of social freedom accorded their male counterparts. Their *Dormitory Handbook* specified weekday curfews ranging from 9:30 P.M. for first-year students to 11:00 P.M. for seniors. On weekends, seniors could stay out until 1:00 A.M., but others had to be in before midnight. Women were required to sign in and sign out for all evening and weekend activities, and those who neglected these procedures faced confinement to rooms or suspension from the university. Daily room inspections by dormitory supervisors ensured that women had their beds made and their belongings orderly. Three unsatisfactory reports resulted in confinement for an entire weekend. During the week and on Sunday, lunch and dinner were seated meals served at assigned tables that began with group singing of the doxology. Women were expected to be punctual and to remain at the table until everyone had completed their meal. Etiquette called for late arrivals to apologize to the hostess before taking a seat. Women were never permitted to take food from the dining room.[27]

In terms of the women's dress regulations, street clothes (excluding slacks) were mandatory at all times on campus and in dining halls. "Shorts are taboo except for play and in your own dorm room." On Sundays and special occasions, "dress-up dresses, hose, heels, hats, and gloves are in order." While sportswear was acceptable at the pool or tennis courts, women were advised to wear beach robes over their swimsuits while walking to and from the pool. The handbook also urged women to take necessary precautions when changing their apparel: "Your rooms are something like fishbowls to the passerby. Please remember to lower your shades when dressing." Beyond matters of dress, women were cautioned against "unlady-like behavior" such as "indiscreet display of affection, use of profane and risqué language, and over-indulgence in alcoholic beverages."[28]

Female students in a dorm room

Resourceful female residents circumvented some of the most onerous restrictions and endured others with a sense of humor. They used balconies as convenient exits and entrances to avoid sign-out and sign-in procedures and wore trench coats to conceal shorts or pajamas during excursions to the upper campus. Their only concern was that a pajama leg might roll down and expose their dress-code transgressions.[29]

At one of their traditional fashion shows in the early 1960s, McFarlin residents lampooned the time-honored dictum that a well-dressed Trinity woman would never appear in public unless she was wearing a hat, gloves, and heels and carrying a purse. One by one the women paraded down the steps into Heidi Lounge attired in outfits representing the finest in modern fashions. As the review drew to a close, a student model appeared at the top of the staircase wearing a broad-brimmed hat, white gloves, and high heels and carrying a purse, but otherwise clad only in a bra and panties. As she slowly descended the stairs, dorm residents cheered, whistled, and applauded.[30]

Despite such occasional challenges to authority, Trinity women in the fifties expressed little interest in feminist issues. The *Trinitonian* published a weekly column entitled "Concerning Women," featuring items on fashion tips and beauty aids, such as how to manicure nails or apply lipstick

Male students in a dorm room

properly, and on table etiquette. Photographs and announcements of weddings, engagements, parties, and dances regularly consumed several pages of the school paper, and the results of beauty contests merited extensive coverage. In one contest, Trinity women vied for the title of "Miss Posture," sponsored by the Women's Recreational Association. Contestants were encouraged to learn correct posture habits "which are so important in achieving poise, self-confidence, and respect of others."[31]

Nevertheless, some Trinity students of the 1950s expressed opinions regarding a number of contemporary issues, including race, anticommunism, loyalty oaths, and presidential campaigns.[32] In 1954, in an open letter in the *Trinitonian*, seven Trinity students challenged university officials to move expeditiously to enroll African-American students in the upcoming fall semester. The students cited Trinity's role as a leader in Christian education as motivation for implementing campus integration. "If the government can go this far," the letter asserted, then Trinity "can do no less than voluntarily lead the way to a true brotherhood of man on the college campus. By admitting Negroes, Trinity can give concrete evidence to the fact that it is Christian in more than name only."[33] Two years later the student association initiated a referendum on desegregation that called for "continued and *immediate* progress of desegregation in social, religious, and academic areas at Trinity University." Seventy-five percent of the Trinity students who participated in the election endorsed the referendum, 12 percent opposed it, and the rest indicated no opinion on the subject.[34]

In another area, student government leaders attempted to reintroduce an honor system similar to the one that had functioned on the Waxahachie campus. Efforts to secure support from the student body during the 1950s, however, proved discouraging. The student court recommended in 1953 that Trinity adopt an honor code, and a subsequent constitution drafted by student government leaders won statewide recognition by the Texas Intercollegiate Student Association for its careful research and applicability to other student governments.[35]

Campus interest, however, never materialized. A questionnaire published in the *Trinitonian* in November 1957 soliciting student input regarding an honor-code proposal failed to receive a single response. In frustration, the editor commented. "We seem to travel in an orbit of expediency here at Trinity. When in doubt we keep our mouths shut. Does anybody care?"[36]

In 1964 student government leaders spearheaded another movement to adopt a campus honor code. Large attendance at an all-school assembly to discuss the subject prompted an ambivalent response from *Trinitonian* editor Joy Cook. Noting that students had conducted the assembly "with a finesse and enthusiasm long absent on the Skyline campus, it actually made Trinity feel like the intellectual center it purports to be."[37] Influenced in part by a lack of faculty support, students resoundingly defeated the measure by a 600 to 110 margin. Advocates for the measure took consolation, however, that the vote represented the largest student participation in recent memory.[38]

As the "baby boomers" arrived on campus in the early 1960s, they displayed little interest in the radical student movements on other college campuses. In the wake of student protests at the University of California at Berkeley in 1964, Trinity students conducted business as usual. While students at nearby St. Mary's University staged rallies and marches protesting police brutality, the Trinity campus remained quiet. "I don't think we'll ever have widespread student awareness at Trinity," said one student. "No one has much energy to lead demonstrations."[39] Responding to this comment, another Trinity student wrote, "I find nothing reactionary, and very little intellectual in the 'student awareness' on the Berkeley campus. If 'awareness' is exemplified only by participating in riots or demonstrations, I hope we remain 'lethargic.'"[40]

Only rarely did world events personally impact campus life. During the

Cuban missile crisis in the fall of 1962, students monitored events closely, aware that because of its military bases, San Antonio was a prime target in case of enemy attack. One student wrote, "We live in an age in which we have five minutes to rush to a bomb shelter to live. For that is how long it would take for a nuclear missile launched from Cuba to reach San Antonio." As tensions heightened and local authorities discussed possible evacuation routes, Thomas informed students that the university was preparing shelter areas with minimum provisions in case an emergency should arise.[41] Upon the resolution of the emergency, some student leaders challenged Trinitonians to become more actively involved in world affairs. The *Trinitonian* staff decided to subscribe to a collegiate news service and to incorporate more national and world news among its campus events.[42]

Social life in the early 1960s featured big-name entertainment brought to the campus by student body president Joe Armstrong. Elected to a precedent-setting two terms (1963–65), Armstrong attracted a variety of talent from the progressive jazz sound of Dave Brubeck to the popular music of the Four Preps and folksong ballads of Josh White. When the New Christy Minstrels performed in 1964, a capacity crowd of more than 3,000 people packed the Sams gymnasium to hear the acclaimed singing group. Armstrong, who later became editor of the *Rolling Stone Magazine*, hailed "the excitement of being part of something that is growing" and stated that big name entertainment "contributed much to the cosmopolitan attitude of the campus."[43]

New events included Parents' Weekend and Bermuda Day. Instituted in 1960, Parents' Weekend included athletic events, theatrical performances, discussions with faculty members, and the president's reception and dinner in the Skyline Dining Room.[44] Bermuda Day, first observed in 1961, featured athletic events, an all-campus picnic, and an opportunity for everyone to wear shorts on the upper campus. Also included in the festivities were fortune-telling booths, a tricycle race around the circle at the Stadium Drive entrance to the campus, and dancing from eight to midnight.[45]

Homecoming weekend in November 1963 featured pep rallies, a football game, and an all-college dance with the Glenn Miller orchestra performing. Shortly after noon on Friday November 22, as students made last minute preparations, everything suddenly fell silent when word reached campus that President John F. Kennedy had been assassinated in Dallas. Kennedy had been in San Antonio the previous day, and a number of Trinity students had viewed the presidential motorcade as it proceeded down Broadway. Excused from classes, students gathered around the flagpole in front of Northrup Hall where Laurie said a brief prayer and ROTC cadets lowered the flag to half-mast. The university cancelled all homecoming events and that evening the Trinity community filled the Ruth Taylor Auditorium for a memorial service.[46]

As they had during previous student generations, intercollegiate athletics, especially football, maintained a prominent place in campus extracurricular activities. Successes or failures on the playing field evoked passionate responses from student supporters. Following a four-game losing streak, including the homecoming contest, during the 1961 season, a group of 300 students held an evening rally during which they burned Coach McElreath in effigy and later hung the tattered remnants on a wall of the student union building.[47] Confronted by these events and longstanding questions regarding the feasibility of supporting a costly football program, the Athletic Board of Control in 1962 stressed the need to "reemphasize the educational value of athletics." To accomplish this goal, the board advocated high academic standards for scholarship student-athletes, increasing participation of nonscholarship student-athletes, realistic budgets, and competition with schools that had similar types of athletic programs and entrance requirements.[48]

Concurring with the recommendations, Trinity trustees approved shifts in athletic personnel that included transferring McElreath to the development office, appointing basketball coach Leslie W. Robinson as athletic director, and naming W. C. "Dub" McElhannon as head football coach. In 1963, after seven years as an independent, Trinity joined the Southland Conference, which included the University of Texas at Arlington, Lamar Technological College in Beaumont, Abilene Christian College, and Arkansas State University. This arrangement continued for the next decade with football teams coached by McElhannon and his successors, Wilson Waites and Earl Gartman.[49]

Coach McElhannon and his staff were the first to recruit African Americans to play intercollegiate athletics at Trinity. In 1964, Lyman Davis, a football and track star and a National Honor Society student at San Antonio Highlands High School, became the first African American to sign a grant-in-aid athletic scholarship at Trinity.[50] Although welcomed by teammates and Trinity fans, Davis and other recruits frequently experienced harsh treatment when they traveled to games in Texas and surrounding states. In silence, they endured taunts, derogatory remarks, and spitting incidents from fans and opposing players.[51]

Even Trinity was not immune from racial tensions. One incident caused considerable discussion and debate on campus. In 1968, student A. D. Arnic clashed with football coach Earl Gartman over a team dress code.

Duncan G. Wimpress,
President (1970–1976)

Duncan and Peggy Wimpress entertaining students
in the Minter House

The Eugenia B. Miller Fountain at its original location near the
Stadium Drive Entrance

Preston G. Northrup Hall and Atrium

Ruth Taylor Theater, c. 1966

Professor Paul Baker with students and staff

Earl C. Sams Memorial Center athletic facility

Solar panels on Sams Center, providing energy for heating and cooling

Students in Ewing Halsell Administrative Studies Center with an IBM 360-44 model computer in the background (c. 1970)

Granted an FCC license in 1976, KRTU initially offered a mixture of rock, jazz, Dixieland, country, and classical music.

Marion Bruce Thomas, Dean of the University (1947–1975)
and Interim President (1950–1951 and 1976–1979)

"His concern for this university and his open willingness to step in
and help in difficult and controversial times are actions
for which we shall all be grateful."
Trinitonian, 6 April 1979

Dedicated in 1978, the new library provided much-needed space
for present holdings and future expansion.

"Man's Evolving Images: In Printing and Writing," a collage by James Sicner,
in the library's circular staircase

Trinity University Board of Trustees, 1978

Left: Gretchen Northrup, Trinity trustee and benefactor
Right: Flora Atherton Crichton, first woman to serve as
chair of the board of trustees (1976–1978)

Ronald K. Calgaard, whose presidency was the longest
in Trinity's history (1979–1999)

Left to right: Trustees Harold Herndon and William Bell
and President Ron Calgaard

At the end of Calgaard's twenty-year presidency, the diplomas of almost
half of Trinity's living alumni/ae bore his name.

Effective classroom teaching was a key ingredient of Trinity's success during the Calgaard era. Here modern language professor Jean Chittenden interacts with students.

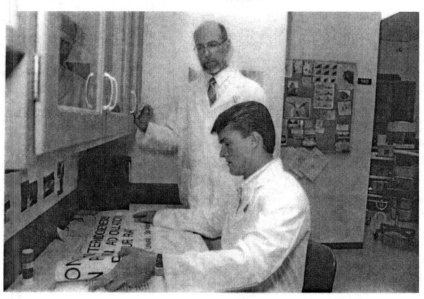

Student and faculty research projects gained Trinity national recognition and encouraged students to pursue graduate studies. Here biology professor Larry Espey supervises research.

William Knox Holt Continuing Education and Conference Center (now Conferences and Special Programs) was dedicated in 1984.

The first floor of the Holt Center provides an attractive setting for meetings and receptions.

The Urban Studies graduate program, directed by Dr. Earl Lewis (right), played a vital role in university and community life. With Lewis are faculty members (left to right) Catherine Powell, Henry Cisneros, and Heywood Sanders.

The Trinity Prize for Excellence in Teaching annually recognizes teachers nominated by the various local school districts. Here Calgaard and Professor John Moore, chair of the Department of Education, honor 1990–91 recipients Joseph Montano (Harlandale ISD) and Veronica Gonzalez (Northside ISD).

Vice President for Student Affairs Coleen Grissom played a formative role in the development of student life and programs for four decades.

University Chaplain Raymond Judd coordinated religious activities, led chapel programs, and counseled students during his thirty-two-year ministry.

The NCAA Division I 1972 championship team went undefeated
in twenty-seven consecutive dual matches.

Donna Stockton and JoAnne Russell celebrate the U.S. Tennis Association
doubles and team championships in 1973.

The Trinity Jazz Band poses for an album cover in Miller Fountain in 1985.

Annual TigerFest Golf Cart Parade

Gartman stipulated that all players had to wear a coat and tie when traveling to games away from home. Arnic, who had adopted the name "Mutapa" as a symbol of racial identity, insisted on wearing a dashiki (African dignity robe) over his dress clothes on such occasions. After several confrontations over the issue, Gartman dismissed Arnic from the team but permitted him to retain his athletic scholarship. The team voted unanimously to endorse Gartman's disciplinary action.[52]

Gartman received widespread support from Trinitonians, most of whom viewed the incident as disciplinary rather than discriminatory. Contributors to the *Trinitonian* criticized Arnic for pressing what they deemed a trivial issue when compared to team unity. One writer questioned the contribution of Arnic's action to the cause of racial equality: "We wonder what a dignity robe and a new name can do to help the plight of the poverty-stricken blacks."[53] Only faculty member William O. Walker Jr. publicly expressed a dissenting opinion. Affirming the importance of identity and pride among African Americans who had been assigned a second-class role in American life, Walker concluded, "Here is one white man's vote of appreciation to Mutapa for affirming his dignity as a black man and for reminding us of how easily values get misplaced in our society."[54]

In addition to racial tensions, Trinity football teams faced stiff competition in the new Southland Conference. Wins did not come easy as Trinity regularly encountered teams with more depth and experience than the Tigers. Nevertheless, a roster of outstanding players entertained loyal Trinity fans whose presence seemed miniscule in the cavernous confines of Alamo Stadium. Two varsity lettermen joined the professional football ranks: Marvin Upshaw as a lineman for the Cleveland Browns and Obert Logan as a defensive specialist for the Dallas Cowboys.

Although Trinity's football fortunes waned, intercollegiate tennis became the vehicle for recognition that the university had so long craved. Referred to by sportswriters as "Tennis Tech," Trinity rose to national prominence with outstanding team and individual performances under the direction of Coach Clarence Mabry. A native Texan and championship tennis player at the University of Texas, Mabry had competed on the professional tour with such players as Jack Kramer, Pancho Gonzales, and Vic Sexias.[55]

Individual performances by Trinity aces such as Chuck McKinley, Frank Froehling, Rod Susman, Butch Newman, Cliff Buchholz, Frank Conner, Bob McKinley, Brian Gottfried, and Dick Stockton captured public attention during the 1960s and early 1970s. Ranked number thirteen in the United States when he entered Trinity as a freshman, Chuck McKin-

Emilie Burrer

ley quickly rose in the national rankings. After a 40–2 victory record at Trinity and a runner-up spot at Wimbledon, he was ranked the number one player in the country in 1962. McKinley won the Wimbledon singles title in 1963 and also led the U.S. Davis Cup team to a world championship in the same year.[56] Bob McKinley, younger brother of Chuck, and Dick Stockton were four-time All-Americans from 1969 to 1972. Stockton, who amassed a 52-7 singles record at Trinity, went on to an outstanding career on the professional circuit, where he acquired a ranking of number eight in the world.[57]

During the same era, women's tennis began to attract attention even though team members did not receive athletic scholarships and lacked adequate coaching. Karen Hantze [Susman] came to Trinity in 1960 ranked as the number two female player in the nation. As a freshman, she won the Wimbledon singles title and shared in a doubles victory in 1961. Emilie Burrer [Foster], who later returned to coach at Trinity, won four national collegiate championships—two in singles and two in doubles—in 1968 and 1969. Led by Burrer, the Trinity women's team won U.S. Tennis Association team championships in 1968 and 1969.[58]

Trinity basketball enjoyed considerable success under coach Leslie

Robinson, who led the Tigers to third place in the NCAA College Division playoffs in 1959–60 and received a second invitation the following year. Robinson resigned in 1964 and was replaced by Bob Polk, formerly of Vanderbilt University.[59] Polk and athletic director Jesse MacLeay recruited Trinity's first African-American basketball players, including Larry Jeffries, Jim Boles, John Lynch, Bill Stokes, and Felix Thruston.[60] Assembling a team composed primarily of first-year students, Polk quickly attained national recognition for Trinity as one of the "top ten" among smaller schools in the country. In 1968, forward Larry Jeffries received Little All-American honors, Trinity placed third in the NCAA College Division Championship, and Polk was named "Coach of the Year."[61]

With the appointment of Houston Wheeler as coach in 1963, Trinity baseball fortunes soared. Under his tutelage Trinity won four Southland Conference championships (1964, 1965, 1966, and 1969) and advanced three times to the NCAA District VI playoffs. In 1965 Wheeler was honored as NCAA District VI coach of the year. Among the talented athletes who played for the Trinity nine during Wheeler's twenty-two-year coaching tenure were several All-Americans, including pitcher Henry Blanks, pitcher-shortstop Jimmy Carter, first baseman Pat Cluney, outfielder Jack Kraus, and third baseman Bill Daffin.[62]

On a smaller scale with limited funding, Trinity initiated sports such as golf, bowling, track, and soccer by the mid-1960s. In 1964 the golf and track teams participated in the first Southland Conference Spring Sports Festival in Abilene.[63] Soccer appeared on the Trinity scene in 1965 when a few students banded together to organize a self-supporting club team.[64] Trinity joined the Texas Collegiate Soccer League and played opponents such as Texas A&M, the University of Texas, St. Mary's University, and Schreiner Institute.[65]

In an effort to secure wider student participation in recreational sports, Athletic Director Jesse MacLeay emphasized intramurals as an integral part of student social life. Although an intramural program had existed for a number of years, it had inadequate facilities, part-time leadership, and a miniscule budget. After the completion of the Sams Center, MacLeay hired Trinity graduate Jim Potter in 1967 to become the university's first full-time intramural director. An outstanding athlete during his undergraduate years, Potter brought energy, enthusiasm, and imagination to his new assignment. Aided by an ability to establish rapport with diverse groups of Trinity students, Potter quickly expanded the existing program to include a variety of new sports and competitive events. By the end of the decade, approximately 70 percent of the student body was participating in one or more intramural activities. Potter continued to direct Trinity's intramural program for thirty-five years and held leadership positions in national intramural organizations.[66]

While intercollegiate athletics and intramurals remained fixtures of campus social life, Trinity students were modifying other longstanding social practices. Class rivalries, once the center of student life, gradually lost their significance as Trinitonians identified more with social clubs, service organizations, and academic interests. Referring to what he called a "Class Myth," a contributor to the *Trinitonian* in 1964 said, "Class officers are elected to preside over non-existent class meetings which are called to discuss imaginary projects." Periodic efforts to revive class identities failed to rouse student interest. By the end of the decade, photographs of class officers and faculty sponsors no longer appeared in the yearbook, the *Mirage*.[67]

Other traditions also succumbed to changing times, such as the homecoming parade, which occurred for the last time in 1960. In its place, students held a carnival on the slab south of McFarlin Dormitory, featuring novelty booths sponsored by social clubs and other organizations.[68] Students no longer learned the alma mater, formerly an important element in freshmen orientation. It would disappear almost completely from ceremonial occasions in the ensuing decade.[69] Even more striking was the demise of the venerable freshman beanie. One upperclassman commented, "it's a sad thing to see a tradition die, but it is a sadder thing to have it laying [*sic*] around, dead and decaying. The only thing to do is to bury it quickly and quietly."[70] The anachronism lingered, however, until University of Texas philosophy professor John Silber addressed first-year students during an orientation session in 1970. While discussing the values of nonconformity, Silber chided Trinity freshmen for wearing what he termed "ridiculous hats." After his remarks, the beanies disappeared, never again to appear on the Trinity campus.[71]

As old customs atrophied, new ones rose to take their place. In 1960 the student government sponsored the first Christmas tree lighting ceremony on the circle in front of the student union building, with prayers, carol singing, and brief remarks by a student government leader.[72] Completion of a reflection pond on upper campus west of the student union building ushered in another new Trinity tradition: ceremonial dunking on occasions such as birthdays, pledging, or other celebrations. The immersions, along with periodic soaping of the water, evoked the displeasure of student life officials but had little effect on student behavior. High maintenance costs and concerns about injuries resulted in the pond being turned into a green area. Undaunted, students found another source in 1966 when the Eugenia B. Miller Fountain was completed at the Stadium Drive entrance just east of Northrup Hall.[73]

Beyond frivolities, Trinity students showed evidence of an increasing social awareness by participating in a variety of community service projects. In 1963 twenty Trinity women volunteered to tutor African-American children at the Ella Austin Home and Hispanic adults at the Inman Christian Center.[74] The following year, the Chi Delta Tau fraternity sponsored a study hall program for African-American students at the Sutton Housing Project on the city's east side. Every weekday afternoon, club members assisted fifty to seventy-five students in improving their writing and reading skills.[75]

Impressed with the results of the Chi Delta Tau project, the student association initiated a Community Service Program in 1965 (today known as Trinity University Voluntary Action Center or TUVAC) to promote on-campus unity and to relate Trinity students to the needs of the community. Financed in part by the Brackenridge and Hogg Foundations, Trinity students conducted study programs at Victoria Courts, Alazan Apache Project, San Juan Homes, Kenwood Project, Cassiano Homes, Lincoln Heights, and the Sutton House. Other volunteer efforts included recreational programs at the House of Neighborly Service and visits to the Brooke Army Medical Center at Fort Sam Houston to talk to wounded veterans, many of whom had served in Vietnam.[76] In 1967 the student association reported that more that 200 Trinity students were working on ten different service projects.[77]

One of San Antonio's most highly regarded volunteer programs had its origins on the Trinity campus during this time period. Louise Locker, chair of the Community Service Committee, began gathering Christmas trees from the dorm rooms in 1968 and giving them to needy families. The next Christmas season she collected letters from the post office addressed to Santa Claus and recruited students to purchase the precise toys requested by the children. With another volunteer dressed up as St. Nicholas, they distributed presents to thirteen families. Today, as "Elf Louise," Locker heads up a volunteer program that serves 32,000 children annually. The recipient of numerous civic awards for her outstanding service, Locker was honored in 2000 as a Distinguished Alumna.[78]

Outside the local community, Trinity students participated in social programs of international dimensions. A number of students became involved in the Cross Roads Africa program founded by an African-American Presbyterian clergyman, James Robinson. Visiting Trinity in the spring of

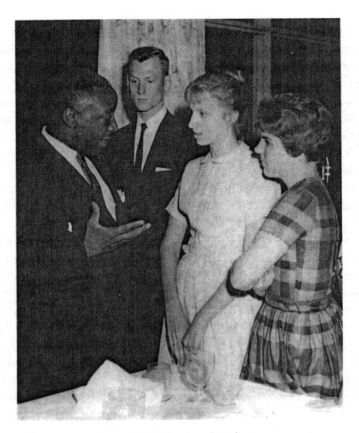

James S. Robinson and students

1961, Robinson reportedly turned the campus "into a beehive of conversation centered on the need, opportunities and inspirations gained from visiting the continent of Africa." The program provided opportunities for American students from a variety of religious, racial, and social backgrounds to visit Africa and become familiar with the social and economic problems facing the continent. Trinity students were among the first in the southwest to volunteer for the program.[79]

In addition to the Cross Roads Africa project, students were attracted to the newly formed Peace Corps. Norman Guerrero was among the vanguard of Trinity volunteers who enlisted to help improve underdeveloped countries and to promote peace. Assigned to a group of indigenous Indians in Peru in 1970, Guerrero's job was to help nomadic farmers maximize their potato yields. At the end of two years, he re-enlisted and served in Paraguay, where he continued to utilize his agricultural expertise. By

2001, Trinity had produced more volunteers for the organization than any other college or university in South Texas. Its ninety-nine participants were nearly double the numbers generated by St. Mary's University, the second-highest ranked institution in the region.[80]

By the mid-1960s, student government leaders were promoting involvement both in campus policy making and in wider national social and political issues. Changes in the organizational structure of the student association, initiated by president Jim Comer in 1966, delegated the responsibility for campus recreation and entertainment such as concerts, movies, receptions, and recitals to the student union board under a director of student activities. Dissolving the Student Senate and incorporating its functions into a unified legislative body freed the Student Council to devote more time to campus issues and interaction with faculty and administrators. In addition, the council controlled the allocation of student government funds for major campus events.[81]

Under the leadership of a series of strong association presidents, such as Jim Jones, Bob McCutcheon, Art Sundstrom, and Bill Hunnicutt, the student association emerged as an effective advocate for student interests and a significant force in shaping academic policies. In an effort to provide informal contacts between students and faculty members, the association initiated a series of faculty-student retreats and study conferences. Other programs included leadership training conferences and a revision of the student orientation program to provide a more challenging introduction to the academic life of the university. Monthly forums where students could meet with administrators, voice their ideas, and discuss controversial issues also encouraged wider student participation in campus issues and activities.[82]

The expulsion of three students in the spring of 1966 heightened students' awareness of their vulnerability in an administrative system that lacked a formal statement of due process and protection of individual rights. The trio had anonymously distributed several issues of an underground paper, "The Tiger's Burp," that attacked university fiscal policies and accused the administration of excessive control over student activities. One headline read, "Five Million Dollars for Buildings: Not One Cent for Education." Stung by what they deemed to be scurrilous and inaccurate journalism, university officials identified the offenders, and, after final examinations were over and most students had departed, the office of student life summarily expelled the three students. Student association president Jim Jones met with Laurie and Thomas to question what he viewed as a denial of free speech. They informed Jones that the anonymity rather than the content of the paper prompted the action. Jones, with administrative support, sent a letter to all Trinity students affirming the administration's assurance of freedom of speech as long as individuals did not exercise that right anonymously.[83]

As a result of the "Tiger's Burp" episode, students became increasingly vocal in their criticism of university's *in loco parentis* policies and practices. Letters in the *Trinitonian* complained about arbitrary rules and vague regulations and noted that the office of student life often handled disciplinary cases without reference to the student court. Some called for a revision of the entire judicial system. "Due process and fair play must be guaranteed," one writer asserted. "Arbitrary action—on the part of the Office of Student Life, the Student Court, or any other judicial body—cannot be allowed to exist." [84] Joining the discussion, philosophy professor Lawrence Kimmel defended the right of students to be governed by law, not a system that operated without specified procedures for review and appeal.[85]

Capitalizing on growing interest in due process, the Faculty Senate and student government leaders initiated a process that in 1969 culminated in the production of a "Joint Statement on Rights and Freedoms of Students," a document that became a model for other universities in the southwest.[86] Trinity trustees accepted the statement "in principle" and left specific expression of freedoms and responsibilities to administrators and students.[87] When completed, the statement included a commitment by the university not to discriminate on the basis of race, creed, or color, protection of students in the classroom from arbitrary evaluations, privacy of student records, rights related to membership in groups and organizations, provisions for student participation in university governing agencies, and procedures related to student discipline. Thurman Adkins, who served for three decades as a staff member in the office of student life, called the Joint Statement the most important student-generated document in the history of the university. With periodic modifications, it continues to serve as a foundational guarantee of student rights in the twenty-first century.[88]

Even before the Joint Statement became official policy, students were effecting changes on academic structures and campus routines. A petition from the student council in 1967 resulted in the introduction of the pass/fail option for courses outside of the general education requirements and the major. Largely through student initiatives, spring vacation, dead week, and reading days were added to the university calendar.[89]

Through the efforts of Trinity's admissions staff, African Americans began to join the ranks of residential students. The first female African American to live on campus, Jacqueline Smith, entered Trinity in 1959 and others soon followed. Some parents withdrew their daughters from Trinity when they encountered African Americans in dormitory suites, and others registered their displeasure with university authorities. Laurie and Thomas handled such complaints by informing unhappy parents that if they did not agree with Trinity's racial policies, then they should look elsewhere for their daughters' educations.[90]

Although generally accepted by their suitemates and other residents, African-American women encountered other issues. Eating at local restaurants, even when accompanied by white students, required an advance call to ensure service. Because interracial dating was not accepted on or off campus, an arrangement between Trinity and Lackland Air Force Base provided one social outlet for African-American female residents. Each week Air Force officials provided transportation for Trinity women to and from Lackland for dances with new recruits.[91]

The appointment of John Narciso as dean of student life in 1959 marked the beginning of expanded programs and efforts to modify traditional disparities between regulations for men and women. The recipient of a Ph.D. in psychology from the University of Texas, Narciso established an off-campus counseling center in 1963 for military veterans and Trinity students at the nearby Mulberry [Street] House and later added a branch office on the upper campus for career counseling.[92]

After the counseling center opened, Narciso chose to serve as its supervisor and stepped down as dean of student life. His successor, J. C. Pool, had varied professional experience, including newspaper administrator, public school teacher, and vocational counselor.[93] About the same time, Coleen Grissom, a recipient of a Ph.D. in English from the University of Texas at Austin, became associate dean of student life. Grissom had served as head resident and counselor for McFarlin Dormitory from 1958 to 1961 before leaving to do graduate work. Possessing exceptional communication and administrative skills, Grissom played a key role in shaping student life policies for nearly four decades.[94]

Grissom discontinued the unpopular practice of sending letters to parents rating their daughters on such qualities as popularity, frequency of dating, study habits, housekeeping, and relationship to the university.[95] Other changes implemented by the Association of Women Students included relaxing sign-in and sign-out procedures and ending regulations that stipulated "acceptable attire" for women students on the upper campus and in residence common areas. However, an "infraction point system," with specified penalties for sign-in, sign-out, and housekeeping violations, remained in effect.[96]

Although few Trinity women identified themselves as feminists, they became more sensitive to gender and equality issues. When the Student Council specified that candidates for the 1961 homecoming queen appear in bathing suits as well as street clothes and formal dress, women strenuously objected. Reconsidering the matter, student council representatives voted to leave the decision up to the candidates, who promptly rejected the idea.[97] The following year, the office of student life established a senior women's honor dormitory in which residents were exempted from curfews and room checks and were required to sign out only when not returning until past midnight or staying overnight off campus. They also had the right to set policies for open houses when males could visit in the residents' living quarters.[98]

Despite rules governing student behavior, Trinity officials were not able to insulate undergraduates from the sexual revolution that swept the country in the 1960s. Although the extent of their participation lacks documentation, some signs showed that the lifestyle of many Trinity students was changing. Commenting on articles in *Time* and *Newsweek* regarding sexual practices in Ivy League colleges and universities, one Trinity student observed that even though Trinitonians liked to think that they were more moral than students in eastern schools, their behavior belied that assumption. "Sneaking out of dorms via the first floor balconies has become the thing to do, along with all night beach parties at Corpus Christi, weekly drinking parties, and having an apartment on the side."[99]

In about the same period, a poll conducted by the *Trinitonian* staff in 1968 indicated that the drug culture had established a presence on the Trinity campus. Approximately 30 percent of students responded to the poll, and about 4 percent of those respondents stated that they regularly or occasionally used marijuana and 10 percent admitted taking LSD or similar substances. Reasons expressed included curiosity, escape from academic stress, and depression, although a number of students indicated that they took drugs "because it feels good and is an enjoyable experience."[100]

While student activism usually affected administrators, the Trinity faculty also experienced the growing influence of students in university affairs. Noting the one-sidedness of a system in which faculty assigned grades but students had no voice in evaluating professors or courses, the student council in 1967 organized a course and teacher evaluation conducted on the basis of voluntary faculty participation. Aided by computer technology, they distributed the results of the evaluations to professors in an effort to promote more effective classes and better communication between professors and students.[101]

For a brief period of time, a free university program flourished on campus. Faculty and students joined together to plan curricula and to discuss crucial intellectual issues and social problems. Professors Lawrence Kimmel, Don Webb, Howard Cave, and Kenneth Kramer joined with students Mikel Miller and Margaret Lindsey in 1969 to plan the project. Courses were free, noncredit, and nongraded and offered students and faculty an opportunity to explore a wide range of learning experiences. Included among the early offerings were classes on birth control, ESP, yoga, Hinduism, interpersonal relationships, computers, chess, conversational Spanish, and Vietnam. Although short lived, the free university program stimulated interaction between faculty and students and provided an outlet for student leadership opportunities.[102]

Along other lines, the student union board initiated the Student Lecture Series in 1967 to bring speakers of national and international renown to campus. The first two featured speakers, Bishop James Pike and Senator Barry Goldwater, attracted large crowds and stimulated considerable discussion and debate on campus. In the case of Pike, a controversial Episcopalian bishop whose allegedly unorthodox theology had offended many churchgoers, students encountered resistance from student life officials who questioned the advisability of bringing a "heretic" to campus. Student body president Jim Jones and Humphrey Bogart, director of student activities, intervened with Laurie to secure approval for Pike's appearance. Amid protests from local church people, Laurie supported the students, hosted a dinner for Pike, and attended the lecture.[103]

Beyond internal relations with administrators and faculty, Trinity students displayed increasing awareness of issues that were impacting campuses nationally. Initial response to the Vietnam conflict reflected the attitudes of the wider military-oriented San Antonio community, where most citizens either supported the war effort or elected not to oppose it publicly. In 1965 the Trinity Young Republicans organization circulated a petition supporting President Lyndon Johnson's Vietnam policies and secured more than 500 signatures. More than 200 Trinitonians participated in a blood drive for servicemen in Southeast Asia sponsored by the International Relations Club and received high praise from the United Military Council of Bexar County for their act of patriotism.[104] As late as 1967, informal campus polls indicated that an overwhelming majority of Trinity students supported the government's policies in Vietnam.[105]

As the U.S. military role in Vietnam shifted from providing assistance to active combat and the draft was extended to college students, Trinity students became more vocal in registering opposition to heightened U. S.

military involvement.[106] They found role models for questioning the Vietnam conflict among some of the younger Trinity faculty members. At monthly meetings sponsored by the student Foreign Policy Association, faculty and students discussed U.S. policies in Vietnam and in other countries overseas.[107] Beyond campus discussions, some Trinity faculty participated in peaceful demonstrations opposing the war.[108]

In concert with a Vietnam moratorium held on campuses throughout the United States, Trinity students in 1969 observed a day-long series of speeches and discussions sponsored by the Student Free Forum and designed to "open up a free expression of dialogue on the campus." Although leaders of the National Vietnam Moratorium Committee urged college students to boycott classes, the Trinity student association rejected that proposal. Instead, following the lead of the Faculty Senate, it strongly encouraged Trinity faculty and students to participate in "meaningful dialogue of current issues." Trinity administrators facilitated the observance by providing space and equipment for the daylong event with the understanding that participants would not attempt to disrupt classes.[109]

On 15 October 1969, several hundred students and faculty gathered in the area around the reflection pond to listen to speakers representing a variety of perspectives on the war and to engage in open discussion and dialogue. Interspersing events with renditions by various local rock bands, the event's leaders scheduled sessions so that students could attend classes and still participate. Although attendance varied throughout the day and represented only a small percentage of the Trinity community, it was a landmark campus happening. Students had acted responsibly in organizing the event and administrators had supported their efforts.[110]

In May 1970, sixty colleges and universities went on strike to protest the United States' invasion of Cambodia. On May 4, members of the National Guard fired on unarmed Kent State University students, killing four and wounding others.[111] Approximately four hundred Trinity students, faculty, and administrators turned out for a brief, informal memorial service led by the president of the student association, Bill Hunnicutt. After the evening event, participants formed a candlelight procession and walked to the Eugenia Miller Fountain, where they gathered in a circle and placed their flickering candles on the ground.[112]

After the group disbanded, about one hundred students chose to walk through Brackenridge Park, joined by Tom Flowers, a representative of the American Friends Service Committee and local political activist who had attended the memorial service. Flowers suggested that the group march to

Student activism peaked during the 1969–70 school year.

Fort Sam Houston to protest military involvement in the Kent State tragedy. With Flowers leading the procession and police cars trailing, the group encountered representatives of the Fourth Army and some military police as they approached base entrance. Informed that they could not proceed, the marchers launched into a song and chant session that quickly turned into a shouting match between the two groups. Finally, about 2:00 A.M., the students retreated from the premises and returned to campus. One of the participants noted later that while some dormitory residents discussed the possibility destroying property and organizing protests, "everyone was wise enough to know it wouldn't do any lasting good."[113]

Student involvement in social, political, and academic issues coincided with a declining interest in traditional campus religious activities. Weekly chapel services and Spiritual Emphasis Week programs were often poorly attended even when religious leaders of national renown were featured speakers. In 1960 Student Christian Council president Mike Price described the campus religious system as "inbred and ineffective, pretty much run by the administration from the top" and lamented that there was "no vital student Christian voice on campus."[114]

Dedication of the Margarite B. Parker Chapel in the spring of 1966 marked the beginning of a new era of religious activities on campus. Located at the heart of the campus between Northrup Hall and the Storch Memorial Library and fronted by the Murchison Tower, the chapel fulfilled one of Laurie's most ardent wishes for a visible religious presence on campus. During its first year of operation, Professor R. Douglas Brackenridge, chair of the Committee on Religious Activities, coordinated chapel programs. In addition to the Wednesday morning services, the chapel conducted occasional Sunday vespers that included traditional worship services and special events such as a jazz mass and supported student-directed groups that invited speakers to discuss contemporary topics in religion and ethics.[115]

Aware that chapel activities required full-time leadership and supervision, Laurie invited Raymond Judd Jr., pastor of the Clarksville, Texas, Presbyterian church, to become Minister-in-Charge of Margarite B. Parker Chapel. A graduate of the class of 1957 and a student leader, he was familiar with the dynamics of campus life and Trinity's relationship with the Synod of Texas.[116] Arriving in San Antonio during the summer of 1967, Judd held this position with distinction for more than thirty years, serving as pastor, counselor, teacher, and friend to the Trinity community.[117]

Once a full-time chaplain was in place, Laurie decided to experiment with Sunday morning chapel services, which called for a re-examination of the relationship between the university and the nearby University Presbyterian Church, the latter originally situated to serve as an unofficial "campus church." Initially, Laurie had assured church officials that Trinity did not intend to compete with their Sunday morning worship services.[118] Response was encouraging, and the services had little impact on attendance at University Presbyterian Church. As a result, ecumenical services became regular Sunday morning occurrences that attracted students, faculty, staff, and members of the wider San Antonio community.[119]

As the 1960s drew to a close, contributors to the *Trinitonian* reflected on their Trinity experiences and the rapidly changing configurations of campus life. Although they remembered the decade as an exciting period of building projects, academic advancements, and social change, some student leaders believed that the "University in the Sun" was only beginning its quest for academic excellence. With Laurie's retirement imminent and Thomas's soon to follow, it was clear that Trinity would soon be directed by a new generation of academic administrators. How they related to student issues and concerns would greatly affect the university's ability to attract and retain a quality student body.

From her perspective as editor of the *Trinitonian*, Karen Abbott made a candid assessment of the university's strengths and weaknesses in 1968.

On the positive side, she noted, "Trinity has a fine location, a beautiful campus, a wide curriculum, some excellent professors and many well-qualified students." Closer scrutiny, however, led her to conclude that Trinity had yet to attain the status of a mature university community. "A school grows like a person," she wrote. "Trinity must pass the adolescent stage of taking each question personally and defensively and secretively. It must take an adult stand where it can reason with students directly—treating them also as adults. With all due respect to Trinity administrators—and we mean that quite sincerely—we would like to suggest that, after 100 years, Trinity's priorities need to be re-examined."[120]

CHAPTER ELEVEN

NEITHER DULL NOR ROUTINE

Whatever the future holds for Trinity, I'm confident that the years ahead
will be neither dull nor routine. Trinity University is on the move.

DUNCAN WIMPRESS, SEPTEMBER 4, 1970

I N CONTRAST TO THE CONTINUITY IN LEADERSHIP under Laurie
and Thomas, Trinity experienced a number of changes in high-level administrators in the 1970s. Before the decade ended, Trinity had three presidents, including one interim, and, following the retirement of Bruce
Thomas, a new vice president for academic affairs. The university also
made major modifications in administrative structures, de-emphasized
intercollegiate athletics, and abandoned its quest for doctoral studies.

In addition to internal changes, rampant inflation and escalating operating expenses during the seventies produced grave crises for higher education in America. Depressed fiscal conditions made it difficult for college
graduates to find employment and fostered doubts among the American
public regarding the value of a college degree. Periodic studies on the financial health of institutions of higher learning issued during the decade
by the Carnegie Commission indicated little hope for an immediate improvement in economic conditions.[1]

As the Laurie presidency drew to a close, the university community exhibited both high expectations and divided loyalties. Accustomed to his
hands-on leadership, a segment that was comfortable with the established
patterns of university operations hoped that the new president would retain much of the previous administration's management style. Others envisioned more collegial and participatory structures that would facilitate
wider involvement in formulating university goals and objectives. Those
faculty and staff who considered Laurie's major contribution to have been

campus construction hoped for a president whose primary concern would be to enhance Trinity's academic reputation.[2]

In keeping with precedent, the presidential search committee consisted solely of trustees, including Laurie, who also was a member of the board. The Faculty Senate appealed to the board of trustees for faculty representation on the search committee. Although the trustees denied the request, they approved the appointment of an *ex officio* Faculty Senate Presidential Selection Committee that would be updated on the progress of the search. Chaired by political science professor Robert Walker, the senate committee met from time to time with individual trustees and reported regularly to the plenary senate.[3]

When the Faculty Senate learned in March 1970 that Duncan Wimpress had been invited to visit the campus as the sole presidential nominee, members passed a resolution stating that they "looked forward to meeting with him to explore areas of mutual interest."[4] After an extended conversation with Wimpress, senators advised the board of trustees that they had reached a consensus regarding the candidate. "[He] is a good choice for the position. We have no substantial reservations." When queried by a colleague as to why the Faculty Senate bothered to convey such a recommendation when the nomination was already a *fait accomplit*, professor Guy Ranson replied, "We are establishing a precedent for future presidential searches. We want to be on record as being involved in the process."[5]

At a press conference on March 13, 1970, chairman of the board of trustees Forrest M. Smith Sr. announced the selection of forty-seven-year-old Duncan Wimpress Jr. as Trinity's fifteenth president. A California native and graduate of the University of Oregon, Wimpress earned an M.A. degree in journalism and political science at the University of Oregon and a Ph.D. in political science at the University of Denver in Colorado. He began his professional career at Whittier College in California, where he served as the director of public relations as well as an instructor in journalism from 1946 to 1951. Subsequently, he served for seven years as the assistant to the president at the Colorado School of Mines and in 1959 was named president of Monticello College in Alton, Illinois.[6]

After five years at Monticello, Wimpress assumed the presidency of nearby Monmouth College, a Presbyterian church-related institution, and held that position until coming to Trinity in 1970. His six-year tenure at Monmouth College, an institution that was similar in many respects to his new charge, had presented issues comparable to those facing Trinity in the 1970s. Although limited by budgetary restrictions, Monmouth had increased enrollment, added new faculty, and improved the physical plant with a new library and a new science center under his leadership. Wimpress presided over the establishment of a covenant relationship between Monmouth and the Synod of Illinois of the United Presbyterian Church in the U.S.A. and guided the college community through a difficult period of student unrest. According to Monmouth historian William Urban, Wimpress was "a firm defender of civil rights and academic freedom" who maintained high academic standards and teaching effectiveness among the faculty during an extremely difficult period in the history of American higher education.[7]

Accompanying Wimpress to San Antonio were his spouse, the former Jean Margaret (Peggy) Skerry of Portland, Oregon, and their three children, Wendy Jo, Victoria Jean, and Scotty. Having served as a presidential spouse at two previous institutions, Peggy Wimpress understood the heavy demands on her time and energy. As hostess in the newly acquired Minter house adjacent to the Trinity campus, Peggy entertained trustees, faculty, students, and other guests on a regular basis. Also active in various civic and social organizations, she functioned as an effective liaison between the university and the wider community.[8]

From the outset, the new president projected an image of modernity and informality. An avid sportsman who skied, golfed, and hunted, Wimpress also played the drums and enjoyed "jam sessions" with student and faculty performers. He traversed the campus in a Corvette Stingray and held a commercial pilot's license with instrument and multiengine ratings. The board of trustees purchased a two-engine Cessna Super Skymaster from Monmouth College to facilitate his extensive travel on university business. Trinity students quickly dubbed the maroon and white plane "Air Wimpress," and the *Trinitonian* featured cartoons of the president dressed in aviator garb at the controls of his aircraft.[9]

In lieu of elaborate festivities, Wimpress elected to mark his inauguration as president in April 1971 during Sunday morning services in the Margarite B. Parker Chapel. "Formal inaugurations can be expensive," Wimpress told the trustees. "They consume faculty and staff man hours and other valuable resources. I'd rather see the money spent on the students."[10] Immediately after the service, members and friends of the Trinity community attended an informal reception in the Great Hall of the Chapman Graduate Center.[11]

In his initial meetings with trustees, Wimpress emphasized the importance of meeting new challenges in the field of higher education. While paying tribute to his predecessor's accomplishments, Wimpress said that

"With all my flying ratings I can't even get off the ground."
The *Trinitonian*, 8 October 1971

the most appropriate memorial to James W. Laurie would be "to work together to make Trinity University an even greater university in the years ahead."[12] To this effect, he appointed a long-range planning committee, which he chaired, composed of students, faculty, and administrators and charged to make recommendations regarding future academic structures and programs. At the same time, Wimpress proposed restructuring trustee committees to bring them more in line with university functions. He also informed the board that he intended to hold the doctoral program in abeyance until he had time to study its viability.[13]

Regarding fiscal affairs, Wimpress emphasized the importance of formulating balanced budgets and avoiding additional debt. Previous budgets, he noted, had been "balanced" using figures of anticipated income from undesignated giving that had not been met. Wimpress wished to present a more realistic assessment of potential income and expenses. He also proposed to give faculty and students access to financial information and to seek their input before finalizing a budget. This represented a major shift from past procedures, in which only a few individuals participated in budget-setting decisions.[14]

Along with these innovations, Wimpress gave departmental chairs more autonomy in determining salary increments for their faculty. For the first time in university history, chairs received an approximate dollar amount budgeted for departmental salaries and had the authority to allocate funds as they saw fit. Although faculty members generally favored the new procedure, some chairs reportedly were less than enthusiastic because they now were required to assume greater accountability than previously, when the vice president for academic affairs and the president had made such decisions.[15]

Working closely with student association president Rex Smith in 1972, Wimpress created the student finance board, composed of five students, two faculty members, and one member each from the office of student life and the business office. The board afforded students a major role in allocating student activity funds. Organizations eligible for funds included the student newspaper, the yearbook, the athletic and intramural programs, and the Student Council. Other organizations could receive financial support if approved by both the Student Finance Board and the Student Council.[16]

Open discussion of university budget priorities precipitated the new administration's first major controversy. Although dissatisfaction with the cost of Trinity's intercollegiate athletics program antedated Wimpress's arrival, the figures now made public revealed that the university expended approximately 7 percent of its operating budget ($400,000) on intercollegiate athletics and that student-athletes received 30 percent of the annual scholarship aid regardless of individual need. When members of the Academic Council (composed of department chairs) learned of the specific numbers in the spring of 1971, they recommended that the administration give serious consideration to modifying or eliminating some areas of intercollegiate athletic activities.[17]

After seeking input from various campus organizations, Wimpress proposed that the university eliminate athletic scholarships, except for men's varsity tennis, which would continue to compete for national recognition. Current athletes who chose to remain at Trinity would retain their scholarships; faculty in the Department of Health, Physical Education, and Recreation would be given the coaching assignments. In order to further reduce costs, he recommended that Trinity play its home games on campus rather than in Alamo Stadium. Such changes would necessitate that Trinity leave the Southland Conference and participate as an independent. Looking ahead, Wimpress said he would take the lead in forming a new intercollegiate conference composed of privately supported institutions with academic goals and financial resources similar to Trinity's. At their board meeting in October 1971, Trinity trustees approved the recommendations and announced their decision at a press conference for local media.[18]

Although Wimpress had broad university support for his proposal, he encountered harsh criticism from student-athletes, coaches, and local

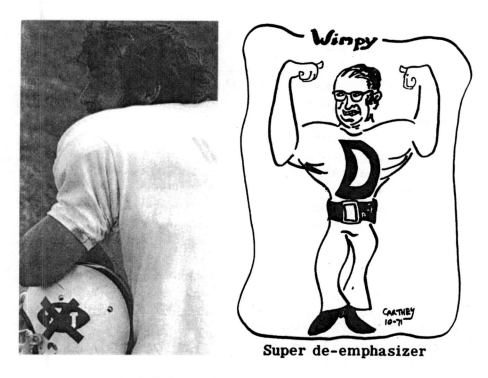

Super de-emphasizer

Football players protested the loss of scholarships.
Left: the *Mirage*, 1972. Right: the *Trinitonian*, 15 October 1971

sportswriters.[19] *San Antonio Express-News* columnist Dan Cook criticized the Trinity president for traversing the country in a $40,000 airplane at a time when the university was severely reducing athletic funds. He accused Wimpress of "taking a slice from the San Antonio sports scene. It's a slice we'd hate to lose."[20] Another sports writer accused Wimpress of establishing "club football" in place of Trinity's long-established tradition of competitive intercollegiate athletics.[21]

Students gave mixed reviews to the new athletic program. Student association president Steve Hudson reported that his membership endorsed this decision, particularly because it would free up funds for other student activities. He also indicated that most students with whom he talked expressed little interest in the decision one way or another.[22] Student-athletes and sports enthusiasts, however, had different views. *Trinitonian* sports editor Tom Landers resigned after writing an editorial condemning the new policy. He claimed that a poll taken by his staff indicated that a majority of students wanted to increase rather than decrease funding of intercollegiate athletics. Contributors to the *Trinitonian* sided with Landers in opposing any change in funding intercollegiate athletics.[23]

In the midst of a successful football season in the Southland Conference, Trinity coaches and players publicly vented their feelings. San Antonio newspapers quoted Coach Gene Offield as saying, "Our players weren't recruited to play club football. They've been abandoned and I support them." After Trinity trustees confirmed the new policy, someone placed a sign in the center of the university practice field that read: "For Sale." Diagonally on the poster in bold letters was the word "SOLD." At the next home game, football players united in silent protest by appearing on the playing field with the university's insignias on their helmets crossed over with black tape, symbolically indicating a double-cross.[24]

Following Offield's resignation as coach and Warren Woodson's resignation as athletic director in 1973, Wimpress appointed basketball coach Pete Murphy, a Trinity graduate and former athlete, to succeed Woodson as athletic director and promoted assistant football coach Gene Norris to the head football coaching position. Norris, who had served as an instructor in the Department of Physical Education since 1961, played football at the University of Illinois and coached high school teams in Michigan prior to coming to Trinity. Students highly regarded both men as teachers and coaches who were committed to making the new program work.[25]

As he had promised, Wimpress played a leading role in establishing the southwest's first nonscholarship and fully coeducational athletic conference. Largely because of his efforts, the Texas Intercollegiate Athletic Association (TIAA) composed of McMurry College, Austin College, Sul Ross State University, Tarleton State University, and Trinity University commenced operations in 1975. The new conference began with only a few sports and some schools still in the process of phasing out athletic scholarships, but eventually it provided competition in eleven sports for both men and women.[26]

The move to nonscholarship intercollegiate athletics also played a role in Trinity's quest for the establishment of a Phi Beta Kappa chapter on campus. The society's visitation team that came to San Antonio in the spring of 1972 was impressed with Trinity's academic progress in recent years, including the Trinity Plan, quality of faculty and student body, library facilities, financial resources, and the recent move to nonscholarship athletics.[27] In August 1973, the Triennial Council of the Chapters of Phi Beta Kappa included Trinity in the fifteen schools that were granted charters. At the time, only four other Texas institutions—the University of Texas at Austin, Rice University, Southern Methodist University, and

Texas Christian University—had chapters. The chair of the visitation team subsequently told Wimpress that the university's stance on intercollegiate athletics had considerable influence on the committee's decision to grant the university a charter.[28]

Wimpress faced another difficult task in implementing Trinity's recently formulated covenant relationship with the Presbyterian church. Denominational leaders found little time to nurture higher education during an extended period of declining membership, extensive budget cuts, and divisive social issues. Moreover, the creation of regional synods in 1972 ended Trinity's exclusive relationship with the Synod of Texas and aligned it with the Synod of the Sun of the United Presbyterian Church in the U.S.A., whose boundaries embraced Texas, Arkansas, Oklahoma, and Louisiana.[29] Under the realignment, Trinity now competed for synodical support with the University of Tulsa and the College of the Ozarks. Working relationships with the Synod of the Red River of the Presbyterian Church in the U.S. also brought Austin College, Austin Presbyterian Theological Seminary, Schreiner Institute, and Arkansas College (now Lyon College) into the constellation of institutions of higher education in the four-state area.[30]

Under the new configuration, the synod rotated its annual meetings, formerly held exclusively on the Trinity campus, among varying locations in all four states.[31] Representation at synod meetings also changed. In the old Synod of Texas, meetings were open to commissioners from every congregation within its bounds; thus, large numbers of people heard the reports on higher education and interacted with university personnel and students. The new Synod of the Sun changed to delegated meetings composed of elected representatives from the constituent presbyteries, which greatly reduced the number of attendees and deprived colleges of the opportunity to speak to a cross section of church membership.[32]

Internally, the university community was ambivalent regarding its church relationship. Laurie, primarily through the force of his personality and his high visibility in denominational circles, had nurtured Trinity's religious heritage and maintained close ties with church officials. Increasingly, however, many Trinity faculty questioned the relevance of a church relationship and viewed it as anachronistic and even hypocritical.[33] In 1973 the University Senate appointed a committee to draft a revised statement of purpose that would more accurately reflect the university's current aims and goals. Adopted by the board of trustees in 1974, the new statement emphasized Trinity's status as an "independent and nonsectarian" university and muted the Christian rhetoric of previous versions.[34]

Even these changes failed to satisfy many faculty and students who thought that all references to "Christian" orientation should be dropped from the statement published in the *Trinity University Catalogue*. Members of the Southern Association of Colleges visitation team in 1975 reported widespread dissatisfaction with Trinity's formal statement of purpose, a document that, in their estimation, reflected a reality that no longer existed. The association team recommended that Trinity reexamine the statement and modify it to conform more closely to university goals and objectives. The decade ended, however, with the statement unchanged and continuing differences of opinion among members of the university community.[35]

In the academic area, Wimpress acted to increase the effectiveness of administrative structures and the quality and diversity of Trinity's student body. Early in 1972, he recommended the establishment of a College of Arts and Sciences to complement the existing business administration, engineering, and graduate schools. Although Bruce Thomas retained supervisory authority over all academic programs, the dean of the College of Arts and Sciences served as chair of five divisional councils: media and fine arts, physical and life sciences, humanities, social and behavioral sciences, and education. When trustees approved the proposed restructuring, Wimpress appointed Associate Dean of Academic Affairs Gail E. Myers to be dean of the new administrative unit. Although not challenging Myers's qualifications, the Faculty Senate expressed concern that the president had not instituted a formal search process.[36]

In other changes, Wimpress replaced the Faculty Senate, composed solely of members of the academic faculty, with a more broadly based University Senate. In the new body, administrative, faculty, and student representatives considered matters brought to it by various university committees or by other faculty or student groups. Senate actions generally had the status of recommendations either to the president or, through him, to the board of trustees. As a member of the University Senate, the president participated in discussions and reported to senate members on decisions made at board meetings.[37]

Two faculty groups, the Academic Council and the Teaching and Research Faculty Commission, dealt with academic policy issues. Composed of all department chairs, twelve administrators, and three students, the Academic Council exercised authority over all courses of instruction, including the approval of new courses and exceptions to stated policies.[38] The inclusion of students in this curricular body marked a departure from previous practice. The Teaching and Research Faculty Commission as-

The Trinity Fact Book (1972) emphasized diversity by including a photograph of an African-American residential student.

sumed responsibility for matters relating to tenure, academic freedom, due process, and employment conditions.[39]

During the Wimpress administration, Trinity placed new emphasis on recruiting minority students, faculty, and staff. In 1970 only 2 percent of undergraduate students were classified as minorities, most of whom were nonresidential Hispanic students who spent little time on campus outside of class.[40] Working closely with local and regional high school counselors, Trinity admissions counselors identified minority students with admissible scholastic records. At the end of the decade, approximately 10 percent of undergraduate students were minorities, but faculty and staff figures remained virtually unchanged at approximately 3 percent.[41]

From the outset of his presidency, Wimpress created opportunities for frequent interaction with faculty and students. Because the faculty's teaching responsibilities limited their meeting times, Wimpress instituted early morning departmental breakfasts for informal conversations and question-and-answer sessions. During the course of each year, he met with all twenty-five departments. Although faculty members appreciated the spirit of the president's initiative, many were not accustomed to arriving on campus in time for 7:00 A.M. breakfasts. In one department, the chair assigned the responsibility of making wake-up calls to departmental colleagues to a member who was known to be a notoriously late riser. He performed flawlessly but went back to sleep and missed the breakfast.[42]

Wimpress hosted forums with students to keep in touch with their viewpoints and to provide them with current information regarding new developments in university planning. Once a month on Sunday evenings, Wimpress invited thirty students to his home for discussion. Students expressed appreciation for his willingness to open his home and listen to their concerns.[43]

In addition to these campus activities, Wimpress traveled widely to participate in regional, national, and international academic and service organizations and to solicit financial support and increase Trinity's visibility in the academic world. In 1973, for example, Wimpress reported that he had made fifty trips to thirty-six cities in eleven states and four foreign countries.[44] Critics would later cite his frequent absences from campus as problematic in terms of hands-on supervision of internal affairs.

Building projects undertaken early in the Wimpress administration enhanced the functionality of the campus. Completion of the Laurie Auditorium and the adjoining Richardson Communications Center in 1971 marked the forty-third structure to be erected on Trinity Hill since the site was first occupied in 1952. Designed by architects O'Neil Ford and Bartlett Cocke and built at a cost of approximately $4.7 million, the five-level, 244,00–square-foot complex included parking facilities, an auditorium with a seating capacity of 3,000, lecture and seminar rooms, offices, and television and radio studios.[45]

During the same year, longtime Trinity supporter, E. M. Stevens, chairman of the board of Great Western Finance Company, gave the university $100,000 to build a new football stadium. The 4,800-seat concrete structure provided Trinity with a permanent home field.[46] Stevens presented the stadium to Wimpress at ceremonies on 9 September 1972, prior to Trinity's first intercollegiate football game on the new field. The Tigers marked the occasion by defeating Southwest Texas State University by a score of 9–7.[47]

Wimpress announced a third major gift in 1971, $1.5 million from

George and Betty Coates to erect a new university center. He also invited students to make suggestions regarding the design and scope of the new building before completing the final blueprints.[48] Architect O'Neill Ford initially proposed constructing the center below the bluff and integrating it above ground with the existing student union. Because of excessive cost, however, Ford decided to raze the adjacent one-story bookstore and office complex to accommodate the center.[49] The new building housed a coffee shop, dining room, and rathskeller (basement restaurant) along with a greatly enlarged bookstore and various recreational and meeting rooms.[50]

While construction of the Coates University Center was in progress, Wimpress revealed plans to raise $5 million to construct a new library, a project he deemed the university's "number one building priority." Noting that the existing library facilities in Storch Memorial Library and the Chapman Graduate Center were rapidly running out of space, Wimpress envisaged a 200,000-square-foot area that would serve the university well into the next century. His ultimate goal was to provide the university with a "futuristic" edifice that could hold one million volumes and seat twelve hundred readers. If donors could not be found to underwrite the entire $5 million, Wimpress indicated that the library might have to be built in stages.[51]

In just a few years, Wimpress appeared to be making an effective transition from the Laurie era and gaining stature in the community as an effective chief executive officer. His handling of the intercollegiate athletics controversy, implementation of a new academic administrative structure, and efforts to continue and expand the campus building projects were acknowledged by the local press as marks of decisive leadership. Despite national trends of declining enrollment and deficit budgets, Trinity's student body continued to increase, and the university annually reported a balanced budget. At a board of trustees meeting in February 1972, chairman Gilbert M. Denman Jr. commended Wimpress for his "vigorous, imaginative leadership of the university" and for his "resolute dedication to the application of sound business principles in the management of Trinity's affairs." The board unanimously supported Denman's resolution.[52]

The 1970s were years of curricular expansion and innovation in which faculty members were encouraged to develop nontraditional courses and to experiment with new methods of pedagogy. Environmental issues captured the interest of Trinity faculty and students. A celebration of Earth Day in 1970 featured a special chapel service, films, lectures, and panel discussions on various environmental issues.[53] In the same year, Trinity faculty approved a new multidisciplinary course entitled "Environmental

Studies: Man's Relationship to a Modern World."[54] In 1972 biology professor Lawrence Espey and engineering science colleague Geoffrey Goring established an environmental science degree program that examined issues such as population growth, resource depletion, pollution, and social stress. Five students received the first degrees in environmental science during the 1973–74 academic year.[55]

The university also implemented a solar energy project that included the installation of solar energy panels on the roof of the Sams Athletic Center and the creation of a cooperative research and training program in solar energy. In 1976 the university secured a $1.2 million grant from the U.S. Energy Research and Development Agency (ERDA) to build a large-scale solar demonstration project. Supervised by Trinity faculty and staff, the project became operational in 1977 and supplied approximately 75 percent of the university's hot water and space heating and cooling requirements for Sams Athletic Center and six residence halls.[56]

As an outgrowth of the solar project, Trinity became the headquarters for a $2.3 million research and training program in solar energy. The ERDA approved a proposal to establish a unified data collection, data analysis, and training program for six states: Texas, Missouri, Oklahoma, Louisiana, Arkansas, and Kansas. The ERDA contributed $1 million to the five-year program with Trinity, St. Louis, and Baylor Universities providing the remaining $1.3 million.[57] The Halsell Foundation contributed funding to support graduate assistantships for outstanding students in the program. Depending on their undergraduate background and specific interests, students could select one of four master of science degree tracks based on a core curriculum of solar energy courses.[58]

Opening of the new Richardson Communications Center enabled the university to expand its offerings in the communication field. The Department of Journalism, Broadcasting, and Film (JBF) offered two degree programs in journalism, one with a broadcast emphasis, and majors in film and broadcasting and in mass communication. New courses offering advanced work in television and film production enabled students to gain valuable hands-on experience in a variety of settings.[59]

After a lengthy effort to obtain funding and an FCC license, in January 1976 Trinity acquired its own radio station, KRTU 91.7 FM, operating at a low-level 50-watt signal. KRTU initially offered a mixture of rock, jazz, Dixieland, country, and classical music that JBF department chair Bill Hays said had "distinctly educational aspects." In addition to recorded music, the programming schedule included a one-hour show called "Studio-B" that featured live music originating from the Richardson Communications Center studios. Acquisition of an Associated Press teletype machine enabled the station to receive news prepared for broadcast rather than the print media. The news department of KRTU offered the special-feature weekly talk show "Night Watch," directed by Jack Landman, a Trinity graduate and department instructor.[60]

In 1974 Trinity initiated a mini-term, an intensive three-week session held during the interim between the end of the spring semester in May and the beginning of the summer session. Devised to attract Trinity students before they left campus for vacation, the program offered students and faculty an opportunity to concentrate on one subject without conflicting time pressures. In addition to on-site classes, courses were held in nine off-campus locations, two in the United States and seven in foreign countries. Among the offerings were a wilderness field trip with biology professor Lawrence Espey, a tour of Russia with history professor Terry Smart, and a trip to Mexico with foreign language professor Ken Taggart.[61]

Other new programs reflected Trinity's interest in cultural diversity. The Department of Education joined with the English, foreign language, and sociology departments to initiate a bilingual/bicultural program designed to prepare future public school teachers to teach in school settings where students were predominantly Hispanic. Certified by the Texas Education Association, the program provided San Antonio school districts with qualified instructors.[62] Underwritten by a grant from the Halsell Foundation, Trinity introduced an Asian Studies Program, initially staffed by a visiting scholar from Malaysia, in 1976. At the same time, the university purchased a widely acclaimed Asian studies book collection, previously owned by Dr. Karl J. Pelzer and housed at Yale University.[63]

In addition to these offerings, Trinity faculty devised courses that had contemporary appeal. English professor William Spinks introduced a course in 1972 that focused on works in science fiction, one of the first such in the country, in which he encouraged students to discuss the role of values in a technological society.[64] History professor Alan Kownslar developed a process of inquiry and values clarification that encouraged students to identify problems, hypothesize answers, and test the validity of their hypotheses. An outgrowth of the course was a series of summer workshops for secondary school teachers who received guidance in how to apply the inquiry method to issues in Texas, U.S., and world history.[65] Psychology department chair Kenneth Kramer created several courses focusing on child psychopathology and community mental health that enabled psychology and sociology majors to gain experience outside traditional classroom settings. Students in these courses underwent eighteen hours of classroom training and sixteen hours of supervised training before being accepted as volunteers and then received credit for volunteer work in such places as the San Antonio Crisis Center and the Bexar County Hospital.[66]

Other Trinity faculty experimented with the concept of team teaching. Professors Richard Bartels (physics) and Ewing Chinn (philosophy) offered a course entitled "Implications of Scientific Thought." Taught from a historical perspective, the course focused on the evolution of thought regarding the subjects of matter, space, and time.[67] Psychology professor Fred Bremner and English professor Bates Hoffer coordinated a course on verbal and nonverbal animal and human language systems. Sessions included communication within the wolf pack, teaching sign language to orangutans and gorillas, and experiments dealing with human and nonverbal communication.[68] In response to a petition signed by more than fifty students, sociology professors O Z White and Richard Machalak offered a course titled "Life in the 'Sixties" that introduced students to a generation identified with the Vietnam war, flower children, and college campus unrest.[69]

One of the most widely discussed team-taught courses during the 1970s was "Human Sexuality," led by professors John Worsham (psychology) and David Oliver (sociology). Offered for the first time in 1976, the course attracted 175 students with many more turned away for lack of space. Utilizing films, lectures, and question-and-answer sessions, Worsham and Oliver explored issues in an open and frank manner. According to Oliver, the teaching team wanted to "help get rid of student hang-ups and apprehensions about sex." The *Trinitonian* reported that the candid nature of the course "roused much talk around campus."[70]

Trinity's computer program accelerated under the leadership of John E. Howland. Prior to 1970, Trinity offered only two computer science courses, numerical analysis in the mathematics department and programming in the engineering department. As chair of the Department of Computing and Information Sciences, Howland recruited faculty and developed the first undergraduate major in computer science in the southwestern United States. In 1972 the department graduated its initial degree candidates and two years later established a master's degree program that attracted considerable student interest.[71]

The installation of six remote APL terminals in August 1970 introduced a new era of computer utilization on campus. In less than a year, more than 500 students and about one-third of the faculty were employing the system for all types of educational activities. By the fall of 1971, twenty-one remote terminals were in use with approximately 5,000 connect hours per month.[72] When a new IBM 370/155 became fully operational in 1972, computer center staff reported that between 800 and 1,000 people used the terminals during a given semester.[73] Not everyone utilized the terminals for academic projects. After receiving complaints from various faculty members, the Computer Center Advisory Committee voted unanimously to remove all existing copies of video games from the university system.[74]

As the decade progressed, computer use on campus became more widespread. The university reached a milestone in 1976 when staff utilized a computer program designed by Howland to write the "Self-Study Report for the Southern Association," the first major Trinity document produced with an on-campus word processor.[75] Other advancements included creation of an online database of admissions information, maintenance of student academic records, and the gradual conversion from manual to computerized checkout of books and periodicals.[76] Only library staff had access to computer terminals, and librarian Robert Houze did not envisage any immediate change. "The day is still in the future, if ever, when students themselves will sit down at the terminals in place of the microfiche or card catalog."[77]

In 1973 Trinity established an auxiliary corporation known as TRINCO to provide computer services on a contract basis to the university and to sell computer time and services to customers in the surrounding community. Instituted largely through the initiative of Vice President for Fiscal Affairs Derwood Hawthorne, TRINCO had total assets in excess of $1 million from the university and from business and offered a broad range of computerized services such as mailing lists, data retrieval, and labeling. Although periodically beset with administrative problems and operational deficits, TRINCO generated revenues that enabled the university to utilize a sophisticated computer system far superior to those normally available on a campus of Trinity's size. The purchase of an IBM 370/3031 model computer in 1979 doubled the speed of the existing equipment and provided students with a more varied range of programs.[78] By the end of the decade, however, mixed reviews from external accrediting agencies and potential IRS problems caused university administrators to rethink the value of retaining the ancillary corporation.[79]

At the graduate level, the administration proposed to abandon its quest for doctoral work and to concentrate on reducing the master's degree programs and improving their quality. The board of trustees concurred and voted to drop the reference to doctoral studies from the university's official statement of purpose.[80] The Graduate Council placed emphasis on cultivating interdisciplinary and professionally oriented programs that constituted terminal degrees for practice in those fields. In 1974, Graduate Dean Leonard Duce announced his impending retirement and his replacement by Charles J. Austin, recipient of an interdisciplinary social science doctorate from the University of Cincinnati. When asked about the future of graduate education at Trinity, Duce expressed uncertainty except to predict that maintenance of high standards would require the university to be very selective in its offerings.[81]

During Austin's tenure as graduate dean (1974–78), the university added degrees in fine arts and Master of Arts degrees in teaching (education combined with history, English, political science, or foreign language), school psychology, gerontology, solar energy studies, and an individualized interdisciplinary program. In addition, the Master of Business Administration (M.B.A.) replaced a previous Master of Science in Business Administration. At the same time, small degree programs in religion, philosophy, health and physical education, and mathematics were discontinued, reducing the number of academic departments offering graduate degrees from twenty-two to eighteen. When Austin resigned in 1978, the administration decided not to appoint a search committee and instead designated the vice president for academic affairs to serve as acting dean.[82]

Along with its degree programs, Trinity expanded its participation in community-oriented services. Under the auspices of Trinity's Department of Speech and Drama, Jearnine Wagner conducted Learning About Learning, a program designed to help children develop their cognitive processes, which she had created as a member of chairman Paul Baker's staff at Baylor University. Incorporated as a foundation in 1972, Learning About Learning extended its services to include teacher training workshops and the production of curricular materials, novelty items, and fun games for commercial markets.[83]

In the fall of 1976, the university launched a continuing education program with Marianne McCarthy, recipient of a Ph.D. degree from Michigan State University, as director. Offering a variety of noncredit courses designed primarily for the wider San Antonio community, McCarthy hoped to attract local and regional residents with courses such as "How to Start a Business and Make it Grow," "Introduction to the Stock Market," "Masterpieces of Oriental Art," "Controversial and Contemporary Writers," and "Transactional Analysis."[84]

Other university-affiliated programs offered services to local residents. Funded by the Office of Health, Education, and Welfare (HEW) and administered by the National Collegiate Athletic Association (NCAA), Trinity conducted a National Youth Sports Program for underprivileged area youth. Participants received instruction in swimming, tennis, baseball, track and field, and other sports skills as well as in character education, drug education, and vocational opportunities. Another popular summer event was the Youth Fitness Program (YFP) that attracted large numbers of area and faculty children. Directed by Jesse MacLeay, the YFP emphasized skills in individual and group sports and promoted qualities of good sportsmanship and cooperation.[85]

The Department of Health and Physical Education administered the Motor Behavior Learning Laboratory, initiated in 1970 by Robert Strauss, a professor in the department. Local neurologists, school counselors, psychiatrists, and other medical professionals referred participants to Trinity's lab. Widely sought as a consultant in special education programs, Strauss combined elements of psychology, special education, and physical education to develop effective training programs for children with motor and learning disabilities and supervised Trinity students as therapists in training.[86]

Wimpress acknowledged Bruce Thomas for playing a key role in much of Trinity's academic progress, especially in the areas of shaping Trinity's curriculum and improving faculty quality. After almost three decades of service to the university, Thomas announced his intention to retire at the end of the 1974–75 academic year. The University Senate described him as "the architect of its academic program, the chief of its faculty, and the conservator of things intellectual," and Wimpress referred to him as "an uncommon man, a wise and innovative builder."[87] In appreciation of his contributions to Trinity, university trustees designated him dean emeritus and named the newly completed high-rise residence hall Thomas Dormitory in his honor.[88]

Wimpress appointed a representative committee of faculty, administrators, and students to conduct a national search for Thomas's successor. The committee recommended J. Norman Parmer, who brought impressive credentials to his role as the university's new chief academic officer. A graduate of Indiana University, Parmer held an M.A in European history from the University of Connecticut and a Ph.D. in Asian history from Cornell University. Parmer had taught at Northern Illinois University and later served as associate dean of faculties at Ohio University before coming to Trinity. In addition, Parmer had served as a Peace Corps director in Malaysia and a division director in Washington, D.C., and published several books and articles on colonial labor policy and administration in Southeast Asia.[89]

Despite outward signs of institutional progress, Wimpress experienced criticism from some trustees who questioned his leadership style of delegation and his fund-raising abilities. Included in that group was William Bell, director of the Chapman Trust, which accounted for approximately two-thirds of Trinity's endowment income. Bell, who had been a member of the Trinity board of trustees since 1967, served on both the finance and executive committees, which formulated key policy decisions for presentation to the plenary board.

Trinity's financial status during the 1970s compared favorably to most small private institutions. The university relied heavily on endowment income to meet annual operating expenses, however, and consequently it was not available for capital growth or special projects. Because of limited funds, Wimpress found it necessary at times to freeze departmental budgets, suspend promotions, and award only nominal salary increases. These practices, during a period of rampant inflation, raised concern among board members that Trinity would lose valued faculty and staff and be limited in its ability to attract quality personnel.[90]

During the closing years of the Laurie presidency, an unusually large distribution from the Chapman Trust had enabled Trinity to pay outstanding bills, become current with its operating budget, and project a balanced budget into the next decade. By 1973, however, surplus funds generated by the Chapman Trust had been consumed due to increased operating expenses and the need to service a debt load that totaled approximately $15 million. Although low-interest government loans for campus buildings accounted for two-thirds of that debt amount and were self-amortizing, trustees had taken out bank loans amounting to $5,250,000 at high interest rates (8.5 percent) to complete the Laurie Auditorium complex and provide cash reserves to cover operating expenses. Unrestricted funds raised annually by the development office were insufficient to cover even interest payments on the university's high-interest debt.[91]

Facing a budget deficit of approximately $1 million during the 1973–74 fiscal year, Trinity escaped financial exigency only because war in the Middle East disrupted the international oil economy and sent domestic oil prices soaring. Income from the Northrup and Cowles Trusts, heavily invested in oil and gas, increased substantially before the inflationary period that followed.[92] In addition, another special distribution from the Chapman Trust in 1974, the result of a tax settlement, enabled Trinity to balance the budget and establish a $1 million operating fund reserve. As a result, Trinity no longer had to borrow each year from local banks and was able to reduce the high-interest debt load.[93]

Throughout this time period, Bell challenged trustees to be more accountable for Trinity's financial needs and urged them not to rely so heavily on the largesse of its various endowment funds. The university, he contended, "simply did not raise enough undesignated funds to meet the needs to balance the budget."[94] Unless they shouldered responsibility for securing a sound financial operation and imposed fiscal restraints, Bell predicted a dire future for the university. In 1973, he told the board, "It is the Chapman belief, that without the infusion of large funds from the James A. Chapman testamentary trust, Trinity University would today be a part of the public University of Texas system. At this time the Chapman Interests see the danger of Trinity University repeating the program that resulted in prior financial difficulties."[95]

Beyond these admonitions, Bell advised trustees not to expect additional sums becoming available from the Chapman Trusts in the near future, including grants from the Leta A. Chapman Trust, established in 1974 at the death of the widow of James Chapman. Income from this new trust, Bell stated, "will not be automatic to beneficiaries, but will be tied to the partnership arrangement for the potential greatness of the recipient institutions." Unless the board and the present administration combined efficiency and frugality with creative fund-raising techniques, Bell warned that Trinity would not benefit from distributions that could amount to as much as $10 million dollars annually.[96]

As the Wimpress administration labored to marshal additional financial resources, it encountered a hostile economic environment. In 1974 skyrocketing utility bills, with electricity up 352 percent and gas 221 percent, resulted in a $300,000 per year increase that had to come out of the operating budget.[97] Even after two years of zero growth in departmental budgets and token salary increments, inflation resulted in an estimated 30–percent decrease in real buying power from current fund resources. In a letter to board chairman Joseph H. Sherrill Jr., Wimpress expressed concern about conditions on campus. "Morale is beginning to be affected, departmental equipment is deteriorating, and a general decline in institutional effectiveness will be felt if this policy continues beyond the next year."[98]

Dissatisfied with the administration's progress toward long-range plans to ensure fiscal stability, the board of trustees, at Bell's initiative, commissioned the New York management firm of Cresap, McCormick, and Paget (CMP) in May 1975 to conduct a comprehensive review of Trinity's academic and supporting programs and to make recommendations for improved administrative organization and management practices. Included in the firm's mandate was an examination of the appropriate role, relationships, and structure of the board of trustees and the design of a process to ensure continuing evaluation and implementation of university policies. Bell noted that a similar study had been conducted at the University of Tulsa with positive results and expressed confidence that Trinity would experience the same benefits.[99]

The commission of the CMP report occurred at a time when Trinity faculty and administrators were making preparations for an upcoming Southern Association ten-year accreditation review. Although this enabled CMP staff to access relevant data and interview key personnel more readily, it also evoked considerable confusion and tension on campus. Several administrators reported that the CMP report had become "a major subject of conversation over the campus, with much speculation and rumor," and was having an adverse effect on community morale.[100]

Amidst an atmosphere of secrecy, board members received the CMP report in October 1975. At a meeting of the University Senate, political science professor Ton DeVos made a motion for the senate to request that the board of trustees make the report available to members of the senate. Before the senators could discuss the motion, Wimpress informed them that the trustees had already decided not to distribute copies of the report but would make the report's summary chapter available for individuals to examine privately in the trustee boardroom.[101]

The CMP report questioned Wimpress's effectiveness as the university's chief executive officer and averred that while Trinity was improving academically, it had a long way to go before it was competitive with select private peer institutions. It also encouraged the board of trustees to assume more responsibility for reviewing administrative organization and effectiveness, setting long-range goals, and participating in fund-raising activities. In effect, the report diminished the president's credibility in the university community and downplayed the significance of his previous accomplishments. Although the report cautioned that trustees should maintain "the desired separation of responsibility for governance and administration," it nevertheless issued the members a mandate to become more deeply involved in the day-to-day management of university affairs.[102]

Although taken back by the severity of the CMP report, Wimpress wrote a detailed reply to the board's executive committee. In response to specific criticisms of his delegating style of leadership, Wimpress acknowledged that apparently it was not as effective as he had thought. While he considered his extensive travel schedule to have been beneficial to Trinity's interests, Wimpress said that he would sell the university aircraft, reduce absences from campus, and spend more time in fund-raising activities. He also agreed to move forward expeditiously with a major administrative reorganization and to formulate long-range goals and objectives with specific plans for their implementation.[103]

At the same time, Wimpress challenged some conclusions reached by the CMP management team. Contrary to the report, Wimpress thought that the university had made substantial progress fiscally and academically under his leadership at a time when many institutions of higher learning were struggling for existence. On balance, he contended, the five years since he had become president in 1970 had been productive years in the life of the university. Trinity's administrators, faculty, and staff should be praised rather than faulted for their sustained efforts to improve the quality of classroom education and campus life. He also disagreed with the recommendation that Trinity should attempt merely to be "a good undergraduate school" serving Texas and the five or six surrounding states rather than seeking national recognition in competition with outstanding peer institutions. Such a goal, he said, "is neither exciting, inspiring, nor practical."[104]

While accepting the CMP report overall as a useful document, Trinity trustees concurred with Wimpress on the issue of national versus regional aspirations. The board's Academic Affairs Committee rejected CMP's recommendations that Trinity concentrate on being a regional university and shelve its plans to construct a new library because the present facilities were adequate. Observing that the report did not present convincing supporting data for these conclusions, trustee Denman reported that the Academic Affairs Committee would make counter-recommendations at an early date.[105]

Although his presidential managerial style had been called into question, Wimpress worked to regain the confidence of the university trustees and restore normality to the troubled campus.[106] By the spring of 1976, Trinity's high-interest debt burden had been halved, and the balance was projected to be reduced to approximately $2 million in the next four or five years. At the same time, the need for undesignated contributions required to balance the budget was only $465,000, the lowest in more than a decade. Trustee James Carroll moved that Wimpress be commended for his administrative accomplishments during a most trying year. The motion was seconded and passed by voice vote.[107]

Despite these encouraging signs, the executive committee of the board of trustees had assumed a major role in university affairs since the CMP report was received. Meeting monthly, the committee closely monitored the president's daily work schedule, formulated objectives and activities, and set deadlines for the completion of administrative reports.[108] The committee gave Wimpress one month to respond in detail to CMP's recommendations and to provide a definite timetable for their implementation. In addition, it required the president to keep detailed records of his various activities, including meetings, appointments, business meals, speeches, weekend activities, out of city travel, and vacations.[109]

The committee also routinely communicated with other administrators without going through the president's office. Trustee correspondence indicates that it requested information directly from various university officials regarding academic and financial information. When the Southern Association accreditation team visited the campus in April 1976, it noted with concern "a pattern of activity within the board of trustees which can be interpreted as interference with the internal management of university affairs" and recommended that the trustees take immediate steps to correct the imbalance. In response, the executive committee justified its increased involvement in university affairs by stating that it was simply following the charge given to it by the plenary board.[110]

Working under severe time constraints, Wimpress moved to implement the major recommendations of the CMP report. He consolidated the offices of public relations, development, alumni, and governmental affairs under the direction of a vice president for university relations, eliminated the position of vice president for student affairs, and assigned Dean of Students Coleen Grissom to report to the vice president for academic affairs. Other administrative changes included the appointment of physics professor Rudolph Gaedke as director of institutional research and the reorganization of the office of academic services to bring more coherence to the functions of student recruitment, admissions, and records.[111]

In February 1976, Wimpress presented a detailed description of proposed institutional goals and objectives to the board of trustees for its approval. The twelve-point statement emphasized the university's intention to be a nationally recognized liberal arts institution with selected professional and graduate programs. It also expressed a commitment to recruit an increasingly higher percentage of superior students of varied backgrounds and to widen its search for outstanding faculty. While stressing the importance of "a background of Christian perspective and concern for human values," the document endorsed a policy of nondiscrimination regarding consideration of race, color, religion, sex, national origin, and age in the selection of faculty, staff, and students.[112]

By June 1976, the university had a new academic administrative structure in place largely through the efforts of Vice President for Academic

Affairs Norman Parmer. Shortly after he arrived on campus in the summer of 1975, Parmer began to formulate a reorganization of Trinity's academic structures and policies that he hoped would anticipate criticisms that might emerge from either the CMP report or the Southern Association visitation team. Forced to expedite procedures in order to meet trustee-imposed deadlines, Parmer submitted a proposal to the general faculty before the end of the 1975–76 academic year.[113]

The new administrative arrangement called for the establishment of six academic divisions, each headed by its own dean. Selected by a committee of peers were internal appointees Richard Burr (business administration), dean of the faculty of business and management studies; John Burke (chemistry), dean of the faculty of engineering and sciences; Gail E. Myers (communications and arts), dean of the faculty of communications and the arts; John H. Moore (education) dean of the faculty of education; George N. Boyd (religion), dean of the faculty of humanities; and Kenneth Kramer (psychology), dean of the faculty of social and behavioral sciences. Along with the graduate dean and dean of students, they functioned as a council of deans under Parmer's direction.[114]

In the new structure, the deans presided over monthly meetings of their respective divisional councils, in which departmental chairs discussed curricular and other divisional or university issues. The deans also had the authority to allocate resources and equipment, participate in hiring, promotion, and tenure decisions, and, in consultation with the vice president for academic affairs, establish comprehensive departmental budgets. The proposal called for the deans to be appointed to five-year terms that normally would not be renewable.[115]

The role of department chairs also changed significantly in the reorganized administrative structure. Rather than having indefinite assignments, chairs served three-year terms that could be renewed by the deans after consulting with department members. Parmer envisaged that chairs would serve six years at the most and then return to full-time teaching, giving others in the department an opportunity to assume leadership roles.[116]

The reorganization structure received a mixed response from faculty and trustees. Some faculty preferred a more centralized administration and others were unhappy with departmental assignments within the divisions. Parmer also encountered opposition from trustees who expressed concern that the new structure diminished the authority of the vice presidents, the president, and to some extent the trustees. Chairman Sherrill recommended approval of the reorganization proposal, noting that it would be reevaluated at the end of three years. He expressed confidence that the faculty would be responsive to leadership and would function efficiently.[117]

During the summer and fall of 1976, Wimpress worked in conjunction with the key administrators and trustees of the Trinity Coordinating Committee for University Planning (TCCUP) to begin implementation of the new university goals and objectives. As discussions progressed, Wimpress hoped to resolve the problems outlined by the board's executive committee before a January 1977 deadline.[118]

In the end, the task proved too daunting. On 17 December 1976, the last day of the fall semester, Wimpress submitted his resignation as president of Trinity University to board chair Flora C. Atherton and simultaneously informed faculty and staff of his decision. In his letter of resignation, Wimpress noted that because Trinity had stabilized financially and had successfully accomplished a major academic reorganization, he deemed the time "especially appropriate for fresh, new leadership to take over and guide the university into the promising years ahead." These facts, he informed Atherton, "coupled with the apparent lack of accord between the Trustee Executive Committee and me regarding management principles and practices, lead me now to submit to you and the board of trustees my resignation as president of Trinity University."[119]

In response, Atherton commended Wimpress for his "vigorous and extensive service" during his six and a half years as president, stated that the board of trustees had appointed him "professor on leave of absence and consultant to the university," and granted him permission to reside in the Minter House for a period of six months.[120] After considering a number of options, Wimpress accepted the position of vice chairman of the board of governors of the Southwest Foundation for Research and Education in San Antonio and was promoted to president in 1982. On his recommendation, the board later changed its name to the Southwest Foundation for Biomedical Research. Wimpress served in this capacity with distinction for ten years until his retirement in 1992.[121]

Reaction to Wimpress's resignation reflected the ambivalence of the university community to his presidency. To many faculty and staff, the decision came as a surprise, especially considering that Trinity had recently received a favorable response from the Southern Association visitation team and that criticisms raised by the CMP report apparently were being addressed. Others expressed relief that the long period of tension had ended and that Trinity could now move forward under new leadership.

When students learned of Wimpress's departure following their return to campus after the Christmas recess, they had few comments. For most undergraduates, the change in leadership had little impact on their daily lives. *Trinitonian* editor Mark Hill, who had clashed with Wimpress on a number of occasions, criticized the ex-president for creating an atmosphere of fear and intimidation, although acknowledging that Wimpress had left Trinity in a better condition than when he assumed the presidency in 1970.[122]

Responding to the editorial, physics professor Fred Loxsom challenged Hill's portrait of Wimpress. While conceding that the president alienated some members of the Trinity community and that faculty members openly disagreed with some of his policies, Loxsom contended that Wimpress never used his position to threaten or punish those with whom he differed. "Some of us feel that Wimpress did a good job as president, that he helped guide Trinity through a difficult period. We are grateful for Wimpress' contribution to Trinity."[123]

Concurrent with Wimpress's resignation, Atherton announced the appointment of retired Dean Bruce Thomas as acting president, the second time that he had been given such an assignment. His leadership abilities and familiarity with university operations signified stability and continuity as a presidential search committee began the process of identifying and interviewing candidates. Thomas frequently received memoranda addressed to "Dean Thomas, Acting President," a combination of titles that reflected both the past and the current realities.[124]

As acting president, Thomas specified his intention not to make any changes in university policies but to provide the incoming president with a smoothly operating organization. What Trinity needs at the moment, he said, "is a breathing spell. Right now, I am walking a very thin line, trying to make a compromise between keeping a holding pattern and keeping the university moving ahead."[125] Initially anticipating a relatively short assignment, Thomas was in office almost two and a half years before a new president arrived. Meanwhile, concerned that the term "acting president" might suggest institutional instability, the board of trustees decided in May 1977 that Thomas should be referred to publicly as "president" until Trinity secured a permanent successor.[126]

During the Thomas interregnum, Parmer acted to implement the recently established university goals and objectives. Parmer was convinced that Trinity needed to upgrade the quality and diversity of incoming students and new faculty and to provide present faculty with adequate facilities and funds to promote their scholarship and research activities. After a period of exceptional growth in terms of campus buildings and enrollment, Trinity needed to attain a new level of academic achievement.

Parmer told university trustees, "While not wishing to cry alarums, I believe that if Trinity remains merely good it will gradually decline."[127]

Parmer moved to reconfigure Trinity's academic profile. Recognizing that existing procedures had been largely ignored or handled informally without adequate documentation, he instituted an annual review process for tenure and promotion that included student course evaluations and peer reviews that involved all tenured department members. Parmer also encouraged departments to be more thorough and comprehensive in their searches for new faculty. In particular, he urged them to recruit candidates from colleges and universities outside the southwest in order to give Trinity a more diverse and broadly experienced faculty.[128]

At the same time, Parmer stressed to trustees the importance of providing funds for faculty research and development. Largely through the support of trustee William Bell and a gift of $200,000 from the Chapman Trust, Trinity made funds available for faculty leaves, special research projects, early retirement, and a distinguished visiting lectureship. When announcing the new program, Bruce Thomas referred to it as "the greatest boost for faculty morale than anything we have done in the last decade."[129]

Cognizant of the importance of adequate library facilities, Parmer opposed the CMP report's recommendation that Trinity defer its plans to build a new library. Working closely with trustee Denman, he prepared a response to the report that convinced university trustees to proceed with the library project. The proposal also included the establishment of an acquisitions budget that would enable library staff to fill gaps in present holdings and to purchase new publications. Endorsed by the board of trustees in 1978, the proposal, which set a goal of raising $10 million over a period of ten years, marked the beginning of a concerted effort to raise the university library to a new standard of excellence.[130]

Dedication of a new $4.5 million library facility, on 7 April 1979, crowned the nearly thirty years of continuous effort by the university to complete its master plan for the Trinity Hill campus. The four-story, 176,280-square-foot building was designed by Trinity architects Ford, Powell & Carson and Bartlett Cocke and Associates to accommodate more than a million volumes and to provide space for audio-visual services and a language laboratory. Two floors were left unfinished for future expansion.[131]

The circular wall surrounding the library's central staircase provided a location for artistic creativity. Trustee Denman suggested that Trinity commission mural artist James Sicner to apply his collage technique to the fif-

J. Norman Parmer, Vice President for Academic Affairs (1975–82)

teen by eighty-foot surfaces (on each side). After two years of research and more than three years of labor, the finished product, "Man's Evolving Images: In Printing and Writing," was ready for viewing. The Mexican calendar stone, the Magna Carta, the Rosetta Stone, the Declaration of Independence, the Gutenberg Bible, the imprint of the first lunar footsteps, and symbols from alphabets of 5,000 languages were only a few of the 800 separate images in the work.[132]

Parmer also spearheaded a movement to reevaluate the Trinity Plan that had served as the general curriculum guide for nearly a decade. While acknowledging the plan's flexibility and freedom of choice, Parmer criticized its cafeteria approach to general education requirements, the wide variation of hours required by faculty advisors, and the difficulty of transfer students trying to fulfill requirements and obtain a degree in a reasonable period of time. In his estimation, the problems of the Trinity Plan were both serious and fundamental and required the creation of a new curriculum that would differ in principle and in detail from the existing program.[133]

After assessing Trinity's curricular needs for more than a year, a committee chaired by history professor Donald Everett proposed a new basic curriculum to become effective in the fall of 1980. Instead of ten goals or areas of study, the plan featured four broad groupings: Arts and Letters,

Humanities, Social Sciences, and Natural and Mathematical Sciences. Entering students had to satisfy competency in English usage either by satisfactory performance on a standardized test or essay administered by the English department or by successful completion of an entry-level English course. Although agreeing in principle with the configuration of the new curriculum, many faculty members expressed displeasure that it did not call for prerequisites in a foreign language or mathematics. As a result, the measure passed by a narrow 92–86 margin, prompting Thomas to direct the curriculum council to restudy suggested modifications and consider their inclusion at a later date.[134]

At the risk of a possible drop in student enrollment, Parmer received approval from university trustees in 1977 to raise admission standards for the coming academic year. Entrance requirements for first-year students were raised from a predicted Trinity GPA of 1.9 to 2.3, and a target goal of 1100 was established for combined SAT scores.[135] By the fall of 1979, the entering class had combined verbal and math SAT scores of approximately 1080, an increase of fifty points over the last two years, second only to Rice University in Texas. According to Director of Academic Services Walter West, 65 percent of students accepted for admission at Trinity actually enrolled, and those who elected to go elsewhere indicated schools such as Stanford, Duke, and Vanderbilt. Trinity was also rejecting a higher percentage of applications than at any time in its history.[136]

In terms of fiscal progress, Vice President for Fiscal Affairs Hawthorne reported that the university continued to reduce its debt load on an annual basis. In October 1977, total liabilities amounted to $8.5 million dollars, down from $14 million in 1975. By 1978 the short-term high-interest notes held by local banks had been paid off, and most of the remaining debt consisted of self-liquidating low-interest federal loans for building construction.[137] With the exception of 6 percent interest paid on money borrowed previously from the endowment fund, the maximum interest paid by the university was 3.5 percent on government-guaranteed loans. By the end of the decade, the endowment totaled approximately $100 million.[138]

Despite some progress in implementing various goals and objectives, Parmer encountered opposition from faculty who were unhappy with the rapid pace of changes in academic policies and structures. While acknowledging that there were certain "faculty anxieties and tensions" due to changes in academic organization and procedures, Parmer thought that such reactions were inevitable during periods of institutional change. He noted that pressures on faculty to complete advanced degrees or face terminal contracts, small or no salary increases for those judged to be poor performers, and necessary reductions in faculty size resulted in "injured feelings, bitterness, and strained relations with administrative officers."[139]

Thomas also questioned the effectiveness of the recent academic restructuring, deeming it to be "too bureaucratic, unnecessary, and impractical" and stating that the resultant proliferation of committee meetings had diverted attention from classroom teaching and student advising. He especially disliked the inclusive feature of the University Senate because he thought it diminished the role of faculty members and denied them a forum where they could meet to represent their interests. To redress the problem, Thomas directed Parmer to disband the University Senate and reinstitute the Faculty Senate.[140] At the same time, he appointed a long-range planning committee to begin discussing future plans rather than waiting until a new president was in place.[141]

Meanwhile, the university community awaited word regarding the selection of a new president. For the first time in Trinity's history, the presidential search committee included faculty as well as trustees. Although students were not represented, the committee welcomed their input regarding desired presidential qualities. Chairman Denman indicated that the committee had not set any deadlines but was moving deliberately in order to find a suitable candidate.[142] By May 1977 Denman reported that approximately 400 applications and nominations had been received and that members were screening dossiers in order to create a short list of four or five candidates.[143] After an extended process that included private interviews with potential finalists, two candidates were invited to visit the Trinity campus in the spring of 1978. After these visits, committee members failed to reach a consensus on either candidate and reported their impasse to the board of trustees. Meeting in executive session, the trustees decided to appoint a new committee and reopen the search.[144]

Chaired by trustee Louis Zbinden, senior minister of First Presbyterian Church in San Antonio, the hunt for a president resumed at an accelerated pace. By the middle of September, the committee had narrowed its interest to two candidates. Based on their campus visits, the committee unanimously selected Ronald K. Calgaard, vice chancellor for academic affairs at the University of Kansas, as its sole nominee, thus ending a search process that had lasted almost two years.[145] At a called meeting on 21 November 1978, the board of trustees confirmed Calgaard's appointment as Trinity's sixteenth president.[146]

With the search concluded, Trinity once again expressed gratitude to Bruce Thomas for services rendered to the university. In a period of two and a half years under his leadership, the school had not lost momentum. Fund-raising for the new library had been completed, the library built and dedicated, and a challenge fund of a half-million dollars for library acquisitions met. The endowment had grown steadily, a new curriculum was written and approved, and admission standards rose—all under a transitional administration.[147]

As someone who knew Trinity well and understood its strengths and weaknesses, Thomas was optimistic regarding the institution's future. He expressed confidence that the university was now in a better position to advance to a higher level of achievement than at any time in its history. "Our financial and our building needs are met. We have good facilities, good students and a good faculty. The question is what we do with it. The greatness is still to come . . . but if we do the job, and have the right leadership, Trinity can rank with any other institution in the country."[148]

CHAPTER TWELVE

STUDENTS OF THE SEVENTIES

In the 50s it was "cool" to actively participate in campus organizations. . . . During the 1960s student attitudes moved to a rebellious, anti-establishment, non-conforming tone. . . . With the 70s apathy hit campus life like a tidal wave. The war was over, radical movements had died and students basically didn't care about much of anything. However, now it is 1978, and a new generation is just around the corner. Although this generation is unique and different, it has picked up many of the strong characteristics of the last three decades.

TRINITONIAN EDITOR ERIN BAKER, 1978

B Y THE EARLY 1970S THE STUDENT ACTIVISM and challenge to authority that dominated college campuses in the previous decade basically had come to a halt. The death of four students in May 1970 at Kent State University dampened the fervor of protests, and the end of the war in Vietnam and cessation of the draft removed some of the issues for unrest. Responses by university administrators to an American Higher Education Survey in 1975 indicated that students appeared to be more constructive and more involved with their studies, and extracurricular activities that had fallen into disfavor in the previous decade were making a vigorous comeback.[1]

In light of a downturn in the economy, students also were noticeably more oriented toward career education than their predecessors. Undergraduates of the 1970s fell at the middle and end of the post–World War II population spurt, when a huge age-cohort entered a saturated job market. As they chose courses, students turned to business, engineering, and scientific and technical fields, rather than the humanities and the social sciences.[2]

Students also displayed little interest in broader social or ideological issues, characteristic of what one historian termed "a return to privatism."[3] Their concerns, if any, focused on issues relating to individual freedom and removal of societal restraints on their personal life styles. Administrators no longer feared student disruption of university operations. Rather, they complained about lack of respect for campus property, non-payment of college bills, increased use of drugs and alcoholic beverages, and "sex folkways disenchanting to donors."[4]

Throughout the decade, Trinity administrators reported little evidence of social unrest and described students as being "more calm and somewhat more conservative." Rather than agitating for power, most students were seeking entertainment and recreation and more assistance in preparing for vocations.[5] University Chaplain Raymond Judd also pointed out a major difference between this generation of Trinity students and those of the past two decades. "[Then] there was a school spirit with which each of us identified. Now there's a club spirit and party spirit, but no school spirit like there was in the 50s and 60s."[6]

Speaking to trustees in 1971, Bruce Thomas said that it had been a good year in regard to student behavior. There had been "a lack of serious disturbances on the campus . . . no student militancy, and good morale among faculty and students."[7] The following year, Dean of Student Life Jay Pool reported that there had been several panty raids and a food fight between two fraternities in the refectory, but he considered none of the incidents to have constituted serious problems. Commenting on student activities, President Wimpress viewed the upsurge of college pranks as a positive rather than a negative sign. Such problems, he explained, were more readily handled than overt clashes between militant students and university authorities.[8]

At times, however, Trinity students showered university officials with more pranks than they could comfortably handle. On several occasions, security personnel were forced to evacuate buildings because of bomb threats called in to the university switchboard. Although campus rumors linked the telephone calls to students facing difficult class examinations, no one was ever apprehended.[9] When campus security officers attempted to crack down on chronic parking offenders in 1973 by placing a locking device called a "Rhino" or "Boot" on the front wheel of their automobiles, Trinity students rose to the occasion. One evening officers affixed the Rhino to a car that belonged to a student who had amassed a large number of tickets. When they returned the next morning, the car had disappeared and the Rhino was secured around a large branch of a nearby oak tree. A handwritten sign attached to the Rhino read: "Don't Fuck With Houdini."[10]

During the same year, individuals identified as "Bonnie and Clyde" broke into the security office and confiscated all existing parking and traffic tickets. The duo slipped a note under the door of the *Trinitonian* office that read, "Students be warned. The Traffic and Security Office no longer has copies of tickets written past years to the present. You have been liberated!" Reporting the episode, *Trinitonian* news editor Brett Hall commented, "Whatever results from Trinity's Watergate . . . the break-in has made Trinity a little more livable."[11]

On another occasion, students organized a contest to jump off the roof and balconies of the Winn residence hall onto mattresses that had been piled on the ground. A crowd of more than 200 stood by and watched the event. Spectators urged contestants to perform increasingly dangerous feats by rating jumps on a scale of one to ten. The event ended when one student missed the target and was rushed to the hospital with serious injuries.[12]

More sustained and troublesome were incidents of campus vandalism and raucous behavior associated with heavy drinking in residence halls. The director of the physical plant, Jud Abernathy, reported repeated incidents of punctured ceiling tiles, discharged fire extinguishers, unrolled fire hoses, ripped out telephones, and damaged money changers. He also described how students frequently gathered in elevators and jumped up and down while they were in transit, causing the mechanisms to stop between floors. Collecting a two-dollar contingency fee per student to create a reserve fund for damages did little to alleviate the problems.[13]

At one party in the Thomas residence hall, attended by an estimated 200 people and fueled by six kegs of beer, students damaged acoustical ceiling tile, vomited in the elevators and hallways, and showered security personnel with beer when they attempted to restore order. The Office of Student Life disciplined the organizers of the party and required them to pay for damages to university property. Grissom, the dean of students, nevertheless argued against changing the alcohol policy or restricting the size of parties. "I am not trying to discourage large parties," she told trustees, "I am trying to encourage responsibility."[14]

Despite such episodes, Trinity students of the 1970s were a diverse group of individuals. Incidents of horseplay, vandalism, and apathy were balanced by academic accomplishment, social concern, and ethical conduct. In many respects, theirs was a pioneering generation that inherited an untested "Joint Statement on Rights and Freedoms of Students" and spent the decade attempting to actualize it. By insisting on the right to "do their own thing," they paved the way for subsequent student generations to enjoy personal freedoms and the right of due process in matters of discipline.

Many Trinity students continued the tradition of social involvement begun in the 1960s through their participation in the Trinity University

TUVAC volunteers working with young people in local detention center, 1977

Voluntary Action Committee (TUVAC). Trinity volunteers worked with child development and tutoring programs in conjunction with local public schools, the Juvenile Detention Center, and the San Antonio Literacy Council. They also served as volunteers in various hospitals and medical facilities and hosted physically challenged and financially deprived children by holding parties and taking them to special events such as circuses and theatrical performances. In 1976, for example, TUVAC leaders reported that more than 300 Trinity students had participated in one or more programs during the academic year.[15]

The decade was marked by changes in student life policies influenced by administrative realignments as well as student organizations. In 1972, Wimpress created the position of vice president for student affairs and elevated Jay Pool to that slot. In his new capacity, Pool devoted his attention primarily to improving the quality of student financial aid and placement programs. The president also promoted Coleen Grissom to dean of student life and placed her in charge of the residence hall program, a move designed to break down the established pattern of dual standards for men and women. Thurman Adkins, coordinator of student activities, was named assistant dean. He had a solid educational background and possessed considerable skills in working with student leaders to coordinate various campus activities.[16]

Under Grissom's direction, a professionally trained residence hall team replaced the traditional "housemother" for women and retired military personnel supervisors for men. Staff members Peg Armstrong, Sandra Ragan, and Leslie Robinson, along with a select group of students who served as residence assistants, interacted with students in a collegial rather than authoritarian manner.[17]

Dissolution of the remnants of *in loco parentis* removed many of the rules and regulations that previously had defined student behavior. Traditional dress codes were no longer enforced. Bare feet and ragged cutoffs emerged as a popular style even during the coldest days of winter.[18] By 1978, the university's dress code had been reduced to two sentences: "Students are encouraged to exercise good taste, judgment and appropriateness in their dress. *Persons who are barefoot will not be permitted in the Dining Hall, Refectory or Coffee Shop.*"[19]

Trinity trustees, however, periodically expressed displeasure over student attire and some wanted to reinstitute a campus dress code. While acknowledging his distaste for current fashions, Jay Pool opposed such restrictions, contending that a dress code would be detrimental to working relationships between students and administrators. He referred to the exemplary work of Student Association President Steve Hudson, whom he described as a "brilliant young man, a diligent worker, and one whose appearance [long hair, beard, and casual attire] betrays his actual conservatism." Board members did not pursue the issue further.[20]

Along with a relaxation of dress codes, Trinity students experienced a change in residence hall rules and regulations. In 1972 the Standards Committee of the Student Association voted to combine the two sets of rules for men and women into one policy for all residents. Although the university continued to honor optional restrictions placed on women by their parents, Adkins indicated that these concessions were gradually being phased out.[21] By the 1976–77 academic year, references to "restricted" and "non-restricted" women no longer appeared in the *Student Handbook*. Visitation hours for both sexes were extended from noon to midnight on Sunday through Thursday and from noon to two in the morning on Friday and Saturday.[22]

The extension of visitation privileges led to an atmosphere of partying in which drinking alcohol and pursuing sexual relationships in the residence hall rooms became increasingly common. In the past, such activities were said to have taken place off campus at drive-in movies or in rented apartments and motel rooms. Grissom reported that a growing number of students partied in their rooms, and, if they did not cause a disturbance, no one reported them. She also noted that more students were spending nights in rooms of friends of the opposite sex.[23]

Creative room remodeling, 1970s

Students were free to reconfigure their living quarters according to individual tastes. They displayed banners, signs, and clotheslines on balcony railings and covered interior walls with exotic posters, hand-painted murals, and abstract works of art. Many enjoyed the novelty of waterbeds although physical plant officials worried about leaks.[24] One imaginative student transformed his room into what he termed "a clubhouse," with an enclosed waterbed and couch. Using two-by-fours and sheetrock, he created a room within a room that provided privacy and comfort. Only budgetary considerations prohibited his installation of colored Plexiglas windows and fur-lined walls.[25]

When the State of Texas lowered the drinking age to eighteen in 1973, students led a movement to end the university's one-hundred-year-old prohibition against the consumption of alcohol on campus.[26] After student

ARHS Is sponsoring an all-school Beer Bust this Saturday evening from 8 p.m. until midnight in the Sams Center Ballroom.
Live music will be provided by Bandango.
Admission is $1.00 for dorm students and $1.50 for town students.
Everybody come for a good time!

The *Trinitonian,*
14 October 1977

life officials expressed apprehension about the proposed change, the University Senate became involved and referred the alcohol issue to an ad hoc committee composed of faculty, students, and administrators. After a seven-month period of discussion and debate, the committee favored removing the ban in order to eliminate the hypocrisy of the present policy and to afford students an opportunity to drink responsibly within the context of their educational environment.[27]

Sanction by the university trustees constituted the students' last hurdle in their quest for campus drinking privileges. Several board members vigorously opposed reversing Trinity's long-standing alcohol policy, citing religious and practical considerations. After extended discussion, however, trustees voted 19 to 2 in favor of the new policy.[28] A *Trinitonian* headline proclaimed, "Trinity Doors Open to the Grapes of Wrath," followed by a story describing the pleasures of drinking beer and wine in dorm rooms and tapping beer kegs at campus parties. Editor Sheri Wolf cautioned, however, that students would have to act responsibly if they hoped to retain their new freedom.[29]

While relaxing alcohol restrictions, university officials continued to prohibit other forms of drug usage. As had previously been the case with drinking alcohol, however, discreetly smoking a joint in the confines of a dorm room rarely evoked a response from resident assistants or security personnel. When the San Antonio Police Department instituted a citywide crackdown on drugs, however, undercover agents arrested several Trinity students for possession of narcotics. An editorial in the *Trinitonian* cautioned students to be wary of unknown people sitting in class or hanging out in the residence halls. "Don't be paranoid," the editorial advised, "just be careful."[30]

In other aspects of residential life, student life officials formulated a plan to gradually end the segregation of male and female students on the east and west sides of the campus that had existed since 1952. Such a move had been advocated by the Southern Association of Colleges and Schools on a number of occasions but had been resisted by trustees who questioned the propriety of "coed dorms," thinking that implied shared rooms and bathroom facilities. Advised that student life personnel were advocating "integrative living," in which men and women lived in the same facility but on different floors, the trustees finally endorsed the relocation.[31]

In the fall of 1970, the Office of Student Life implemented a program of coeducational dormitories on a voluntary basis. Trinity's first experiment with shared living arrangements assigned 115 sophomore and junior women to the third floor of Winn and all three floors of East (now Calvert). Seventy-two men occupied the North dormitory in the women's residential complex. Initial problems were minor, and the number of informal contacts between men and women students in groups—at meals, in the lounges, and on the lawns greatly increased.[32]

Two years later, student life officials proposed moving women into Murchison Dormitory. Murchison had been a popular choice of male athletes and clusters of fraternity brothers, and when residents learned of relocation plans, they formed a united front of opposition. Their protests culminated in a nocturnal gathering on the residence hall lawn, where they torched university furniture, played music, and read poetry around the bonfire. Security officers watched the scene from a distance, but they filed no charges against the protesters.[33]

Aware of divided student sentiment regarding relocation, Grissom moved judiciously to achieve the goal of integrated campus living. As the process continued, student resistance diminished. Both men and women reported favorable experiences with the new system, and incoming students accepted it as normal. By 1979 females occupied Murchison West, and male students lived in Isabel and South. Men and women both were housed in Beze and North residence halls, although on different floors. Grissom reported that "integrative relocation" had many pluses, including improved security and a decrease in the rowdiness that had characterized the all-male dorms.[34]

The relocation controversy, however, re-emerged in another venue that had wider repercussions for the university community. During a performance at Sing Song in the spring of 1977, Theta Tau Upsilon fraternity members spoofed the administration's dormitory location policies in a presentation that some members of the audience, including acting President Thomas, deemed "obscene and vulgar and reflecting discredit on Trinity University." Acting unilaterally, Thomas placed the Thetas on probation and prohibited their participation in Sing Song or any other campus social activities.[35]

Theta president Robin Ruff appealed Thomas's decision, citing both content of the performance and procedural grounds. He noted that definitions of obscenity varied greatly and that Thomas had failed to specify precisely how he defined the term and what elements constituted obscenity. Most importantly, Thomas had convicted and sentenced the Thetas without a hearing, disregarding the "Joint Statement on Rights and Freedoms of Students." "We feel that this is entirely unjust," Ruff asserted, "and violates the very principle of democratic justice."[36]

Trinitonian editor Mark Hill rallied to the Theta's cause, referring to the controversy as the "most important student issue to arise this year." If students allowed Thomas's suspension to stand unchallenged, Hill believed that all student organizations and all individual students were in danger of having their "speech, actions and opinions judged just as arbitrarily by the man who sits in the president's office." Besides, Hill argued, according to contemporary standards, the Theta's act did not even merit a good six on an obscenity scale of one to ten.[37]

In response to student appeals, Thomas reconsidered his decision. He rescinded the censure and informed the Thetas that their privileges had been restored. Admitting that he should have discussed the issue with the fraternity before taking any action, Thomas said, "I have withdrawn the letter entirely. It was the only fair thing to do." For Trinity students, the president's retraction constituted a vindication of their rights and a reminder to university officials that Trinity students would not acquiesce to disciplinary actions undertaken without due process.[38]

Other changes occurred in the management of university residential life services. When Blanche King retired as director of food services in 1973, Trinity outsourced the operations to Aramark Food Service Corporation. While maintaining previous standards, Aramark offered extended hours of service and added new items to the menu such as pizza, burritos, and a variety of desserts.[39] At the same time, Trinity engaged Mercury Management to assume responsibility for housekeeping services in residence halls and other campus buildings. The outside enterprise provided employee benefits not available under Trinity management, offered a higher pay scale, and opened positions once available only to men to both sexes.[40]

Beyond the confines of their residence halls, Trinity students had multiple options for off-campus entertainment. Favorite establishments in the immediate vicinity included the Stables, the Crystal Pistol, Hipps Bubble Room, Kelly's Pub, the Garter, and Pearl Brewery, where free drinks were served.[41] For many Trinity students, the Crystal Pistol was "a second home," where they played pool and pinball, danced, ate popcorn, and drank beer.[42] By the late seventies, however, the Pistol began to attract a different clientele, so students gravitated to the Bombay Bicycle Club, located adjacent to campus on the edge of Brackenridge Park.[43]

For a number of years, the Theta Tau Upsilon fraternity sponsored a Friday afternoon happy hour in the nearby pavilion in Olmos Park Basin. The weekly event enabled students to drink as much beer as they wanted for a nominal fee: $1.50 for men and $1.00 for women.[44] So-called "Woodsies," outdoor parties held along the Guadalupe River or at Canyon Lake, featured kegs of beer and impromptu swims. Most fraternities scheduled at least one "Coast Trip" to beaches along the southern coast of Texas at Corpus Christi, Port Aransas, or Padre Island.[45]

On campus, the Trinity Student Activity Board (SAB) offered a variety of concerts, dances, and other social events to keep students entertained. A "gross-out weekend" featured gross costume and booth contests judged by the audience prior to a midnight showing of the film "Pink Flamingos." Winners received a free keg of beer.[46] The SAB also sponsored a toga party modeled after the movie "Animal House." Approximately 400 students, draped in bed sheets or other costumes, crowded the Coates Center's Rathskeller. At midnight, they watched the *Rocky Horror Picture Show.*[47]

For several years the SAB and various off-campus organizations sponsored rock concerts in Laurie Auditorium that drew capacity crowds from both campus and community. Trinity officials eventually ended non–Trinity-sponsored rock concerts because of alleged widespread use of drugs and consumption of alcohol on premises and destruction of university property. Wimpress said that members of the San Antonio Police Department told him, "if you want to go to smoke some joints and drink a half-gallon of wine, Laurie concerts were a good place to have some fun."[48]

On the academic level, the SAB sponsored events that brought a wide range of nationally known figures to the Trinity campus. Included were speakers such as anti-war spokesman Daniel Ellsberg, consumer rights advocate Ralph Nader, comedian and political rights activist Dick Gregory, and poet Lawrence Ferlinghetti. The Last Lectures Series, sponsored by a local chapter of the national honor society Mortar Board, regularly drew large audiences. By invitation, respected Trinity professors were invited to address students as though this were his or her last opportunity to speak.[49]

Music continued to play a prominent role in student activities. The annual spring choir tour generated favorable publicity for the university and gave students an opportunity to perform in locations outside San Antonio. Usually the tours were regional, hosted by Presbyterian churches, but in 1973 the choir flew to Yugoslavia under the sponsorship of the Ambassadors for Friendship Agency in New York. The forty-member choir presented concerts in factories, youth clubs, hotels, restaurants, and city parks and on street corners throughout the country. During one outdoor performance in Sarajevo, several journalists interpreted Latin words in a song to be of a religious character. They summoned local police, who arrested choir director Claude Zetty for illegally attracting crowds and singing church music in a public venue. After intensive questioning, authorities released Zetty but advised him to monitor future selections more carefully.[50]

The annual pops concert, initiated in 1970, incorporated a blend of contemporary and traditional music. In 1974 the program featured a rock band, drawn from members of the choir, who performed songs by John Lennon and Paul McCartney, Jim Croce, Stephen Stills, Jimmy Webb, Loggins and Messina, and the Moody Blues.[51] Performances by the Trinity University Community Orchestra, the University Band, the Chamber Singers, the Chapel Choir, the Parker Handbell Choir, and the Collegium Musicum rounded out Trinity's diverse musical programs.[52]

Although Trinity's sororities and fraternities played important roles in campus social life, their memberships declined during the 1970s.[53] Counterculture alternatives to social clubs flourished briefly during this time period, including the Phi Zappa Krappas and the Tappa Kegga Beers. The former, named in honor of rock musician Frank Zappa, termed itself an "unofficial co-ed fratority" whose goals were "to perpetuate a spirit of

unity, fellowship and krap" and "to conquer alienation through liquor."[54] More subdued but no less critical, the Tappa Keggas consisted of a group of women on the second floor of Highrise (later Thomas) who existed solely to buy drinks for financially strapped students.[55]

In contrast to the waning interest in social clubs, the number of recognized honorary, academic, political, and service organizations increased during the 1970s. In addition to university-sponsored organizations such as those in athletics, music, and publications, the *Student Handbook* for 1978–79 listed more than sixty groups.[56] Included were the American So-

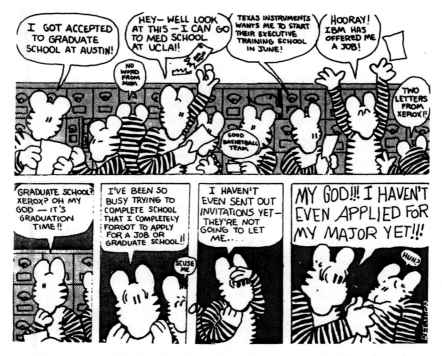

The cartoons of Jon Regnier (class of 1980) captured student lifestyles and
critiqued administrative policies. Opposite, top: the *Trinitonian*,
26 January 1979; opposite, bottom: the *Trinitonian*, 11 November 1977;
above: the *Trinitonian*, 17 April 1979

ciety for Personnel Administration, Alpha Phi Omega (service fraternity),
Campus Crusade, Compass Club, Scuba Club, Film Club, Chi Alpha (re-
ligious), Association for Childhood Education, Baptist Student Union,
Trinity Flyers Club, Rugby Football Club, Model United Nations Club,
Trinity University Players (drama), and Women in Communications.[57]

Students of the seventies were lukewarm in their support of intercollegiate athletics. Various efforts to promote school spirit and increase attendance at athletic contests proved futile. Pep rallies, tailgate parties, postgame dances, and the revival of traditional homecoming king and queen
ceremonies failed to draw students to intercollegiate athletics contests.[58]
To bolster attendance, the university offered free admission to Air Force
trainees at Lackland Air Force Base, who came by chartered bus for home
football games. Through the auspices of TUVAC, groups of disadvantaged
students, chaperoned by Trinity students, also attended games.[59] The
Sperm Squad first appeared on the scene at homecoming festivities in the

fall of 1976. Self-described as "a not-so-scientific phenomenon designed to startle, amuse, and repulse" and to promote school spirit at football games, the group derived its inspiration from the Woody Allen movie, *Everything You Always Wanted to Know About Sex But Were Afraid to Ask*. Students dressed in all white support hose, shorts, T-shirt, hat, and towel. They selected one player on the football team to be their "favorite" and cheered vociferously anytime he was involved in a play. Lineman Dave Sanders was the first "chosen one," and the group initially adopted the name of "Sanders' Raiders" in his honor.[60]

Growing steadily in numbers and audacity, the Sperm became an unofficial homecoming tradition. The group subsequently added female counterparts known as the Ova and paraded on the track at halftime with antics and gyrations that some spectators found offensive or obscene. Even one of the Sperm's founders, David Wright, admitted that many people thought the Sperm were disgusting, but he was undeterred by such comments.[61] Over the years, opposition to their performances mounted among various segments of the university community, including students, faculty, staff, and alumni. In 1989 Trinity administrators prohibited the group from entering the stadium and threatened expulsion to those who disobeyed the order. As a result, the group disbanded and the tradition ended.[62]

Guided by veteran coaches Gene Norris (football), Pete Murphy (basketball), and Houston Wheeler (baseball), Trinity began to participate in the new nonscholarship TIAA conference in 1976. In football, Trinity won its first conference championship since 1955 with a 4–0 record in 1976 against conference foes.[63] Basketball and baseball teams, playing long seasons against mostly scholarship opponents, never attained the success that they had achieved during the previous decades.[64]

A trap and skeet program coached by Tom Hanzel, who was also Trinity's director of personnel, commenced in 1970 and quickly gained national prominence. Marksmen Ricky Pope, Robert Paxton, Pat Bartel, and John Shima and female shooters Carla Brundage and Sheri Confer enabled Trinity teams to claim national collegiate titles in 1975, 1976, 1977, and 1980. In addition to the collegiate laurels, the sharpshooters won some nineteen individual world championships and seven Texas skeet crowns before Hanzel's retirement in 1985.[65]

Tennis continued to be a major attraction on the Trinity campus. Trinity's men's tennis team captured the NCAA championship in 1972. Not since 1959 had the national championship gone to anyone other than the University of California at Los Angeles (UCLA) or the University of South-

The Sperm and Ova became a Trinity tradition during the 1970s and 1980s.

ern California (USC). The title closed a season that saw Trinity record 27 straight dual match victories, the nation's only perfect 1972 season record by a major tennis university. During a televised match between Trinity and the visiting national powerhouse USC, the Trinity team (led by Dick Stockton, Bob McKinley, Brian Gottfried, and Paul Gerkin) received a standing ovation from the more than 3,000 fans who filled the stadium, stood on the roofs of nearby buildings, and sat in trees. Trinity won two of the final three doubles matches to upset the heavily favored USC Trojans.[66]

When Clarence Mabry retired in 1974, Bob McKinley returned to coach Trinity's men's tennis squad to a 219–57 record from 1975 through 1984. Named the NCAA Coach of the Year in 1977, his teams reached the NCAA championship match in both 1977 and 1979. During his tenure at Trinity, he coached seven All-Americans, including Bill Scanlon, who won the NCAA men's singles championship in 1976, and Erick Iskersky and Ben McCown, who won the doubles title in 1979. By 1986, seventy-two Trinity players had been selected for All-America teams since 1963, a remarkable achievement in collegiate tennis for a school of Trinity's size.[67]

Some of the most memorable contests of the 1970s occurred during the intense rivalry between Trinity and Stanford University, both recognized powers in Division I tennis. When Stanford played Trinity in San Antonio in 1978, the event featured a matchup between Trinity's Larry Gottfried and Stanford's John McEnroe in which Gottfried handed McEnroe his only defeat while an undergraduate at Stanford.[68]

Following the passage of Title IX legislation, which mandated equality of funding for both sexes, Trinity was among the first NCAA institutions in Texas to award athletic scholarships to female tennis players. In 1973, Trinity varsity tennis players Val Franta, Mary Hamm, JoAnne Russell, and Donna Stockton became the first recipients of such awards.[69] The women's team, coached by Marilyn Rindfuss, won the U.S. Tennis Association team championships in 1973, 1975, and 1976. Stephanie Tolleson won the national singles title in 1975, and JoAnne Russell and Donna Stockton took first place in doubles that same year. In 1978 Anne Smith gained All-America honors and later pursued a professional tennis career.[70]

Other women's sports flourished under the leadership of Libby Johnson, who served as assistant athletic director in charge of women's athletics and, for a number of years, coached basketball, volleyball, and softball. After playing for several years on an extramural basis, Trinity women opened the 1974 volleyball season as a member of the Texas Association of Intercollegiate Athletics for Women, an equivalent of the men's NCAA. Before she left Trinity in 1981, Johnson's teams had won six basketball, four volleyball, and four softball city collegiate championships.[71]

Women also assumed other roles in athletics previously occupied solely by males. Coach Gene Norris appointed Kara Christian in 1974 to be the first female student manager of the football team in Trinity's long history.[72] In another precedent-breaking action, Claudia White became the first female sports editor of the *Trinitonian*. In announcing her appointment, White commented, "I suppose Trinity athletes thought the 'Simon Pure' adoption was the final blow to their Herculean endeavors. Well, here's another—me."[73]

Despite success on the playing field, women athletes operated in the shadow of their male counterparts. Complaining about the *Trinitonian's* lack of coverage of women's sports, a group of Trinity's female athletes referred to themselves as "mysteries" and "unknown entities." "We tire of the seemingly intentional omission of our often successful attempts at competitive team sports."[74] Although she acknowledged that athletic director Pete Murphy had been "accommodating" to her teams, Johnson observed that even with the growing popularity of women's sports, their budgets and recognition did not equal that of their male counterparts.[75]

Intramural sports continued to flourish on the Trinity campus. Both men and women participated in a program that regularly attracted more than 70 percent of the student body. Intramurals director Jim Potter supervised a growing list of activities, with coed sports such as flag football, basketball, tennis, and softball among the most popular offerings. Intra-

Frisbee was a popular sport on campus. The *Mirage*, 1977

mural contests also drew large crowds, especially at championship games or during traditional rivalries. The annual homecoming Triniteers–Bengal Lancers flag football game, for example, often drew a larger following than most intercollegiate athletic contests.[76]

One recreational sport developed independently of the intramural program. Ardent Frisbee golf enthusiasts designed an eighteen-hole course that embraced both the lower and upper levels of the campus. Players threw Frisbees at designated landmarks such as a mailbox, light-post, or tree trunk, with favorite targets being campus statuary, especially the bronze busts of Earl Sams and George Storch. According to student lore, *Trinitonian* editor Mark Hill organized the first on-site Frisbee golf tournament in 1972, an event that featured a round-robin elimination contest.[77] In 1973 the founding fathers of Frisbee golf held an invitational tournament that offered an enormous gold-painted Frisbee as the first-place prize. In addition to golf, the event featured other throwing contests, a victory keg in the Rathskeller, and the crowning of a Frisbee queen.[78] Three years later, The Frisbee Golf Association of the United States designated Trinity as an official tournament site.[79]

Although not an organized sport, the streaking mania hit the Trinity campus during the 1970s. One evening before the beginning of the 1974 spring break, a staged streaking event behind Thomas Hall attracted a group of about 400 students and several local television crews. Under the glare of the news crews' floodlights, Trinity streakers, some on foot, others on bicycles, one on the roof of an automobile, and a male and female couple on a motorcycle, went by. Then a group of about twenty men came rushing down from Shook Avenue, which borders the campus, waving underwear before disappearing into the darkness. When it became apparent that the show was over, the crowd disbanded and the TV crews hurried to make the late news shows.[80]

One of the most daring streaking exhibitions occurred in 1979 during parents' weekend. In the midst of a musical number, three naked men entered from the wings and scurried across the stage. As spectators laughed, cheered, and applauded, the performers stood momentarily dumbfounded, unable to sing, but when the accompanist resumed the music, they went on with the show. Afterwards, mistress of ceremonies Coleen Grissom remarked, "If you've seen one, you've seen them all."[81]

As on other campuses throughout the country, Trinity students displayed waning interest in wider societal issues. A national moratorium against the war in Vietnam in the spring of 1971 evoked little enthusiasm compared with the one held several years earlier. A week prior to the moratorium, the *Trinitonian* reported, "No one [had] asked, written, or perhaps, cared about the Moratorium." Student Association President Steve Hudson stated that student government officers had made no plans for the event but would be willing to cooperate "if someone else took the initiative."[82] At the last moment, a group of Trinity students arranged for a succession of speakers to address war issues on the esplanade adjacent to the student union building. Never large, the crowd dwindled to a handful of students as the day progressed. One senior who briefly observed the event from a distance said, "I'm just not interested anymore; it wasn't worthwhile."[83]

Students also showed a declining commitment to traditional campus religious activities. Many either came to Trinity with little religious background or elected to participate in local churches rather than the university's chapel programs. Despite an active program, Chaplain Judd found it difficult to attract a cross section of students to worship services, Bible studies, lectures, and retreats. The university dropped Wednesday chapel in 1973 but maintained Sunday morning worship services for both student and community participants. The traditional baccalaureate ceremony was abandoned three years later, replaced by a voluntary chapel service dedicated to seniors on the last Sunday of the academic year.[84]

In contrast to their lack of enthusiasm for traditional religious organizations, Trinity students showed a growing interest in eastern religions and in practices such as yoga and meditation. The Student's International Meditation Society organized in 1972 to promote the practice of transcendental meditation (TM), as taught by Maharishi Mahesh Yogi. According to Trinity freshman Milton Clark, TM opened one's awareness to "the field of creative intelligence," which promoted clearer thinking and greater comprehension.[85] Adherents of diverse groups such as the International Society for Krishna Consciousness (ISKCON), the Unification Church, and the Children of God periodically visited the campus, talking informally with students and speaking in religion and sociology classes. Most visible were the saffron-robed Hare Krishnas, devotees of a Hindu group who chanted their rhythmic devotional mantra to the accompaniment of drums and tambourines.[86]

Student leaders' efforts to create interest in campus governance issues evoked little response from the student body. Despite widespread publicity, only two students showed up to attend a public hearing in 1974 on a proposed constitutional revision. Observing the attendance, *Trinitonian* columnist Brett Hall commented, "It seems no one has an opinion about anything anymore. Just give the students movies, concerts, a radio station, a booze party here and there, and that's all they want."[87] The following year, a speak-out organized to hear candidates present their platforms for Student Senate races attracted only one student. Even some of the candidates failed to attend. After waiting fifteen minutes, someone said, "Let's go get drunk." The chair reluctantly conceded. "Let's give it up," she said, "there's no point in staying."[88]

Some student leaders attributed the lack of interest in campus governance to insensitivity on the part of administrators who failed to give students a real voice in policy decisions.[89] Another explanation was that administrators formulated rules and regulations in order to placate parents and benefactors and then appeased students by not enforcing them. According to this rationale, students remained uninvolved because they were permitted to do as they pleased as long as they did not infringe on the rights of others.[90]

The *Mirage* also fell victim to student disinterest, inadequate financial support, and lack of effective supervision during the 1970s. Early in the decade, students engaged in a heated debate regarding the value of publishing a yearbook, a university tradition that stretched back more than half a century. Although some students stressed the value of having a verbal and pictorial record of their college experience, many echoed the sen-

The *Trinitonian*, 15 September 1978

timents of Student Association President Rex Smith, who argued that his student generation was not interested in memories of old alma mater. "I want the money from any activity fee to go to something that can be enjoyed and something that might be beneficial at this time—not in the distant future."[91]

Against this backdrop of waning student interest, the student finance board decided in 1973 to reallocate most of the publication funds to enhance the *Trinitonian* rather than support a yearbook. Operating on the assumption that this would likely be the last *Mirage*, editor Joe E. Harmes and his staff (Jack Landman, Naomi Shihab, David Norris, and Oscar Williams III) published two controversial magazine-style editions of the yearbook that were devoid of traditional photographs and records of campus activities.[92] Although some applauded the volumes as artistic and creative, the overall response was negative.[93] Managing editor Landman admitted that their counterculture venture was designed to provoke rather than please its intended audience. "It offended people in every walk of life on campus. It offended administrators. It offended teachers. It offended students. It blasted at everybody."[94]

During the next three years, volunteer editors attempted to publish editions of the *Mirage* solely on subscription sales and advertising revenues. In the process, however, they incurred debts that the university eventually was forced to absorb.[95] As a result, the Publications Committee decided not to publish the *Mirage* for the 1978–79 school year and considered the possibility of shutting down operations permanently.[96] In 1979 and 1980, student volunteers produced slender volumes entitled *Images* that provided some glimpses of campus life and a few photographs of graduating seniors. Publication of the *Mirage* resumed in 1981 after the board of trustees approved an increase in the student activity fee to accommodate the publication of a yearbook. For the first time in nearly a decade, the *Mirage* was completed on time and under budget.[97]

Despite the prevalence of campus apathy, Trinity students responded to issues that had personal, local, or regional implications. Following a decision by the Academic Council to reduce the number of reading days preceding final examinations from two to one, 800 students signed a petition protesting the action.[98] They also filed a protest after university staff members searched residence halls during spring break, confiscating refectory silverware and informing security of stolen street signs. Three hundred and fifteen students charged university housing, maintenance, and security personnel with failure to obtain search warrants and threatened legal action against the university. Acting president Thomas agreed with the protesters and ordered an immediate end to such practices.[99]

In a related campus issue, Trinity students opposed the construction of McAllister Freeway, whose proposed route, a part of which would connect downtown and the international airport, was in close proximity to residence halls on the university's eastern boundaries. Solicited by members of Trinity's recently formed Sierra Club, some 500 Trinity students signed petitions in 1970 opposing the freeway, and a small group of Trinitonians joined other San Antonio residents in a vigil on the proposed right of way. Delayed by litigation and lack of funding, the freeway project remained in limbo for almost a decade. During that interim, the Trinity Sierra Club disbanded and student interest dwindled.[100]

Trinity students also participated in a statewide effort to secure "full adult status" for 18- to 20-year-old voters. Working in conjunction with the Texas Intercollegiate Student Association (TISA), the Student Affairs Committee of the Student Council circulated petitions that asked the Texas legislature for the right to consume and possess alcoholic beverages, the privilege to serve on juries, and the right to adult status in their relationships as students within institutions of higher learning. Don Davis, coordinator of the TISA project at Trinity, organized a door-to-door petition drive in the residence halls and set up a booth in the student union to reach town students.[101] As a result, more than 600 Trinity students and a number of faculty members signed the petitions.[102]

Trinity women expressed growing interest in feminist issues, especially in the area of vocational choices. The San Antonio chapter of the National Organization for Women (NOW) periodically held assertiveness training clinics and seminars in conjunction with the University Center.[103] Commenting on women's new awareness of potential career roles, Trinity graduate student Martha Calloway said, "We have begun to realize that careers are abundant and we can shape our future without regard to the past."[104] A debate on "Femininity vs. Feminism," sponsored by Trinity's Speech Activities Program, drew an enthusiastic crowd to the Coates Center multipurpose room. Subtitled "Beauty versus the Bitches," the debate featured four speakers, two on each side.[105]

Increasing numbers of role models on campus encouraged Trinity women to broaden their vision of vocational choices. Senior female faculty members such as Linda Anooshian (psychology), Jean Chittenden (foreign languages), Linda Hall (history), Shirley Rushing (health, physical education, and athletics), and Frances Swinny (speech and drama) were highly regarded as teachers and assumed leadership roles in various university committees. In 1976 San Antonio resident Flora C. Atherton, a former national committeewoman for the Republican Party, became the first woman to serve as chair of the board of trustees. The following year Elizabeth Luce Moore, chair of the State University of New York Board of Regents, gave the commencement address to Trinity graduates, the first woman to do so.[106]

The first public discussion of sexual orientation issues at Trinity occurred in 1978 when several students (identified only by initials in the *Trinitonian*) professed their homosexuality in response to singer Anita Bryant's widely publicized opposition to the gay rights movement.[107] All agreed that Bryant had a right to express her belief but contended that she should be held accountable "for the lives she destroys or alters in a negative way." They also charged that Christian churches did little to satisfy gays' needs in terms of spiritual guidance and support.[108]

In a follow-up letter to the *Trinitonian*, one of the male students, whose comments appeared in the initial article, provided his name and expressed regret that the article did not adequately convey their sense of alienation from the student body. He affirmed that the time had come when gay and lesbian students should form a gay student association to provide mutual support and to interpret their lifestyle to the straight community. He invited students interested in joining with others "in finding a way to be gay" to contact him at their convenience.[109]

The same issue of the *Trinitonian* featured an interview with Trinity sociologist O Z White, who condemned the prevalent homophobia in American society. "Gay people will receive their rights," he said, "but I don't believe it will be in my lifetime."[110] Breaking conventional taboos, White invited three lesbian women to speak to his class on sex roles.[111]

Even though their numbers remained small, Hispanic and African-American students created organizations for mutual support and promotion of minority issues. Hispanics formed the Trinity Association for Chicano Students (TACS) in 1970. Describing the new group as "a non-militant organization concerning itself with people not ideologies," TACS President George Anchondo issued a set of proposals that included hiring Chicano admissions counselors, recruiting Chicano faculty, creating an interdepartmental Chicano studies program, and substantially increasing the number of residential Hispanic students. The election of Homero Garza as president of the Student Association added to the visibility of the group.[112]

"The common problem of the Chicano in the U.S. is the identity crisis. He is a person that is classified as white by the census, but because he is darker than most Anglos or speaks with an accent, he is designated as a minority. He is discriminated against because he desires to maintain his native language, customs and traditions. . . . We reject the notion of subjugating our heritage in order to rise in the American society. Instead we present you, the Anglo, with the challenge of accepting us as equal human beings."

"Brown Reflections," the *Trinitonian*, 24 April 1970

As its membership grew, TACS became more proactive in the political arena. When recruiters for the National Labor Relations Board visited campus, Hispanic students organized a protest to express their displeasure with governmental indifference to minority issues.[113] On another occasion, they rallied to support migrant workers in the Southwest and California. Supported by the Student Council, TACS urged Trinity food-service personnel to serve only union produce in the refectory. When food-service supervisors failed to cooperate, student leaders organized a boycott of nonunion lettuce and invited a United Farm Worker's unionist to visit the campus. Their efforts ultimately ended in the compromise that the university would serve both union and nonunion lettuce, with each being clearly marked.[114]

Following a similar pattern, Trinity African Americans organized in 1971 with a charter membership of thirty students to create the Black Efforts of Trinity (BET). Asserting that Trinity's institutional structures were "racist from the top down," BET founders set forth a list of grievances that called for African-American–oriented courses and recruitment of African Americans to administrative, managerial, coaching, and secretarial positions.[115] Under the guidance of professors Earl Lewis (urban studies) and Guy Ranson (religion), BET sponsored Trinity's first Black Heritage celebration in February 1973 in conjunction with National Black History week. The event featured poetry readings, art exhibits, and modern dance and karate demonstrations.[116]

"When I reflect on my stay on Trinity Hill my thoughts immediately turn to the phrase 'it's a white world.' It's not a dull white, beginning to fade into gray or light brown as the influences of other racial and ethnic groups are felt; it is a sterile, lifeless and all pervasive white. . . . Being Black at Trinity Hill means many things. . . . Black is watching students drool over the Temptations or Supremes, and refusing to speak to you. Black is seeing more potential for a faculty revolt because of a paucity of concerned students than a student revolt. . . . Black is being patronized by a campus 'liberal' who apparently thinks that speaking to a Black is being open minded. . . . Black is waiting on Trinity University to have a soul transplant. Think about it."

"Black Reflections," the *Trinitonian*, 24 April 1970

Despite making progress in promoting racial harmony on campus, African-American students reported incidents of harassment and isolation that continued to diminish their university experience.[117] A series of incidents in 1977 and 1978 in which unidentified parties targeted African-American students with death threats and racial slurs evoked strong responses from university officials and campus organizations. In addition to increased security measures in residence halls, the Faculty Senate recommended sustained efforts to institute race relations dialogues between students and faculty and to provide individual counseling for victims of racial attacks. No further incidents of racial harassment were reported during the remainder of the school year.[118]

As the decade drew to a close, some Trinitonians reflected on the impact of their student generation on campus life and the world at large. One student described the late 1970s as a throwback to the 1950s: a conservative manner of dress, evident in khaki pants, oxford cloth shirts, and more traditional styles in women's fashions; conservatism in political ideologies; and a return to traditional entertainments such as toga parties and homecoming celebrations. Most evident was the prevailing indifference toward social problems that did not directly affect the everyday lives of upper-middle-class Americans. "Trinity in the late 60s was an anachronism, and in essence, it seems to me that Trinity University never really left the 50s. And here we are 20 years later."[119]

On a more optimistic note, *Trinitonian* editor Erin Baker observed that a new and unique student generation was emerging out of the 1970s, one that had assimilated major characteristics of the last three decades. The high level of participation in all types of social activities and campus organizations of the 1950s, the demand for students' rights and representation of the 1960s, and the "you do your thing and I'll do mine" of the 1970s were meshing to produce a new breed of involved, mature, and independent students. She expressed hope that if this trend continued, the Trinity student body would play an increasingly important role in the shaping of campus values and intellectual activities in the closing decades of the twentieth century.[120]

CHAPTER THIRTEEN

AN AGENDA FOR EXCELLENCE

The mission, indeed the destiny, of Trinity University is to become one of
the nation's leading small universities emphasizing the liberal arts with its
major commitment to excellence in undergraduate education.

RONALD K. CALGAARD, JANUARY 1981

RONALD K. CALGAARD HIT THE TRINITY CAMPUS with the intensity of a Kansas tornado. Unlike a tempestuous and short-lived funnel
cloud, however, he brought a directed and sustained energy that dramatically altered the institution's academic image. During the last two decades
of the century, he relentlessly pursued the goal of transforming Trinity
from a reputable regional institution into a nationally acclaimed, well-
endowed, primarily undergraduate, residential university. Largely through
his focused vision and adept management, he helped Trinity attain and
solidify that objective.

Calgaard's upbringing, educational training, and professional experiences prepared him well for the Trinity presidency. Of Norwegian ancestry, Calgaard was raised in Joice, Iowa, in a close-knit family noted for its
work ethic and Lutheran piety. In high school, from which he graduated
as class valedictorian, Calgaard participated in a variety of activities, including debate, student government, choir, drama, and basketball. After
graduation, Calgaard enrolled at nearby Luther College, a small church-
related institution where he majored in economics and philosophy, graduating summa cum laude in 1959.[1]

Initially intending to pursue a law career, Calgaard was awarded a
Woodrow Wilson Graduate Fellowship and elected to attend the University of Iowa. While working on an M.A. and Ph.D. in economics, Calgaard attended teach-ins on Vietnam, taught undergraduate classes, and
observed the dynamics of campus politics in a large public institution.

After completing a dissertation on economic planning in underdeveloped countries, he received his doctorate in 1963 and accepted a position as assistant professor of economics at the University of Kansas in Lawrence. From 1965 to 1967, he was on leave as a postdoctoral fellow in Latin American studies in Santiago, Chile, on a grant from the Social Science Research Council/American Council of Learned Societies.[2]

During his tenure in Kansas, Calgaard rose rapidly as an academician and administrator, attaining the rank of professor in 1972. He combined a successful teaching career with an active role in faculty governance, serving as chair of the University Senate executive committee, president of the faculty, and president of the local chapter of the American Association of University Professors (AAUP). From 1970 to 1974, he served as associate dean of the College of Liberal Arts and Sciences and as associate vice chancellor for outreach for one year. In 1975, at the age of forty-one, he accepted the appointment of vice chancellor for academic affairs, the position he left to become president of Trinity University.[3]

In the 1970s, the University of Kansas was marked by student unrest over the Kent State shootings and the war in Vietnam. During this period, Calgaard forged an administrative style characterized by a firm grasp of fiscal operations and an ability to make decisions quickly and decisively. He soon realized that whoever controlled the budget made most of the policy decisions, and this awareness affected his choice of administrative positions. He also learned that he could not please all constituencies of the academic community. "People weren't going to like all the decisions you made. The best you could hope for was that whether they liked them or not, there would be some respect; that your yes was a yes, and your no was a no, and that they could depend on that. Sometimes people would rather have an answer that they don't like than no answer at all."[4]

When Trinity's presidential search committee sought background information on Calgaard, they found unanimity among his Kansas colleagues regarding his administrative skills, describing him as a person prepared to deal with budgetary issues and one who could make decisions and implement them effectively. One respondent said, "He is tough but sensitive and he knows how to get things done. Overall he is a very fair, informed, and involved administrator." Queried about possible weaknesses in his leadership abilities, another colleague hesitated and then said, "It may be impatience. He is a quick thinker and responds possibly too quickly or shows a bit of frustration with those whose thought processes work more slowly, but he is not the type of person who 'shoots from the hip.'"[5]

Following his acceptance of the presidency in November 1978 but before establishing residence in San Antonio in June 1979, Calgaard visited the campus three days each month. He inspected every building, including residence halls, storage areas, and physical plant facilities. Calgaard also began to associate names and faces so that by the time he actually assumed the presidency, he could personally greet most faculty, staff, administrators, and trustees by name. During the same time frame, he read voraciously, perusing Trinity histories, self-studies, financial records, trustee minutes, and committee reports in order to familiarize himself with university policies and procedures. His rapidly acquired knowledge of university operations impressed everyone, including Harold Herndon, chair of the board of trustees, who told a local newspaper reporter, "Ron knows more about this school right now than anyone I've known in years."[6]

Calgaard's spouse, Gene (Genie) Flom Calgaard, and their two children, Lisa (14) and Kent (10), accompanied the new president to San Antonio. The Calgaards had first met as undergraduates at Luther College, where Genie was majoring in elementary education. Coming from similar backgrounds and sharing many common interests, they cultivated a relationship that led to marriage and an enduring partnership of love and mutual respect. According to Genie, she and Ron had a simple working agreement: "You do what you do best, and I'll do what I do best, and we'll try to do the other things together."[7] Although members of Trinity's search committee were impressed with Ron Calgaard's academic credentials, they were also captivated by Genie's outgoing personality and consummate social skills. Committee member Paul Smith told the board in 1978 that "we really want Genie to come to be our first lady, and we hope she brings Ron with her."[8]

The Trinity presidency attracted Ron Calgaard for a number of reasons. During his years at the University of Kansas, he had grown convinced that undergraduate institutions represented the most significant and challenging areas in the field of higher education and that private institutions had a better opportunity to develop more effective undergraduate studies than did large public universities. Given Trinity's decision to forego doctoral studies and to eliminate some of its weakest master's degree programs, Calgaard thought that the university had an opportunity to offer an attractive mixture of undergraduate liberal arts and selected professional programs. With disciplined leadership, he predicted that Trinity could compete for outstanding students and rise in the academic world.[9]

In accepting the presidency of Trinity, Calgaard acknowledged that he had inherited an institution with exceptional fiscal resources, an attractive physical plant, a competent and dedicated faculty, and an increasingly se-

Ron and Genie Calgaard

lect student body. He credited the work of his predecessors, especially James Laurie and Bruce Thomas, with moving Trinity from a barren campus on the brink of closure to a respected regional university. "It was a lot easier to persuade the board and potential donors that we could go from where we were in 1979 to become a really first-rate institution than when Jim Laurie was out trying to sell his dream. There wasn't much there to sell."[10]

At the same time, Calgaard thought that the university had not clearly articulated its mission as an educational institution. Shortly after becoming president, he received a letter from a trustee stating that the board wanted to create the finest academic university in the Southwest, but, the writer noted, "The term most frequently heard at Board meetings is 'academic excellence,' but I'm not sure we all know what it means."[11] When Calgaard asked the board what kind of university it wanted, members invariably answered "a better one." Beyond those words, they could provide no clear direction about what "better" might mean except that, given Trinity's institutional resources, they believed something more needed to be achieved.[12]

Addressing the lack of institutional focus, Calgaard emphasized to university trustees the necessity of developing clearly defined goals and objectives. "Unless you are willing to take the risk of establishing specific targets," he said, "you will probably not be very successful in moving your institution to any new plateau of academic progress." At the same time, he stressed the importance of having a specific plan for obtaining the necessary financial resources and the willingness to be candid in assessing successes and failures.[13]

In order to reach its goal of academic excellence, Calgaard recommended that Trinity concentrate on becoming a premier undergraduate liberal arts university with selected professional programs and curtail its graduate offerings. During a period when many schools were seeking to increase enrollment, Trinity would decrease its size, increase its tuition, and become more selective in its admissions process. Simultaneously, the university would recruit faculty with degrees from nationally regarded educational institutions in order to challenge the projected new generation of Trinity students. In short, Calgaard proposed to make Trinity one of the top undergraduate liberal arts colleges in the United States, and he intended to accomplish this feat within a decade.[14]

Calgaard quickly established himself as a "hands-on" administrator—both hands. Nothing of consequence happened at Trinity without his knowledge and approval. Twenty years of memoranda and correspondence indicate that he monitored decision-making processes at all administrative levels and vetoed or approved projects and strategies based on his evaluation of how they contributed to the overall mission of the university. At the same time, he maintained a keen interest in national trends in higher education, especially those related to demographics and economic factors. This ability to focus simultaneously on the micro and macro dimensions of university life contributed to his accomplishments at Trinity University.[15]

Impelled by Calgaard's energy and his long workdays, the pulse of Trinity heightened. Even on weekends, Calgaard was on campus, eager to talk about his vision for the university. Some faculty members and administrators at work in their offices closed their doors, drew their blinds, and dimmed their lights to avoid a potentially lengthy presidential visit.[16] Religion professor Paula Cooey said that the new president gave "omnipresence a whole new meaning," and Coleen Grissom commented, "I have never known anyone with such stamina, focus, and loyalty. It's intimidating, exhausting, and inspiring."[17]

Having a conversation with Ron Calgaard was a unique experience. It was like playing Ping-Pong except that he was the only one who had a paddle. You had to bounce balls off his paddle. Conversations were never frivolous or unfocused and almost never involved small talk. They invariably were directed to campus activities or to political, social, economic, or other issues related to higher education. He had strong convictions on these subjects and articulated them with clarity and authority.[18]

Calgaard's penchant for communication carried over into the public arena. Usually speaking without a manuscript and often without notes, he was adept at crafting his remarks to fit particular situations. Gifted with a resonant speaking voice, Calgaard impressed audiences with his kaleidoscopic knowledge and his passion for Trinity. Frequently called on to introduce international and national figures, he did so in a relaxed and confident manner. At ease in both formal and informal social situations, he mixed well with people and made a favorable impression on potential benefactors and supporters.[19]

Calgaard, who was a chain-smoker at the time, maintained such a hectic pace during his first few years as president that trustees became concerned about his health, so much so that members of the executive committee thought it advisable for Calgaard to have a complete medical examination. Despite good results, the trustees urged him to slow down and relax. In a letter to Calgaard, board chairman Herndon wrote, "I would emphasize that the major concern voiced by those who had a part of the decision making, it was expressed universally that we think you are spending too many late hours in your office."[20]

Calgaard nevertheless continued his work habits and assembled a list of specific goals for the university to achieve in the next decade. He also shaped his presidential inauguration to highlight his view of Trinity's institutional mission. The two-day event opened with a four-hour symposium entitled "The Nature of Liberal Education" and carried over into inaugural ceremonies that were conducted with a flourish of academic pageantry.[21] In his inaugural address, Calgaard called for a renewed commitment to undergraduate liberal education as an enriching and unifying element in our culture. Trinity's mission, Calgaard affirmed, was to help students "communicate effectively, to read and to think critically, to acquire some appreciation of our history, our literature, and some sensitivity to aesthetic values."[22]

Calgaard also emphasized the importance of balancing Trinity's identity as a private liberal arts institution with its roots as a church-related university. He announced that the board of trustees had established, at his urging, a church relations committee, the first such committee in the university's history, and had affirmed its intent to strengthen denominational ties, to support efforts to promote spiritual life on campus, and to maintain a ceremonial religious presence at public observances such as commencements and convocations.[23]

Trustee Harold Herndon and Calgaard at inauguration ceremonies

One of Calgaard's initial tasks was to establish a clear line of demarcation between presidential duties and trustee responsibilities. Coming into an environment in which individual trustees were involved in day-to-day university operations, Calgaard openly clarified his understanding of the relationship between the board of trustees and the administration. "It is the role of the board to develop general policy. It is the role of the administration to administer these policies. . . . I would hope the board would leave the administrative details to the administration. Its function is to appoint the leadership, establish the policies, and expect accountability."[24] Meeting privately with various trustees, Calgaard stressed that when the trustees were not in plenary session, they should not speak for the institution. At the same time, he also promised that he would keep them fully informed about developments at the university in terms of both problems and accomplishments.[25]

Building on this new understanding, Calgaard forged a harmonious working relationship with the university trustees that lasted throughout his tenure at Trinity. During his presidency, he benefited from the leadership of board chairs Harold D. Herndon (1978–84), William H. Bell (1984–87), Richard W. Calvert (1987–90), Walter F. Brown (1990–94), Paul H. Smith (1994–97), and James F. Dicke II (1997–2000). Calgaard and the university community referred to Harold Herndon, who served two consecutive terms, as "Mr. Trinity" for his enthusiastic leadership.[26]

Calgaard also established one of his closest personal relationships with William H. Bell, who also served as trustee for the various funds of the extensive Chapman endowments. Dating back to the Laurie years, the interaction between the Chapman Foundation and the university had been strained at times. Early in his presidency, Calgaard held frank conversations with Bell regarding how best to establish an association that would be acceptable to the Chapman interests and beneficial to the university. Together they reached a verbal agreement that stabilized endowment income and allowed for the promotion of a variety of capital projects and improvements. This bond of respect and mutual admiration between Bell and Calgaard contributed to Trinity's fiscal stability and financial growth over the years. Because of their friendship, Trinity's investment committee was periodically invited to visit Tulsa to observe the management of the Chapman trusts and to share information about Trinity's operations.[27]

Bell and Calgaard agreed on a formula for distributing Chapman funds that enabled the university to implement a balanced budget rather than operating under an unpredictable and fluctuating income. The two parties agreed that income from the 1949 Chapman trust would be an unrestricted distribution to fund the university's operating budget. Distributions from the larger 1966 trust would be in two apportionments. The first $3.5 million ($875,000 per quarter) would go into the operating budget as an unrestricted grant. Everything above that ($2 million to $3 million) would be dedicated to special projects, such as buildings, scholarships, and endowed professorships. Income from the Leta Chapman Trust, of which Trinity had no proprietary rights, was negotiated annually between the two men. Ten percent (approximately $300,000) regularly went for operation of the Chapman Center and the remainder for a variety of mutually-agreed-on projects. In establishing the agreement, Bell and Calgaard encouraged the trustees to raise matching funds for capital projects so that the board members would be participants rather than spectators in the development process.[28]

Although Trinity had no control over the investment strategies of the Chapman trusts, it had responsibility for other funds that accounted for approximately half of the university's endowment income. One of Calgaard's first steps to improve the university's fiscal situation was to limit the disbursement of endowment income to 5 or 6 percent annually so that the corpus of the endowment would grow and offset the effects of inflation. Noting that the university had historically invested heavily in gas and oil stock, Calgaard moved to diversify investments and adopted a "moderate-risk posture" that sacrificed some potential opportunities for gain during rising markets in order to avoid large short-term declines during falling markets.[29]

Concurrently, the trustees agreed to a new form of investment management that would replace the board investment committee, which met monthly to make decisions on the purchase and sale of stocks. In its stead, Calgaard recommended that a group of professional managers, each with different investment strategies, be hired to administer the endowment assets under board oversight. The board concurred and hired four managers who handled approximately $100 million of Trinity's money. The various managers, evaluated on a quarterly basis, were continued or terminated based on their individual performances. In the long run, putting endowment funds in the hands of experienced professionals enabled Trinity to achieve greater diversification and to experience favorable returns on its investments. By the end of the century, the market value of Trinity's endowment had increased to approximately $600 million.[30]

Noting that Trinity's tuition and fees were substantially lower than the national higher education price index during the last decade, Calgaard recommended that they be raised immediately by 16 percent. He also projected subsequent increases in order to produce funds for general university operations rather than tapping endowment income for such purposes. At the same time, he urged that every effort be made to provide more scholarship aid to students of modest economic means so that rising tuition would not deny them access to private higher education.[31]

Aware that Calgaard's institutional vision could not be implemented without sufficient financial undergirding, the board of trustees unanimously agreed in 1981 to launch a $48.5-million capital campaign. Trustee Richard Calvert announced that the ambitious project, entitled "A Commitment to Distinction," included $6 million for faculty recruitment and an additional $3 million for projects such as academic leaves, research, and curriculum development. Another $6 million was designated for a scholarship endowment to enable Trinity to recruit talented students regardless of their economic background. The campaign also proposed to raise $16.5 million for library acquisitions and laboratory equipment, $9 million for academic facility maintenance, $5 million for renovation and new construction of residence halls, and $1 million for an endowment to support the Parker Chapel program. In addition to the basic academic elements, the project called for $2 million to initiate a program of special lectures, concerts, and other cultural events that would enrich community life.[32]

Murchison Tower at night

Ron and Genie Calgaard, 1999

Calgaard leaving last commencement exercises in 1999;
photo Express-News Publishing Company

Four Trinity presidents (1999); left to right: John R. Brazil, Ronald K. Calgaard, G. Duncan Wimpress, and Marion Bruce Thomas

President John R. Brazil and Janice H. Brazil

Trinity University Board of Trustees, 2003
(For individual identifications, see appendix.)

Members of the Trinity community leaving Memorial Service
on 11 September 2001

Students, faculty, and staff give blood in response to 9/11 disaster.

General Colin Powell, Distinguished Lecture Series speaker in 1995

Author Margaret Atwood, (second from right),
Stieren Arts and Enrichment Series speaker,
with Trinity students in 1989

Trinity's annual community Christmas concert in Laurie Auditorium

Trinity faculty, staff, and students participate in San Antonio's
2002 Battle of Flowers Parade.

Information Commons in Coates Library

Computer technology in the classroom

Cabaret, the first musical in the new Stieren Theater, April 2000.
Photo Tim Francis, Department of Speech and Drama.

Trinity University Choir visits former Waxahachie campus. Alumnus Chapman
Middleton kneeling front, Scott MacPherson, University Choir Director,
kneeling right second row.

Henry Moore's sculpture, *Large Interior Form*, enhances the area
adjacent to the Coates esplanade.

Graduates of the Class of 2004 celebrate with Hepworth's
Coversation with Magic Stones in the background.

Interior of Margarite B. Parker Chapel

Trinity campus viewed from Olmos Tower Condominiums

Spring wildflowers in upper campus jogging trail area.
Photo, Michael Schweitzer, Trinity University Physical Plant.

New Northrup Hall viewed from Stadium Drive

Eugenia B. Miller Fountain in new location west of Northrup Hall

South campus recreational area

William H. Bell Athletic Center

Trinity's NCAA Division III National Champions, left to right: Women's Basketball 2003 (Allison Wooley and Coach Becky Geyer); Men's Soccer 2003 (Chris Quinn and Coach Paul McGinlay; Women's and Men's Tennis 2000 (Lindsay Smith, Coach Butch Newman, and Russell McMindes). Athletic Director Bob King at back.

Coach Steve Mohr and the Trinity football team celebrate the SCAC Football Championship in 2001. Trinity won ten consecutive conference championships (1993–2003).

Sunset on Trinity Campus

Chairman Richard Calvert, Herndon, and Calgaard mark the
beginning of a $48.5-million campaign.

With support from trustees, staff, alumni, and faculty, the capital campaign committee solicited contributions from a wide variety of potential donors throughout the country. Leading by example throughout the grueling three-year campaign, Calgaard committed considerable time and energy to fund-raising in addition to his usual presidential duties. At a dinner meeting in May 1984, the board held a victory celebration to mark the campaign's successful completion. According to Calgaard, Trinity's trustees and their related sources contributed approximately half of the total sum raised, an indication of their commitment to the university and its programs.[33]

In addition to his fiscal initiatives, Calgaard moved to reconfigure the administrative structure that had been established during the previous decade. Calgaard favored a model with a strong office of academic affairs that was responsible for both graduate and undergraduate operations. His overall plans for a unified faculty did not include separate schools such as engineering and business. He also considered the divisional deans to be senior staff members rather than professional school administrators with curricular and admissions authority.[34]

Calgaard delegated the task of proposing a new organizational model to a faculty and administrative committee chaired by Frank Kersnowski, a senior professor in the Department of English. After seeking input from various campus constituencies, the committee recommended reducing the six academic divisions and a division of graduate studies to four academic divisions (Humanities and Arts; Behavioral Sciences; Business and Administrative Studies; and Sciences, Mathematics, and Engineering) led by deans who would be responsible for undergraduate and graduate programs in their divisions. The divisions would be accountable to the Office of the Vice President for Academic Affairs. To improve the effectiveness of academic operations, the committee proposed the appointment of an associate vice president for academic affairs who would supervise summer school, continuing education, and grant-sponsored research. In addition, the report urged that faculty be involved in the selection and periodic evaluation of academic administrators, including the president, vice president for academic affairs, deans, and department chairs.[35]

In another initiative, Calgaard recommended that the Faculty Senate establish a commission on promotion and tenure in order to give faculty the responsibility for recommendations to the administration on promotion and tenure decisions. The commission consisted of faculty representatives elected from each of the academic divisions and three additional faculty members elected at-large, with the vice president for academic affairs serving as a nonvoting chair. Candidates for tenure and/or promotion submitted materials pertaining to their teaching, scholarship, and service along with recommendations from peers and external referees. After deliberations, the commission would forward its recommendations to the president, who made the final determination.[36] The faculty and the board of trustees approved the recommendations, and the new structure went into effect in June 1980.[37]

In conjunction with the reorganization process, Calgaard began to assemble a cadre of administrators who were committed to his institutional goals and would emulate his work ethic. With few exceptions, they served throughout his presidency. Coleen Grissom remained as dean of student affairs and would later be promoted to vice president for student affairs, the first woman at Trinity to attain such status. New arrivals included Craig McCoy, vice president for fiscal affairs; Marc Raney, vice president for development; and James S. Vinson, vice president for academic affairs. When Vinson left in 1987, Edward C. Roy Jr., a professor in Trinity's Department of Geology (now Department of Geosciences), was appointed to fill the position. In other academic personnel changes, Charles B. (Chuck) White, a member of the Department of Psychology, replaced Robert Stepsis as associate vice president for academic affairs when the latter accepted a position at another university. Assistant registrar Richard Elliott succeeded Burford Higgins, who retired, as registrar, and veteran staff member Alberta (Doodie) Meyer, replaced Russell Gossage as director of admissions, with Gossage continuing to serve the university in alumni affairs and as a development officer.[38]

Essential to the success of Calgaard's academic agenda was the university's ability to attract and retain an outstanding student body. Meyer headed up a corps of field representatives who traversed the country in search of quality students. In 1982 she formed the Trinity Admissions Council (TAC), a group of student volunteers who worked with the admissions staff to contact prospective high school students and to host their campus visits. Beginning with 50 students, the group attained a membership of nearly 500 and proved to be an effective recruiting device. Meyer was also active in professional circles, serving as president of the National Association for College Admission Counseling (NACAC) and establishing close relationships with high school counselors throughout the country.[39]

Utilizing a number of strategies, Calgaard instituted changes in the university's admissions process. Instead of a policy of continuous acceptance that permitted students to apply as late as during the registration process, the university set early decision dates and a deadline for the closing of applications. In granting admission credits, the university also raised advanced placement score requirements to be more in line with peer institutions. In 1984 the average SAT score had risen to approximately 1185, and more than 80 percent of the entering class was in the top 8 percent of their high school graduating class. After peaking at 1230 in 1987, SAT average scores leveled off at 1200 by the end of the decade. During the same time period, attrition rates among first-year students declined from 22 percent to less than 13 percent.[40]

Trinity also substantially reduced the number of transfer students accepted for admission to the university. Prior to Calgaard's arrival, Trinity annually enrolled 300 to 500 transfer students, many of whom were less prepared academically than those who entered as first-year students. The university now required all transfer students to meet the increased academic standards and to earn their last sixty hours of credit at Trinity. By 1986 the number of transfer students had dropped to about seventy annually, and before the end of the decade the annual number ranged between thirty-five and fifty.[41]

National competition for minority students with high SAT scores and outstanding high school records was keen. Despite aggressive recruiting, the percentage of minority students dropped from 17.7 percent to 9.5 percent between 1980 and 1983. Nevertheless, Calgaard remained adamant about maintaining the university's admissions standards.[42] Committed to diversity on campus, however, Calgaard appointed an Advisory Committee for Minority Recruitment and budgeted approximately $300,000 to be available in the general grant category for minority recruitment. The committee produced a report in 1984 entitled "Diversity for Excellence" that included plans to raise and maintain the presence of minorities at Trinity. Regarding students, the committee called for effective publication of the university's renewed commitment to minority recruitment, a substantial increase in financial aid for minority students, a targeted and personalized recruitment strategy, flexible selection criteria, and the development of programs designed to nurture and retain minority students once they matriculated at Trinity.[43]

Concerted efforts by students, faculty, and staff, along with the commitment of additional financial resources for scholarships and financial aid for minorities, produced positive results. Within a few years, minority percentages began to increase and by the end of the decade showed considerable improvement. In 1990, Director of Institutional Research Michael Yost reported that the entering class had a 21 percent ethnic minority component, the highest ever in Trinity's history.[44]

In addition to heightened admission requirements, Trinity aggressively recruited National Merit Scholars to improve the admissions pool and to capture public attention. In 1981, Trinity offered full tuition to any National Merit finalist, and eleven accepted. Two years later, the entering class included 54 National Merit Scholars, and in 1984 the number soared to 120, an incredible number for a school of Trinity's size.[45] In addition, the new Murchison Scholarships provided ten entering students each year with full tuition grants for four years of undergraduate studies at Trinity. As a result, the university received wide acclaim as an emerging academic institution in newspapers, trade journals, and magazines such as the *New York Times, Wall Street Journal, Forbes Magazine, Chronicle of Higher Education, Time,* and *U.S. News and World Report.* Calgaard appeared on local, regional, and national television, including an interview with David Hartman on ABC's "Good Morning America" program.[46]

To reinforce the university's changing national image, Calgaard decided in 1982 to withdraw Trinity from the Texas Intercollegiate Athletic Association, a National Association of Intercollegiate Athletics (NAIA) conference, and join the nonscholarship Division III of the National College Athletic Association (NCAA) in order to play teams with similar educational and athletic philosophies. When an effort to create a conference restricted to private institutions failed, Trinity was forced to play as an independent.[47] Trinity elected, however, to continue to participate in NCAA Division I scholarship tennis.[48]

The university also attained heightened visibility through the establishment of a variety of lecture series that brought nationally and internationally recognized scholars, artists, journalists, and political leaders to the Trinity campus. The Distinguished Lecture Series, instituted in 1979 and later funded by trustee Walter F. Brown and his spouse Lenora, brought figures such as Carl Sagan, Bill Moyers, Patricia Roberts Harris, Colin Powell, Desmond Tutu, Helmut Schmidt, and Jean Kirkpatrick to Laurie Auditorium. The Atherton Lecture series, begun in 1982 and funded by trustee Flora C. Atherton, focused on national and international politics and attracted participants such as former presidents George Bush, Jimmy Carter, and Gerald Ford. Trustee Arthur Stieren and his spouse Jane funded the Stieren Arts and Enrichment Series that enabled the university to bring many well-known figures in the arts for performances, lectures, colloquia, and classroom discussions. Among their number were Margaret Atwood, Ken Burns, John Updike, Liv Ullmann, John Corigliano, Nicholas Wolsterstorff, Claire Bloom, Toni Morrison, and Henry Louis Gates Jr. San Antonio business leaders were invited to attend Trinity's Policy Maker Breakfasts to hear speakers such as Malcolm S. Forbes, Carl Rowan, Walter Mondale, Robert McNamara, and Robert S. Strauss.[49]

Beyond these strategies, Calgaard emphasized the importance of a well-groomed and striking campus as an effective recruiting device, both for prospective students and for faculty and staff. He believed that a visitor's first impression of the institution often would be based on the general appearance of the facilities rather than on the quality of the faculty, the average SAT scores, or the number of volumes in the library. After touring the campus, he decided to develop a physical facilities planning process for the next decade formulated on the answer to two basic questions: "What kinds of activities and programs will we be offering on the campus in the next decade, and what kinds of physical facilities do we really need to carry out these programs?"[50]

Perambulating the campus early in the morning, Ron and Genie Calgaard maintained a sharp eye for detractions, such as malfunctioning sprinkler heads, overflowing waste receptacles, and unsightly landscaping. His subsequent memos to appropriate staff members were frequent and explicit: "There is a very bad spot in the landscaping at the southwest corner of the Mabee Dining Hall. It is very visible and unattractive. . . . There is mildew on the concrete at the football stadium and tennis courts. . . . The front doors of the Chapman Center are in very poor condition. The doors either need to be replaced or refinished as soon as possible. . . . Please see that the manhole covers around the campus are painted dark green. . . . The recital hall in Ruth Taylor is a minor disaster, an embarrassment. Many of the seats are torn and almost all of the seats are badly worn. Take care of this at once."[51]

In regard to student accommodations, Calgaard deemed it imperative that the university provide attractive, secure, and well-ordered residential halls. During his initial tours of campus residence halls, Calgaard saw buildings that were run down due to deferred maintenance, theft, and vandalism. He immediately committed financial resources to undertake major residence hall renovations. During the next several summers, physical plant staff and outside contractors repaired, repainted, and refurbished residence hall rooms. The construction of a parking garage and new physical plant facilities added to the functionality of the residential complex.[52]

When Calgaard arrived on campus in the summer of 1979, he encountered a cadre of students who were accustomed to wide-ranging freedom in residence halls and other social venues. The rapid demise of *in loco parentis* during the previous decade and the right to legally consume alcohol at age eighteen had contributed to a campus environment of partying and irresponsible behavior.[53] Contractual security employees were ineffective in identifying and reporting offenders of university regulations, and understaffed student life personnel were unable to enforce existing codes of conduct.[54]

Calgaard severed relationships with the local security agency and established a university security and safety office with its own director and certified peace officers. This move gave the university more control over the quality of its security force and encouraged greater continuity of personnel. By the end of the decade, Trinity had thirty employees on its security and safety staff who provided service twenty-four hours a day, seven days a week, with a budget approaching $900,000 annually.[55]

Along with establishing new security arrangements, Calgaard and Grissom monitored the hiring of an expanded professional residence hall staff and charged them with enforcing rules and regulations, revitalizing the residence hall judicial court, and initiating educational programs to promote responsible social behavior. He interviewed candidates for these positions and emphasized the importance of hands-on supervision of all aspects of residence hall life. If they were not willing and able to enforce university regulations, he advised them to look elsewhere for employment.[56]

At the same time, Calgaard directed the University Standards Committee to formulate new regulations for campus residence halls. The university began requiring students to sign an agreement that outlined their relationship as renters with the institution as landlord. Violations of the agreement could lead to expulsion, probation, or removal from the residence hall. Major offenses included destruction of property or vandalism, refusal to present identification or follow an administrative order, use of fireworks, possession of weapons, indecent or obscene behavior, and unauthorized entry onto university property. According to Grissom, the university based these regulations on three areas of concern: "danger to others or self, infringement on privacy, and degree of blatancy."[57]

The rules also prohibited activities that students had previously taken for granted. They were not allowed to redecorate or paint residence hall rooms and were required to maintain their balconies "in a neat, uncluttered manner," an edict that banned hanging laundry or banners in public view. Residence hall roofs, where students frequently gathered to sunbathe or watch athletic events, were placed off limits. Moreover, beer kegs were no longer permitted in residence hall rooms, hallways, or balconies. Parties had to be registered with the Office of Student Affairs and held in designated areas. Such events could be scheduled only on Friday or Saturday evenings and were subject to a midnight curfew. A similar set of rules covered off-campus parties.[58]

The University Standards Committee also developed guidelines to regulate traditional fraternity and sorority pledging activities that jeopardized the physical safety of students and exposed the university to potential litigation. Previous policy statements such as "any behavior which can do mental or bodily harm" or "which can be offensive to the dignity of an individual" had left considerable room for interpretation.[59] The new guidelines specifically prohibited practices such as "walks" or any form of calisthenics or exercise and the required consumption of any food or substance as part of a pledge program. They were subsequently modified to forbid the wearing of costumes or carrying of paraphernalia that could be construed as sexist, racist, or disruptive.[60]

By 1984 Calgaard deemed the time propitious for Trinity to take steps to become a residential, rather than a mixed residential-commuter, campus community. The trustees approved, requiring all first-year students to live on campus in university residence halls beginning with the 1985–86 academic year. Trustees subsequently extended this to include sophomores (1988) and juniors (1992), with only seniors given the option to live off campus. By the end of the century, approximately 75 percent of Trinity's student body lived on campus.[61] In retrospect, Calgaard considered this decision to be one of the most significant steps undertaken by the board of trustees to reconfigure Trinity's academic image.[62]

Nevertheless, Calgaard encountered opposition from students, parents, and alumni, who viewed the requirements as restrictive, expensive, and exclusionary. Alumni in particular argued that such restrictions would make it fiscally difficult for some local students to attend Trinity and would reinforce the university's long-standing image as a country club school that catered to wealthy families. Calgaard defended his decision by citing the dramatic increase in the university's budget for financial aid and by advising critics not to confuse "residential" with "country club." Trinity's demanding academic environment, he contended, dispelled any residual impressions that students enrolled primarily to socialize rather than to receive an education.[63]

As the number of residential students increased, university trustees commissioned building projects totaling more than $15 million in order to provide adequate accommodations. The student dining hall (renamed Mabee Hall) was renovated and expanded in 1985 and food services were upgraded. Construction of the Verna McLean (1985) and the Dick and Peggy Prassel Residence Halls (1988) raised the number of buildings available to house students on campus to fourteen. In addition, a commitment to improve the quality of residential life resulted in a $6 million renovation and expansion of the Coates University Center in 1987.[64]

Although student recruitment received more national attention, Trinity devoted as much internal energy and effort, as well as considerable resources, to obtaining a diverse faculty of skilled teachers and productive scholars. Calgaard recognized that Trinity had an excellent faculty when he assumed the presidency, but he pointed to heavy teaching loads and the lack of faculty development funds as obstacles to their scholarly production. Now that more resources were available, he expected the faculty to pursue their research interests. He drew a distinction between an atmosphere of "publish or perish" and a context in which teaching faculty members must also be first-rate scholars. This entailed staying abreast of developments within the profession, knowing the literature in one's field of specialization, and communicating such information to students and colleagues.[65]

Calgaard set high standards for faculty recruitment and created incentives to attract an array of outstanding candidates to the Trinity campus. By means of a national search process that involved the participation of tenured department members, deans, the vice president for academic affairs, and the president, Trinity added forty new full-time faculty during a period of declining student enrollment. At the same time, the number of part-time faculty dropped substantially, a trend counter to many peer institutions that were employing adjunct and part-time instructors as a cost-cutting measure.[66]

A low turnover rate of faculty and a highly competitive job market, however, made it difficult to attract minority candidates. In 1984 Trinity had only ten ethnic-minority members (4.3 percent) out of a faculty of 229. Urban studies professor Earl Lewis, Trinity's lone African-American faculty member, described the numbers of minority students and faculty persons as "alarmingly low and declining steadily," and Hispanic sociology professor Edward Murguia observed that the university campus was a place where black and brown faces were visible only among groundskeepers and service crews who were employed to conduct housekeeping chores.[67]

Calgaard realized that Trinity had not made as much progress in recruiting minority faculty as he had desired, but, in a response to Professor Murguia, he noted that the university had achieved some success in hiring a growing number of minority professional and administrative staff members.[68] Moreover, the university was slowly increasing the percentage of women holding faculty positions (43, or 18.8 percent) and had created a standing committee on the recruitment of women and minorities.[69]

Most faculty members hired during the 1980s were young scholars in the early years of their professional careers who were attracted to Trinity by Calgaard's vision of quality undergraduate education. In addition to a commitment to scholarly research and publication, they brought enthusiasm for intellectual interaction with students and a willingness to experiment with new teaching methodologies. Many assumed leadership roles in their departments and in various aspects of campus life. Included among the new faculty were eighteen endowed distinguished professorships. Calgaard had recommended and the trustees had approved the distinguished professor program, viewing it as another means of enhancing Trinity's scholarly reputation in the wider academic world. Representing a variety of disciplines, these senior professors taught undergraduate classes, conducted research, and served on university committees.[70]

During the hiring processes, Calgaard personally interviewed all candidates who visited campus in order to assess their compatibility with Trinity's dual academic emphasis on classroom teaching and scholarly research. Calgaard would also raise the subject of Trinity's relationship with the Presbyterian church to ascertain whether they were comfortable with the university's traditional ties. When queried about whether he scrupulously followed this procedure, he replied, "I am almost certain that nobody got hired at Trinity who wasn't aware of our church relationship. Nobody."[71]

In order to create more equity in evaluating faculty performance, the university developed a system of annual reviews that used explicitly stated criteria and procedures for merit salary increases. Previously, faculty salaries had been based on far fewer formal requirements, and decisions were less obviously related to the performance of faculty members overall.[72] In addition, following a three-year process initiated by students and implemented by the faculty and student senates, the general faculty in 1983 approved university-wide mandatory student evaluations to be used for formative faculty self-improvement and summative merit salary, reappointment, promotion, and tenure purposes.[73]

At about the same time that more participatory and formal evaluation procedures were being developed, Calgaard addressed the issue of faculty compensation. During the decade from 1979 to 1989 the average faculty salary rose from $23,000 to more than $44,000, an increase of more than 90 percent when many small private institutions were freezing salaries or were unable to keep pace with inflation.[74] Calgaard also established a general faculty development program from more than $6.5 million in endowment funds provided by gifts from the Chapman trusts and the estate of Norine R. Murchison. Academic leaves and summer research stipends were awarded to faculty based on recommendations from the department and dean and on evaluations by the Faculty Development Committee (FDC).[75] In order to attract and retain talented, nontenured junior faculty, the university created fifteen junior faculty fellowships that provided renewable summer stipends to facilitate their scholarship and research. At the same time, it allocated funds to departments and deans for further faculty development as well as support for summer workshops.[76]

In a number of departments, Trinity faculty engaged in cooperative research projects with undergraduates in order to develop the students' investigative skills and stimulate their interest in graduate work. An article in the *New York Times*, which focused on the state of undergraduate research in the country, cited Trinity in 1990 for doing effective work with undergraduate students.[77] Among others, faculty in the departments of biology, chemistry, computer science, mathematics, and engineering science worked with students on topics such as immune systems in marsupials, chemical electric transfer systems, mathematical modeling, pollution control and waste management, and cardiovascular system dynamics. A number of Trinity students served as coauthor of published articles with

Mandatory student evaluations of faculty were approved.
The *Trinitonian,* 14 November 1980

their professors and received fellowship grants in recognition of their research expertise.[78]

In 1984 Calgaard announced the establishment of the Z. T. Scott Faculty Fellowship, awarded annually to a faculty member in recognition of his/her excellence in teaching and advising. Funded by a gift from Trinity alumnus Richard M. Kleberg III in memory of his grandparents, the fellowship consisted of cash awards of $5,000 and $3,000 for professional development. Honorees of this continuing award are recognized at brief ceremonies during the spring commencement exercises. The first recipient of the award, Frances Richter Swinny, professor in the Department of Speech and Drama, began her association with Trinity on the Woodlawn campus. Throughout her career, Swinny, combined expertise in the classroom with personal attention to advising, sponsorship of student organizations, and sustained contact with alumni.[79]

To tie Trinity into closer relationships with the community, Calgaard also endorsed and provided financial support for a proposal by John Moore, chair of Trinity's Department of Education, to recognize San Antonio area public school teachers for their outstanding contributions to education. In 1981 the university instituted the Trinity Prize for Excellence in Teaching, funded annually by the university with assistance from the H.E.B. Foundation and the *San Antonio Express-News* and given to two teachers nominated by the various school districts at a ceremony held on the Trinity campus.[80] The Trinity Department of Education also received a renewable grant from the federal government to establish an Upward Bound unit on the Trinity campus. This program, first begun in the 1960s during President Lyndon Johnson's "war on poverty," identifies participants with college potential who are recommended primarily by high school teachers and counselors. Students participate in classes, counseling sessions, and field trips on Saturdays or in a program in which they live on campus for six weeks.[81]

Recognizing the importance of a superior library for undergraduate and faculty research, Calgaard encouraged the board of trustees to make a philosophical and financial commitment to ensure that Trinity's library would become one of the finest undergraduate depositories in the country. A committee chaired by trustee Gilbert M. Denman Jr. urged that $8 million for the purchase of books and periodicals be allocated over and above amounts normally budgeted for acquisitions.[82] As a result, the university raised its annual budget for acquisitions from about $300,000 to $1.2 million, giving Trinity the highest expenditure per student for a library of any non-Ph.D.-granting institution in the country.[83] By the close of the decade, holdings of books and periodicals in the Elizabeth Coates Maddux Library (later renamed the Elizabeth Huth Coates Library) numbered more than 650,000 and were continuing to expand. Because of its extensive collection, the library was utilized not only by members of the Trinity community but by students and faculty from other academic institutions in the area as well as by the general public.[84]

Calgaard authorized other improvement projects in the 1980s that underscored Trinity's academic goals and aspirations. Opening an additional floor of the library added 40,000 square feet of space to provide room for the library's expanding collection of books and periodicals. New laboratory facilities for the Department of Chemistry in the Moody Engineering Building, a suite of offices for the Department of Mathematics in Marrs McLean Science Center, modernization of the Richardson Communication Center, and space for offices and classrooms in the Chapman Graduate Center for the Departments of Business Administration, Economics, and Health Care Administration enhanced the working environment for faculty and students.[85]

In addition to building and renovation projects, two major works of art given to the university by Arthur and Jane Stieren added to the ambiance of the campus. Sculpted by internationally renowned Dame Barbara Hepworth, "A Conversation with Magic Stones," a cluster of metallic shapes on the upper campus south of the library, provided a gathering place for students to study and converse. The second, a Sir Henry Moore sculpture called "Large Interior Form," an improvisational depiction of a woman's femininity, was situated adjacent to the Coates esplanade.[86]

In tandem with efforts to improve the quality of the students, faculty, and facilities, the university engaged in extensive curricular modification. Early on, Calgaard ordered an intensive scrutiny of Trinity's graduate programs to ascertain their relevance to the university's institutional mission. Detailed reports by senior administrators indicated that, with few exceptions, the programs were of poor quality and had been experiencing negative enrollment trends for a number of years. Entrance requirements were vague and not uniformly applied, most students were part-time and often ill prepared for graduate study, and many enrolled in undergraduate classes that required only an additional paper to receive graduate credit.[87]

Based largely on the results of these studies, the faculty voted to eliminate most of the existing master's degree programs. From a high of twenty-two master's degrees offered prior to 1979, the number was reduced to five by the end of the century: the Master of Arts (Education: School Psychology), the Master of Arts in Teaching, the Master of Education (Education: School Administration), and the Master of Science (Accounting and Health Care Administration).[88] A commission on graduate studies attended to curricular matters, and the dean of behavioral and administrative studies, who reported to the vice president for academic affairs, served as administrator of the programs. These changes clarified uncertainties about the future of Trinity's graduate program that had existed for almost two decades and reflected the university's primary commitment to undergraduate education.[89]

In 1983 the faculty embarked on a three-year quest to create a new undergraduate general curriculum. Noting that the previous curriculum had been adopted by a narrow vote and reflected considerable ambivalence among faculty members, committee chair and member of the economics faculty Richard Butler emphasized that the time was appropriate for a comprehensive reconsideration of curricular matters. Calling for a concerted effort to "establish Trinity's intellectual identity," Butler told the faculty assembly that "whatever we do about curriculum will have a great deal to say about Trinity's image to the rest of the world."[90]

After a participatory discussion of theoretical and practical considerations, in the fall of 1985 the Trinity faculty overwhelmingly approved a new common curriculum designed to provide each Trinity student with a basis for understanding the varied dimensions of human knowledge and experience.[91] The curriculum centered on a cluster of "understandings" that emphasized student exposure to eastern and western cultures, epistemology, values, physical and social sciences, and aesthetic experience and artistic creativity. A range of courses gave students a variety of options in fulfilling the understandings.[92]

In addition to the understandings, the new curriculum featured a freshman (later called first-year) seminar and a writing workshop, which was staffed by faculty in the Department of English. The seminar proved to be one of the most successful components of the new curriculum. Taught by faculty from all academic divisions, the seminars were limited to fifteen students and designed around common themes such as "freedom and responsibility" and "progress." An innovative addition to the program was the employment of upper-class students as peer tutors, selected by the Office of Academic Affairs, to assist first-year students in developing skills in speaking, writing, and critical thinking. Other requirements of the new curriculum included modern languages, computer skills, and lifetime sports or fitness requirements.[93]

Beyond the common curriculum, the Trinity faculty produced a number of programmatic changes, including the creation of new departments and courses, the reconfiguration of degree majors, and the elimination of several programs. Supported by university funding, a team of faculty members created the first integrative course in the Trinity curriculum. Offered initially in 1982, the interdisciplinary course "Human Quest: Explorations in Western Culture" was team-taught. Utilizing plenary lecture sessions that employed a variety of multimedia techniques and small group discussions, the course proved to be popular with students. Later, another group of faculty created a parallel "Asian Quest" course that focused similarly on elements of eastern culture.[94]

Responding to the shift in institutional mission, a number of professionally oriented departments reinforced the university's emphasis on a liberal arts curriculum. In 1982 the Department of Urban Studies introduced a new nonprofessional major and minor at the undergraduate level that was designed to acquaint students with the urban environment in which they lived. Courses such as "Religion in the City" and "Urbanism and Social Institutions" taught by historians and sociologists provided a broad interdepartmental perspective.[95] Two years later, the Department of Communication devised a curriculum that provided students with a basis to understand media's impact from a variety of viewpoints. Instead of utilizing traditional industry categories such as broadcast and print journalism, advertising, and public relations, the new curriculum featured four broad areas: media studies and theory, media management and research, media writing, and media production.[96]

When Paul Baker, architect of Trinity's drama program, retired in 1977, the Department of Speech and Drama entered a period of restructuring that lasted more than a decade. Under Baker, the department was weighted toward a professional production-oriented theater program closely affiliated with the Dallas Theater Center. The university subsequently ended its relationship with the Dallas Theater Center, dropped the master's degree in fine arts from its graduate curriculum, and developed a program that featured speech, drama, and forensics components. With Calgaard's support, the department revived Trinity's participation in local, regional, and national debate competitions.[97]

Classical studies entered the Trinity curriculum in 1988 under the leadership of Colin Wells, the T. Frank Murchison Distinguished Professor of Classical Studies. The new department offered interdisciplinary majors in ancient Mediterranean studies, Greek, Latin, and classical languages. Opportunities to participate in archaeological excavations during the summer months gave students hands-on experience with methodology and occasions for intercultural activities. The art history, philosophy, history, political science, religion, sociology and anthropology, and speech and drama departments provided students with a variety of related courses.[98]

Supported by a grant from the National Endowment for the Humanities and additional assistance from the Chapman trust, the Department of Education developed a humanities-centered major for elementary education teachers to help prepare them to fill the many roles of their profession. The new curriculum included eight required humanities courses, a cluster of new humanities courses developed especially for the program, a redesigned set of education courses and requirements, and general electives.[99]

The Department of Education Chair John Moore also instituted a five-year Master of Arts in Teaching degree in 1991 that replaced the traditional sequence of undergraduate teaching methods courses and changed the locus of study from Trinity classrooms to one of six professional development schools in the area. The program required an academic major in the student's selected teaching field and a full year of a teaching internship in a public school setting in addition to classes designed to complement their field experiences and introduce them to educational issues.[100] Ernest Boyer, president of the Carnegie Foundation for the Advancement of Teaching, said that Trinity's program was "one of the most impressive efforts in the nation" in terms of recruiting, training, and renewing teachers.[101]

Following the dedication of the William Knox Holt Continuing Education and Conference Center in 1984, the continuing education program (later called Continuing Education and Conferences and then Conferences and Special Programs), under director Ann Knoebel, increased emphasis on summer conferences that brought numerous visitors and increased revenue to campus. During the summer of 1989, for example, Trinity attracted more than 10,000 people from all fifty states and 120 countries, 7,500 of whom stayed in university residence halls. Groups included the National Conference in Undergraduate Research, World Council of Churches, Officers Advance Course for the United States 5th Army, U.S. Junior Olympics, and the Student Council Conference. These programs not only generated revenue of more than $1 million for the general budget but also served as a recruiting tool in introducing Trinity to many visitors.[102]

Along with the initiatives, Calgaard discontinued a number of programs that he considered inappropriate to the overall institutional mission. One of the first was TRINCO, the university computer operation that, in addition to servicing academic and administrative computing needs on campus, solicited commercial clients. Citing a history of deficit operations, high turnover of professional and operations staff, and general dissatisfaction among campus users of the quality of service rendered, Calgaard engineered a transition from the incorporated TRINCO to a wholly university-funded computer center under the supervision of the Office of Academic Affairs. Hampered by contractual obligations and other legal technicalities, however, the process took five years to reach completion. On 31 December 1985, TRINCO ceased to exist as a corporation, and the Trinity University Computer Center commenced operations.[103]

After careful consideration, the faculty voted to phase out a number of academic programs during the early 1980s, including the homebuilding department and programs in gerontology and solar energy. During the same time frame, the university dropped the May mini-term and condensed the traditional two-semester summer school program into one six-week session.[104] The program that was conducted by the Department of Education in conjunction with nearby Sunshine Cottage to train teachers for hearing-impaired children closed in 1987 after more than a quarter century of operation. Lessening participation in the program among Trinity's elementary education majors was a prominent factor in this decision. About the same time, Trinity ceased to sponsor the Motor Behavior Laboratory directed by Robert Strauss of the Department of Health, Physical Education, and Athletics. Although deemed a valuable community service project, the laboratory had never been fully included in the university's instructional or research programs.[105]

The ROTC program, a university fixture since moving to Trinity Hill in 1952, ceased operations at the close of the 1990–91 academic year. Prompted by a general cutback in the army reserve program throughout the country, the move spelled the end of the Department of Military Science. Trinity students who wished to continue in the military reserve program were given the opportunity to cross-enroll in the Air Force ROTC unit at the University of Texas in San Antonio.[106]

The decade also saw the demise of the Trinity University Press after more than a quarter-century of publishing books and monographs in a variety of scholarly fields. Its publishing opportunities were limited due to a lack of adequate endowment, and Calgaard had ambivalent feelings regarding the appropriateness of maintaining a university press at an institution that was centered primarily on undergraduate education. After postponing closure for several years in hopes that funding could be secured, Calgaard announced that the press would cease operations at the end of the 1988–89 fiscal year.[107]

The rapidity of change over a short period of time that was introduced by Calgaard generated unrest and dissent in virtually all segments of the university community. Summing up her impressions of the 1985–86 academic year, Grissom said, "This was the year for me in which the rapidly changing nature of the Trinity University student body became strikingly clear. It was also the year in which I had to acknowledge the truth of a prediction made by Ronald Calgaard several years ago. 'When the university really becomes what the Board of Trustees and administration have determined it will become, everyone here now won't like it.'"[108]

At times, Calgaard's aggressive leadership style exacerbated campus tensions. Students in particular felt excluded from the university's decision-making processes, especially when new policies impacted directly on their everyday lives. Echoing the sentiments of many of his peers, one student expressed his frustration with "the numerous not-so-subtle changes" that were occurring "too fast, with little consideration for students' input."[109] In a similar vein, other students charged that Calgaard was so intent on building Trinity's image that he had little interest in student participation in campus governance. "There is a profound and accompanying sense of frustration, one of impotence, if you will, that I see and hear among students. Many think and feel, deep down, that regardless of their opinions the university's administration will continue to set policy in what seems a thoughtless, headstrong way."[110]

Trinitonian cartoons frequently reflected student unrest during the 1980s.
Left: 31 January 1986; right: 22 April 1988

Students also complained that Trinity was losing its ambiance as a place where undergraduates had adequate time both for study and socializing. A senior resident assistant lamented the change that had taken place on campus during her four years at Trinity (1980–84). "The focus of the university has shifted, and the atmosphere, once casual, has become competitive." While the quality of students had improved, the new academic ethos had "choked student life," leaving little time for interaction and reflection. "The seniors still try to enjoy life and do well," she said, "while the freshmen simply try to outdo one another."[111]

While Calgaard agreed on the importance of the social environment, he insisted that students should be able to meet the university's academic demands and still find time for nonacademic activities. In response to a student letter, Calgaard wrote, "I believe that the first priority of any quality college or university is to offer demanding academic programs. Academic excellence should and must be the number one priority. This in no way means that the university is unconcerned with the social and personal growth of its students. . . . I believe that the best academic environments exist where students and faculty work very hard and play hard."[112]

Following a succession of unpopular administrative policy decisions involving things such as heightened restrictions on alcohol consumption, increased tuition rates, mandatory residence requirements, and the denial of official status to a gay and lesbian support group, student unrest erupted into a series of protests. In particular, the latter decision evoked heated discussion and debate on campus among students, faculty, and staff.[113] The Student Association conducted an investigation of the sequence of events and concluded that the group had been granted and then unjustly denied official recognition by the administration. Several petitions by the gay support group requesting a reversal of the administrative decision failed to win approval. With the issue of recognition unresolved after almost two years of negotiations, Grissom appointed a task force to study the problem and make recommendations for change.[114]

Before the task force could complete its work, however, students took matters into their own hands. In November 1985, some 150 students representing a variety of campus organizations, along with several professors, gathered in Northrup Hall to confront the trustees who were in session in the boardroom. Bearing a petition signed by 400 students and brandishing signs bearing slogans such as "Is Trinity for the Students or the Trustees?" "Liberal Arts but NOT Liberal Thinking," and "Who's Afraid of the Big Bad Board?," they called for recognition of the gay support group. Given the traditionally quiescent demeanor of Trinity students, the protests stirred the campus and captured the attention of the local media. A reporter described the demonstration as "very cooperative and orderly," and the *Trinitonian* hailed it as welcome sign that Trinity students had finally roused from their extended lethargy.[115]

A few months later, students rallied to protest a revised alcohol policy, designed to be in compliance with state legislation that raised the legal drinking age to twenty-one. Consumption of alcohol on campus was restricted to the rooms of legal-age students in two designated residence halls, and alcohol advertisements were no longer permitted in university publications. Discussion expanded to include objections to an administrative proposal to create several first-year-only residence halls and the university's stance on the gay and lesbian support group. A group of some 200 students converged on administrators' homes on Oakmont, ending up at Calgaard's front door. Calgaard emerged, listened to the complaints, and talked to the students for about half an hour before the group voluntarily dispersed.[116]

To address their concerns, Calgaard initiated monthly forums in which students and administrators engaged in dialogue on campus issues and discussed ways to improve working relationships between the two parties. At the initial forum, Grissom announced that the task force on student organization recognition had developed a policy rationale and proposed a three-tiered configuration of sponsored, recognized, and registered organizations with varying privileges for each group. The gay support group was included in the registered category, consisting of "voluntary associations of students having no special relation with the University except through the Office of Student Affairs."[117] Later reduced to two categories (sponsored and recognized), the policy eventually proved to be a workable system of maintaining a balance between university standards and student autonomy.[118]

In other actions, Calgaard endorsed a proposal by the Student Association to add students as nonvoting members of three trustee committees (Building and Grounds, Religious Life, and Student Affairs), and Grissom awarded a revitalized Student Court more responsibility in handling discipline cases that formerly had been adjudicated primarily by administrators.[119]

Calgaard's administrative style affected his relationships with faculty and staff as well as with students. He could be abrasive, demanding, critical, and, at times, volatile. His temper surfaced on occasions when he encountered what he deemed ignorance, ineptitude, or indolence. Colleagues who periodically experienced his outbursts learned to back off, listen to his impassioned orations, and wait for an opportunity to continue the conversation. Sometimes the tirades would be brief, but not infrequently they would extend over a period of time. The most commonly repeated joke around campus was, "Do you think Calgaard has high blood pressure?" The answer: "No, but he is a carrier."[120]

Once Calgaard decided on a course of action, he was usually unbending to change. Those closest to him knew that if they wished to make a suggestion, they had better have their arguments well in hand and be prepared to answer his penetrating questions. One administrator recalled his first encounter with Calgaard when he stopped by the president's office to suggest a change in admissions procedures that he thought might facilitate recruitment of new students. Launching a barrage of criticisms, Calgaard systematically demolished the proposal, leaving the fledgling administrator shaken and dubious about his future at Trinity. A colleague advised him to accept the encounter as a learning experience. "Never venture a proposal unless you are prepared to stand your ground and defend it vigorously."[121]

Calgaard's zeal to do what he deemed best for Trinity sometimes led to

Sociology professor Edward Murguia protests in support of a gay
and lesbian student group. The *Mirage*, 1986

confrontations with faculty who thought he was acting unilaterally rather
than following established procedures. On one occasion, Calgaard appointed Louis J. (Lou) Fox, former San Antonio city manager, as a visiting professor and acting chair of the Department of Urban Studies (later
the Department of Urban Administration) without a formal search
process. The Faculty Senate thought that the president had overstepped
his presidential authority. In response, Calgaard pointed out that the *University Faculty and Contract Staff Handbook* gave him the power to hire
interim or visiting professors and that he had acted accordingly. Nevertheless, Robert Blystone, chair of the Faculty Senate, termed the action "a
dangerous precedent." He told a student reporter, "Dr. Calgaard has a
very powerful personality, a very strong set of beliefs, and a strong sense
of direction. I sometimes wish he would let the faculty share his vision."[122]

Calgaard and Admissions Director Doodie Meyer clashed in 1987 over
a change in admissions policy instituted by the president. Cognizant that
federal and state funds for student financial aid had been steadily declining and shifting from grants to loans, Calgaard had increased the university's contribution to financial aid almost 700 percent over an eight-year
period. Even so, Trinity was still not able to meet all the financial needs of
every student accepted for admission. Although the National Association
for College Admission Counseling (NACAC) had an official policy of

"need blind" admission, Calgaard decided to adopt a "need-conscious" posture at Trinity. The university would not admit students unless it could fully fund them by means of loans, grants, and scholarships. He directed Meyer to inform families of prospective students that they would need to share with the university in meeting tuition expenses and that Trinity would look at the financial aid circumstances of a small percentage of students, those with relatively weak academic records and very large needs for financial aid (excluding minorities), before making admission decisions.[123]

Citing what she termed "philosophical differences" and "moral and professional considerations," Meyer refused to implement Calgaard's directive and went public with her opposition to the new policy. The ensuing controversy, which students immediately termed "Doodie-Gate," engulfed the university with sustained debate and unfavorable national publicity and resulted in a depleted admissions staff. In January 1988, Calgaard dismissed Meyer as director and other admissions staff resignations quickly followed. Later in the spring, members of the Trinity Admissions Council (TAC) resigned en masse in an expression of support for Meyer, leaving the university admissions program in a state of turmoil.[124] Although the effects did not abate quickly, the admissions office gradually stabilized under new leadership. NACAC subsequently modified its stance on the need-blind admission criterion from a "must" to a "should" status in its "Statement of Principles" and recognized the rights of those with differing judgments.[125]

Despite initiatives to support faculty research and teaching, the rapid change in the composition and quality of the general faculty and administrative staff also resulted in considerable unrest among the faculty. On the one hand, junior members felt that they were being held to higher standards than senior faculty who had been hired when scholarship played a less significant role in merit evaluations. On the other hand, the growing importance of scholarly research and publication created tensions among some senior faculty members who either had difficulty adjusting to new expectations or felt undervalued for their contributions. Perceiving a dichotomy of treatment between B.C. (Before Calgaard) and A.C. (After Calgaard) appointees, longtime faculty complained that many of the newcomers acted as if nothing of significance had been accomplished at Trinity prior to 1979.[126]

Nevertheless, Calgaard earned respect for his informed decisions and exemplary work ethic. Faculty and staff also valued his acknowledgment of their loyalty, hard work, and accomplishments. If he could mete out criticism, he could also dispense praise. During the course of the academic year, Calgaard routinely sent complimentary and supportive handwritten notes to faculty and staff members whose outstanding performance caught his attention. When dealing with personal problems of students, faculty, and staff, Calgaard revealed a side of his personality that was not visible to the wider community. On numerous occasions, he responded sympathetically and constructively to individuals who faced physical, mental, or fiscal problems. In such situations, Calgaard granted exceptions to policy based on the particular circumstances of each case. He quietly granted staff members who had substance-abuse problems leaves for treatment and rehabilitation. When a faculty member left the university without notice and abandoned his spouse and children, Calgaard extended the tuition remission to the children despite no legal obligation to do so. On another occasion, when a spouse of a faculty member was undergoing an experimental treatment not covered by Trinity's medical plan, he authorized an interest-free loan with payments spread out over a period of years. Other faculty members have related how Calgaard counseled them during periods of personal and professional anxiety, listened attentively, and offered support.[127]

Even though student leaders frequently disagreed with presidential policies, they acknowledged Calgaard's openness and willingness to explain the rationale of his decisions. They also appreciated his efforts to improve the quality of campus life by renovating residence halls, upgrading the Coates University Center, and providing funds for social activities. On a personal level, students occasionally had an opportunity to observe that Calgaard's gruff exterior often masked a concern for them as individuals. To cite only one example, his early morning visit to Calvert residents during the trauma of a student suicide evoked an appreciative response from a resident assistant: "I know that the residents of third floor and the remainder of the student body are touched and proud that they have an administrator who cares deeply enough for his students to personally lend his support in time of crisis. I think you've instilled in them the feeling that this school and its staff, from the highest position to the lowest, view the life of each student as a personal responsibility."[128]

Notwithstanding Calgaard's intense administrative style, even those who opposed some of the president's decisions recognized his positive impact on the university's progress toward academic excellence. In a short span of time, Trinity had established a new institutional identity and radiated a spirit of confidence in the future. Robert Blanchard, the chair of the Department of Communication who came to Trinity at the outset of the

Calgaard administration, expressed the feelings of many of his colleagues: "While I've been here, I've seen the relentless and consistent pursuit of a vision to a degree I've never seen in 25 years of higher education."[129]

Beyond the campus, Calgaard received accolades from a variety of sources for his role in the university's meteoric rise in the field of undergraduate education. Selected in 1986 as one of the one hundred most effective college presidents in a poll conducted by the Council for Advancement and Support of Education, Calgaard was cited for his successful pursuit of a well-defined institutional mission. His alma mater, Luther College, and Texas Lutheran College awarded him honorary degrees for his dynamic leadership in elevating Trinity's status locally, regionally, and nationally. A feature article on education in the magazine *U.S. News and World Report* noted Trinity's "dramatic turnaround in the past decade, evolving from what was once considered an educational country club for privileged white suburbanites to one of the nation's most challenging and highly regarded regional universities." The magazine ranked as Trinity the best regional university in the West in the categories of quality of student body and faculty, academic excellence, financial resources, and ability to retain students.[130]

As Calgaard's first decade of leadership drew to a close, some observers speculated that he was ready to move on to other challenges. Calgaard himself on at least one occasion had informed trustees that "in the not too distant future" the time would come for him to explore different career opportunities and for Trinity to have new leadership with new energy and vision.[131] Periodically, he had permitted his name to be considered as a presidential candidate at other educational institutions and had been offered positions at several large universities.[132] After extended conversations with various board members who urged Calgaard to remain at Trinity, he agreed to a renewable four-year contract, but set 1999 as an absolute termination date that would round out a twenty-year Trinity career.[133]

Calgaard has credited the combined efforts of trustees, faculty, and staff with playing significant roles in Trinity's achievements of the 1980s. In particular, he has cited the trustees for their financial commitments to the university and their willingness to take risks in order to attain the goals and objectives of their ambitious agenda. "There are few institutions whose governing boards would be willing to do what we did— shrink the size and scope of the institution at a time when neither were fashionable."[134]

At the same time, he reminded the trustees that much remained to be done. Referring to a *Trinitonian* article from 1988 that urged the administration to continue its pursuit of excellence, Calgaard concluded: "We have come a long way. Together we have made rather enormous progress, but it is no time to rest on our laurels. It is a good time to find out how we can get from where we are to where we might hope to be in all dimensions of life in the institution: the academic life, social life, its concern for quality of life and development of individuals on this campus."[135]

CHAPTER FOURTEEN

ADVANCING TOWARD MATURITY

Trinity's mature years, its truly mature years, are still in the future. This is now, and will be even more in the next decade, one of the truly great undergraduate institutions of higher education in America. Trinity has people who want that to occur, and who are committed to give up their time, their talents, and their treasures to make it possible.

RONALD K. CALGAARD, JANUARY 1999

TEN YEARS OF RAPID CHANGE under Ronald Calgaard had taxed the university community's intellectual, psychological, and physical resources, and many were wary of another such period of institutional transformation. Even the president was not immune from the fatigue that seemed to engulf the campus. Addressing the board of trustees in 1989, Calgaard acknowledged that he looked forward to a time when the university could "work on building traditions instead of working so hard on transitions" and could refine rather than reconstitute its goals and objectives.[1]

Calgaard generally planned to build on previous accomplishments rather than to promote dramatic programmatic and administrative innovation in the 1990s. Most important to him was to continue to recruit and retain excellent undergraduate students and a talented faculty and staff. He proposed that the university maintain the current size of the student body (approximately 2,500) and faculty (about 230) while adding to the endowment, raising the level of financial aid for students, and increasing compensation for faculty and staff. At the same time, he wanted the institution to improve the percentages of minorities on campus in light of the declines experienced in the 1980s.[2]

Along with such goals, Calgaard stressed the importance of what he termed "efforts to build a greater sense of community," a subject that had been on his mind for quite some time.[3] From the outset of his presidency, Calgaard had articulated an essential link between the classroom experience and the wider learning environment, but now he wanted to focus even more attention on building community among students, faculty, and staff. This emphasis would largely influence program choices and the allocation of financial resources during the last ten years of his presidency.

Although academic changes during the 1990s were fewer than in the previous decade, the faculty and administration continued the quest toward excellence in undergraduate education. In 1991 Trinity faculty modified the structure, membership, and procedures of the University Curriculum Council (UCC) in order to increase faculty participation in oversight of the curriculum and to speed up the processes of routine change. Under the new bylaws, the UCC had fewer members, met more frequently, and utilized consent and discussion agendas. It also encouraged individual faculty to participate in curricular decision making, and, accordingly, the Faculty Assembly scheduled more stated meetings in which the faculty could debate curricular issues.[4]

In 1993 the Faculty Senate initiated a standing committee of the university, the Teaching and Learning Committee, in order to assess the general status and needs of teaching and learning. The committee encouraged reflection and discussion regarding ways to improve teaching methodologies by periodically holding seminars and workshops and by inviting innovative educators to share their experiences with Trinity faculty.[5]

The common curriculum continued to govern the undergraduate program but was periodically reevaluated and modified. One such change was the inclusion of an additional three-hour requirement in the area of world cultures, intended to increase Trinity students' familiarity with diversity. Faculty dropped the common-theme approach to the first-year seminar and permitted instructors to select interdisciplinary topics of their own choosing. Other changes provided students with more flexibility in course selection to fulfill their understandings.[6]

Along with adjustments to the common curriculum, Trinity faculty created a number of new programs. By the end of the decade Trinity offered interdisciplinary minors such as American intercultural studies, cognitive science, communication management, environmental studies, international studies, linguistics, medieval studies (later, medieval and Renaissance studies), and women's studies.[7] In 1990 the department of modern languages and literatures introduced courses in Chinese and Japanese language, literature, and culture. Chinese studies eventually developed into an academic major with courses cross-listed in history, philosophy, and religion.[8] In 1996 the university inaugurated the Languages Across the Curriculum program, a group of one-hour courses on specialized subjects taught in a language other than English. Professors in several departments, including communication, economics, history, modern languages and literatures, and sociology and anthropology taught courses listed under international studies. Some of the first courses offered were "La económica mexicana (The Mexican Economy)," "Perspectivas Contemporáneas de América Latina (Latin American Perspectives)," and "La telenovela en América Latina," in which students learned about Mexican culture through the medium of Mexican televison soap operas.[9]

Study abroad and international studies programs became an increasingly important component of the university's curriculum. Under the leadership of George Boyd, dean of humanities and arts and director of study abroad, and Nancy Ericksen, study abroad counselor, Trinity entered into a number of consortia that enabled students to study abroad in all disciplines and in many different languages and countries. Participation increased from 38 students in 1981–82 to 200 by 1999–2000.[10] The International Studies Program, created in 1986 out of the preceding International and Comparative Studies Program, shifted its orientation from the social sciences to language and culture. Under the supervision of history professor Donald Clark, the program received funds from the president for faculty summer seminars on internationalization, Confucianism, and a traveling seminar to Mexico City.[11]

Some first-year seminars, as well as courses in sociology, psychology, and religion, facilitated student learning outside the traditional classroom setting by incorporating local fieldwork experiences into the syllabus. Education majors participated in service projects at local public schools. Field trips to the Texas-Mexico border and to interior sites also gave students first-hand opportunities to become better informed about contemporary social, economic, and political issues affecting the Hispanic population in the United States and Mexico.[12]

A growing number of professors employed group projects as a major component of their undergraduate courses. Divided into teams, students conducted research on specified topics, prepared class presentations, and wrote papers describing their projects, requiring organizational and group dynamic skills.[13] Business administration professor Philip Cooley offered a student-managed investment fund that provided upper-division students the opportunity to administer an actual investment portfolio. Utilizing $500,000 allocated by Trinity's board of trustees, students voted by secret ballot on proposed purchases or sales of stocks, and each decision required a two-thirds majority.[14]

Faculty continued to have opportunities for research and publication funded by university stipends and academic leaves. Calgaard insisted, however, that these programs were not entitlements and that they be based on peer-evaluated proposals and produce quantifiable results. Citing problems relating to inadequate common curriculum course offerings and excessive employment of part-time replacements, he limited funded academic and administrative leaves to 10 percent of the full-time faculty. The Faculty Senate objected to this restriction, contending that curricular needs were being met and that part-time replacements represented no serious fiscal burden. Although discussions continued up to the time of Calgaard's retirement, the policy remained unchanged.[15]

Strongly supported by Calgaard and Vice President for Academic Affairs Ed Roy, Trinity became a member of the Associated Colleges of the South (ACS) in 1992, formed the previous year by a consortium of liberal arts institutions located in twelve southern states.[16] Following early efforts to improve the quality of international program offerings, the ACS broadened its scope to include activities such as seminars and projects for faculty enrichment, staff development activities, and cooperation in environmental studies. A $1.5-million grant from the Andrew W. Mellon Foundation in 1995 enabled the ACS to assist faculty in making more effective use of technology in the classroom by sponsoring workshops on programs in archaeology, calculus, chemistry, classics, economics, and humanities. In 1996, aided by another Mellon grant, the ACS created the Palladian Alliance, an electronic virtual library program that allowed students and faculty access to an expanded set of indices and periodicals.[17]

Although Trinity's full-time faculty size remained fairly constant, its composition altered as a large number of senior faculty members retired, some because of personal choice and some with incentives. The first group of retirements occurred in the spring of 1991 when ten faculty members ended their teaching careers.[18] Between 1997 and 2000, twenty-four senior faculty members left the university.[19]

Despite periodic fluctuations in enrollment, Trinity continued to attract talented students who excelled in the classroom and participated in extracurricular activities. The average SAT scores remained steady at approximately 1200 (1275 after "recentering" in 1996), and 48 percent of the class that entered in 1998 was in the top 10 percent of their high school class. After graduation, approximately 40 percent of Trinity students entered graduate and professional programs at home or abroad.[20] In 1996 Trinity senior Ana Unruh, a chemistry major and geosciences minor, became the first Trinity student to be designated a Rhodes Scholar and studied at Oxford University in England.[21]

In terms of racial-ethnic diversity, Trinity's minority enrollment in the 1990s held steady at approximately 20 percent, a figure that compared favorably with most of its peer institutions.[22] This was achieved despite a ruling in 1996 by the 5th U.S. Circuit Court of Appeals (Hopwood vs. Texas) that the University of Texas at Austin School of Law could not consider race in admissions decisions to maintain diverse enrollment or to remedy past discrimination.[23] Although the Hopwood case did not involve private colleges and did not address the issue of minority scholarships, Trinity lawyers advised the administration that it would be prudent to suspend them rather than face a multimillion-dollar court challenge. Other leading private universities in Texas took the same actions.[24]

During the 1990s, Student Association leaders lobbied to add the category of sexual orientation to the university's antidiscrimination policy, which was contained in the "Joint Statement on Rights and Freedoms of Students." Despite support from the general faculty, administrators and trustees rejected the change.[25] Calgaard argued that because federal law did not require the inclusion of sexual orientation, its presence in the joint statement would make the university vulnerable to litigation. If challenged, the university would be required to produce information it did not possess and would not want to collect. In lieu of such a policy, trustees voted in 1997 to reaffirm the inclusion of sexual orientation in the university's harassment policy and to include it in Trinity's recruiting and admissions literature as well as in the *Student Handbook*.[26] In the same year, the university began to include the names of domestic partners in the directory of faculty, staff, and students published annually by the Office of Public Relations.[27]

In response to student and faculty requests, Calgaard officially sanctioned a celebration of Martin Luther King Jr. Day in 1997. Rather than declare a holiday from classes, the university sponsored a week of activities to honor the civil rights leader. Clarence Page, Pulitzer Prize–winning and nationally syndicated columnist with the *Chicago Tribune*, was the keynote speaker. Page discussed the legacy and relevance of King's teaching. Other events included a campus march patterned after the Birmingham march, readings and skits on the Coates esplanade by the Trinity University Players, and movies. The following year, civil rights activist Julian Bond addressed a capacity audience in Laurie Auditorium.[28]

Religious diversity also flourished on campus during the 1990s. Surveys of religious preferences of first-year students conducted during the decade indicated that Trinity students came from a variety of religious backgrounds. In 1996 approximately 25 percent were Roman Catholic and 30

Keynote speaker Julian Bond
at Martin Luther King Jr.
celebration

percent were Protestant (Baptist, Episcopalian, Lutheran, Methodist, Presbyterian, and United Church of Christ). Other Christian traditions with
adherents among the student body were Eastern Orthodox and the Latter-
day Saints (Mormons). Also represented were members of Buddhist, Mus-
lim, and Jewish faiths who established campus support groups and sponsored various religious and cultural events. A growing number of Trinity
students (17 percent) indicated that they had no religious preference, a
trend reflected in national studies as well.[29]

Diversity impacted religious studies as well as student composition. In
the early 1960s, the Department of Religion was staffed by five men, all
ordained Presbyterian ministers who taught required Bible courses and a
few electives that dealt almost exclusively with the Christian religion,
trained professionals in the field of Christian education, and counseled
students who planned to attend theological seminaries. Presently, the department has only one ordained member and includes male and female
scholars of varied backgrounds with expertise in fields such as South and
East Asian religions, Islam, and the psychology of religion. The department now offers a wide range of courses in the academic study of religion
designed to enable students to deepen their understanding of various religious traditions.[30]

In the area of fiscal affairs, Calgaard continued to implement a detailed
line-item budget based on a system of projecting revenues and maintain-

ing tight controls on expenditures that virtually eliminated the university's debt burden. Under the scrutiny of the board of trustees, the university's professional investment managers continued to increase the value of university-controlled endowment funds.[31] Although Calgaard initially had contemplated a second major capital campaign in the 1990s, he chose instead to focus on targeted fund-raising projects such as building renovations, campus expansion, scholarship and chapel endowment, and information technology enhancement.[32]

Several major physical plant renovations were completed, and a schedule of preventative maintenance closely followed during the last decade of the century. In 1989, the trustees authorized the expenditure of $15 million to transform the Earl W. Sams Center into a comprehensive athletic and recreational complex. Renovated and refurbished at a cost of $5.1 million dollars in 1995, the Marrs McLean Science Center housed the offices, classrooms, and laboratories of the departments of mathematics, geosciences, and physics, as well as an instructional biology laboratory and several chemistry research laboratories. Completion of the first floor of the Maddux Library in 1997 provided space for instructional media services, a computer laboratory, an electronic classroom, microfilm readers, and additional bookshelves.[33]

Made possible by a contribution of $3.2 million from Trinity benefactors Jane and Arthur Stieren, Theater One in the Ruth Taylor complex underwent extensive renovation, including a new sound and light system, an orchestra pit, and an expanded seating capacity of 500. Dedicated and renamed the Jane and Arthur Stieren Theater in April 1999, the facility serves as a site for both drama offerings and other public gatherings.[34]

For several years, university trustees explored the possibilities of either renovating Northrup Hall or erecting a new administration building and classroom complex. After a series of studies, the board decided to raze Northrup Hall and replace it with a new structure estimated to cost between $15 and $20 million. Given the proximity of Calgaard's retirement and the need to develop a comprehensive master plan for the building, the board eventually specified that construction would not begin until a new president was in place and funding had been secured.[35]

To ensure the ongoing operation of the religious life programs on campus, Calgaard initiated a financial campaign to create an endowment for the Margarite B. Parker Chapel.[36] In 1999 he announced that $4 million had been raised to support the position of chaplain, the maintenance of the Parker Chapel, and the continuance of an active program. The Chapman Foundation, the estate of Bishop Everett T. Jones, and gifts from trustees, alumni, and friends of the university supplied substantial sums.[37]

In the area of information technology, Trinity made notable progress despite concerns by the president regarding its applicability to personalized undergraduate education. He feared an excessive dependence on computers, often saying that if Trinity substituted "high tech" for "high touch," the university would diminish interaction between the faculty and staff and the students and their families.[38] While many professionals viewed cell phones and laptops as vital aids, Calgaard eschewed such technological paraphernalia. His presidential office contained neither a desktop computer nor a typewriter. Instead, he communicated in pencil or pen on lined notepads and relied on the secretarial staff to transfer his longhand into readable print. Underlined among the qualifications for potential members of the president's staff was the sentence, "Must be able to read the president's handwriting."[39]

Associate Vice President for Academic Affairs Charles (Chuck) White played a key role in promoting the advancement of information technology at Trinity. Working closely with staff member Lawrence (Larry) Gindler, later director of the computing center, White wished to replace the university's mainframe computer system with a more flexible network of interactive personal computers.[40] When a decision was made in 1991 to wire the campus with fiber optic cable to accommodate a new telephone system, White and Gindler lobbied successfully to increase the cable capacity so that it could handle future information technology needs. Calgaard excluded residence halls from the project, however, citing expense factors and computer security concerns as major obstacles.[41]

In 1992, as Trinity prepared to move into the new century, Calgaard appointed a special committee to study the university's technology needs. Chaired by White, the Computing 2000 Committee developed a unified strategy for technological development that envisioned a campus fully equipped to cope with the new information age.[42] Influenced by the report, Calgaard extended the lower campus project to wire all residence hall rooms with cable television, telephone, and Internet connections. With his endorsement, the university trustees committed $1.4 million to bring modern technology to the entire campus in time for the opening of the 1996–97 academic year.[43] Coleen Grissom lightheartedly took some credit for the president's decision. "I finally got a metaphor across to him that made sense. I told him that cable TV to these students was like indoor plumbing to my generation."[44]

With the cable network in place, information technology continued to make advances as the decade drew to a close. The final stages of the transfer from a mainframe to a distributed computing environment were completed in 1997. At that time, White reported that Trinity had 930 personal computers on campus in faculty offices, laboratories, and administrative offices. The new system enabled the university to integrate all of the data from admissions, financial aid, fiscal affairs, and the registrar and facilitated the expansion of electronic classrooms. By 1998 thirteen such classrooms allowed professors to utilize Internet resources and produce multimedia presentations.[45]

While the advancement of Trinity's academic profile continued to be a high priority, Calgaard channeled a great deal of energy into his efforts to promote the enhancement of campus community. His interest reflected trends in undergraduate higher education that were emerging during the late 1980s. A study by Ernest L. Boyer, for example, conducted under the auspices of the Carnegie Foundation for the Advancement of Teaching and released in 1987 generated widespread discussion among college administrators and faculty. Among other problems, Boyer identified a great separation between academic and social life on campuses despite lip service given to the importance of the campus as a community.[46]

In a convocation address in 1993, Calgaard referred several times to Boyer's book when discussing his understanding of Trinity's mission. Emphasizing the importance of liberal education in the context of a residential community, Calgaard affirmed that what went on in residence halls, on playing fields, and in extracurricular activities were all part of the learning experience. "In this community," he said, "as we learn to live together, although we come from varied backgrounds, different socio-economic circumstances, different races and cultures, we begin in this small place to do what must be done to build some sense of community, to build some respect for others."[47] In what he termed "a participation model," Calgaard envisioned a residential campus where faculty, staff, and students frequently shared common experiences at lectures, concerts, athletic events, and other social gatherings and engaged in social and civic activities in the wider San Antonio community.[48]

The Calgaards diligently modeled his conception of community. There were few activities on the university's calendar that they missed, especially theater productions, music recitals, lectures, and athletic contests, as well as countless other academic and social occasions. Both Ron and Genie Calgaard were also active in local civic and national professional organizations.

His involvements included service as a trustee or member of the advisory councils of the Southwest Research Institute, the San Antonio Art Institute, San Antonio Symphony, San Antonio Education Partnership, San Antonio Holocaust Commission, San Antonio World Trade Association, Texas Military Institute, University of Texas Health Science Center, and the Higher Education Council of San Antonio. In 1996 he was the first university president to head the San Antonio and Bexar County United Way Annual Campaign and continued to serve on its board and executive committee. Calgaard was an ordained elder at First Presbyterian Church, served on the session, taught church school classes, and handled key committee assignments.

Beyond the local community, Calgaard acquired a reputation as a resourceful leader possessed with exceptional management skills and fundraising abilities. During his Trinity presidency, Calgaard served on national educational boards such as the American Association for Higher Education, Association of American Colleges and Universities, Association of Governing Boards, Association of Presbyterian Colleges and Universities, the American Council on Education, the National Endowment for the Humanities, the Institute of European Studies, and the World Affairs Council.[49]

Genie Calgaard maintained a high profile in San Antonio, serving on boards and agencies such as the Southwest Foundation Auxiliary and the Cancer Center Council and as an ordained deacon at First Presbyterian Church, where she was actively involved in the church's pastoral care program.[50] Her commitment and her service to the Trinity community led the board of trustees, at the initiative of William Bell, to appoint her as a special assistant to the board in 1987 and provide her with an annual stipend, marking the first time in university history that a presidential spouse had been so recognized.[51]

Cognizant of the role that intercollegiate athletics could play in fostering school spirit and traditions, Calgaard reassessed Trinity's athletic program and its contribution to the university's overall mission. He determined that the institution would have an intercollegiate athletics program that did not offer scholarships and would seek entry into an athletic conference composed of peer academic institutions. This decision spelled the end of Division I tennis, Trinity's only scholarship sport, bringing to a close a tradition that had endured for more than four decades. Using the financial resources then devoted to tennis, along with additional funding, Calgaard developed a competitive athletic program that could attract the interest and support of the campus community.[52]

The decision to terminate Trinity's participation in NCAA Division I tennis evoked a storm of protest from students, athletes, and alumni and generated considerable interest in the local print and television media. An angry crowd of students greeted university trustees who were assembling for the board meeting in October 1990 to vote on the issue, pelted them with tennis balls, and chanted, "Rights are rights and Ron is wrong." Despite a petition signed by 900 students protesting the action, the board of trustees unanimously supported Calgaard's recommendation to abolish scholarship tennis. Male and female students currently holding scholarships were given three choices: (1) keep their scholarships at Trinity but not play tennis; (2) give up their athletic scholarships and continue playing tennis at Trinity; or (3) transfer to another university.[53]

Trinity joined the College Athletic Conference (CAC) and began participating in a number of sports during the 1989–90 season. At the time, the CAC consisted of Rhodes College, Centre College, Fisk University, the University of the South (Sewanee), Millsaps College, and Trinity. The conference initially had only male sports, but Calgaard spearheaded a movement to include female sports in the total program. In 1991 the conference changed its name to the Southern Collegiate Athletic Conference (SCAC) and granted the men's and women's teams of the member universities equal opportunities to compete for conference championships.[54]

Under the leadership of Athletic Director Gene Norris and his successor, Robert (Bob) King, who came to Trinity from Millsaps College in 1993, the university expanded its athletic program to include eighteen sports. The women's programs featured basketball, cross country, golf, soccer, softball, swimming and diving, tennis, track and field, and volleyball. In men's sports, Trinity fielded teams in baseball, basketball, cross country, football, golf, soccer, swimming and diving, tennis, track and field. Other offerings included intramurals, recreation programs for faculty, staff, and students, club sports, and cheerleader and dance team programs.[55]

The renewed emphasis on intercollegiate athletics as well as the institution's academic standards had major implications for the university's physical education program. In the past, student-athletes tended to concentrate on physical education, but the current group was spread out among the academic majors. Faculty members of the Department of Physical Education had formerly also served as athletics coaches. As Trinity expanded its intercollegiate athletics program, coaches who were hired became professional contract staff who taught activity courses in the department in addition to their coaching assignments.[56]

Along with improving the quality of intercollegiate athletics and intramurals, Calgaard wished to create more recreational facilities. He envi-

Students protesting
end of NCAA
Division I tennis

sioned expanding the campus southward to embrace a six-acre residential
area bounded by Kings Court, Mulberry, and Ancona Avenues. Through
the services of a local real estate agent, the university purchased property
in the neighborhood over a period of time. By the spring of 1986, Trinity
had acquired sufficient real estate to create a recreational green space for
the expansion of the school's playing fields and intramural activities.[57]

For a time, it appeared that the south campus project might never become a reality. When the university announced its intention to remove approximately thirty homes to make room for athletic fields, residents of the
Monte Vista Historical District mobilized to oppose the plan. Accusing
Trinity of having a "robber baron mentality," some Monte Vista constituents said that the project would "massacre the neighborhood."[58] The
controversy between the university and the Monte Vista residents dragged
on for more than a year before the San Antonio Historical Review Board
approved the proposed athletic complex in December 1988. Trinity agreed
to move a number of houses to new locations and accepted restrictions on
future expansion in the neighborhood for a period of twenty-five years.[59]

Nevertheless, a lone homeowner refused to sell his property to the university unless it would meet his asking price of almost a half million dollars. When negotiations reached an impasse, Calgaard pressed forward
with an alternative plan for a smaller recreational area that left the house
intact but isolated on a cul-de-sac. Faced with this reality, the homeown-

er capitulated and enabled Trinity to proceed with its plans for a comprehensive recreational area.[60]

At ceremonies held on 4 October 1990, university officials dedicated the lower campus addition, which was funded by the Houston Endowment Inc. and named in honor of Houston philanthropist, Jesse H. Jones. The centerpiece of the $11-million project was the Meadows Pavilion, which was surrounded by a softball diamond, a soccer field, basketball courts, a sand volleyball court, intramural fields, and a jogging trail.[61]

In 1992 Trinity opened the William H. Bell Athletic Center, a state-of-the-art athletic complex named in appreciation of trustee William H. Bell, an enthusiastic supporter of the new athletic program. The 185,000–square-foot structure, erected at a cost of $15 million, contained two gymnasiums, racquetball and squash courts, a fitness center, a training room, a dance and aerobics studio, classrooms, meeting rooms, offices, and a natatorium. In addition, the university added outdoor athletic fields and a new track and field facility and renovated the baseball, football, and softball fields and the outdoor swimming pool.[62]

In short order, the rejuvenated athletic program began to show positive results in terms of team victories, school spirit, and student retention. After winning their first-ever SCAC championships in the spring of 1992 in men's and women's tennis, the Tigers were victorious in six different sports and captured the SCAC President's Trophy that was awarded annually to the school with the best overall conference sports record. Trinity continued to win conference championships over the next several seasons and moved to another level of success in the 1997–98 school year when seven sports advanced to the NCAA Division III Playoffs. During the next two years, Trinity teams increased their participation in the postseason by sending fourteen teams to various levels of NCAA playoffs and placed among the top ten in the Sears Cup, a National Association of College Directors of Athletics (NACDA) ranking of the most successful Division III sports programs in the nation. To culminate the 1999–2000 season, the men's and women's tennis teams became the first teams in Division III history to win national tennis titles in the same season.[63]

While realizing these achievements, retention and graduation rates were higher among student-athletes than those of the general student population, and student-athletes' grade point averages were comparable. A study conducted during the 1999–2000 athletic season, one of the most successful seasons in school history, revealed that the grade point average of the student-athlete population differed by less than one-tenth of a percent from that of the general student population. Trinity also placed 103

The Calgaards entertaining

student-athletes on the SCAC academic honor roll, more than any other conference school. Between 1995 and 2001, sixteen male and female athletes received NCAA postgraduate scholarships (worth $5,000 each) in recognition of their academic accomplishments.[64]

Calgaard also recognized the role that Trinity alumni could play in developing a wider sense of community by maintaining close ties with the university. To facilitate contacts, he increased the professional staff in the alumni office and provided it financial resources. He initiated the reconstitution of the National Alumni Board, which reactivated the Distinguished Alumnus Award, an alumni chapter system, and an alumni weekend. Ron and Genie Calgaard regularly attended the annual Waxahachie Alumni/ae Reunion and formed close relationships with the participants.[65]

On a more personal level, the Calgaards held social events to encourage a spirit of community. Throughout the school year, they hosted groups of faculty and staff and their spouses or guests for informal dinners in their Oakmont residence, allowing opportunities for social interaction not always possible during the regular workday.[66] At the beginning of the school year, new faculty and staff and their respective department chairs and supervisors attended a welcome dinner in the Great Hall of the Chapman Center following a social hour in the president's home. Tenure and promotion recipients were similarly honored toward the end of the school year. In addition, the Calgaards annually hosted a Sunday brunch for retired faculty and staff at which the president updated participants on developments at the university and provided an opportunity for discussion.[67]

Other events brought the university community into contact with students, parents, and campus visitors. Every year, the Calgaards held an open house for new students and their parents, greeting each family personally as they entered their home. At this occasion, faculty and staff were also invited to greet the newcomers and answer questions. To facilitate social mixing at graduation ceremonies, Calgaard moved the time of the spring commencement from Saturday evening to Saturday morning. The graduate commencement took place at 9:00 A.M. and the undergraduate ceremonies at 10:30 A.M. After these events, a catered lunch was held at the Bell Athletic Center for the graduates and their families, as well as faculty and staff.[68]

Another Calgaard innovation was the creation of the SuperFund, an annual grant of $25,000 to be used at the discretion of Vice President Grissom to encourage a sense of community and to celebrate multiculturalism.[69] During its first year of operation (1987–88), the fund supported parties, dances, and symposia and enabled student leaders to attend various student leadership conferences. It also funded Black History Month, senior disorientation, all-school study breaks, and paid for an outdoor sand-filled volleyball court and barbecue grills on the south campus recreational area.[70] According to Director of Student Activities Peter Neville, Trinity's SuperFund elicited widespread appreciation of the generous financial support for student programs among his colleagues at other universities.[71]

An annual service award ceremony followed by a reception acknowledged the contributions of all Trinity employees with fifteen, twenty, twenty-five, and more years of service.[72] A special award recognized individuals for outstanding accomplishments in their areas of expertise. The Rhea Fern Malsbury Memorial Award, named in honor of Fern Malsbury, who served as the assistant to presidents Wimpress, Thomas, and Calgaard, was given annually to a contract staff member in recognition of "initiative and creativity in resolving difficulties and in improving services, and positive and wide ranging contributions to enhancing the quality of life throughout the University community." The first recipient of the award in 1990 was Pedro D. Vasquez Sr., event and delivery supervisor in the physical plant services. Vasquez was known throughout the Trinity community for his responsibility, efficiency, and cooperative spirit.[73]

Levi "Knock" Knight

The Helen Heare McKinley Classified Employee Excellence Award established in 1998 recognized university employees for their "exemplary attitude, innovation, and work ethic." The donor, who had attended Trinity at Waxahachie and San Antonio, stipulated that the award be given personally by the president at an informal ceremony in his office. The first recipient was Patricia Cardenas, who had served as senior secretary in the Department of Modern Languages for more than twenty years.[74]

Calgaard also originated the idea of a Hall of Fame to honor former Trinity athletes at ceremonies held annually during Alumni Weekend. He hoped that the occasion would help to link past generations of student-athletes with their contemporary counterparts. At the inaugural event in 1999, Trinity honored former coaches Clarence Mabry (tennis) and Houston Wheeler (baseball); former tennis players Bob McKinley, Dick Stockton, Anne Smith, and Chuck McKinley (deceased); Alvin Beal and Obert Logan (football), Larry Jeffries (basketball), and Todd Bender (trap and skeet).[75] The accomplishments of each honoree are noted on special plaques mounted on the Hall of Fame wall in the Bell Athletic Center.[76]

In addition to Clarence Mabry, the only other non-Trinity graduate presently in the Hall of Fame is Levi "Knock" Knight, who served as an athletic trainer for more than thirty-five years. Knight was one of the first African-American trainers to work at a predominantly white university when he joined the Trinity staff in 1946. Skilled in his profession, Knight was also a counselor and confidant to generations of Trinity students who appreciated his wisdom, sincerity, and humanity. When Knight died in 2001, former Trinity athlete and present university trustee Walter Huntley expressed his gratitude for Knight's influence: "It is very difficult to quantify Knock's contributions to Trinity and to the people there. They're immeasurable."[77]

Other programs initiated in the 1990s related to Trinity employees and the wider community. A new health plan, Trinity University Voluntary Employee Benefit Association (VEBA), became operative in 1990, giving individuals more flexibility in the selection of physicians and hospitals. In 1992 Trinity received a grant from the National Fitness Campaign under the sponsorship of Santa Rosa Hospital to help reduce the incidence of cardiovascular disease. Administered by personnel services staff, the program emphasized a holistic approach to the concept of wellness that encouraged employees to become actively involved in achieving total fitness. Included in its offerings were brown bag seminars, exercise activities, medical screenings, and newsletters and bulletins.[78]

Trinity's music program served as a vehicle for integrating Trinity with the San Antonio community. With Calgaard's support, the Department of Music under the chairmanship of Andrew Mihalso held its first annual Christmas concert in 1994, an event that featured the wind symphony, handbell choir, Trinity choir, chapel choir, and the symphony orchestra in a program of Christmas music. Admission was free and open to the public, and from its inception the concert drew capacity crowds. The concert continues as one of Trinity's community traditions.[79]

Late in the 1990s, Calgaard commissioned music professor Timothy Kramer to create a new version of the university's alma mater. The former alma mater had not been sung at campus events since the early 1960s, and Kramer sought to create a song that had "vitality but a singable melody." His revised version took its impetus from the Trinity bell peal conceived by composer William Thornton, former chair of the department of music. "We Sing to Thee" was first performed publicly in February 1999 by the university choir at the annual president's dinner honoring the Trinity Associates.[80]

With reluctance, in 1994 Calgaard terminated the all-university opening academic convocation, which he had begun early in his presidency. Originally an evening event and later shifted to a morning setting, Calgaard wanted the convocation to introduce a note of academic pageantry and intellectual reflection at the beginning of the school year. The event, however, failed to capture the interest either of students or faculty in sufficient numbers to warrant its continuation.[81]

The *Trinitonian*, 31 October 1980

In concert with presidential initiatives, Grissom and her staff devoted time and resources to encourage community building within the student body. Their efforts took place in the context of sustained tensions between administrators and students primarily in regard to issues of freedom and responsibility. Adversarial relationships, which dated back to the previous decade, impacted negatively on the development of shared goals and mutual understanding.[82]

When the Gulf War erupted in 1991, several Trinity students displayed flags on their balconies to show support for the coalition forces in Iraq. Initially, Grissom was unwilling to make an exception to the balcony policy, citing a concern that the display of flags could become a source of divisiveness on campus. Subsequently, however, after seeking student opinion on the subject, she permitted flags and banners to be displayed either in support of or in opposition to the war.[83]

In response to the growing AIDS crisis, Trinity adopted guidelines affirming that AIDS victims or carriers should not be excluded from social, educational, or cultural activities and emphasized the importance of ongoing AIDS awareness education.[84] Although the guidelines advocated the

The *Trinitonian,* 21 April 1989

use of condoms as an effective method of disease prevention, they contained no provision for making them available on campus. Grissom maintained that the university had no legal, moral, or ethical responsibilities to distribute condoms and questioned the feasibility of selling them in the university bookstore.[85] Students and administrators debated the issue of condom distribution for several years, with the Student Association pressing university officials to make condoms available on campus either for sale or *gratis.* In 1993 the administration agreed to distribute condoms free of charge at the health service dispensary, with funding coming from private donations rather than university accounts. Students requesting condoms for the first time were required to meet with a registered nurse and receive information about safe-sex practices.[86]

An administrative decision to heighten university oversight of campus publications in 1991 evoked charges of censorship and violations of the joint statement from the Student Association. In particular, association leaders objected to changes in funding procedures and to the appointment of a professional advisor to work with the *Trinitonian* and *Mirage* staffs. In support of the new guidelines, Calgaard acknowledged student concerns about censorship but argued that there was a greater danger of student editors acting irresponsibly without guidance and supervision. Student fears about censorship subsided as the new advisor, Vickie Ashwill, helped staff members to improve the professionalism and quality of the publications without editorial interference.[87]

By far the most troubling issue for administrators, as in previous decades, was how to address the illegal consumption and abuse of alcohol by Trinity students. Despite thoughtful planning and ample publicity, alcohol-free activities on campus failed to attract many students, who tended to congregate at unsupervised off-campus parties where drink was readily available to everyone regardless of age.[88] The student affairs staff sponsored educational programs to promote respect for the law and moderation in alcohol consumption and encouraged student organization leaders to take more responsibility for group behavior. Offenders were disciplined through the Student Court with punishment meted out according to the severity and extent of the violations.[89]

The preponderance of alcohol infractions had been associated with unofficial and unregulated off-campus parties sponsored by university fraternities and sororities. A series of incidents during the late 1980s involving hazing and alcohol resulted in brawls and injuries. In 1987 Grissom disbanded the Bengal Lancers for a year after an accident in which two men were injured during initiation rites.[90] During the same year, she placed the Triniteers (or Teers) on restricted status for the remainder of the spring semester for an alcohol violation at an off-campus pre-rush party.[91] Two years later, the same group was again placed on probation when a pledge dressed in a Nazi costume as part of pledge activities, which triggered a negative response from the Trinity and San Antonio communities.[92]

The situation worsened in 1991 when a Triniteer pledge died in an automobile accident on his way to a fraternity retreat. Prior to the accident, the group had allegedly held a party where members consumed two half-kegs of beer. Grissom revoked the organization's charter, canceled all pledge activities for the year, and instituted a permanent ban on pledging. In a letter to fraternity and sorority leaders, she emphasized the administration's intention to hold them accountable for following university rules: "No activity that has even the hint of intimidating or threatening a student with ostracism, mental stress, shame, or humiliation will be tolerated."[93]

Subsequent incidents of alcohol violations and altercations between members of different fraternities caused administrators to consider disbanding all Greek organizations. Concerted efforts by Grissom and the student affairs staff, however, helped the groups re-evaluate their activities and make them more consonant with the university's mission.[94] By means of new organizational structures and revised orientation programs, traditional pledging practices were de-emphasized and educational and integrative activities were encouraged.[95]

Despite ongoing administrative-student tensions, many Trinity undergraduates showed an increasing awareness of the importance of community building. The inauguration of Volunteer Awareness Week (VAW) in 1989 marked the beginning of concerted efforts by TUVAC and other service groups to rekindle the social responsibility that had declined during the 1980s.[96] In 1992, 500 students volunteered more than 1,000 hours in a seven-day period, rebuilding homes and recycling products. Reporting that during the previous year Trinity students had donated nearly 17,000 hours to service projects, TUVAC Director Drew Scheberle concluded, "So don't let anyone tell you that Trinity students are apathetic."[97]

Throughout the decade, TUVAC volunteers participated in many programs in the San Antonio community. More than 500 students were involved in programs such as the children's shelter, elderly visitation, juvenile detention, and the Bridge, a halfway house for teenagers. Others were active in newly established programs assisting AIDS victims at the San Antonio AIDS Foundation, the homeless at the San Antonio Metropolitan Ministry, battered women at the Women's Shelter, and mentally challenged young people (Best Buddies).[98]

Other student organizations cooperated with TUVAC in various activities in addition to their own service projects. The 100-member Trinity chapter of Alpha Phi Omega (APO), a national coed service fraternity, held an annual blood drive for the Bexar County Blood Bank and supported organizations such as the United Way Junior Forum, Mission Road Developmental Center, and Boy Scouts. The Association of Residence Hall Students conducted a food drive for the San Antonio Food Bank, and the Catholic student group cosponsored a blood drive and tutored elementary students in local schools. Another volunteer group affiliated with the National Student Campaign Against Hunger and Homelessness raised $1,000 to support national and local charities.[99]

Trinity's intercollegiate athletics program spawned a number of community-building initiatives. Sponsored by the Omega Phi and Gamma Chi Delta organizations and supported by a grant from the SuperFund, Midnight Madness quickly became a popular student tradition. The opening session in 1992 attracted a crowd of 800 basketball enthusiasts who watched Calgaard and Grissom coach opposing teams. Noting that women's basketball was not represented in the initial event, Trinity women's basketball team member Yanika Daniels protested the omission and told student reporters that she was "going to keep raising hell until somebody gets it right." The following year the program featured both men's and women's basketball.[100]

In 1995 the Association of Student Representatives (ASR) raised

$2,000 to purchase a victory bell to boost school spirit at athletic contests. Money from the SuperFund paid for a cart to transport the bell.[101] The following year the ASR asked the administration to fund the purchase of a life-sized tiger statue to be located in the vicinity of the Bell Center. Thanks to a gift from the Chapman Trusts, a 1,000–pound bronze statue symbolizing Trinity's pride and spirit was dedicated at unveiling ceremonies in April 1999.[102]

Other student-centered programs encouraged interaction among members of the Trinity community. The Playfair/Tower Party held at the beginning of every school year featured food, live music, and a rare opportunity for students to climb the Murchison Tower. The weeklong Rites of Spring culminated in an all-day Springfest and Shrimp Boil. Senior Disorientation, a series of events created to give seniors a college finale and to provide them with valuable post-graduation information, was a popular attraction. Activities varied from year to year but usually featured educational seminars, a talent show, and a "Last Great Reception" in the Great Hall, at which faculty honored upcoming graduates. A number of seniors signed up for the Wine, Dine, and Act Fine dinners hosted by Genie Calgaard where they acquired tips about social etiquette during a seven-course meal.[103]

Events sponsored by residential life staff became fixtures in the growing list of student activities, including Spurs Night Out, at which Trinity students, faculty, and staff attended a San Antonio Spurs basketball game. At the beginning of each school year, students competed for a trophy for their residence hall in Hallympics, held before the commencement of intramural sports.[104] Although not officially sponsored by residential life staff, student traditions such as the Primal Scream, a gathering of students at midnight on the eve of final exams, the Ghosts of Calvert Halloween Run, and birthday immersions in the Miller Fountain retained places in Trinity student traditions.[105]

Reflecting on the effectiveness of their community-building efforts, both Calgaard and Grissom admitted that the results were mixed. They acknowledged that community-oriented goals were more elusive to articulate, more difficult to execute, and more problematic to evaluate than those designed to raise academic standards and meet fiscal needs. Nevertheless, they were gratified at indications of some positive results. The reconfigured intercollegiate athletics program proved to be effective both as a recruitment and retention device. Increasing numbers of students participated in local community service projects and worked to promote school spirit. Faculty and staff awards and various social events recognized service and provided opportunities for social interaction. Relationships between Trinity and the San Antonio community improved considerably due in part to the Calgaards' extensive involvement in civic affairs and to the university's cultural contributions through its lecture series and musical events.

On the negative side, Calgaard and Grissom regretted that they had not succeeded in convincing a higher percentage of faculty, staff, and students to appear at athletic contests, music recitals and concerts, distinguished lectures, and all-school events sponsored by student organizations. Despite generous funding, extensive publicity, and outstanding programming, university events rarely attracted large numbers of the Trinity community. On many occasions, more people from the general public attended lectures and concerts than from campus constituencies.

To a considerable extent, the results experienced at Trinity were repeated on campuses throughout the country. Administrative goals of "total involvement" were counter to national changes in campus culture. Undergraduates lived in a different demographical, social, economic, and technological world, which made them less dependent on campus sources of entertainment and also consumed much of their free time. Multiculturalism, diversity, and political correctness led students to seek community in groups that focused on particular issues and stifled initiatives for more inclusive campus organizations and social events.[106] By the end of the decade, Trinity had more than a hundred student organizations with narrowly defined academic, social, religious, political, and recreational goals and activities. As one Trinity student expressed it, "Not everybody wants to be friends with, or even friendly to, everyone else on this campus. And that's OK."[107]

Moreover, some students attributed their lack of interest in supporting campus community programs to the fact that the programs were imposed by administrators rather than by undergraduate initiatives. Among others, one Trinity student compared residential life programs to driving automobiles with "Student Driver" signs on the doors and "an administrator sitting in the passenger seat with a foot on the chicken brake, telling us how fast to go, where to turn and when to stop."[108]

Most faculty and staff members considered the administration's expectations regarding their community involvement to be unrealistic. Faculty commitments to classroom teaching, research and publication, advising, and committee responsibilities absorbed much of their time and energy and limited opportunities for out-of-class interaction with students. In addition, many younger faculty and staff shared parenting responsibilities with working spouses that consumed much of their free time. Unlike previous decades when Trinity personnel lived in close proximity to campus, many chose long commutes in order to have affordable housing in good school districts. As a result, they were not inclined to return to campus for evening or weekend events.[109]

The search for community is ongoing, taxing the ingenuity and involvement of university leadership at all levels. Aware of the difficulty of the task, Grissom noted, "Community cannot be mandated. Maybe it can be encouraged and modeled."[110] What to encourage and how to model, however, continue to be discussed and debated.

At the beginning of the decade, Calgaard had informed the trustees that he would not serve beyond the 1998–99 academic year. In March 1998 he made this decision public. Nevertheless, he vowed to carry out his presidential responsibilities with the same vigor as in previous years. "I intend to be active," he told reporters, "and I intend to run this University just as I have until the 31st day of May of 1999."[111] Concurrent with Calgaard's announcement, the university's trustees established a committee to select a new chief executive officer.[112]

At the same time, other key administrators announced their intention either to retire, to return to the classroom, or to accept employment elsewhere. Richard Elliott, the university registrar since 1980, resigned in 1999 to pursue a career in information services. After thirty-two years of service as university chaplain, Raymond Judd retired at the end of the 1998–99 academic year, and Vice President for Academic Affairs Edward C. Roy relinquished his position in 1999 and returned to the Department of Geosciences as the Gertrude and Walter Pyron Distinguished Professor of Geology. Executive Director of Admissions and Financial Aid George Boyd retired at the end of the 1999–2000 academic year. After assisting the transition into the new presidency and taking a year's leave of absence, Vice President for Student Affairs Coleen Grissom became a full-time faculty member in the Department of English in the fall of 2001.

As the president's retirement date approached, the Calgaards were the recipients of various receptions and parties honoring their many contributions to Trinity and the San Antonio community. In 1998 the San Antonio Board of Prevent Blindness Texas honored him with a "People of Vision" Award, and he was the recipient of the San Antonio Academy's W. T. Bondurant Sr. Distinguished Humanitarian Award.[113] The following year, Calgaard was inducted into the San Antonio Business Hall of Fame in recognition of his leadership and community support.[114] At a reception on the Coates esplanade, students, faculty, and staff honored the Calgaards for their service to the university. As the couple sat side by side on the stage,

Distinguished Service Award, 1999; left to right: Calgaard, Crichton, and Denman

senior Mark Tucker and junior Greg Tasian co-emceed the presentation of gifts from departments, offices, athletic teams, and Greek organizations.[115]

At his last trustee meeting, Calgaard reflected on his career at Trinity and the people who had contributed to the university's growth and development. He emphasized that the accomplishments during his presidency had been due to "a shared vision and not just somebody's temporary whim." Paying tribute to his predecessors, he pointed to the portraits of former trustees and presidents and said, "I feel I am a kind of bridge in some ways, because I am certainly the last Trinity president who will have known almost all the people whose portraits grace the wall, who made a difference, who made Trinity."[116]

In regard to his own contributions, Calgaard admitted that Trinity was not perfect and never would be, "But it is better than what it was, and for that I feel grateful." When asked to describe his most satisfying accomplishment as president, he responded, "Developing and implementing an institutional mission to have a nationally prominent, primarily undergraduate, mostly liberal arts institution. We have made rather dramatic progress in that direction, and I find that personally most satisfying."[117]

Commencement exercises on 8 May 1999, marked Calgaard's last ceremonial performance as university president. He handed 428 diplomas to graduates and presented distinguished service awards to two longtime trustees, Flora Cameron Crichton and Gilbert M. Denman Jr., and was himself a recipient of the award. At the end of his twenty-year presidency, the longest in Trinity's history, almost half of all living Trinity alumni bore the name of Ronald K. Calgaard on their diplomas.

In his closing remarks, Calgaard urged students to choose vocations that would give meaning to their lives and to seek opportunities for service to community and country. "One of the joys of my life is that I have done almost everyday something I enjoy doing. I've been working at a Trinity degree a little longer than the rest of you. Most of you have managed to do this in four or five years. It has taken me twenty, but I intend to graduate today. And I can only hope for you, as we both plan for some changes in our lives and for some new futures, an exciting, an interesting, and a rewarding time."[118]

INTO A NEW CENTURY

In the late 1970s the vision for Trinity University was transformational:
to make a good university into an excellent university. . . . The vision for
Trinity University at the beginning of the twenty-first century must also be
transformational: to make an excellent university an outstanding university
and take it into the front ranks of American's finest smaller colleges and
universities, less by changing in kind than by accelerating changes in
degree, less by changing *what* Trinity is than by concentrating intently
on *how well* it fulfills its mission.

JOHN R. BRAZIL, FEBRUARY 2002

O N THE CUSP OF A NEW CENTURY, Trinity University trustees prepared for a presidential search, a task they had not undertaken in twenty
years. Chaired by trustee Robert McClane and assisted by a national consulting firm, the search committee announced its quest for an individual
who would "build upon what has already been accomplished, and who
would expand the University's vision for the next Century." The committee had no forewarning, however, of the events of 11 September 2001,
when terrorists struck the World Trade Center Towers and the Pentagon
with devastating loss of life and property. Whoever was called to be president of Trinity University would soon face an environment of global
turmoil marked by economic instability, terrorist attacks, and conflicts
among nations.

After reviewing 150 nominations and applications, the committee
unanimously selected nominee John R. Brazil, president of Bradley University in Illinois and professor of English, to become Trinity's next chief
executive officer. Committee members were impressed with his enthusiasm
for classroom teaching, his collegial style of leadership, and his fiscal and
academic accomplishments at Bradley.[1] Public announcement of the appointment was made in December 1998 when Brazil visited the Trinity
campus to meet with university trustees, administrators, faculty, staff, and
students. Speaking to an overflow audience in the Chapman Auditorium,
Brazil emphasized that he had no preconceived agenda for radical change.

"I do not come to Trinity with a blueprint or a prescription for excellence. It's principally a question of refinement."[2]

Brazil came to Trinity as an established scholar, teacher, writer, and administrator. Prior to Bradley, Brazil had served as chancellor and professor of English at the University of Massachusetts at Dartmouth (originally Southeastern Massachusetts University) from 1984 to 1992. Earlier, he had been associated with San Jose State University in California, where he coordinated the American studies program and rose through the academic ranks from lecturer to professor of humanities and American studies over the course of eleven years. While at San Jose State, Brazil held the positions of executive-assistant to the president, associate academic vice president for undergraduate studies, and interim academic vice president.[3]

Brazil was raised in a family environment that fostered reading, inquiry, and community service. His father, Burton R. Brazil, earned a Ph.D. in political science from Stanford University and held faculty and administrative posts at San Jose State University in California. He also served for a time as mayor of Saratoga, California. His mother, Helen Douglas Brazil, a college graduate, worked as a bank officer and was active in community life. As a result of his upbringing, Brazil's intellectual interests were always broad and interdisciplinary, a trait that would help him as an administrator to understand the complexities of various academic disciplines.[4]

Brazil earned a A.B. in history at Stanford University in 1968 but studied widely in the fields of political science, philosophy, English, and social sciences. After Stanford, Brazil attended Yale University, where he received two degrees in American studies: a Master of Philosophy (1972) and a Ph.D. (1975). In 1980 he was a Fulbright senior scholar in English and American studies at the University of Sydney, Australia. A member of Phi Beta Kappa and Phi Kappa Phi honor societies, Brazil had published in scholarly journals such as the *American Quarterly, Twentieth-Century Literary Criticism, American Literary Realism,* and *Mississippi Quarterly.*[5]

While at Bradley, Brazil's community service included membership on the board of directors of Caterpillar, the Methodist Medical Center of Illinois, the National Association of Independent Colleges and Universities, the Central Illinois Light Company, and the Missouri Valley Conference Presidents Council, as well as on other educational boards and agencies. In San Antonio, Brazil has served on the board of directors of the United Way of San Antonio and Bexar County and of the Independent Colleges and Universities of Texas, Inc. In addition, he is a board member and member of the Executive Committee of the National Association of Independent Colleges and Universities and of the Association of Presbyterian

Colleges and Universities and a board member of the Texas Research Park Foundation.[6]

His spouse, Janice Hosking Brazil, quickly became involved in campus community life. One of her first initiatives was to sponsor a contest for Trinity students to design the university's annual holiday card. She also developed programs for trustees' spouses who accompanied members to board meetings, such as presentations by Trinity faculty and community excursions that included visits to art galleries, craft centers, and other cultural venues. A published poet and an avid learner, Brazil enrolled in Spanish classes at Trinity. She regularly hosts students, faculty, trustees, and guests for luncheons, dinners, and receptions at her home and participates in other campus and community events.[7]

The university community and distinguished visitors gathered on 12 February 2000, to inaugurate Brazil as Trinity's seventeenth president. The previous day, a symposium in the Stieren Theater on "Trinity University and the Changing Landscape of Higher Education" was introduced by a lecture and visual presentation on Trinity's history by religion professor R. Douglas Brackenridge. Keynote speaker Kathleen Hall Jamieson, professor and dean of the Annenberg School for Communication and director of the Annenberg Public Policy Center at the University of Pennsylvania, spoke on "Higher Education: Fostering Citizenship and Civility in High Tech Times," followed by a panel of Trinity faculty and students who reflected on the symposium's theme.[8]

In his inaugural address, Brazil paid tribute to the men and women whose talents and tenacity had enabled Trinity to reach its present level of accomplishments. At the same time, he challenged the university community to strive to achieve and sustain even higher levels of institutional stature. "We must design and deliver an education that satisfies both our students' need to make a living and their need to live a life rich in purpose and permeated with meaning. We must do this based on the understanding that these are not separate needs separately satisfied. They are integral, inseparable parts of a larger need that can only be fully addressed by an integrated, interanimating attention to both."[9]

One of Brazil's first tasks was to fill vacant positions in Trinity's administrative leadership. After a national search in 1999–2000, he appointed Michael Fischer, formerly dean of the College of Arts and Sciences at the University of New Mexico, as vice president for academic affairs. Fischer earned a B.A. in English from Princeton University and a Ph.D. from Northwestern University before beginning his teaching and administrative career at the University of New Mexico. As vice president for student affairs, Brazil selected Gage Paine, who holds a Ph.D. from the University of Texas at Austin and a J.D. from Texas Tech University and who served as associate vice president for student affairs and dean of student life at Southern Methodist University.[10]

Convinced that Trinity needed strong focused leadership in the area of information technology and management, Brazil created the position of vice president for information resources and administrative affairs and appointed Charles B. White, former Trinity associate vice president for academic affairs, to lead the new division. The structure centralized the administration of the computing center, the registrar's office, the library, the telephone and cable systems, and the conferences and special programs.[11]

Other Brazil appointments included dean of admissions and financial aid Christopher J. Ellertson, who held a similar position at Whitman College; and Registrar Alfred Rodriguez Jr., whose past experience included registrar and admissions work at Baylor College of Medicine, Texas Tech University Health Sciences Center, and the University of Houston. They were joined by chaplain Stephen R. Nickle, a veteran of campus ministry at Maryville College in Tennessee, and university librarian Diane Graves, formerly dean of library and information services at Hollins College in Virginia.[12] In addition, Brazil began the process of hiring new faculty to replace the recent retirees and to fill new positions. By the beginning of the 2003–2004 academic year, Brazil had approved the appointment of sixty-nine replacement faculty members and authorized the creation of twelve new faculty positions.[13]

In a document entitled "Ends and Means," Brazil identified a series of initiatives that he believed would enable the university both to enhance current operations and to find new ways to fulfill its institutional mission.[14] Prominent on his list, in addition to curricular reform, were improving methods of recruitment and retention of faculty and students, acquiring critical technology and information resources, strengthening alumni engagement and support, upgrading physical facilities, and securing adequate financial resources.[15]

Brazil also commissioned the firm of Lipman Hearne, Inc., of Chicago to develop a long-term integrated marketing plan for the university. At the center of the new program is a way of describing Trinity's distinctiveness, value, and purpose in terms of benefits for students and, by extension, for alumni, parents, and other higher education audiences. Presented to the university in 2002, the program is presently in its early stages of implementation.[16] In the spring of 2003 with the assistance of a representative university committee, the Office of Public Relations unveiled a new university logo featuring the outline of Murchison Tower partially enclosed in an oval-shaped mark and typographic treatment of the university's name. While maintaining continuity with the past, the new logo is intended to "reinforce the University's qualities, attributes, and promises." At the same time, the university changed its address from 715 Stadium Drive to One Trinity Place.[17]

While developing long-range plans, Brazil also took steps in the academic arena. He encouraged the Trinity faculty to undertake an intensive evaluation of the common curriculum that had been in place for fifteen years. In 2002 the faculty approved a new basic curriculum that offered students greater flexibility in fulfilling understandings (reduced from six to five) and facilitated majoring simultaneously in two disciplines. Other features included individually created interdisciplinary majors, a "Senior Experience" with four options (thesis, major capstone course, integrative research project, or interdisciplinary seminar), and a "Summer Experience" program offering opportunities for intensive courses and activities such as special topics, educational tours, and experimental learning.[18]

In 2000, Brazil announced the reinstitution of Trinity University Press, which had ceased operations in 1989, and commissioned a search for a director. The process culminated with the appointment of Barbara Ras, who has extensive publishing experience: principal editor, University of California Press; managing editor, North Point Press; and assistant director and executive editor, University of Georgia Press. Funded by a $2.9-million grant from the Ewing Halsell Foundation, the press anticipates publishing six to eight books annually with a primary focus on regional works, but also seeking to attract authors from the national and international scholarly communities.[19]

Responding to student interest, the Office of Academic Affairs appointed an ad hoc Academic Honor Code Committee to explore establishing an honor code at Trinity.[20] In February 2003, the faculty approved the implementation of an honor code to be phased in over a period of three years. The code requires that incoming students sign an agreement to abide by the academic honor code policy and provides for a student honor council to hear cases involving alleged infractions against the code and to determine sanctions in cases in which a violation has occurred.[21]

Under the Brazil administration, Trinity's information technology resources have grown at a rapid pace during the opening years of the new century. The computer has become the most important communication device on the campus, with e-mail now the primary means of written communication, and most students and many faculty and staff also own cellular telephones. In addition to a high-speed network and cable television services, residential students have access to movies and a campus television channel with student programming.[22]

With the support of the Chapman Trust, the university opened a new teleconferencing facility and added two computer science classrooms, a digital art laboratory, and a communications media facility to the university's technological infrastructure. Faculty members increasingly have access to electronic classrooms and new courseware for providing course materials and class communication opportunities online. By 2001 degree audits were online, and the registrar's office successfully completed Trinity's first completely online course registration utilizing the web-based interactive software system locally known as TigerPAWS (PAWS = Personal Assistant Web Services). Students registered from their desktops, from advisors' offices, and in some cases from study-abroad locations as far away as Australia and Eastern Europe.[23]

Digital resources have transformed the library from primarily a repository of print materials into a gateway to hundreds of electronic resources. The library has developed a wireless network and acquired video and audio streaming technology with grants from the State of Texas, and a $1.3-million gift from the Priddy Charitable Trust with an additional $100,000 from the Olin Foundation has enabled Trinity to create an information commons area on the third floor. In addition, the installation of a new coffee and beverage kiosk and seating area (Java City) has contributed to a busier library and increased circulation of print materials.[24]

Recognizing Trinity's adept application of technology and its commitment to expanding the boundaries of teaching, learning, and research, the New Media Consortium, a nonprofit organization that targets emerging technologies in colleges, universities, and museums, designated Trinity as a New Media Center in May 2003. Trinity joined 125 institutions, including highly regarded universities such as Princeton, Yale, UCLA, the University of Texas, the University of Richmond, and Carleton College, that have received the designation of excellence in the consortium's ten-year history.[25]

Following an assessment of university needs, Trinity trustees decided to finance construction of a new Northrup Hall over a period of thirty years by issuing a tax-exempt bonds of approximately $30 million. A competition among architectural firms was held to design a building that would blend the activities of faculty, staff, and students, address the front entrance to the university, provide sufficient parking, and create a mall-like atmosphere through the center of the campus.[26] From four finalists, the trustees chose the New York firm of Robert A. M. Stern Architects. They deemed that the proposed design, "two relatively narrow four-story wings connected by a central lobby on each floor and a glass-enclosed grand staircase that runs through the entire building," best complemented the existing campus architecture and integrated academic and administrative areas. Faculty and staff vacated Northup Hall in May 2002 and the building was subsequently razed. Construction commenced in July and offices began to be occupied in March 2004.[27]

Despite a substantial endowment ($586 million in 1999) and basically debt-free status, the university faced fiscal challenges as it moved into the new century. During the previous decade, Trinity's endowment growth had not kept pace with comparable private educational institutions, falling from forty-fourth nationally to the mid-seventies. To facilitate endowment growth, Brazil decreased the spending rate of endowment income from 6 percent to 5 percent, increased asset allocation diversification, brought in a national consulting firm to monitor investment managers, and began preparations for a major capital campaign. Although in recent years economic downturns and a declining stock market have adversely affected institutional endowments nationwide, the university's annual budget has continued to grow at about 4 percent per year, while experiencing no layoffs or cutbacks.[28]

From the outset of his presidency, Brazil established close relationships with students and indicated a desire to give them a wider role in university governance. As a symbolic first step, he climbed the Murchison Tower during the annual first-year orientation Tower Party and greeted the students who also chose to make the climb. Subsequently, Brazil has maintained a practice of informally lunching with students in Mabee Dining Hall and inviting groups to his home for conversation and refreshments. One summer, he and Janice accompanied Trinity students on a geology field trip to Big Bend National Park, where they participated in the learning experience and interacted socially.[29]

To foster the integration of student social life and academic life, Brazil commissioned a representative Task Force on the Quality of Student Life to ascertain problem areas and to make recommendations for improvements.[30] In May 2001, after interviewing more than 400 students, faculty, and staff, the task force presented fourteen recommendations for implementation, ranging from identifying opportunities for student self-governance to initiatives for improving academic advising, new student orientation, and campus diversity. Some of the recommendations were already in the process of being addressed by the time the report was approved.[31]

The routines of campus life came to a sudden halt on 11 September 2001, when news of the terrorists attacks on the World Trade Center Towers and the Pentagon interrupted scheduled programming on radio and television. As the tragedy unfolded, the campus community gathered around television sets to watch the continuous coverage. Brazil cancelled afternoon classes, enabling more than 600 people to attend a prayer service in Margarite B. Parker Chapel led by Chaplain Nickle and Father John Keefer, chaplain to the Catholic Student Union.[32] In a memorandum to the campus community, Brazil called for resolve in facing the crisis. "Tomorrow is a new day, and although individually and as a nation we will struggle for a long time to comprehend what has happened and find a way to constructively respond to it, classes will resume tomorrow and the business of the University will go forward. The confusion, fear, and disruption that is the fodder of terrorists will not control our lives. Together we will best serve ourselves and others by refusing to give in and by continuing our lives."[33]

Students returned to class the following day. On 14 September, which was designated a national day of prayer and remembrance by President George W. Bush, a panel of Trinity faculty discussed national security issues, ethnic stereotypes, and continuing media coverage at a forum in Chapman Auditorium. That evening, community members gathered for a prayer service in the chapel, followed by a candlelight vigil.[34]

The university community responded in other ways to assist victims of the terrorist attacks. Students, faculty, and staff supported a campus blood drive that had been previously planned by Alpha Phi Omega. Before bags and supplies were depleted, 150 pints of blood were donated in two days. Three student organizations acting under an umbrella group called Trinity Cares launched a campus fund drive to support the relief effort headed by the American Red Cross. Exceeding its initial goal of $8,000, the group sent the national agency a check for $11,700 on 26 September. Leaders of the Association of Student Representatives distributed blue lapel ribbons to be worn in honor of those killed or injured in the terrorist attacks.[35]

Moving forward after 9/11, Brazil approved the appointment of several new staff positions in the Office of Student Affairs, including a coordinator of student activities for diversity and service programming and a full-time director of career services. The former is charged with general promotion and program planning and serves as advisor to TUVAC and the Trinity Multi-Cultural Network. The latter is responsible for advising students individually on careers, developing vocational workshops, and establishing networks with Trinity alumni.[36]

A reconfigured and extended student orientation program offered intellectually engaging activities and opportunities to explore the university's urban environment. In 2002, events included an academic fair, lectures by Trinity faculty, and a keynote address by Richard Light, author of *Making the Most of College*, which incoming students had read over the summer. In addition, students could sign up for a driving tour of San Antonio, a shopping trip, and TUVAC community service projects.[37]

Addressing another major student issue, an Alcohol Task Force consisting of students, faculty, and staff discussed ways to alter the university's alcohol policy. In response to their recommendations, Brazil approved the experimental establishment of the on-campus Tigers' Pub, where students over twenty-one years old can be served beer and wine. This environment offers a place where administrators, faculty, staff, and students can socialize.[38]

Trinity's intercollegiate athletic program continued its success in the Southern Collegiate Athletic Conference competition and in NCAA Division III. During the 2000–01 and 2001–02 seasons, seven Trinity teams advanced to the national playoffs, three of which made it to the NCAA quarterfinals or better. The National Association of Collegiate Directors of Athletics honored Trinity's Bob King in 2000 as the Division III Athletic Director of the Year in the Western Region. The fall of 2002 was the best fall season in the history of Trinity University athletics. Football, men's soccer, women's soccer, and volleyball all were in the NCAA semifinals, the first time in NCAA history (any division) for one school to place those four sports in the semifinals in one semester. The football team advanced to the Division III national championship game, the Amos Alonzo Stagg Bowl, winning a school-record fourteen games during the season. The men's and women's soccer teams both finished as semifinalists, losing by one goal in each game.[39]

Other accomplishments in recent years have solidified the university's reputation for producing exceptional athletic teams. In 2003, Trinity's women's basketball team won its first NCAA Division III national title by defeating Eastern Connecticut State University 60–58 in the championship game. During the same year, Trinity's men's soccer team defeated the Drew University Rangers 2–1 to win the Division III national championship. Boasting an undefeated season, the Tigers became the first Texas team to win an NCAA soccer championship in any division, men's or women's.[40]

While preparing for the future, the university paused to remember its past. In 2002, Trinity observed three anniversaries: the one-hundredth anniversary of the move from Tehuacana to Waxahachie; the sixtieth anniversary of the move from Waxahachie to San Antonio; and the fiftieth anniversary of the move from the Woodlawn Campus to the present location. On 22 September 2002, the university community gathered on the Tower Plaza to celebrate Trinity's sixty years in San Antonio. The evening began with a service of thanksgiving in the Parker Chapel, followed by refreshments, music, and presentations by various civic dignitaries. The evening culminated with the official illumination of the Murchison Tower. To further mark the occasion, the university initiated a fund drive to purchase books for the San Antonio Public Library as a gesture of appreciation for the important role that the city has played in Trinity's development.[41]

In the fall of 1902, two months after the university had departed for Waxahachie, Jake Hodges, Trinity class of 1877, visited the deserted Tehuacana campus. Traversing the familiar scenes of his student days, Hodges reported that he found "melancholy pleasure" in everything he saw, recalling the names of students, faculty, and townspeople who had helped to sharpen his intellect and shape his character. In the silence of the abandoned hillside campus, Hodges recalled when Tehuacana bustled with energy and activity and made an apt observation. "It should be no new thought that Trinity University was never Tehuacana nor Tehuacana Trinity University; and it is quite as true now that Trinity University is not Waxahachie nor Waxahachie Trinity University. The house is neither the family, nor the younger children neither more nor less the family than are the older ones. We are one forever."[42]

As it has in the past, Trinity faces both challenges and opportunities in the days that lie ahead. Its future as an educational institution will be determined by creativity rather than by geography, by renewal rather than by removal, and by people rather than by property. President Brazil's words make a fitting ending to this Tale of Three Cities. "We must not let our sense of accomplishment obscure our sense of potential."[43]

APPENDIX

Presidents of Trinity University

1. William E. Beeson 1869–1882
   Robert W. Pitman* 1877–1878
   Samuel T. Anderson*. 1882–1883
2. Benjamin G. McLeskey 1883–1885
3. Luther A. Johnson. 1885–1889
4. John L. Dickens. 1889–1890
5. Benjamin. D. Cockrill 1890–1896
   Luther A. Johnson ** 1896–1900
   Samuel L. Hornbeak** 1900–1901
6. Jesse Anderson. 1901–1902
7. Leonidas C. Kirkes 1902–1904
8. Archelaus E. Turner. 1904–1906
9. Samuel L. Hornbeak 1907–1921
10. John H. Burma 1921–1933
    Samuel L. Hornbeak* 1933–1934
11. Raymond H. Leach 1934–1937
12. Frank L. Wear 1937–1942
13. Monroe G. Everett. 1942–1950
    M. Bruce Thomas* 1950–1951
14. James W. Laurie. 1951–1970
15. Duncan G. Wimpress. 1970–1977
    M. Bruce Thomas* 1977–1979
16. Ronald K. Calgaard. 1979–1999
17. John R. Brazil 1999–2010
18. Dennis A. Ahlburg. 2010–2015
19. Danny J. Anderson. 2015–

*Acting President during interim
**Chairman of the Faculty during interim

Board of Trustees 2003

Back row left to right: Gaines Voigt, Steve P. Mach, Peter M. Holt, Thomas R. Semmes, Walter R. Huntley, Jr., L. Herbert Stumberg, Jr., John C. Korbell, Jack L. Stotts, John D. Thornton, David K. Straus, James F. Dicke II

Seated left to right: Reverend Judy R. Fletcher, Clarkson P. Moseley, Sharon J. Bell, Charles T. Sunderland, George C. (Tim) Hixon, Barbara W. Pierce, Emilio Nicolas, Phyllis Browning, Neil M. Chur, Lissa Walls Vahldiek, Douglas D. Hawthorne

On couch left to right: Robert S. McClane, Chair; John R. Brazil, President

Not pictured: Walter F. Brown, Richard W. Calvert, Flora C. Crichton, Gilbert M. Denman, Jr., Gen. Robert T. Herres, USAF (ret.), James W. Jones IV, Richard M. Kleberg III, Marshall B. Miller, Jr., John J. Roberts, Paul H. Smith, Irene S. Wischer, Louis H. Zbinden

NOTES

Notes to Preface

1. The ideas about space are derived from Sidney E. Mead, *The Lively Experiment* (New York, Evanston, and London, 1963), 1–15.

2. For a concise summary of Presbyterian denominational history in the United States, see James H. Smylie, *A Brief History of Presbyterians* (Louisville, Kentucky, 1996).

Notes to Chapter One

1. Rupert N. Richardson, Adrian Anderson, and Ernest Wallace, *Texas, The Lone Star State*, 6th ed. (Englewood Cliffs, N.J., 1993), 125–147, 165.

2. For a concise background of Cumberland Presbyterian origins, see Walter Posey, *Frontier Mission: A History of Religion West of the Southern Appalachians to 1861* (Lexington, Ky., 1966), 64–80.

3. Ben M. Barrus, Milton L. Baughn, and Thomas H. Campbell, *A People Called Cumberland Presbyterians* (Memphis, Tn., 1972), 213–215.

4. Barrus, Baughn, and Campbell, *A People Called Cumberland Presbyterians*, 225–227. See also J. V. Stephens, "A Historical Sketch of the Educational Spirit and Interests of the Cumberland Presbyterian Church," *The Cumberland Presbyterian*, 3 March 1900, 13–15.

5. For an overview of Bacon's career, see R. Douglas Brackenridge, *Voice in the Wilderness: A History of the Cumberland Presbyterian Church in Texas* (San Antonio, 1968), 13–46.

6. Minutes of the Texas Presbytery of the Cumberland Presbyterian Church, 2 October 1840. Hereafter, Texas Presbytery Minutes (CP). Later figures are derived from compiled statistics of Texas, Brazos, and Colorado Synod Minutes. Common to all

Presbyterian denominations is a system of interconnected governing bodies beginning locally with church sessions (elders elected by individual congregations) and ascending to presbyteries (a group of congregations in a specific geographical area), synods (a group of presbyteries in a specific geographical area), and an annual General Assembly consisting of commissioners elected by the various presbyteries.

7. *The Texas Presbyterian,* 18 October 1851; Minutes of the Red River Presbytery of the Cumberland Presbyterian Church, 16 November 1854.

8. Minutes of the Buffalo Gap Presbytery of the Cumberland Presbyterian Church, 27 June and 12 December 1885. For other examples of ministerial poverty, see Brackenridge, *Voice in the Wilderness,* 57–58, 102–103. As late as 1900, a survey of Cumberland Presbyterian clergy revealed that most pastors received only about $400–$500 annual salary and were dependent on farming, teaching, or other occupational skills to support their families. W. B. Farr, "Some Startling Statistics," *St. Louis Observer,* 25 October 1895: 4.

9. Texas Presbytery Minutes (CP), 28 November 1837.

10. Bosque Academy, for example, was endorsed by Brazos Synod even though it functioned as a private institution. Texas Presbytery Minutes (CP), 1846: 42; Minutes of the Brazos Synod of the Cumberland Presbyterian Church, 1854: 121. Hereafter, Brazos Synod Minutes (CP). Early presbytery and synod records do not always give a precise date for their sessions. For example, the date of the opening session is frequently referred to as "the first Thursday after the second Sunday in October." In such instances, the year and the page number of the minutes are given. When the date can clearly be ascertained by day, month, and year, a precise reference is given.

11. The histories of the three schools are independent except that some funds and equipment from the three schools were donated to Trinity and some faculty from the predecessor institutions later joined the staff of the new university.

12. For background on organizational structures of nineteenth-century Presbyterian colleges, see C. Harvey Geiger, *The Program of Higher Education of the Presbyterian Church in the United States of America* (Cedar Rapids, Ia., 1940), 83–89.

13. Brazos Synod Minutes (CP), 1849: 4. See also Fred H. Ford and J. L. Brown, *Larissa* (New Orleans, 1951), 31–39.

14. Christopher Long, "Larissa," in Ron Tyler, Douglas E. Barnett, Roy R. Barkley, Penelope C. Anderson, and Mark F. Odintz (eds.), *The New Handbook of Texas* 6 vols. (Austin, 1996), IV, 80.

15. Brazos Synod Minutes (CP), 4 February and 13 October 1855.

16. *The Texas Presbyterian,* 1 May 1852: 4. The school opened in 1852 but had a short life due to financial difficulties. For biographical information on Yoakum, see Nellie Jean Evans, "A History of Larissa College," Master's thesis (University of Texas at Austin, 1941), 51–55.

17. Brazos Synod Minutes (CP), 1856: 62–63, 70–71. Records indicate that funds for the theological department never materialized, and the project was abandoned.

18. *The Banner of Peace,* 19 July 1860: 4.

19. Evans, "A History of Larissa College," 74–75, and Thomas Campbell, *A History of the Cumberland Presbyterian Church in Texas,* (Nashville, Tn., 1936), 93–94.

20. Brazos Synod Minutes (CP), 1855: 49–50; 1856: 73–74; 1867: 261.

21. William R. Hogan, *The Texas Republic: A Social and Economic History* (Nor-

man, Ok., 1946), 149–155. See also William S. Red, *History of the Presbyterian Church in Texas* (Austin, 1936), 222–225.

22. Richardson, Anderson, and Wallace, *Texas, The Lone Star State*, 6th ed., 194.

23. Minutes of the Colorado Presbytery of the Cumberland Presbyterian Church, 29 September 1848 and 7 March 1857.

24. Minutes of the Colorado Synod of the Cumberland Presbyterian Church, 1859: 46–48; 1862: 70.

25. Samuel L. Hornbeak, "Trinity University: Project of Pioneers" (typescript, n.d.), 2, Trinity University Archives; William B. Preston, "Sketches of Early Days in Trinity University" (typescript, n.d.), 5–7, Trinity University Archives. Hereafter, TU Archives.

26. Texas Synod Minutes (CP), 1851: 68, 71, 73; 1869: 240. See also Carl L. McFarland, "Chapel Hill College," in Tyler et al. (eds.), *The New Handbook of Texas*, II, 77.

27. Texas Synod Minutes (CP), 1854: 89–90; 1858: 143.

28. *The Banner of Peace*, 17 July 1852: 2. In the class of 1857 were W. B. Ward, S. M. Ward, J. A. Ward, N. O. Bradford, and J. A. Corley.

29. Texas Synod Minutes (CP), 1860: 176; 1865: 209; Hornbeak, "Trinity University: Project of Pioneers," 3; Evans, "A History of Larissa College," 22–23. Some secondary sources indicate that Beeson did not resume his position as president following the Civil War. Evans cites a letter from Beeson to the contrary. See also J. A. Ward, "Chapel Hill College," *The Banner of Peace*, 25 July 1867: 1.

30. A. J. McGown, "Letter from Texas," *The Banner of Peace*, 6 September 1866: 1 and 13 December 1866: 1.

31. Richardson, Anderson, and Wallace, *Texas, The Lone Star State*, 6th ed., 240–241.

32. Richard Beard, "The Economy of our Colleges," *The Banner of Peace*, 6 February 1868: 2; 27 February 1868: 2; 23 April 1868: 2.

33. J. V. Stephens, "Our Schools," *The Cumberland Presbyterian*, 21 June 1900: 777–778. Stephens received the material for this article from Professor B. D. Bodenhamer of Trinity University. For brief biographies of Haynes and Bone, see John Collier, "Rev. Andrew Jackson Haynes," *The Cumberland Presbyterian*, 7 April 1898: 1264–1265, and "The Late Rev. H. F. Bone, D. D.," *The Presbyterian Advance*, 13 September 1917: 2.

34. Brazos Synod Minutes (CP), 1866: 160–161.

35. *Dallas Herald*, 30 November 1867.

36. Sources vary regarding how the $25,000 was to be constituted. According to some sources, it was to be $25,000 in gold. See "Meeting of the Synod of Brazos," *The Banner of Peace*, 10 December 1868: 1. Yet, according to the same synod minutes of a later date, it was described as "donations in money and property and buildings" amounting to $25,000. Brazos Synod Minutes (CP), 1869: 196. Apparently the latter was the case because Trinity did not have $25,000 in hand when it commenced operations.

37. Colorado Synod Minutes (CP), 1868: 110; Brazos Synod Minutes (CP), 1868: 187; I. C. Phillips, "Meeting of the Synod of Brazos," *The Banner of Peace*, 10 December 1868: 1.

38. A. J. Haynes, "A Letter From Texas," *The Banner of Peace*, 29 August 1867:

1. See also Campbell, *The Cumberland Presbyterian Church in Texas*, 86–89. In addition, the editor of the *Dallas Herald* reported that several businessmen had agreed to contribute a thousand dollars each and that others were expressing interest in the project. "The University," *Dallas Herald*, 14 December 1867. The Cumberland Presbyterians were members of Red Oak Presbytery, which had decided in 1866 that Dallas should be the location of the new university. See Haynes, "A Letter From Texas," 1.

39. "Trinity University[:] A Brief History." A Foreword to the Minutes of the Board of Trustees of Trinity University, I: 2–4. Hereafter, the Minutes of the Board of Trustees of Trinity University are referred to as Board of Trustees Minutes.

40. Ray A. Walter, *A History of Limestone County* (Austin, 1959), 37–39, 114–115; Donald E. Everett, *Trinity University: A Record of One Hundred Years* (San Antonio, 1968), 1–3.

41. The story is told in several sources with varying wording of the inscription. See L. Clay Collier, "Trinity University," *The Cumberland Presbyterian*, 10 July 1890: 1; D. S. Bodenhamer, "Trinity University Commencement," *The Cumberland Presbyterian*, 13 June 1895: 756. For a brief biography of Sanders, see Campbell, *History of the Cumberland Presbyterian Church in Texas*, 74–75.

42. "Report to the Three Synods," *The Cumberland Presbyterian*, 22 July 1875: 4.

43. Walter, *A History of Limestone County*, 37–38.

44. Everett, *Trinity University*, 8–11.

45. "Waxahachie and Its Surroundings," *Dallas Herald*, 31 July 1869.

46. Margaret L. Felty, "Waxahachie, Texas," in Tyler et al. (eds.), *The New Handbook of Texas*, VI, 854–855; *A History of Waxahachie, Texas, and Citizens National Bank* (Waxahachie, 1968), 3–15.

47. "The Presbyterian College," *Dallas Herald*, 28 November 1868.

48. For example, Hornbeak, "Trinity University: Project of Pioneers," 7–8. Although unknown to committee members at the time, the proffered land would later be worth millions of dollars, when Dallas became one of the southwest's great commercial centers.

49. Brazos Synod Minutes (CP), 1869: 196–197; Colorado Synod Minutes (CP), 1969: 123; Eugenia Reiwald, "Trinity University: Aspects of the Tehuacana Period," Master's thesis (Trinity University, 1964), 14–18.

50. Stearns Scarbrough, "Round Rock, Texas," in Tyler et al. (eds.), *The New Handbook of Texas*, V, 697; Mary Starr Barkley, *A History of Central Texas* (Austin, 1970), 208–209.

51. Board of Trustees Minutes, "A Brief History," I: 2. Another primary account written by W. G. L. Quaite says, "after a full and impartial investigation of the claims of the different localities bidding for the University, it was located by a unanimous vote at Tehuacana." "The Cumberland Presbyterian University," *Dallas Herald*, 8 May 1869. Among others, Dallas supporters were unhappy about the selection of Tehuacana. Editor Swindells commented, "The location made certainly has one advantage, that of being central, but aside from this there are no other requisites about the place selected that we can think of, except that of a liberal subscription." "Cumberland Presbyterian University," *Dallas Herald*, 1 May 1869.

52. Board of Trustees Minutes, "A Brief History," I: 2.

53. "Death of Thomas B. Wilson," *The Banner of Peace*, 8 July 1873: 4; Yetta

Graham Mitchell, "The History of Trinity University from 1869–1934," Master's thesis (Southern Methodist University, 1936), 39.

54. Board of Trustees Minutes, "A Brief History," I: 2–4; Texas Synod Minutes (CP), 2–3 November 1870.

55. Preston, "Sketches of Early Days in Trinity University," 3–4. Preston attended Trinity in the 1870s and wrote his narrative early in the twentieth century. Other books and theses cite Preston or give no precise reference. Occasionally writers have connected the name with the three predecessor colleges, but there is no historical basis to that claim.

56. J. H. Wofford, "Trinity University," *The Banner of Peace*, 12 April 1870: 2.

57. Board of Trustees Minutes, 1 May, 19 May, and 13 July 1869.

58. Board of Trustees Minutes, 19 May and 13 July 1869. See also "Items from Colorado, Texas, and Brazos Synods," *The Banner of Peace*, 2 December 1869: 1. The first trustees were J. S. Wills, D. M. Prendergast, J. M. Love, H. A. Boyd, J. H. Roberts, S. B. Campbell, D. R. Oliphant, J. H. Bell, and Mark M. Burgess. Officers were J. S. Wills, president; James M. Love, treasurer; and H. A. Boyd, secretary.

NOTES TO CHAPTER TWO

1. Brazos Synod Minutes (CP), 1869: 199–200; Texas Synod Minutes (CP), 2–3 November 1870. Secondary sources vary regarding the number of students who enrolled the first day. Campbell, *History of the Presbyterian Church in Texas*, 101, says two students attended. Hornbeak, "Trinity University: Project of Pioneers," 11, reports thirteen students in attendance. The primary sources (Synod minutes) state that seven students were present.

2. *First Annual Catalogue of Trinity University* (1869–70), 4–6, 11. Hereafter, *TU Catalogue* with date. All catalogues are in the Trinity University Archives. The catalogue changed its title in the twentieth century, using *Courses of Study Bulletin* and then just *Courses of Study*.

3. *TU Catalogue* (1869–70): 11.

4. *TU Catalogue* (1869–70): 16.

5. *TU Catalogue* (1869–70): 3; (1870–71): 4.

6. "Our Dead Heroes: President W. E. Beeson," *The Cumberland Presbyterian*, 10 December 1896: 4–5.

7. W. P. Bone to R. D. Bone (typescript copy), 20 September 1879, Bone Family Letters, TU Archives. Hereafter, Bone Letters. The originals are in the archives of Stephen F. Austin University, Nacogdoches, Texas.

8. Benjamin Spencer, "William E. Beeson," *The Cumberland Presbyterian*, 10 December 1896: 4.

9. W. B. Preston, "Some Presbyterian Pioneers," *The Presbyterian Advance*, 30 November 1916: 16.

10. Hornbeak, "Trinity University: Project of Pioneers," 36. See also "Our Dead Heroes," 4–5.

11. *TU Catalogue* (1869–70): 17. In 1875 Trinity trustees applied successfully for support from the Texas Public School Fund to educate primary, grammar, and preparatory students. The University received fifty cents per month for each qualified resident student. Board of Trustees Minutes, 27 February 1875.

12. Hornbeak, "Trinity University: Project of Pioneers," 29; *TU Catalogue* (1899–1900): 13.

13. *TU Catalogue* (1877–78): 5–12.

14. *TU Catalogue* (1869–70: 11–16; (1880–81): 14. Women who were not sufficiently prepared for college work took preliminary courses for a year. These included orthography, writing, primary geography, reading, mental arithmetic, and history of the United States.

15. For background on this movement, see Roger Geiger, ed., *The American College in the Nineteenth Century* (Nashville, 2000): 127–152.

16. *TU Catalogue* (1875–76): 22.

17. *TU Catalogue* (1877–78): 12.

18. *TU Catalogue* (1873–74): 25–27; (1875–76): 26; (1876–77): 23.

19. *TU Catalogue* (1877–78): 22; Hornbeak, "Trinity University: Project of Pioneers," 15–16, 25–26. Included among the law school graduates were A. C. Prendergast, prominent Waco lawyer who served as an Associate Justice of the Court of Criminal Appeals in Austin; and Truman H. Conner, who held the position of chief justice of the Court of Civil Appeals in Fort Worth for more than a quarter of a century.

20. Board of Trustees Minutes, 23 March 1872.

21. Board of Trustees Minutes, 8 June and 1 July 1876. In 1901 the Dallas Medical College organized as the medical department of Trinity University. An attempt to merge the Dallas Medical College in 1902 with the University of Dallas failed. Trinity dissolved its relationship with the medical college in 1903 because the standard of work was not acceptable. The medical college reorganized, but merged in 1904 with the Baylor University College of Medicine. See *Field and Laboratory Papers from the Science Division of Southern Methodist University* (October, 1952): 134–135, and Synod of Texas Minutes (CP), 7–21 September 1903: 36.

22. Brazos Synod Minutes (CP), 1869: 201.

23. E. B. Crisman, "Trinity University Endowment," *The Cumberland Presbyterian*, 14 April 1881: 1. In a report to Brazos Synod, the trustees acknowledged, "the fact is, there is little or no endowment." See Brazos Synod Minutes (CP), 7 October 1879. See also Reiwald, "Trinity University: Aspects of the Tehuacana Period," 41–42.

24. J. H. Wofford, "Texas Correspondence," *The Cumberland Presbyterian*, 25 July 1878: 1, and "To the Friends of Trinity University," 19 August 1875: 1.

25. E. B. Crisman, "Trinity University," *The Cumberland Presbyterian*, 11 November 1880: 2. Another tactic was to ask Trinity supporters to donate their paid scholarships to the school, to convert perpetual ones into two limited ones, or to pay tuition for a few years. See J. H. Wofford, "Texas Items," *The Cumberland Presbyterian*, 13 June 1878: 5.

26. Texas Synod Minutes (CP), 2–3 November 1870; Reiwald, "Trinity University: Aspects of the Tehuacana Period," 45.

27. Colorado Synod Minutes (CP), 1871: 150–151.

28. Hornbeak, "Trinity University: Project of Pioneers," 30–31.

29. Board of Trustees Minutes, 2 May 1873.

30. Board of Trustees Minutes, 20 June 1873.

31. Brazos Synod Minutes (CP), 1877: 49.

32. Board of Trustees Minutes, 27 July and 23 September 1871.

33. Hornbeak, "Trinity University: Project of Pioneers," 15–16.

34. Board of Trustees Minutes, 8 October 1870 and 1 February 1871.

35. Board of Trustees Minutes, 8 April 1871.

36. Board of Trustees Minutes, 29 June and 3 August 1871.

37. Brazos Synod Minutes (CP), 1873: 274; "Our Schools," *The Cumberland Presbyterian,* 22 July 1875: 4.

38. Each year in their report to the Cumberland synods, Trinity trustees requested financial assistance in order to complete work on the building.

39. Frederick Eby, *The Development of Education in Texas* (New York, 1925), 143–145. In 1865 the trustees of Waco University became the first to accept the mixing of sexes in classes on the recommendation of President Rufus C. Burleson.

40. For arguments, see "Co-education," *The Cumberland Presbyterian,* 30 August 1877: 1, and "Co-education of the Sexes," 20 June 1878: 4. For general background, see John S. Brubacher and Willis Rudy, *Higher Education in Transition,* 4th ed. (New Brunswick and London, 1997), 66–68.

41. Brazos Synod Minutes (CP), 1869: 199.

42. Board of Trustees Minutes, 23 October 1871.

43. Texas Synod Minutes (CP), 4–6 October 1872.

44. Brazos Synod Minutes (CP), 1873: 268. The full text of the petition is given in these minutes.

45. Brazos Synod Minutes (CP), 1873: 271–272.

46. Colorado Synod Minutes (CP), 1873: 170–171; Texas Synod Minutes (CP), 1873: 115–116; Brazos Synod Minutes (CP), 1873: 292–293.

47. Board of Trustees Minutes, 24 February 1877.

48. *The Cumberland Presbyterian,* 24 August 1889: 12.

49. *TU Catalogue* (1896–97): 6–7.

50. Brazos Synod Minutes (CP), 6–8 October 1877. My assumption in this narrative is that the "troubles" centered on Beeson's relationship with the literary department faculty members. Efforts to find corroborating evidence in sources other than official records have to this point in time proved unsuccessful. It is also possible that the controversy involved differences of opinion regarding coeducation, but this does not seem likely, given the faculty's previous unanimous resolution supporting the practice. Unfortunately, Beeson papers, once noted as being in the Trinity University Archives, are missing. They might provide more specific information regarding the issues involved in the dispute.

51. Board of Trustees Minutes, 2 September 1876.

52. Board of Trustees Minutes, 23 September 1876.

53. Board of Trustees Minutes, 23 December 1876.

54. Board of Trustees Minutes, 27 January 1877.

55. Board of Trustees Minutes, 10 and 24 February 1877.

56. Board of Trustees Minutes, 24 March 1877.

57. Board of Trustees Minutes, 12 April 1877.

58. Board of Trustees Minutes, 25 August 1877.

59. Board of Trustees Minutes, 31 August 1877.

60. Board of Trustees Minutes, 11 June and 24 November 1877 and 11 June 1878.

61. Texas Synod Minutes (CP), October 1877: 182.

62. Board of Trustees Minutes, 11 June 1877 and 11 June 1878; Annual Report to the Three Synods, October 1878, Box 1, Tehuacana Papers, TU Archives. Hereafter, Tehuacana Papers.

63. Figures from *TU Catalogue* (1900–01): 50–57.

64. W. P. Bone to R. D. Bone, 15 November 1879, Bone Letters.

65. W. P. Bone to R. D. Bone, 23 February 1880, Bone Letters.

66. S. M. Templeton to R. D. Bone, 18 October 1879, Bone Letters. For another student's perspective, see V. W. Grubbs, *Practical Prohibition* (Greenville, TX, 1887): 9–17.

67. S. M. Templeton to R. D. Bone, 17 May 1881, Bone Letters.

68. *TU Catalogue* (1869–70): 15.

69. Winstead P. Bone to Jessie N. Bone, 4 October 1879, Bone Letters.

70. *TU Catalogue* (1881–82): 18–19.

71. *TU Catalogue* (1875–76): 29.

72. *TU Catalogue* (1875–76): 30.

73. *TU Catalogue* (1871–72): 28–29.

74. *TU Catalogue* (1881–82): 19.

75. *TU Catalogue* (1874–75): 32–33. These regulations are included in all early catalogues. The account of the meeting is taken from a letter written by a Trinity student to his parents. See Luther P. Sears to parents (photocopy), 15 December 1878, TU Archives.

76. "Items from Trinity," *The Cumberland Presbyterian*, 20 April 1885: 2. On another occasion, a Trinity student wrote, "We had a glorious meeting last night. I never saw anything equal to it. I don't believe I ever saw as many happy people in my life at one time. Four conversions night before and seven last night—eleven in all." W. P. Bone to R. D. Bone, 27 October 1882, Bone Letters.

77. Brubacher and Rudy, *Higher Education in Transition*, 84–99. See also Light Townsend Cummins, *Austin College: A Sesquicentennial History, 1849–1999* (Austin, 1999), 39–40.

78. Information taken from a letter [c. 1880] written by Hudson to B. G. McLeskey, president of Trinity University, Box 1, Tehuacana Papers.

79. Hornbeak, "Trinity University: Project of Pioneers," 38.

80. *TU Catalogue* (1871–72): 25–26.

81. *TU Catalogue* (1872–73): 23; (1874–75): 22.

82. William Hudson, "Examining Students in Trinity University," *The Cumberland Presbyterian*, 4 March 1875: 1; 1 April 1875: 2.

83. Winstead Bone to Robert D. Bone, 30 January 1880, Bone Letters.

84. Jessie Bone to Robert D. Bone, 12 and 30 September 1882, Bone Letters.

85. William Hudson, "Examining Students in Trinity University," *The Cumberland Presbyterian*, 1 April 1875: 2.

86. S. T. Anderson to R. G. McLeskey, 17 August 1885, TU Archives. The Board later dismissed Anderson after complaints from several parents who said they would not patronize the school if Anderson remained.

87. On occasion faculty reminded the students that the literary societies were not autonomous. In 1897 the board of trustees noted that it was the prerogative of the faculty "to amend or abolish any program submitted to them, to make suggestions to the societies and to do whatever in their judgment will promote the usefulness of

the societies as organic parts of the University." Board of Trustees Minutes, 1 June 1897.

88. Brubacher and Rudy, *Higher Education in Transition*, 47.

89. *TU Catalogue* (1896–97): 42–43.

90. B. E. Looney, "Student Life in Trinity University, 1891–1894," 20 September 1958, Box 2, Tehuacana Papers.

91. Ratio-Genic Society "Critic's Book," Box 1, Tehuacana Papers.

92. H. P. Bone to R. D. Bone, 18 October and 29 November 1879, Bone Letters.

93. John Bone to Mrs. G. M. Bone, 13 November 1898, Bone Letters.

94. *Trinity Collegian* (June 1877): 4, TU Archives. Two additional issues have been preserved in this collection.

95. Mitchell, "The History of Trinity University from 1869–1934," 35; J. H. Wofford, "Trinity University," *The Cumberland Presbyterian*, 27 June 1878: 5; *The Trinity Herald* (March 1885): 1.

96. *TU Catalogue* (1896–97): 10, 43–44.

97. Board of Trustees Minutes, 23 December 1882.

98. Board of Trustees Minutes, 20 march 1883. The *TU Catalogue* stated that the penalty for participating in a secret society was expulsion. *TU Catalogue* (1883–84): 29.

99. D. S. Bodenhamer, "Trinity University Commencement," *The Cumberland Presbyterian*, 13 June 1895: 756; "President William S. Beeson," *The Cumberland Presbyterian*, 10 December 1896; 4–5.

100. Jesse Bone to R. D. Bone, 12 September and 2 November 1882, Bone Letters.

101. "Trinity University," *The Cumberland Presbyterian*, 22 September 1882: 1.

Notes to Chapter Three

1. In private correspondence, trustee N. A. Davis said that if the new president (McLeskey) could raise money for endowment, then people would be content to have the school stay in Tehuacana. "But if not," he said, "I am of the opinion that it will be made appear that the university has friends that are not satisfied with what the Board has done and Tehuacana will feel it. For if we cannot endow at Tehuacana, let us go where we can." N. A. Davis to J. R. Kirkpatrick, 11 August 1885, Box 1, Tehuacana Papers.

2. Board of Trustees Minutes, 9 September 1882.

3. D. S. Bodenhamer, "The Rev. B. G. McLeskey, D.D.," *The Cumberland Presbyterian*, 6 May 1886: 2. The program for ministerial students featured "rigid drilling in all those things pertaining to clerical and pulpit manners. We preach a sermon, read a scripture lesson, read hymns and take general lessons in manners. This new feature is a supply which has not come too soon, for many of our boys cannot go to Lebanon." *Trinity Herald*, April 1884: 6.

4. Hornbeak, "Trinity University: Project of Pioneers," 40.

5. Board of Trustees Minutes, 10 January 1884.

6. Board of Trustees Minutes, 3 June 1884.

7. Board of Trustees Minutes, 8 June 1885. The *TU Catalogue* for 1883–84 listed five vacancies in the collegiate department and two in the music and art departments.

8. Board of Trustees Minutes, 9 September 1885.

9. The *Texas Observer* began publication in 1879 as a vehicle for promoting Trinity University and the Cumberland Presbyterian Church in Texas. Initially published in Tehuacana, it was moved to Dallas and the name was changed to the *Texas Cumberland Presbyterian*.

10. J. D. Kirkpatrick to E. B. Crisman, 10 March 1883, and J. R. Brown to E. B. Crisman, 11 March 1883, Box 1, Tehuacana Papers.

11. J. H. Wofford to B. G. McLeskey, 4 August 1885, Box 1, Tehuacana Papers.

12. Board of Trustees Minutes, 9 September 1885.

13. Board of Trustees Minutes, 31 October 1885; 3 February 1886.

14. For a background of this period, see Christopher J. Lucas, *American Higher Education: A History* (NY, 1994), 139–184.

15. "Luther Apelles Johnson," *Trinitonian*, January 1901: 42, in L. A. Johnson Presidential Papers, TU Archives.

16. Charles A. Harper, *A Century of Public Teacher Education* (Westport, Ct., 1970), 80–86, 124–126.

17. "Trinity University," *St. Louis Observer*, 16 July 1896: 6; Hornbeak, "Trinity University: Project of Pioneers," 41.

18. *TU Catalogue* (1885–86): 12; "Trinity University," *St. Louis Observer*, 16 July 1896: 6.

19. D. M. Harris, "Trinity University," *The Cumberland Presbyterian*, 30 July 1885: 4.

20. *TU Catalogue* (1885–86): 14. Subsequently, this information was included in the university catalogue as a money-saving measure.

21. *TU Catalogue* (1886–87): 24–25.

22. *TU Catalogue* (1885–86): 19–21.

23. *TU Catalogue* (1886–87): 23; (1887–88): 21–22.

24. Board of Trustees Minutes, 7 June 1887.

25. *TU Catalogue* (1888–89): 2.

26. *TU Catalogue* (1889–90): 16–31.

27. Board of Trustees Minutes, 7 June 1887.

28. *TU Catalogue* (1896–97): 11, 18–19. For a concise description of the Trinity curriculum in the 1890s, see "Trinity University," *St. Louis Observer,* 16 July 1896: 5. For background on the elective controversy, see Brubacher and Rudy, *Higher Education in Transition,* 100–115.

29. Frederick Rudolph, *The American College and University: A History* (New York, 1962), 348–352.

30. Board of Trustees Minutes, 31 May 1893 and 29 May 1895. See also Hornbeak, "Trinity University: Project of Pioneers," 41. Johnson credits trustee N. A. Davis with being instrumental in convincing board members to adopt the new policy. L A. Johnson, "Chaplain N. A. Davis," *The Cumberland Presbyterian,* 17 and 24 January 1895.

31. "Editorials," *Trinitonian*, March 1901: 146–147.

32. Luther Apelles Johnson, "The Work and Place of Denominational Colleges and Universities," pamphlet (Nashville, Tn., 1897), 27. On one occasion Johnson found it necessary to distance himself publicly from Harper's endorsement of the application of higher criticism to Biblical studies. While acknowledging that he was familiar with the application of higher criticism to the study of profane literature, Johnson assured

readers of the *St. Louis Observer* in 1894 that he had not accepted any of Harper's conclusions regarding Biblical criticism. "I believe I have too much of the scientific and scholastic spirit to form precipitately any views contrary to those I have always held." L. A. Johnson, "An Explanation," *St. Louis Observer*, 26 April 1894: 5.

33. *Minutes of the General Assembly of the Cumberland Presbyterian Church,* 1892: 35.

34. Board of Trustees Minutes, 1 June 1892; *Minutes of the Synod of Texas of the Cumberland Presbyterian Church Synod of Texas Minutes (CP),* 1892: 14. Hereafter, *Synod of Texas Minutes (CP).*

35. Board of Trustees Minutes, 1 June 1898.

36. Johnson, "The Work and Place of Denominational Colleges and Universities," 28.

37. Board of Trustees Minutes, 2 May 1889.

38. Board of Trustees Minutes, 18 September 1889 and 23 January 1890.

39. Board of Trustees Minutes, 2 June 1890.

40. Board of Trustees Minutes, 2 June 1890.

41. Hornbeak, "Trinity University: Project of Pioneers," 42.

42. *TU Catalogue* (1890–91): 7–8.

43. *TU Catalogue* (1891–92): 10–11. Variations in dress occurred from time to time, but changes were only minor.

44. Originally known as Rule Ten, it was most frequently listed in the catalogues as Rule Nine. See, for example, *TU Catalogue* (1890–91): 7 and (1893–94): 7.

45. "Yvetta Graham Mitchell, "Social Life at Trinity University in 1869," *Trinitonian,* 5 May 1944; Everett, *Trinity University,* 28–29.

46. *Waxahachie Daily Light,* 17 April 1928; Everett, *Trinity University,* 30.

47. Mary Newton Beskow, "Trinity in Old Tehuacana Days," 2 October 1958, Box 1, Tehuacana Papers; Everett, *Trinity University,* 30. Despite faculty supervision, male and female students managed to get together. "Had a time this afternoon, in spite of the ninth rule. Just after our C. E. closed, Sterling & myself went over to the bluff with Adelaide & Lillie. We sure had a jolly good time. Don't think any one of the Profs saw us as they attended the wedding this afternoon." John N. Bone to Mrs. G. M. Bone, 30 April 1899, Bone Letters.

48. Melvina Watkins, "Rule Ten," 7 October 1958, Box 1, Tehuacana Papers; Everett, *Trinity University,* 29.

49. Daisy McKinney Perry, "Trinity at Tehuacana," 13 October 1958, Box 1, Tehuacana Papers; Everett, *Trinity University,* 32.

50. John Bone to Mrs. G. M. Bone, 20 November 1898, Bone Letters. A Trinity student from the early 1890s stated, "There's wasn't very much liquor drunk there. You just didn't have it at all. Of course, at a school like that there would be some boys who would drink but there was very little drinking going on among our folks out there." Morgan Baker Remembers Trinity at Tehuacana (typescript, n.d [c. 1965]), Box 1, Tehuacana Papers.

51. Hornbeak, "Trinity University: Project of Pioneers," 31.

52. Everett, *Trinity University,* 32.

53. Brubacher and Rudy, *Higher Education in Transition,* 122.

54. Board of Trustees Minutes, 27 May and 1 June 1898, Appendix A (Faculty Report).

55. Board of Trustees Minutes 31 May 1898.

56. *Trinitonian* (March 1901):147.

57. "Trinity University," *The Cumberland Presbyterian*, 26 April 1900: 17; Cummins, *Austin College*, 136–37.

58. *Trinity Exponent*, April 1888: 1–7, TU Archives. Only a few issues from the period 1888–90 have survived.

59. Minutes of the Timothean Society, passim, Box 2, Tehuacana Papers. The name of the society derives from First Timothy 2:15, "Study to show thyself approved unto God, a workman that needeth not to be ashamed, rightly dividing the word of truth."

60. William Hudson, "Trinity University Expedition," *The Cumberland Presbyterian*, 23 July 1885: 2 and 30 July 1885: 4.

61. William Hudson, "Trinity University's Exploring Expedition," *The Cumberland Presbyterian*, 10 September 1885: 2. See also issues dated 6, 13, and 20 August.

62. "Trinity University," *The Cumberland Presbyterian*, 13 August 1901: 21. On a number of occasions, Campbell and a Trinity choral group visited area churches and made presentations. In Mexia, the local newspaper reported, "the music was fully up to the high standard already established by the profession in his musical entertainments. Especially good was the solo by Professor Campbell." "The Lecture," *Mexia Evening News*, 9 May 1900: 2.

63. Brubacher and Rudy, *Higher Education in Transition*, 132–133.

64. "University Notes," *Trinitonian*, March 1901: 153.

65. John Bone to J. R. Bone, 25 September 1898, Bone Letters.

66. B. E. Looney to Clarkie Patton Harrison, 23 October 1962, TU Archives. For a background on intercollegiate athletics, see Rudolph, *The American College and University*, 390–391. Believing that collegiate sports fostered community spirit and developed individual character, President Harper in 1892 hired Amos Alonzo Stagg as football coach and awarded him professional rank and tenure.

67. George P. Stoker, "First Football Captain Sees Tigers Play Cowboys," 29 October 1953, in "Tales of Tehuacana," Box 1, Tehuacana Papers.

68. The name Warriors derives from the Tehuacana tribe of Native Americans who had lived and hunted in the vicinity before white settlers came to the area.

69. "Athletics," *Trinitonian*, February 1901: 95–99; William L. Jordan, "Football history of Trinity University," Box 1, Waxahachie Papers, TU Archives.

70. "University Notes," *Trinitonian* (March 1901): 153; Looney to Harrison, 23 October 1962.

71. Marla Pierson, "Ivory Tower in Mesquite Patch," *Waco-Tribune Herald*, 5 October 1996. It is possible, however, that basketball first came to Tehuacana after 1902 when Westminster College occupied the campus. Primary sources in the archives give no indication of basketball being played during Trinity's occupancy of the Tehuacana campus.

72. *Synod of Texas Minutes (CP)*, 13–18 September 1888: 22.

73. *Synod of Texas Minutes (CP)*, 17–21 September 1891: 18.

74. *TU Catalogue* (1890–91): 5; Board of Trustees Minutes, 1 June 1897; Vivian E. Smyrl, "Tehuacana, Texas," in Tyler, et al. (eds.), *The New Handbook of Texas*, VI, 236. Rail service to Tehuacana was completed in 1903 when the Trinity and Brazos Valley Railway finished its track between Cleburne and Mexia, passing through

Tehuacana. Tehuacana lost its rail service during World War II, and the line never reopened.

75. Hornbeak, "Trinity University: Project of Pioneers," 25.

76. *TU Catalogue* (1896–97): 9; *Minutes of the Synod of Texas (CP)*, 13–17 September 1894: 37 and 12–16 September 1895: 39.

77. "Trinity University," *St. Louis Observer*, 16 July 1896: 3–7. The article was reproduced and distributed by the university to reach a wider audience in Texas.

78. D. M. Harris, "In Texas," *St. Louis Observer*, 19 November 1896: 3.

79. "Eighth Annual Report of the Educational Commission of the Cumberland Presbyterian Church," in *Minutes of the General Assembly of the Presbyterian Church in the United States of America*, 1902, II: 113–115. Although Trinity employed an agent to solicit funds in Texas for the Million Dollar Endowment Movement, the results were disappointing, and trustees abandoned the project. See "The Progress and Present Condition of the Endowment," *The Cumberland Presbyterian*, 9 August 1900: 126; "Education in Texas," 31 January 1901: 147.

80. During its last twelve years in Tehuacana, tuition was unchanged: $20 for preparatory students and $25 for collegiate students.

81. "Unveiling of the Monument of Dr. L. A. Johnson," *The Cumberland Presbyterian*, 12 June 1902: 757; Board of Trustees Minutes, 19 July 1900.

82. *Synod of Texas Minutes (CP)*, 15–19 November 1900: 44.

83. *Waxahachie Enterprise* 23 November 1900.

84. *Synod of Texas Minutes (CP)*, 15–19 November 1900: 42; "Waxahachie and Trinity University," *The Cumberland Presbyterian*, 28 March 1901: 403.

85. *Synod of Texas Minutes (CP)*, 12–16 September 1901: 15.

86. *Waxahachie Enterprise*, 28 June 1901.

87. *Synod of Texas Minutes (CP)*, 12–16 September 1901: 15.

88. *Synod of Texas Minutes (CP)*, 12–16 September 1901: 23; Board of Trustees Minutes, 30 September 1901.

89. Walter, *A History of Limestone County*, 119–120; Patrick Pearson, "Original Tehuacana Campus Undergoes Renovation," *Trinitonian*, 24 February 1995: 11. In 1916 Westminster became a junior college and was later affiliated with Southwestern University in Georgetown, Texas. From 1953 to 1972, the Congregational Methodist denomination operated the Westminster College and Bible Institute on the premises, but the property then passed into private hands.

90. Cited in "Trinity University," *The Cumberland Presbyterian*, 19 April 1902: 465.

91. Robert Bone to Nevie Bone, undated [c. 1900–01], Bone Letters.

92. Jesse Anderson to Board of Trustees, 21 October 1901, Box 1, Tehuacana Papers. Anderson submitted his resignation to the trustees on 21 October 1901 but stayed for the remainder of the academic year. He returned to the University of Chicago for additional graduate work and later served the Cumberland Presbyterian Church in Hubbard City, Texas. See David S. Bodenhamer, "In Memory of Rev. Jesse Anderson, A. M., Ph.D.," *The Cumberland Presbyterian*, 9 November 1905: 538–539.

93. Board of Trustees Minutes, 7 January 1902.

94. "Trinity's Cornerstone Laying," *The Cumberland Presbyterian*, 3 April 1902: 43.

95. Everett, *Trinity University*, 55–56; *Waxahachie Enterprise*, 21 March 1902.

96. "Trinity University," *The Cumberland Presbyterian,* 5 June 1902: 29–30.

97. "Trinity University Commencement Exercises," *The Cumberland Presbyterian,* 12 June 1902: 751.

98. Ibid.

Notes to Chapter Four

1. "Trinity University," *Waxahachie Enterprise,* 6 December 1901. Ira Landrith, a prominent Cumberland Presbyterian Church executive and candidate for the Trinity presidency, made the statement.

2. *TU Catalogue* (1902): 15.

3. Waxahachie leaders promised that if Trinity came to their city, they would spearhead a movement to close all saloons in Ellis County. "Church News," *The Cumberland Presbyterian,* 30 August 1902: 497; *Trinity University Bulletin* (August 1911): 4. Hereafter, *TU Bulletin.*

4. See, for example, "One Hundred Lashes," *Waxahachie Enterprise,* 15 September 1905, and "Burning of Steven Davis at the Stake," 15 September 1905. Perpetrators of the burning said, "This is no mob. This is a gathering of gentlemanly citizens of Ellis County who believe in the protection of their wives and daughters by making examples of the black brutes who violate the sanctity of a home."

5. These generalizations are based on an examination of yearbook photographs and enrollment surnames as well as interviews with Waxahachie alumni/ae.

6. Hornbeak, "Trinity University: Project of Pioneers," 50–51.

7. Hornbeak, "Trinity University: Project of Pioneers," 53.

8. Board of Trustees Minutes, 1 June 1903.

9. "The Opening of Trinity University," *The Cumberland Presbyterian,* 23 October 1902: 461.

10. Board of Trustees Minutes, 6 November 1902.

11. Board of Trustees Minutes, 1 June 1903.

12. Hornbeak, "Trinity University: Project of Pioneers," 53–54.

13. Hornbeak, "Trinity University: Project of Pioneers," 54–55.

14. Hornbeak, "Trinity University: Project of Pioneers," 55.

15. Hornbeak, "Trinity University: Project of Pioneers," 56.

16. *Minutes of the Synod of Texas of the Presbyterian Church in the U.S.A.,* 1913: 13. Hereafter, *Synod of Texas Minutes (PCUSA).*

17. Hornbeak, "Trinity University: Project of Pioneers," 57. See also "Trinity University," *The Cumberland Presbyterian,* 16 June 1904: 763.

18. Hornbeak, "Trinity University: Project of Pioneers," 59–60; "Trinity University," *The Cumberland Presbyterian,* 30 June 1904: 827.

19. "The Presidency Declined," *Waxahachie Enterprise,* 7 June 1904.

20. Hornbeak, "Trinity University: Project of Pioneers," 59.

21. The decline of clergy presidents at private institutions began in the last decade of the nineteenth century; Denison in 1889, Illinois College in 1892, Yale in 1899, Princeton in 1902, and Marietta in 1913 exemplify this trend. See Rudolph, *The American College and University,* 419–420.

22. "Notes from Trinity University," *The Cumberland Presbyterian,* 5 January

1907: 27; D. S. Bodenhammer, "Trinity University," *The Cumberland Presbyterian,* 27 July 1905: 91.

23. "Inauguration and Dedication at Trinity University," *The Cumberland Presbyterian,* 4 May 1905: 570–571.

24. *Synod of Texas Minutes (CP),* 1905, Appendix A: 30.

25. Hornbeak, "Trinity University: Project of Pioneers," 78.

26. Board of Trustees Minutes, 5 May 1905.

27. Board of Trustees Minutes, 5 April 1906.

28. *TU Catalogue* (1907–08): 16. Despite references to modern facilities, toilet and bath facilities were located in an exterior building about twenty-five yards from the main building.

29. James H. Smylie, *A Brief History of the Presbyterians* (Louisville, Ky., 1996): 107.

30. For a full description of the reunion controversy, see Brackenridge, *Voice in the Wilderness,* 133–162.

31. "Aid Given to Trinity University from 1906–1922," Record Group (RG) 32-27-12, Presbyterian Historical Society Archives (Philadelphia, Pa.). Hereafter, PHS Archives.

32. For historical background on the Board of College Aid, see C. Harve Geiger, *The Program of Higher Education of the Presbyterian Church,* 83–102. At the Presbyterian College Union meetings, participants discussed topics such as "Present Educational Agencies and Their Functions," "The Honor System," "Principles to be Followed in Selecting Professors," and "Should All Teachers be Voting Members of the Faculty?"

33. Barrus, Baughn, and Campbell, *A People Called Cumberland Presbyterians,* 323–379.

34. *The Texas Cumberland Presbyterian,* 1 April 1907: 2. Turner frequently acknowledged that the "union question" had a debilitating effect on his efforts to raise money.

35. "The Texas Presbyterian University, Report of the Dallas Commercial Club," 19 October 1905, RG 32-27-3, PHS Archives.

36. W. H. Claggett to James Dickson, 1 January 1906, 29 August and 14 September 1907, and 1 January 1908, RG 32-27-3, PHS Archives. Additional correspondence on this subject can be found in the same record group.

37. J. S. Dickson to W. H. Claggett, 31 May 1907, RG 32-27-3, PHS Archives.

38. Samuel L. Hornbeak to J. S. Dickson, 12 May 1908, RG 32-27-3, PHS Archives.

39. Board of Trustees Minutes, 5 April 1907; W. H. Claggett to J. S. Dickson, 14 September 1907, RG 32-27-3, PHS Archives. Turner subsequently became president of Hastings College in Nebraska and later returned to Lincoln University as chief executive officer. In 1930, at seventy years of age, Turner was ordained to the gospel ministry and served as pastor in various churches in Illinois until his death in 1938. Hornbeak, "Trinity University: Project of Pioneers," 78–79.

40. Board of Trustees Minutes, 20 June 1908.

41. Hornbeak, "Trinity University: Project of Pioneers," 80.

42. Hornbeak, "Trinity University: Project of Pioneers," 81.

43. Hornbeak, "Trinity University: Project of Pioneers," 81–82.

44. Board of Trustees Minutes, 3 June 1908.

45. Hornbeak, "Trinity University: Project of Pioneers," 84.

46. *TU Catalogue* (1908–09): 26–27.

47. *TU Catalogue* (1907–08): 25. Trinity faculty allowed electives "but [did] not allow freedom of election to the extent of permitting the student to take continually the line of least resistance."

48. *Mirage* (1912): n.p.

49. *TU Catalogue* (1905): 33–52. For a discussion of the rise of the elective principle, see Rudolph, *The American College and University*, 287–306.

50. *TU Catalogue* (1903–04): 25; (1904): 24; (1907–08): 23–24.

51. *TU Catalogue* (1915–16): 82.

52. *TU Catalogue* (1922–23): 28–29.

53. *TU Catalogue* (1908–09): 51; (1917–18): 59.

54. *TU Bulletin* (September 1909): 3–4.

55. *TU Bulletin* (February 1910): 4.

56. *TU Catalogue* (1918): 57–58, 61.

57. *TU Catalogue* (1907–08): 51–52; (1919): 67.

58. *TU Bulletin* (August 1917): 1–3.

59. *TU Catalogue* (1910): 4; Board of Trustees Minutes, 3 June 1911 and 4 June 1912. Initially Hornbeak appointed a part-time athletic director for young men at an annual salary of $500.

60. *TU Bulletin* (February 1915): 2–3; (April 1917): 23.

61. *TU Bulletin* (June 1918): 2; (September 1918): 1–4. Patriotism flourished on the Trinity campus during World War I. Women made surgical dressings and knitted sweaters in Drane Hall, the YMCA raised $1,700 for a "Friendship War Fund," and the student body collected $125 to erect a seventy-five foot metal flagpole and flag in front of the administration building. Trinity faculty dedicated the 1918 catalogue "to our boys in khaki," citing the Biblical verse, "Greater love hath no man than this, that a man lay down his life for his friend." See *TU Bulletin* (December 1917): 4; *TU Catalogue* (1918): 1.

62. Samuel L. Hornbeak to James Clarke, 20 December 1918, RG 32-27-13, PHS Archives. For information regarding the military program, see *TU Bulletin* (September 1918): 1–4.

63. Theresa R. Simms, "History of Trinity University Library," June 1960, n.p., Box 00–01, TU Archives. In 1918 the only references books in the library were a *Webster's New International Dictionary, Hastings Dictionary of the Bible, The Encyclopedia Britannica* (13th ed.), *Hastings Encyclopedia of Religion and Ethics,* and *Schaff-Herzon Encyclopedia of Religious Knowledge.* The library did not have a line item in the budget until 1932 (and then only $500). Prior to that time, it relied on donations from individuals and church groups.

64. *Synod of Texas Minutes (PCUSA),* 1914: 53–54.

65. Hornbeak to James E. Clarke, 14 June 1919, RG 32-27-11, PHS Archives.

66. Hornbeak to C. H. French, 21 July 1915, RG 32-27-10, PHS Archives.

67. Hornbeak to J. S. Dickson, 20 July 1908, RG 32-27-6, PHS Archives. In response to the question, "Has it [Trinity] in its faculty only such teachers as can be regarded as exerting a definitely Christian influence over the students?" Hornbeak replied, "It has only such teachers from Coach of Athletics to president." Board of College Aid Financial Aid Form, 1910–11, RG 32-32-7, PHS Archives.

68. *TU Bulletin* (September 1905): 251.

69. "Institutional Survey," 1920, n.p., RG 32-27-11, PHS Archives.

70. L. J. Berry, "In Appreciation of Dr. D. S. Bodenhamer," "Trinity Recollections, 1903–1920," TU Archives.

71. *Synod of Texas Minutes (PCUSA)*, 1914: 53; Board of Trustees Minutes, 4 April 1914; Hornbeak, "Trinity University: Project of Pioneers," 43–44. Bodenhamer's pension was exceptional. Trinity had no pension provisions during the Waxahachie years. When asked, "What does the institution do when its men are too old to work?" Hornbeak responded, "It has in some instances been compelled to dismiss them from service." See Samuel L. Hornbeak, "A Brief Statement of Facts Concerning Trinity University," 31 May 1910: 3, RG 32-27-7, PHS Archives.

72. Board of Trustees Minutes (Executive Committee), 26 April 1911. Hereafter, Board of Trustees Ex. Com. Minutes.

73. *Synod of Texas Minutes (PCUSA)*, 1912: 48, 59–60.

74. Hornbeak, "Trinity University: Project of Pioneers," 89.

75. "Trinity Closes Successful Year," *Waxahachie Daily Light*, 7 June 1911; Hornbeak, "Trinity University: Project of Pioneers," 88–89.

76. "Dedication of Drane Hall," *Waxahachie Evening Herald*, 27 April 1912.

77. *Synod of Texas Minutes (PCUSA)*, 1912: 59–60; *TU Catalogue* (1914): 101.

78. Samuel L. Hornbeak, "A Brief Statement of Facts Concerning Trinity University," May 1910, passim, RG 32-27-7, PHS Archives.

79. *Synod of Texas Minutes (PCUSA)*, 1914: 56.

80. Hornbeak to James Clarke, 18 February 1914, RG 32-27-9, PHS Archives.

81. Hornbeak to Robert McKenzie, 5 September 1914, RG 32-27-9, PHS Archives.

82. "Trinity University Celebration," *Waxahachie Daily Light*, 9 January 1915.

83. Hornbeak to James Clarke, 25 October 1916, RG 32-27-10, PHS Archives.

84. Hornbeak to James Clarke, 29 May 1915, RG 32-27-9, PHS Archives.

85. Hornbeak to Robert McKenzie, 24 April 1917, RG 32-27-10, PHS Archives.

86. *Synod of Texas Minutes (PCUSA)*, 1917: 97.

87. *Synod of Texas Minutes (PCUSA)*, 1919: 70–71.

88. Board of Trustees Minutes, 14 February 1928.

89. Hornbeak, "Trinity University: Project of Pioneers," 99; *Synod of Texas Minutes (PCUSA)*, 1918: 6–8.

90. "Fiftieth Commencement of Trinity University," *TU Bulletin*, 15 May 1919: 1.

91. Hornbeak to James Clarke, 14 June 1919, RG 32-27-11, PHS Archives.

92. Hornbeak to James Clarke, 20 June and 18 September 1919, RG 32-27-11, PHS Archives.

93. Hornbeak to Edgar P. Hill, 21 January 1919, RG 32-27-11, PHS Archives.

94. Hornbeak to James Clarke, 18 September 1919, RG 32-27-11, PHS Archives.

95. *Synod of Texas Minutes (PCUSA)*, 1919: 72–73.

96. Hornbeak to Calvin H. French, 7 June 1917, RG 32-27-11, PHS Archives.

97. James Clarke to Edgar P. Hill, 4 April 1919, RG 32-27-11, PHS Archives.

98. *Waxahachie Daily Light*, 11 February 1920; Board of Trustees Minutes, 8 June 1920.

99. Board of Trustees Minutes, 11 February 1919. According to Trinity's annual

report to the Presbyterian General Board of Education in 1920, the university's productive endowment was $178,624 and approximately $50,000 was listed as unproductive. Record Group 32-27-11, PHS Archives.

100. Hornbeak, "Trinity University: Project of Pioneers," 125–126. During Hornbeak's tenure as president, more students graduated than during any other continuous period of twenty-four years. The graduates included 5 lawyers, 4 physicians, 10 theological students, 22 ministers, 4 foreign missionaries, and 104 teachers. *TU Catalogue* (February 1919): 1.

101. Hornbeak, "Trinity University: Project of Pioneers," 45.

Notes to Chapter Five

1. Rudolph, *The American College and University*, 355–359. "Students of both sexes are allowed to meet in the classroom and the chapel and are a mutual restraint and inspiration. They have, however, separate boarding places, and separate grounds." *TU Catalogue* (1903): 10. The only student protest noted in official university records occurred in 1903 when President Kirkes encountered what was termed "an uprising of the students." No additional information is provided except that it dealt with a case of disciplining a female student. See Board of Trustees Minutes, 23 April 1903.

2. Rudolph, *The American College and University*, 454. In 1922 the Trinity faculty appointed a committee "to consider carefully the whole matter of the use of automobiles by students, especially their use during the two weeks of commencement." Trinity University Faculty Minutes 1922–55, 12 December 1922, TU Archives. Hereafter, Faculty Minutes with date. The following year the faculty ruled that "no boarding student be permitted to keep a car in Waxahachie for personal use." Faculty Minutes, 25 January 1923.

3. Rudolph, *The American College and University*, 357–358.

4. "Trinity University," *The Cumberland Presbyterian*, 30 October 1902: 497. Trinity yearbooks always provided fully illustrated coverage of football followed by a section entitled "Minor Sports" for all other athletic teams. See *Mirage* (1927): 137.

5. *TU Bulletin* (15 January 1903): 81.

6. *TU Catalogue* (1902–03): 55; (1904): 69.

7. "Athletics," *Trinitonian*, October 1902: 44–45.

8. Joe Rugel, "Forerunner of the Cotton Bowl Series," in "Trinity Recollections" (typescript, 1903–1920), n.p., Box 1, Waxahachie Papers.

9. "Athletics," *Trinitonian*, November 1902: 72. The student editor described a game in which one man caught his opponent and bit off a piece of his hand. He was ejected from the game.

10. "Our Football Team," *Trinitonian*, December 1903: 9.

11. "Complimentary Reception," *Trinitonian*, December 1904: 18–19.

12. "Trinity Football Team Will Play Austin College," *Waxahachie Daily Light*, 27 November 1916. Interurban streetcars left at 8:00 A.M. and returned at 6:00 P.M. and cost $1.50.

13. Rudolph, *The American College and University*, 373–393.

14. *TU Catalogue* (1906): 76; "Athletic Department," *Trinitonian*, December 1906: 20; "Football Season Here," *Waxahachie Daily Light*, 21 September 1906.

15. *TU Catalogue* (1907): 77–78.

16. "Tennis," *Trinitonian*, October 1906: 21.

17. "University Notes," *Trinitonian*, November 1906: 20; "Waxahachie, Texas," *The Cumberland Presbyterian*, 18 October 1906: 505.

18. Board of Trustees Minutes, 11 February 1919.

19. "Campus Sensed Greatness," *Trinity Today* (October 1975): 1–2.

20. Board of Trustees Minutes, 13 January 1930. Trinity paid Holton a salary of $4,000, a thousand dollars more than Hornbeak, the senior professor on campus. Board of Trustees Minutes, 8 February 1927.

21. *Synod of Texas Minutes (PCUSA)*, 1930: 59, 66.

22. *Synod of Texas Minutes (PCUSA)*, 1934: 59; 1935: 54.

23. Board of Trustees Minutes, 9 February 1937; 10 and 18 May 1939; Minutes of Meeting of College Presidents and Athletic Representatives of the Texas Conference, 20 April 1941: 2. University officials periodically had problems with the behavior of athletes living in the T House. President Wear said that such behavior caused the university to have a bad image with neighborhood residents.

24. *Mirage* (1928): 98; (1929): 74.

25. Walter Cunningham, "Trinity 3 Texas A&M 0" in "Trinity Recollections, 1869–1950," typescript, n.p. Box 1, Waxahachie Papers.

26. "When Detroit Tigers Meet the Giants," *Waxahachie Daily News*, 23 March 1916.

27. "Trinity Player Signed by Tigers," *Waxahachie Daily News*, 4 April 1916.

28. "Trinity Team Ready for Game," *Waxahachie Daily News*, 27 September 1916.

29. The Tiger logo was used extensively for the first time in the 1922 *Mirage*.

30. "University Notes," *Trinitonian*, October 1902: 44–45.

31. Grace Herring Haynes, "Athletics at Trinity 1907–1911" in "Trinity Recollections, 1869–1950."

32. "Trinity Team Ready for Game," *Waxahachie Daily News*, 27 September 1916.

33. "Pep Rally," *Trinitonian*, 7 October 1919: 1–2.

34. *Mirage* (1940): 130.

35. *Mirage* (1937): n.p. Despite declining interest, Trinity cheerleaders continued the tradition of rallies and parades to encourage school spirit. During a pep rally in 1937, students formed a parade at the university and marched through the streets to the town square where they sang rousing fight songs, culminating with the alma mater. "Dynamic Pep," *Trinitonian*, 2 October 1937: 1.

36. *TU Bulletin* (1913): 6–7; *Trinitonian*, October 1914: 28.

37. *TU Catalogue* (1922): 77.

38. Miriam Clark, "Social Life in Trinity University," *Trinitonian*, April 1908: 12.

39. "Trinity Stag Roundup," *Waxahachie Daily Light*, 22 September 1916. In 1924 the Trinity faculty prohibited the Stag Roundup and other initiatory ceremonies that impacted negatively on "the good name and reputation of the institution." Faculty Minutes, 15 October 1924.

40. "Impressive Swing-In Affair," *Trinitonian*, 27 September 1940: 3.

41. "Swing Out Will be at Drane Hall," *Trinitonian*, 18 May 1940: 3.

42. Miriam Clark, "Social Life in Trinity University," *Trinitonian*, October 1914: 13.

43. "Founders Day Program Made," *Trinitonian*, 9 April 1932: 1; "Field Day, Chapel Program, and Banquet to Feature Annual Founders Day," 19 April 1934: 1.

44. "Trinitonian Rates Year's News Stories," *Trinitonian*, 25 May 1939: 1. May Day, another spring tradition, consisted of the coronation of a May queen, maypole dances, and a concluding banquet. See photographs in *The Presbyterian Advance*, 8 July 1915: 13.

45. "Ivy Day," *Trinitonian*, May 1907: 24. Another longstanding Trinity tradition was sitting on the green benches scattered throughout the campus, exchanging ideas, disseminating gossip, and "bull throwing" in general. When Trinity moved to San Antonio, the benches were transported to the new location. See "How About the Green Benches?" *Trinitonian*, 4 December 1942: 2.

46. "Texas Tidings," *The Presbyterian Advance*, 17 June 1915: 18.

47. *TU Catalogue* (1903–04): 13. Over the years this restriction was gradually eased. In 1922 women were permitted to meet guests at trains "properly chaperoned," and in 1931 they could do so "with approval from the Dean of Women." Subsequent catalogues omit references to this particular rule.

48. *TU Catalogue* (1903–04): 13–14. The *TU Catalogue* for 1922–23, p. 19, specified only that women use "simplicity in dress."

49. Miriam Clark, "Social Life in Trinity University," *Trinitonian*, April 1908: 12–13.

50. "Editorials," *Trinitonian*, 30 September 1932: 2.

51. *TU Catalogue* (1915): 114–15. The point system was dropped in 1923. Students were required to complete an extracurricular activity form and submit it to the dean, who could make decisions regarding student overloads. Faculty Minutes, 22 November 1923. Later the faculty instituted "Dead Week" at the end of the semester, when there were to be no student social activities, no tests, no papers assigned, and no rehearsals or extra class sessions. Faculty Minutes, 3 June 1941.

52. *Mirage* (1924): 86; (1937): n.p.; "Blue Key Chapter Undertakes Many Activities," *Trinitonian*, 15 May 1931: 2.

53. *Mirage* (1924): 84.

54. *Mirage* (1924): 90–92, 100.

55. *TU Catalogue* (1910): 95.

56. *Mirage* (1924): 78. The group also conducted field trips to various publishing organizations during the course of the school year. "Script Crafters Visit *Dallas News*," *Trinitonian*, 17 May 1923: 1–2.

57. *Mirage* (1925): 95. Music and drama organizations also flourished during this time period. Glee clubs, quartets, orchestra, band, and choir were among the options open to students. The Players Club, a student drama group, presented several plays during the academic year. See *Mirage* (1924): 85.

58. *Mirage* (1924): 89, 94, 97; (1927): 99–101; (1937): n.p.

59. *Mirage* (1924): 72–73.

60. *Student Handbook*, 1911–12. Some examples of the literary yells: "Tonight, Tonight! We'll have a fight, Tomorrow you'll be sore, Because the Looney Loving Cup Will be with you no more," and "Fe-fo-fi-fum, Philo-Sapphos on the run. What's the use of making a fuss, The Loving Cup belongs to us." See Hazel Gibbons Papers, Box 98-9, TU Archives.

61. *TU Catalogue* (1923–24): 101; (1926–27): 87.

62. *Mirage* (1924): 88.

63. The privilege was also extended to the editor-in-chief and the business manager of the *Trinitonian* and the *Mirage*. Faculty Minutes, 17 May 1923.

64. *Mirage* (1922): 101.

65. Faculty Minutes, 1 May 1924; *Mirage* (1927): 89.

66. *TU Catalogue* (1905): 108.

67. *TU Bulletin* (January 1919): 1–2; (May 1919): 1. In 1925 Trinity reported that 7,557 students had matriculated and 687 graduated (366 men and 321 women). *TU Catalogue* (1925–26): 12.

68. *TU Catalogue* (1930–31): 111.

69. *TU Catalogue* (1914): 97.

70. *Synod of Texas Minutes (PCUSA)*, 1938: 52–53.

71. *Mirage* (1925): 84.

72. "History of the Upper Room," *Trinitonian*, 20 November 1942: 2.

73. *Synod of Texas Minutes (PCUSA)*, 1939: 57.

74. "As a gesture of cooperation," the faculty agreed to lighten the scholastic load during the week so that students could attend the evening services "without endangering their class standing." "Spiritual Emphasis Week Begins," *Trinitonian*, 1 February 1936: 1.

75. *Synod of Texas Minutes (PCUSA)*, 1938: 52–53.

76. Burma to E. F. Hallenbeck, 31 January 1925, Box 6, Folder 32, Burma Correspondence. Hereafter, Burma Corres.

77. *Synod of Texas Minutes (PCUSA)*, 1930: 63. The university did not implement the recommendation.

78. "First Trinitonian Published as a Magazine," *Trinitonian*, 19 April 1934: 1.

79. *TU Bulletin*, 1 June 1912: 2.

80. Rudolph, *The American College and University*, 369–370.

81. A copy of the original student constitution can be found in Mitchell, "The History of Trinity University from 1869–1934," Appendix X, 188–194.

82. Mitchell, "The History of Trinity University from 1869–1934," 190–192. The bylaws specified "All students are expected to conduct themselves, at all times, as ladies and gentlemen. All students are expected to do nothing that will reflect upon the good name of the university. Unnecessary noise shall be prohibited on the campus and in the Administration building during class hours. No smoking is allowed on campus."

83. Faculty Minutes, 3 April 1923.

84. Faculty Minutes, 14 March and 2 May 1927. See also minutes of 9 December 1929, when a student was put on probation for cheating on a paper and given no credit for the assignment.

85. Faculty Minutes, 14 November 1932. In 1925 students and faculty formed the Joint Welfare Council to deal with violations of the honor code. See Faculty Minutes, 20 February and 3 May 1925.

86. Drane Fellowship Hall Minutes, 18 November 1924, Box 1, Waxahachie Papers.

87. Drane Fellowship Hall Minutes, 19 March 1924.

88. Drane Fellowship Hall Minutes, 14 January 1927.

89. Drane Fellowship Hall Minutes, 1 March 1926; Faculty Minutes, 3 March 1926.

90. Drane Fellowship Hall Minutes, 3 November 1925. By the 1930s, cases of discipline had considerably diminished. The most frequent admonition from the dean of women was to be more careful about signing in and out.

91. Faculty Minutes, 7 and 25 November and 4 and 9 December 1929. The loitering rule was relaxed in April 1930. Faculty also amended a catalogue statement concerning immoral conduct by striking out the word "usually" so that the statement read, "Immoral conduct such as drinking, gambling, and licentiousness, is [usually] subject to the severest discipline, which is suspension, or expulsion from college." Faculty Minutes, 10 March 1930.

92. Faculty Minutes, 16, 17, and 18 April 1930.

93. "Campus Comment," *Trinitonian*, 29 February 1930: 2; Faculty Minutes, 13 and 28 January, 14 April, and 12 May 1930. Some minor changes were made in the student constitution, but the honor code remained intact.

94. In 1918 the faculty deemed hazing offenses sufficiently serious to warrant a pronouncement that "the evils of hazing and class rushes are specifically forbidden" and that students engaging in such practices would be subject to suspension. To ensure compliance, school officials required students entering Trinity to sign a pledge that they would not participate in hazing activities. *TU Catalogue* (1918): 27.

95. One incident involved kidnapping a group of freshmen, beating them with brooms, and leaving them bound, gagged, and locked in an abandoned jail in a nearby town. Burma to T. W. Davidson, 9 September 1924, Box 5, Folder 24; Burma to A. L Groves, 29 March 1924, Box 5, Folder 27; and Burma to W. C. Pennington, 20 April 1925, Box 6, Folder 38, Burma Corres. See also W. C. Pennington to Burma, 19 April 1925, Box 6, Folder 38.

96. Faculty Minutes, 30 March 1926 and 1 October 1928.

97. Faculty Minutes, 25 October 1933.

98. Faculty Minutes, 26 October and 13 November 1933. Faculty members decided to ignore the chapel demonstration and take no action.

99. *TU Catalogue* (1935–36): 30.

100. "Freshman Regulations," *Trinitonian*, 21 March 1934. In 1939 the faculty forbade students to climb the water tower and paint class numerals. See Faculty Minutes, 12 September and 2 October 1939.

101. "How About Hazing?" *Trinitonian*, 27 September 1940: 2.

102. "Freshmen Loaf, Think, Study and Court," *Trinitonian*, 10 May 1934: 1, 3.

103. "Who is the Most Outstanding Man Alive?" *Trinitonian*, 18 February 1939: 1–2.

104. "Trinity Frosh Are Third-Termers," *Trinitonian*, 27 September 1940: 1.

105. "The Real Danger," *Trinitonian*, 18 May 1940: 2; "Hitler and Propaganda," *Trinitonian*, 18 February 1939: 2.

106. "Trinity Frosh Are Third-Termers," *Trinitonian*, 27 September 1940: 1.

107. "Trinity University," *The Presbyterian Advance,* 24 August 1917: 4. A graduate of the class of 1934 wrote, "I do not regret one minute that I have spent at Trinity, for I feel that I have been educated in more ways than just through books. I have learned to be independent in financial ways, and I have learned to make decisions for myself without so much aid of others. "Four Years with the Class of 1934," *Trinitonian,* 26 May 1934: 3.

108. James A. Spivey, interview with R. Douglas Brackenridge, 23 July 1999,

Oral History Collection, Trinity University Archives. Hereafter, interviews with the author are marked by "interview with RDB."

NOTES TO CHAPTER SIX

1. Burma to W. H. Claggett, 30 June 1925, Box 5, Folder 24, Burma Corres.; Mitchell, "The History of Trinity University from 1869–1934," 105–107. Throughout the Waxahachie period it is difficult to ascertain the basis on which university officials calculated endowment figures. It appears that they were sometimes overly optimistic about the value of property holdings and other investments. Moreover, they repeatedly borrowed from the endowment corpus and were unable to repay the money. Figures should always be taken as approximate rather than exact.

2. Burma, "Speech to Faculty," 24 September 1922, Box 2, Folder 6, Burma Corres.

3. "Texas Tidings," *The Presbyterian Advance,* 24 February 1916: 22; Hornbeak, "Trinity University: Project of Pioneers," 128–129.

4. "Texas Tidings," *The Presbyterian Advance,* 27 May 1920: 14.

5. Whenever a pulpit became vacant in the Synod of Texas, church members turned to Burma for advice in seeking a replacement. A high percentage of his correspondence deals with congregational, presbytery, and synod activities.

6. Burma, "Speech to the Faculty," 24 September 1922.

7. Burma to A. C. Bigger, 14 February 1924, Box 2, Folder 8, Burma Corres. The book in question was by Durant Drake, *Problems of Religion* (Boston and New York, 1916). Despite this action, Burma rejected fundamentalism and sided with Harry Emerson Fosdick, the well-known liberal preacher of the day. In a letter to a friend, Burma said, "Fosdick is the greatest living prophet in America and is doing more to give thinking people and young people a belief with convictions back of it than all the fundamentalists combined are doing." Burma to R. L. Irving, 6 March 1923, Box 3, Folder 14, Burma Corres.

8. Burma, "Speech to the Faculty," 24 September 1922. Burma's correspondence indicates that he gave considerable attention to the needs of students, especially those who were having difficulty academically or financially. Learning that a student had taken her trunk with her when she left for Christmas holidays, Burma wrote to her, "I sincerely trust this does not mean that you contemplate dropping out of school. I hope to see you back bright and early on January 6th." Burma to Katherine Culp, 24 December 1924, Box 2, Folder 7, Burma Corres.

9. In hiring a home economics teacher, Burma specified that "she ought to be a southern woman and a Christian, and, since Trinity University is a Presbyterian institution, a Presbyterian would not be amiss." Burma to M. C. Vicars, 26 March 1924, Box 2, Folder 7, Burma Corres.

10. Burma to W. E. Jones, 4 January 1923, Box 3, Folder 14, Burma Corres.

11. Burma to Florence M. Foster, 30 July 1928, Box 9, Folder 52; and Burma to Frederick E. Stockwell, 3 March 1931, Box 10, Folder 61, Burma Corres.

12. Burma wrote to Mrs. Chapman, "All of us really feel that this gracious gift through your beloved husband has marked the dawning of a new day for Trinity University. Just how much it has meant and will mean eternity alone can reveal." Burma to Mrs. P. A. Chapman, 23 September 1924, Box 2, Folder 7, Burma Corres.

13. Faculty Minutes, 11 June 1923; *Synod of Texas Minutes (PCUSA),* 1924:

42–43. Burma reported in 1924 that Trinity's active endowment was $415,315 and that the institution had an accumulated deficit of $43,000, which included debts on buildings. Burma to James Clarke, 29 March 1924, Box 2, Folder 9, Burma Corres.

14. Faculty Minutes, 8 June 1924; *TU Catalogue* (1928–29): 43–44.

15. Burma to Thomas W. Synnott, 20 November 1929, Box 9, Folder 57, Burma Corres.

16. Burma to Charles B. Lipman, 23 September 1924, Box 2, Folder 8; and Burma to A. C. Biggar, 14 February 1924, Box 2, Folder 9, Burma Corres. For a comprehensive history of the Southern Association, see James D. Miller, *A Centennial History of the Southern Association of Colleges and Schools* (Decatur, Ga., 1998). Chapter Two, "Shaping Society, Shaped by Society," is particularly insightful for the conditions under which Trinity joined the association.

17. Burma to Frederick E. Stockwell, 29 March 1924, Box 2, Folder 9; and Burma to E. E. Moore, 18 September 1925, Box 6, Folder 36, Burma Corres.

18. Illion T. Jones to Burma, 23 December 1925, Box 6, Folder 23; and Burma to H. L. Jamieson, 24 December 1926, Box 8, Folder 45, Burma Corres.

19. *TU Catalogue* (1929–30): 17; Mitchell, "The History of Trinity University from 1869–1934," 105–107.

20. *TU Catalogue* (1929–30): 17; *Synod of Texas Minutes (PCUSA)*, 1928: 56–58. The board advanced $12,000 from endowment funds pending sale of the Watkins property. Because of declining property values, however, the farm remained unsold during the Depression. See Burma to Frederick E. Stockwell, 1 October 1932, 32-32-13, PHS.

21. Hornbeak, "Trinity University: Project of Pioneers," 135–136; Mitchell, "The History of Trinity University from 1869–1934," 108; James A. Spivey, interview with RDB, 21 July 1999.

22. Burma to R. W. Norris, 14 November 1929, Box 9, Folder 26, Burma Corres.

23. Hornbeak, "Trinity University: Project of Pioneers," 136. In 1934 Trinity purchased three nearby homes for male residential students designated as the Franklin E. Haynes Home, the Freshman House, and the T House (for athletes). *TU Catalogue* (1939–40): 12.

24. Faculty Minutes, 11 March and 27 September 1931; Raymond Leach to Harold M. Robinson, 7 June 1934, RG 32-45-13, PHS Archives.

25. Trustees Papers, Box 007, TU Archives.

26. Board of Trustees Minutes, 12 February 1935; *Synod of Texas Minutes (PCUSA)*, 1934: 60; 1935: 57. Between 1935 and 1943, the federal government spent more than $93 million dollars on the higher education of 620,000 students, motivated more by temporary economic considerations than by any long-term plan to aid college students. See Brubacher and Rudy, *Higher Education in Transition*, 230–231.

27. *Synod of Texas Minutes (PCUSA)*, 1932: 60–61. Much of the endowment was vested in real estate that plummeted in value during the Depression decade. Foreclosures did little to alleviate the cash-flow problem that the university was experiencing.

28. Board of Trustees Minutes, 30 June 1933.

29. "Reverend Leach, New Trinity University President," *Trinitonian*, 21 February 1934: 1–2.

30. Hornbeak, "Trinity University: Project of Pioneers," 144.

31. Leach to H. L. Robinson, 24 October 1934, RG 32-27-13, PHS Archives. Trinity's investment policy was to invest in loans on real estate property in Ellis County. Board of Trustees Minutes, 12 February 1924.

32. A. H. Burnett to William L. Young, 18 September 1934, RG 32-27-13, PHS Archives.

33. "Announcement Regarding Dancing," 7 January 1925, Box 6, Folder 23, Burma Corres. Eight students were suspended for violating the rule forbidding boarding students to attend dances, but because it was the first offense under the new regulation, the faculty gave them a suspended sentence, carrying with it the loss of all privileges. Faculty Minutes, 16 March 1925.

34. Faculty Minutes, 21 February 1929. The committee presented a list of fourteen recommendations, none of which included dancing on campus. Faculty Minutes, 21 March 1929.

35. Faculty Minutes, 27 October 1932; Board of Trustees Minutes, 29 October 1932.

36. Faculty Minutes, 3 March 1933; Board of Trustees Minutes, 14 March 1933.

37. Faculty Minutes 5 November 1934 and 23 January 1935.

38. "Blue Key News Flashes" (December 1934): 1, RG 32-27-16, PHS Archives. See also *Mirage* (1935): 31.

39. "Should Trinity Students Dance?" *Trinitonian*, 1 May 1935: 2.

40. S. M. Templeton to Raymond Leach, 15 December 1934 and 23 January 1935; Raymond Leach to S. M. Templeton, 7 January 1935. Copies of these letters are found on pages 245–249 of Board of Trustees Minutes. Some of Leach's correspondents supported his stance on dancing mostly on the pragmatic grounds that students would dance with or without administrative permission. One supporter wrote, "In response to the argument advanced that no one has decided to be a missionary or a minister while dancing, I would reply that I know of no record of a person having decided for the ministry or to the Christian life while engaged in playing a game of football, a game of tennis, or a game of basketball." Hasting Harris to Leach, 11 February 1935, RG 32-27-13, PHS Archives.

41. "Should Trinity Students Dance?" *Trinitonian*, 1 May 1935: 2.

42. Board of Trustees Minutes, 22 October 1935.

43. *Synod of Texas Minutes (PCUSA)*, 1935: 16, 35; "Regulations," *Trinitonian*, 10 November 1941. Regulations set forth by Dean Davis specified that the word *dance* not be used in headlines or any articles describing social events.

44. In 1932 Burma reported that, in order to maintain full membership in the Southern Association, Trinity needed to raise the salaries of department heads and increase the library budget from $2,000 to $5,000 annually. He said that they were meeting the minimum requirements in other areas "except possibly in the matter of endowment." Board of Trustees Minutes, 15 March 1932. See also letter of J. R. McCain, chairman of the Committee on Triennial Reports, to Raymond Leach, 4 January 1934, in Board of Trustees Minutes, 12 February 1935.

45. Raymond Leach to Harold M. Robinson, 14 February 1936, RG 32-27-13, PHS Archives.

46. C. C. Carmichael to Paul J. Schwab, 5 January 1937, RG 32-27-13, PHS Archives.

47. In 1938 the library was moved to the basement of Drane Hall, where students

had adequate study facilities and access to the enlarged collection of books and periodicals. See *Synod of Texas Minutes (PCUSA)*, 1939: 60.

48. Board of Trustees Minutes, 10 May 1939. President Wear told a gathering of Texas Conference athletic representatives that Trinity had an annual deficit of $10,000 in football and that he wished that all schools in the conference would drop the sport. See "Minutes of the Meeting of College Presidents and Athletic Representatives of the Texas Conference," 20 April 1940," n.p., Austin College Merger Folders, Papers of President Wear. Hereafter, Wear Papers.

49. *Synod of Texas Minutes (PCUSA)*, 1941: 57; Trinity Faculty Minutes, 8 December 1941.

50. Raymond H. Leach to William L. Young, 1 October 1934, RG 32-27-13, PHS Archives.

51. Board of Trustees Minutes, 17 June 1936.

52. "Biography of Frank Lucian Wear," Box 1, Folder 1, Wear Papers.

53. Mitchell, "The History of Trinity University from 1869–1934," 115.

54. *TU Catalogue* (1925–26): 29–34. Operating on a three-term school year with Saturday classes, Trinity required 180 term-hours of credit, forty-five of them in the major.

55. *TU Catalogue* (1934–35): 25–64.

56. "Trinity Campus Biography," *Trinitonian*, 18 May 1940: 2.

57. Josephine Lumpkins Moore, "Autobiography," Box 1, Waxahachie Papers. Other courses initiated by Schwab, such as "The Ancestry of the English Bible" and "Inter-Testament History," reflect a critical-historical approach to the Bible. See *TU Catalogue* (1929–30): 40.

58. Board of Trustees Minutes, 12 February 1935; *Synod of Texas Minutes (PCUSA)*, 1935: 55. Schwab also encouraged faculty to attend meetings of educational associations and learned societies and to participate in panels and presentations. In 1935 he reported that one or more faculty members had represented Trinity at twenty-two such conferences during the year. *Synod of Texas Minutes (PCUSA)*, 1935: 51.

59. Faculty Minutes, 1 November 1923.

60. James A. Spivey, interview with RDB, 23 July 1999. Spivey attended Trinity from 1929 to 1933 and participated in the chapel program.

61. "T.U. Biology Class Conducts Survey," *Trinitonian*, 17 May 1923: 1.

62. *Synod of Texas Minutes (PCUSA)*, 1938: 54.

63. "Aviation Is Introduced at Trinity University," *Trinitonian*, 27 September 1940: 1; "All Trinity Flyers Have Made First Solo," *Trinitonian*, 15 November 1940: 1. See also *Synod of Texas Minutes (PCUSA)*, 1940: 57; 1941: 58.

64. Faculty Minutes, 13 May 1935; *Synod of Texas Minutes (PCUSA)*, 1935: 52.

65. "High I.Q.," *Trinitonian*, 9 October 1937: 1. A survey taken in 1920 asked current students why they came to Trinity. The most frequent reason given was "parents favored this college," followed by "recommendation of pastor or former student," a relative who previously attended the school, and coeducation. See "Advertising Survey," Box 2, Folder 7, Burma Corres.

66. Faculty Minutes, 2 December 1940.

67. "Many TU Graduates Continue Study," *Trinitonian*, 27 February 1936: 4.

68. *TU Catalogue* (1939–40): 14.

69. "Chapel Speakers," *Trinitonian*, 10 May 1934: 2.

70. In 1937 Trinity required attendance three times a week and allowed six absences a semester. After the seventh absence, students were placed on academic probation, and, for each additional absence, they were suspended for one week. The faculty suspended a student who "absented himself from Chapel exercises an excessive number of times . . . and has shown a defiant attitude toward it." Faculty Minutes, 28 February 1924.

71. Faculty Minutes, 19 May and 13 September 1937; "Will It Work?" *Trinitonian*, 2 October 1937: 2.

72. Faculty Minutes, 1 May 1939; *TU Catalogue* (1940–41): 38; *Synod of Texas Minutes (PCUSA)*, 1941: 58. The weekly services were led by faculty and designed to provide "genuinely religious inspiration and expression."

73. *Synod of Texas Minutes (PCUSA)*, 1939: 62–63. Financial figures revealed a net loss of $21,710.88 from operations in the year ending 30 June 1939, and the trend continued until Trinity's final year in Waxahachie.

74. *Synod of Texas Minutes (PCUSA)*, 1939: 39. My narrative tracing the merger negotiations between Austin College and Trinity University relies heavily on the work of Donald Everett's *History of Trinity University: The First Hundred Years*, Chapter IX. Readers interested in a more detailed account of this failed merger should consult Everett's work. For a description of events from an Austin College perspective, see Cummins, *Austin College*, 251–259.

75. Cummins, *Austin College*, 79–104.

76. For example, the U.S.A. Church endorsed a racially inclusive society and permitted the ordination of women as deacons and elders, and the U.S. Church accepted segregation as a cultural norm and denied women the right to any ordained office.

77. Board of Trustees Minutes, 14 November 1940; *Synod of Texas Minutes (PCUSA)*, 1940: 26–28.

78. "Dual Merger Explained," *Trinitonian*, 15 October 1940: 2.

79. *Synod of Texas Minutes (PCUSA)*, 1941: 35–37.

80. "Question: Merger of Austin College and Trinity University" (typescript, October 21, 1941), 2–3, Austin College folders, Wear Papers. According to President Tucker, many Austin College board members looked unfavorably on the proposed move to San Antonio. Writing to Arthur V. Boand, Tucker said, "You will have to remember that these are mostly North Texas men who look upon San Antonio as the center of Catholic rule, of Communistic activity, and of what one man called 'the rottenest government in Texas.' San Antonio will be a hard sell." E. B. Tucker to Arthur V. Boand, 28 March 1941, Austin College Folders, Wear Papers.

81. *Synod of Texas Minutes (PCUSA)*, 1941: 41.

82. Arthur V. Boand to James W. Laurie, 4 October 1962, Box 1, Waxahachie Papers.

83. Ibid.

84. Ibid.; University Committee of the San Antonio Chamber of Commerce, "Presentation Book," 122, TU Archives.

85. "Minutes, Board of Directors, San Antonio Chamber of Commerce," 25 March 1941, TU Archives.

86. "Minutes, Board of Directors, San Antonio Chamber of Commerce," 24 November 1941, TU Archives.

87. Everett, *History of Trinity University*, 123.

88. "Minutes, Special Meeting of Board of Directors, San Antonio Chamber of Commerce," 8 December 1941.

89. *Synod of Texas Minutes (PCUSA)*, 1942: 17. Shortly after the meeting, President Tucker of Austin College wrote a letter to committee members expressing doubts that the merger could be financed on a sound basis and urging that all merger activities cease for the duration of the war. E. B. Tucker to T. Thomsen, 13 December 1941, Austin College folders, Wear Papers.

90. Minutes of the Joint Committee of Austin College and Trinity University, 8 January 1942, Wear Papers.

91. *Synod of Texas Minutes (PCUSA)*, 1942: 20–25.

92. "Minutes, Board of Directors, San Antonio Chamber of Commerce," 24 November 1942.

93. "Greater Trinity Reared in San Antonio," *San Antonio Express*, 28 February 1942.

94. "Trinity University," *San Antonio Express*, 23 August 1942 (special insert).

Notes to Chapter Seven

1. T. R. Fehrenbach, "San Antonio," *The New Texas Handbook*, V, 796–797.

2. Edward Rian, "Trinity in the City of the Alamo" (typescript, n.d., n.p.), TU Archives.

3. Board of Trustees Minutes, 29 June 1942.

4. "Biographical Information," Monroe G. Everett Papers, TU Archives. Hereafter, Monroe Everett Papers.

5. Board of Trustees Minutes, 1 and 8 June 1942.

6. "Outline of the Proposed Basis of Merger, Austin College and Trinity University," Board of Trustees Minutes, 14 January 1943. The school would be known as either Trinity and Austin University or Austin and Trinity University.

7. For details, see Everett, *Trinity University*, 140–143, and Cummins, *Austin College*, 255–257.

8. Everett, *Trinity University*, 143.

9. Faculty Minutes, 5 October, 2 November, and 9 December 1942; 5 March 1943.

10. Board of Trustees Minutes, 8 April 1946. The *TU Catalogue* contained the following statement: "Any student who shows a persistent spirit of disobedience will not be permitted to remain as a member of the University family. A student who is manifestly out of harmony with the ideals of this institution may be dismissed without specific charges." *TU Catalogue* (1946–47): 47.

11. "Article," *Trinitonian*, 20 October 1942; Board of Trustees Minutes, 4 October 1944.

12. "Exhibit A-1," Board of Trustees Minutes, 18 May 1943.

13. "Exhibit A-1," Board of Trustees Minutes, 18 May 1943.

14. "University in the Sun," *Texas Parade* (April 1969): 4.

15. "Lonely Looies," *Trinitonian*, 24 March 1944: 2.

16. See, for example, columns in the *Trinitonian* on 8 October 1943, 24 March, 5 May, and 29 September 1944.

17. Ernie Pyle, "Captain Waskow's Men Say Goodbye," *Reader's Digest* (March 1944): 53–54, and "Courageous Captain," *Time Magazine* (17 January 1944): 24.

18. "Heels All-Campus Hosts," *Trinitonian*, 3 December 1943: 1.

19. "Student Stages Seasonal Festival," *Trinitonian*, 12 October 1945: 2.

20. "Less Than Half the Students Organized," *Trinitonian*, 15 February 1946: 2.

21. "Extracurricular," *Trinitonian*, 9 February 1944: 2.

22. Board of Trustees Minutes, 12 and 15 May 1946; "Health Board Suspends All Meetings," *Trinitonian*, 25 May 1946: 1.

23. Everett, *Trinity University*, 148–149.

24. *Synod of Texas Minutes (PCUSA)*, 16 October 1946: 9–10.

25. Board of Trustees Minutes, 16 May and 8 October 1947.

26. Board of Trustees Minutes, 12 May 1948.

27. "Dr. Paul J. Schwab Resigns," *Trinitonian*, 7 February 1947: 1; "Trinity's New Class Schedule," *Trinitonian*, 3 July 1947: 2.

28. Everett to M. C. Huntley, 20 February 1947, Monroe Everett Papers.

29. "Dr. Bruce Thomas, Dean," *Trinitonian*, 19 September 47: 7. See also Everett to Rasmus Thomsen, 1 May 1947, Monroe Everett Papers.

30. "Tex Taylor New Public Relations Officer," *Trinitonian*, 19 September 1947: 8.

31. *Synod of Texas Minutes (PCUSA)*, 1946: 63. Two years later, Trinity had ninety-one faculty of whom eighteen held a Ph.D. degree and forty-five a master's degree. Twenty-five percent of the faculty possessed bachelor's degrees. *Synod of Texas Minutes (PCUSA)*, 1948: 51.

32. Margaret Shannon, interview with RDB, 9 March 2000.

33. Everett, *Trinity University*, 190–191; Board of Trustees Ex. Com. Minutes, 7 August 1947.

34. Board of Trustees Minutes, 12 October 1949 and 11 May 1950. Admission requirements were flexible. Applicants with a bachelor's degree from an accredited institution with at least a B grade average could be admitted in full standing, others provisionally; graduates from unaccredited institutions could be admitted provisionally and receive full standing after successful completion of twelve hours of course work; college seniors with twelve hours or less remaining for their undergraduate degree were eligible to take some graduate courses. *TU Graduate Bulletin* (1951–52): 9–10.

35. "Report of the Chairman of the Graduate Council," Board of Trustees Minutes, 10 May 1951. See also Board of Trustees Minutes, 11 May 1950 and 6 May 1952.

36. J. Hoytt Boles to Monroe G. Everett, 27 April 1945 and 14 January 1946, Monroe Everett Papers. Students also clamored for the resumption of intercollegiate athletics. See "Let's Go Trinity," *Trinitonian*, 19 April 1946: 2.

37. Everett to Rasmus Thomsen, 24 January 1946, Monroe Everett Papers. Everett also said, "A dozen coaches with as many football teams will not make an outstanding, agreeable student out of a few psychopathic cases we have on campus."

38. "Trinity's First Football Season," *Trinitonian*, 6 December 1946: 6.

39. Board of Trustees Minutes, 16 May 1947.

40. "He Wants Home Grid Games," *Trinitonian*, 21 November 1947, 6; Everett, *Trinity University*, 155–157.

41. "New Athletic Director," *Trinitonian*, 24 September 1948: 4. James had

played tackle on the noted Praying Colonels of Centre College from 1918 to 1921 when they defeated Harvard and other eastern colleges.

42. "Uncle Bill James Confident," *Trinitonian*, 15 October 1948: 4; "Four Big LSC Colleges," *Trinitonian*, 7 February 1949: 4.

43. Glenna McCord, interview with RDB, 6 January 1999.

44. "Athletic Budget," Board of Trustees Minutes, 5 May 1949 and 6 May 1952.

45. "Freshman Participation Now Voluntary," *Trinitonian*, 29 September 1945: 1.

46. "Freshman's Last Stand," *Trinitonian* 12 October 1948: 1; "The Fish Struck Before Dawn," *Trinitonian*, 31 October 1950: 1.

47. "Constitution Explained," *Trinitonian* 19 March 1948: 2; "Proposed Constitution," *Trinitonian*, 16 April 1948: 4.

48. "Trinity Pioneers in Student Government," *Trinitonian*, 13 January 1950: 2.

49. *Mirage*, 1945: 75.

50. *Mirage*, 1947: 102.

51. *Mirage*, 1947: 124.

52. *Mirage*, 1947: 124.

53. "Trinity Finds Its Radio Voice," *Trinitonian*, 12 May 1950: 1.

54. "Texas High Schools Send Delegates," *Trinitonian*, 20 March 1950: 1; "Speech Tournament," *Trinitonian*, 4 March 1955: 1. The Scriptcrafters from the Waxahachie campus merged with the Sigma Tau Delta of the University of San Antonio campus to form the Gamma Delta Chapter of the national college writers' organization. Their major function was to sponsor the annual poetry conference, which began in Waxahachie in 1927. See "Scriptcrafters Merge," *Trinitonian*, 12 February 1948: 1; "Scriptcrafters to Sponsor Annual Poetry Meet," *Trinitonian*, 22 March 1946: 3.

55. "Thirteen Debaters Claim Placements," *Trinitonian*, 7 December 1947: 1.

56. "Students, Faculty, Begin Series," *Trinitonian*, 16 December 1949: 1. See also "Trinity Trio," *Trinity* magazine (Fall 2002): 42.

57. "TV Set Will Be Installed," *Trinitonian*, 21 February 1951: 1; "Careful Please," *Trinitonian*, 19 January 1951: 2.

58. Students frequently commented on the inequity and hypocrisy of the system. See "Justice on a Bus," *Trinitonian*, 19 April 1946: 2; "Sarcasm vs. Race Issue," *Trinitonian*, 5 March 1948: 4.

59. "Civil Rights Program," *Trinitonian*, 25 March 1948: 2.

60. "The Impending Decision," *Trinitonian*, 21 January 1949: 2; "Racial Analysis," *Trinitonian*, 21 May 1948: 4.

61. "Negro Delegates Lead Discussion," *Trinitonian*, 19 March 1948: 1.

62. "Bethune Guest Speaker," *Trinitonian*, 7 May 1948: 1. Another program on the Radio Forum was, "Are We Solving the Race Problem in Texas," *Trinitonian*, 21 January 1949: 1.

63. "All Alone and Blue," *Trinitonian*, 19 January 1951: 2.

64. "Can We Exercise Freedom," *Trinitonian*, 27 April 1951: 2.

65. "Trinity Students and the Truman-MacArthur Tilt," *Trinitonian*, 20 April 1951: 2; "Newsitorials," *Trinitonian*, 27 April 1951: 2.

66. Board of Trustees Minutes, 14 January 1943. In January 1945 Trinity officials implemented a program of Sunday morning church services on campus that might lead to the establishment of a Presbyterian Church on or near the Woodlawn Cam-

pus. Everett expressed hope that such would become a strong church serving the neighborhood even if Trinity moved to a new location. Lack of adequate funding and a poor attendance resulted in a decision to abandon the project. See Everett to J. Hoytt Boles, 2 January 1945, and J. Hoytt Boles to Gerald Blackburn, 24 March 1945, Monroe Everett Papers.

67. Kenneth Reeves, "Survey Report on Expressions of Christian Influence at Trinity University," 4 February 1952: 7, PHS Archives.

68. "The Chapel Corner," *Trinitonian*, 26 September 1947: 2.

69. "Offices to Close," *Trinitonian*, 7 February 1947: 2; "Two Weekly Obligations," *Trinitonian*, 21 November 1947: 4.

70. Reeves, "Survey Report," 7. Reeves characterized the Trinity students as "religiously conservative, evangelical, uncritical, but idealistic and activistic toward all good causes."

71. "From Missions to Trinity," *Trinitonian*, 8 October 1948: 2. See also "The Hour is 11 O' Clock," *Trinitonian*, 6 February 1948: 4, and "Something To Be Done," *Trinitonian*, 27 February 1948: 2.

72. "KYFM To Broadcast," *Trinitonian*, 4 February 1949: 1.

73. "History of the Upper Room," *Trinitonian*, 20 February 1948: 3; Board of Trustees Minutes, 4 October 1950.

74. Rasmus Thomsen to Everett, 5 March 1947, and Thomsen to E. Fay Campbell, 5 October 1946, Monroe Everett Papers.

75. T. Jasper Manton to Thomas Wilbanks, 2 July 1951, Personnel Committee Papers, TU Archives. The synod retained the right to approve the election of trustees, but in practice the slate of nominees presented by the university was rarely challenged.

76. T. Jasper Manton to Donald H. Stewart, 14 October 1949, Personnel Committee Papers, TU Archives.

77. T. Frank Murchison to T. Jasper Manton, 17 October 1949.

78. Everett to Rasmus Thomsen, 5 June 1946, Monroe Everett Papers.

79. *TU Catalogue* (1935–36): 10–11 and (1951–52): 26–27. See also Reeves, "Survey Report," 4–5.

80. Everett to Rasmus Thomsen, 20 May 1947, Monroe Everett Papers.

81. J. Hoytt Boles to Monroe G. Everett, 23 November 1948, and J. Hoytt Boles to E. Fay Campbell, 29 November 1948, Monroe Everett Papers.

82. Board of Trustees Minutes, 20 October 1942 and 14 May 1943.

83. "Planning Committee Report," Board of Trustees Minutes, 10 May 1944.

84. "Report on Campus Site," Board of Trustees Minutes, 11 July 1944.

85. "Minutes of the Special Site and Planning Committee," 14 September 1944; Board of Trustees Minutes, 4 October 1944. Voting in favor of the Alamo Stadium site were trustees Calvert, Murchison, Napier, Hunsdon, Wheeler, and Everett. Voting in favor of the San Pedro site were Frost, Brown, Miller, and Fitzhugh.

86. "City to Trade 50 Acres," *San Antonio Express*, 1 November 1944. The City Council approved a deed of exchange in which San Antonio gained title to the lots at the corner of Bandera Road and Woodlawn Avenue and Trinity received fifty acres near Alamo Stadium.

87. Board of Trustees Minutes, 9 May 1945; Minutes of the Special Campus Site and Planning Committee," 10 September 1945. For a more detailed description of various pieces of property, see Everett, *Trinity University*, 171–172.

88. *They Were Right*, Trinity Brochure (1948): 22–23, TU Archives.

89. Board of Trustees Minutes, 9 May 1945. See also Mary Carolyn Hollers George, *O'Neil Ford, Architect* (College Station, Tx., 1992): 93–97.

90. *They Were Right*: 24.

91. Board of Trustees Ex. Com. Minutes, 13 November 1947.

92. Board of Trustees Minutes, 16 May 1947.

93. Board of Trustees Minutes, 29 September 1948.

94. "New Campus Roof Raising Begins," *Trinitonian*, 3 April 1950: 1. For a more technical description of the process, see "Trinity University," *Architectural Forum* (September 1951), 1–8.

95. "University in the Sun," *Texas Parade* (April 1969): n.p. Box 90-41, TU Archives.

96. Board of Trustees Ex. Com. Minutes, 16 January 1949. From 1949 until his death in 1982, Ford was involved in the design of more than forty buildings on the Trinity campus. Cocke and Ford formed a joint venture partnership doing business under the name of Trinity Architects. See David Dillon, *The Architecture of O'Neil Ford* (Austin, Tx., 1999), 58–59. Even though the architects expected the campus to expand rapidly, they placed the first buildings rather close together in order to block future administrations from erecting a "great central monument" that would destroy the architectural integrity of the unique campus setting. For an excellent description of the campus design, see "Another Look At Trinity," *Architectural Forum* (March 1955): 130–136.

97. Board of Trustees Minutes, 5 May and 12 October 1949; Board of Trustees Ex. Com. Minutes, 18 November 1949.

98. "Pep Rally Slated," *Trinitonian*, 17 October 1947: 1.

99. Board of Trustees Minutes, 29 September 1948.

100. "500 Attend Dedication," *Trinitonian*, 29 April 1949: 1.

101. "Administration-Classroom Building," *Trinitonian*, 27 January 1951: 1.

102. "New Campus Roof Raising," *Trinitonian*, 14 April 1950: 1.

103. Bruce Thomas, interview with RDB, 19 January 2000. This oft-repeated story has many variations, including the erroneous statement that it was James W. Laurie rather than Everett who participated in the event. Although most accounts relate that the men stood under the slab and photographers recorded the scene, I have not uncovered any such photographs. The narrative heightened with retelling. One account says that the two men crawled under the slab when it was only forty inches above the ground. See "University in the Sun," *Texas Parade* (April 1969): n.p., Box 90-41, TU Archives.

104. "Tickets Go On Sale," *Trinitonian*, 4 May 1951: 1; "Tommy Dorsey Band To Arrive," *Trinitonian*, 11 May 1951: 1.

105. Board of Trustees Ex. Com. Minutes, 11 August 1950 and 25 January 1951.

106. Board of Trustees Minutes, 11 May 1950.

107. Board of Trustees Minutes, 12 October 1949 and 11 May 1950. See also Bruce Thomas, interview with RDB, 6 July 1998.

108. Board of Trustees Minutes, 11 May 1950.

109. Board of Trustees Ex. Com. Minutes, 25 January 1951. Chapman set up the trust to ensure that the corpus would continue to grow. To achieve this goal, he stipulated that beneficiaries would receive half their allotted share for ten years and then

a third for the next five years. According to this procedure, he projected that the trust would be worth about $10 million within fifteen years.

NOTES TO CHAPTER EIGHT

1. "Trinity Future Major Subject," *San Antonio Express-News*, 9 December 1953.

2. T. Jasper Manton to Paul C. Payne, 4 May 1951, Personnel Committee Papers, TU Archives. Hereafter, Personnel Com. Papers.

3. T. Jasper Manton to Clint Small, 11 January 1951, Personnel Com. Papers. From Manton's perspective, it was imperative that the next president inspire the confidence and support of the church. "This was scarcely true of the last administration. Dr. Everett, who had many frailties, was possibly at his poorest in public relations, and especially with the church." T. Jasper Manton to Thomas Wilbanks, 6 July 1951, Personnel Com. Papers.

4. R. Douglas Brackenridge, *Beckoning Frontiers: A Biography of James W. Laurie* (San Antonio, Tx., 1976), 105–108. See also R. Douglas Brackenridge, *Eugene Carson Blake: Prophet With Portfolio* (New York, 1978).

5. Paul C. Payne to T. Jasper Manton, 11 June 1951, Personnel Com. Papers. It is interesting to speculate how the histories of the denomination and Trinity University would have been different if Laurie had won the Stated Clerk's position and Blake had come to Trinity. Both men had exceptional leadership abilities but differed in theological perspectives and administrative styles.

6. For additional biographical information on the Lauries, see Brackenridge, *Beckoning Frontiers*.

7. Dorothy Laurie, interview with RDB, 8 July 1971.

8. James W. Laurie to Jean Laurie, n.d., cited in Brackenridge, *Beckoning Frontiers*, 146.

9. Brackenridge, *Beckoning Frontiers*, 181–186. The text of the sermon is given in full.

10. Brackenridge, *Beckoning Frontiers*, 110–111. Unfortunately, these notebooks were inadvertently destroyed several years ago when many of the Laurie papers were temporarily stored in the Sams Center. To my knowledge, I am the only person other than Laurie who ever saw the notebooks. The consistency with which he maintained the discipline of self-examination and reflection over a long period of time indicates that this was a deeply engrained spiritual discipline.

11. Brackenridge, *Beckoning Frontiers*, 111.

12. Leon Taylor, interview with RDB, 17 July 1973.

13. Gene Robinson, interview with RDB, 10 December 1973.

14. Board of Trustees Ex. Com. Minutes, 25 January 1951.

15. Board of Trustees Minutes, 6 May 1952.

16. Board of Trustees Minutes (Building Committee), 14 April 1952. See also Everett, *Trinity University*, 179–180.

17. Board of Trustees Minutes, 12 May 1948 and 11 May 1950.

18. Board of Trustees Minutes, 6 May 1952.

19. Board of Trustees Minutes, 29 September 1948; Board of Trustees Ex. Com. Minutes, 25 January 1951.

20. Board of Trustees Minutes, 6 May and 19 September 1952. Conscientious objectors were protected and exempted from the military requirement.

21. "Transfer Firms to Aid in Trek," *Trinitonian*, 21 March 1952: 1; Board of Trustees Minutes, 31 July 1952. The move received attention from newspapers, magazines, radio, television, and newsreels throughout the United States. Actually, the move took much longer than one day. Transfer of library books began three weeks before the publicized moving day, and movement of furniture and other equipment continued for several days afterward.

22. Nancy Cook, "On Trinity Hill," *Trinity* magazine (Summer 1982): 16.

23. Ibid.

24. Brackenridge, *Beckoning Frontiers*, 149.

25. "Trinity Wears New Look," *Trinitonian*, 16 May 1952: 3; "Trinity Library," *Trinitonian*, 25 September 1953: 4; Board of Trustees Minutes, 31 July 1952.

26. In some instances, the single telephone served two offices and six faculty members. The telephone was passed back and forth through a hole cut in the wall between the two offices. For a number of years, the entire physical education department shared one small office in Northrup Hall and conducted activity classes on an outdoor concrete slab located on the lower campus.

27. These situations existed when the author came to the campus in 1962. Conditions improved shortly thereafter.

28. Brackenridge, *Beckoning Frontiers*, 120.

29. All of this is the personal experience of the author. Others too numerous to mention would verify these observations.

30. "Large Number of Delegates," *Trinitonian*, 3 October: 1952: 1; "Dr. Laurie Installed," *Trinitonian*, 10 October 1952: 1.

31. James W. Laurie, "How You Make History," n.d., Laurie Papers, TU Archives. Hereafter, Laurie Papers. In his letters to university trustees, Laurie was always candid about the importance of raising money for Trinity. When one trustee was re-elected to the Board, Laurie congratulated him and then said, "We are very happy to have your continuing interest and counsel and, of course, expect in addition volumes of students and buckets full of money from New Mexico." James W. Laurie to Robert Boshen, 26 October 1956, Trustees Correspondence (Boshen), Box 0–14, TU Archives.

32. Everett, *Trinity University*, 195–196.

33. Everett, *Trinity University*, 192–193.

34. Everett, *Trinity University*, 194–195.

35. Report on Visit to Trinity University, 7–10 November 1965, Institutional Self-Study and Periodic Visitation Program, pp. 14–19, TU Archives. Hereafter, 1965 Southern Association Visitation Team Report. The Southern Association team recommended that "the revaluation of financial structure be given top priority in the institution's thinking."

36. James W. Laurie to Henry Coffield, 5 June 1953, Trustees Correspondence (Coffield), Box 0-14, TU Archives.

37. Nancy Cook, "Notes on Interviews with Trinity Administrators," n.d. [c. 1977], n.p., Box 86-49, TU Archives. The source of this story was Leon Taylor.

38. Cook, "Notes on Interviews with Trinity Administrators," n.p.

39. John Burke, conversation with RDB, June 2000. The author also had conver-

sations with Derwood Hawthorne, who confirmed this story and gave other examples of unsuccessful efforts to restrain Laurie's spending. He admitted, however, that Laurie always managed to raise the necessary funds to see the projects to completion.

40. Everett, *Trinity University*, 190.

41. Faculty Minutes, 29 January 1953.

42. Board of Trustees Minutes, 6 October 1954.

43. Board of Trustees Minutes, 16 February 1955.

44. Bruce Thomas, interview with RDB, 21 February 2001.

45. Board of Trustees Minutes, 9 May 1956.

46. Board of Trustees Minutes, 9 May 1956; Bruce Thomas, interview with RDB, 8 February 2001. In 1958 Thomas reported that nine new African-American students were attending Trinity but that neither they nor any previously admitted African-American students were living in the dormitories. Board of Trustees Minutes, 15 October 1958.

47. Board of Trustees Minutes, 8 May 1957. Laurie was aware that the appointment of Miller would not be favorably received among some leaders in the Synod of Texas. He selected Arch Underwood, a prominent Presbyterian layman from Amarillo, as a vice president of the board in order to "balance the ticket." See James W. Laurie to Arch Underwood, 30 April 1957, Trustees Correspondence (Underwood), Box 0-16, TU Archives.

48. Presbyterian clergyman Thomas J. Wilbanks, who was a member of the board at the time of Miller's election, stated privately that it was "through him [Miller] that the dichotomy between Trinity at San Antonio and the Presbyterian Church which started Trinity in the first place" was created. Wilbanks also quoted another Presbyterian board member who said, "I don't know what I am doing here. It seems to me that Trinity is no longer Christian but Chamber of Commerce." Thomas J. Wilbanks to Thomas G. Wilbanks, 27 February 1985, Trustees Correspondence, Box 0-16, TU Archives.

49. Board of Trustees Minutes, 8 May 1957; "Trustee Dies," *Trinitonian*, 20 November 1964: 1. See also *TU Catalogue* (1960–61): 198. Other early female board members included Mrs. H. Lutcher Brown (1944), Margarite B. Parker (1945), Margaret Kampmann (1946), and Susan Griffiths (1954).

50. "Trinity University Report of Institutional Self-Study for the Commission on Colleges of the Southern Association of Colleges and Schools" (October 1965): 148, TU Archives. Hereafter, 1965 Self-Study.

51. 1965 Self-Study: 150.

52. Board of Trustees Minutes, 4 October 1944.

53. Faculty Minutes, 12 September 1952.

54. Faculty Minutes, 23 and 28 April 1953. The Faculty Senate would be involved only with administrative decisions to terminate faculty members who already had attained tenure, and such cases were to be referred to the Faculty Senate only "for consideration and advice."

55. Recommendations for promotion were presented to the Faculty Senate by the president and dean in consultation with the respective department chairs. After open discussion, a two-thirds vote by secret ballot was required to validate a promotion recommendation.

56. Standards for promotion to full professor included "established reputation as a teacher, demonstration in teaching of imagination and ability to organize material, worth to the institution on a basis other than his work in his specific specialization alone, and a Ph.D. or the equivalent."

57. Board of Trustees Minutes, 20 February 1957. There was a three-year gap between the commencement of the faculty policy and the approval by the board of trustees.

58. One exception that was approved permitted the administration to issue contracts to instructors beyond the probationary period without conveying tenure, provided that the faculty member agreed to the arrangement. Trinity University Faculty Senate Minutes, 16 February 1954, Box 90-15, TU Archives. Hereafter, Faculty Senate Minutes.

59. Faculty Senate Minutes, 5 February 1957. The administration continued to present appointments above the rank of assistant professor to the Faculty Senate for approval. Otherwise, hiring, tenure, and promotion decisions were the prerogative of the dean and the president with an opportunity for input from the department chair. See "Southern Association Report Form" (1957): 8–9.

60. 1965 Self-Study: 101–104.

61. "Trinity to offer New Course," *Trinitonian*, 5 February 1952: 1.

62. "Engineering Science Field," *Trinitonian*, 17 February 1961: 1; 1965 Self-Study, 102–103.

63. Stacy Maloney, "Southwest Foundation for Biomedical Research," in Tyler, et al. (eds.) *The New Texas Handbook*, V, 1172–1173.

64. *TU Catalogue* (1961–62): 26.

65. Faculty Minutes, 27 April 1954; Board of Trustees Executive and Finance Committee Minutes, 31 July 1968. Hereafter, Board of Trustees Ex. and Fin. Com. Minutes. Founded in 1947, the agency originally met in the servants' quarters of the Landa Estate but moved to its present location on Tuleta Avenue in 1953. The teachers use an oral method of instruction rather than sign language so that students can eventually attend public schools.

66. "Religious Affiliation of Students at Trinity University," Board of Trustees Minutes, 15 October 1958.

67. Board of Trustees Minutes, 20 February 1957; Trinity University Interim Report to the Southern Association (1959): 31 (attachment).

68. *TU Catalogue* (1952–53): 26–27.

69. *TU Catalogue* (1953–54): 13.

70. James W. Laurie, "Five Years on Trinity Hill and a Look at the Future," Board of Trustees Minutes, 13 May 1957: 1–3.

71. Bruce Thomas, interview with RDB, 3 April 2001, and personal observation of the author.

72. Paul Walthall, interview with RDB, 24 September 1973; Brackenridge, *Beckoning Frontiers*, 120–121.

73. Bruce Thomas, interview with RDB, 10 April 2001. See also Allen's account of the episode in a manuscript, "Carlton and Barbara Allen" (typescript, n.d.), TU Archives.

74. Raymond Judd, interview with RDB, 26 July 1973. As an example of Laurie's "meddling" in student affairs, he vetoed the choice of a class ring because he did not like the design. In spite of student protests, Laurie's selection prevailed.

75. "Thomas Resigns," *Trinitonian*, 17 January 1958: 1; Bruce Thomas, interview with RDB, 10 April 2001.

76. Board of Trustees Minutes, 15 January 1958.

77. "Hawthorne New Business Manager," *Trinitonian*, 21 February 1958: 1.

78. "Replacement of Dean," *Trinitonian*, 7 February 1958: 1.

79. Bruce Thomas, interview with RDB, 3 and 10 April 2001.

80. Brackenridge, *Beckoning Frontiers*, 123–124.

81. "Laurie Recovers," *Trinitonian*, 18 December 1959: 7.

82. Brackenridge, *Beckoning Frontiers*, 125.

83. Brackenridge, *Beckoning Frontiers*, 123.

84. Raymond Judd, interview with RDB, 26 July 1973; Leon Taylor, interview with RDB, 17 July 1973.

85. "Trinity Drops Thriller," *Trinitonian*, 4 October 1953: 4.

86. "Lee Roy Arrives," *Trinitonian*, 18 September 1953: 1. Following Lee Roy's demise, the tradition continued with his year-old cub, Lee Roy II. See "TU Mascot Dies," 2 March 1962: 1; "Lee Roy II Joins," *Trinitonian*, 14 September 1962: 2.

87. "Texas Sports Writers Choose Mac," *Trinitonian*, 7 January 1955: 4; "Trinity Advances," *Trinitonian*, 5 October 1955: 2.

88. "T. F. Murchison Dies," *Trinitonian*, 18 November 1955: 1.

89. Board of Trustees Ex. Com. Minutes, 18 July 1956.

90. "Tiger Program in Error," *Trinitonian*, 16 December 1960: 1.

91. Board of Trustees Minutes, 8 May 1957.

92. Board of Trustees Minutes, 12 February 1958.

93. *San Antonio News*, 27 May 1959.

94. *San Antonio Express*, 14 November 1960. Laurie had played a leading role in helping to integrate local restaurants, including Earl Abel's, a popular gathering place for north side residents and Trinity students.

95. "Decade of Noise," *Trinitonian*, 8 December 1961: 3; *TU Catalogue* (1961–62): 12–19.

96. Board of Trustees Minutes, 11 October 1961. In 1961 the Northrup Trust had a book value of $1.5 million.

97. "In Memoriam," *Trinity* magazine (Summer 1988): 8.

98. Everett, *Trinity University*, 187–188.

99. *San Antonio News*, 6 December 1961.

NOTES TO CHAPTER NINE

1. The phrase appears to have been the creation of Leon "Tex" Taylor and was widely used in university publications throughout the decade.

2. Brackenridge, *Beckoning Frontiers*, 133.

3. Everett, *Trinity University*, 198.

4. George, *O'Neil Ford, Architect*, 98–99.

5. Dillon, *The Architecture of O'Neil Ford*, 69–70.

6. Board of Trustees Ex. and Fin. Committee Minutes, 24 January 1968.

7. Board of Trustees Minutes, 11 December 1969. In order to start construction, however, Trinity had to increase its debt load, which already exceeded $5 million.

Trustees William Bell and Andrew Cowles registered their disapproval of incurring additional debt.

8. Board of Trustees Minutes, 12 October 1967.

9. Fifth Year Report of Trinity University to the Southern Association of Colleges and Schools, 1971: 3–4. Hereafter, 1971 Fifth Year Report.

10. Board of Trustees Minutes, 8 May 1963.

11. Observations of the author.

12. "Smoky Stover Injured," *Trinitonian*, 16 September 1960: 1.

13. "Mon Cherie," *Trinitonian*, 24 September 1965: 2; "Strict Building Closing Times," *Trinitonian*, 8 October 1965: 8; "Smithmen Guard Campus," *Trinitonian*, 10 May 1968: 2.

14. "Digital Computer Added to Math Department," *Trinitonian*, 2 December 1960: 2; *TU Catalogue* (1961–62): 15.

15. Prior to this time, the H. B. Zachry Company provided Trinity with essential computer time (4 to 6 A.M.) for payroll and other essential computerized activities. Board of Trustees Ex. and Fin. Com. Minutes, 1 January 1967.

16. "Computer Used," *Trinitonian*, 10 May 1968: 1; Board of Trustees Ex. and Fin. Com. Minutes, 15 September 1968.

17. "Computer Center Receives Grant," *Trinitonian*, 9 December 1966: 8; Board of Trustees Ex. and Fin. Com. Minutes, 1 January 1967; Board of Trustees Minutes, 8 February 1968.

18. "Southern Association Report Form" (1954): 10, TU Archives. High school students in the bottom quarter of their class were accepted on probation if the admissions committee determined that "extenuating circumstances" accounted for their low grades. Transfer students from accredited colleges with grades of C or above were routinely accepted, and those from unaccredited institutions received credit for previous work after completing a year of satisfactory residence at Trinity.

19. 1965 Self-Study: 82–83.

20. 1971 Fifth Year Report: 9–10.

21. Board of Trustees Minutes, 12 October 1966. In 1959 approximately 77 percent of admitted male and female students scored below 500 on the verbal portion of the SAT examination. In 1964, only 49 percent of males and 34 percent of females were in this category. 1965 Self-Study: 86.

22. 1965 Self-Study: 95.

23. Board of Trustees Minutes, 11 May 1966; 1971 Fifth Year Report: 23.

24. Conversations with a number of faculty members hired during the 1960s confirm this generalization. Among the faculty who provided leadership during this period and made career commitments to Trinity were Jean S. Chittenden (Foreign Languages), Guy H. Ranson (Religion), Richard Gentry (Journalism), Geoffrey E. Goring (Engineering Science), John Brantley (English), Frederick Bremner (Psychology), Robert Strauss (Physical Education), George N. Boyd (Religion), Ewing Chinn (Philosophy), Richard A. Cooper (Mathematics), Joe C. Davis (Economics), Donald G. McGannon (Geology), Kenneth Kramer (Psychology), O Z White (Sociology), William O. Walker Jr. (Religion), Harold Murray (Biology), William Thornton (Music), Jesse H. McLeay (Physical Education), R. Douglas Brackenridge (Religion), Anelise Duncan (Foreign Languages), Philip J. Evett (Art), Richard D. Woods (Foreign Languages), Herb Treat (Engineering Science), Jim Potter (Physical Education),

William A. Bristow (Art), Ton DeVos (Political Science), Frank L. Kersnowski (English), Benjamin F. Plummer (Chemistry), Richard A. Bartels (Physics), Lawrence L. Espey (Biology), Gene Norris (Physical Education), John A. Burke Jr. (Chemistry), Rudolph M. Gaedke (Physics), Rosalind Phillips (Music), L. Tucker Gibson (Political Science), Shirley Rushing (Physical Education), David L. Middleton (English), Terry L. Smart (History), Robert S. Walker (Political Science), Gerald R. Benjamin (Music), Francisco O. Garcia-Treto (Religion), Lawrence D. Kimmel (Philosophy), John H. Moore (Education), and Edward C. Roy Jr. (Geology).

25. Both stories were told to the author by the parties involved a number of years ago. The Department of Religion was an exception to this general policy. Laurie preferred that members of that department be ordained Presbyterian clergy. Even so, in 1964 he approved appointment of a Baptist clergyman who earned his doctorate at Princeton Theological Seminary.

26. Board of Trustees Minutes, 13 May 1964. Thomas observed that for the first time Trinity was beginning to fulfill a major function of a university, "the production of new knowledge through research."

27. Board of Trustees Minutes, 13 May 1964; "Trinity Professor Wins Award," *Trinitonian*, 2 December 1964: 1.

28. Sandra Hooge, editor, "*Centennial Publication*" (November 1969), Box 90-41, TU Archives.

29. The Southern Association team in 1965 deemed faculty governance as "awkward in several respects. . . . The many faculty advisory committees function in a poorly defined peripheral area, without clearly stated objectives or regularly scheduled meetings. The Senate exists as a court of appeal, but meets seldom and does not initiate business. From a faculty standpoint this arrangement results in an individual sense of being cut off from the realm of discussion or decision making, with no clear channels of communication." 1965 Self-Study: 21–22.

30. Jean Chittenden, interview with RDB, 10 August 1999.

31. Ibid.

32. "Stanage to Leave," *Trinitonian*, 14 December 1967: 9.

33. "Academic Freedom Is Topic," *Trinitonian*, 6 January 1968: 5.

34. Faculty Senate Minutes, 19 January and 1 March 1968. See also Everett, *Trinity University*, 201.

35. "Faculty Approves New Constitution," *Trinitonian*, 11 October 1968: 1; Trinity University Report of Institutional Self-Study for the Commission on Colleges of the Southern Association of Colleges and Schools (February 1976): 148, TU Archives. Hereafter, 1976 Self-Study. American Association of University Professors (AAUP) documents were used as a model for the new constitution and for tenure and promotion documents. Members of the local AAUP chapter played leading roles in this process and in curricular revision.

36. Board of Trustees Ex. Com. Minutes, 31 July 1968.

37. Board of Trustees Minutes, 11 December 1968; "Faculty Approves New Constitution," *Trinitonian*, 11 October 1968: 1.

38. 1976 Self-Study: 376. The initial amounts were $1,500 in 1963 and $5,000 in 1965. Most grants were small, consisting of a few hundred dollars for items such as travel and typing of manuscripts.

39. Everett, *Trinity University*, 203.

40. Jay B. Clark, "The Odyssey of a University Library," *The Journal of Library History* (April 1970): 125–127.

41. Clark, "Odyssey of a University Library," 128.

42. 1971 Fifth Year Report: 29–35.

43. Clark, "Odyssey of a University Library," 128–129; Board of Trustees Minutes, 14 October 1964. In 1965 the Southern Association visitation team identified the library as an area in which Trinity needed to make considerable improvement. See 1965 Southern Association Visitation Team Report.

44. 1965 Self-Study: 108–110; "An Intense Education," *Trinitonian*, 17 September 1965: 4.

45. This was the first comprehensive self-study conducted by the university since it was accredited in 1925. Prior to 1965, Trinity had reported periodically on particular areas considered to be problematic by the Southern Association. In 1966 the association accredited Trinity for the next decade. Board of Trustees Minutes, 9 February 1966 and 8 February 1967.

46. "New Curriculum Approved," *Trinitonian*, 6 October 1967; *TU Catalogue* (1968–69): 68–75. At the same time, Trinity faculty dropped the requirement that candidates for graduation must "give evidence of maintaining worthy moral standards." Faculty Minutes, 4 January 1967.

47. Minutes of the Academic Council, 21 March 1975.

48. The *Mirage* (1967: 71) featured a photograph of McGannon wiping perspiration from his face after one of his lectures. "The professor's efforts do not go unnoticed by students. Last year he was given an ovation for his final lecture."

49. "Baker, Baylor Boast Amazing Drama Firsts," *Trinitonian*, 15 March 1963: 3.

50. "Baker and Five Associates Come to TU," *Trinitonian*, 15 March 1963: 1. For biographical background on Baker, see Board of Trustees Minutes, 14 May 1958.

51. "Creativity Elements," *Trinitonian*, 22 April 1966: 5; Paul Baker, *Integration of Abilities: Exercises for Creative Growth* (San Antonio, Tx., 1972), vii–xv. Positive responses from students over the years indicated that the course was helpful in deepening their appreciation of life far beyond the particular dimensions of their professions or occupations.

52. "Professor Writes Article," *Trinitonian*, 14 November 1969: 5; David Burkett, conversations with RDB, February 2001. Burkett also teamed with colleague John Narciso to write *Declare Yourself: Discovering the Me in Relationships* (New York, 1975), a book that was based in part on the experience of teaching the mass communications course.

53. *TU Catalogue* (1961–62): 67.

54. *TU Catalogue* (1966–67): 133; "Two Misunderstood Doctors," *Trinitonian* (15 April 1977): 1.

55. "Music Appreciation," *Trinitonian*, 10 January 1958: 2.

56. "Electronic Education Instituted," *Trinitonian*, 14 April 1961: 8; Board of Trustees Minutes, 14 February 1962.

57. Board of Trustees Minutes, 15 October 1958 and 7 October 1959.

58. McCutcheon emphasized the need for additional faculty at the graduate level and increased emphasis on research and productive scholarship. He also stressed the importance of increased library resources and improved administration, including more careful supervision of admission procedures, comprehension examinations, and

preparation of theses. "Interim Report," Board of Trustees Ex. Com. Minutes, 24 April 1959.

59. Board of Trustees Minutes, 7 October 1959. Laurie and Bruce Thomas signed the report, but Laurie was the driving force behind the move toward an expanded graduate program.

60. "Duce Will Direct Graduate School," *Trinitonian*, 1 April 1960: 1; "Report of the Dean of the Graduate School," Board of Trustees Minutes, 10 May 1961.

61. 1965 Self-Study: 315–317.

62. 1971 Fifth Year Report: 15–16.

63. Board of Trustees Ex. and Fin. Com. Minutes, 31 July 1968; "Urban Studies to Begin," *Trinitonian*, 2 May 1969: 5. See also 1971 Fifth Year Report: 17–18.

64. Board of Trustees Ex. Com. Minutes, 22 January 1962; "The Program of Dedication Chapman Graduate Center," Box 90-41, TU Archives.

65. The information about Chapman's attitude toward Laurie is derived from Jeanne Ronda, who interviewed Chapman's lawyers regarding this subject. She is presently working on a history of the Chapman Foundation. Jeanne Ronda to RDB, 10 June 2000. Chapman did, however, reduce the total corpus of the trust by taking $8 million from his estate and drawing up $2 million trusts for four new beneficiaries.

66. "Chapman Leaves Trinity Fund," *Trinitonian*, 21 October 1966: 1. The official figure was $110 million, of which Trinity's share was $27.5 million. Second Follow-Up Report for the Institutional Self-Study and Periodic Visitation Program, 6 September 1968: 7, TU Archives.

67. 1965 Southern Association Visitation Team Report: 48; Board of Trustees Minutes, 9 February 1966.

68. Board of Trustees Minutes, 12 October 1967.

69. Leonard Duce, "A Report on the Graduate Program at Trinity University," Board of Trustees Minutes, 12 February 1969.

70. Professors Harold T. Davis (mathematics) and Donald E. Everett (history) were the individuals chiefly responsible for bringing the press to San Antonio. Everett initially served as managing editor.

71. "Math Work Published," *Trinitonian*, 1 December 1962: 2; "Trinity University Press," 12 October 1967: 3.

72. "Background and Description of Trinity University Press" (typescript, n.d.), Box 90-49, TU Archives.

73. Technically, Trinity trustees held university assets in trust for the synod. If the university were to sell its property and cease operations, for example, the assets would revert to the denomination. Conversely, if the university closed with more liabilities than assets, the denomination would have some responsibility for the debts.

74. "The Church and Higher Education," *Minutes of the General Assembly of the United Presbyterian Church*, 1961, I: 149–182. Hereafter, *Minutes (GAUPC)*. The document stated that modern church-related colleges should not be based on indoctrination or curtailment of academic freedom, but on academic excellence undergirded by competent faculty and quality curricula. "If the education offered does not demand the highest standards of excellence, it had better not be offered in the name of the church and the Christian faith."

75. "Administrative Guidelines for Colleges Related to the United Presbyterian Church," *Minutes (GAUPC)*, 1963, I: 135–137. For background on changing church

relationships, see Bradley J. Longfield and George M. Marsden, "Presbyterian Colleges in Twentieth-Century America," in Milton J Coalter, John M. Mulder, and Louis B. Weeks, *The Pluralistic Vision: Presbyterians and Mainstream Protestant Education and Leadership* (Louisville, Ky., 1992): 99–124.

76. "Recommendations Relating to Higher Education," *Minutes (GAUPC)*, 1965, I: 131–137. Church-related institutions were also receiving pressures from accrediting agencies to remove any implied authority over the trustees of the university. Board of Trustees Minutes, 11 December 1967.

77. "Synod Relations to the Colleges," *Minutes (GAUPC)*, I: 1968: 163–164.

78. Board of Trustees Ex. and Fin. Com. Minutes, 24 January 1968.

79. Board of Trustees Minutes, 7 May 1969; Board of Trustees Ex. and Fin. Committee Minutes, 16 April 1969.

80. "Centennial Festivities Begin," *Trinitonian*, 19 April 1968: 1, 5; "Waxahachie Cornerstone," *Trinitonian*, 13 September 1968: 1.

81. "Follow the Sun," *Trinitonian*, 9 May 1969: 3.

82. Board of Trustees Minutes, 11 December 1968; "His Place in the Sun," *Trinitonian*, 21 February 1969: 2. Laurie was an ex officio member of the search committee. He would play a key role in the selection of his successor.

83. Board of Trustees Minutes, 26 October 1969. Laurie and Duce conferred with University of Texas officials regarding the future of graduate work in San Antonio. By 1970 Trinity listed twenty-one graduate programs, an increase of ten since the beginning of the previous decade.

84. Board of Trustees Minutes, 15 October 1969.

85. Philip Detweiler, "State of the Senate Message," in Faculty Senate Minutes, 11 March 1970.

86. Board of Trustees Minutes, 11 December 1968 and 15 October 1969. See also "R.O.T.C. voluntary," *Trinitonian*, 11 April 1969: 1.

87. Board of Trustees Minutes, 25 February 1970.

88. Faculty Senate Minutes, 9 May 1969.

89. Duncan Wimpress, interview with RDB, 27 October 1999.

90. James W. Laurie, "The Beginning of Wisdom," 8–10, Box 90-41, TU Archives.

91. Brackenridge, *Beckoning Frontiers*, 149.

92. Ibid.

93. Ibid., 149–150; Board of Trustees Minutes, 13 May 1970. Initially the building was named in honor of both President and Mrs. Laurie. Following the death of her husband, Dorothy Laurie requested that her name be dropped from the title, and the board concurred with her request. Board of Trustees Minutes, 14 May 1971.

94. Brackenridge, *Beckoning Frontiers*, 154.

95. "Personable Inspiration," *Trinitonian*, 17 September 1965: 12.

Notes to Chapter Ten

1. Subject to criticism by many faculty and alumni who deemed the term inappropriate and misleading, Trinity abandoned the terminology and the logo in the late 1970s.

2. Helen Lefkowitz Horowitz, *Campus Life: Undergraduate Cultures from the End of the Eighteenth Century to the Present* (Chicago and London, 1987): 220–221.

3. Horowitz, *Campus Life*, 223–224.

4. Jim Jones, interview with RDB, 10 February 2001; *Trinitonian*, "Nostalgia Strikes," 31 October 1973: 3.

5. "Dashing Through the Snow," *Trinitonian*, 11 April 1975: 7; "Busch Recalls High Points of Long Journalism Career," *Trinitonian*, 14 April 1978: 4; personal observations of author.

6. J. Newton Rayzor to James W. Laurie, 11 April 1966: 2, Box 9, "Trustees General," Wimpress Papers.

7. Arthur Sundstrom, interview with RDB, 23 July 2001.

8. "Personable Inspiration," *Trinitonian*, 17 September 1965: 12.

9. Faculty Minutes, 10 September 1952; Everett, *Trinity University*, 180–181.

10. "Unfinished Campus Topsy-Turvy Routine," *San Antonio Light*, 28 September 1952. The cost per student for three meals each day was two dollars.

11. Brackenridge, *Beckoning Frontiers*, 118.

12. Thurman Adkins, interview with RDB, 21 July 1999.

13. "Social Regulations Procedures," *Trinitonian*, 25 September 1953: 3.

14. "Homecoming Celebration," *Trinitonian*, 5 November 1954: 1; "Gala Floats," *Trinitonian*, 11 November 1955: 1. In 1960 the Student Council dispensed with the annual homecoming parade and substituted a county fair that was held on the slab. "TU Traditions Oriented by Student Government," *Trinitonian*, 8 December 1961: 2. See also "Suddenly, It's the Color of Yesteryear," *Trinitonian*, 22 November 1963: 2–3. If Trinity won the contest, students enjoyed a holiday from classes the following Monday. After the game, students attended a dance, and the weekend concluded on Sunday with dormitory open houses and a faculty music recital.

15. "Trinity Float," *Trinitonian*, 13 April 1906: 1.

16. "Trinity Salutes Founders' Day," *Trinitonian*, 27 April 1956: 1.

17. "Tigerland Coronation," *Trinitonian*, 25 March 1955: 1.

18. "Junior-Senior Prom," *Trinitonian*, 11 May 1956: 1.

19. "Inter-Class Activities Program," *Trinitonian*, 18 September 1953: 2.

20. "Inter-Class Activities" *Trinitonian*, 18 September 1955: 2.

21. "Open Letter to Trinity Students," *Trinitonian*, 1 October 1954: 2; "Administrative Council Minutes," *Trinitonian*, 24 September 1954: 1.

22. *Trinity University Student Handbook* (1956–57): 51, Box 85-17. TU Archives. First-year students were asked to wear beanies with their name and class sign above the bill. Upper-class students were asked to wear nametags of designated colors representing the sophomore, junior, and senior classes.

23. "Congratulations Fish," *Trinitonian*, 5 October 1955: 2.

24. "Dean Reaffirms Hazing Policy," *Trinitonian*, 11 December 1959: 2; "Inter-Club Council Formed," *Trinitonian*, 13 January 1961: 1. See also *Mirage* (1965): 132–153.

25. "School Sing Song," *Trinitonian*, 17 January 1958: 1; "Spurs Awarded Trophy," *Trinitonian*, 15 April 1958: 1. Updated information supplied by Pete Neville, director of Coates Center Student Activities.

26. *Men's Residential Handbook* (1967–68), Box 85-17, TU Archives.

27. *McFarlin Dormitory Handbook for Resident Women* (1955–56), Box 85-17, TU Archives.

28. Ibid.

29. Coleen Grissom, interview with RDB, 11 August 1999.

30. Ibid.

31. "Trinity Posture Contest," *Trinitonian*, 5 November 1954: 3.

32. The Nixon-Kennedy election generated considerable interest on the Trinity campus. Although the students favored Nixon by a 60-40 margin, they did not think that religion should be an important factor in selecting a candidate. "Nixon Wins Campus Poll," *Trinitonian*, 26 February 1960: 8; "No Part in the Campaign," *Trinitonian*, 23 September 1960: 8.

33. "What Will Trinity Do?" *Trinitonian*, 21 May 1954: 2. Signing the letter were students Bob Benton, Herman Harren, Kenneth McCall, Dink Reese, Jim Sanders, Jack Stotts, and Derk Swain.

34. "New Staff Fills Posts," *Trinitonian*, 4 May 1956: 1.

35. "Student Senate Report," *Trinitonian*, 17 February 1958: 2; "Honor System Is Trophy Winner," *Trinitonian*, 7 March 1958: 1.

36. "Student Court Proposes Honor System," *Trinitonian*, 17 August 1953: 2; "What Is an Honor System?" *Trinitonian*, 22 November 1957: 2; "Wake Up 'Lil Student Body," *Trinitonian*, 6 December 1957: 2.

37. "Cook's Short Orders," *Trinitonian*, 24 March 1964: 2.

38. "Faculty Pessimism," *Trinitonian*, 14 February 1964: 4; "Voters Trounce Honor Proposal," *Trinitonian*, 26 March 1964: 1.

39. "Trinity University: Aware or Asleep?" *Trinitonian*, 30 April 1964: 2.

40. "Trinity University: Aware or Asleep?" *Trinitonian*, 7 May 1964: 2.

41. *Trinitonian*, 22 October 1962: 1.

42. "Isolation Trends," *Trinitonian*, 2 November 1962: 2. One student wrote, "It takes a national crisis to lift the blinders off our eyes for a few moments." Referring to Trinity as the "Lift-Slab Sanctuary," he said that students lived in "a private little world of empty reflection ponds and overactive sprinkling systems."

43. "Minstrels Fulfill Their Mission," *Trinitonian*, 2 October 1964: 1; "Spirit of the Skyline Campus," *Trinitonian*, 6 November 1964: 8–9; "Laud and Honor," *Trinitonian*, 13 November 1964: 2.

44. "Annual Parents' Weekend," *Trinitonian*, 22 April 1960: 1.

45. "Bermuda Day," *Trinitonian*, 17 April 1962: 1. The event died in the early 1970s when dress codes were abolished and students could dress as they pleased on the upper campus.

46. "Homecoming Eclipsed by History," *Trinitonian*, 6 December 1963: 6.

47. "Mac in a Crack," *Trinitonian*, 3 November 1961: 7; "T.U. Phenomena," *Trinitonian*, 3 November 1961: 8.

48. Board of Trustees Minutes, 14 February 1962; "Trustees Approve Athletic Program," *Trinitonian*, 16 February 1962: 6; "McElreath Transferred," *Trinitonian*, 23 February 1962: 6. During the first five years of the decade, deficits from the athletic program, primarily due to football, were $84,900, $90,500, $48,000, $42,000, and $52,000, respectively. Southern Association Visitation Team Report (1965): 14–15. The visitation team recommended that football be eliminated and other sports be emphasized.

49. "TU Athletic Teams," *Trinitonian*, 22 March 1963: 1.

50. Other outstanding African-American student-athletes from this era included Marvin Upshaw, A. D. Arnic, and Clyde Glossom.

51. Experience of author; Gene Norris, interview with RDB, 10 May 2001.

52. "What's in a Name," *Trinitonian*, 27 September 1968: 2.

53. "Suspended," *Trinitonian*, 27 September 1968: 6.

54. "Letters to the Editor," *Trinitonian*, 11 October 1968: 2.

55. "Mabry's Tennis Theory," *Trinitonian*, 17 May 1963: 10. Between 1957 and 1963 Mabry compiled a 105–8 record at Trinity.

56. "McKinley Ends Career," *Trinitonian*, 10 May 1963: 7.

57. James Hill, "Trinity Tennis," memorandum to RDB, 14 May 2001. Frank Conner, presently a member of the PGA Senior Tour, is one of only two men to have played in both the U.S. Open Golf and Tennis Championships.

58. Nixon, "The Tigers' Tale," *Trinity* magazine (Spring 1986): 17; "Trinity University 1975 National Women's Collegiate Tennis Championships Fact Booklet," Wimpress Papers, Box 4.

59. Nixon, "The Tigers' Tale," *Trinity* magazine (Spring 1986): 16.

60. "Former Vanderbilt Coach," *Trinitonian*, 9 April 1965: 1.

61. "NCAA Tournament Ends," *Trinitonian*, 22 March 1968: 1. The following year Trinity won the Southland Conference championship. During his Trinity career (1965–69), Jeffries produced a total of 2,454 points in 97 games, a record that still stands.

62. Ibid.

63. *Mirage* (1964): 114–115.

64. "Tiger Sports," *Mirage* (August 1968): 72.

65. "Soccer Newest Sport," *Mirage* (1967): 164; "Tiger Team Opens Season," *Trinitonian*, 27 September 1968: 7.

66. "New Intramural System," *Trinitonian*, 24 September 1965: 7; "Potter for Student Participation," 20 October 1967: 6; "Potter Uplifts Intramurals," *Trinitonian*, 22 November 1974: 10.

67. "Class Myth," *Trinitonian*, 5 April 1964: 2.

68. "The Color of Yesteryear," *Trinitonian*, 22 November 1963: 3.

69. "Hail What?" *Trinitonian*, 2 October 1964; "Faculty Talks: Dialogue," *Trinitonian*, 16 September 1966: 4. One student suggested that the alma mater should "die a merciful death, never to plague a school function again."

70. "The Beanie: Rest in Peace," *Trinitonian*, 16 October 1964: 2; "A Tradition of Degradation," *Trinitonian*, 23 September 1966: 2.

71. Thurman Adkins, interview with RDB, 22 July 1999. Others who attended the orientation session confirm this story.

72. "Christmas Spirit Sparked by a New Trinity Tradition," *Trinitonian*, 2 December 1960: 1. In support of the new tradition, Dean Champion extended the curfew for freshman and sophomore women to 11:00 P.M. for the occasion.

73. "Homecoming Schedule," *Trinitonian*, 8 October 1968: 8; "Hazing in Proper Perspective," *Trinitonian*, 23 February 1968: 2.

74. "Trinity Coeds Donate Time," *Trinitonian*, 18 December 1963: 2.

75. "Chi Delta Tau Service Project," *Trinitonian*, 30 October 1964: 8.

76. "Tutoring Planned," *Trinitonian*, 8 October 1965: 1.

77. "Student Association Banquet," *Trinitonian*, 7 April 1967: 2.

78. "Volunteer Santas," *Trinitonian*, 10 December 1976: 3; Susie Gonzalez, "Louise Locker—aka 'Elf Louise,'" *Trinity* magazine (Fall 2000): 33.

79. "Cross Roaders Selected," *Trinitonian*, 11 December 1959: 2; "Africa Needs

Education," *Trinitonian*, 7 April 1961: 3. See also "Crossroads Memorable Summer," *Trinitonian*, 24 October 1969: 5.

80. Matt Flores, "Peace Corps to honor Trinity," *San Antonio Express-News*, 20 March 2001.

81. "Students Vote on Gov't Change," *Trinitonian*, 25 February 1966: 1; "Students Give Approval," *Trinitonian*, 4 March 1966: 1. At this time, the Student Council began to provide salaries for student body officers.

82. "Student Council Plans," *Trinitonian*, 30 September 1966: 1; "High Hopes for Forum," *Trinitonian*, 1 December 1967: 2; "Trinity University Student Association," *Mirage* (1967): 179.

83. Jim Jones, interview with RDB, 10 February 2001.

84. "Due Process Long Overdue," *Trinitonian*, 22 September 1967: 2.

85. "Due Process: A Rebuttal," *Trinitonian*, 13 October 1967: 3.

86. "Council Views Rights Statement," *Trinitonian*, 17 November 1967: 1.

87. Board of Trustees Minutes, 11 December 1968; Art Sundstrom, interview with RDB, 23 July 2001; "Council, Trustees Approve Statement," *Trinitonian*, 16 December 1968: 1.

88. Thurman Adkins, interview with RDB, 21 July 1999.

89. "First Pass-Fail System," *Trinitonian*, 13 September 1967: 1; "Faculty Reminded of Reading Days," *Trinitonian*, 31 January 1970: 1.

90. Coleen Grissom, interview with RDB, 11 August 1999.

91. Ibid.

92. "Career Counseling," *Trinitonian*, 21 March 1975: 3.

93. "J. C. Pool Selected," *Trinitonian*, 25 September 1964: 8.

94. "Former Counselor Receives Deanship," *Trinitonian*, 26 April 1963: 1; "A Remarkable Woman," *Trinitonian*, 29 March 1963: 5.

95. "Letter to the Editor," *Trinitonian*, 18 December 1963; *Trinity University Handbook for Resident Women* (1969–70): 9–11.

96. *Student Handbook* (1969–70): 40–42. Regulations for men were also relaxed during this time period.

97. "Heard Around Campus," *Trinitonian*, 3 November 1961: 2. Assistant Dean of Student Life Charles Pickering expressed indifference to the issue, but commented to a *Trinitonian* reporter that "if choosing the Homecoming Queen was going to be a big event, why not go all the way, including their appearing in a bathing suit."

98. *Trinity University Handbook for Resident Women* (1969–70): 8.

99. "Sex Habits," *Trinitonian*, 1 May 1964: 4.

100. "4% Grass—Why?" *Trinitonian*, 5 April 1968: 2; "The LSD Users," *Trinitonian*, 19 April 1968: 2. The following year, local police arrested four Trinity students for possession of marijuana and theft of over $100 from interstate shipments. University authorities cooperated with the arrest. "Students Arrested," *Trinitonian*, 15 December 1969: 1.

101. "Faculty Evaluations Scheduled," *Trinitonian*, 17 March 1967: 2; "Second Study Planned," *Trinitonian*, 14 December 1967: 1. The evaluations were for faculty eyes only and not used for salary or promotion purposes.

102. "Program Is Initiated," *Trinitonian*, 7 November 1969: 1; "Introduction to the Concept of a Free University," *Trinitonian*, 30 January 1970: 2; "Free University Topics Announced," *Trinitonian*, 13 February 1970: 1. The program continued to

be popular until the mid-1970s when student interest began to wane and continuing education provided courses in these areas.

103. Jim Jones to R. Douglas Brackenridge, 14 June 1973; "Controversial Bishop Pike," *Trinitonian*, 23 April 1967: 1; *Mirage* (January 1968): 44. A consummate politician, Laurie moved the lecture from the chapel to the Sams Center, thus assuaging some of the opposition to the event.

104. "Viet Nam War or No?" *Trinitonian*, 26 February 1965: 2.

105. "Trinity Students Support War," *Trinitonian*, 24 February 1967: 1.

106. "Viet Nam War or No?" *Trinitonian*, 25 February 1965: 2; "Waking Up Is Hard to Do," *Trinitonian*, 12 November 1965: 2. By 1968 a campus poll determined that 56 percent of Trinity students considered the war to be immoral. "Trinitonians Give Opinion," *Trinitonian*, 22 November 1968: 1.

107. "Great Decisions," *Trinitonian*, 10 February 1967: 8; "Walker Denounces Policy," *Trinitonian*, 14 December 1967: 1.

108. For example, "Dr. Walker Participates," *Trinitonian*, 17 February 1967: 8.

109. Faculty Senate Minutes, 1 October 1969; "Moratorium Held October 15," *Trinitonian*, 10 October 1969: 1. In contrast to Trinity officials, administrators at San Antonio College asked teachers to administer tests on Wednesday so that students could not hold a moratorium on campus.

110. "Post-Moratorium," *Trinitonian*, 17 October 1969: 2. Thomas agreed that the event had been conducted in "an appropriate and relevant manner."

111. Horowitz, *Campus Life*, 220–244.

112. "Non-Violent Services at Trinity," *Trinitonian*, 8 May 1970: 1.

113. Ibid., 2.

114. "Campus Christians," *Trinitonian*, 8 April 1960: 4; personal observations of author.

115. "Sunday Evening Conversations, Chapel Services," *Trinitonian*, 12 November 1965: 1. Vesper services varied greatly in format. At one service the Trinity choir accompanied by a combo of Trinity students combined traditional elements such as Gregorian chants that modulated into jazz. See "Jazz Mass," *Trinitonian*, 4 April 1966: 1.

116. Laurie avoided use of the term "university chaplain." A decade passed before Judd was awarded that title.

117. "Students-Faculty Discuss Aims," *Trinitonian*, 23 February 2968: 4; "The Right Emphasis," *Trinitonian*, 23 February 1968: 2.

118. "Chapel Plans Made," *Trinitonian*, 15 September 1967: 5.

119. From personal experience. Shortly after Sunday morning services began, the university utilized the free ten-to-eleven morning hour on Monday, Wednesday, and Friday for classes. These periods had previously been used for activities such as committee meetings, chapel, and ROTC.

120. "A Second Century," *Trinitonian*, 26 April 1968: 2.

Notes to Chapter Eleven

1. Brubacher, *Higher Education in Transition*, 382–384. See also Lewis B. Mayhew, "The Steady Seventies, "*The Journal of Higher Education*," XLV (March 1974): 163–173.

2. Observations of the author.

3. Philip Detweiler, "The State of the Senate," Faculty Senate Minutes, 3 March 1970. As president of the Faculty Senate, Detweiler thought that the body should be more involved in the formulation, interpretation, and implementation of general university policy. Referring to participation in the presidential search process, Detweiler said, "This, though a modest venture, *was* involvement."

4. Faculty Senate Minutes, 3 March 1970. Professor Guy Ranson wrote in the margin of the archival minutes, "effective and inoffensive way of saying that we want to participate."

5. Faculty Senate Minutes, 7 and 9 March 1970; William O. Walker Jr., interview with RDB, 26 July 2001.

6. Board of Trustees Minutes, 13 March 1970; "Dr. Wimpress Takes Presidency," *Trinitonian*, 31 July 1970: 3.

7. William Urban, *A History of Monmouth College through its Fifth Quarter-Century* (Monmouth, Il., 1979): 128–134, 166–189. Wimpress was Trinity's third president who was not a minister and the third president with previous experience as the head of a college or university. The two previous nonministerial presidents were Archelaus Turner (1904–07) and Samuel Hornbeak (1908–20). Turner and Trinity's first president, William Beeson (1869–82), both had served as college presidents before coming to Trinity.

8. Duncan Wimpress, telephone conversation with RDB, 6 November 2001.

9. Jeff James, "Dr. Duncan Wimpress," *Business San Antonio* (August 1998): 35–37.

10. Board of Trustees Minutes, 14 October 1970.

11. "Wimpress Requests Small Inauguration," *Trinitonian*, 23 April 1971: 1; "Presidential Inauguration," *Trinitonian*, 30 April 1971: 6.

12. Board of Trustees Minutes, 14 May 1971.

13. Board of Trustees Minutes, 14 October 1970 and 5 February 1971. The new committees were Academic Affairs, Student Life, Business, Development and Alumni, and Nominations and By-Laws.

14. Board of Trustees Minutes, 14 October 1970. Wimpress continued this practice throughout his presidency. See "Room and Board Increase," *Trinitonian*, 22 November 1974: 3.

15. Board of Trustees Minutes, 11 October 1972 and 9 February 1973. Salary decisions were subject to review by the vice president for academic affairs.

16. "Proposed Finance Board," *Trinitonian*, 19 November 1971: 3; "Financiers Dole Out Cash," *Trinitonian*, 28 September 1973: 1.

17. Academic Council Minutes, 14 May 1971, Box 90-15, TU Archives. Formerly the Curriculum Committee, the name was changed to the Academic Council in 1970. In 1976, the Academic Council was renamed the Curriculum Council.

18. Board of Trustees Minutes, 13 October 1971; "No More Scholarships," *San Antonio Express-News*, 14 October 1971.

19. The proposal was supported by the Faculty Senate, the Academic Council, the Student Council, and the Athletic Council. Board of Trustees Minutes, 13 October 1971; "Student Council Athletic Statement," *Trinitonian*, 15 October 1971: 5.

20. *San Antonio Express-News*, 11 October 1971. See also "Wimpress Center of Controversy," *San Antonio Express-News*, 10 October 1971.

21. Karl O'Quinn, "Morning Line," *San Antonio Express-News*, 13 October 1971.

22. "Student Council Athletic Statement," *Trinitonian*, 15 October 1971: 5.

23. "The Sensuous Sport," *Trinitonian*, 22 October 1971: 11. See also "Viewpoints," *Trinitonian*, 8 October 1971: 2.

24. "Board of Trustees Decides," *Trinitonian*, 15 October 1971: 5; Barry Robinson, "Day to Remember," *San Antonio Express-News*, 14 October 1971; Barry Robinson, "The Great Ripoff," *Mirage* (1972): 144–145. See also "Trinity Athletics—Ahead of Our Time?" *Trinitonian*, 2 April 1976: 2.

25. Board of Trustees Minutes, 8 February 1974; "Norris at Helm," *Trinitonian*, 8 February 1974: 10; "New Regime," *Trinitonian*, 16 April 1974: 9.

26. Board of Trustees Minutes, 8 May 1976. See also "Board Decides," *Trinitonian*, 15 October 1971: 5 and "TIAA on the Way," *Trinitonian*, 10 September 1976: 11.

27. Jess Carnes, "How Phi Beta Kappa Came to Trinity," *Mirage* (Spring 1974): 34.

28. Duncan Wimpress, interview with RDB, 27 October 1999; Board of Trustees Minutes, 9 February 1973; Carnes, "How Phi Beta Kappa Came to Trinity," 34. About the same time, Trinity also received a charter for Mortar Board, a senior women's honorary organization. See Board of Trustees Minutes, 11 October 1972.

29. The United Presbyterian Church in the U.S.A. Synod of Texas met for the last time on the Trinity campus on 7–8 June 1972.

30. Judy Fletcher, memorandum to RDB, 14 January 2002. Fletcher is the chief executive officer of the Synod of the Sun.

31. Board of Trustees Minutes, 13 May 1972.

32. Samuel M. Junkin, "Texas Presbyterian Institutions of Higher Education in the 20th Century," *Proceedings of the Presbyterian Historical Society of the Southwest* (March 2000): 83–96.

33. One faculty member said, "The university can't masquerade as something it's not. It would be a mistake to assume that all of Trinity's faculty, administration, and students are practicing Christians, and that one of the purposes of Trinity is to profess and promote the Christian faith." "Trinity Has New Purpose," *Trinitonian*, 25 October 1974: 4.

34. *TU Catalogue* (1975–76): 14–15. See also 1976 Self-Study: 5–6. In part, trustees felt the need to change the statement of purpose to accommodate the university's reception of Tuition Equalization Grants awarded by the state for Texas residents who elected to attend a private institution. In 1976 Trinity was receiving more than half a million dollars annually in scholarship aid from this source. See Board of Trustees Minutes, 19 October 1974.

35. 1976 Self-Study: 6–7. Wimpress favored retaining Christian references in the statement of purpose. See Board of Trustees Ex. Com. Minutes, 3 January 1976.

36. "Reorganization Creates New Titles," *Trinitonian*, 17 March 1972: 4; Faculty Senate Minutes, 23 February and 16 March 1972.

37. 1976 Self-Study: 147–148.

38. Students, however, had no voting rights. They participated in discussions as advisors to support and represent student interests. See "Creation of Classes," *Trinitonian*, 3 December 1971: 4.

39. 1976 Self-Study: 148. The Board of Trustees approved the new academic structure on 19 October 1974. See also "Faculty Considers Constitution," *Trinitonian*, 22 September 1972: 1. In 1974 the commission formalized procedures for de-

partments to recommend new appointments and for evaluations of probationary faculty. Essentially, the document specified the participation of chairs and tenured faculty in hiring, tenure, and promotion decisions before they were referred to appropriate administrators. Not all departments adhered to the procedures, however, and administrative monitoring of departments was uneven. See Faculty Senate Minutes, 23 February 1972.

40. Other figures include 0 percent for technicians and 14 percent for office and clerical staff. On the other hand, minorities accounted for 64 percent of the skilled craftsmen, 80 percent of the semiskilled operatives, and 99 percent of the unskilled laborers and service workers. "Trinity University Minority Work Force," Box 8, Wimpress Papers, TU Archives; "Compliance Report of Institutions of Higher Education" (Trinity University, Fall 1972), Box 1, Wimpress Papers. Of the undergraduates, 44 were African American, 208 Hispanic, and 6 Asian American. Graduate students were categorized as 26 African American, 67 Hispanic, and 1 Asian American.

41. Figures supplied by Trinity's Office of Institutional Research, 18 February 2002.

42. Sarah Burke, conversation with RDB, 7 September 2001.

43. Charles Kenworthy, "An Interview with Duncan Wimpress," *San Antonio Magazine* (January 1971): 22; "The Best Kept Secrets," *Trinitonian*, 25 January 1974: 1.

44. Board of Trustees Minutes, 9 February 1973.

45. Board of Trustees Minutes, 14 October 1971; "Auditorium Dedication," *Trinitonian*, 22 October 1971: 1, 5.

46. "Stevens Contributes Funds for Stadium," *Trinitonian*, 11 February 1972: 1.

47. "New Stadium Initiated," *Trinitonian*, 8 September 1972: 5; "Tigers Edge SWT," *Trinitonian*, 15 September 1972: 7.

48. "Trinity Receives New Center," *Trinitonian*, 5 November 1971: 1; "Student Opinion," *Trinitonian*, 5 September 1971: 6.

49. "Architect Ford Talks About New Center," *Trinitonian*, 17 November 1972: 1. The new location broke with the original master plan that called for keeping the view from Northrup Hall open to the city.

50. "Coates Center Dedication," *Trinitonian*, 19 October 1973: 2. Interior finishing work took an additional six months.

51. "Wimpress Seeks New Building," *Trinitonian*, 23 March 1973: 7.

52. Board of Trustees Minutes, 4 February 1972; Gilbert Denman Jr. to Duncan Wimpress, 20 March 1972, Box 2, Wimpress Papers.

53. "Events Scheduled for Earth Day," *Trinitonian*, 17 April 1970: 1.

54. "Faculty Organizes New Trinity Course, *Trinitonian*, 20 March 1970: 1.

55. "Academic Council Approves Program," *Trinitonian*, 14 April 1972: 3; report by Cresap, McCormick, and Paget, "Trinity University: A Study of Long-Range Plans and Administrative Organization" (October 1975) II: 18–19. Hereafter, CMP report. A copy of the report is in the TU archives.

56. "Trinity University Solar Energy Project," 1–2, Box 4, Wimpress Papers.

57. "Solar Project Nation's Largest," *Trinitonian*, 9 September 1977: 1; "Solar Project," *Trinitonian*, 7 November 1975: 5.

58. *Trinity University Graduate School Bulletin* (1977–78): 106–107; *Prospectives for Progress, A Report of the President of Trinity University for the 1975–76 Year*, 25, Box 1, Wimpress Papers. Hereafter, *Prospectives for Progress.*

59. "Communications Courses to be Offered," *Trinitonian*, 4 February 1972: 3; "Journalism Revamp Complete," *Trinitonian*, 27 April 1973: 3. In 1972 Trinity purchased a fully equipped mobile television unit and began doing remote TV productions, primarily community service productions on invitation and without pay. In 1976 a commercial television company in Dallas sued Trinity for creating unfair competition and being in conflict with its status as a nonprofit, church-affiliated institution. Trinity subsequently settled the issue out of court and sold the mobile unit. See Board of Trustees Ex. Com. Minutes, 12 November 1976, and "Lawsuit Hits Trinity," *Trinitonian*, 29 October 1976: 1.

60. Board of Trustees Minutes, 16 October 1976; "Ye Gods! A Radio Station," *Trinitonian*, 30 January 1976: 3.

61. Board of Trustees Minutes, 8 February 1974; "Mini-term Offered," *Trinitonian*, 14 February 1975: 1.

62. "Bi-lingual Program," *Trinitonian*, 10 October 1975: 1.

63. Board of Trustees Minutes, 6 February 1976.

64. "Spinks Sparks Value Exchange," *Trinitonian*, 10 March 1978: 9.

65. "Kownslar Outlines Teaching," *Trinitonian*, 3 February 1978: 12; Kownslar, conversation with RDB, February 18, 2002.

66. "Courses Offer Hands-on Experience," *Trinitonian*, 21 November 1975: 5.

67. "Philosophy, Physics Merge," *Trinitonian*, 3 December 1971: 1.

68. "Unusual Communication Course," *Trinitonian*, 30 March 1979: 4.

69. "White Takes Students to the 'Sixties' Era," *Trinitonian*, 2 December 1977: 3.

70. "Students Explore Sexuality in Class," *Trinitonian*, 5 November 1976: 5.

71. *CMP Report*, II: 16; Trinity University Computer Science Department General Information Bulletin, 30 July 2001: 2.

72. 1971 Fifth Year Report, 39–40.

73. "Center Installs New Computer," 28 January 1972: 3.

74. Minutes of the Computer Center Advisory Committee, 8 December 1975, Box 8, Wimpress Papers.

75. 1976 Self-Study: Acknowledgments.

76. Minutes of Vice Presidents' Meeting, 30 August 1976, Box 5, Wimpress Papers.

77. "Trinity Libraries to Modernize Operations," *Trinitonian*, 10 February 1978: 5. Houze was more optimistic about the installation of detectors at exit gates, although he cautioned, "Whether belt buckles and keys will trip the alarm, remains to be seen."

78. "TU Installs New Computer," *Trinitonian*, 6 February 1979: 5.

79. 1976 Self-Study: 102–108; CMP Report IV: 39–42; Board of Trustees Minutes, 19 October 1974. See also "Students Programmed Out of Computer Center," *Trinitonian*, 21 November 1975: 1.

80. "Joint Long Range Planning Committee Year-end Report" (December 1974), Box 4, Wimpress Papers.

81. "Grads: In the Nature of the Beast," *Trinitonian*, 16 November 1973: 3; "Dean's Study Shapes Future," *Trinitonian*, 13 September 1974: 4.

82. Charles J. Austin, "Graduate Education at Trinity University," 1–8, Thomas Papers; "Parmer fills position," *Trinitonian*, 17 November 1978: 8.

83. "Creative Aspects of Learning," *Trinitonian*, 7 December 1973: 8; "S.A. Youths," *Trinitonian*, 3 May 1974: 9.

84. "Continuing Education Offers Courses," *Trinitonian*, 3 September 1976: 3.

85. Even as adults, former participants report fond memories of the program, especially the mass motor ball game when they waited apprehensively for "Mr. Stocking Face" to appear and barrage them with a seemingly endless supply of balls.

86. "Motor Skills Lab," *Trinitonian*, 21 October 1977: 5.

87. "Thomas Retires," *Trinitonian*, 2 May 1975: 3.

88. Board of Trustees Minutes, 20 October 1973 and 7 February 1975; "Thomas retiring," *Trinitonian*, 2 May 1975: 3; "Bruce Thomas Hall Dedication," 6 April 1974, Box 1, Wimpress Papers.

89. Board of Trustees Ex. Com. Minutes, 12 November 1974; "Search ends," *Trinitonian*, 15 November 1974; "Parmer's arrival," *Trinitonian*, 3 July 1975: 1.

90. Board of Trustees Minutes, 12 May 1973.

91. Board of Trustees Minutes, 18 October 1975.

92. Board of Trustees Minutes, 20 October 1973. In order initially to balance the budget, the Finance Committee recommended that $200,000 designated to repay university indebtedness be diverted to cover operating expenses. A number of trustees, including James Calvert and C. W. Miller, expressed dissatisfaction with the decision not to lower the debt. Trustees Calvert and Negley abstained from voting as a way of registering their disapproval of the budget.

93. Board of Trustees Minutes, 6 February 1976.

94. Board of Trustees Minutes, 18 October 1975.

95. William Bell, memorandum, Board of Trustees Minutes, 12 May 1973. Bell also asserted that leadership in connection with the fiscal operation of the university was a trustee responsibility. The administration, from his perspective, was to deal primarily with academic matters.

96. Board of Trustees Minutes, 6 February 1976. Provisions of the Leta Chapman Trust stated that Trinity could receive "up to ten percent" of the distributions at the discretion of the trustee. In other words, the trustee could elect not to give Trinity anything if he or she deemed that the university had not been functioning efficiently.

97. "Skyrocketing Utility Bills," *Trinitonian*, 25 October 1974: 1.

98. Duncan Wimpress to Joseph F. Sherrill, Jr., 4 February 1974, Box 1, Wimpress Papers. See also Board of Trustees Minutes, 8 February 1974.

99. Board of Trustees Minutes, 10 May 1975.

100. Minutes of Deans' Meetings, 20 October 1975, Box 5, Wimpress Papers. See also "Studies probe Trinity's strengths," *Trinitonian*, 26 September 1975: 2.

101. University Senate Minutes, 29 October 1975. Although DeVos withdrew his motion, he expressed hope that the trustees would take no action on the report until there had been adequate time for discussion between the faculty and the administration. See "Rumors, Hot Debate," *Trinitonian*, 31 October 1975: 1; Board of Trustees Minutes, 6 February 1976.

102. *CMP Report*, III: 17. For example, the report recommended that the executive committee, under the leadership of the chairman of the board, closely monitor and evaluate the president's performance and "act decisively and promptly if and when the performance of the president and the needs of the university diverge" (III: 9). See also "Trustees evaluating CMP recommendations," *Trinitonian*, 21 November 1975: 9.

103. Wimpress, Response, 2, 10.

104. Wimpress, Response, 2, 7.

105. Board of Trustees Minutes, 18 October 1975.

106. Ibid.

107. Board of Trustees Minutes, 8 May 1976.

108. Board of Trustees Minutes, 18 October 1975; Board of Trustees Ex. Com. Minutes, 6 February 1976. Chaired by Joseph H. Sherrill Jr., the committee consisted of Flora Holt Atherton, William H. Bell, Harold D. Herndon, Everett H. Jones, and Clarkson P. Moseley.

109. Board of Trustees Ex. Com. Minutes, 17 October 1975; Box 8, Wimpress Papers.

110. "Report of the Southern Association Visitation Team" (6–19 April 1976): 2–3, Box 5, Wimpress Papers; Board of Trustees Ex. Com. Minutes, 29 January 1976. Not all trustees shared the perspective of the Executive Committee. During a discussion of the role of trustees in the life of the university, trustee Paul Howell, a Houston business executive, reminded board members that Trinity was a combination educational, eleemosynary, and educational institution and that simple business techniques were not appropriate. Howell complimented Wimpress for his success in fundraising and administrative abilities. Board of Trustees Minutes, 8 May 1976.

111. *Prospectives for Progress,*23.

112. Board of Trustees Minutes, 6 February 1976; Board of Trustees Ex. Com. Minutes, 29 January 1976.

113. Parmer informed trustees that some faculty members were experiencing "stress and anxieties" due to the recent reorganization and was concerned that they might bring their viewpoints to individual trustees. He expressed confidence that once the reorganization got underway, tensions would diminish. Board of Trustees Minutes (Fiscal Affairs Com.), 11 October 1976. See also "Reorganization sparks debate," *Trinitonian*, 26 March 1976: 3.

114. *Prospectives for Progress*, 8–9. For more detailed information on the new academic structure, see Board of Trustees Minutes, 8 May 1976, Board of Trustees Ex. Com. Minutes, 5 May 1976, and "Six Deans appointed," *Trinitonian*, 30 April 1976: 9.

115. Board of Trustees Ex. Com. Minutes, 14 April 1976.

116. Ibid.

117. Board of Trustees Minutes, 8 May 1976.

118. Duncan Wimpress to Rudolph M. Gaedke, 1 December 1976, Box 8, Wimpress Papers.

119. Duncan Wimpress to Flora H. Atherton, 17 December 1976, Box 5, Wimpress Papers; Board of Trustees Minutes, 4 February 1977.

120. "Wimpress Resigns," *Trinitonian*, 14 January 1977: 1.

121. "Who Is Duncan Wimpress?" *Southwest Foundation Reporter* (August 1977): 1–2; Duncan Wimpress, interview with RDB, 27 October 1999. See also Jeff James, "Doctor Duncan Wimpress, Both Sides of Philanthropy," *Business San Antonio* (August 1998): 35–37.

122. Mark Hill, "Students Should Benefit From Change," *Trinitonian*, 14 January 1977: 2.

123. "Prof Criticizes Editor," *Trinitonian*, 11 February 1977: 2. Hill was not cowed by Loxsom's response. He maintained that his analysis of Wimpress had been

confirmed by a cross section of "administrative/faculty types." As for Loxsom, Hill had these words: "May the electrons in the atoms of your mustache be attacked and annihilated by an unruly cloud of positrons. Light may travel at the same speed, no matter what your frame of reference; but for political affairs you'd do well to stick to your own inertial system."

124. Box 1, Bruce Thomas Interim President Papers.

125. "Thomas Is President," *Trinitonian*, 14 January 1977: 2; Board of Trustees Minutes, 4 February 1977.

126. Board of Trustees Minutes, 14 May 1977.

127. Board of Trustees Minutes, 8 May 1976 and 14 May 1977.

128. J. Norman Parmer, interview with RDB, 19 February 1999.

129. Board of Trustees Minutes, 7 October 1977.

130. J. Norman Parmer, interview with RDB, 19 February 1999; Board of Trustees Minutes, 27 October 1978.

131. "Library dedication," *Trinitonian*, 6 April 1979: 1.

132. "Library Grows with Campaign Gifts," *Trinity* magazine (Spring 1982): 16–17.

133. Board of Trustees Minutes, 14 May 1977 and 16 February 1979.

134. "School Revises Curriculum," *Trinitonian*, 13 October 1978; "General Faculty Approves," *Trinitonian*, 16 February 1979: 1.

135. Board of Trustees Minutes, 10 May 1978; Board of Trustees Ex. Com. Minutes, 3 June 1977.

136. "TU Re-evaluates Academic Reputation," *Trinitonian*, 30 March 1979: 9; Board of Trustees Minutes, 11 May 1979. At the same time, in 1977, Trinity reported the largest number of transfer students (317) in its history. Board of Trustees Minutes, 16 November 1977.

137. The remaining debt was $3.5 million on dormitories, $200,000 on Moody Engineering Building, $700,000 on Cowles Life Science Building, and $2.5 million on Laurie Auditorium, all at 3.5 percent interest. Board of Trustees Ex. Com. Minutes, 11 August 1978.

138. Board of Trustees Minutes, 8 May 1976 and 4 February and 8 May 1977. Endowment figure supplied by Director of Information Services, April 2003.

139. Vice Presidents' Meetings Notes, 7 October 1976: 3 and 13 October: 2, Box 9, Wimpress Papers.

140. Board of Trustees Minutes, 8 February 1978; Bruce Thomas, "A Suggestion for Modifying the Academic Organization," 3 January 1988, Box 2, Thomas Papers.

141. Board of Trustees Ex. Com. Minutes, 11 August 1978. See also Bruce Thomas, "Comments on Academic Reorganization," memorandum to Walter West, 2 February 1979, and "The Academic Organization of the University," 27 September 1978, Box 1, Thomas Papers.

142. "Committee members listed," *Trinitonian*, 4 February 1977: 1.

143. Board of Tustees Ex. Com. Minutes, 14 November and 22 June 1977.

144. Board of Trustees Minutes, 10 May 1978.

145. "Trinity Gets New President," *Trinitonian*, 1 December 1978: 1.

146. Board of Trustees Minutes, 21 November 1978.

147. Board of Trustees Minutes, 20 October 1978 and 11 May 1979.

148. "TU: Changes in Latitudes, Attitudes," *Trinitonian*, 21 April 1978: 5.

1. Howard R. Bowen and W. John Minter, *Private Higher Education: First Annual Report on Finances and Educational Trends in the Private Sector of American Higher Education* (Washington, D.C., 1975): 43–44.

2. Horowitz, *Campus Life*, 248–249. In 1977 the most popular declared majors at Trinity were business administration and journalism, broadcast, and film, followed by engineering, computer and engineering science, biology, and speech and drama. "Popular Majors," *Trinitonian*, 11 November 1977: 11.

3. Horowitz, *Campus Life*, 251.

4. Horowitz, *Campus Life*, 250; Bowen and Minter, *Private Higher Education*, 44. A survey in 1979 showed that roughly half of college students believed that premarital sex was "ok if people like each other" and approved of couples living together before marriage.

5. Board of Trustees Minutes, 9 February and 20 October 1973 and 11 May 1974.

6. "Raymond E. Judd," *Trinitonian*, 27 September 1974: 2.

7. Board of Trustees Minutes, 5 February 1971.

8. Board of Trustees Minutes, 13 May 1972 and 12 May 1973. For a tongue-in-cheek description of the new Trinity student of the 1970s, see John Brantley, "Famous Among the Barns: An Anthropomorphic View of the Trinity Student," *Mirage* (Fall 1973): 14–16.

9. "Bomb Scares," *Trinitonian*, 21 March 1975: 1.

10. "Parking Rules Stiffen," *Trinitonian*, 1 September 1972: 1. Faculty members Kenneth Hummel and Darwin Peek of the mathematics department contributed their recollections of this event to the author.

11. "Ticket Caper Unsolved," *Trinitonian*, 27 April 1973: 1.

12. "Dorm Jumping Contest," *Trinitonian*, 28 October 1977: 2; "Jumping Contest," *Trinitonian*, 28 October 1977: 8.

13. "It May Be Funny," *Trinitonian*, 15 November 1974: 1.

14. "TU Holds Party Hosts Responsible," *Trinitonian*, 6 October 1978: 1, 6.

15. "TUVAC Works," *Trinitonian*, 8 November 1974: 2; "TUVAC Offers," *Trinitonian*, 14 February 1975: 5; "TUVAC Has Active Year," *Trinitonian*, 22 October 1976: 4.

16. Board of Trustees Minutes, 13 May 1972. Following a recommendation of the CMP Report, Wimpress later abolished Pool's position and placed Grissom in charge of student affairs at the dean's rank. See Chapter Eleven for details.

17. Thurman Adkins, interview with RDB, 22 July 1999.

18. Observations of author. Although faculty displayed restraint in adopting modern dress, their classroom attire became more casual, and male hairstyles cautiously mimicked their student counterparts.

19. *Student Handbook* (1978–79): 3.

20. Board of Trustees Minutes, 14 May 1971.

21. "Committee Plans Changes," *Trinitonian*, 28 April 1972: 3.

22. *Student Handbook* (1976–77): 60. The last reference to visitation hours appears in the 1977–78 handbook.

23. Annual Report of the Associate Dean of Student Life (1970–71): 5–6, Box 8,

Wimpress Papers; "Revision of Dorm Visitation Policy," *Trinitonian*, 15 October 1971: 3.

24. "Waterbeds Make Waves," *Trinitonian*, 22 October 1971: 9.

25. "Imaginative Student Transforms his Room," *Trinitonian*, 4 February 1972: 9.

26. "New Liquor Law," *Trinitonian*, 7 September 1973: 5.

27. University Senate Minutes, 22 March 1974; "Alcohol Discussed," *Trinitonian*, 30 November 1973: 1; "Senate Gives Nod to Alcohol," *Trinitonian*, 29 March 1974: 1.

28. Board of Trustees Minutes, 7 February 1975.

29. "Trinity Doors Open to the Grapes of Wrath," *Trinitonian*, 25 October 1974: 3. Under a license obtained by TRINCO, Trinity students opened a pub in 1978 in the University Center that operated from seven to ten on Wednesday and Thursday evenings and featured music furnished by local talent. See "Rathskeller Opens," *Trinitonian*, 3 November 1978: 3.

30. "Editorial," *Trinitonian*, 4 February 1972: 6.

31. 1976 Report of the Southern Association Visiting Team: 30; "Murchison Dorm Is First," *Trinitonian*, 25 February 1977: 6.

32. Board of Trustees Minutes, 14 October 1970; "Residence Relocation to Begin Next Fall," *Trinitonian*, 6 February 1970: 1.

33. "University Forum," *Trinitonian*, 28 October 1977: 1.

34. "Integrative Relocation," *Trinitonian*, 30 March 1979: 1.

35. A copy of Thomas's letter appeared in the *Trinitonian*, 15 April 1977: 1.

36. "The Thetas State Their Case," *Trinitonian*, 15 April 1977: 1.

37. "Theta Case Vital to Students," *Trinitonian*, 15 April 1977: 1.

38. "'Vulgar' Thetas Get Apology," *Trinitonian*, 22 April 1977: 1.

39. "New Food Service," *Trinitonian*, 29 June 1973: 1.

40. "Dormitories Get New Mr. Clean," *Trinitonian*, 26 October 1973: 5. Trinity periodically changed managers. In 1975, Trinity trustees approved a voluntary retirement plan for full-time staff who had served the university for at least three years. Board of Trustees Minutes, 7 February 1975.

41. "The Most Important Joint," *Trinitonian*, 7 September 1973: 8.

42. "Crystal Pistol," *Trinitonian*, 11 October 1974: 5. For students who opted to party quietly in their dorm rooms, the standard fare reportedly was assorted party nuts and bottles of Bacardi Rum. It was not uncommon for couples to get together to watch TV, eat pizza, and "enjoy a few hugs and osculations." *Trinitonian*, "The Most Important Joint": 8.

43. "Pistol Provides Second Home for Students," *Trinitonian*, 3 December 1971: 9; "Bombay Bereft of Bar Banality," *Trinitonian*, 1 February 1974: 6; "Past, Present Reflected at Bombay," *Trinitonian*, 28 April 1978: 9.

44. "Thetas Plan Return of Happy Hour," *Trinitonian*, 25 February 1972: 8.

45. "The Nighttime," *Trinitonian*, 23 March 1973: 2.

46. "Gross-Out Weekend," *Trinitonian*, 19 April 1974: 7.

47. "Toga! Toga! Toga!" *Trinitonian*, 20 October 1978: 8.

48. "Concert Ban," *Trinitonian*, 26 January 1973: 1; "Concert Ban Lifted," *Trinitonian*, 9 February 1973: 1.

49. "Last Lecture," *Trinitonian*, 24 October 1975: 1; Annual Report of Associate Dean of Student Life, 1970–71, Box 8, Wimpress Papers.

50. "Choir Performs," *Trinitonian*, 29 June 1973: 2. During the nation's bicentennial year, the choir toured southern and eastern seaboard states and visited the nation's capital. At the invitation of then Secretary of Defense Donald Rumsfeld, a relative of Trinity choir member Jim Rumsfeld, the choir presented a concert in the Pentagon. "Choir Tour," *Trinitonian*, 19 March 1976: 5.

51. "Fifth-Annual Pops Concert," *Trinitonian*, 25 October 1974: 7.

52. *Student Handbook* (1978–79): 22–23.

53. "Considering Clubs," *Trinitonian*, 7 December 1973: 2.

54. "Phi Zappas," *Trinitonian*, 15 February 1974: 1.

55. "Tappa Kegga Beer," *Trinitonian*, 22 February 1974: 9.

56. Adjusting to guidelines established by Title IX legislation, Mortar Board (senior women), Blue Key (junior and senior men), and Alpha Lambda Delta (first year and sophomore women) admitted both men and women to their respective organizations. Board of Trustees Minutes, 18 October 1975; "Women Admitted," *Trinitonian*, 19 September 1975: 1.

57. *Student Handbook* (1978–79): 24–30; Board of Trustees Minutes, 11 May 1976; "New Club," *Trinitonian*, 24 January 1974: 3.

58. "Homecoming Court," *Trinitonian*, 29 October 1976: 9. The tradition had been dropped in 1971 due to lack of student interest.

59. "Flyboys Bring Spirit," *Trinitonian*, 26 October 1973: 7.

60. "Sperm Take the Field," *Trinitonian*, 3 November 1978: 7.

61. "Sperm Provide Climax," *Trinitonian*, 26 October 1979: 9.

62. "Letters to Editor," *Trinitonian*, 20 November 1987: 2; "Football Tradition," *Trinitonian*, 28 October 1988: 16, and "Letters to Editor," 29 September 1989: 10; "Proud To Be a Sperm," *Trinitonian*, 4 November 1988: 12; "Letters to Editor," *Trinitonian*, 6 October 1989: 12.

63. "TU Is New Champ," *Trinitonian*, 12 November 1976: 10.

64. Because the TIAA conference did not include baseball, Trinity's teams played as independents in that sport.

65. "Trap and Skeet," *Trinitonian*, 22 October 1976: 11; "Shooters Win Again," *Trinitonian*, 30 April 1976. See also Harry Nixon, "The Tigers' Tale," *Trinity* magazine (Spring 1986): 18.

66. Lee Scheide, "Czar of Tennis," *San Antonio Express-News*, 21 January 2001; *National Champions: The Story of Tennis at Trinity University* (University Publication, 1972), Wimpress Papers (Athletics).

67. Nixon, "The Tigers' Tale," 17; Jennifer Bellis, "Back on Top," *San Antonio Express-News*, 13 May 2001.

68. "Tennis Tradition Relived," *Trinitonian*, 2 October 1987: 21.

69. "Women in NCAA," *Trinitonian*, 7 September 1973: 11.

70. James Hill, "Trinity Tennis," memorandum to RDB, 14 May 2001.

71. Harry Nixon, "The Tigers' Tale": 17–18. Among the outstanding athletes of the era were Patti McBee, Terry Hailey, Val Stein, Betsy Chenault, Jill Harenberg, and Teresa Machu.

72. "Females Pioneer," *Trinitonian*, 27 September 1974: 9.

73. "Ms. Invades Sports," *Trinitonian*, 9 February 1973: 7. Betsy Gerhardt assumed the same position during the 1976–77 school year.

74. "Neglected Jocketts," *Trinitonian*, 17 November 1978: 2.

75. "Volleyball Season Opens," *Trinitonian*, 20 September 1974: 5; "A Look at Women's Sports," *Trinitonian*, 2 April 1976: 14. During the 1977–78 school year, the basketball allotment for men was three times that spent on women. "Who Pays," *Trinitonian*, 4 February 1977: 4; "Co-Eds Want Team," *Trinitonian*, 8 November 1974: 10.

76. *Mirage* (1977): 95; "Intramurals," *Trinitonian*, 6 February 1976: 7.

77. "Frisbee-Golf Tourney Set," *Trinitonian*, 3 November 1972: 11.

78. "Wait a Minute," *Trinitonian*, 23 February 1973: 7; "Frisbee Tournament," *Trinitonian*, 14 September 1973: 5. In addition to Hill, the founding fathers reportedly were David Hutchinson, Rich Anderson, and Jeff Woolford.

79. "Frisbee Golf Association Sanctions Tourney," *Trinitonian*, 10 September 1976: 6; "Frisbee Golf Tournament Set for Sunday," *Trinitonian*, 14 October 1977: 10.

80. "The Decline and Fall of Streaking," *Trinitonian*, 24 March 74: 2; "Remember When," *Trinitonian*, 11 October 1974: 1. The following evening a lone streaker ran through the Coates Center game room screaming at the top of his lungs, but he received little response from the few students in attendance. Another streaker also appeared at the 1975 homecoming football game. "It's Homecoming," *Trinitonian*, 5 November 1976: 13.

81. "Streakers Surprise Audience," *Trinitonian*, 16 April 1979: 3.

82. "Moratorium Called: Trinity Remains Silent," *Trinitonian*, 30 April 1971: 6.

83. "Trinity Moratorium a Success?," *Trinitonian*, 7 May 1971: 1.

84. Board of Trustees Minutes, 12 May 1973.

85. "Advocate Discusses Meditation," *Trinitonian*, 17 November 1972: 5.

86. During this same time period, the Department of Religion hired a faculty member in Asian religions who offered introductory courses in various eastern religious traditions.

87. Brett Hall, "You're Gonna Miss Us," *Trinitonian*, 1 February 1974: 1.

88. "Election Today," *Trinitonian*, 3 October 1975: 1.

89. "Student Council: How Effective Is Student Government?" *Trinitonian*, 1 December 1972: 7.

90. "What's the Matter," *Trinitonian*, 18 January 1974: 3.

91. "Council Reps Disclose Opinions," *Trinitonian*, 22 October 1971: 7.

92. "Mirage Problems," *Trinitonian*, 16 February 1979: 6.

93. "Mirage Still in Hot Water," *Trinitonian*, 1 March 1974: 5; "Previous Debts Continue to Haunt Mirage," *Trinitonian*, 28 April 1978: 3.

94. "Mirage Problems Trace Back," *Trinitonian*, 16 February 1979: 6.

95. "The Mirage, an Epilogue," *Trinitonian*, 15 September 1978: 2; "1975 Annual," *Trinitonian*, 1 November 1974: 7.

96. "Finance Board Stab-Axes Yearbook," *Trinitonian*, 15 September 1978: 1.

97. *Mirage* (1981): 138.

98. Minutes of the Academic Council, 3 May 1973.

99. "Students Protest Room Search," *Trinitonian*, 28 April 1978: 1.

100. "Northwest Expressway Studied," *Trinitonian*, 23 October 1970: 7; "Students Circulate Petitions," *Trinitonian*, 13 November 1970: 5; "Expressway History," *Trinitonian*, 13 September 1974: 3.

101. "Petition to Advocate Adult Status," *Trinitonian*, 4 February 1972: 3.

102. "Adult Status Petition Drive," *Trinitonian*, 18 February 1972: 3.

103. "Women's Assertiveness Urged," *Trinitonian*, 14 November 1975: 5.

104. "Women Aware of Career Roles," *Trinitonian*, 16 February 1973: 7; "'Ms.' Spreads Women's Lib Message," *Trinitonian*, 4 February 1972: 9.

105. "Femininity v. Feminism," *Trinitonian*, 21 October 1977: 1. Another debate addressed the topic, "Resolved: Marriage is an Unnecessary Institution." Endorsing contractual agreements, students made three proposals: (1) all heterosexual relationships between consenting adults should be legalized; (2) all states should legalize contractual living conditions between two people; and (3) all states should remove the term *illegitimacy* from state statutes. "Marriage: to Knot or not to Knot," *Trinitonian*, 7 April 1978: 1.

106. "Woman to Speak at Graduation," *Trinitonian*, 29 April 1977: 8.

107. Dudley Clendinen, "Anita Bryant," *St. Petersburg Times On Line Floridian*, 28 November 1999.

108. "Trinity Gays Speak Out," *Trinitonian*, 24 February 1978: 8.

109. "Student Advocates Gay Association," *Trinitonian*, 10 March 1978: 2. A reference to the term *faggot* in a movie review prompted a letter to the *Trinitonian* protesting the use of such prejudicial language. "Backtalk," *Trinitonian*, 21 February 1975: 7.

110. "Sociologist Views Gay as Lifestyle," *Trinitonian*, 24 February 1978: 8.

111. "Trio Talks to Sociology Class," *Trinitonian*, 14 April 1978: 8.

112. "Chicanos on Campus," *Trinitonian*, 25 September 1970: 4; "Chicano Proposals," *Trinitonian*, 13 November 1970: 2.

113. Board of Trustees Minutes, 13 May 1972.

114. "Boycott to Eliminate Non-Union Lettuce," *Trinitonian*, 22 September 1972: 1; "Boycott Canvases Support," *Trinitonian*, 13 October 1972: 1; "Boycott Reaches Trinity," *Trinitonian*, 16 November 1973: 1. The boycott proved to be short-lived. "Union Lettuce," *Trinitonian*, 22 November 1974: 4.

115. "Black Students Plan Meeting," *Trinitonian*, 16 April 1971: 2; "Blacks Organizing," *Trinitonian*, 23 April 1971: 2. The group was originally known as the Black Students Organization but changed its name to BET the following year. See also "Black Students List Demands," *Trinitonian*, 7 May 1971: 12.

116. "Black Heritage Day," *Trinitonian*, 13 April 1973: 2. The celebration later became a weeklong event featuring book displays, lectures, music, and a worship service in the university chapel. "Black Heritage Week," *Trinitonian*, 6 February 1976: 1.

117. "Trinity Blacks Establish Own Identity," *Trinitonian*, 21 September 1973: 7; "Trinity's Queens," *Trinitonian*, 5 September 1975: 7; "Funding Racism," *Trinitonian*, 12 September 1975: 1.

118. "Resolution Concerning University Action in Regard to Racist Threats and Intimidation of Trinity University Black Students," Box 01-23, Thomas Presidential Papers; Board of Trustees Minutes, 11 May 1979; "Racial events spark media coverage," *Trinitonian*, 8 December 1978: 1.

119. "Apathy: A Recurring Trinity Theme," *Trinitonian*, 10 November 1978: 5.

120. "The Beauty, the Brawn, and the Party," *Trinitonian*, 3 November 1978: 3.

1. Ronald K. Calgaard, interview with RDB, 1 December 2001.

2. Ibid.

3. "Biographical Information, Ronald K.Calgaard," Records 10, Calgaard Presidential Papers, TU Archives. Hereafter, Calgaard Papers.

4. Calgaard, interview with RDB and Lois Boyd, 26 November 1988.

5. Elden T. Smith to Trinity University Search Committee, 18 August 1978, Records 10, Calgaard Papers.

6. "Trustees Play Major Role," *Trinitonian,* 30 November 1979: 1.

7. Genie Calgaard, interview with RDB, 4 December 2001.

8. "Genie First Lady," *Trinitonian,* 29 April 1983: 10–11.

9. Calgaard, interview with RDB, 1 December 2001.

10. Calgaard, interview with RDB, 1 December 2001. The market value of the endowment had increased from $60 million in 1976 to more than $100 million by 1980 and the endowment income rose from $4.9 million to $8.5 million over the same time period. Report of the Institutional Self-Study for the Commission on Colleges of the Southern Association of Colleges and Schools (1986): 3. Hereafter, 1986 Self-Study.

11. Calgaard, interview with RDB, 1 December 2001; David J. Straus to Ronald K. Calgaard, 22 November 1978, Records 10, Calgaard Papers.

12. Calgaard, interview with RDB, 1 December 2001.

13. Ronald Calgaard, "Expanding Roles, New Directions, and New Expectations," typescript (22 June 1986), Records 10, Calgaard Papers.

14. Ibid.

15. Generalizations based on reading of Calgaard's presidential papers in the university archives.

16. Personal observations of author as well as information from a number of faculty and administrators on various occasions.

17. "Grissom Comments," *Trinitonian,* 20 January 1995: 12.

18. The Ping-Pong simile was initially related to me by Frank H. Heinze in reference to Eugene Carson Blake. Having known both Blake and Calgaard personally, I think the saying is equally applicable to both. For Blake reference, see Brackenridge, *Eugene Carson Blake: Prophet with Portfolio,* xv.

19. Personal observations of author.

20. Harold Herndon to Ronald Calgaard, 20 April 1982, Records 10, Calgaard Papers.

21. "Presidential Inauguration," Records 2, Calgaard Papers.

22. Ronald Calgaard, "Draft of Inaugural Speech," Records 10, Calgaard Papers.

23. Ibid.; Board of Trustees Minutes, 14 February 1980; Ronald Calgaard, "Outline of Chapel Address," 22 August 1982, Records 11, Calgaard Papers. In 1981 Calgaard established a Christian Renewal Endowment Fund dedicated to renewed Christian commitment and growing Christian discipleship and service. Income from the fund was to be used to provide support beyond what was ordinarily budgeted by the university for lectures, retreats, and other programs to encourage renewal. "Endowment Fund for Christian Renewal," Records 11, Calgaard papers.

24. "Newest Candidate Visits," *Trinitonian,* 10 November 1978: 1 and 4.

25. Calgaard, interview with RDB, 1 December 2001.

26. "Herndon Carrying the Bag," *Trinitonian,* 28 September 1984: 6; Board of Trustees Minutes, 11 May 1984. He also lightened meetings and public gatherings with a unique sense of humor. At the dinner for faculty and staff opening the academic year, Herndon led the gathering in singing "School Days." During one slow-moving board meeting, he unexpectedly blew a whistle to rouse nodding participants. According to eyewitnesses, Calgaard, who was sitting next to Herndon, was so startled that he literally jumped out of his seat.

27. Board of Trustees Minutes, 6 May 1988.

28. Calgaard, interview with RDB, 1 December 2001.

29. Board of Trustees Minutes, 7 October 1983; Calgaard, interview with RDB, 1 December 2001.

30. Board of Trustees Minutes, 13 May 1983, 7 February 1986, 4 May 1990, and 4 October 1991; Calgaard, interview with RDB, 10 December 2001.

31. Board of Trustees Minutes, 9 May 1980.

32. Board of Trustees Minutes, 8 May 1981; *Trinity University News,* 9 October 1981, Records 11, Calgaard Papers.

33. "Trinity Celebrates Campaign Victory," *San Antonio Express-News,* 12 May 1984.

34. Calgaard, interview with RDB, 10 December 2001.

35. Board of Trustees Ex. Com. Minutes, 7 September 1979. The full committee report can be found attached to the 12 October 1979 plenary session minutes.

36. "Committee Readies Tenure Requests," *Trinitonian,* 6 February 1981: 4; Report of the Institutional Self-Study of Trinity University to the Commission on Colleges of the Southern Association of Colleges and Schools (1996): 95. Hereafter, 1996 Self-Study. During Calgaard's tenure as president, commission recommendations were accepted with very few exceptions.

37. "Academic Reorganization," *Trinitonian,* 25 January 1980: 1; Board of Trustees Minutes (Academic Affairs Com.), 11 February 1982.

38. Public Relations Folders, Box 86: 10, TU Archives.

39. "TAC Faces Change," *Trinitonian,* 8 February 1988: 1, 6.

40. "Freshmen Score Record Statistics," *Trinitonian,* 31 August 1984: 1, 3; *A Decade of Emergence: Trinity University 1980–1990:* 6, TU Archives. Hereafter, *Decade of Emergence.*

41. Michael Yost to Ronald Calgaard, 16 December 1988, Records 22, Calgaard Papers; *Decade of Emergence,* 6. Prior to Calgaard's tenure, most years more than 50 percent of the graduating class consisted of either transfer or commuter students, some of whom had taken only 30 hours of class work at Trinity.

42. "You do not enhance anything by including students who will not do well." Ronald Calgaard to Edward Roy, 28 August 1989, Records 4, Calgaard Papers.

43. "Committee Seeks Minority Recruitment," *Trinitonian,* 17 February 1984: 1; Board of Trustees Minutes, 10 May 1985. Trinity increased its commitment to minority causes in 1988 by housing a branch office of the Tomas Rivera Center, a national institute for the study of public policy and its effects on Hispanic populations. See "Trinity Provides Home," *Trinitonian,* 23 September 1988: 1 and 8.

44. "Calgaard Brings Changes," *Trinitonian,* 7 September 1990: 4.

45. Information supplied by Diane Saphire, associate vice president for Information Resources, Trinity University. After 1984, the number of National Merit Scholars began to decline. By the end of the decade, Trinity had 52 in the entering class.

46. A sampling of articles can be found in Records 27 and 28, Calgaard Papers.

47. Ronald Calgaard to Harry Fritz, 4 August 1982, Records 6, Calgaard Papers; "New Schedules," *Trinitonian,* 3 September 1982: 7.

48. At the time, NCAA permitted Division III schools to play one sport in the Division I or II scholarship categories. Trinity was the only school in the country to avail itself of this exception in the area of tennis.

49. "International Speakers Visit Trinity," *Trinity Magazine* (Spring 1984): 10–11; "Trinity seeks nation's elite," *Trinitonian,* 9 February 1983: 6; "Trinity University," *Educational Record* (Fall 1986): 27–28.

50. Ronald Calgaard, "A President Looks at Facilities Management," *Facilities Manager* (Winter 1978): 12–15, Records 10, Calgaard Papers.

51. These examples are taken from various memoranda in Records 20, Calgaard Papers. Before approving any maintenance or improvement project, Calgaard meticulously examined cost estimates and queried staff regarding possible alternatives and potential problems. He typically added 30 to 50 percent to cost estimates in order to prevent budget overruns.

52. *Decade of Emergence,* 16–17.

53. "Calgaard Pursues Job," *Trinitonian,* 15 February 1980: 1; "Game Room Bomb Threat," *Trinitonian,* 25 April 1980: 1; "Prank Bomb Threat," *Trinitonian,* 11 September 1981: 1.

54. Board of Trustees Minutes, 12 October 1979; Board of Trustees Ex. Com. Minutes, 26 September 1980. Grissom reported that she received daily reports on instances of disturbances, vandalism, and trashing of residence hall areas, but not accompanied by names of the persons responsible. Grissom, Annual Report to President, 1979–80: 5, Records 31, Calgaard Papers.

55. Craig McCoy, Fiscal Affairs Report, Administrative Retreat July 1991, Records 4, Calgaard Papers.

56. Thurman Adkins, interview with RDB, 21 July 1999.

57. *Student Handbook* (1981–82): 30. See also "Residence Hall Rules," *Trinitonian,* 25 September 1981: 1; "Armstrong Explains Rules," *Trinitonian,* 25 September 1981: 1, 5.

58. *Student Handbook* (1981–82): 28, 32; *Student Handbook* (1983–84): 12–13.

59. *Student Handbook* (1978–79): 36.

60. *Student Handbook* (1981–82): 27; "Policies Concerning Pledging Activities," Records 31, Calgaard Papers; "Grissom Writes Open Letter," *Trinitonian,* 19 April 1993: 13.

61. *Decade of Emergence,* 11.

62. Administrative/Staff Retreat Notes, Records 4, Calgaard Papers.

63. Correspondence in Calgaard's papers indicates that he had to defend his decision on numerous occasions. For example, John A. Poteet to Ronald Calgaard, 29 February 1984, and Ronald Calgaard to John A. Poteet, 29 February 1984, Records 5, Calgaard Papers.

64. *Decade of Emergence,* 15. When Calgaard noted that the pillars outside the Coates Center had been painted in a variety of bright colors that he deemed inappro-

priate for the setting, he acted quickly. The next day, university painters transformed them into a uniform shade of green that blended with the landscape.

65. "Tenure Delicate Subject," *Trinitonian*, 5 November 1982: 3.

66. The number of faculty in tenured or tenure-track positions increased from 195 to 230, and the student-faculty ratio decreased from more than 15 to 1 in 1979 to 11 to 1 in 1986–87. Ronald Calgaard, "A Brief Review of Developments at Trinity University," 6 April 1987, Records 9, Calgaard Papers.

67. "Campus Faces Minority Decline," *Trinitonian*, 4 November 1983: 1, 8; "No Progress," *Trinitonian*, 18 November 1983: 1.

68. Ronald Calgaard to Edward Murguia, 12 November 1983, Records 32, Calgaard Papers.

69. "Diversity for Excellence: A Statement of Purpose and a Plan of Action for Increasing and Maintaining the Presence of Minorities at Trinity University" (April 1985): 22, in Board of Trustees Minutes, 10 May 1985. Hereafter, "Diversity for Excellence." In a confidential memorandum to Vice President for Academic Affairs James Vinson, Calgaard directed him to give priority to filling new faculty positions with qualified women and minorities. Ronald Calgaard to James Vinson, 24 September 1984, Records 32, Calgaard Papers.

70. By the end of the century, Trinity had twenty-two funded distinguished professorships. "Changes During President Ronald Calgaard's Tenure," Office of Public Relations, n.d., Records 10, Calgaard Papers.

71. Calgaard, interview with RDB, 10 December 2001.

72. Initially the administration allotted a percentage increase for the department, and the chairs evaluated faculty and assigned a percentage increment, ranking the faculty members as high, medium, and low. In 1995 the process was modified to shift the initial determination of the salary increment from the departmental chair to the dean. See 1996 Self-Study: 94–95.

73. "Mandatory Student Evaluations," *Trinitonian*, 18 September 1981: 1; "General Faculty Approves," *Trinitonian*, 26 February 1982: 1 and 3; "Student Evaluations Approved," *Trinitonian*, 29 April 1983: 3.

74. *Decade of Emergence*, 6.

75. 1996 Self-Study: 97.

76. *Decade of Emergence*, 10. The junior faculty fellowship program elicited national recognition. See "Research Fellowships," *The Chronicle of Higher Education*, 18 December 1985: 19.

77. "Students as Catalysts," *New York Times*, 2 December 1990.

78. Board of Trustees Ex. Com. Minutes, 9 April 1987; "Trinity Takes Lead," *Trinitonian*, 26 January 1990: 7.

79. Ronald Calgaard to Richard M. Kleberg, 26 April 1984, Records 11, Calgaard Papers; 1986 Self-Study: 64–65. Subsequent recipients include Donald E. Everett (history), Robert V. Blystone (biology), Andrew Mihalso (music), William A. Bristow (art), John H. Moore (education), Nancy S. Mills (chemistry), Victoria Aarons (English), Mahbub Uddin (engineering science), R. Douglas Brackenridge (religion), Lawrence D. Kimmel (philosophy), Frank L. (Char) Miller (history), C. Mackenzie Brown (religion), Matthew D. Stroud (modern languages and literature), Gerald N. Pitts (computer science), Richard V. Butler (economics), L. Brooks Hill (speech and drama), and Jorge G. Gonzalez (economics).

80. "TU Shines Light on Top Teachers," *Trinitonian*, 29 March 85: 5.

81. "Upward Bound," *Trinitonian*, 15 March 1985: 8; "Upward Bound Aims High," *Trinitonian*, 24 February 1989: 9. Joyce McQueen, a Trinity graduate, has served as Upward Bound program director since its inception in 1980.

82. Board of Trustees Minutes, 11 October 1980. A comparative study of eighty-six peer institutions and libraries from the Higher Education Data Sharing Consortium conducted in 1989 revealed that Trinity's library budget (8.2 percent of general budget) was almost twice the average of all the institutions. The number of volumes added to the library in 1988 was higher than that of any of the other institutions in the study. Michael Yost to Richard W. Calvert, 1 June 1989, Record 21, Calgaard Papers.

83. Michael Yost to Ronald Calgaard, 16 December 1988, Records 22, Calgaard Papers.

84. *Decade of Emergence*, 12–13; Board of Trustees Minutes, 8 February 1991; 1996 Self-Study: 131–133. See also "Library Grows," *Trinity Magazine* (Spring 1982): 8–17. Following the death of benefactor Elizabeth Coates Maddux in 1996, the library, at her previous request, was renamed the Elizabeth Huth Coates Library.

85. *Decade of Emergence*, 17–18.

86. Board of Trustees Minutes, 7 February 1983; "Statues Add Stature," *Trinitonian*, 2 September 1983: 12; "Statues on Campus," *Mirage* (1988): 32.

87. Walter West to Ronald Calgaard, 28 October and 30 December 1980, Records 30, Calgaard Papers; Michael Yost to Ronald Calgaard, 29 November 1984, Records 21, Calgaard Papers.

88. *Trinity University Graduate Studies Bulletin* (1990–91): 12; 1986 Self-Study: 74–76; 1996 Self-Study: 3.

89. *Trinity University Courses of Study (1999–2000)*: 43; Stephen Tucker, telephone conversation with RDB, 12 January 2003.

90. "Committee to Revise General Curriculum," *Trinitonian*, 4 November 1983: 1.

91. "Q&A TU Vice President Vinson," *Trinitonian*, 27 March 1987: 7, 12.

92. *TU Catalogue* (1986–87): 25–28. An understanding on major institutional systems was never implemented and was later dropped.

93. *TU Catalogue* (1986–87): 23–24; "Peer Tutor Organizers," *Trinitonian*, 22 November 1991. The administration of the peer tutor program was originally handled by the Department of English but was shifted to the Office of Academic Affairs in 1988.

94. "Common Curriculum Reports," Records 13, Calgaard Papers. The initial faculty team included Francisco O. Garcia-Treto (religion), Karl Kregor (English), Bruce Chamberlain (music), Henry Graham (art), and Gary Kates (history).

95. "Urban Studies," *Trinitonian*, 12 November 1982: 4.

96. Department of Communication Self-Study (1995): 4–5; Department of Communication, Records 11, Calgaard Papers. In 1984 the Department of Art History was constituted as distinct from studio art.

97. Department of Speech and Drama Self-Study (1995): 1–8; Brooks Hill, interview with RDB, 11 June 2002.

98. Classical Studies, Records 11, Calgaard Papers.

99. Thomas C. Greaves to Joan Matthews, 2 October 1986, Records 4, Calgaard Papers.

100. Department of Education Self-Study (1995): 2–3.

101. "Teacher Education at Trinity University," *Wall Street Journal*, 27 December 1991. Beyond degree programs, the department initiated a cooperative relationship in 1991 with San Antonio area public schools to improve the quality of classroom instruction. The program, known initially as the Alliance for Better Schools and later as Smart Schools for San Antonio's Future, has proved to be highly successful and well received within the San Antonio community. See Department of Education Self-Study (1995): 61–62.

102. 1986 Self-Study: 92–93; "Education Continues at Holt," *Trinitonian*, 11 April 1986: 5; "Trinity a Summer Hot Spot," *Trinitonian*, 21 April 1989: 13.

103. Documents relating to the operation and closure of TRINCO can be found in Records 14, Calgaard Papers. See also Board of Trustees Minutes, 8 October 1982 and 11 October 1985; "Computer Center Engages," *Trinitonian*, 10 October 1980.

104. 1986 Self-Study: 61.

105. For background on these programs, see correspondence and historical material in Records 5 and 6, Calgaard Papers.

106. "Army Budgets Cut," *Trinitonian*, 31 August 1990: 1. This arrangement continued until UTSA dropped its program a decade later.

107. Board of Trustees Minutes, 11 October 1985; Board of Trustees Minutes (Academic Affairs Com.), 7 February 1985 and 6 February 1986.

108. Grissom, Annual Report, 1985–86, Records 31, Calgaard Papers.

109. "Too Much, Too Soon," *Trinitonian*, 31 January 1986: 3.

110. "Open Letter to Calgaard," *Trinitonian*, 30 November 1985: 4.

111. "What Did Santa Bring?" *Trinitonian*, 30 November 1984: 8.

112. Ronald Calgaard to Vicki Gratton, 4 June 1982, Records 32, Calgaard Papers.

113. Board of Trustees Minutes, 10 February 1984. Grissom made a detailed report of the events leading up to the administrative decision. See also "Gay Support Group," *Trinitonian*, 27 January 1984: 1.

114. "Report: Recognition of Gays Removed," *Trinitonian*, 17 February 1984: 1, 5; "GLSG Status Denial," *Trinitonian*, 22 February 1985: 3; "Gay Group Turned Down," *Trinitonian*, 15 February 1985: 1; "Ad Hoc Committee," *Trinitonian*, 29 October 1993: 2.

115. "150 Trinity Students Protest," *San Antonio Express-News*, 9 November 1985; "Students United," *Trinitonian*, 15 November 1985: 3; *Mirage* (1986): 73.

116. "Students Visit House of Calgaard," *Trinitonian*, 31 January 1986: 1.

117. *Student Handbook* (1986–87): 8–14. Sponsored organizations were defined as ones "directly related to the purposes and functions of Trinity University as set out in the *Statement of Institutional Mission* and approved by the Board of Trustees." *Student Handbook* (1988–89): 38–44.

118. "Administration Approves," *Trinitonian*, 21 January 1994: 1, 7.

119. Board of Trustees Minutes, February 1986; "Student Association Organizations," Records 31, Calgaard Papers. Initially, the ASR recommended student appointees to the president, but over a period of time it became standard procedure for one of the chapel deacons to serve on the Religious Life Committee and for Student Affairs representatives to be selected by Grissom. See also Grissom, "Annual Report," 1988–89, 3, Calgaard Papers.

120. Personal observations of author, confirmed by interviews with numerous

staff members. The response is attributed to Bob Stepsis, associate vice president for academic affairs.

121. Charles B. White, interview with RDB, 25 June 2002.

122. "Faculty Opposes Appointment," *Trinitonian,* 10 November 1989: 1, 8.

123. Ronald Calgaard and Edward Roy, "Memorandum to Students, Faculty, and Staff," 22 February 1988, Records 5, Calgaard Papers. See also Board of Trustees Minutes, 12 February 1988.

124. Meyer initiated court action against the university alleging defamation of character and other irregularities in the handling of her case. The matter was later settled out of court and the proceedings sealed. Board of Trustees Ex. Com. Minutes, 14 April 1989.

125. George Boyd to Nancy S. Stevens, 23 January 1996, Records 5, Calgaard Papers. See also Bobby D. Schrade to Ronald Calgaard, 22 July 1988, and Ronald Calgaard to Bobby D. Schrade, 2 August 1988, Records 5, Calgaard Papers.

126. Personal experience of author, confirmed by conversations with other faculty members.

127. Knowledge gained by author through personal observation and conversations with various faculty and staff. Some examples of correspondence can be found in Records 31, Calgaard Papers.

128. Kathleen French to Ronald Calgaard, n.d. [c. September 1982], Records 9, Calgaard Papers.

129. "Wonder Years," *Trinitonian,* 28 April 1989: 1, 3.

130. Martha Tack to Ronald Calgaard, 27 October 1986, Records 9, Calgaard Papers; "We're Number One," *Trinitonian,* 13 October 1989: 1.

131. "Is He Ready to Move On?" *San Antonio Express-News,* 16 October 1989; Board of Trustees Minutes, 1 May 1987.

132. Calgaard, interview with RDB, 17 December 2001.

133. Calgaard, interview with RDB, 17 December 2001.

134. Ronald Calgaard, "Review and Summary of the 1986 Self-Study" (typescript), 10 October 1986, Records 9, Calgaard Papers.

135. Board of Trustees Minutes, 7 October 1988; "Trinity Can't Rest on its Laurels," *Trinitonian,* 7 October 1988: 15.

Notes to Chapter Fourteen

1. Board of Trustees Minutes, 6 October 1989.

2. Ronald Calgaard, "Institutional Goals for the 1990s," Records 4, Calgaard Papers.

3. Ronald Calgaard to Coleen Grissom, 17 August 1987, Records 9, Calgaard Papers.

4. 1995 Self-Study: 44.

5. 1995 Self-Study: 45.

6. "Faculty Switch Understanding," *Trinitonian,* 3 November 1989: 4.

7. 1986 Self-Study: 45.

8. "Japanese Perspectives" and "Chinese Studies," *Trinitonian,* 31 August 1990: 13.

9. "LAC Courses," *Trinitonian,* 13 October 1995: 3; "Students Learn," *Trinitonian,* 21 November 1997: 7.

10. "Statistics on Study Abroad," Study Abroad Office, 2003; Self-Study of the Study Abroad Program (1995): 2–4.

11. Donald Clark, interview with RDB, 23 January 2003; Self-Study of the International Studies Program, (1995): 1–2. Study Abroad and International Studies combined in 2000 with shared office space, an increased staff, and a significantly enlarged budget.

12. "TUVAC Tries," *Trinitonian,* 12 April 1996: 3; "Globalization Hits Trinity Classrooms," *Trinitonian,* 26 February 1999: 8. For a sampling of courses, see "Fall Service Curriculum List," Student Association's Memorandum 1994, Records 32, Calgaard Papers.

13. "Group Projects," *Trinitonian,* 7 November 1997: 8.

14. "Investment Class," *Trinitonian,* 3 April 1998: 8; "Students Use Stock Smarts," *Trinitonian,* 19 February 1999: 3. During the first several years of its operation, the collective investments of the class matched or outperformed the Dow Jones industrial average.

15. Documents and correspondence relating to this discussion can be found in Records 19 and 29, Calgaard Papers.

16. Board of Trustees Minutes, 4 October 1991.

17. *ACS: A Ten-Year Retrospective* (Atlanta, Ga., 1992): n.p. See also *ACS: The Next Five Years* (Atlanta, Ga., 2002): 8–9. Presently, the members of the ACS in addition to Trinity are Birmingham-Southern College, Centenary College of Louisiana, Centre College, Davidson College, Furman University, Hendrix College, Millsaps College, Morehouse College, Rhodes College, Rollins College, Southwestern University, Spelman College, University of Richmond, University of the South, and Washington and Lee University.

18. "Ten Faculty Members," *Trinitonian,* 19 April 1991: 3.

19. Statistics supplied by the Office of Institutional Research. Like most private institutions of higher education, approximately 80 percent of Trinity faculty was tenured. The retirements reduced that percentage.

20. *Trinity University: A Twenty-Year Report 1979–1999:* n.p. The "recentering" of SAT scores in 1996 raised scores approximately 75 points.

21. "Unruh Named," *Trinitonian,* 26 January 1996: 1, 5. In addition to an outstanding academic record, Unruh was president of Mortar Board and the Chemistry Club, an all-conference soccer player, and an assistant coach of a women's club soccer team.

22. *Trinity University Fact Book* (2000–2001): 27.

23. In 1992 Cheryl Hopwood and three other Anglo students challenged their rejection from the University of Texas Law School when the university admitted minorities judged to be less qualified. See "Hopwood vs. Texas: Timeline of Events," http://www.law.utexas.edu/hopwood/timeline.html.

24. "Trinity Suspends Minority Scholarships," *Trinitonian,* 6 March 1997: 1, 3; "Trinity Will Follow Morales," *Trinitonian,* 4 April 1997: 1, 3; "Minority Enrollment Holds Steady," *Trinitonian,* 19 September 1997: 1. A recent Supreme Court decision (Grutter vs. Bollinger, et al., June 2003) ruled that race can be used in university admission decisions. However, the narrowly divided court placed limits on how much of a factor race can play in giving minority students an advantage in the admissions process. For details, see http://www.npr.org/news/specials/michigan.

25. "Wanted: Anti-Discrimination Policy," *Trinitonian*, 3 December 1993: 1, 3; "Sexual Orientation Amendment," *Trinitonian*, 25 February 1994: 1, 6.

26. Board of Trustees Minutes, 3 October 1997, "Sexual Orientation Amendment Denied," *Trinitonian*, 25 February 1994: 1; "Faculty Assembly Supports," *Trinitonian*, 8 April 1994: 1, 8.

27. "Partners Make Directory," *Trinitonian*, 31 October 1997: 1, 3.

28. "Trinity Plans MLK Day," *Trinitonian*, 6 December 1996: 1, 3; "Students Celebrate," *Trinitonian*, 24 January 1997: 2. About 100 students showed up for the march, but few faculty members or administrators were in attendance.

29. "Religious Diversity," *Trinitonian*, 4 September 1998: 6; Trinity University Fact Book (1993–94): 8 and (1998–99): 11.

30. Department of Religion Self-Study, 1995: 1–3; William O. Walker Jr., "Defining the Role of Religious Studies at Trinity," *Trinity* magazine (Winter 1986): 15–16. For an interesting case study of the evolution of a department of religion in a church-related institution, see Dale Robb, "Miami University 1809–2002: From Presbyterian Enterprise to Public Institution," *Journal of Presbyterian History* (Spring 2003): 35–54.

31. In 1994 Calgaard reported that asset allocations had changed from a balanced managed style to one that was 70 percent equity and 30 percent fixed income. Money managers over the previous three years had an average return of 14.5 percent. Board of Trustees Minutes, 29 April 1994.

32. Fiscal Affairs Report, Administrative Retreat 1991, Records 4, Calgaard Papers. In 1987 Calgaard told trustees that the university should plan for another major capital campaign in the early 1990s to provide funds for physical facilities and the continued growth of unrestricted endowment. Board of Trustees Minutes, 6 April 1987.

33. Board of Trustees Ex. Com. Minutes, 9 February 1989; "Rededication of the Marrs McLean Science Center Brochure," 5 October 1995, Box 91-3, TU Archives; "Library Expands," *Trinitonian*, 29 August 1997: 4.

34. "The New Look," *Trinitonian*, 27 August 1999: 1; "Long Live Richard III," *Trinitonian*, 12 November 1999: 14.

35. Board of Trustees Minutes, 3 October 1997 and 13 February and 1 May 1998.

36. Board of Trustees Minutes, 2 October 1992.

37. Board of Trustees Minutes, 1 May 1998.

38. Ronald Calgaard to John Dickey and Charles White, 30 July 1991, Records 4, Calgaard Papers; Administrative Staff Retreat Notes, 2 July 1998.

39. Calgaard, interview with RDB, 1 December 2001; "Secretarial Job Description," Records 25, Calgaard Papers.

40. "Computer System Antiquated," *Trinitonian*, 16 November 1990: 1.

41. "TUCC Gets Upper Campus," *Trinitonian*, 29 October 1993: 9; "Calgaard Shares Thoughts," *Trinitonian*, 17 March 1995: 5. By 1991 the Trinity library had installed an integrated online system that enabled users to locate books and periodicals by author, title, subject, or key word. See Robert Blystone, "Instructional Technology," *Trinity Today* (Summer 1998): 11–14.

42. Board of Trustees Minutes (Academic Affairs Com.), 4 February 1993; "Report of the Computing 2000 Committee," Records 4, Calgaard Papers.

43. Board of Trustees Minutes, 10 February 1995; "University Installs," *Trinitonian*, 26 January 1996: 2.

44. "Trinity Campus Plugs," *Trinitonian*, 24 August 1996: 3.

45. Board of Trustees Minutes (Academic Affairs Com.), 13 February 1997. At the same time, Trinity's Information Technology Committee approved official guidelines for students who desired to design and publish web pages on the university site. "New Web Policy," *Trinitonian*, 4 October 1996: 1, 2.

46. Ernest Boyer, *College: The Undergraduate Experience in America* (New York, 1987): 1–2.

47. Ronald Calgaard, transcript of convocation address, 2 September 1993, Records 3 Calgaard Papers.

48. Calgaard, interview with RDB, 1 December 2001.

49. "Biographical Information, Ronald K. Calgaard," Records 10, Calgaard Papers.

50. *Trinity University News*, 9 March 1998, Office of Public Relations.

51. Genie Calgaard, interview with RDB, 4 December 2001. Bell had attended a national meeting of university trustees where the subject of spouse compensation was a subject of discussion. Aware that other universities were compensating spouses for their varied contributions to university life, Bell thought that the practice should be inaugurated at Trinity.

52. Ronald Calgaard and Ed Roy, "Memorandum to Trinity University Faculty, Staff, and Students," 8 October 1990, Records 31, Calgaard Papers; Calgaard, interview with RDB, 10 December 2001.

53. Board of Trustees Minutes, 5 October 1990; "Division One Falls," *Trinitonian*, 12 October 1990: 1. See also retrospective article by Heather Todd, "Decisions, Decisions . . .," *Trinity* magazine (Spring 1998): 20–23.

54. "Conference Sports," *Trinitonian*, 2 September 1988: 1; "Tigers Entering Conference," *Trinitonian*, 1 September 1989: 13; Trinity University Intercollegiate Athletics Self-Study, 1990–95: 1–2. Presently, the members of the conference in addition to Trinity are Centre College, DePauw University, Hendrix College, Millsaps College, Oglethorpe University, Rhodes College, Rose-Hulman Institute of Technology, University of the South at Sewanee, and Southwestern University.

55. Trinity University Intercollegiate Athletics Self-Study, 1990–95: 2–3; "Four Years Four Bells," *Trinitonian*, 25 April 1997: 16; "Excellence in Athletics," *Trinitonian*, 28 August 1998: 34.

56. Calgaard, interview with RDB, 10 December 2001. Today only one physical education professor remains as a tenured faculty member.

57. Board of Trustees Minutes (Academic Affairs Com.), 4 May 1988; Board of Trustees Minutes (plenary), 10 February 1989. With funds donated by trustee Gilbert M. Denman, Jr., the university constructed a three-quarter-mile jogging track on a twelve-acre site on the northeast corner of the campus. See "Joggers to Make Tracks," *Trinitonian*, 18 April 1983: 7.

58. "Angry Monte Vista Dwellers," *San Antonio Express-News*, 14 July 1987.

59. David Anthony Richelieu, "Board Ok's Trinity Athletic Expansion," *San Antonio Express-News*, 14 March 1989.

60. Board of Trustees Minutes, 5 October 1990.

61. "Southern Celebration," *Trinitonian*, 5 October 1990: 8. Correspondence and newspaper clippings relating to the south campus development can be found in Calgaard Papers, Records 9.

62. "Bell Center Unveiled," *Trinitonian,* 22 August 1992: 39.

63. Justin Parker (sports information director), memorandum to RDB, 26 October 2002. Additions to the coaching staff included Charles Brock, men's basketball; Steve Mohr, football; Jeff Brown, baseball; Paul McGinlay, men's soccer; Nick Cowell, women's soccer; Becky Geyer, women's basketball; and John Ryan, men's and women's swimming and diving. They joined incumbents Julie Jenkins, women's volleyball, and Butch Newman, men's and women's tennis.

64. Ibid.; Robert King to RDB, 30 December 2002. See also "Hear Us Roar," *Trinity Today* (Fall 2000): 5.

65. "Alumni Association Activity Since 1982," (Alumni Office typescript, n.d. [c. 1990]: n.p.; Bonnie Flake, interview with RDB, 23 January 2003.

66. Calgaard, interview with RDB, 1 December 2001.

67. Calgaard, interview with RDB, 1 December 2001; Records 17, Calgaard Papers. The Calgaards ceased to host the annual fall faculty and staff dinner, which had featured themes such as a Mexican fiesta, western rodeo, or French Riviera vacation. In 1992 a southern hospitality motif described as a "Plantation Party" was deemed "racially insensitive" by a number of faculty members who declined their invitations. As hosts, the Calgaards were offended by the manner of the response and its implications of racism on their part. Editorials in the *Trinitonian* commented on the event and called for more sensitivity to issues of race, gender, and ethnicity. See "Editorial," *Trinitonian,* 18 September 1992: 10; "Racial Sensitivity Abounds," *Trinitonian,* 29 September 1992: 12.

68. Board of Trustees Minutes, 2 October 1987.

69. "Student Affairs Gets Superfund," *Trinitonian,* 30 October 1987: 1, 22.

70. Grissom, Annual Report, 7 June 1989: n.p. See also her Annual Reports, 3 June 1992 and 31 May 1996.

71. Pete Neville, interview with RDB, 30 April 2002.

72. "Service Awards," Records 26, Calgaard Papers. The program began in April 1987.

73. Board of Trustees Minutes, 1 May 1987; "Nominations for the Rhea Fern Malsbury Memorial Award 2002," Malsbury Award Committee, memorandum. Other recipients included Russell Gossage, Sug Zowarka, Lois Human, Janet Waltman, Lois Boyd, Kathryn Soupiset, Cindy McGraw, Karen Risley, Joyce Penland, Nancy Ericksen, John Greene, and Carmen Garza.

74. "Call for Nominations for the Helen Heare McKinley Award, June 2002," and "Cardenas Receives McKinley," *Trinitonian,* 4 December 1998: 3. Subsequent recipients included Joseph Leard, Barbara Weatherman, Thomas DeFayette, Lydia Cervantes, Esther Villegas, Larry Loessin, Sonia Mireles, Claudette Reese, E. J. "Tiny" Johnson, Janice Sabec, Reginald Lyro, Susie Dubose, Sylvia De La O, Juan Carrasco, Lupe Cobarubia, Gilbert Vasquez, Pete Vasquez Jr., and Robert Miller.

75. "Ten Tiger Athletes," *Trinity Today* (Spring 2000): 12–13.

76. "Athletic Hall of Fame," *Trinitonian,* 22 October 1999: 23. Subsequent recipients included Emilie Burrer Foster (tennis), Frank Conner (tennis and golf), Frank Froehling (tennis), Levi "Knock" Knight (athletic trainer), Gretchen Rush Magers (tennis), and Marvin Upshaw (football).

77. David Flores, "'Knock' Was a Pioneer," *San Antonio Express-News,* 23 March 2001; "Knock Trains Tradition," *Trinitonian,* 3 December 1986: 11, 12.

78. Board of Trustees Minutes (Academic Affairs Com.), 7 February 1991; "Wellness Program," Records 26, Calgaard Papers.

79. "First-ever Christmas Concert," *Trinitonian,* 2 December 1994: 1; "Christmas concert," Malsbury Award Committee, 1 December 1995: 1.

80. "We Sing to Thee," Records 25, Calgaard Papers; Timothy Kramer, telephone conversation with RDB, 12 September 2002.

81. Coleen Grissom to Ronald Calgaard, 23 September 1986, Records 31, Calgaard Papers.

82. For background, see Student Affairs, Administrative Retreat, 10 July 1991, Records 4, Calgaard Papers.

83. "The Flag Was Still There," *Trinitonian,* 1 February 1991: 1; "Grissom Approves," *Trinitonian,* 15 February 1991: 1, 7.

84. "AIDS Issues To Be Explored," *Trinitonian,* 14 October 1988: 1, 11. Grissom expressed concern that Trinity might be perceived as condoning premarital sex if condoms were readily available on campus or be subject to litigation if students claimed they had received faulty condoms.

85. Coleen Grissom to Ad Hoc Committee on AIDS, 11 April 1989, Records 31, Calgaard Papers. See also "Modern Love," *Trinitonian,* 18 October 1988: 11; "Trinity Needs Condoms," *Trinitonian,* 28 October 1988: 15.

86. "Condom Conundrum Quelled," *Trinitonian,* 19 November 1993: 6; "Free condoms," *Trinitonian,* 1 November 1996: 10.

87. "Campus Debates Advisor," *Trinitonian,* 29 September 1989: 1, 7; "Students Strike Back," *Trinitonian,* 23 February 1990: 9; "Register Stalled," *Trinitonian,* 6 December 1991: 2. See also relevant correspondence and reports in Records 13, Calgaard Papers.

88. "Parties to Suffer," *Trinitonian,* 5 April 1986: 3; Grissom, Annual Report, 3 June 1993: 5.

89. Grissom, Annual Report, 31 May 1996: 4.

90. "Lancers Disbanded," *Trinitonian,* 5 March 1987: 1; "President Rejects Appeal," *Trinitonian,* 27 March 1987: 3; "Lancers Return," *Trinitonian,* 9 September 1988: 1, 8.

91. "Alcohol Violation," *Trinitonian* 30 January 1987: 1.

92. "Teers on Probation," *Trinitonian,* 14 April 189: 1 and 8; "Calgaard Reinstates Pledging Ban," *Trinitonian,* 15 September 1989: 1, 6.

93. "Teers Disbanded," *Trinitonian,* 1 March 1991: 1, 3; "Pledging Banned," *Trinitonian,* 1 March 91: 1, 7. See also, "Grissom Writes Open Letter," *Trinitonian,* 19 April 1993: 13; "New Programs," *Trinitonian, Trinitonian,* 6 March 1992: 3. In 1991 the Triniteers successfully petitioned for reinstatement as a fraternity.

94. Board of Trustees Minutes, 6 October 1995, "Fight Threatens Greeks," *Trinitonian,* 22 September 1995: 1, 2; "17 Students Charged," *Trinitonian,* 29 March 1996: 1, 9.

95. "Greeks Recommend Reforms," *Trinitonian,* 24 January 1997: 1, 3; Coleen Grissom, "Fraternity and Sorority New Member Orientation," memorandum to Trinity University Faculty, 8 February 1999, Records 32, Calgaard Papers. A combined Greek Council for sororities and fraternities replaced the former Inter-Fraternity Council and the Trinity Sorority Council in 1999.

96. "TUVAC Confronts," *Trinitonian*, 8 September 1989: 5. For background, see Levine, *When Fear and Hope Collide*, 36–42.

97. "School Spirit," *Trinitonian*, 6 November 1992: 8.

98. "TUVAC Outlines Plans," *Trinitonian*, 9 September 1994: 4; "Alternative Spring Break," *Trinitonian*, 3 February 1995: 13; "TUVAC Program," *Trinitonian*, 2 October 1998: 5; "Trinity Groups Clean," *Trinitonian*, 16 October 1998: 3.

99. "Community Service Activities," Records 31, Calgaard Papers; "Save Raises Funds," *Trinitonian*, 2 February 1990: 4,; "TUVAC and Co-sponsor Expand Services," *Trinitonian*, 15 November 1996: 10.

100. "Women's Basketball," *Trinitonian*, 5 November 1993: 9; "Midnight Madness," *Trinitonian*, 4 November 1994: 21.

101. "Trinity Rings in a New Tradition," *Trinitonian*, 26 August 1995: 11.

102. "Tiger Sculpture," *Trinity Today* (Fall 1999): 9; "ASR on the prowl," *Trinitonian*, 4 October 1996: 1–2.

103. "Students Get Disoriented," *Trinitonian*, 16 April 1987: 2–3; "Last Great Whine," *Trinitonian*, 23 April 1999: 10; "Senior Orientation Brings Closure," *Trinity Today* (Summer 1998): 6–7.

104. "Hallympics," *Trinitonian*, 9 September 1994: 2.

105. "Who Says Trinity Has No Traditions?" *Trinitonian*, 6 November 1998: 11.

106. Levine, *When Hope and Fear Collide*, 11.

107. "Community: Take it or Leave it," *Trinitonian*, 9 September 1994: 11. Grissom expressed concern about the tendency of Trinity students to form into exclusive cliques. "Most troubling to me is my growing awareness that if a student does not get into a clique in the first year, he/she remains left out and excluded throughout the undergraduate experience." Annual Report, 3 June 1993: 3.

108. "Administrators Can Experience," *Trinitonian*, 7 October 1984: 11. See also "Progress Toward Community," *Trinitonian*, 9 October 1987: 11, and "Community: Take it or Leave it," *Trinitonian*, 9 September 1994: 11.

109. Grissom, Annual Report 1996–97: 1, Records 26, Calgaard Papers.

110. Coleen Grissom, "Community Key Word," Trinitonian, 22 August 1992: 29.

111. "Calgaard Announces Retirement," Trinitonian, 20 March 1998: 1; "It's Been a Joy," Trinitonian, 3 April 1998: 1.

112. Board of Trustees Minutes, 1 May 1998.

113. Biographical Information, Ronald K. Calgaard, Records 10, Calgaard Papers.

114. "Calgaard Joins," Trinitonian, 22 January 1999: 7.

115. "Afternoon Bash," Trinitonian, 15 April 1999: 2.

116. Board of Trustees Minutes, 30 April 1999.

117. Calgaard, notes of interview with Sharon Schweitzer, Records 2, Calgaard Papers.

118. Calgaard, transcript of remarks at commencement, 8 May 1999, Records 8, Calgaard Papers.

Notes to Epilogue

1. Mary Denny, "Meet the Brazils," *Trinity* magazine (Fall 1999): 15.

2. "Trustees Pick New President," *Trinitonian*, 22 January 1999: 2–3, and recollections of author.

3. "John R. Brazil Accepts Appointment," *Trinity* magazine (Spring 1999): 5.

4. John R. Brazil, interview with RDB, 11 April 2002.

5. Ibid.; "John R. Brazil Accepts Appointment," *Trinity* magazine (Spring 1999): 5.

6. John R. Brazil, curriculum vita, January 2003, Office of the President.

7. Janice Brazil, interview with RDB, 27 February 2003. The Brazils have two children: son Adrian, a Bradley graduate who works in the finance field, and daughter Morgan, who is in law practice in San Antonio.

8. "Scenes from an Inauguration," *Trinity* magazine (Spring 2000): 14–15; "Mission Accomplished," *Trinitonian*, 18 February 2000: 2.

9. John R. Brazil, "Inaugural Address," 12 February 2002.

10. "Three New VP's," *Trinitonian*, 19 August 2000: 3.

11. President's Report, Board of Trustees Minutes, 29 April 2000; "Administration Restructure," *Trinitonian*, 23 February 2001: 2–3. Relieved of responsibilities for the library, registrar's office, and information services, Vice President Fischer recommended eliminating the positions of division deans so that department chairs could interact directly with his office. Brazil concurred and approved the appointment of two new associate vice presidents for academic affairs, one to oversee faculty recruitment and development and the other budget and research. An existing vice presidential position continued to supervise curriculum and student issues.

12. Board of Trustees Minutes, "President's Report," 29 April 2000; "Nickel, Rodriguez, Ellertson," *Trinitonian*, 19 August 2000: 4; "University Librarian," *Trinity* magazine (Fall 2001): 7.

13. Statistics from Diane G. Saphire, associate vice president for information resources, January 2003.

14. John R. Brazil, "President's Letter," *Trinity* magazine, (Spring 2001): 5.

15. President's Report, Board of Trustees Minutes, 16 February 2002.

16. Board of Board of Trustees Minutes, 10 February 2001 and 16 February 2002; "Trinity University Marketing Plan," April 2002, Office of Public Relations.

17. "Trinity University Graphic Identity Program," (Spring 2002), Office of Public Relations.

18. "Curricular Reform Proposal," Faculty Assembly Minutes, 15 November 2002; "Ideas Gel," *Trinitonian*, 4 February 2000: 2; "UCC Proposal," *Trinitonian*, 22 November 2002: 1, 2. The five understandings are Cultural Heritage, Arts and Literature, Human Social Interaction, Quantitative Reasoning, and Natural Science and Technology.

19. "President's Report," Board of Trustees Minutes, 16 May 2002; "Trinity University Press," *Trinitonian*, 1 March 2001: 3 and 5; "University Press," *Trinitonian*, 30 August 2002: 6.

20. "Modified Academic Honor Code," *Trinity* magazine (Fall 2002): 6.

21. Faculty Assembly Minutes, 21 February 2003; "Students Seek Honor Code," *Trinitonian*, 13 September 2002: 1, 4; "Modified Academic Code," *Trinity* magazine (Fall 2001): 6.

22. Charles White, memorandum to Trinity Faculty, 31 July 2001.

23. Board of Trustees Minutes, 5 May 2001.

24. Board of Trustees Minutes, 13 October 2001.

25. "Trinity University News Release," Office of Public Relations, 24 May 2003.

26. Board of Trustees Minutes, 10 February 2001; Craig McCoy to RDB, 22 January 2003.

27. Board of Trustees Minutes, 10 February 2001; Board of Trustees Minutes (Fiscal Affairs Com.), 13 October 2000 and 9 February 2001. See also "Architect Chosen," *Trinity* magazine (Spring 2001): 7.

28. Board of Trustees Minutes, 29 April 2000 and 13 October 2001; Craig McCoy to RDB, 22 January 2003. According to Vice President for Fiscal Affairs Craig McCoy, the endowment was approximately $675 million in April 2004.

29. "First Impression," *Trinitonian*, 27 August 1999: 2; Janice Brazil, interview with RDB, 27 February 2003. One student observed, "He stops to talk to students, eats in the dining halls, and shows a general love for the university." "Editorial," *Trinitonian*, 19 August 2000: 10.

30. "Students React to Brazil," *Trinitonian*, 22 January 1999: 2.

31. "Final Report: Task Force on the Quality of Student Life," 24 May 2001, Office of Student Affairs; Board of Trustees Minutes (Student Affairs Com.), 12 October 2001. For example, residence hall rules were liberalized, a monthly newsletter was created to keep students better informed about campus issues, and classes were suspended in order to permit students to celebrate Martin Luther King Jr. Day.

32. Susie P. Gonzalez, "Trinity Action," *Trinity* magazine (Fall 2001): 17–18.

33. John Brazil, memorandum to the Trinity community, 11 September 2001; Board of Trustees Minutes, 13 October 2001, Appendix.

34. Gonzalez, "Trinity Action," *Trinity* magazine: 18.

35. Ibid., 18–19.

36. "TMN Diversity Proposal," *Trinitonian*, 31 August 2001: 2; "JaNay Queen," *Trinitonian*, 20 September 2002: 2; "Administration Acts," *Trinitonian*, 28 September 2002: 4.

37. "Revised NSO," *Trinitonian*, 23 August 2002: 1–2.

38. "Task Force," *Trinitonian*, 1 November 2002: 3; "Aramark to Serve Alcohol," *Trinitonian*, 30 August 2002: 2.

39. Justin Parker, sports information director, to RDB, 10 February 2003.

40. *San Antonio Express-News*, 23 March 2003; *Trinity* magazine (Fall 2003): 15.

41. "Celebration Marks," *Trinitonian*, 20 September 2002: 2; "President's Report," *Trinitonian*, 4 May 2002: 2.

42. "A Visit to Tehuacana Hills," *The Cumberland Presbyterian*, 30 October 1902: 493.

43. Denny, "Meet the Brazils," *Trinity* magazine: 17.

SELECTED BIBLIOGRAPHY

THIS HISTORY RELIES HEAVILY on university archival sources such as board of trustee minutes; presidential papers; faculty assembly, faculty senate, and university curriculum council minutes; the faculty and contract staff handbook; university catalogues (under different titles, such as Courses of Study Bulletin and just Courses of Study); accreditation, reaccreditation and self-study reports; institutional research office data; student newspapers and yearbooks; committee reports; memoranda and correspondence; historical narratives; personal papers; scrapbooks; newspaper sources; and various in-house pamphlets and brochures. Numerous individual and group oral history interviews have been conducted with Trinity trustees, faculty, staff, and students. Tapes of these interviews, which are restricted, will be deposited in the university archives. The notes for each chapter provide specific information regarding the title and location of the documents used in writing this narrative.

In addition to the university archives, useful information regarding Trinity's early history can be found in the archives of the Presbyterian Historical Society in Philadelphia, Pennsylvania, and of the Historical Foundation of the Cumberland Presbyterian Church in Memphis, Tennessee. Much of the material in Philadelphia consists of denominational governing body minutes and correspondence between the university and denominational officials, including annual statistical reports to the Board of College Aid and its successors. The archives in both Philadelphia and Memphis have microfilm or hard copies of denominational newspapers not otherwise readily available to researchers.

Institutional Minutes, Reports, and Papers

Annual Report of the Board of Christian Education of the Presbyterian Church in the United States of America

Annual Report of the Board of College Aid of the Presbyterian Church in the United States of America

Annual Report of the Board of General Education of the Presbyterian Church in the United States of America

Minutes of the Brazos Synod of the Cumberland Presbyterian Church

Minutes of the Buffalo Gap Presbytery of the Cumberland Presbyterian Church

Minutes of the Colorado Presbytery of the Cumberland Presbyterian Church

Minutes of the Colorado Synod of the Cumberland Presbyterian Church

Minutes of the General Assembly of the Cumberland Presbyterian Church

Minutes of the General Assembly of the Presbyterian Church (U.S.A.)

Minutes of the General Assembly of the United Presbyterian Church in the United States of America

Minutes of the Red River Presbytery of the Cumberland Presbyterian Church

Minutes of the Synod of Texas of the Cumberland Presbyterian Church

Minutes of the Synod of Texas of the Presbyterian Church in the United States of America

Minutes of the Synod of Texas of the United Presbyterian Church in the United States of America

Minutes of the Synod of the Sun of the Presbyterian Church (U.S.A.)

Minutes of the Synod of the Sun of the United Presbyterian Church in the United States of America

Minutes of the Texas Presbytery of the Cumberland Presbyterian Church

Minutes of the Texas Synod of the Cumberland Presbyterian Church

Minutes of the Trinity University Board of Trustees

Minutes of the Trinity University Faculty Assembly

Minutes of Trinity University Curriculum Council

Newspapers and Periodicals

Mexia Evening News

San Antonio Express

San Antonio Express-News

San Antonio Light

San Antonio News

St. Louis Observer

The Banner of Peace

Cumberland Presbyterian (Cumberland Historical Foundation archives)

Dallas Herald

Mirage

Presbyterian Advance (Presbyterian Historical Society archives)

Texas Observer (later titled *Texas Cumberland Presbyterian*)

Texas Presbyterian
Trinitonian
Waxahachie Daily Light
Waxahachie Enterprise

BOOKS

Balmer, Randall, and Fitzmier, J. *The Presbyterians.* Westport, CT: Greenwood Press, 1993.

Astin, Alexander W. *What Matters in College? Four Critical Years Revisited.* San Francisco: Jossey-Bass Publishers, 1993.

Barkley, Mary Starr. *A History of Central Texas.* Austin, TX: Austin Printing Company, 1970.

Barrus, Ben M., Baughn, Milton L., and Campbell, Thomas H. *A People Called Cumberland Presbyterians.* Memphis, TN: Frontier Press, 1972.

Bowen, Howard R., and Minter, W. John. *Private Higher Education: First Annual Report on Finances and Educational Trends in the Private Sector of American Higher Education.* Washington, DC: Government Printing Office, 1975.

Boyer, Ernest L. *Scholarship Reconsidered: Priorities of the Professoriate.* San Francisco: Jossey-Bass Inc., 1990.

———. *College: The Undergraduate Experience in America.* New York: Harper and Row, 1987.

Brackenridge, R. Douglas. *Beckoning Frontiers: A Biography of James W. Laurie.* San Antonio, TX: Trinity University Press, 1976.

———. *Voice in the Wilderness: A History of the Cumberland Presbyterian Church in Texas.* San Antonio, TX: Trinity University Press, 1968.

Brubacher, John S., and Rudy, Willis. *Higher Education in Transition,* 4th ed. New Brunswick, NJ: Transaction Publishers, 1997.

Campbell, Thomas. *History of the Cumberland Presbyterian Church in Texas.* Nashville, TN: Cumberland Presbyterian Publishing House, 1936.

Cummins, Light Townsend. *Austin College: A Sesquicentennial History 1849–1999.* Austin, TX: Eakin Press, 1999.

Cuninggim, Merrimon, *Church-Related Higher Education.* Valley Forge, PA: Abingdon Press, 1978.

———. *Uneasy Partners: The Church and the College.* Nashville, TN: Abingdon Press, 1994.

Dillon, David. *The Architecture of O'Neil Ford.* Austin, TX: University of Texas Press, 1999.

Eby, Frederick. *The Development of Education in Texas.* New York: Macmillan, 1925.

Everett, Donald E. *Trinity University: A Record of One Hundred Years.* San Antonio, TX: Trinity University Press, 1968.

Geiger, C. Harvey. *The Program of Higher Education of the Presbyterian Church in the United States of America.* Cedar Rapids, IA: Laurance Press, 1940.

Geiger, Roger L., ed. *The American College in the Nineteenth Century.* Nashville, TN: Vanderbilt University Press, 2000.

George, Mary Carolyn Hollers. *O'Neil Ford, Architect.* College Station, TX: Texas A&M Press, 1992.

Harper, Charles A. *A Century of Public Teacher Education.* Westport, CT: Greenwood Press, 1970.

Hofstadter, Richard, and Smith, Wilson. *American Higher Education: A Documentary History,* 2 vols. Chicago: University of Chicago Press, 1961.

Hogan, William R. *The Texas Republic: A Social and Economic History.* Norman, OK: University of Oklahoma Press, 1946.

Horowitz, Helen Lefkowitz. *Campus Life: Undergraduate Cultures From the End of the Eighteenth Century to the Present.* Chicago: University of Chicago Press, 1987.

Hughes, Jonathan. *American Economic History,* 3rd ed. New York: HarperCollins Publishers, 1990.

Lane, J. J. *History of Education in Texas.* Washington, DC: Government Printing Office, 1903.

Levine, Arthur. *When Hope and Fear Collide: A Portrait of Today's College Student.* San Francisco: Jossey-Bass Publishers, 1998.

Levine, Arthur. *When Dreams and Heroes Died: A Portrait of Today's College Student.* San Francisco: Jossey-Bass Publishers, 1980.

———. *Higher Learning in America: 1980–2000.* Baltimore: Johns Hopkins University Press, 1993.

Longfield, Bradley J., and Marsden, George M. "Presbyterian Colleges in Twentieth-Century America." In Milton J Coalter, John M. Mulder, and Louis B. Weeks, eds., *The Pluralistic Vision: Presbyterians and Mainstream Protestant Education and Leadership.* Louisville, KY: Westminster/John Knox Press, 1992.

Lucas, Christopher J. *American Higher Education: A History.* New York: St. Martins Press, 1994.

McDonnold, B. W. *History of the Cumberland Presbyterian Church.* Nashville, TN: Board of Publication of the Cumberland Presbyterian Church, 1888.

Paschal Jr., George H., and Benner Judith A. *One Hundred Years of Challenge and Change: A History of the Synod of Texas of the United Presbyterian Church in the U.S.A.* San Antonio, TX: Trinity University Press, 1968.

Posey, Walter. *Frontier Mission: A History of Religion West of the Southern Appalachians to 1861.* Lexington, KY: University of Kentucky Press, 1966.

Red, William S. *History of the Presbyterian Church in Texas.* Austin, TX: Steck Company, 1936.

Richardson, Rupert N., Anderson, Adrian, and Wallace, Ernest. *Texas, The Lone Star State,* 6th ed. Englewood Cliffs, NJ: Prentice-Hall, 1993.

Ringenberg, William C., *The Christian College: A History of Protestant Higher Education in America.* Grand Rapids, MI: Eerdmans, 1984.

Rudolph, Frederick. *The American College and University: A History.* New York: Knopf Publishers, 1962.

Smylie, James H. *A Brief History of the Presbyterians*. Louisville, KY: Geneva Press, 1996.

Tewksbury, Donald G. *The Founding of American Colleges and Universities Before the Civil War*. 1932. Reprint, Hamden, CT: Archon Books, 1965.

Tyler, Ron, Barnett, Douglas E., Barkley, Roy R., Anderson, Penelope C., and Odintz, Mark F., eds. *The New Handbook of Texas*, 6 vols. Austin, TX: Texas State Historical Association, 1996.

Urban, William. *A History of Monmouth College Through Its Fifth Quarter-Century*. Monmouth, IL: privately printed, 1979.

Walter, Ray A. *A History of Limestone County*. Austin: Austin Printing Company, 1959.

ARTICLES

Junkin, Samuel M. "Texas Presbyterian Institutions of Higher Education in the 20th Century," *Proceedings of the Presbyterian Historical Society of the Southwest* (March 2000): 83–96.

DISSERTATIONS AND THESES

Evans, Nellie Jean. "A History of Larissa College." Master's thesis, University of Texas at Austin, 1941.

Hetherington, Ann. "The Story of Relocation in San Antonio, Texas." Master's thesis, University of Texas at Austin, 1965.

Mason, Blanche M. "Trinity University: The Waxahachie Period." Master's thesis, Trinity University, 1966.

Mitchell, Yetta Graham. "The History of Trinity University from 1869–1934." Master's thesis, Southern Methodist University, 1936.

Reiwald, Eugenia. "Trinity University: Aspects of the Tehuacana Period." Master's thesis, Trinity University, 1964.

INDEX

Page numbers in italics have photographs or illustrations. The abbreviation "pl."
refers to unnumbered plates found between the indicated pages.

enrollment of, 20
faculty of, 18, 21, 33, 45, 50, 67, *pl.*
    114–15
faculty salaries and, 25, 33
graduation rate for, 34, 41
opening of, 20
presidents of, *pl. 114–15*
religion and, 36, 41, 53
relocation movement for, 62–64, 66–67
scholarships and, 25, 26, 27
student accommodations for, 20–21,
    53, 64
student body of, 45–46, *pl. 114–15*
student organizations and, 38–41, 59–60
tuition for, 22, 23
Television, 162, 219
Templeton, M. B., 75
Templeton, S. M., 34, 67
Templeton, Samuel L., 132
Tennis
    Tehuacana era, 62, 63
    Waxahachie era, 101
    Trinity Hill era, *pl. 194–95 and*
        242–243, 243, 244, 262, 302–4,
        pl. 322–23, 327, 357–58, 359,
        360
Tenure, 191–92, 212–13, 284
Texas A&M University, 99, 101, 102–3
Texas Association of Intercollegiate
    Athletics for Women, 304
Texas Christian University, 99, 109–10
Texas Collegiate Soccer League, 245
Texas Conference, 102
Texas Fairemont Seminary, 93
Texas Hall, 106
Texas Intercollegiate Athletic Association
    (TIAA), 264, 302, 326
Texas Intercollegiate Student Association
    (TISA), 161, 309
Texas Presbyterian University (proposed),
    82
Texas Presbytery, Cumberland Presbyter-
    ian Church, 6
Texas State Oratorical Association, 59
Texas Synod, Cumberland Presbyterian
    Church, 6, 7, 10, 12–13, 18, 25,
    29–30, 62

Theta Tau Upsilon, 236, 297, 298
Thomas, M. Bruce, *pl. 194–95*, 216,
    242–43, and 322–23
    as acting president after Everett, 174–77
    as acting president after Wimpress, 283,
        285–88, 297, 309
    background of, 156
    faculty's relationship with, 211–13
    graduate education and, 158, 219
    integration and, 188–90
    promotion of, to vice president, 226
    resumes position as dean, 197
    retirement of, 275
    ROTC and, 181
    students' relationship with, 231, 249–50
    terms of, 385
    on Texas Commission on Higher Educa-
        tion, 196
    Trinity Plan and, 216
Thomas Dormitory, 275
Thomsen, Rasmus, 159, 165–67, 386
Thornton, John D., 387
Thornton, William, 364
Thruston, Felix, 245
Tiger Club, 133
TigerFest Golf Cart Parade, *pl. 242–43*
Tigerland Coronation, 172, 234
TigerPaws, 379
"Tiger's Burp," 249–50
Tigers' Pub, 382
Timothean Society, 59–60
Title IX, 303–4
Tolleson, Stephanie, 304
Town Club, 108, 234
Track, 245
Transcendental meditation (TM), 307
Transfer students, 325
Trap and skeet, 302
TRINCO, 273, 338
Triniteers, 218, 236, 305, 367
Trinitonian, 59, 108, 113, 114, 164,
    256–57, 308, 366
Trinity Admissions Council (TAC), 325,
    344
Trinity Association for Chicano Students
    (TACS), 311–12
Trinity Booster's Club, 171

Design and Composition: Barbara Jellow
Typefaces: Sabon text, Centaur display
Printer/Binder: Thomson-Shore, Inc.

CPSIA information can be obtained at www.ICGtesting.com
Printed in the USA
LVOW10s2353050516

486834LV00006B/10/P